CRITICAL PRAISE FOR ETHICS IN PSYCHOTHERAPY AND COUNSELING

(Continued from the outside back cover)

"[The 5th edition] is a must for every clinician's bookshelf!"
—**Beverly Greene**, Ph.D., ABPP, Professor of Psychology, St. John's University

"In the evolution of thought about ethics, and the continuing expansion of technology, Pope and Vasquez do more than keep up with the times in this 5th edition of their landmark book – they stay ahead of the curve. This up-to-date volume, packed with useful and thought-provoking case illustrations, belongs on the shelf of every practicing psychologist and educator."
—**Douglas C. Haldeman**, Ph.D., John F. Kennedy University

"*Ethics in Psychotherapy and Counseling* has always been the volume I turn to when confronted with a complex risk management question. It has never let me down. As changes in technology and the changes in the health care system precipitated by the Affordable Care Act accelerate; mental health professionals will be confronting, with little guidance, unique problems with considerable ethical ambiguity. In this time of rapid change, this comprehensive but down to earth [5th edition] will become an even more essential resource."
—**Eric Harris**, JD, Ph.D., Risk Management Consultant, The Trust (formerly American Psychological Association Insurance Trust)

This is the kind of book that stretches the reader to be their best selves, that gets us looking inside to better comprehend our paths to difficult decisions and wise choices. This is one that I'll be recommending to colleagues and friends.
—**Laura S. Brown**, Ph.D., ABPP, Director, Fremont Community Therapy Project

"In the Fifth Edition of this essential text, Pope and Vasquez build on the strengths of previous versions and add many new ways of framing ethical issues in practice and research in psychology. They continue to underpin their ethical ideas with the belief that most psychologists are conscientious and caring individuals, committed to ethical behavior. Nevertheless a host of misunderstandings, fallacies, and cognitive traps foil good decision-making. A major purpose of the book is to explain and sort through such potential problems to improve ethical judgment."
—**Patrick O'Neill**, Ph.D., former President, Canadian Psychological Association

"[The new 5th edition] is a wonderful resource that should be found on the bookshelf of every practicing clinician. Pope and Vasquez' practical approach to ethics and the thorough coverage of current areas of risk and confusion make this a valuable must read. I applaud them on their thorough coverage of the areas of interstate practice, mental health practice in the digital age, multiple relationships and related psychology "hot topics." Bravo!"

–**Jeffrey N. Younggren**, Ph.D., Clinical Professor, UCLA School of Medicine

"This landmark 5th edition by Pope and Vasquez continues their fine tradition of outstanding scholarship, day-to-day practicality, and responsiveness to the ever changing health care environment of the 21st century. *Ethical Intelligence* nicely captures the manner in which clinicians of today must grapple with psychotherapy's complex realities. Brilliant, readily readable, and inspirational."

–**Pat DeLeon**, Ph.D., former President, American Psychological Association.

"Leading ethics scholars, Pope and Vasquez, in the 5th edition of their book, *Ethics in Psychotherapy and Counseling: A practical guide*, instantly draw the reader in much like a mystery writer does. They quickly engage our minds with ethical dilemmas that are powerful, intriguing and believable. We wonder how the cases will turn out. They never tell but they then take us through a world of ethics that causes us to explore the real meaning of ethics from the inside out. The book will encourage readers to understand written ethical codes and understand what their own moral compass would dictate in such complex situations. I have used previous editions of the book and will surely use this one as it is even better."

–**Rosie Bingham**, Ph.D., former President, APA Division 17 (Society of Counseling Psychology); recipient of the 2015 APA Award for Distinguished Professional Contributions to Institutional Practice

"A splendid book.... This is essential reading for all those in psychotherapy and related fields."

–**Clifford Stromberg**, Esq., Partner, Healthcare Law, Hogan & Hartson, Washington, DC

"This stirring and stimulating [5th edition] represents a must read invitation for professionals and students alike who aspire to respond in an ethically intelligent way to circumstances and situations for which often there are no easy solutions."

–**William D. Parham**, Ph.D., ABPP, Professor, Counseling Program School of Education Loyola Marymount University Past-President, APA Division 17 (Society of Counseling Psychology)

"This newly revised fifth edition of Pope and Vasquez' very comprehensive *Ethics in Psychotherapy and Counseling* goes far beyond a legalistic or 'memorize the ethics code' view of ethics. In fact, the title of this book could easily be Ethics for the Real World. It is a very practical, realistic, and thought provoking book that guides readers to develop the attitudes, perspectives, and skills needed to successfully address the many ethical challenges and dilemmas that we each are likely to be confronted by in the increasingly complex world of the practice of psychology."

–**Jeffrey E. Barnett**, Psy.D., ABPP, Professor of Psychology Associate Dean for Graduate Programs and the Social Sciences Loyola University Maryland

"Pope and Vasquez just keep getting better. The fifth edition offers solid up-to-date information and data that all practitioners must master, couched in a most engaging format that disappoints only because each punchy, absorbing chapter has to end. Readers are kept thinking not only about challenging decision-making but also about who they are or should aspire to be as self-reflective, competent practitioners."

–**Patricia Keith-Spiegel**, Ph.D., former Chair, American Psychological Association Ethics Committee

"This book had become a must-read resource for psychotherapists and counselors across disciplines. The 5th edition has updated and expanded coverage by including extensive coverage of new digital technologies and practical approaches to addressing the related concerns of privacy and practice across jurisdictions. They also include significant new material on critical thinking and avoiding fads or pseudoscientific practices. New chapters on moral distress/courage and strengthening ethics in organizations will also prove quite valuable to clinicians as we find new roles in integrated health and accountable care contexts. Pope and Vasquez have made this highly valued resource more useful, timely, and necessary."

–**Gerald P. Koocher**, Ph.D., ABPP, Dean, College of Science and Health, DePaul University; former President, American Psychological Association

"An excellent blend of case law, research evidence, down-to-earth principles and practical examples from two authors with outstanding expertise. Promotes valuable understanding through case illustrations, self-directed exercises, and thoughtful discussion of such issues as cultural diversity."

–**Dick Suinn**, Ph.D., former President, American Psychological Association

"Fresh clear thinking about ethics in practice seen from the eyes of psychologists and counselors nearly doubles the enriching number of pages and areas covered in this 5th edition over the prior edition. Therapists will feel comfortable in relating to humane, non-technocratic writings."

–**Jack G Wiggins**, Ph.D., former President, American Psychological Association

"This superb reference belongs in every psychology training program's curriculum and on every psychologist's bookshelf."

–**Lillian Comas-Diaz**, Ph.D., former President, APA Division of Psychologists in Independent Practice

"It should be part of every therapist's basic library."

–**Allen Webb**, Ph.D., ABPP, former President, American Board of Professional Psychology

"I love this book! And so will therapists, supervisors and trainees. In fact, it really should be required reading for every mental professional and aspiring professional . . . . And it is a fun read to boot!"

–**Stephen J. Ceci**, Ph.D., H.L. Carr Professor of Psychology, Cornell University

"The quite unique accomplishment of [the new 5th edition] is that as essential concepts (e.g., diversity and multiculturalism) and practical matters (e.g., assessing suicidal risk) are comprehensively presented, important contemporary topics are introduced. These emerging and timely subjects of pseudoscience and academic legends, fallacies in reasoning, the power of words, moral distress and courage, and ethics in organizations are but a few that will not be found in any other single ethics source. The originality, breadth, and richness of this leading edge work make it an essential reading for mental health professionals."

–**Linda F. Campbell**, Ph.D., The University of Georgia

Ethics in Psychotherapy and Counseling

Ethics in Psychotherapy and Counseling

A Practical Guide, Fifth Edition

MEL

WILEY

Published by John Wiley & Sons, Inc., Hoboken, New Jersey.
Published simultaneously in Canada.

For general information on our other products and services, please contact our Customer Care Department within the U.S. at 800-956-7739, outside the U.S. at 317-572-3986, or fax 317-572-4002.

Wiley publishes in a variety of print and electronic formats and by print-on-demand. Some material included with standard print versions of this book may not be included in e-books or in print-on-demand. If this book refers to media such as a CD or DVD that is not included in the version you purchased, you may download this material at http://booksupport.wiley.com. For more information about Wiley products, visit www.wiley.com.

Library of Congress Cataloging-in-Publication Data

Pope, Kenneth S.
  Ethics in psychotherapy and counseling : a practical guide / Kenneth S. Pope, Melba J. T. Vasquez. — Fifth edition.
      pages cm
  Includes bibliographical references and index.
  ISBN 978-1-119-19544-3 (pbk.) ISBN 978-1-119-19545-0 (epdf) ISBN 978-1-119-19546-7 (epub)
  1. Counseling psychologists — Professional ethics. 2. Psychotherapists — Professional ethics.
  3. Counseling psychology — Moral and ethical aspects. 4. Psychotherapy — Moral and ethical aspects.
  5. Counseling psychologist and client. I. Vasquez, Melba Jean Trinidad. II. Title.
  BF636.67.P67 2016
  174′.91583 — dc23

                              2015033566

Cover design: Wiley

Printed in the United States of America

FIFTH EDITION

HB Printing   10 9 8 7 6 5 4 3 2 1
PB Printing   10 9 8 7 6 5 4 3 2 1

CONTENTS

DEDICATION

To those who show me and others that life can be more than we
thought; who bring laughter, hope, and help to those without; who do
the right thing when no one is looking and the cost is high; who don't
shrug and turn away; whose lives are bridges, ladders, lighthouses,
lifeboats, and sanctuaries for those hurting and in need; and especially
to Hanna, Phil, Utah, Joe, Judy, Ed, Katherine, Pete, Henry, and Mary
Ann, for decades of making me laugh, cry, sing, and dream; most of all
to my wife Karen, the love of my life, who makes every moment magic.

— Ken Pope

To my friends, colleagues, clients, students, and family, from whom I
have learned tremendously; especially my spouse and best friend, Jim
H. Miller, and mother, Ofelia Vasquez Philo.

— Melba Vasquez

ACKNOWLEDGMENTS

W e are deeply indebted to all those who contributed directly or indirectly to this book. We are grateful to all but have space to mention only a few. Ray Arsenault, Linda Campbell, Ursula Delworth, Barry Farber, Lisa Grossman, Kate Hays, Loralie Lawson, Karen Olio, Carole Sinclaire, and Janet Sonne are among those who read drafts of the current or previous editions and offered valuable suggestions for improvements.

We asked a number of prominent therapists with expertise in recognizing and responding to suicidal risk to discuss pitfalls of work in this area. Chapter 25 presents the advice that each of these experts gives to readers. We thank those who contributed discussions: David Barlow, Danny Brom, Marla Craig, Jessica Henderson Daniel, the late Norman Farberow, the late Erika Fromm, Rosa Garci-Peltoniemi, Jesse Geller, Don Hiroto, Nadine Kaslow, the late Helen Block Lewis, Marsha Linehan, Ricardo Munoz, Michael Peck, David Rudd, Gary Schoener, the late Hans Strupp, and Danny Wedding.

We received exceptionally skillful and generous help from Rebecca McGovern and Xenia Lisanevich of Jossey-Bass Publishers in preparing the first edition; from Alan Rinzler, Katie Levine, Margaret Sebold, Joanne Clapp Fullagar, and Paula Goldstein of Jossey-Bass Publishers and Rachel Anderson of Satellite Publishing Services in preparing the second edition; from Alan Rinzler, Carol Hartland, Seth Schwartz, and Jennifer Wenzel of Jossey-Bass Publishers, along with Beverly Harrison Miller, in preparing the third edition; from Patricia Rossi, Fiona Brown, and Kate Lindsay in preparing the fourth edition; and from Marquita Flemming, Melinda Noack, Elisha Benjamin, and Brian Grimm in preparing this fifth edition.

PREFACE

Welcome to the fifth edition! Creative innovation, surprising research findings, landmark legal decisions, demographic changes, and new perspectives continue to bring change to the field of psychotherapy and to ethical standards, theory, and practice. We've updated all the chapters in this new edition and have expanded the book from the fourth edition's 21 chapters to the current 27 to discuss those changes.

The poor, unloved preface has gained sad notoriety as the least-read part of most books. We'll keep this one short — limiting it to only one item (a note on terminology) — in hopes of inspiring you to read on, set yourself apart from the crowd, and gain elite status as a reader of the preface.

A NOTE ON TERMINOLOGY

This book discusses ethical issues that confront psychologists working as psychotherapists, other kinds of therapists (e.g., behavior therapists), and counselors. For brevity and convenience, we often use just one of these terms — rather than some hyphenated form of all three — in a sentence. Similarly, some therapists identify those to whom they provide services as clients; others use the term patients. Again, for brevity and convenience, we have used these terms interchangeably throughout the book.

Ethics in Psychotherapy and Counseling

Chapter 1

STRENGTHENING ETHICAL INTELLIGENCE

What Do I Do Now?

- I'm staring at this insurance form, wondering if I should get creative with the diagnosis. They won't cover this new patient's condition, but he can't get the help he desperately needs without the coverage.
- Thought I'd hit the jackpot when my new grad school therapy supervisor turned out to be nationally known and his recommendation to be key to the rest of my career, but she's telling me to do things that are ethically shifty.
- She's sitting here in front of me, crying and telling me I'm her last hope because her husband beats her, but there are no shelter beds open and she can't go to the police because her husband's a decorated police captain.
- The physician down the hall is a quack, but as long as I refer my patients to him, he sends me enough referrals to pay my bills.

Doing psychotherapy confronts us with constant challenges. Each ethical challenge, large or small, subtle or staring us in the face, brings a tangle of questions. Is there a "right" thing to do? If so, how do I find out what it is? How do I actually go about doing it? What makes it right? Who says so? If I do it, what will happen to the patient? to me? to innocent — and not-so-innocent — bystanders?

We wrestle with personal questions that are hard to admit to ourselves or others. What am I tempted to do? What could I get away with? Would doing the right thing cost too much? make people mad at me? get me sued? get me fired? Would doing the wrong thing be all that bad? Would anyone find out? What would happen to me if they did? What if I'm not strong enough, not "good" enough to do the right thing? Can I duck this one and stick someone else with it?

These stinging questions always lead back to the basic question: *What do I do now?*

Ethical intelligence helps us answer that question. It brings into focus how our choices affect the lives of our patients, our colleagues, and the public. It frees us from the sticky webs of habit, fatigue, fallacy, dogma, carelessness, hurry, and stress. It wakes us to new possibilities.

This book's purpose is to help readers find better answers to that basic question — *What do I do now?* — by strengthening ethical intelligence. This book will disappoint those readers looking for an ethics cookbook, an authority pointing out the right answer for every occasion. We believe that approach fails in the real world, leading us to blunder with confidence.

Ethical intelligence, like emotional intelligence (Boyatzis, Gaskin, & Wei, 2015; Goleman, 1995; J. D. Mayer, Salovey, & Caruso, 2004; Salovey & Mayer, 1990), draws on both intrapersonal and interpersonal forms of intelligence. It empowers us to bring an informed awareness to the ethical challenges, pitfalls, and opportunities that we face in each unique, constantly changing situation and to make the best choices. Different writers approach the term *ethical intelligence* from diverse perspectives, in different contexts (e.g., Opincar, 2013; Prozesky, 2007; Sternberg, 2010; Wickham & O'Donohue, 2012). We emphasize eight basic assumptions about ethical intelligence.

> Ethical intelligence is an active process of continuous awareness that involves constant questioning and personal responsibility.

Conflicts with managed care companies, the urgency of patients' needs, the lack of adequate support, the possibility of formal complaints, mind-deadening routines, endless paperwork, worrying about making ends meet, exhaustion, and so much else can muffle our responsiveness and dull our sense of responsibility. Those challenges can overwhelm us, distract us, drain us, and lull us into ethical sleep. Our work requires constant alertness and mindful awareness of the ethical implications of what we choose to do and not do.

Ethical intelligence means setting aside arrogance. All of us have weaknesses, vulnerabilities, and blind spots — it comes with being human. The stark differences are not so much between those with many flaws and those with few but between those who are freely open to themselves and others about how their own shortcomings affect their work and those who tend to see others as their inferiors. Chapter 12, "Competence and the Human Therapist," explores some of these themes.

Ethical intelligence depends on our ability to take care of ourselves, to recognize when fear, anger, boredom, resentment, sadness, hopelessness, or anxiety hurt our work, and to do something about it. Chapter 13, "Creating — and Using — Strategies for Self-Care," offers ideas on how we can recognize when our lack of enthusiasm, resilience, meaning, and joy makes us less effective, and suggests steps to prevent that from happening or to turn things around when it is happening.

> Awareness of ethical codes is crucial, but formal codes cannot take the place of an active, thoughtful, creative approach to our ethical responsibilities.

Ethical intelligence is intelligent ethics, informed by pouring over the ethics codes that bear on our work. But formal standards and guidelines are no substitute for an active, deliberative, and creative approach to our ethical responsibilities. Codes prompt, guide, and inform our ethical consideration; they do not shut it down or take its place.

Ethical intelligence never allows us to follow a code in a rote, thoughtless manner. Each new client, whatever his or her similarities to previous clients, is unique. Each situation is unique and constantly changing — time and events never stand still. Our theoretical orientation, our community and the client's community, our culture and the client's culture, and so many other contexts shape what we see and what we make of what we see. Each ethical choice must take these contexts into account.

Codes can steer us away from clearly unethical approaches. They can shine a light on key values and concerns. But they cannot tell us what form these values and concerns will take. Standards and guidelines can set forth essential tasks or point to aspirational goals, but they never show us the best way to carry out those tasks and realize those goals with a unique client facing unique problems in a specific time and place with limited resources. Ethical decision making is a process and codes are only one part of that process.

> Awareness of laws is crucial, but legal standards should not be confused with ethical responsibilities.

A risk in the emphasis on legal standards is that meeting legal standards, which for some can mean finding ways around those standards (a.k.a. looking for loopholes), can start to replace ethical behavior. This practice is a high art in the political arena. Caught betraying the public trust, politicians often insist they did nothing wrong because no law was broken. (When it turns out that a law *was* broken, they admit that their enemies are harping on a mere "technical violation of the law.") Ethical intelligence avoids the comfortable trap of aiming low, of striving only to get by without breaking any law.

Ethical intelligence stays alert to possible conflicts between our ethical and our legal duties. These conflicts are discussed in Chapter 15, "Codes and Complaints in Context."

An overly exclusive focus on legal standards discourages ethical responsibility. Practicing "defensive therapy" — making risk management our main focus — can cause us to lose sight of our ethical responsibilities and the ethical consequences of what we say and do. When we originally discussed this tendency to confuse legal and ethical issues a quarter of a century ago in this book's first edition, the tendency had already begun to spread widely. It shows no signs of slowing down.

We believe that the overwhelming majority of therapists and counselors are conscientious, dedicated, caring individuals, committed to ethical behavior. But none of us is infallible.

All of us can — and do — make mistakes, overlook something important, work from a limited perspective, reach conclusions that are wrong, hold tight to a cherished belief that is misguided. We're aware of many barriers between us and our best work, but we may underestimate or overlook some of those barriers. Part of our responsibility is to question ourselves: What if I'm wrong about this? Is there something I'm overlooking? Could there be another way of understanding this situation? Are there other possibilities? Can I come up with a more creative, more effective, better way of responding?

Many of us find it easier to question the ethics of others than to question what we ourselves value, believe, and do. It is worth noticing if we often find ourselves stewing over just how ethically weak, dense, or shady others are while sparing ourselves from a searching self-assessment.

It is a red flag if we spend more time trying to point out other people's weaknesses, flaws, mistakes, ethical blindness, destructive actions, or hopeless stupidity than we spend questioning and challenging ourselves in positive, effective, and productive ways that awaken us to new perspectives and possibilities. Questioning ourselves is at least as important as questioning others.

Most of us find it easier to question ourselves on those intriguing topics we know we don't understand, that we stumble onto with confusion, uncertainty, and doubt. The harder but more helpful work is to question ourselves about our casual certainties. What have we taken for granted and accepted without challenge? Nothing can be placed off limits for this questioning.

Certainties are hard to give up, especially when they feel like they are part of who we are. They become landmarks, helping us make sense of the world, guiding our steps. But perhaps an always-reliable theoretical orientation begins distorting our view of a new patient, leading us to interventions that make things worse. Or having always prided ourselves on the soundness of our psychological evaluations, we keep rereading our draft report in a case in which an unbiased description of our findings may bring about a tragic injustice, harming many innocent people, and begin to wonder if our feelings for the client led us to shade the truth. Or the heart of our internship has been the supervision, and we've made it a point to tell the supervisor everything important about every patient, except about getting so turned on with that one patient, the one who is not very vulnerable at all and does not really need therapy, the one we keep having fantasies of asking out after waiting a reasonable time after termination and then, if all goes well, proposing to.

Questioning our certainties means seeking out and listening respectfully to those who disagree with us and engaging them in openly exchanging views. It means actively searching out articles and books that challenge — and sometimes attack — our assumptions, beliefs, and practices.

We must follow this questioning wherever it leads, even if we venture into territories that some might view as politically incorrect or — much harder for most of us — "psychologically incorrect" (Pope, Sonne, & Greene, 2006).

> We often encounter ethical dilemmas without clear and easy answers.

As we try to help people who come to us because they are hurting and in need, we confront overwhelming needs unmatched by adequate resources, conflicting responsibilities that seem impossible to reconcile, frustrating limits to our understanding and interventions, and countless other challenges. We may be the only person a desperate client can turn to, and we may be jerked every which way by values, events, limited time, and limited options. Our best efforts to sort through such challenges may lead us to a thoughtful, informed conclusion about the most ethical path that is in stark contradiction to the thoughtful, informed conclusion of a best friend, a formal consultant, our attorney, or the professional groups we belong to.

In the midst of these limitations, conflicts, disagreements, and complexities, we must make the best choices we can. We must each struggle to answer the question: What do I do now? And each of us must take responsibility for our decisions. We cannot shift personal responsibility for what we decide and what we do to another person, group, law, code, or custom. There is no escape from these struggles. They are part of our work.

> We and our clients do not live in a vacuum.

We act in accordance with an ethic of social justice. We open our eyes to how discrimination, hatred, injustice, beatings, slavery, jail, starvation, torture, or genocide — based on factors like race, religion, culture, gender, sexual orientation, politics — affect us, our clients, our supervisees, and the world we live and work in. We search for the most ethical response to social injustice. We don't shrug our shoulders and turn away.

Chapter 2

ETHICS IN REAL LIFE

Grad School Didn't Prepare Us for This

Even the simplest ethical concept, standard, or guideline can fool us. We hear it in class. We read it in the code. We understand it. We could explain it on a test, give a lecture on it, or help a jury understand it during a cross-examination.

We know the concept, standard, or guideline, but it fools us when it shows up unexpected in the messiness of real life. It comes dressed in different clothes, and we don't recognize it.

Therapy offers countless challenges to recognizing when and where a specific ethical concept, standard, or guideline might be helpful or vital. One reason is that concepts, standards, and guidelines tend to be abstract, often very general, and sometimes ambiguous. Another reason is that psychotherapy can be such a complex set of interactions between two unique people. Yet another is that psychotherapy can serve as the intense focus of need, hope, risk, and expectation. Lives can be at stake.

Therapy holds out the promise of help for people who are hurting and in need. It can change lives.

Clients can discover their strengths. They can change course toward a more meaningful life. They can confront loss, tragedy, hopelessness, and the end of life in ways that do not leave them numb or paralyzed. They can discover what brings them joy and what sustains them in hard times. They can start to trust, or trust more wisely. They can learn new behaviors in therapy and how to teach themselves new behaviors after therapy ends. They can question what they always believed was unquestionable. They can find out what matters most to them and stop wasting time. They can become happier, or at least less miserable. They can become better able, as Freud noted, to love and to work.

As therapists, we hold great responsibilities. What we do can make a difference in whether a client loses hope and commits suicide or chooses to live, whether a battered spouse finds shelter or returns to someone who may kill, and whether an anorexic teen chooses health or starves to death. Even new therapists know that dramatic examples tell only part of the story. So many people come to us facing what seem to be minor, hard-to-define problems, yet the hard, risky, unpredictable twists and turns of therapy can lead to more meaningful, effective, fulfilling lives.

In the midst of this work as it actually happens in real life, it can be hard to recognize those moments when an abstract ethical concept, standard, or guideline is relevant.

This chapter provides seven examples of those moments as they happen in the messy textures of real life. None is based on a specific case (and none of the people are based on actual clinicians or patients), but each represents the kinds of challenges that therapists and counselors face.

The seven clinicians were trying to do their best. Readers may disagree over whether each clinician met the highest or even minimal ethical standards, and such disagreements can form the focus of classroom, case conference, supervision, or related discussions. In at least one or two instances, you may believe that what the clinician did was perfectly reasonable and perhaps even showed courage and sensitivity. In some cases, you may believe that important information is missing. But what each clinician did or failed to do triggered a formal complaint.

COMPUTER COINCIDENCES

What happened to these therapists was so traumatic that even though they are fictional characters and never existed, they fled into other lines of work and to this day have never auditioned for another fictional scenario, even for a minor role as a walk-on. We empathize with their wish not to be recognized and agreed to their demand for anonymity in this hypothetical scenario.

The catastrophes started when one of them hit the Send button on his computer.

For many years these therapists enjoyed their small and very successful group practice. Then they modernized, bringing in state-of-the-art computers, elegantly networked and equipped with cutting-edge software that saved time, coordinated schedules, and made their work much easier.

Until one day the first therapist hit the Send button.

He had organized all the electronic records of one of his patients, who was involved in litigation, to e-mail to the patient's attorney. He had gathered the billing records, psychological testing results, records of therapy sessions, as well as the background records (employment, disability, and others).

The therapist gave one last look and hit the Send button.

It was only after watching his computer send off the records that he noticed he had used the wrong address. The records were not resting in the inbox of the patient's attorney but were sparking interest on a large Internet discussion list that was listed right next to the attorney in the therapist's address book. A few months later the therapist received an old-fashioned paper document from the patient's attorney. The paper was legal sized.

By a far-fetched coincidence typical of hypothetical scenarios, the second therapist walked into the first therapist's office just as the first therapist hit the fatal Send button. The second therapist said: "Can you believe it!? I'm being sued, and it's all because of my computer! When my patient temporarily moved to the East Coast for a sabbatical, we thought it best to continue treatment, but because of the time difference and our heavy schedules, we couldn't find a time when we could both talk, so we decided to communicate by e-mail. But then she got mad at me about something and filed complaints against me in the other state! So now they're saying I was providing psychological services in that state without being licensed there and that I failed to follow that state's rules and regulations about . . . well, you'd have to read the complaints her attorney has filed with the licensing board, the courts, and the ethics committee. It's terrible! I don't know what I'm going to do!"

As if sensing that another wild coincidence was needed to keep the story moving, the third therapist rushed into the first therapist's office at just that moment and cried, "You won't believe what happened! I got hit with a formal notice that I'm being sued! Somehow a virus or Trojan or worm or one of those things got into my computer and took my files — you know, all my confidential case files — and sent them to everyone listed in my address book and to all the other addresses in my computer's memory. What do I do now?"

On cue, the fourth therapist ran into the room and wailed, "Help! I'm in such trouble! One of my patients is involved in a nasty lawsuit, and I received a court order to produce all my records. The patient had given me consent to turn them over because she and her attorney believe they will be the key to their winning the case. So I sat down to print them out and . . . they're gone! My hard drive crashed, and when I hired a company to rescue what they could, they retrieved some records but all the files for that patient are gone. What do I do now?"

Although the room was getting crowded, the fifth therapist slouched in, collapsed in a chair, and announced, "I'm doomed. I kept all my records on my laptop. But while I was at lunch today, someone broke into my car and stole my laptop. Then I got worse news. I thought at least the files would be safe because I encrypted them, but a colleague just told me that since the program I used to encrypt and unencrypt them is on that computer and since many thieves have software that enables them to get past passwords and gain use of the encryption program, it would be pretty easy for a hacker to unencrypt my files."

When the final member of their group practice failed to show up with bad news, they grew concerned and went down the hall to her office. She was sitting at her desk with a big smile spreading across her face. She chirped, "I can't tell you how good I feel! I've been so concerned about keeping records on my computer that I finally decided it just wasn't worth the worry. I printed out all my records, made extra copies that I put in my safe deposit box, and got rid of my computer. It was such a good move for me. I haven't felt this good in days."

It was only months later that she discovered, as she read the complaint filed against her, that she had done a poor job of trying to erase her hard drive before selling her computer. The person who had bought it had little trouble retrieving the supposedly erased files and reading all the details about her patients.

LIFE IN CHAOS

Professor Alvarez, a 45-year-old physics professor, has never before sought psychotherapy. He shows up for his first appointment with Dr. Brinks. Professor Alvarez says that his life is in chaos. He was granted full professor status about a year ago, and about a month after that, his wife suddenly left him to live with another man. He plunged into a deep depression. About four months ago, he began to feel anxious and have trouble concentrating. He feels he needs someone to talk to so that he can figure out what happened. Professor Alvarez and Dr. Brinks agree to meet twice a week for outpatient psychotherapy.

During the first few sessions, Professor Alvarez says that he feels relieved that he can talk about his problems, but is still jittery. During the next few months, he begins talking about some pretty terrible things that happened to him when he was a child. He says that he is having even more trouble concentrating. Dr. Brinks assures him that this is not surprising; problems concentrating often become temporarily worse when a patient starts confronting difficult issues. She suggests that they begin meeting three times a week. Professor Alvarez agrees.

A month later, Professor Alvarez collapses and is rushed to the hospital, where he is pronounced dead on arrival. An autopsy reveals that a small tumor had been pressing against a blood vessel in his brain. When the vessel burst, he died.

Months after Professor Alvarez's death, Dr. Brinks learns that Professor Alvarez's relatives are pursuing a formal complaint against her with the state ethics committee and suing her for malpractice. The ethics complaint and the malpractice suit claim that she was grossly negligent in diagnosing Professor Alvarez in that she had failed to take any step to rule out organic causes for Professor Alvarez's concentration difficulties, had not applied any of the principles and procedures of the profession of psychology to identify organic impairment, and had not referred Professor Alvarez for evaluation by a neuropsychologist or to a physician for a medical examination.

Therapists and counselors in ethics and malpractice workshops (who would probably not constitute a random sample of practicing psychologists) who have reviewed this scenario have tended to conclude that Dr. Brinks may have been practicing beyond the range of her competence and violated some of the fundamental standards of assessment (see Chapter 20).

EVALUATING CHILDREN

Ms. Cain brings her two daughters, ages 4 and 6, to Dr. Durrenberger for a psychological evaluation. She reports that they have become upset during the past few months. They have nightmares and wet their beds. She suspects that the problem may have something to do with their last visit to their father, who lives out of state.

Dr. Durrenberger schedules three sessions in which he sees Ms. Cain and her two children together and three individual sessions with each daughter. While preparing his report, he receives a subpoena to testify in a civil suit that Ms. Cain is filing against her ex-husband. She is suing for custody of her children. During the trial, Dr. Durrenberger testifies that the daughters seem, on the basis of interviews and psychological tests, to have a stronger, more positive relationship with their mother. He gives his professional opinion that the children would be better off with their mother and that she should be given custody.

Mr. Cain files an ethics complaint, a civil suit, and a licensing complaint against Dr. Durrenberger. Mr. Cain claims that Dr. Durrenberger failed to obtain informed consent to conduct the assessments. When Mr. and Ms. Cain had divorced 2 years previously, the court had granted Mr. Cain legal custody of the daughters but granted Ms. Cain visitation rights. (Ms. Cain had arranged for the assessments of the children during a long summer visit.)

Mr. Cain also claimed that Dr. Durrenberger made a formal recommendation about custody placement without trying to interview Mr. Cain. Mr. Cain's attorney called two expert witnesses to testify that no custody recommendation should be made without interviewing both parents. They also testified that Dr. Durrenberger should not have served as both therapist and forensic evaluator. Dr. Durrenberger clearly had not reviewed the Guidelines for Evaluation of Child Custody in Family Law Proceedings (American Psychological Association [APA], 2010b).

Although laws regarding rights of custodial and noncustodial parents differ from state to state and province to province, ethics and malpractice workshop participants tend to conclude that Dr. Durrenberger failed to fulfill his ethical (and, in many states, legal) responsibility to obtain adequate informed consent from the relevant parent (see Chapter 19) and that he had failed to conduct an adequate assessment to justify his conclusions and recommendations (see Chapter 20).

THE FATAL DISEASE

When George, a 22-year-old college student, began psychotherapy with Dr. Hightower, he told the doctor that he was suffering from a fatal disease. Two months into therapy, George felt that he trusted his therapist enough to tell her that the disease was AIDS.

During the next 18 months, therapy focused on George's losing battle with his illness and his preparations to die. After two stays in the hospital for pneumonia, George informed Dr. Hightower that he knew he would not survive his next hospitalization. He had done independent research and talked with his physicians, and he was sure that if pneumonia struck again, it would inflict a long, painful death.

George said that when that time came, he wanted to die in the off-campus apartment he had lived in since he came to college — *not* in the hospital. When he felt himself getting sicker, he would take a fatal dose of drugs he had bought on the street.

Dr. Hightower tried to talk him out of this plan, but George refused to discuss it and said that if Dr. Hightower continued to bring up the subject, he would quit therapy. Convinced that George would quit therapy rather than discuss his plan, Dr. Hightower chose to offer kindness, caring, and support — rather than confrontation and argument — to a patient who seemed to have only a few months to live.

Four months later, Dr. Hightower found out that George had taken his life. Within the next month, Dr. Hightower became the defendant in two civil suits. George's family claimed that Dr. Hightower, knowing that George planned to take his own life, failed to take reasonable and adequate steps to prevent the suicide, did not notify any third parties of the suicide plan, did not ask George to get rid of the fatal drugs, and did not use hospitalization to prevent the suicide.

George's lover filed the other suit, claiming that he did not know that George had been suffering from AIDS. Two expert witnesses testified that Dr. Hightower, knowing that George had both a fatal sexually transmitted disease and a lover, had a duty to take reasonable steps to try to protect the lover.

This scenario has been one of the most agonizing and controversial for the therapists who struggle with it at ethics and malpractice workshops. Some believe that Dr. Hightower acted in the most humane, sensitive, and ethical manner. Others believe that she was wrong to accept, without more vigorous challenge, George's decision to take his own life. In this sense, it illustrates the dilemmas we face when confronted with a suicidal individual (see Chapter 25). It also shows the problems we sometimes face trying to balance — ethically, legally, clinically, or practically — confidentiality (see Chapter 24) and risks to third parties.

Many would argue that the main goal of therapy when suicide is an issue is to defuse the potentially lethal situation. According to this view, we have a professional duty to try to prevent patients from harming themselves, a duty that may include in extreme cases taking steps to hospitalize patients against their will through civil commitment.

Others would argue that therapists must respect the client's autonomy even if that includes the client's decision to commit suicide. Some would accord this "right to die" to any client. Others would recognize it only in certain extreme situations (e.g., if the client is suffering from a painful and terminal disease). Some would draw the line at accepting a client's decision to commit suicide and taking no steps to interfere with the client's self-destructive acts. Others would consider actively assisting the person to die.

These agonizing, controversial issues have become especially difficult for some who provide mental health services to those with AIDS (Burke, 2014; Downs, 2015; Kooyman & Barret, 2009; Pope & Morin, 1990), as in this vignette. As is so often the case, the ethical and clinical issues are interwoven with legal standards. Laws addressing assisted suicide raise an extremely broad and diverse array of complex issues and stir controversy (see, e.g., Attaran, 2015; Gamondi, Borasio, Limoni, Preston, & Payne, 2014; Glascock, 2009; Gostin, 2006; Isenberg-Grzeda & Ellis, 2015; S. M. Johnson, Cramer, Conroy, & Gardner, 2014; Kleespies, 2004; Lindblad, Lofmark, & Lynoe, 2008; Lulé et al., 2014; Lyall, 2009; Nock, 2014).

THE MECHANIC

Ms. Huang, whose family had moved from mainland China to the United States 15 years ago, is a 45-year-old automobile mechanic. She agreed, at the strong urging of her employer, to seek psychotherapy for difficulties that seem to affect her work. She shows up late, often phones in sick, and seems distracted. She complains to her new therapist, Dr. Jackson, about how hard it is to cope with both psychomotor epilepsy, which has been controlled through medication, and her progressive diabetes, which also requires medical care.

Although she has no real experience treating those from the Chinese culture or those with chronic medical conditions such as epilepsy and progressive diabetes, Dr. Jackson begins work with Ms. Huang. She meets with her on a regular basis for 3 months but never feels that a solid working alliance is developing. After 3 months, Ms. Huang abruptly quits therapy. She has not paid for the past six sessions.

Two weeks later, Dr. Jackson receives a request to send Ms. Huang's treatment records to her new therapist. Dr. Jackson notifies Ms. Huang that she will not forward the records until the bill has been paid in full.

Sometime later, Dr. Jackson receives notice that the American Psychological Association Ethics Committee is investigating an ethics complaint against her and that she has been sued for malpractice. The complaints allege that Dr. Jackson had been practicing outside her areas of competence because she had received no education, training, or supervised experience in treating people from the Chinese culture or those with multiple serious and chronic medical diseases.

The complaints also allege that Ms. Huang had never adequately understood the nature of treatment, as evidenced by the lack of any written informed consent. Finally, the complaints allege that "holding records hostage" for payment violated Ms. Huang's welfare and deprived her subsequent therapist of having prompt and comprehensive information for Ms. Huang's treatment.

Participants in ethics and malpractice workshops, asked to assume the role of an ethics committee to review this scenario, often conclude that Dr. Jackson was acting without adequate competence to treat someone from a different culture (see Chapter 23) or with a chronic medical condition, had failed to obtain adequate informed consent in regard to a clear description and understanding of Dr. Jackson's fee structure, and had abused the power as former therapist in refusing to release records because of an unpaid bill.

THE POSTDOCTORAL EXPERIENCE

Dr. Larson serves as executive director and clinical chief of staff at the Golden Internship Health Maintenance Organization (HMO). For 1 year, he closely supervises an outstanding postdoc, Dr. Marshall. The supervisee shows great potential, working with a range of patients who respond positively to her interventions. After completing her postdoc and becoming licensed, Dr. Marshall goes into business for herself, opening an office several blocks from Golden Internship Health Maintenance Organization.

Dr. Larson tells Dr. Marshall that she must transfer all patients to other center therapists before terminating her work at the HMO. All of the patients who can afford her fee schedule, however, decide to continue in therapy with Dr. Marshall. The patients who cannot afford Dr. Marshall's fee schedule are assigned to new therapists at the center.

Dr. Larson hires an attorney to sue Dr. Marshall, asserting that she unethically exploited the HMO by stealing patients and engaging in deceptive practices. He files ethics and licensing complaints against her, charging that she had refused to follow his supervision in regard to the patients and pointed out that he, as the clinical supervisor of this trainee, had been both clinically and legally responsible for the patients. He refuses to turn over the patients' charts to Dr. Marshall or to certify to various associations to which she has applied for membership that she has successfully completed her internship.

Dr. Marshall countersues, claiming that Dr. Larson is engaging in illegal restraint of trade and failing to act in the patients' best interests. The patients, she asserts, have formed an intense transference and an effective working alliance with her; to lose their therapist would be clinically damaging and not in their best interests. She files ethics and licensing complaints against Dr. Larson, charging that his refusal to deliver copies of the patients' charts when presented with the patients' signed requests and authorizations violated Health Insurance Portability and Accountability Act (HIPAA) and professional standards. She also alleges that his refusal to certify that she completed her postdoctoral requirement violated legal and ethical standards.

Some of the patients sue the HMO, Dr. Larson, and Dr. Marshall, charging that the conflict and the legal actions (in which their cases are put at issue without their consent) have been damaging to their therapy.

Workshop participants often conclude that both Dr. Larson and Dr. Marshall have behaved unethically in terms of misusing their power (see Chapter 9), failing to clarify in advance the conclusion of Dr. Marshall's work with the patients (see Chapters 18 and 19), and neglecting to address these issues adequately in the supervision contract (see Chapter 27).

STAYING SOBER

In therapy for 1 year with Dr. Franks, Mr. Edwards is an alcoholic and drank heavily for 4 years prior to the therapy. Dr. Franks uses a psychodynamic approach and incorporates behavioral techniques designed to address the drinking problem.

Two months into therapy, when it became clear that outpatient psychotherapy alone was not effective, Mr. Edwards agreed to attend Alcoholics Anonymous (AA) meetings in addition to his therapy. During the past 9 months of therapy, Mr. Edwards had usually stayed sober, suffering only two relapses, each time falling off the wagon for a long weekend.

Now, a year into therapy, Mr. Edwards suffers a third relapse. He shows up at the session with several drinks under his belt. During the session, Dr. Franks and Mr. Edwards conclude that some of the troubling material that has been emerging in the therapy had led Mr. Edwards to begin drinking again. At the end of the session, Mr. Edwards feels that he has gained some additional insight into why he drank. He plans to go straight from the session to an AA meeting.

One month later, Dr. Franks opens the door to his waiting room and a stranger thrusts papers into his hand. That's how he found out he was being sued. On his way from the therapy session to the AA meeting, Mr. Edwards had run a red light, smashing into a mother carrying her baby in the crosswalk. The suit alleged that the therapist knew or should have known his patient to be dangerous on the evening of the accident and should have taken reasonable steps to prevent him from driving that night. It also alleges that Dr. Franks should have taken reasonable steps to prevent Mr. Edwards from driving at all until his alcoholism no longer constituted a danger to the public.

Although workshop participants tend to fault Dr. Franks for not adequately assessing his client's condition and the danger that the client's driving in that condition would constitute for the public, there was a common empathic response, as with many of the other scenarios. Clinicians tend to identify with Dr. Franks and think, "That could be me."

Struck by the challenges these hypothetical clinicians face, we wonder if we would do any better if we were in their place.

Because this book's approach emphasizes personal responsibility and the need — as these seven scenarios illustrate — to think clearly about the responsibilities emerging in each new situation, Chapters 4 through 8 focus on critical thinking.

Chapter 3

THE HUMAN THERAPIST AND THE (SOMETIMES) INHUMAN RELATIONSHIP

Being Absent in the Present

Terms like *respect* don't get no respect. We rarely dignify vague, hard-to-define generalities like *respect* and *dignity* with a second glance. We sail right past them in ethics codes on our way to get guidance on practical specifics like consent, confidentiality, fees, or multiple relationships. But professional associations like the American Psychological Association (APA) and the Canadian Psychological Association (CPA) emphasize them as fundamental.

For APA, "Respect for People's Rights and Dignity" is one of the five basic principles. APA's ethics code states that

> Psychologists respect the dignity and worth of all people, and the rights of individuals to privacy, confidentiality, and self-determination. Psychologists are aware that special safeguards may be necessary to protect the rights and welfare of persons or communities whose vulnerabilities impair autonomous decision making. Psychologists are aware of and respect cultural, individual, and role differences, including those based on age, gender, gender identity, race, ethnicity, culture, national origin, religion, sexual orientation, disability, language, and socioeconomic status, and consider these factors when working with members of such groups. Psychologists try to eliminate the effect on their work of biases based on those factors, and they do not knowingly participate in or condone activities of others based upon such prejudices. (APA, 2010a, Principle E)

17

CPA makes "Respect for the Dignity of Persons" the first of four basic principles, the one generally given the most weight. The draft of the fourth edition of the CPA code emphasizes that "this principle, with its emphasis on inherent worth, non-discrimination, moral rights, and distributive justice, generally should be given the highest weight, except in circumstances in which there is a clear and imminent danger of bodily harm to someone" (CPA, 2015).

When we strengthen our ethical intelligence we fine-tune our skills at catching ourselves whenever we fail to fully respect the dignity of our patients, perhaps by not paying careful attention to them. Most of us learn about this failure when we're on the receiving end. Has any reader led a charmed life free of the sinking realization that the other person, supposedly there to help, was either not showing us the basic respect of paying attention or seemed intent on slowing or blocking our getting the help we need? Consider the following scenes to see if any feel familiar.

You walk into the store to buy a new coat and (good!) there are no other customers — just four sales clerks near the back of the store telling each other jokes — so you should be able to get in and out of there without standing in line to check out. You go over to the coats but no sales person comes over to ask if you need help. You pick out the coat you want, try it on to make sure it fits, and walk over to the register. The sales clerks seem blissfully unaware of your existence, even after you clear your throat a couple of times. Finally, you say, "I'd like to buy this coat. Would one of you be able to check me out?" The sales clerk nearest you turns around to see who's talking, looking at you as if you'd burped loudly at a formal dinner. The clerk holds up an index finger, indicating that your opportunity to give the store your money will come soon and you should show some patience. Finally, one of the longest jokes in recorded history reaches its long-anticipated punch line, and not too long after, you have left the store with your new coat. Another "satisfied" customer.

■ ■ ■

You (calling a clinic near closing time to reach your child's pediatrician before he leaves the country on a 2-week vacation): Hi, I'm hoping to reach Dr. Guzman before he heads for the airport. My child has come down with something and no one knows her like Dr. Guzman. Any chance he's still there?

Receptionist: Oh, I just saw him packing his briefcase in his office. Let me run catch him before he leaves and I have to chase him across the parking lot! [puts you on hold]

[You wait. And wait. You see in your mind's eye the old movie convention of clock hands whirring around to show the passage of time. Then you see calendar pages flying off the wall. And then finally!]

Receptionist: What were you waiting for? Oh, I'm sorry, he left a while ago.

■ ■ ■

You on the phone to tech support: Hi, I'm hoping you can help me get my Internet connection up and running again quickly because I've got an Internet session scheduled for a homebound patient in 5 minutes. Let me tell you what I've already tried so that we can save time not going through those initial steps. I've tried disconnecting everything from my router, unplugging it from the wall socket, waiting 10 seconds, then plugging it again, and reconnecting everything. Then I tried checking all the settings on my computer to make sure they were correct. Then I made sure my computer didn't have a virus that was messing things up. Anything else we could try?

Tech support: I am so sorry you are having trouble with our company's services, but I am sure that I will be able to help you reconnect to the Internet. Let's start with this: First, please disconnect everything from your router, unplug it from the electrical socket, and wait about 10 seconds before we plug everything back in to see if that works.

■ ■ ■

Anyone who speaks to you using sentences that begin "No offense intended but . . . ," "I hope you won't take this the wrong way but . . . ," or "With all due respect, . . . "

For most of us, realizing that others are cutting us short on respect and dignity comes easier than realizing when we are doing it to others. What is completely understandable under the circumstances and hardly worth noticing when we do it is, when someone does it to us, arrogance, intentional disrespect, veiled hostility, a personality disorder, a lack of human decency, and part of a pattern of high crimes and misdemeanors.

This ethical responsibility slips so easily from our awareness. Even if treating others with full respect for their dignity is our goal and our custom, we face countless obstacles. Here is a small sample:

Diagnostic categories We work in a world in which most of us must manage the DSM, the ICD, insurance forms, and other forces that draw our attention to diagnostic categories and invite us to think of our patients in terms of which diagnostic labels apply. The powerful language of labels can distort or blot out completely the person behind the label. Some clinicians, particularly in inpatient and forensic settings, may stop using the patient's name entirely and use only the label, often in a way that seems to lack respect or dignity (e.g., "Time to see if that schizophrenic is ready for a home visit. You gotta be careful with schizos").

Financial concerns We also work in a world where most of us must pay the bills and many of us face financial pressures. If we are in independent practice, the gain or loss of one patient, particularly one who promptly pays our full fee, can mark the difference in whether we're in the red or black that month and whether we can pay the office rent and our other bills on time. When each patient fee can produce such an immediate powerful impact, it is hard not to have financial issues weighing on our mind as we decide whether this long-term patient is ready for termination or whether we're truly competent to work with that new patient we just screened.

Fatigue When we're tired, it's hard to pay full attention to our patients, to take in what they may be telling us between the lines of what they say, and to respond sensitively. When we're dragging through the day, it's easy to be short with others, to take things the wrong way, and to miss what's important.

Personal Predispositions, Preferences, and Prejudices We all have them — certain things we like and, of course, dislike about other people. Each of us could get a good start on our own private list of negative reactions by completing the following sentences as many ways as possible with complete honesty and without censoring ourselves:

- I can't stand it when someone...
- I'd rather not be around someone who...
- The worst kind of person is someone who...
- The people who are responsible for more trouble in the world than anyone else are the...
- The kind of person I'd least like to be seated next to on a long car trip is...
- It's not politically correct to say it, but personally...

Our personal list may include negative emotional reactions evoked solely by someone's membership in certain categories based on

- Religion
- Politics
- Race
- Skin color
- Ethnic group
- Weight
- Intelligence
- Education
- Mental health status or disorder
- Country of origin or current citizenship
- Income (or lack of it)
- Occupation
- Physical ability or disability
- Mental ability or disability
- Sexual orientation
- Gender identity
- Speech (e.g., whether the person makes grammatical errors, uses slang unfamiliar to us, speaks our language with an accent)

- ○ Age (e.g., someone who is very old)
- ○ Dress
- ○ Personal hygiene

These negative emotional reactions based solely on such categories have the potential to choke off our respect for the dignity of that person.

This chapter is a reminder that treating others with respect for their dignity is a basic ethic of our profession, one easily overlooked but facing countless challenges. None of us is perfect in this area. All of us will fall short more than once over the course of a career: It will suddenly strike us that we've been sitting with a patient for most of a therapy session and for most of that time our mind has been elsewhere; we'll breathe a deep sigh of relief as we terminate a patient, realizing that we never liked the person, never invested much in the therapy, and feel joy that we're rid of that person; a patient will say something that somehow breaks through our shell and we'll discover that some time ago we'd lost our sense of shared humanity with someone who'd started to seem like a stranger. The Golden Rule is useful here, no less so for being a cliché: We must strive to treat our patients and others with the same respect for their dignity that wish to receive from others.

Chapter 4

AVOIDING PSEUDOSCIENCE, FADS, AND ACADEMIC URBAN LEGENDS

The art of psychotherapy uses the tools of science to guide us toward interventions most likely to help a particular person and away from interventions that are harmful, too risky, or a waste of time. A fundamental psychotherapy ethic is to keep our work grounded in current science. The APA code emphasizes, "Psychologists' work is based upon established scientific and professional knowledge of the discipline" (APA, 2010a, section 2.04). The 2015 draft of the 4th edition of the CPA code reminds us that psychologists "keep themselves up to date with a broad range of relevant knowledge, research methods, techniques, and technologies and their impact on individuals and groups (e.g., couples, families, organizations, communities and peoples), through the reading of relevant literature, peer consultation, and continuing education activities, in order that their practice, teaching and research activities will benefit and not harm others" (CPA, 2015, Section II.9).

Staying abreast of the current science is no easy task. The challenges are daunting. Our knowledge can die a quick death at the hands of new research that disproves what we thought was true, guides new interpretations that replace misunderstandings, and reveals better ways of helping people. Our field's wealth of journals, each constantly releasing new articles, contributes to this rapid rate of change in the state of the art and science. Almost a half century ago Dubin (1972) noted that the "outpouring of publications [in psychology] creates an obsolescence situation of staggering proportions" (p. 487),

22

estimated that the half-life of what psychologists know at any given time is around 10 to 12 years, and recommended that about 20% of a professional's time should focus on updating. (We will pause here until most therapists finish laughing. We'll also answer the question that may have popped into readers' minds: No, Dubin's article did not tell therapists where they could find the extra time in their schedules to do this updating.)

As the field continues to grow, research increases, new journals sprout, and the half-life of knowledge in our field continues to shrink. Neimeyer, Taylor, and Rozensky (2012), for example, reported a Delphi Poll suggesting that "the expected half-life of knowledge in professional psychology was expected to shrink from its current level of 8.80 years to 7.07 years within the next 10 years. This represents a predicted 20% decrease over the course of the next decade" (p. 368). A follow-up study found the overall durability of knowledge across all areas within specialties in professional psychology to vary from a high of 18.37 years (psychoanalysis) to a low of 7.58 years (clinical health psychology) with the overall durability of knowledge across all areas being 8.68 years (Neimeyer, Taylor, Rozensky, & Cox, 2014).

We face another challenge in the increasing tendency of theories to avoid adequate testing against other theories that might better explain the data. Bruce Bower (2013) wrote:

> In its idealized form, science resembles a championship boxing match. Theories square off.... Under the stern eyes of a host of referees, one theory triumphs by best explaining available evidence — at least until the next bout. But in the real world, science sometimes works more like a fashion show. Researchers clothe plausible explanations of experimental findings in glittery statistical suits and gowns. These gussied-up hypotheses charm journal editors and attract media coverage with carefully orchestrated runway struts, never having to battle competitors.

It is not just that we often get the first word — often making a lasting impact — of new "findings" from press releases, newspaper articles (which may quote only supporters), and television segments. Researchers tend to avoid competing theories, focusing closely on experimental data and statistical tests of their own favored theory. Walter Mischel (2008) referred to this tendency as the *toothbrush problem*: "Psychologists treat other peoples' theories like toothbrushes — no self-respecting person wants to use anyone else's.... Even the structure of our disciplines and sub-disciplines, rooted in what made sense a century ago when psychology departments formed, feed the toothbrush drive and undermine current efforts to build a cumulative psychological science."

Fiedler, Kutzner, and Kutzner (2012) noted our field's unfortunate emphasis on "statistical tests of causal models (while ignoring alternative theoretical models)" (p. 664). They cite the story of Clever Hans, a horse that had repeatedly demonstrated in various tests an apparent ability to perform mathematical calculations:

> Even the most compelling evidence (large n, small α) that the horse named Hans provided correct responses to calculation tasks could not prove that the horse could do math in its head. The genius of Oskar Pfungst (Pfungst, Stumpf, & Rahn, 1911) was to consider β errors. He tested Hans under novel conditions (e.g., varying the testers' body language) that others — among them famed psychologist Carl Stumpf — had not dreamed of as being relevant. (p. 664)

Another challenge sounds like an old time horror movie title: *The Myth That Will Not Die!* Some theories, studies, and approaches that have been discredited continue to live on and mislead us. We meet these myths in secondary sources, lectures, and expert testimony. Olio and Cornell (1998) described these as *academic urban legends*. They provided detailed documentation to demonstrate how an "imperfect narrative . . . and pseudoscientific conclusions have been uncritically accepted and repeated in the literature, thus becoming an academic version of an urban legend" (p. 1195). Rekdal (2014) subsequently described what happened when these hardy academic urban legends met the Internet and computerized databases:

> The digital revolution has certainly made it easier to expose and debunk myths, but it has also created opportunities for new and remarkably efficient academic shortcuts, highly attractive and tempting not just in milieus characterized by increasing publication pressure and more concerned with quantity than quality, but also for groups and individuals strongly involved in rhetorics of demarcation of science, but less concerned with following the scientific principles they claim to defend. Some academic urban legends may perish in the new digital academic environment, but others will thrive and have ideal conditions for explosive growth. (p. 651)

Many of these myths not only survive repeated debunking but continue to thrive. Lilienfeld, Marshall, Todd, and Shane (2014) note that "repeatedly stating that a claim is incorrect can, paradoxically, generate a 'familiarity backfire effect,' whereby the claim comes to be accepted as true merely because it has been heard many times."

An active approach helps ground us in the current science — actively seeking out new theory, research, and practices relevant to our work; actively reading and listening to critics of our own current beliefs and practices; actively questioning new claims (Pope, 1996, 1997, 1998).

Open, active, constant questioning of all new claims is as important as seeking them out. "Uncritical acceptance of scientific claims may be as damaging as reflexive rejection. Science, policy, and education suffer when the vigorous authoritative promotion of claims fails to meet vigorous critical examination" (Pope, 1996, p. 957). Some claims flourish free of rigorous questioning because they enjoy the support of prevailing scientific paradigms, historical contexts, authoritative sponsors, and the bandwagon effect (Mednick, 1989; Pope, 1996, 1997, 1998). Making sure no claims we encounter escape critical evaluation can begin by asking the basic questions we learned in graduate school for each new study. Here are a few examples:

- How many participants? Were there enough for the statistical power of the inferential statistics?
- How were the participants selected? A random sample? A sample of convenience? A call for volunteers posted on the Internet? A call for volunteers in an undergraduate introductory psychology course?
- How representative were the participants for the particular study? For the study's stated purposes, conclusions, and claims were there any limitations or potential biasing factors such as age, gender, race, ethnicity, culture, background, language, sexual orientation, or physical or mental abilities and disabilities?
- Did the study do a good job of exploring potential confounding factors? Were the factors identified, discussed, and taken account of in the design and inferences drawn from the study? Can you think of any that might have been missed?
- Did the interpretation of the results mistake correlation for causation? Few cautions are so well-known in our field and yet it is surprising how often this confusion sneaks into the conclusions we draw.
- Could the study's funding or sponsorship have played an unfortunate role in framing the hypotheses, choosing measures or comparison groups, selecting the statistical tests, or reporting the results? For example, meta-analyses and other systematic reviews have found that drug studies that are sponsored by the drug's manufacturer are associated with significantly more favorable results for the sponsor's drug than drug studies that are independently sponsored (see, e.g., Bhandari et al., 2004; Flacco et al. 2015; Kelly et al., 2006; Krauth, Anglemyer, Philipps, & Bero, 2014; Lexchin, Bero, Djulbegovic, & Clark, 2003; Lundh, Sismondo, Lexchin, Busuioc, & Bero, 2012).

The next three chapters expand the discussion of critical thinking beyond this chapter's focus on research. Those chapters focus on three aspects of critical thinking we can use to strengthen our ethical intelligence: judgment ("Ethical Judgment Under Uncertainty and Pressure: Critical Thinking About Heuristics, Authorities, and Groups"), reasoning ("26 Logical Fallacies in Ethical Reasoning"), and language ("Using and Misusing Words to Reveal and Conceal").

Chapter 5

ETHICAL JUDGMENT UNDER UNCERTAINTY AND PRESSURE

Critical Thinking About Heuristics, Authorities, and Groups

The little-known club of ethically perfect therapists — those with errorless ethical judgment and fallacy-free ethical reasoning — is so exclusive that no one ever qualifies for membership.

Most of us know we're not cut out for that club. We accept the obvious: We all have weaknesses. We fail to see something in our ethical blind spots. We misjudge how an ethical principle applies to a specific situation. We rush past a red flag. Our ethical reasoning adds 2 plus 2 and comes up with 4,938. It happens to all of us from time to time.

We have weaknesses, but we can work to strengthen them. One good place to start is how we think about ethics. The more we notice how we think about ethics, the more we can think critically about our own ethical judgment, reasoning, language, and justifications. As we work to spot and understand patterns of ethical thinking that tug us off course, we discover we are thinking more clearly and gaining the skill to pull ourselves back from common missteps. As psychologist and Nobel Prize for Economics recipient Daniel Kahneman (2011) put it: "The proof that you truly understand a pattern of behavior is that you know how to reverse it" (p. 133). This is the first of four chapters focusing on facets of critical thinking: judgment, reasoning, language, and justifications.

Ethics requires judgment. We confront ethical challenges that are rarely simple, obvious, and easy. Subtle ethical issues sneak by unnoticed. Ethical crises appear in a clash of competing needs, expectations, and values. Scarce time and resources narrow our options. No one can effectively apply the principles in the ethics code or other sources of guidance to real-life situations in an automatic, unthinking, or rote manner. There is no paint-by-numbers approach that works. This chapter explores five factors that can draw our ethical judgment off track: cognitive commitments, authorities, groups, WYSIATI (What You See Is All There Is), and imaginative illusions.

COGNITIVE COMMITMENTS

New theories, methods, or interventions that challenge dogma, people in power, or "the way we've always done it" can run into resistance, ridicule, and minds shut tight. Barbara McClintock knew what that was like. A distinguished scientist, she discovered genetic transposition ("jumping genes"), a stunning advance that earned her dismissive ridicule and ostracism from colleagues for two decades. When others finally caught up with her and began to grasp the brilliance of her discovery, she described what she had lived through at the banquet when she accepted the 1983 Nobel Prize for Physiology or Medicine:

> [My work] revealed a genetic phenomenon that was totally at odds with the dogma of the times, the mid-nineteen forties. Recently, with the general acceptance of this phenomenon, I have been asked...just how I felt during the long period when my work was ignored, dismissed, or aroused frustration.... [My theory] was much too radical for the time.... [During those years] I was not invited to give lectures or seminars, except on rare occasions, or to serve on committees or panels, or to perform other scientists' duties. ("Barbara McClintock — Banquet Speech," 1983)

History furnishes all too many examples of those labeled lightweights, fools, fanatics, true believers, pseudoscientists, quacks, frauds, or heretics: Galileo Galilei, Muhammad ibn Zakariya al-Razi, Ruth Sager, Ignaz Semmelweis, to name but a few (for additional information and examples, see Hajdu, 2007; Kohlstedt, 2004; Reynolds, 2004; Solon, 2012). We admire these brave souls; at least once the rest of us have caught up to them we see what their commitment to an unpopular idea has cost them. Their unwavering loyalty to what they believe to be true, their persistence in looking for evidence to support their vision, and their determination to hold onto their belief despite the resistance it arouses inspire us.

But this commitment to an approach, theory, or idea can throw our judgment off course in two major ways: by falling prey to either the logical mistake of affirming the consequent or the inferential mistake of confirmation bias.

The logical fallacy of affirming the consequent, which will be discussed in the following chapter, "26 Common Logical Fallacies in Ethical Reasoning," invites us to assume that *because* our idea evokes resistance, ridicule, or refutation, we must be on the right track. Then we come up with reasons for the opposition: Our idea is too radical for those rooted in the status quo, too brilliant for our contemporaries, too threatening to those in power. Carl Sagan defused this kind of fallacy: "The fact that some geniuses were laughed at does not imply that all who are laughed at are geniuses . . . . They laughed at Fulton, they laughed at the Wright brothers. But they also laughed at Bozo the Clown" (1979, p. 64).

For a good description of the biased judgment that can be caused by cognitive commitment, we turn first to Francis Bacon, who wrote in 1620:

> The human understanding when it has once adopted an opinion . . . draws all things else to support and agree with it. And though there be a greater number and weight of instances to be found on the other side, yet these it either neglects or despises, or else by some distinction sets aside and rejects . . . . This mischief insinuate[s] itself into philosophy and the sciences; in which the first conclusion colors and brings into conformity with itself all that come after. (1955, p. 472)

Evans (1989) noted that "confirmation bias is perhaps the best known and most widely accepted notion of inferential error." The notion "is that human beings have a fundamental tendency to seek information consistent with their current beliefs, theories or hypotheses and to avoid the collection of potentially falsifying evidence" (p. 41).

Cognitive and social psychology have explored how this influence takes different forms. Kurt Lewin (1976; see also Gold, 1999) examined how committing to a decision often seems to freeze the mind, hardening it against reconsideration. Ellen Langer (1989), summarizing the research she and her colleagues had conducted (e.g., Chanowitz & Langer, 1981), described the common process of

> forming a mindset when we first encounter something and then clinging to it when we reencounter that same thing. Because such mindsets form before we do much reflection, we call them premature cognitive commitments . . . . The mindless individual is committed to one predetermined use of the information, and other possible uses are not explored. (p. 22)

Leon Festinger's experiments focused on how commitment to an approach, theory, or idea leads to a screening out of any information that would lead to cognitive dissonance. The commitment means that there would be "less emphasis on objectivity and there is more partiality and bias in the way in which the person views and evaluates the alternatives" (1964, p. 155; see also de Vries, Byrne, & Kehoe, 2015; Frey & Schulz-Hardt, 2001; Guazzini, Yoneki, & Gronchi, 2015; C. Hill, Memon, & McGeorge, 2008; Munro &

Stansbury, 2009; Stice, Rohde, Butryn, Menke, & Marti, 2015; Tschan et al., 2009).

Our vulnerability to this bias creates a responsibility to question our own views, whether snap judgments or long-held beliefs. We can balance our loyalty to our judgments if we search relentlessly for facts that do not fit, listen openly to those who disagree, and constantly ask ourselves what the other possibilities are. Otherwise we can end up clinging so tightly to our ethical certainties that we do not notice contradictory information, better possibilities, and the consequences of our own missteps. Once again, Carl Sagan (1991) offers sound advice, recommending

> an exquisite balance between . . . skeptical scrutiny of all hypotheses that are served up to us and . . . great openness to new ideas . . . . If you are only skeptical, then no new ideas make it through to you . . . . If you are open to the point of gullibility and have not an ounce of skeptical sense . . . , then you cannot distinguish the useful ideas from the worthless ones. (pp. 4–5)

AUTHORITIES

When puzzling over an ethical dilemma, we often turn to authorities. The law, a supervisor, and the ethics code can provide invaluable help. We misuse these resources, however, if we use them to short-circuit our ethical judgment. We cannot avoid an ethical struggle by focusing only on the law and claiming, "It violates no law [or the law requires it] so it must be ethical." We cannot shrug off ethical responsibility by explaining that we were just following what our supervisor told us to do. We cannot hide behind ethics codes as refuge from an active, creative search for the most ethical response. Although authorities play countless constructive roles in our society, the psychological literature — not to mention history itself — shows the dangers of overreliance on and unquestioning obedience to authority (see, for example, Darley, 1995; Ent & Baumeister, 2014, 2015; Haslam, Loughnan, & Perry, 2014; Meeus & Raaijmakers, 1986, 1995; Staub, 2014).

Awareness of ethics codes, laws, and professional guidelines is crucial to competence in the area of ethics. These documents prompt, guide, and inform our ethical consideration. They do not take the place of our thoughtful consideration. We can apply them effectively in a rote, thoughtless manner. Each new client, whatever his or her similarities to previous clients, is a unique individual. Each situation also is unique and is likely to change significantly over time. Authoritative documents may prohibit some acts as clearly unethical. They may call our attention to ethical concerns in different areas of practice, but they cannot tell us how these concerns will manifest themselves in a particular clinical situation. They may set forth essential tasks that we must fulfill, but they cannot tell us how we can accomplish these tasks with a unique client facing unique problems. We cannot hide from these struggles.

GROUPS

Like authorities, groups are a valuable resource. They can provide support, diverse views, the opportunity to work together on an ethical dilemma, and relief from the sense of isolation. But—like authorities—certain group processes can work to block sound ethical judgment. We get ourselves into trouble when we allow groups to shield us from ethical struggles and the sense of ethical responsibility.

Psychologist Paul Meehl (1977) wrote a fascinating essay we recommend to all of this book's readers—"Why I Do Not Attend Case Conferences." He pointed out the "groupthink process" (p. 228) that discourages sound judgment and may be familiar to all of us:

> In one respect the clinical case conference is no different from other academic group phenomena such as committee meetings, in that many intelligent, educated, sane, rational persons seem to undergo a kind of intellectual deterioration when they gather around a table in one room. (p. 227)

Psychologist Irving Janis (1972) studied ways in which groupthink clouds our judgment. Janis and Mann (1977, pp. 130–131) identified the eight symptoms of groupthink, adapted next, to emphasize their effects on ethical judgment:

1. An illusion of invulnerability, shared by most or all members, which creates excessive optimism and encourages taking extreme risks
2. Collective efforts to rationalize in order to discount warnings
3. An unquestioned belief in the group's inherent high ethics, leading members to underestimate their ethical responsibilities or the negative consequences of their behavior
4. Stereotyped views of those who disagree about ethical issues, encouraging group members to disparage the motives, intelligence, heart, or good faith of those who disagree with the group's views
5. Pressure on any group member who dissents or raises serious questions about the group's views or behavior
6. Self-stifling of deviations from the group's approach; an inclination of each member to deny, discount, or minimize doubts or counterarguments
7. The illusion of virtual unanimity, created by self-stifling and assuming that silence means consent
8. Some members taking on the role of "mindguard[s]—members who protect the group from adverse information that might shatter their shared complacency about the effectiveness and morality of their decisions."

In addition, we tend to form groups in a we/they dichotomy, which leads to a subconscious (and sometimes conscious) automatic categorization of people in our *in-groups*, those with whom we identify, and our *out-groups*, those whom we see as being outside our realm of identification. People in our in-groups are more highly valued, more trusted, and engender greater cooperation as opposed to competition. We have more compassion for those in our in-group than those in our out-group and are more likely to endorse and support those in this category. On the other hand, people in our out-groups are implicitly conceptualized as "they." We often tend to treat out-group members in negative ways (Cikara, Bruneau, Van Bavel, & Saxe, 2014; Dovidio & Gaertner, 2010; Gilead & Liberman, 2014; Ito, 2013; Opotow, 1990, 1995, 2005, 2012).

These in-group/out-group dynamics can have unfortunate effects on the way we welcome and provide psychological services to members we've placed in the out-group category. They also affect how we behave toward our colleagues and new ideas that might lead us to change our mind, even when in- and out-groups are defined by disagreements over ideas. Psychologist Steven Pinker (2006) wrote:

> People have a nasty habit of clustering in coalitions, professing certain beliefs as badges of their commitment to the coalition and treating rival coalitions as intellectually unfit and morally depraved. Debates between members of the coalitions can make things even worse, because when the other side fails to capitulate to one's devastating arguments, it only proves they are immune to reason.... New ideas, nuanced ideas, hybrid ideas — and sometimes dangerous ideas — often have trouble getting a hearing against these group-bonding convictions.

WYSIATI

In his foreword to the second edition of *What Therapists Don't Talk About and Why: Understanding Taboos That Hurt Us and Our Clients* (Pope, Sonne, & Greene, 2006), former American Psychological Association president Gerry Koocher tells of a fascinating public confession he sometimes makes:

> On occasion, I tell my students and professional audiences that I once spent an entire psychotherapy session holding hands with a 26-year-old woman together in a quiet darkened room. That disclosure usually elicits more than a few gasps and grimaces. When I add that I could not bring myself to end the session after 50 minutes and stayed with the young woman holding hands for another half hour, and when I add the fact that I never billed for the extra time, eyes roll. (p. xxii)

It is easy to understand why most listeners are both shocked and critical. A prominent ethicist and former APA president is describing what seems clearly to be his mishandling of a sexualized relationship with a patient. But he is not really making a confession. He's illustrating how easily we make false judgments under uncertainty when we do not know the whole story but assume that we do.

Koocher fills in some of the missing information:

> Then I explain that the young woman had cystic fibrosis with severe pulmonary disease and panic-inducing air hunger. She had to struggle through three breaths on an oxygen line before she could speak a sentence. I had come into her room, sat down by her bedside, and asked how I might help her. She grabbed my hand and said, "Don't let go." When the time came for another appointment, I called a nurse to take my place. (p. xxii)

The missing facts lead us to very different judgments about the clinician's behavior and what is actually going on in that quiet, darkened room.

As therapists, we are constantly called on to make judgments without access to complete information. We can't duck our responsibility to step up and provide knowledgeable and competent help, especially in emergencies. We do the best we can, knowing that in some situations we cannot know all the relevant information. The critical misjudgment springs up when we lose awareness that we do not have all the facts.

Daniel Kahneman (2011) described this mistake as belief in WYSIATI: What You See Is All There Is. We all face this hazard as we make judgments under uncertainty and time pressures based on sometimes necessarily incomplete information. Confirmation bias can harden our WYSIATI misjudgments into confidently held certainties that find their way into patient charts, treatment plans, disability evaluations, pre-employment assessments, and courtroom testimony and legal opinions. These certainties screen out or reshape everything the patient says or does that does not fit the misjudgment.

Our judgment that a colleague's behavior violates ethical standards might change if we did not assume that WYSIATI. We might revise our WYSIATI interpretation of an IQ score and report of psychological assessment involving standardized instruments if we knew that the man had forgotten to take his meds or bring his glasses, that a woman had been threatened by an abusive partner the night before and was afraid he'd show up when she left the assessment, or that a child had been up all night because his parents were fighting and he'd had no breakfast before the testing — but the person conducting the assessment had not been aware of these factors, had neglected to ask, and had not mentioned any of them in the assessment report. Perhaps we remember doing things that might seem highly questionable, wrong, or outrageous to others if they did not know the whole story.

IMAGINATIVE ILLUSIONS

Our imagination is an invaluable resource. We can imagine different ways to apply ethical principles to a specific situation and what the likely outcomes might be. We can use imagination to place ourselves, however partially and imperfectly, in the shoes of a supervisee or colleague who did not handle an ethical issue the way (we think) we would. We can imagine how different software and hardware combinations for handling appointments, billing, and clinical records would protect against data breaches of confidential information when fully installed and running full time month after month in our practice setting, what might go wrong with each, and whether there is a reliable fix for potential problems.

We open ourselves for trouble when we forget that our imagination and the judgments it shapes are prone to common forms of bias. Here are a few:

Hindsight Bias

Also known as "Monday morning quarterbacking" or "I knew it all along," hindsight bias is our tendency to imagine, once we know how an event turned out, that we would have much better predictions than we actually would have had we not known the outcome (Arkes, Faust, Guilmette, & Hart, 1988; Fischhoff, 1975; Fischhoff & Beyth, 1975; Kahneman, 2011; Wood, 1978). Perhaps we are members of a hospital peer review committee, an ethics committee, or an expert witness considering a colleague's choice when faced with an ethical dilemma. If we know that the choice ended in disaster, we might imagine that we ourselves would've chosen more wisely another course had we faced the same dilemma. Imagining that the colleague lacks the sound judgment that we would've used in that situation may have unfortunate consequences for judging our poor colleague's choice.

Correspondence Bias

Also called the fundamental attribution error (Ross, 1977), correspondence bias leads us to downplay or ignore entirely situational influences when judging someone else's behavior, imagining the behavior to be caused by the individual's personality, attitudes, or character, while often attributing our own less-than-admirable behaviors to the situation, a bias that tends to be more prevalent in Western countries (Bauman & Skitka, 2010; Blanchard-Fields, Chen, Horhota, & Wang, 2007; E. E. Jones, 1979; Ross & Nisbett, 2011; Stockus & Walter, 2015). We cut an ethical corner because we were under a lot of pressure, in a hurry, or sleep deprived; other people do the same thing because they are dishonest, basically unethical, or lack integrity.

False Consensus

Also called egocentric bias, false consensus bias is our tendency to imagine that other people are more like us than they really are, and that our behaviors are more appropriate and more common than alternate behaviors (Mullen et al., 1985; Ross, Greene, & House, 1977; Windschitl, Bruchmann, Scherer, & McEvoy, 2013). Our vulnerability to this bias underscores the importance of checking carefully with patients during the informed consent process to make sure we are not assuming that they share our assumptions, our values, and our preferences. It highlights the importance of consultation that can strengthen our awareness of how our imagination is leading us toward biased judgments. It shows how "everybody does it" and similar spins on ethically questionable decisions deserve careful scrutiny.

Status Quo Bias

A bias toward the status quo often tends to run through our judgments and decision making (Kahneman, Knetsch, & Thaler, 1991; Nebel, 2015; Proudfoot & Kay, 2014). This bias makes it hard for us to give weight to ethical choices that will force major changes in our lives or, once we make such a choice, to follow through on it. Familiarity, habits, a resistance to change, and "the way we've always done it" can, under some circumstances, be powerful enemies of clear thinking. This tendency to stick with the way things are now may join forces with related common tendency in making judgments and decisions: omission bias.

Omission Bias

If two of our options cause equally terrible outcomes and if one involves doing something and the other involves doing nothing, we have a tendency to gravitate toward the one that involves inaction and view ourselves as less responsible for the terrible outcome (E. K. Chung, Kim, & Sohn, 2014; Spranca, Minsk, & Baron, 1991). Sins of omission often seem less culpable than sins of commission, even when they lead to identical outcomes. In our imagination, the active doing of something seems more causally related to the bad outcome than our doing nothing whatsoever.

Optimistic Bias

Daniel Kahneman (2011) wrote that "in terms of its consequences for decisions, the optimistic bias may well be the most significant of the cognitive biases" (p. 255). We have a tendency to believe that our decisions carry less risk than they actually do, that our judgments and decisions are more likely to be borne out than is justified, that options and opportunities are more favorable than an objective assessment warrants. When we fall prey to the *planning fallacy*, a result of optimistic bias, we imagine that we will accomplish our plans more easily, more quickly, more successfully than they will likely work out. Of course, that is if they *do* work out. Optimistic bias makes it hard to imagine that we will meet any obstacles, encounter delays, get distracted, or tire out.

Narrative Bias

Narrative bias leads us to construct or believe narratives that explain why events happen by oversimplifying and overinterpreting. Nassim Taleb (2010) writes:

> The narrative fallacy addresses our limited ability to look at sequences of facts without weaving an explanation into them, or, equivalently, forcing a logical link, an *arrow of relationship*, upon them. Explanations bind facts together. They make them all the more easily remembered; they help them *make more sense*. Where this propensity can go wrong is when it increases our *impression of understanding*. (p. 43; italics in original)

Many other factors such as anchoring, availability, halo effects, outcome bias, past experience, and representativeness, to name but a few, can of course distort our ethical judgment and decision making. We recommend Bushyhead and Christensen-Szalanski (1980); Connolly, Arkes, and Hammond (2000); Gilovich, Griffin, and Kahneman (2002); Kahneman (2011); Kahneman and Klein (2009); Kane & Webster (2013); Rosenzweig (2014); Taleb (2010); Taleb and Blyth (2011); and Tversky and Kahneman (1974) as wonderful resources for those wishing to learn more in this area.

We can strengthen our ethical decision making if we remain aware that these factors can sometimes serve us well but other times sweep us off course in our inferences. Errors in ethical reasoning, the focus of the next chapter, can also send us in the wrong direction.

Chapter 6

26 LOGICAL FALLACIES IN ETHICAL REASONING*

L ogical fallacies sneak up in camouflage. They slide into the background and blend in with some of our best reasoning. They fool us with misdirection. We fall for their dazzling demonstrations that adding apples and oranges equals somewhere in the neighborhood of green beans.

Here are 26 logical fallacies — with a brief description and example of each — that can send ethical reasoning off track. No one is magically immune to them. They trip up all of us at one time or another.

1. AD HOC RATIONALIZATION

In this fallacy, an explanatory factor, condition, or reason is set forth without validity to counter a specific objection or argument in order to defend one's original assertion, hypothesis, findings, or conclusion.

Example

In the following example, Dr. A uses ad hoc rationalization when questioned by Dr. B:

> Dr A: My paper-and-pencil test of intelligence is better than any of the others.
> Dr B: But in that recent study, it showed no reliability or validity.

* This chapter is adapted from "Common Logical Fallacies in Psychology: 26 Types & Examples" by Kenneth S. Pope, Ph.D., ABPP. [© copyright K.S. Pope, 2003, 2010, 2012, 2014]. It is available online at http://kspope.com/fallacies/fallacies.php.

Dr A: I'm sure they scored it incorrectly.

Dr B: They brought in two other teams to make sure the scoring was done correctly.

Dr A: The researcher was probably one of my rivals, someone who wanted to do me in.

Dr B: Actually, it's your best friend who has been your biggest supporter for decades.

Dr A: Well, no wonder! He had to lean over backward to make my test look bad so that he wouldn't be accused of favoritism!

2. AD HOMINEM OR AD FEMINAM

The argumentum ad hominem or ad feminam attempts to discredit an argument or position by drawing attention to characteristics of the person who is making the argument or who holds the position.

Example

"The research and reasoning that supposedly supports [or that supposedly discredits] this intervention are a joke. The researchers are people who are not methodologically sophisticated and there have been rumors — I have no idea whether they're true or not — that they faked some of the data. The advocates [or opponents] of this intervention are the worst kind of sloppy thinkers. They are fanatical adherents who already have their minds made up; they've become true believers in their cause. They make arguments only a stupid person would accept, and mistakes in reasoning that would make an undergrad psych major blush. These are not the kind of people who deserve to be taken seriously."

3. AFFIRMING THE CONSEQUENT

This fallacy takes the form of

If x, then y.
y.
Therefore, x.

Example

"People who are psychotic act in a bizarre manner. This person acts in a bizarre manner. Therefore, this person is psychotic."

Alternate example: "If this client is competent to stand trial, she will certainly know the answers to at least 80% of the questions on this standardized test. She knows the answers to 87% of the test questions. Therefore, she is competent to stand trial."

4. APPEAL TO IGNORANCE (AD IGNORANTIUM)

The appeal to ignorance fallacy takes the form of

There is no (or insufficient) evidence establishing that x is false. Therefore, x is true.

Example

"In the 6 years that I have been practicing my new and improved brand of cognitive-humanistic-dynamic-behavioral-deconstructive-metaregressive-deontological psychotherapy (now with biofeedback!), which I developed, there has not been one published study showing that it fails to work or that it has ever harmed a patient. It is clearly one of the safest and most effective interventions ever devised."

5. ARGUMENT TO LOGIC (ARGUMENTUM AD LOGICAM)

The argument to logic fallacy takes the form of assuming that a proposition must be false because an argument offered in support of that proposition was fallacious.

Example

"This new test seemed so promising, but the three studies that supported its validity turned out to have critical methodological flaws, so the test is probably not valid."

6. BEGGING THE QUESTION (PETITIO PRINCIPII)

This fallacy, one of the fallacies of circularity, takes the form of arguments or other statements that simply assume or restate their own truth rather than providing relevant evidence and logical arguments.

Example

Sometimes this fallacy literally takes the form of a question, such as, "Has your psychology department stopped teaching that ineffective approach to therapy yet?" (The question assumes — and a "yes" or "no" response to the question affirms — that the approach is ineffective.) Or: "Why must you always take positions that are so unscientific?" (The question assumes that all of the person's positions are unscientific.) Sometimes this fallacy takes the form of a statement such as "No one can deny that [my theoretical orientation] is the only valid theoretical orientation" or "It must be acknowledged that [whatever psychological test battery I use] is the only legitimate test battery." Sometimes it takes the form of a logical argument, such as, "My new method of conducting meta-analyses is the most valid there is because it is the only one capable of such validity, the only one that has ever approached such validity, and the only one that is so completely valid."

7. COMPOSITION FALLACY

This fallacy takes the form of assuming that a group possesses the characteristics of its individual members.

Example

"Several years ago, a group of 10 psychologists started a psychology training program. Each of those psychologists is efficient, effective, and highly regarded. Their training program must be efficient, effective, and highly regarded."

8. DENYING THE ANTECEDENT

This fallacy takes the form of

> If x, then y.
> Not x.
> Therefore, not y.

Example

"If this test were based on fraudulent norms, then it would be invalid. But the norms are not fraudulent. Therefore, this test is valid."

9. DISJUNCTIVE FALLACY

This fallacy takes the form of

> Either x or y.
> x.
> Therefore, not y.

Example

"These test results are clearly wrong, and it must be either because the client was malingering or because I bungled the test administration. Taking another look at the test manual, I see now that I bungled the test administration. Therefore, the client was not malingering."

10. DIVISION FALLACY

The division fallacy or decomposition fallacy takes the form of assuming that the members of a group possess the characteristics of the group.

Example

"This clinic sure makes a lot of money. Each of the psychologists who work there must earn a large income."

11. EXISTENTIAL FALLACY

The existential fallacy begins with two universal premises and draws a specific conclusion from them. The two premises may be true, but that does not logically establish the existence of any members in the categories they represent.

Example

"I currently have as patients in my practice all the patients in this town who are willing and able to pay $5,000 per session for long-term twice-weekly therapy. If you buy my practice, all my clients will be included. Therefore, if you buy my practice you will then have at least some patients willing and able to pay $5,000 per session for long-term twice-weekly therapy."

12. FALSE ANALOGY

The false or faulty analogy fallacy takes the form of argument by analogy in which the comparison is misleading in at least one important aspect.

Example

"There were wonderful psychologists who passed away several decades ago. If they could be effective in what they did without reading any of the studies or other articles that have been published in the past several decades, there's no need for me to read any of those works in order to be effective."

13. FALSE CONTINUUM

In this fallacy, the absence of a clear, definitive marker separating a continuum into two mutually exclusive groups proves that there is no difference between the two extremes on the continuum.

Example

"In many cases you can't really tell whether patients are improving because of what the therapist is doing or because of the placebo effect — there's a fuzzy line separating the two — so we must conclude that they are actually the same mechanism of improvement."

14. FALSE DILEMMA

Also known as the either/or fallacy or the fallacy of false choices, this fallacy takes the form of acknowledging only two (one of which is usually extreme) options from a continuum or other array of possibilities.

Example

"Either we accept the findings of this study demonstrating that this new intervention is the best to be used for this disorder, or we must no longer call ourselves scientists, psychologists, or reasonable people."

15. FALSE EQUIVALENCE

In this fallacy, the fact that two items share a characteristic or are linked by some similarity demonstrates that they are equivalent.

Example

"Most of my testimony about the defendant was the opposite of what I actually believe but I'll bet there are no expert witnesses who have always told the truth from the time they were old enough to talk, so I'm no less honest than they are."

16. GENETIC FALLACY

In this fallacy, whether a proposition is true or false is deduced or inferred from the proposition's origin.

Example

"This theory originally occurred to a scientist in the form of a dream; therefore it cannot be valid."

Example

"Since it was a deathbed confession, it must be true."

17. GOLDEN MEAN FALLACY

The fallacy of the Golden Mean (or fallacy of compromise, or fallacy of moderation) takes the form of assuming that the most valid conclusion is that which accepts the best compromise between two competing positions.

Example

"In our psychology department, half of the faculty believe that a behavioral approach is the only valid approach; the other half believe that the only valid approach is psychodynamic. Obviously, the most valid approach must be one that incorporates both behavioral and psychodynamic elements."

18. IGNORATIO ELENCHI

This fallacy takes the form of assuming that an argument, whether or not internally valid, proves a particular point when in fact it misses the point at issue.

Example

"There is zero doubt that she has the condition. She scored high on two separate diagnostic tests for it, and both tests have shown extremely high validity. That proves she has it."

Example

"I don't see how you can believe he is not guilty of that crime. He's a terrible person and I can prove it. In fact, several years ago he was convicted of that same kind of crime."

19. MISTAKING DEDUCTIVE VALIDITY FOR TRUTH

This fallacy takes the form of assuming that because an argument is a logical syllogism, the conclusion must be true. It ignores the possibility that the premises of the argument may be false.

Example

"I just read a book that proves that the book's author can do much better than any psychological test at finding out if someone is malingering. The book's author reviews the literature showing that no psychological test is perfect at identifying malingering. All have at least some false positives and false negatives. But the author has a new method of identifying malingerers. All he does is listen to the sound of their voice as they say a sentence or two. And he included in the book a chart showing that by using this method he has never been wrong in hundreds of cases. That proves his method is better than using psychological tests."

20. NATURALISTIC FALLACY

The naturalistic fallacy takes the form of logically deducing values (e.g., what is good, best, right, ethical, or moral) based only on statements of fact.

Example

"There is no intervention for victims of domestic violence that has more empirical support from controlled studies than this one. It is clear that this is the right way to address this problem and we should all be providing this therapy whenever victims of domestic violence come to us for help."

21. NOMINAL FALLACY

The nominal fallacy is the mistake of assuming that because we have given a name to something, we have explained it.

Example

> Therapist A: I just don't care about my patient anymore. I don't pay attention to what they say. I show up late for sessions. I don't care if they show up. I ask them if they'd rather we just use the session playing a game of tennis or sharing a cup of coffee. I don't keep records.
> Therapist B: You have a classic case of burnout!
> Therapist A: But why am I doing all these things?
> Therapist B: Because you're burned out.

22. POST HOC, ERGO PROPTER HOC (AFTER THIS, THEREFORE ON ACCOUNT OF THIS)

The post hoc, ergo propter hoc fallacy takes the form of confusing correlation with causation and concluding that because y follows x, then y must be a result of x.

Example

"My new sport psychology intervention works! I chose the player with the lowest batting average based on the last game from each of the teams in our amateur baseball league. Then I gave each of them my 5-minute intervention. And almost all of them improved their batting average in the next game!" (Note: This example may also involve the statistical phenomenon of regression to the mean.)

23. RED HERRING

This fallacy takes the form of introducing or focusing on irrelevant information with the specific intention of misleading the audience by distracting them from the valid evidence and reasoning. (It is this specific intention to mislead that sets it apart from the ignoratio elenchi fallacy.) It takes its name from the strategy of dragging a herring or other fish across the path to distract hounds and other tracking dogs and to throw them off the scent of whatever they were searching for.

Example

"Some of you have objected to the new test batteries that were purchased for our program, alleging that they have no demonstrable validity, were not adequately normed for the kind of clients we see, and are unusable for clients who are physically disabled. What you have conveniently failed to mention, however, is that they cost less than a third of the price for the other tests we had been using, are much easier to learn, and can be administered and scored in less than half the time of the tests we used to use."

24. SLIPPERY SLOPE (ALSO KNOWN AS THE CAMEL'S NOSE FALLACY)

The slippery slope fallacy is a form of the non causa pro causa (mistaking a non-cause as a cause) and the non sequitur (it does not follow), which claims (without proof) that A inevitably must cause B, and B can have no other outcome than C, and C is sufficient cause for D, and D must lead to E, and E must produce F, and so on, and because the last link in the supposedly causal chain is undesirable, therefore the first step is undesirable.

Example

"If the government allows psychologists to prescribe medications, there will be no basis to block them from obtaining competence and legal authority to conduct other traditionally medical procedures such as diagnosing minor skin irritations, treating a sprained ankle, setting a broken bone, and performing neurosurgery." Or: "Never reduce a fee for any patient for any reason or else you'll find yourself constantly reducing fees for everyone, everyone will take advantage of you, your patients will lose respect for you and for therapy, and you'll lose money and go bankrupt."

25. STRAW PERSON

The straw person — or straw man or straw woman — fallacy takes the form of mischaracterizing someone else's position in a way that makes it weaker, false, or ridiculous.

Example

"Those who believe in behavior modification obviously want to try to control everyone by subjecting them to rewards and punishments."

26. YOU TOO! (TU QUOQUE)

This fallacy takes the form of distracting attention from error or weakness by claiming that an opposing argument, person, or position has the same error or weakness.

Example

"I have been accused of using an ad hominem approach in trying to defend my research. But those who attack my research and me are also using ad hominem. And they started it!"

Chapter 7

USING AND MISUSING WORDS TO REVEAL AND CONCEAL

L anguage shapes the way we experience the world. What we call things matters. Critical thinking requires paying attention to the words we use to describe, communicate, and think. One friend darkens our day by telling us about a despicable unethical psychologist, a law breaker who had deprived a defendant of his right to a fair trial and showed no remorse. Another friend lifts our hearts by mentioning a psychologist so committed to her ethical values that she went to extraordinary lengths to "do no harm" to her client, even at great cost to herself. Both friends describe the same psychologist: a therapist who refused a court order — even though it meant spending time in jail and facing ethics and licensing complaints — to provide her therapy records to an attorney representing the client's husband in a criminal trial. The husband had threaten to kill the client and her children and the records contained information that might enable the husband to discover the current residence of the client and her children, the identities of mutual friends who had helped the woman escape to a place of refuge, the names of those who were providing the woman and her children with food and other resources until they could start a new life, and so on. As Rhoda Unger (1998) reminds us: "Description is always from someone's point of view and hence is always evaluative" (p. 140).

An executive director hesitates to fire therapists who helped found a clinic and stayed loyal through the lean years. Can she push these colleagues out the door and cut off their income just to make more money by hiring less qualified therapists for lower pay? She finds it easier when she throws a word blanket over what she does and the people she does it to. She can use language to block our view. She banishes words like *firing* and *colleagues* along with the names of the people who will disappear from the scene. Office memos mention a "multitude of unfortunate but inescapable factors necessitating a substantial but temporary reduction in force in order to maximize competitive preparedness and responsiveness in a volatile and challenging marketplace." Press releases hail an "innovative and state-of-the-art intervention and development strategy of providing maximum direction, safety, and assistance activity during the discrete transitional process steps associated with the temporary downsizing implementation phase and the arrangement of management-directed outplacement services." (This means the company has hired armed guards to escort each therapist out of the building, help carry any belongings, and make sure the therapist does not reenter the building.)

These descriptions hide what she is doing and the people she is doing it to. Language can deceive by design. It conceals, misdirects, and creates the verbal equivalent of optical illusions. But even when used with the best of intentions, careless or bloated language makes it hard to think clearly. Many of us have gone missing in professional articles, last seen slogging our way through a paragraph packed with professional jargon, clichés, and not-quite-right words.

In his classic essay, "Politics and the English Language," George Orwell (1946) rewrote a widely quoted biblical passage in what he called "modern English." Here's the original passage from Ecclesiastes (9:11) in the King James Bible:

> I returned and saw under the sun, that the race is not to the swift, nor the battle to the strong, neither yet bread to the wise, nor yet riches to men of understanding, nor yet favor to men of skill; but time and chance happeneth to them all.

See if Orwell's translation reminds you of any professional articles, lectures, or discussions: "Objective consideration of contemporary phenomena compels the conclusion that success or failure in competitive activities exhibits no tendency to be commensurate with innate capacity, but that a considerable element of the unpredictable must invariably be taken into account" (Orwell, 1946, p. 163).

Too often we lose sight of ethical issues as they disappear in clouds of clichés, jargon, deceptive words, and careless language. Reading more carefully strengthens our ethical intelligence, helping us to notice when words point our attention toward small details and rush us along, hoping we won't see the big picture. We read more thoughtfully, noticing when words push us to assume, accept, and conclude instead of stop and question.

This section looks at common language patterns that hide or confuse ethical issues, responsibilities, or consequences. We present the patterns in extreme form that makes them easier to recognize and remember. If we learn these basic patterns in simplified form, we can spot them more easily when they try to sneak by us in the busy rush of our day-to-day work.

Most of us will find it easy to remember seeing these patterns in the newspaper, on television, and during our professional meetings. What is much harder — but more useful — is to try to remember when we ourselves have fallen into these patterns.

Orwell emphasized how universal and persistent these word tricks are. He notes that they "are a continuous temptation, a packet of aspirin always at one's elbow. Look back through this essay, and for certain you will find that I have again and again committed the very faults I am protesting against" (1946, p. 168).

We start with Jack, our hypothetical therapist, who did something unethical, was caught and disciplined, knows what he did was wrong, is sorry, and wants to make a public statement to take responsibility and apologize. Here is what Jack did: He stole therapy records of the clinic's famous clients, altered them to make it look as if the clients had described lurid sexual activity to their therapists, and then sold the records to tabloids.

In his public statement, Jack says:

> I stole the patient files, added some lies to them, and sold them. I have no excuses or explanations. I am solely responsible. I knew it was wrong and would hurt innocent people who trusted the clinic, and I did it anyway because I wanted the money. I apologize to everyone, especially to those whom I've hurt. I will do whatever I can to try to make things right.

Here are some alternate statements that show common language patterns that can interfere with clear thinking about ethics. As in the prior section on logical fallacies, there is a brief description and example of each pattern.

SUBSTITUTE THE GENERAL FOR THE SPECIFIC

In this pattern, both the specific individual and the specific act disappear. A description of a general category of acts and a vague reference in the third person replace (and hide) the specifics. Jack might say: "I believe that everyone knows that taking a patient's file without the patient's permission and using it for some purpose for which it was not intended is wrong. Anyone who does something like that is out of line."

USE A CONDITIONAL FRAME FOR CONSEQUENCES

The speaker shifts the focus to the question of whether the acts affected anyone. The apology is made contingent on how others reacted or were affected. Example: "If my actions harmed, or even just offended, anyone — and I can well understand how that could happen — I apologize."

USE DENIED MOTIVATION AS MISDIRECTION

Instead of honestly stating the motivation, the speaker seeks self-exoneration by talking about what the motivation was not. Denying an irrelevant charge that no one has made can be an effective rhetorical tactic. The denials are often true. For example, the person who repeatedly embezzles pension funds, uses substandard materials to build high-rises, speeds while drunk, and stresses that he or she never meant to hurt anyone was probably not acting with the intention of making other people suffer. Example: "I can honestly say that at no time during these unfortunate events with the clinic records did I ever intend for anyone to be hurt."

USE THE ABSTRACT LANGUAGE OF TECHNICALITIES

The speaker translates people and events into abstractions, using the jargon of technicalities. Jack could say:

I know that many of you have heard rumors and you deserve to know what happened. I want to acknowledge publicly, in closing this unfortunate chapter, that I did not fulfill all requirements in the JCAHO [Joint Commission on Accreditation of Healthcare Organizations] manual for the handling of charts. There were instances in which I reviewed and added information without following all the bureaucratic specifications for identifying the source of additional material, and I did not always follow the precise procedures for obtaining informed consent for release of information in transferring these charts to individuals who lacked proper authorization to receive them. I regret my lack of attention to JCAHO and similar regulations, and I assure everyone that I will be reviewing those regulatory specifications and will make every attempt to conform to those guidelines in the future.

USE THE PASSIVE VOICE

The speaker disappears. Things are done without reference to who does them. Jack would say:

I know that all of you, like me, want to know the results of the extensive, no-holds-barred investigation that was conducted in the light of recent allegations. I have been authorized to provide you with a complete report of the findings. Regrettably, the investigation confirmed that some files were taken without authorization, were altered, and were provided to those who should not have received them. Both the policies of our own clinic and the regulations of external authorities were violated. We wish to assure everyone that appropriate actions will be taken so that the problems will be addressed. Relevant steps have already been taken toward remedying this situation.

MAKE UNIMPORTANT BY CONTRASTING WITH WHAT DID NOT OCCUR

The speaker anchors the presentation in scenarios of extreme consequences that did not occur. The contrast makes whatever may have happened seem trivial. Here is Jack's statement:

> All of us have been concerned about the effects of recent events. As you know, allegations led to thorough investigations by several agencies. These investigations are now concluded. Let me assure you that regardless of what you may have heard, no patient died or even suffered any physical injury whatsoever, whether chronic or acute, significant or trivial. I believe that some of you have been concerned that some of the patients might, as a result of these events, become distraught and take their own lives. However, I want to assure each and every one of you that no patient has committed suicide or, to the best of our knowledge, threatened or attempted suicide. As a final note, I believe that some of you were distressed that the events may have involved serious criminal behavior of the kind exemplified by what our state terms a Class A felony. However — and I want to emphasize this! — not only were there no charges of Class A felonies for anyone involved in this sequence of events, but no one from the district attorney's office ever mentioned even the remote possibility of such charges. Although I think any of us might acknowledge that perhaps things might have been handled a bit better, it is important — and an issue of fundamental fairness — to keep what happened in perspective, to avoid the witch hunt mentality, and to remember that none of us is perfect. Thank you for your time and attention.

REPLACE INTENTIONAL UNETHICAL BEHAVIOR WITH THE LANGUAGE OF ACCIDENTS, MISFORTUNE, AND MISTAKES

The speaker fails to mention making a conscious decision to profit by stealing charts, filling them with lies, and selling them to the highest bidder, which would strike most people as unethical. The description makes the speaker a victim of being an imperfect human, of lacking omniscience and infallibility. The speaker pushes the acts into the category of those random, inevitable mistakes that afflict us all and are beyond our control. At worst, they are a matter of having fumbled a matter of judgment, although, if this construction is examined closely, it seems to assume that almost anyone would have difficulty judging whether stealing charts, inserting bogus material that will hurt patients, and selling them to those who will publish them is ethical. This may not be quite as hard a judgment as the rhetoric implies. Here is how Jack would use that tactic:

I wanted to address the unfortunate events that have troubled us all lately, so that you would understand what occurred and why. To my great regret, I have realized now in hindsight — hindsight being 20–20 — that in handling clinic records, I made some mistakes. I'm sure you all know how I feel about this, and I hope you will be understanding and chalk this unfortunate error in judgment up to youthful indiscretion, to my tendency to want to take on a little too much so that this clinic will function as well as possible, and to a momentary lapse of attention in the crush of daily demands that I face as clinic director. All of us make mistakes in our work here, and I want you to know how sorry I am for this misstep.

SMOTHER THE EVENTS IN THE LANGUAGE OF ATTACK

Assuming that the best defense is a good offense, the speaker avoids responsibility by attacking others. Whatever the speaker may have done becomes trivial or justifiable in light of the terrible things other people have done. The language of attack stirs up emotional responses. It works against people joining together to examine the facts and their implications and sets people against each other, dividing them into "us" (the good people, unjustly attacked) and "them" (the bad people, who deserve what we can dish out). The speaker's rhetoric serves to draw listeners into his or her camp and to ridicule or intimidate those who are on the other side (i.e., the enemy). The rhetoric encourages listeners to evaluate claims not in terms of whether they are valid and relevant but in terms of whether they support the listener's loyalty to one side.

Jack comes out swinging:

> Thank you for coming today. I will take just a few minutes of your time with the following statement about the recent events in which I have had to endure the most vicious attacks. It is a sad sign of our "take no responsibility" culture that several patients who came to our clinic in need and were not turned away have shown their gratitude for all we have done for them by trying to gain publicity for themselves — their 15 minutes of fame — and to enrich themselves at our expense by filing formal complaints. This is one of the most destructive aspects of the modern mind-set: It's all me-me-me, without thinking of how such complaints might affect the rest of us who have dedicated our lives to healing the sick, comforting those in need, and helping those who turn to us in their hour of crisis. The selfishness of such formal complaints is hard to comprehend. These scurrilous complaints rob us of the time and resources that we would otherwise use to provide services to those who have nowhere else to turn. And it is for those people who have so little and suffer so much that this clinic has resolved to fight these complaints with every resource we can muster. We have hired some of the most skilled and successful attorneys

that this nation has yet produced, and they have already filed countercharges in civil court. The support staff aiding these attorneys have discovered, in the course of their extensive background research, some facts about those who filed complaints against us that I believe will surprise the public and place these vicious complaints in their proper perspective. I've been asked by our attorneys not to reveal that material at this time, but I assure you that our attorneys will present it at the proper time — in court — should these complaints go to trial. Again, pursuant to the advice of our attorneys, I will have no more comment on this matter at this time. Thank you for your time and attention.

Chapter 8

ETHICS PLACEBOS, CONS, AND CREATIVE CHEATING: A USER'S GUIDE

*E*thics placebos (Pope, 2015b) are what all of us are tempted to reach for when we need fast, effective relief from the heartburn of an upsetting ethical challenge. Part of us *wants* to do the right thing, of course, but doing something else calls our name seductively because that other path is so much safer, easier, simpler, quicker, more popular, more profitable, or more fun. Ethics placebos switch the process from searching for and then choosing the most ethical response to taking what we want to do and finding ways to justify it.

In some cases we may need to take industrial-strength ethics placebos, but we can usually find a way to do almost anything we really want to do and to do it with at least a temporarily soothed conscience. The most common ethics placebos can spin the most questionable behaviors into *seemingly* ethical ideals, though of course they are simply excuses for engaging in ethical questionable or unethical behavior.

To restate a major theme of this book, we believe that the overwhelming majority of psychologists are conscientious, caring individuals, committed to ethical behavior. We also believe that none of us is infallible and that perhaps all of us, at one time or another, have been tempted to reach for at least a few of these ethics placebos and might be able extend the list of brands. Many of the false justifications appeared in previous editions of this book, and some were added when the list appeared in *What Therapists Don't Talk About and*

Why: Understanding Taboos That Hurt Us and Our Clients (Pope, Sonne, & Greene, 2006):

- It's not unethical as long as a managed care administrator or insurance case reviewer required or suggested it.
- It's not unethical if the professional association you belong to allows it.
- It's not unethical if an ethics code never mentions the concept, term, or act.
- It's not unethical as long as no law was broken.
- It's not unethical if we can use the passive voice and look ahead. If someone discovers that our c.v. is full of degrees we never earned, positions we never held, and awards we never received, all we need to do is nondefensively acknowledge that mistakes were made and it's time to move on.
- It's not unethical as long as we can name others who do the same thing.
- It's not unethical as long as no one else is perfect. Hey, everyone makes mistakes! So I'm sorry I borrowed your laptop with all your dissertation data and clinical notes on it and it got stolen out of my car, but it could happen to anyone, no one's perfect, so don't make a big deal out of it. Just file a claim with your insurance company and, hey, you'll even get a new one! Wouldn't that be lucky! Want to get a brewski?
- It's not unethical as long as we didn't mean to hurt anyone.
- It's not unethical even if our acts have caused harm as long as the person we harmed had it coming, provoked us, deserved it, was really asking for it, or practically forced us to do it — or, failing that, has not behaved perfectly, is in some way unlikable, or is acting unreasonably.
- It's not unethical as long as there is no body of universally accepted, methodologically perfect (i.e., without any flaws, weaknesses, or limitations) studies showing — without any doubt whatsoever — that exactly what we did was the necessary and sufficient proximate cause of harm to the client and that the client would otherwise be free of all physical and psychological problems, difficulties, or challenges. This view was succinctly stated by a member of the Texas pesticide regulatory board charged with protecting Texas citizens against undue risks from pesticides. In discussing chlordane, a chemical used to kill termites, one member said, "Sure, it's going to kill a lot of people, but they may be dying of something else anyway" ("Perspectives," *Newsweek*, April 23, 1990, p. 17).
- It's not unethical if we could not (or did not) anticipate the unintended consequences of our acts.
- It's not unethical if we see it in the context of everything the person ever did — in which case, it is only a drop in the bucket. For example, it may seem as if a therapist who has submitted hundreds of thousands of dollars' worth of bogus insurance claims for patients he never saw might

have behaved "unethically." However, as attorneys and others representing such professionals often point out, it was completely inconsistent with the high ethics manifest in every other part of the person's life (that we know about), and insignificant in the context of the unbelievable good that this person has done and continues to do.

- It's not unethical if we can say any of the following about it (feel free to extend the list):
  ○ "What else could I do?"
  ○ "Anyone else would've done the same thing."
  ○ "It came from the heart."
  ○ "I listened to my soul."
  ○ "I went with my gut."
  ○ "It was the smart thing to do."
  ○ "It was just common sense."
  ○ "I just knew that's what the client needed."
  ○ "Look, I was just stuck between a rock and a hard place."
  ○ "I'd do the same thing again if I had it to do over."
  ○ "It worked before."
  ○ "What's the big deal?"
- It's not unethical if we have written an article, chapter, or book about it.
- It's not unethical as long as we were under a lot of stress. No fair-minded person would hold us accountable when it is clear that it was the stress we were under — along with all sorts of other powerful factors — that must be held responsible.
- It's not unethical as long as no one ever complained about it.
- It's not unethical as long as we know that the people involved in enforcing standards (e.g., licensing boards or administrative law judges) are dishonest, stupid, destructive, and extremist; are unlike us in some significant way; or are conspiring against us.
- It's not unethical as long as we felt under a lot of pressure to do it from our supervisor, the chair of our training program, or someone else in authority.
- It's not unethical as long as it results in a higher income or more prestige (i.e., is necessary).
- It's not unethical if we're victims. Claiming tragic victim status is easy: We can always use one of two traditional scapegoats — (1) our anything-goes society, which lacks clear standards and leaves us ethically adrift; or, conversely, (2) our coercive, intolerant society, which tyrannizes us with "political correctness," dumbs us down, and controls us like children. Imagine, for example, we are arrested for speeding while drunk, and the person whose car we hit presses vengeful charges against us. We show ourselves as the real victim by pointing out that some politically correct, self-serving tyrants have hijacked the legal system and unfairly

demonized drunk driving. These powerful people of bad character and evil motivation refuse to acknowledge that most speeding while drunk is not only harmless — actuarial studies show that only a small percentage of the instances of drunk speeding actually result in harm to people or property — but also sometimes unavoidable, profoundly ethical, and a social good, getting drivers to their destinations faster and in better spirits. We stress that any studies seeming to show drunk speeding is harmful are not just unscientific (e.g., none randomly assigns drivers to drunk speeding and nondrunk speeding conditions) but hopelessly biased (e.g., focusing on measures of harm but failing to include measures sensitive to the numerous benefits of drunk speeding).

- It's not unethical as long as it would be almost impossible to do things another way.
- It's not unethical as long as there are books, articles, or papers claiming that it is the right thing to do.
- It's not unethical as long as we can find a consultant who says it's okay.

Remaining mindfully aware of the ways that each of us as individuals may be vulnerable — particularly at times of stress or fatigue, of great temptation, or of temporary weakness — to these cognitive strategies may be an important aspect of our ability to respond ethically to difficult, complex, constantly evolving situations, particularly at moments when we are not at our best.

These reminders may help us to resist temptation and keep searching for the most ethical response to our work's complex, constantly changing challenges.

Chapter 9

TRUST, POWER, AND CARING

Psychotherapy is a remarkable venture. It puts to work three diverse phenomena — trust, power, and caring — to help people. We face the ethical challenge of understanding, respecting, and handling carefully all three.

TRUST

When we apply to states and provinces for professional status via licensure and certification, we accept the responsibility that comes with that status. Society expects us to be trustworthy, to avoid abusing the trust that people place in us. Society depends on us to fulfill that trust for the good of our clients as well as society. (Ethical dilemmas can arise from the clash between the client's interests and society's interests, or between the client's interests and the therapist's interests.) In return for assuming a role in which the safety, well-being, and ultimate good of clients is to be held as a sacred trust, we are entitled to the roles, privileges, and power that governments and society entrust to professionals.

This concept of trust is key to understanding the context in which clients enter into a working relationship with us. Clients rightfully expect or desperately hope that they can trust us. Many fear we might betray their trust. Some agonize over trust issues. Others find trust barriers almost insurmountable. Still others come to therapy unaware of how their problems trusting others have made it hard for them to love, work, thrive, and enjoy life.

This common event shines a light on the trust underlying therapy: Clients can walk into the consulting room of an absolute stranger and begin saying things that they would say to no one else. We therapists may ask questions that would get us slapped, punched, or sued if we asked them outside of therapy.

What patients tell us in confidence carries both healing and, if the confidentiality is violated, harmful potential. This potential has prompted virtually all states and provinces to recognize some form of professional confidentiality and therapist–patient privilege. Laws prevent therapists, with some specific exceptions, from talking to others about what clients tell them during therapy (see Chapter 24).

Therapy, like surgery, relies on trust. Surgery patients allow themselves to be physically opened up in the hope that their condition will improve. They trust surgeons not to take advantage of their vulnerability to harm or exploit them. Therapy patients undergo a process of psychological opening up in the hope that their condition will improve. They trust us not to harm or exploit them.

Freud (1952) noticed this similarity. He wrote that the newly developed "talking therapy" was "comparable to a surgical operation" (p. 467) and emphasized that "the transference especially . . . is a dangerous instrument. . . . If a knife will not cut, neither will it serve a surgeon" (p. 471).

Recognizing and respecting the potential harm that could result from psychotherapy was, according to Freud (1963), essential:

> It is grossly to undervalue both the origins and the practical significance of the psychoneuroses to suppose that these disorders are to be removed by pottering about with a few harmless remedies. . . . Psychoanalysis . . . is not afraid to handle the most dangerous forces in the mind and set them to work for the benefit of the patient. (p. 179)

Our personal responsibility includes respecting our clients' trust that we will do nothing that places them at risk for harm.

When we betray our clients' trust, we can cause deep, pervasive, and lasting damage. Mann and Winer (1991), discussing the ways that exploitation of trust can harm patients, quote Adrienne Rich:

> When we discover that someone we trusted can be trusted no longer, it forces us to reexamine the whole instinct and concept of trust. For a while, we are thrust back into some bleak, jutting ledge . . . in a world before kinship, or naming, or tenderness exist; we are brought close to formlessness. (p. 325)

We all face the challenge of understanding what the careless handling of trust can mean for the person who is the client. Our clients do not live their lives in abstractions like "fiduciary relationships" and "social good." Trusting us is deeply personal.

POWER

The trust that society and individual clients give to therapists is a source of power — for example, the power to respect and value that trust or to abuse and betray. The role of therapist holds power ranging from superficial to profound, from fleeting to enduring. The following sections look at seven forms of power: power given by the state; power to name and define; power of testimony; power of knowledge; power of expectation; power created by the therapist; and the inherent power differential.

Power Conferred by the State

State and provincial licensing confers power. Licensed professionals can do things that people without a license cannot.

With patients' consent, surgeons can cut human beings wide open and remove internal organs, anesthesiologists can drug them until they are unconscious, and many therapists can administer mind- or mood-altering drugs to them, all with the law's authorization.

People will take off their clothes and willingly (well, somewhat willingly) submit to all sorts of indignities during a medical examination. They let physicians do things to them that they would not dream of letting anyone else do.

Similarly, clients will open up and allow us as therapists to explore private aspects of their cognitive and emotional lives, including their history, fantasies, hopes, and fears. Clients will tell us their most guarded secrets, material shared with literally no one else. We can ask questions off-limits to others.

States and provinces recognize the importance of protecting clients against the misuse of this power to violate privacy. Except in certain instances, we are legally required to keep confidential what we have learned about their clients through the professional relationship. Holding private information about our clients gives us power (see Chapter 24).

Through licensing, governments also invest us with the power of state-recognized authority to affect our clients' lives. We have the power to make decisions (subject to judicial review) about our clients' civil liberties. In some cases, we have the power to determine whether a person constitutes an immediate danger to the life of someone else and should be held against his or her will for observation or treatment. Alan Stone (1978), professor of law and psychiatry at Harvard University and a former president of the American Psychiatric Association, noted that in the 1950s the United States incarcerated more of its citizens against their will for mental health purposes than any other country, and that the abuse of this power later led to extensive reforms and formal safeguards.

Power to Name and Define

We hold the power of naming and defining. To diagnose someone is to exercise power. In one of the most widely cited psychological research studies, "On Being Sane in Insane Places," Rosenhan (1973) wrote, "Such labels, conferred by mental health professionals, are as influential on the patient as they are on his relatives and friends, and it should not surprise anyone that the diagnosis acts on all of them as a self-fulfilling prophesy. Eventually, the patient himself accepts the diagnosis, with all of its surplus meanings and expectations, and behaves accordingly" (p. 254; see also Frances, 2013; Greenberg, 2013; Heingartner, 2009; Langer & Abelson, 1974; Martinez, Piff, Mendoza-Denton, & Hinshaw, 2011; Mednick, 1989; Murphy, 1976; Pope, 1996; Pope, Butcher, & Seelen, 2006; Reiser & Levenson, 1984; Scribner, 2001; Slater, 2004).

Caplan's description (1995) of psychiatrist Bruno Bettelheim's analysis of student protesters reveals the potential power of diagnosis and other forms of clinical naming to affect how we view people:

> In the turbulent 1960s, Bettelheim... told the United States Congress of his findings: student anti-war protesters who charged the University of Chicago with complicity in the war machine had no serious political agenda; they were acting out an unresolved Oedipal conflict by attacking the university as a surrogate father. (p. 277)

Power of Testimony

We possess authority to affect lives through our testimony as experts in the civil and criminal courts and through similar judicial or administrative proceedings. Our testimony may help determine whether someone convicted of murder is executed. It may be the deciding factor in whether a parent gains or loses custody of a child. It may shape a jury's view of whether a defendant was capable of committing a crime, was likely to have committed it, was legally sane at the time the crime was committed, or is likely to commit similar crimes in the future. It may lead a jury to believe that an uncle sexually abused a young child or that the child either imagined the abuse or was coached as part of a custody dispute. Our testimony may convince a jury that the plaintiff is an innocent victim of a needless trauma who is suffering severe and chronic harm or is a chronic liar, a gold digger, or a malingerer.

Power of Knowledge

Our role as therapist holds power beyond the power that a license creates. We hold power that comes from knowledge. We study human behavior and the factors that affect motivation, decision, and action. We learn methods to bring about change. Maintaining a constant, respectful awareness of the power flowing from knowledge and expertise is essential to avoid the subtle ways of manipulating and exploiting clients.

Power of Expectation

The process of psychotherapy itself creates and uses different forms of power. Most therapies recognize the force of the client's expectation that the therapist's interventions will be able to induce beneficial change. One aspect of this expectation is the placebo effect, a factor that must be taken into account when studying the efficacy and effectiveness of interventions. The client's investing the therapist with power to help bring about change can become a significant part of the change process itself.

Conversely, the therapist's expectations, including optimism and belief in the client's capacity to change, are powerful as well. Miller (2014) conducted research on the efficacy of specific treatments for substance abusers versus common factors. He found that therapist belief that the client could change mattered significantly. How you do therapy matters, and the ability to convey empathy, care and belief in the client significantly affects outcome.

The therapist often becomes invested with other important meanings as well. Psychodynamic theory, for example, describes a process termed *transference*: Clients transfer feelings, attachments, or styles of relationship associated with figures from their past, such as parents, onto the therapist. Deep feelings, such as love, rejection, shame, guilt, longing for approval, dependence, panic, and neediness — each perhaps representing the unfinished business of development or traumatic experiences needing understanding and healing — originally experienced within an early relationship may emerge in the therapist–client relationship in ways that tend to shock and overwhelm the client.

Our potential to elicit such profound feelings — simply by serving as a therapist — and to "feel" to the client as if we were a figure from the client's past (with the client frequently functioning as if he or she were at an earlier stage of development) represent the sometimes surprising aspects of our power to affect their clients.

The concept of transference grew out of the psychodynamic framework, but empirical studies suggest that it may be relevant to nonpsychodynamic therapies as well (see, e.g., Beach & Power, 1996; Gelso & Bhatia, 2012; Hoglend, 2014; Tellides et al., 2008).

Therapist-Created Power

In some approaches, the therapist works to create specific kinds of power. A family therapist may unbalance the equilibrium and alliances among family members. A behavior therapist may create a hospital ward or halfway house in which desirable behaviors bring a rewarding response from the staff (perhaps in the form of tokens that can be exchanged for goods or privileges); the power of the therapist and staff is used to control, or at least influence, the client's behavior.

Psychologist Laura Brown (1994b) describes another domain of the therapist's power:

> The therapist also has the power to engage in certain defining behaviors that are real and concrete. She sets the fee; decides the time, place, and circumstances of the meeting; and determines what she will share about herself and not disclose. Even when she allows some leeway in negotiating these and similar points, this allowance proceeds from the implicit understanding that it is within the therapist's power to give, and to take away, such compromises. (p. 111)

Inherent Power Differential

The power differential is inherent in psychotherapy. Although some approaches emphasize egalitarian ideals in which therapist and client are equal, such goals are viewed only within a narrowly limited context of the relationship. In truly equal relationships, in which there is no appreciable power differential, there is no designation of one member as "therapist" in relation to the other member, there is no fee charged by one member to the other for the relationship, there is no designation of the activity as "professional" (and falling within the scope of a professional liability policy), there is no license possessed by one member allowing initiation of a 72-hour hold on the other, and so on. A defining attribute of the professional is the recognition, understanding, and careful handling of the considerable power — and the personal responsibility for that power — inherent in the role.

CARING

Both the individual client and society recognize the diverse powers of the professional role and place their trust in us to use those powers to help — never to harm or exploit. We must match with our caring the trust that society and the individual client give to us. Only within a context of caring — specifically, caring about the client's well-being — are our professional status and powers justified.

Historically, charging high fees did not create or define professional status, nor did spending long years in training or reaching a high level of skill. The professional's defining characteristic was an ethic of placing the client's well-being foremost and not allowing professional judgment or services to be drawn off course by one's own needs.

The touchstone for the approaches discussed in this book is caring for and about our clients. This book's concept of caring avoids passive, empty sentimentality. Caring includes responding to a client's legitimate needs and recognizing that the client must never be exploited. It also includes assuming personal responsibility for working to help and to avoid harming or endangering our clients.

Unfortunately, this concept may not receive adequate attention in graduate training programs. As Seymour Sarason (1985) wrote:

> On the surface, trainees accept the need for objectivity — it does have the ring of science, and its importance can be illustrated with examples of the baleful consequences of "emotional over-involvement" — but internally there is a struggle, as one of my students put it, "between what your heart says you should say and do and what theory and your supervisor say you should say and do." Many trainees give up the struggle but there are some who continue to feel that in striving to maintain the stance of objectivity they are robbing themselves and their clients of something of therapeutic value. The trainee's struggle, which supervisors gloss over as a normal developmental phase that trainees grow out of, points to an omission in psychological-psychiatric theories. Those theories never concern themselves with caring and compassion. What does it mean to be caring and compassionate? When do caring and compassion arise as feelings? What inhibits or facilitates their expression? Why do people differ so widely in having such feelings and the ways they express them? It is, of course, implicit in all of these theories that these feelings are crucial in human development, but the reader would be surprised how little attention is given to their phenomenology and consequences (positive and negative). (p. 168; see also Fan & Lin, 2013; Lolak, 2013; Pope, Sonne, & Greene, 2006; Pope, Sonne, & Holroyd, 1993; Pope & Tabachnick, 1993, 1994)

Sarason made some excellent recommendations for how to encourage and develop caring, compassion, and empathy in clinical training programs, and more recently other innovative approaches have begun to emerge (see, for example, "Compassion Resources for Therapists & Counselors," 2015; "Empathy Resources for Therapists & Counselors," 2015; Kelm, Womer, Walter, & Feudtner, 2014; Misra-Hebert et al., 2012; Ozcan, Oflaz, & Bakir, 2012).

We still have a long way to go in ensuring that clinical training programs, internships, professional organizations, clinics, hospitals, and other settings are doing all they can to support caring, compassion, and empathy among clinicians. Unfortunately, there is evidence that such qualities may actually decline in some settings (see, for example, Hegazi & Wilson, 2013).

Caring about clients and what happens to them is one of the strongest foundations for the formal rules and regulations that are society's attempt to hold us accountable, but it also encourages us to look beyond those generalities. Caring is a foundation of our personal responsibilities as therapists.

Chapter 10

MORAL DISTRESS AND MORAL COURAGE

Thinking about doing the right thing can leave us feeling alone, afraid, or helpless. We've thought through an ethical dilemma and have found the right path. And yet... the path seems blocked. Doing what we believe is right is prohibited by clinic policy, the hospital director, our employment contract, the insurance company, the budget, our colleagues with whom we collaborate to provide care to a patient, the licensing board, or some other external constraint.

We hate — or at least feel uncomfortable with — the idea that we are about to take part in something we know is wrong or to stand aside and let it happen. But to do what is right scares us. We feel frozen, powerless. Doing the right thing might cost us our job, our license, our reputation. Or it might have no effect at all: No matter what we do, we cannot stop something that is deeply wrong — our only choice is to take part reluctantly, to witness the inevitable, or to turn a blind eye and deaf ear to something deeply wrong.

This chapter's purpose is to call attention to a threat to ethical behavior that differs from so many others we face in our work. The vast majority of therapists devote themselves to the ethical path and always strive to do the right thing. But we're all human and we all fall short at least some of the time. Fatigue, carelessness, misperceptions, misinformation, misjudgments, fallacies, pride, and impatience are only some of the hazards that trip up all of us at one time or another, causing us to overlook the most effective ethical response. You can probably name several others off the top of your head without pausing too long to think about it.

All those hazards can cloud our ethical vision, causing us to miss what is clearly the most ethical response. Standing in contrast to these barriers to seeing the ethical path are those external pressures convincing us we cannot set foot on that path in a particular time and place. Consider these examples:

- As you show up at the clinic where you've provided outpatient therapy for the past 6 years, the chief administrative officer summons you to her office and informs you that due to a critical financial situation, the CEO and Board of Directors have ordered an emergency restructuring, effective immediately. You are to report now to their satellite clinic across town to assume new duties. Your current patients — some of whom are struggling with thoughts of suicide, some of whom you've diagnosed as suffering from borderline personality disorder, and some of whom struggle with difficulties trusting a therapist — will be assigned to other clinic therapists. You will not be able to meet with them before they meet with their new therapists, will no longer have access to their charts, and will no longer be allowed to communicate with them while they form working relationships with their new therapists.

  You state as diplomatically as possible your concerns about not only ethical but also clinical problems with that approach. However, the chief administrative officer cuts you off, tells you that she and the CEO have thought through this plan carefully, that the extraordinary financial pressures call for extraordinary steps to keep the organization afloat, and that if you are unable to accept the new position as it has been laid out for you, she will unfortunately and with great sadness and reluctance, need to act immediately to hire your replacement. In an extremely tight job market, you need this job to support yourself and your family, especially since you're a single parent.

- You are the graduate student representative on the admissions committee for a small clinical psychology department. As the folders pass from person to person, you notice an outstanding candidate who indicates, in her biographical sketch, that she is a Muslim. When the folder reaches the hypersensitive, opinionated, and dictatorial — and that's on his good days — chair of the clinical program, he tosses it aside and says, "Not while I'm chair of the program! I don't want to see our building blown up because someone didn't like her grades. So officially let's just write down in our notes that her academic interests are not a good match for our program." One of the other faculty members chuckles and nods her head; the others laugh.

  You remain silent, burying your face in one of the other folders as if you're reading intently, hoping nobody will pay any attention to you, realizing that to speak up within the context of this faculty would doom your prospects of success in the program. You also realize that if you let anyone outside the room know what just happened and there is any sort of complaint, publicity, or controversy, every faculty member will know the source of the leak.

Yet you believe what happened is deeply wrong — a violation of ethics, justice, fairness, legal standards, and the clinical program's own stated policies. You believe the right thing to do is to speak up, and yet... you hesitate, not wanting to face what will happen to you if you do. You ask yourself if you would find it easier to do the right thing if rather than Muslim applicants who were banned from the program in practice, though not in formal policies or public statements of inclusion and openness, it had been LGBT applicants, Black applicants, Latina or Latino applicants, Jewish applicants, applicants who were older than 50, applicants whose biographies described their activities in extreme right-wing causes, or applicants whose biographies described their activities in extreme left-wing causes.

• After taking out a large loan to support yourself during a 6-month dry spell in your employment, you finally find a new job. You begin your first day of work at a well-regarded managed care system. Your supervisor explains that you'll be doing intakes in the mental health department. You'll be evaluating everyone showing up to ask for psychological services. Although the company touts their comprehensive mental health services, the supervisor tells you that you are to place everyone you can on a waiting list and warns you to be sure to write in your notes that your psychological evaluation showed no urgent needs for professional care. All others, he says, are to be assigned to one of the large therapy groups meeting every other week. For those, he directs you to write that your psychological evaluation showed that group therapy was most appropriate for a patient with this particular set of clinical needs.

When you gently but firmly raise concerns about why this approach is wrong on so many levels, he says, "Look, just between you and me — and don't quote me on this or I'll deny I ever said it — I know what you're talking about. But this company has been in business a long time and this is their business model. They quickly 'reorganize' any time they want to get rid of someone who is not on board with the way they want things handled. If you fail even once to do what I'm telling you today, you'll get a terrible weekly evaluation in your file, though it'll list other reasons for why you're not a good employee. If you fail to do it a second time, you'll be gone within a few days."

Those three examples represent what is often called *moral distress*. Andrew Jameton, professor in the University of Nebraska College of Public Health, pioneered the use of this term in his classic book on nursing ethics, defining it as what happens "when one knows the right thing to do, but institutional constraints make it nearly impossible to pursue the right course of action" (1984, p. 6). He distinguished it from other ethical quandaries:

The experience of moral distress can be distinguished from the experience of moral dilemmas. In moral distress, a nurse knows the morally right course of action to take, but institutional structure and conflicts with other co-workers create obstacles. A nurse who fails to act in the face of obstacles also may have reactive distress in addition to the initial distress. Both kinds of distress pose dilemmas about individual and collective moral responsibility. (Jameton, 1992, p. 542; see also Jameton, 1984)

Much of the early work on moral distress in clinical work focused on nursing. The American Association of Critical-Care Nurses' Position Statement on Moral Distress (2012; see also Rittenmeyer & Huffman, 2009) summarized some major themes of over a quarter century of research in this area and their implications:

Moral distress is a key issue affecting the workplace environment. Research demonstrates that moral distress is a significant cause of emotional suffering among nurses and contributes to loss of nurses from the workforce. Further, it threatens the quality of patient care. In recognition of these harmful effects, the provision of education and tools to address and manage moral distress in the work environment is imperative and will lead to essential improvements in patient care and outcomes.

When an organization inflicts moral distress on its members, the cause may go beyond the constraints created by one or a few individuals (e.g., a CEO, a supervisor). The organization's goals and values may create an ethical culture that clashes with some clinicians' deepest professional and personal values. Humphries and Woods (2015) wrote: "Moral distress is inevitable in an ethical climate where the organization's main priorities are perceived by nursing staff to be budget and patient throughput, rather than patient safety and care."

Although much of the research on moral distress has focused on organizational settings, therapists who are in independent practice may encounter it in other forms. Kälvemark, Höglund, Hansson, Westerholm, and Arnetz (2004) noted that "moral distress does not occur only as a consequence of institutional constraints... [but also as a result of other constraints such as] legal regulations" (p. 1075).

The neutral clinical language that typically describes moral distress may drain it of impact as our eyes pass over it on the page. Fourie (2015), for example, writes that "moral distress should be understood as a specific psychological response to morally challenging situations such as those of moral constraint or moral conflict, or both" (p. 91). Shay, in contrast, uses the term *moral injury* when describing what can happen to combat soldiers who are ordered to do something they believe is not morally right. He writes of the "the soul wound inflicted by doing something that violates one's own ethics, ideals, or attachments" (Shay, 2012, p. 57; see also Shay, 2002). Similarly, Litz et al. (2009) describe the pervasive harm we can suffer when we fail to do the right thing in important situations: "Potentially morally injurious events, such as perpetrating, failing to prevent, or bearing witness to acts that transgress deeply held moral beliefs and expectations may be deleterious in the long-term, emotionally, psychologically, behaviorally, spiritually, and socially (what we label as *moral injury*)" (p. 695).

The deep moral distress that occurs when external forces push heavily against our commitment to do the right thing finds its way into many settings, including oncology and hematology (Lazzarin, Biondi, & Di Mauro, 2012); pediatrics (Sauerland, Marotta, Peinemann, Berndt, & Robichaux, 2015); intensive care (Hamric & Blackhall, 2007); health system management (Mitton, Peacock, Storch, Smith, & Cornelissen, 2011); health promotion (Sunderland, Harris, Johnstone, Del Fabbro, & Kendall, 2015); community research (Sunderland, Catalano, Kendall, McAuliffe, & Chenoweth, 2010); and academia (Ganske, 2010).

If you experience moral distress, you are far from alone. "Moral distress is a common experience for clinicians, regardless of profession" (Whitehead, Herbertson, Hamric, Epstein, & Fisher, 2014, p. 117; see also Kälvemark et al., 2004). Studies chart its occurrence among psychologists (see, for example, Austin, Rankel, Kagan, Bergum, & Lemermeyer, 2005) and psychiatrists (see, for example, Austin, Kagan, Rankel, & Bergum, 2008).

How do psychologists respond to moral distress? A study conducted by Austin and colleagues (2005) found six major ways of handling the experience:

1. Remaining silent
2. Taking a stand
3. Acting in secret
4. Sustaining the self by focusing on work with patients
5. Reaching out to colleagues for support
6. Leaving

The field can respond to moral distress by discussing it in graduate school, internships, continuing education courses, and professional conferences so that clinicians and clinicians in training learn about the phenomenon and its causes and can recognize it in themselves and others. We can develop supportive networks to help those experiencing moral distress to connect with each other and with additional sources of help. We can work to strengthen the ethics of organizations that inflict moral distress on their members, the focus of another chapter in this book.

But responding ethically and effectively to moral distress when we confront it in our individual lives will always require moral courage. We conclude this chapter with a striking profile in courage: A psychologist who took on a massive organization to protect his patients and was fired before ultimately prevailing.

"The Psychologist as Whistle Blower: A Case Study" tells in careful and vivid detail of an individual's long and hard struggle to do the right thing, and the roles that the Veterans Administration, professional associations, the Civil Service Commission, and others played. The following excerpts, as they appeared over almost four decades ago, show us all what true courage can look like — and do — in the face of moral distress and overwhelming odds.

THE PSYCHOLOGIST AS WHISTLE BLOWER: A CASE STUDY

(This study is reprinted with permission from the American Psychological Association from Simon, G. C. (1978). The psychologist as whistle blower: A case study. *Professional Psychology: Research and practice, 9,* 322–340.)

Although whistle blowing is an issue of wide social relevance, it has particular significance for psychologists, and other professionals, who are salaried employees. Because they occupy two statuses simultaneously, professional and bureaucrat, the opportunities for conflict between the demands of their conscience and those of their organization are greatly increased in comparison to other employees. The separation between employer and client may force a choice between loyalty to the organization and loyalty to professional ethics, a situation not faced by the traditional self-employed professional. The resolution of such conflicts may require the psychologist either to acquiesce in professionally unconscionable practices or to expose the practices publicly. Thus, whistle blowing, for psychologists, may not only be a matter of personal conscience but a professional responsibility as well....

It is also a matter of high personal risk. Intense economic and organizational pressures appear to have successfully stifled much internal dissent and to have maintained whistle blowing as a rare and personally costly response (Committee on Scientific Freedom and Responsibility, 1975; Nader, Petkas, & Blackwell, 1972; Peters & Branch, 1972). As a result, both the public and the profession stand to suffer. Clients and the community at large may be subjected to unnecessary danger or expense while psychology's ability to function as an independent, autonomous profession is attenuated. Psychologists, therefore, have an important stake in what happens to their colleagues who become whistle blowers. Accordingly, it is important to document publicly cases, such as the one described below, in which psychologists allege that they have received punitive treatment for following the dictates of their professional conscience. Documentation of such cases may contribute to a climate of opinion and an awareness of needed social or professional changes that will reduce the likelihood that institutional power will be abused in the future.

Background

In February 1971, a serious earthquake struck Southern California. Although there were relatively few deaths, there was extensive property damage. Especially hard hit were several Veterans Administration (VA) hospitals. As a result of the damage, the VA launched a general survey of structural stability of other hospitals in the area. Among those surveyed were Brentwood Hospital, Wadsworth Hospital, and the Extended Care Hospital, three administratively separate facilities sharing the grounds of the National Military Home in west Los Angeles adjacent to the campus of the University of California (UCLA). Although these three hospitals had come through the earthquake unscathed, the VA announced nearly 1 year later that engineering tests indicated that a number of buildings might be unsafe in the event of another major earthquake. Therefore, these buildings were ordered closed.

Building 156, which housed the Adult Restoration Program at the Extended Care Hospital, was one of the buildings ordered closed. Donald Spiegel, a PhD psychologist who was chief of the program, received the news on January 14, 1972, a Friday. Over the weekend, unbeknown to Spiegel, paperwork was completed allowing the majority of the patients in the program to be discharged from the hospital. When he returned to work, Spiegel was asked by George Gillick, the physician who was Chief of Staff, to begin "evacuating" his patients into the community immediately. Gillick, who had been considering phasing out the restoration program even before the engineering test results were in, wanted the patients moved out quickly. However, because most of his patients were older single men without social or family ties to the community, satisfactory places for them to live outside of the hospital were not readily available. Nevertheless, on Wednesday, January 19, Gillick informed Spiegel that he was dissatisfied with the latter's "lack of progress" and instructed him to discharge all the remaining patients within 1 week.

Spiegel was to discharge 5 patients that day, 10 the next day, 15 the day after that, and so on, so that before the end of the 7th day all 120 remaining patients would be out of the hospital. Spiegel, however, did not believe that he could meet these daily quotas without seriously jeopardizing the lives and well-being of his patients, particularly the elderly ones. Accordingly 2 days later, on January 21, he asked Gillick during a staff meeting to reconsider the quota system. Gillick responded by summarily removing Spiegel from his position as Chief of the Adult Restoration Program and ordering him to report to the head of the psychology service for new duties. Later the same day he appointed Edward O'Neil, a physician, as the new chief. In the meantime, someone informed a television reporter of what had happened, and that night Spiegel was shown on television criticizing the VA's hasty patient evacuation as he cleaned out his desk.

Having reported to the psychology service, Spiegel spent the next 5 days waiting for a new assignment. Finally, on January 26, he was detailed to the "women's cottage" to counsel women who were about to be discharged or transferred to a VA facility in Virginia. Again, it seemed to Spiegel that patients were being moved out of the hospital precipitously. Elderly women with serious medical problems who had lived at the hospital for many years were being uprooted suddenly. Convinced that the hospital's methods could lead to the deaths of some of these patients, Spiegel tried to have the procedures modified. When neither the hospital director nor chief of staff responded to his appeals, Spiegel appeared at a January 28 press conference arranged by the California State Psychological Association. Although agreeing that unsafe building conditions made it necessary to move the patients, Spiegel insisted that the "chaotic" manner in which their relocation was being carried out was as life threatening as another earthquake. He added, according to an article that appeared in the Los Angeles Times (Nelson, 1972) that psychologists were "concerned about a system which permits the imposition of administrative fiat on professional personnel for taking a stand against orders which would clearly damage patients or be detrimental to their welfare" (p. 1). Additional publicity was generated by patients who picketed the hospital in opposition to the relocations and Spiegel's removal from the restoration program.

O'Neil, meanwhile, continued evacuating Building 156. In contrast to Spiegel, he was given no quotas to meet, and (perhaps as a result of the publicity given Spiegel's charges) he was allowed to transfer some of the patients to other buildings on the hospital's grounds, an option not made available to Spiegel. By the beginning of March the issue had become moot. All of the residents of Building 156 had been relocated and Spiegel, now attached to the psychology service, was at work on other projects. In addition, the final touches were being put on the administrative consolidation of Wadsworth Hospital and Extended Care Hospital into the Wadsworth Hospital Center that had been occasioned by the decision to close some of the buildings and relocate the patients.

Then on March 8, 1972, 7 weeks after Spiegel had been relieved of his position with the restoration program, a teletype message arrived from the VA central office in Washington, DC, ordering Spiegel to transfer to the VA hospital in Temple, Texas. The order indicated that the resettlement of many former Wadsworth Hospital Center patients to this installation required a reallocation of professional personnel "for the good of the service."

Spiegel, however, interpreted his transfer order as retaliation for his efforts to protect his patients. Since he had considerable seniority as an 18-year employee of the VA, any legitimate need for additional personnel at this facility, he reasoned, could have been accomplished by transferring any one of several other Wadsworth psychologists with less seniority. Moreover, transferring to Temple, Texas, a much less desirable location, would have caused a profound disruption in his personal and professional life. Consequently, he decided to fight the order. Seeking assistance in every available quarter, he contacted a number of groups including the California State Psychological Association, the American Psychological Association (APA), and the American Federation of Government Employees (AFGE), which filed a grievance in his behalf.

The VA responded to his protests by offering him a second choice. He was told that he could go to the Outpatient Clinic in downtown Los Angeles instead of transferring to Texas. Spiegel, who had spent the immediately preceding 13 years in a Research Psychologist position at Brentwood Hospital, discovered that his clinic responsibilities would involve providing full-time clinical services. In addition he would be unable to continue working on a research project funded jointly by the VA and the National Institute of Mental Health of which he was the principal investigator. Accordingly, on March 22 he turned down the VA's second offer. The VA then promptly reinstated its original demand that he move to Temple, Texas, by May 1. Spiegel reiterated his unwillingness to relocate there, and so May 1 came and went and Spiegel remained in Los Angeles. As a result, on May 19 he was informed by John J. Cox, Director of the VA's Southern California District, that he would be "separated" from the VA as of June 2, 1972.

The AFGE immediately filed an appeal to Cox's directive with the Civil Service Commission (CSC) charging that Spiegel's job rights had been violated. The CSC agreed to hold a hearing on Spiegel's appeal, but it was not until nearly 6 months later, on November 14, that the hearing was held. It lasted for 2 days. Testimony was taken from Spiegel, Gillick, Cox, and others, including . . . the VA's head psychologist. Then 5 months later the CSC's San Francisco Regional Office . . . ruled that the "arbitrary selection of the appellant for reassignment to the VA Hospital at Temple was improper" and overturned Spiegel's removal.

The VA appealed the decision of the regional office to the CSC's court of last resort, the Board of Appeals and Review. Unlike the regional office, the board did not deal with the question of whether the VA had violated certain procedural rules (e.g., seniority) in attempting to transfer Spiegel away from the Wadsworth Hospital Center. Instead, the board . . . in effect ruled that a federal agency has the authority to take whatever actions "as may be administratively desirable" as long as the action is "for the good of the service." It decided, therefore, that Spiegel's transfer "was not unreasonable, arbitrary or capricious, but was effected for such cause as will promote the efficiency of the service" and overturned the decision of the regional office . . . .

Convinced of the merits of his case, Spiegel and the AFGE refused to accept the board decision. Accordingly, they decided to pursue the issue in the federal courts. After numerous delays, AFGE attorneys filed suit against the VA in the U.S. Court of Claims in October 1974. Brought into the case for the first time, the Justice Department and the VA's own General Counsel's office advised that the VA should enter into negotiations with Spiegel's representatives. The VA agreed and action on the suit was postponed during the interim.

Finally in February 1975, the VA agreed to an out-of-court settlement that reinstated Spiegel with full back pay and, in effect, acknowledged that it had acted wrongly in trying to transfer him. On March 2, 1975, nearly 3 full years after he refused to accept what he regarded as a punitive transfer, Spiegel returned to Brentwood Hospital.

Bureaucratic-Professional Conflict

Spiegel's battle with the VA is an engrossing story, but it is more than simply another tale of David and Goliath. It illustrates the need for further attention to a number of important issues that should be of concern to psychologists, individually and collectively. For instance, what are the ethical obligations of a psychologist whose employer and clients are locked in a conflict? What assistance — moral, political, or financial — is available to psychologists caught in a conflict of this sort? And how can psychologists maintain their *professional* standing when they abandon the traditional model of independent practice and become salaried employees?

It is important to realize, then, that the dispute between Spiegel and his VA superiors is fundamentally a conflict of bureaucratic and professional values, especially the definition of authority. One of the distinguishing features of a bureaucracy is the hierarchical distribution of power and authority according to which subordinates are expected to follow the directives of their organizational superiors. A profession, on the other hand, is organized in a manner that emphasizes the autonomy of each individual member to act according to the dictates of his or her professional judgment. Consequently, when a professional is a salaried member of a bureaucracy, there is a necessary tension between the authority of the organization and the professional's own judgment (Blau & Scott, 1962). This tension may be kept in check by defining separate spheres of influence. Thus, professionals may accept the authority of the organization in, say, operational issues, such as the scheduling of client assignment. In return, the organization recognizes the right of professionals to decide, for instance, the type of treatment or service that is to be administered (cf. Abrahamson, 1967; Scott, 1969). In other words, although professionals may be subordinate to one another in organizational matters as a consequence of their different bureaucratic ranks, all are equal when it comes to matters of professional practice (e.g., patient care).

In refusing to move his patients out of the hospital as rapidly as the hospital director wished, Spiegel was asserting his professional autonomy and responsibility. In removing him as restoration program chief and later ordering him to another installation, the VA was attempting to reassert its authority and ensure future conformity to its policies. However, because of legal assistance from the AFGE and the accessibility of the federal courts, the VA's effort failed. This case is worthy, therefore, not merely because professional judgment and organizational policy differed but because the professional prevailed in his refusal to comply with orders that violated his professional integrity. The implications of this conflict may be better appreciated by examining the issues and the responses of the key parties more closely.

The Transfer

Why was Spiegel ordered to Temple, Texas? According to the VA, there was an urgent need for another psychologist at Temple since the Texas facility was in the process of receiving 102 patients from the Wadsworth Hospital Center and was already suffering from a vacant psychologist position. The agency's legal representative at Spiegel's CSC hearing maintained that "patient care was the primary and moving (sic) reason for the transfer of Dr. Spiegel to Temple." . . . Spiegel did not contest the need for another psychologist at Temple, but he did not agree that he should be the one or that he was the most qualified. The VA, on the other hand, not only maintained that Spiegel was highly qualified for the post but that he was virtually without peers. [The VA's Head Psychologist], who had accepted responsibility for selecting Spiegel to go to Texas, was asked by Spiegel's AFGE representative, George Boss, why he had chosen Spiegel and not someone else:

> Boss: If there was such an urgent need for the specialized qualifications of a Research Psychologists, are you, in effect stating that there are no other Research Psychologists qualified to fill the job at Temple, Texas?
> [The VA's Head Psychologist]: The position is open, and I'm not aware of any psychologists with the qualifications of Dr. Spiegel to fill that position.
> Boss: Am I to understand that Dr. Spiegel is the only individual psychologist in the Veteran's Administration that's qualified to do this job in Temple, Texas?
> [The VA's Head Psychologist]: That's what I have indicated; that Dr. Spiegel had qualifications that could optimally fit this situation . . . .

Cox. . . , VA's Southern California District director, in his letter of appeal to the CSC Board of Appeals and Review chairman, provided 15 citations from the transcript of the CSC hearing that he indicated testified to Spiegel's "extra-ordinary combinations of skills."

Since [the VA's Head Psychologist] maintained that patient needs at Temple required the immediate attention of a well-qualified psychologist, Boss was puzzled that [the VA's Head Psychologist] had not assigned another psychologist to Temple after Spiegel was fired:

> Then, in turn, would you explain why you have not selected another individual to fill the job in Temple, Texas?
> [The VA's Head Psychologist]: For the simple reason we are not aware of anyone with these qualifications to go there . . . .

In other words, Spiegel was ordered to Texas because he alone had the requisite qualifications to meet the needs of the Temple patients, and since, by definition, his talents were unique, there was no other VA psychologist that [the VA's Head Psychologist] could send to Temple. Spiegel and Boss found this reasoning "curious."

In his argument before the CSC hearing examiner, Boss pointed out several other curious aspects that appeared to contradict the VA's claim that patient care was "the moving reason" for Spiegel's transfer. First of all, following his refusal to go to Texas, [the VA's Head Psychologist] had offered Spiegel the alternative of moving to the Outpatient Clinic in downtown Los Angeles. If the Temple patients truly required Spiegel's talents, and his alone, why was he offered a transfer to the Los Angeles clinic? The reason, according to Cox, was that the Los Angeles clinic also needed Spiegel's "unique and specialized qualifications" and that the VA central office felt a "sense of compassion" for the personal disruption transfer would cause Spiegel and his wife, a professor of psychology at San Fernando Valley State College . . . . Second, [the VA's Head Psychologist]'s involvement in the transfer was highly unusual. VA administrators testified that transfers are typically initiated by the local administrative authorities, not the central office. In this case, however, the central office intervened directly and without consulting the administration of Wadsworth Hospital Center or the chief psychologists at either Temple or the Los Angeles Outpatient Clinic. Third, Boss pointed out that Spiegel could have been transferred back to Brentwood Hospital, his original station, but this alternative was rejected by the VA. Finally, Boss argued that the transfer of Elizabeth Hecht, a Wadsworth psychologist who had "volunteered" to go to Temple in order to avoid losing her job through a reduction in force, alleviated the need to send Spiegel there. (Later the AFGE would claim that the VA was attempting to transfer Spiegel to a supervisory position that was already "encumbered" by Hecht and another psychologist at Temple, a state of affairs definitely in violation of CSC regulations.)

If the VA's explanations for Spiegel's transfer were specious, what were the real reasons? According to Spiegel, it was a mixture of inter-professional rivalry and bureaucratic spleen. Spiegel was appointed Chief of the Adult Restoration Program by a social worker serving as hospital director in an acting capacity, who died shortly after making the appointment. About the same time, Gillick was appointed chief of staff. According to Spiegel, Gillick, a physician, was unhappy with the idea of a non-MD heading the restoration program (Spiegel's predecessor and successor were physicians), and therefore, he refused to approve Spiegel's position description and subsequently ousted him as restoration chief. His transfer,

Spiegel charged, was in retaliation for his criticism of the hospital's administration and the unfavorable publicity that followed his removal. Spiegel felt that the VA was more interested in removing him from Extended Care Hospital (later Wadsworth Hospital Center) and in punishing him for his public dissent than it was in meeting its personnel requirements.

Spiegel's charge that his public criticism of the VA was related to his transfer order was flatly denied by VA officials. [The VA's Head Psychologist] has testified that the news stories did not influence his judgment in proposing Spiegel's transfer. He and other VA officials acknowledged that they were aware of the media reports relating Spiegel's criticism, but they insisted that they maintained a detached attitude toward these reports, as indicated by this exchange between Cox and Boss:

> Boss: What was the substance of your discussion with the VACO [VA central office] concerning that article in the paper?
>
> Cox: If I recall correctly, I believe in my discussion with officials in Washington it was to the effect that with all the trauma that we were going through out here in transferring our patients to various parts of the country, we didn't need further articles of this type to disrupt our patients any further.
>
> Boss: Then your discussion was critical of the information furnished by Dr. Spiegel to the press?
>
> Cox: I wouldn't call it critical. I would say it was *informative....*

In addition to questioning the cogency of the VA's explanations for his transfer, Spiegel also challenged the procedural legitimacy of the actions taken against him. He claimed that his removal as head of the restoration program constituted a "reduction in rank" since he no longer reported directly to the chief of staff. And as this change was accomplished without the usual elements of due process that are called for by CSC regulations, he argued that it should be considered invalid. For similar reasons, he maintained that his transfer to Texas violated both "reduction-in-rank" (since again he would be one level further down the organizational chain of command) and "reduction-in-force" regulations — the latter because he had been given no opportunity to exercise his right to "bump" someone of lower seniority. Therefore, since the VA had acted improperly, he argued, these adverse actions should be nullified.

Legal Maneuvers

The formal discussions of these points are not only arcane and exceedingly technical, they have a distinctly Alice-in-Wonderland quality. For instance, the VA argued that Spiegel's rank was not reduced because he had never "really" been restoration chief. The VA's position was that even though (a) Extended Care Hospital distributed a memo announcing Spiegel's appointment as Chief of the Adult Restoration Program, (b) the hospital director signed an organizational chart which showed that Spiegel reported directly to the chief of staff (Gillick), and (c) Spiegel in fact functioned as restoration chief for approximately 6 months, Spiegel's supervisor (Gillick) had never signed his official position description. Since CSC regulations require all government employees to have an approved position description relevant to their duties, the VA claimed that Spiegel had never legally been restoration chief. Therefore, they argued, they could not have improperly reduced his rank since he had never truly held the chief's position.

Furthermore, the fact that Gillick did not issue a personnel action (Form 50) when he removed Spiegel was cited as additional evidence that Spiegel had never occupied a rank higher than "psychologist." (Spiegel, of course, felt that this omission merely represented an additional violation of his job rights.) According to the federal suit filed by the AFGE . . . , this line of reasoning would be tantamount to arguing that a municipality could never prosecute someone for driving without a license because driving is legally defined as "an action which requires the issuance of a driver's license."

Spiegel's lawyers, however, were not unwilling to turn this tortured logic to the benefit of their client. Thus, they argued that if it were true that Spiegel had never truly been chief at Extended Care Hospital because he did not have a duly signed position description for his duties there, it must also be true that his transfer from his original position ("research psychologist") at Brentwood had never been consummated. Therefore, the VA's termination order was procedurally defective since it fired him from a position that he had never held (i.e., "psychologist" at Extended Care Hospital).

An even more bizarre twist developed over the grievance that had been lodged in Spiegel's behalf by the AFGE shortly after Gillick removed him as restoration chief. The grievance was filed by William McPeak, an AFGE official, in a letter to Jaffrey, Director of Wadsworth Hospital Center. Unfortunately, a few days after writing Jaffrey, McPeak died. Jaffrey then decided not to follow up on the grievance on the grounds that the VA did not "know" who now exercised Spiegel's power of attorney. Later, after the period for filing a grievance had passed and in response to the union's insistence that something be done about Spiegel's grievance, Jaffrey wrote a letter to the (deceased) McPeak citing his demise as the reason for the hospital's failure to act on the grievance. This state of affairs led the CSC San Francisco Regional Office . . . to rule "the fact that the appellant's representative died within a few days after writing the letter does not absolve the agency of their responsibility to take some positive and affirmative action on this grievance."

Like its answer to Spiegel's charges that he had been improperly reduced in rank, the VA's response to the charge that it had violated his rights under reduction-in-force regulations was based on a highly technical interpretation of the facts. VA officials acknowledged that a reorganization was underway at the time that Spiegel was ordered to Texas. They also acknowledged that "general" notices were sent in February 1972 to over 700 employees announcing that there would be a reduction in the number of staff needed at Wadsworth, and that several psychologists (not including Spiegel and others with high seniority) received these notices. In addition, they acknowledged that the personnel officer had indicated "unofficially" in the employees newsletter that there were eight "surplus" psychologists.

Following these announcements, one psychologist applied for retirement, two resigned, and six (including Elizabeth Hecht, who went to Temple, and two who went to Brentwood) transferred to other stations. As a result of these individual moves, the VA claimed that the problem of "surplus" psychologists was solved without resort to the issuance of individual reduction-in-force notices. And since individual notices had never been issued, the VA argued that a reduction in force did not formally exist in the Psychology Service by the time that the central office transmitted its order for Spiegel to transfer to Texas.

The CSC Board of Appeals and Review, which has come under attack for adopting a reflexively "pro-management" position (cf. Vaughn, 1975), accepted all of the VA's contentions. Overruling the regional office, the board decided that the VA had not violated CSC reduction-in-force procedures in ordering Spiegel to move to Texas or to leave the service, and it agreed with the VA that Spiegel had not suffered a reduction in rank. Accordingly, it refused to order the VA to reinstate Spiegel.

At this point Spiegel and the AFGE went into federal court. They repeated their claims that the VA's actions toward Spiegel were punitive and in violation of CSC regulations. They also charged that the CSC board's decision represented "an improper, arbitrary and capricious interpretation of the Federal Personnel Manual in violation of the . . . U.S. Constitution." . . . Shortly thereafter the V A contacted Spiegel's representatives to seek an out-of-court settlement. No official explanation of this decision has been offered; however, VA officials (who have asked not to be identified) have indicated that the reason for this change in position was the agency's belated realization that the actions taken against Spiegel had been improper, and they didn't think that their case would stand up in court.

Although Spiegel has now won his job back, the basic issues remain unresolved. There have been no changes in policies governing professional roles in the VA or administrative discretion in ordering transfers. As a result, according to Dale Tresidder . . . , Director of the VA Evaluation and Systems Service in Washington, "It could happen all over again."

The Profession's Response

Spiegel's abrupt dismissal as Chief of the Adult Restoration Program came at a time when the public was just becoming aware of [California's] plan to close down the state's mental hospitals. Only 2 days before, the California State Employees Association had released a 17-page report charging that thousands of people had been dumped out of state hospitals into unequipped "board and care" homes or hotels for transients (Endicott, 1972). According to Karl Pottharst . . . , President of the California State Psychological Association (CSPA) at the time, the CSPA Board of Directors were concerned about the apparent breakdown in mental health care. They had, for example, decided to join a lobbying effort at the state capitol to halt further hospital closings. Pottharst, however, felt that more was required. He wanted "to find some way to bring to public attention the barely visible plight of mental patients" who were being precipitously pushed out of state hospitals . . . . Despite assurance of CSPA moral support, efforts to encourage some of the psychologists in the state system to speak out publicly were unsuccessful because the latter were afraid that they would be transferred or lose their jobs if they did. Consequently, upon learning of Spiegel's ouster, Pottharst immediately contacted him and asked him to appear at a news conference called by CSPA and to describe the plight of his patients.

According to Pottharst, another problem in addition to job insecurity that impeded the mobilization of the state-employed psychologists was the lack of clearly defined ethical principles and precedents. Neither the *Ethical Standards* of Psychologists (APA, 1972a) nor the Guidelines for Conditions of Employment for Psychologists (APA, 1972b) seemed to provide clear direction to psychologists torn between loyalty to their clients and loyalty to their employer. Accordingly, Pottharst...wrote to Richard Brooks, then Chairman of the CPA Committee on Ethics and Professional Responsibility, to charge the committee "with the task of defining a professionally responsible and ethical position with regard to the issues raised in this situation (i.e., patient dumping) in time for reporting to the CSPA Board of Directors at its June meeting." The committee, however, did not carry out this mandate.

Pottharst wrote a number of other letters during this period concerning Spiegel. Included among these was a letter to S. Don Schultz, then Chairman of the APA Board of Professional Affairs asking that the board direct its Committee on Academic Freedom and Conditions of Employment (CAFCOE) to investigate what had happened to Spiegel. Schultz...wrote back that it would be best if Spiegel himself filed a complaint with CAFCOE and requested an investigation. He also suggested that Pottharst formally request the Task Force on Standards for Providers of Psychological Services to review the situation. However, he expressed doubt that either unit would be able to take action prior to the board's next meeting, 2 months away. This turned out to be the case. Although Schultz did inform the board of his correspondence with Pottharst, it took no action.

Spiegel, meanwhile, had acted upon Schultz's advice and had filed a complaint with CAFCOE, which by this time included the issue of his transfer in addition to his removal as restoration chief. Although F. Nowell Jones, Chairman of CAFCOE, called him several times shortly after he submitted his complaint, Spiegel soon began to doubt the wisdom of having requested APA's intervention. Overall, APA seemed unresponsive and ineffectual, and its procedures for handling his grievance seemed slow and cumbersome. Finally, fearing the CAFCOE's investigators might lack the experience or skill to get at the truth or would interfere in some way with the defense being prepared by his lawyers, Spiegel decided to disengage himself from the committee. Consequently, when APA Central Office staff wrote requesting information and indicated that his case would be considered closed unless this information was received, he did not respond. Inexplicably, he failed to give his reason and APA, for its part, did not inquire into it. The committee...simply voted to close the case.

The Loneliness of Whistle Blowing

The reaction of the other hospital employees has left Spiegel nonplussed. After he was ordered to Texas, but before he was actually separated, Spiegel reported that many staff people would come up to him to express their support and to "leak" information to him on what the administration was planning next. When he returned to his job, many people came up to congratulate him and to tell him how happy they were that a person could successfully stand up to them. Despite the positive reception that he received upon his return and prior to his leaving, none of the staff contacted him during his hiatus. "I assumed that the people who are tied into the system were afraid, but I really don't know," he says....

Had it not been for George Katz, a Wadsworth psychologist fired along with Spiegel when he too refused to accept a transfer, and the AFGE, Spiegel indicated that it would have been very difficult psychologically. He and Katz were in frequent contact comparing their similar situations. The AFGE, he said . . . was "really marvelous. There was always someone there you could talk to. And they were always willing to try something." (Spiegel had not always been a union supporter. It wasn't until after he had received his transfer order and had received the immediate backing of local union representatives that he joined the union.) . . .

In view of the publicity surrounding his case and the considerable brouhaha that it generated, Spiegel assumed that everyone would have known about it. Not so. Soon after his return to the hospital after an absence of nearly 3 years, he ran into an old colleague. "Where have you been?" the other researcher asked, "I haven't seen you around in a while."

Chapter 11

THE ETHICS OF TELETHERAPY, INTERNET THERAPY, AND OTHER DIGITAL WORK

Challenges of the New Technologies

Technology creates new ways to reach our patients. Distance disappears and barriers fall. We can start and end therapy without ever being in the same room with our patient. Hawn (2009) wrote in "Take Two Aspirin and Tweet Me in the Morning: How Twitter, Facebook, and Other Social Media Are Reshaping Health Care": "Across the health-care industry, from large hospital networks to patient support groups, new media tools like weblogs, instant messaging platforms, video chat, and social networks are reengineering the way doctors and patients interact" (p. 361; see also Fischer & Soyez, 2015). The new technologies can change how we work with our patients and what treatments we provide. Mohr (2009) noted: "Existing and emerging telecommunications technologies not only allow us to extend access to mental health care, but they also provide opportunities to develop fundamentally new treatment paradigms" (p. 343).

This brave new digital world of clinical possibilities brings with it ethical challenges (Appelbaum & Kopelman, 2014; Drum & Littleton, 2014; Jordan et al., 2014; F. W. Kaslow, Patterson, & Gottlieb, 2011; Lindinger-Sternart & Piazza, 2014; Lustgarten, 2015). For example, as digital records, communication, and storage moves toward cloud-based technology, Lustgarten (2015) provides a thoughtful analysis of the ethical challenges, along with advantages, that the cloud brings to clinical work. One challenge is keeping digital data secure. Blumenthall and McGraw (2015) noted:

> The personal health information of patients . . . is not safe, and it needs to be . . . . If patients have concerns that their digitized personal health information will be compromised, they will resist sharing it via electronic means . . . . Concerned patients may also withhold sensitive information about issues such as mental health, substance abuse, human immunodeficiency virus status, and genetic predispositions. Surveys suggest this may already be happening to some degree. (p. 1424)

This chapter takes a look at clinical work in the digital world, ethical challenges of working in that world, and a set of questions that can help us think through how to meet those challenges in our own clinical work.

Consider these vignettes:

- Roberto lives in a small Florida town and uses a wheelchair to get around. He does not own a car. Feeling lonely and trapped in a job he hates, he is ready to begin therapy again. Ten years ago a cognitive behavioral therapist had helped him after he had been in a serious car wreck. Wanting to work with a cognitive behavior therapist again, he discovers that the closest CBT office is over 2 hours away. The distance is impractical: He could not take that much time off work even if he could find someone to drive him there and back once or twice a week. He decides to search the web, examining professional sites, consulting referral databases, and following leads. Within days he has found Dr. Spillane, a psychologist specializing in CBT who will provide therapy online. During a 45-minute session each week, they each sit at their computers, using webcams and their computers' audio systems to communicate with each other.

- Dr. Mosley's third patient of the day is Edgar, a young man with an impulse control disorder and a history of violence and alcohol abuse. It is Edgar's sixth session and he seems starkly different. He is flushed, agitated, and clearly not sober. He begins speaking loudly and is soon screaming. His company downsized and fired him 4 days ago. The bank won't give him a loan he needs to tide him over. It seems everyone is against him. This morning he found evidence that his best friend, a man he had often mentioned in therapy — their families shared a vacation each year and often went on weekend hiking and camping trips together — had been sleeping with Edgar's wife. Edgar gets up and begins pacing as he talks about how a man just could not put up with something like this, that he would put a stop to it and make his friend pay. He seems to get more and more worked up. He stops pacing and turns to face Dr. Mosely: "I'm going to get a gun and kill him and all his family right now." Edgar is out the door before Dr. Mosely has any chance of stopping him.

She runs to her phone, calls 911, and tells the police her patient's name, intentions, and home address, and that he had been clear that he was going straight to a gun shop and then to murder his friend and the friend's family. She does not know the name of the friend. She then calls Edgar's home phone, hoping someone there will be able to identify the friend, but there is no answer. She sits down at her computer and Googles her patient's full name. She finds his Facebook page, which includes vacation photos and the name of Edgar's friend. She uses that name to find the friend's phone number, which she gives to the police, who are able to contact the family and protect them until they find Edgar and place him on a 72-hour hold in a locked facility for a psychological evaluation.

- Dr. Christie is the only therapist in a very remote rural setting. A man who just moved there from Rwanda contacts him because his 13-year-old daughter is distraught and depressed. She refuses to tell her family why she is upset but tells her father that she needs to see a therapist. The problem is that although the father can speak a little English, his daughter speaks only Swahili. The daughter will say nothing to the therapist if her father is to serve as translator. No one else in the area speaks both Swahili and English. Dr. Christie begins searching the web and soon finds someone fluent in both Swahili and English who has been trained to serve as a translator in mental health settings. She is aware of the sensitive issues and intense emotional reactions that can arise, the need for rapport and precise translation, potential problems due to cultural differences and regional dialect, and confidentiality requirements. During each of Dr. Christie's sessions with the daughter, the translator will join them in videoconference.

- Jean is a born-again Christian who tries to live her life in accordance with the Bible. Profoundly depressed, she talks with her pastor, who prays with her, provides spiritual guidance, and suggests that meeting with a therapist might be helpful. There are three therapists in her town. She schedules an initial session with each but never feels comfortable talking with them and does not feel that they understand, appreciate, or perhaps even respect her beliefs. She asks her pastor for help in finding a therapist who shares her religious beliefs. Her pastor asks the church hierarchy and his fellow pastors for help, and a week later he provides Jean with the name of a therapist, Dr. Salter, who is a member of another church in the same denomination who will meet with her weekly via videophone. Though Jean does not have a videophone and does not even own a computer, the pastor will let her use the church's videophone in one of the church offices once a week.

These vignettes illustrate just a few of the many benefits that digital technologies provide to us and our patients. But the benefits come with costs, risks, and occasional disasters.

RISKS, DOWNSIDES, AND DISASTERS

Digital technologies take confidential information that was once confined to a paper chart kept under lock and key and spread it over electronic networks. Carelessness, human error, and hacker ingenuity make these networks vulnerable to a growing cascade of breaches. Liu, Musen, and Chou (2015) reported that 29 million records containing confidential patient information had already been breached between 2010 and 2013. Wike (2014) noted that "roughly 1 in 10 Americans . . . have been affected by big data breaches" of their private health information.

Policies promising privacy often fail to deliver in practice. Freeny (2007) wrote:

> The gravitation to an electronic medical record promises much greater speed and efficiency in using client medical information in critical situations. However, it is a direction that also contains great confidentiality compromises for the client as the world has gone global in distributing confidential information. Unfortunately, mental health clinicians are largely ignorant of the full ramifications of these new initiatives. The HIPAA privacy rules suggested that the bar would be raised for clinical privacy, but, in fact, the standards were significantly lowered. (p. 13; see also Alonso-Zaldivar, 2008; Richards, 2009)

Sometimes those policing privacy fail to follow the rules they enforce on others. In 2014, the Canadian Broadcasting Corporation reported that the Office of the Privacy Commissioner of Canada had lost an unencrypted hard drive with private data on hundreds of people (E. Chung, 2014). The report noted that "the information on the hard drive dates back 12 years, even though a government-wide policy says records of this kind aren't supposed to be kept for more than seven" (E. Chung, 2014).And sometimes patient information has been kept in databases without informed consent. Those who maintain the databases may react strongly against those who object. The *British Medical Journal* reported that a "junior doctor . . . was excluded from work for five years after she objected to the inclusion of patients' medical records, including her own, on research databases without consent" (Dyer, 2008, p. 63).

As we house confidential patient information in distant servers, send it through many networks, and carry it around in our laptops and personal digital assistants, it becomes ever more vulnerable to theft and other forms of loss. Here are just a few examples:

- The Toronto *Globe & Mail* reported that "Alberta Health Minister Fred Horne said Wednesday he is 'outraged' a laptop containing key information on 620,000 patients was stolen four months ago but only now brought to his department's attention. The information includes unencrypted names, birthdates, health card numbers, billing codes, billing amounts and diagnostic codes for patients" (D. Bennett, 2014).

• Reuters reported that "a data security breach of Montana's state health records has compromised the Social Security numbers and other personal information of some 1.3 million people, but the full extent of damage from the intrusion is unclear" (Zuckerman, 2014).

• The Canadian Broadcasting Corporation released an article stating: "This latest breach of privacy is the fifth to come to light at Eastern Health since 2012. In July 2012, Eastern Health dealt with the largest privacy breach in the province's history.... [Beverley Clarke, vice-president of privacy for Eastern Health,] indicated that some in the workforce don't get how significant the issue is. 'All 13,000 employees, I guess, truly do not understand yet that in fact this is inappropriate,' Clarke said" ("Insider Tipped Eastern Health to Latest Privacy Breach," 2014).

• The *Wall Street Journal* reported that "Anthem Inc., the country's second-biggest health insurer, said hackers broke into a database containing personal information for about 80 million of its customers and employees" (Matthews & Yadron, 2015).

• According to the Canadian Broadcasting Corporation, "The personal-health data of millions of British Columbians has been accessed without proper authorization." ("B.C. Privacy Breach Shows Millions Affected," 2013).

• Federal News Radio reported that "Veterans Affairs sustained another data breach, putting more than 7,000 veterans at risk of identity theft" (Miller, 2014).

• Community Health Systems, according to the *Wall Street Journal*, announced that "its computer network was a target of an external criminal cyberattack...that affected data related to some 4.5 million individuals" (McCarthy, 2014).

Chapter 24 focuses on maintaining patient privacy and confidentiality, but it is worth noting here that clinicians need to know the relevant laws and regulations in this area, such as the U.S. Privacy Act of 1974 and its amendments (e.g., the Computer Matching and Privacy Protection Act of 1988), the U.S. Health Insurance Portability and Accountability Act of 1996 (HIPAA) and its amendments, the Canadian Privacy Act of 1982, the Canadian Personal Information and Electronics Document Act (PIPEDA), and Section 8 of the Canadian Charter of Rights and Freedoms (see Pope, 2014).

Technology presents other potential problems. Clinicians' careless tweets, blogs, and posts to social media sites have piled up unprofessional public comments about patients, colleagues, and settings (see, e.g., Kesselhiem, Batra,

Belmonte, Boland, & McGregor, 2014). These public comments can affect clinicians' careers. Jain (2009) wrote:

> In an e-mail to students and faculty of Harvard Medical School, Dean for Medical Education Jules Dienstag wrote: "Caution is recommended . . . in using social networking sites such as Facebook or MySpace. Items that represent unprofessional behavior that are posted by you on such networking sites reflect poorly on you and the medical profession. Such items may become public and could subject you to unintended exposure and consequences." At the Drexel University College of Medicine, medical students are warned about the possibility that information placed on social-networking sites might influence the fate of their applications for postgraduate training: "Programs/employers are increasingly gaining access to social networking sites such as Facebook and MySpace to see what they can learn about candidates." Although legal questions surrounding the relationship between clinical medicine and social networking are as yet undefined, there are obvious concerns for individuals and institutions, since their Internet presence makes clinicians' attitudes and activities increasingly visible. (p. 650; see also Dolan, 2009; McCoy, 2009)

Ponce and colleagues (2013) found that almost half of residency applicants had created Facebook profiles and that 16% of these profiles included unprofessional content.

Rubenstein (2008) described another kind of problem that occurred with a social networking site: "Two workers at University of New Mexico Hospital were fired for using their cellphone cameras to take shots of patients in treatment, then posting the pics on MySpace."

One of the most fascinating accounts of a clinician undone through his use of technology involved an Ivy League–educated physician on trial for malpractice. During cross-examination, he was suddenly asked if he was "Flea." As the *Boston Globe* (Saltzman, 2007) reported:

> Flea, jurors in the case didn't know, was the screen name for a blogger who had written often and at length about a trial remarkably similar to the one that was going on in the courtroom that day.
>
> In his blog, Flea had ridiculed the plaintiff's case and the plaintiff's lawyer. He had revealed the defense strategy. He had accused members of the jury of dozing.
>
> With the jury looking on in puzzlement, Lindeman admitted that he was, in fact, Flea.
>
> The next morning, on May 15, he agreed to pay what members of Boston's tight-knit legal community describe as a substantial settlement — case closed.

Digital technologies also provide the opportunity to make information about psychological tests — including the test items themselves and scoring guides — widely available to anyone who can access the Internet. Schultz and Loving (2012) found that of the top 88 websites offering information about the Rorschach, 19% posed a direct threat to test security (see also Hartmann & Hartmann, 2014). A controversial instance involved Wikipedia. Cohen (2009) reported that "the online encyclopedia Wikipedia has been engulfed in a furious debate involving psychologists who are angry that the 10 original Rorschach plates are reproduced online, along with common responses for each." LoBello and Zachar (2007) found that

> psychological test materials are available on eBay. Overall, about half of the test items listed for sale did not specify any restrictions on purchases. The sale of test manuals containing the administration procedures and responses to items represents the greatest potential breach of test security. However, even when test manuals were offered for sale, almost 40% of these items were listed without purchase restrictions. (p. 69)

The tests they found for sale on the Internet included the Wechsler Adult Intelligence Scale — Revised, Wechsler-Bellevue Intelligence Scale, Wechsler Individual Achievement Test, Wechsler Preschool and Primary Scale of Intelligence — Revised, Wechsler Memory Scale-Revised, Rorschach, Thematic Apperception Test, Minnesota Multiphasic Personality Inventory, Minnesota Multiphasic Personality Inventory — Adolescent, and Behavior Assessment System for Children — Second Edition. For examples involving other tests, see Bauer and McCaffrey (2006).

FIVE SPECIAL PITFALLS

The risks, downsides, and disasters reviewed to this point — along with the six potential disasters described in Chapter 2's section "Computer Coincidences" — shine a light on areas requiring special awareness. The following vignettes illustrate five of the most common pitfalls clinicians encounter in the digital world.

Pitfall 1

Skeptical at first about trying to conduct therapy sessions over the Internet — he used his simple computer only for e-mail — Dr. Chandler had finally decided to develop a niche practice of working with patients using webcams. Not trusting his limited computer skills, he hired his neighbor's daughter, a Massachusetts Institute of Technology graduate student home for a 2-week break, to select a comprehensive system, install it for him, and teach him how to use it. She spent the first week buying and installing the components. She spent the second week teaching him the system's wonders: how to use the webcam to talk with another person, how to record the sessions, how to keep his patient information and treatment files in digital form, how to use the system's scheduling software, and how to back up all his data using an independent hard drive. When Dr. Chandler felt confident he knew how to operate the comprehensive system she'd created, she uploaded a website announcing his services and allowing people to request appointments and pay in advance using credit cards or PayPal.

Within months he had six clients, one of whom was Philip, a fragile, shy, anxious ballet dancer. Philip felt that no one really listened to him but was also afraid to talk honestly with others about himself. He would refer indirectly to his "secrets," suggesting that if anyone knew what he was really like, they'd hate him and never speak to him again. It took Philip months to work up the courage and trust to tell Dr. Chandler what he had never told another soul. He had barely gotten his secret out before he began sobbing, unable to continue. It was at this moment that Dr. Chandler's system crashed.

It was only later that afternoon, after he'd finally found a computer specialist in the yellow pages who made emergency office visits, that he learned that the data kept on his computer was gone. A new computer worm had systematically erased and repeatedly overwritten his schedule, his billing records, his patient contact information and files, his recorded sessions, and the award acceptance address he'd written for the convention next week when he was to receive the Niche Practitioner of the Year honor from his state psychological association.

This, however, was not the worst of it. The worst of it was when the computer specialist pointed out that because he'd left the independent hard drive on which he made his backups plugged into the main system "for convenience," the worm had been able to access it, erase it, and overwrite the disk repeatedly, making any attempt to rescue the original data hopeless. All of his data, including his backup copies, were gone.

Dr. Chandler wanted to contact Philip right away, to tell him what had happened and to find out how he was, but because he no longer had any contact information, it was some time before he was able to track him down.

Dr. Chandler's adventures in Internet therapy illustrate an important reality: It is not just therapists who are both fallible and vulnerable; so are our computers. An important part of using computers in a therapy practice is evaluating carefully when and how they can fail and preparing for those failures.

Pitfall 2

Dr. Doyle was tired of it all. In solo practice, she sat in the same chair in the same room most of the day, getting very little exercise. She was exhausted by the end of the day and didn't feel like doing much of anything except going home, eating dinner, and going to bed.

On impulse, she signed up for a noon beginner's class in belly dancing. It changed her life. She loved it. She looked forward to it every day, and every afternoon she felt energized. She knew she was becoming more fit, building stamina, and toning her muscles. But mainly belly dancing brought joy to her life.

A woman in her class told her about a belly dancing website. You could sign up and become part of a discussion list. Members shared their love of belly dancing and traded information about dances, costumes, courses, and festivals. Dr. Doyle visited the website and signed up.

It was only later that Dr. Doyle learned that by signing up, she had agreed to allow the organization to access her computer's address book. It used the names to send invitations to join the belly dancing list to everyone in her address book. The invitations mentioned her name and were written ambiguously so that recipients might assume they came from her. Her address book contained the names of her current and former therapy patients, attorneys she'd been in contact with for cases in which they'd be deposing and cross-examining her as an expert witness, a former boyfriend, various colleagues including members of the state licensing board, her rabbi, and her bank's loan officer to whom she'd applied for some funds to tide her over.

Dr. Doyle's misfortune shows the hazards of not understanding the implications of participating in cyberactivities such as joining lists or providing information on websites. Many of us become used to reflexively clicking "agree" without reading all the dull boilerplate and legalese of policy statements when we install new software. That reflex takes over when we journey around the web. And even if we read every statement before agreeing, many of them may not cover material that is crucial to us in making informed decisions and avoiding disasters.

Pitfall 3

Dr. Hammett had been working via video with a girl in her midteens for close to 3 months. Her parents lived in a remote area, were desperate to find some way to help her, but were unable to travel on a regular basis to a therapist's office. The girl was homeschooled and highly intelligent. Dr. Hammett was sure that one of her problems was loneliness: She spent most of her time in her room, painstakingly creating stop-action videos, which she refused to share with Dr. Hammett, saying only that she always put them on the web and that he could find them if he was really interested.

Attempts to engage her in conversation, to encourage her to talk, or to ask any kind of questions were met with sullen evasions or passive-aggressive comments. It took time to gain her trust.

The session she finally started talking, she began telling Dr. Hammett how much she hated him. He was like almost everyone else in her life. He did not listen. He didn't care about her. He just wanted to control her. He said stupid things. She hated him.

It wasn't the most comfortable session for Dr. Hammett, but he felt very good about the breakthrough. She was expressing what was going on inside her in a very honest and direct way. The real work had begun.

It was only several days later that Dr. Hammett's friends and colleagues alerted him to how he was becoming an international sensation. When he typed his name into Google and followed the links, he discovered what his patient had done.

She had been recording their sessions, and had posted a clever short video, "My Experience of Therapy with Dr. Hammett," on YouTube. Her video had gone viral.

The video showed segment after segment of her saying something she'd never said during the session but had recorded later for her video. After each segment, she'd inserted a clip of something Dr. Hammett had said during their sessions, taken completely out of context and chosen because it made him look like a fool.

One segment showed her saying, "Dr. Hammett, I feel like no one listens to me, no one hears what I really say," followed by a clip of something he'd said when the audio feed had been temporarily interrupted: "I can see you but I can't hear anything you're saying."

Another segment showed her saying, "My parents are only interested in my always-perfect brother; he's all they want to talk about. It's like no one is interested in me; I don't even exist," followed by Dr. Hammett saying, "I wonder if we could talk about your brother."

Another showed her yelling, "I can't take it anymore! I'm going to hang myself with this noose!" followed by him smiling and saying "What a wonderful idea! I was hoping you would! I think this is a good time to end our session."

Dr. Hammett discovered a growing number of alternate versions of his patient's video gaining popularity on the web. Kids had downloaded the video, making copies, and replaced his actual patient with themselves as the patient, making up new lines for him to respond to, each boy or girl trying to create a funnier or more outrageous version.

Stunned and enraged at what his patient was doing to his dignity, image, and reputation, Dr. Hammett grabbed the phone and called the city's most powerful law firm, making an appointment that afternoon with the firm's most feared and successful litigator.

Quickly taking a seat in the litigator's office that afternoon, Dr. Hammett explained the decision and his intention not only to take legal action to have the videos taken down but also to sue his patient for every penny her family had.

Accustomed to listening to outraged people consumed with a molten determination to sue, the attorney listened with the patience of someone who charged $500 an hour for consultation. He explained the difficulties of legal action against something that was clearly satire and likely protected by the First Amendment, the significant expenses — expenses that Dr. Hammett would have to pay out of his own pocket — involved in preparing for and conducting a trial, the fact that filing suit would make the videos more popular than ever, the problems of dealing with the many jurisdictions — some outside the United States — from which different kids had uploaded their versions of the video, and what would happen to his reputation if the media began portraying him as someone suing parents for not stopping his child patient from making fun of him.

Dr. Hammett had been unaware of how the technology he used had changed the nature of his practice, affected the privacy of what he said and did as a therapist in his own office, and given tools to his patients that could be used in ways he had not imagined.

Pitfall 4

Dr. MacDonald had worked as hard as anyone else in his graduate training program, and his transcripts were as good as anyone else's who graduated that year. He'd worked with some of the program's best professors, and they seemed to like him. He'd gotten into a good internship and done well. His supervisors had praised his skills and invited him to stay on an extra year so that he could be licensed by the time he was ready to look for a position as a clinician in the student counseling center at one of the universities.

He found entry-level openings for a counselor at 10 centers and submitted applications, making sure all the transcripts, letters of recommendation, and other materials arrived before the deadline. What surprised him was that not one of the schools called him for an initial interview.

He had a very rough year after leaving his internship setting, able to find a clinical job — but not in a university counseling center — only after 10 months of searching.

It was only after he'd been licensed for almost three years that a friend who'd been working at a university counseling center explained why he'd had such a hard time finding work.

Dr. MacDonald had become well known among psychologists on the Internet, and not in a particularly good way. He posted frequently on psychology lists, pointing out mistakes in his colleagues' messages, ridiculing questions as stupid or naive, and insulting anyone who disagreed with him. He was especially hard on students and on colleagues who did not belong to the particular list on which he was posting.

Dr. MacDonald was unaware of how his posts, which he thought were so effective in shaping opinions about other people, actually shaped how people viewed him. He did not realize that the reputation he created in cyberspace might play a role in how future employers and members of hiring committees viewed him as a job candidate.

Pitfall 5

Dr. James had a thriving videoconferencing therapy practice. She had set up her website so that applicants, who created a user name and password, filled out applications. When she found an appropriate candidate for therapy, the patient scheduled an appointment and paid (using a credit card or PayPal) via the website. At the scheduled time, she and the patient met via webcam for each therapy session.

One of her most interesting patients was a young software engineer who had become independently wealthy when he sold his company to a large corporation. His problems were mainly indecision about what he now wanted to do with his life and his travel schedule (he had to fly to other countries to troubleshoot their implementation of the software products his company made — he was obligated to travel as one of the contractual stipulations to the corporation that had bought his company).

Three months into the treatment, Dr. James received an unpleasant letter, sent registered mail, return receipt requested, from an attorney in a distant state. She discovered that the patient was actually a minor whose parents were involved in a bitter divorce. The lawyer, representing one of the parents, wanted to know why Dr. James was providing treatment to a minor without the informed consent of the boy's parent. He also wanted to know why Dr. James was providing services that required a license when a check with the state licensing board showed that Dr. James was not licensed to practice in the state where the boy lived and was receiving treatment. He asked Dr. James to send the boy's assessment and treatment records to him within the next 5 business days. Soon after, Dr. James learned that the boy was not a software engineer and had never owned his own business. He was in high school and worked part time at a fast food outlet. The boy apparently believed his fantasies and suffered from a serious psychological disorder. However, Dr. James had not recognized the disorder, conducted an adequate assessment, or provided the appropriate treatment.

Dr. James's focus on the wonders of website and videoconferencing technologies led her to overlook the responsibilities they bring with them. She failed to notice that the webcam's power to let her work with patients in distant states and provinces meant that she needed to be familiar with and comply with the relevant laws and regulations. Working within the framework of videoconferencing seemed to distract her from doing the kind of careful assessment she no doubt would have conducted had she been working with the client in person.

QUESTIONS TO ASSESS USES OF DIGITAL MEDIA

The following questions and responses may be helpful in avoiding pitfalls, strengthening ethical intelligence, and meeting the challenges of working in the digital world.

Where Is the Computer?

Some readers may have visited clinics and seen confidential information about patients on a computer screen. One of the first questions to ask is: When this computer is on, who can see the screen? Can anyone who is not authorized see patient names or other sensitive information on the screen? This can be a problem for those who work with confidential information on portable computers during long flights or in terminals, waiting rooms, and other public spaces.

When the computer is unattended — whether for only a few minutes or overnight — is there a secure barrier between it and anyone who might want to access it or steal it? If you were to offer someone a considerable sum of money to access the computer without authorization or to steal it, how confident are you that you would not lose your money?

Is the Computer Protected From Hackers?

If the computer is hooked up to the Internet, a software or hardware firewall can help protect against unauthorized entry. Note the word *help*. No method of protection is foolproof. All have strengths but also vulnerabilities. The more layers of protection you use, the more secure your confidential data will be. If one or two layers fail to block unauthorized entry, others may work. Like a house with many locks and forms of security, a well-protected computer may discourage all but the most determined and skilled hackers.

Is the Computer Protected From Malicious Code That Can Access Confidential Information?

When computers connect to the Internet, they are vulnerable. Security hardware and software can lower but not remove the vulnerability. Viruses, Trojans, worms, and other malware continue to find more devious paths to fool a computer's defenses. E-mails formatted in HTML can mask malicious code. E-mail attachments can infect a computer before they are opened. A visit to a website may result in a malicious program downloading into the computer without the user's knowledge. These programs can look for a computer's most sensitive files (e.g., those that fit the patterns of social security numbers, credit card numbers, passwords, financial statements; those that contain words like *private, confidential, clinical,* or *medical*). They can transmit those files to a temporary throwaway address in another country, post them on an anonymous website, or send them to every e-mail address in your computer's memory.

One approach to protecting confidential information on a computer is a two-step process: (1) keep several layers of protection on the computer and (2) keep the information encrypted on a removable medium (such as a portable external hard drive, CD, or DVD). The removable medium would always be kept secure and would be hooked up to the computer only when the therapist is using it.

An approach that offers more protection is to use one computer for connecting with the Internet and storing nonconfidential data and a separate computer that is never hooked up to the Internet or other networks to store confidential information. Because the confidential information is stored on a completely isolated, stand-alone computer, there is no wired or wireless link from it to any network and it cannot transmit data to unauthorized recipients.

Is Your Computer Protected From Viruses and Other Malware?

Do you have a good antivirus program? Do you maintain it by installing the company's new virus definitions?

Is the Computer Protected Using a Strong Password?

If someone finds a computer unattended or steals it, a system of passwords can make it difficult to access confidential information. Loading the operating system when turning on the computer, gaining access to a set of files, and opening a particular file can be made contingent on passwords.

Words do not make the most secure passwords. Dictionary programs are readily available to hackers, who use them to enter a password-protected computer. A password is likely to block password-breaking software if it has a combination of lowercase letters, uppercase letters, and symbols and if it runs at least 12 characters long.

Any password is useless if someone who is determined to access your computer sees it written down somewhere. Someone sitting at your computer and attempting to gain unauthorized access is likely to look through the papers on and in your desk (including under the keyboard and on the monitor) to see if the password has been jotted down.

Is Confidential Information Encrypted?

While passwords can limit access to information by unsophisticated users (assuming you have a strong password and do not leave it written on a slip of paper by your computer), hackers can easily get around those passwords and read, steal, alter, or destroy the information. However, even if someone defeats your password protection, he or she will still face a formidable layer of protection if your computer's files are encrypted. Encryption scrambles or camouflages information (e.g., progress notes, billing information) by changing it into a form that makes it extremely hard for those without the encryption key to restore to readable form. Apple, Microsoft, and other makers of the major computer operating systems as well as other companies (e.g., PGP at www.pgp.com) provide software programs that will encrypt files. However, the free hard disk encryption programs that come with the Apple and Microsoft operating systems are *not* turned on by default—you have to turn on these disk encryption programs for them to start the encryption protection—and only a tiny minority of users turn them on (Goodman, 2015).

In an excellent article, psychologist Samuel Lustgarten (2015) gives us solid advice:

> Encrypt Everything. If possible, every client record and communication should be encrypted. When mobile devices are used for client contact (i.e., text messages and/or e-mails), it is important to consider the phone's encryption capabilities. Currently, iPhones, with a good password, can be encrypted and protected from password attacks for about 5.5 years (Apple Inc., 2014b). It is also possible for iPhones to encrypt iMessages (text messages between iPhones), which would only be accessible between sender and recipient.

How Are Confidential Files Deleted?

On most computers, using the Delete key to get rid of a file leaves virtually all of the file on the hard disk, where it can be retrieved easily by an inexpensive data recovery program. To dispose confidential files, it is useful to use some form of secure deleting, such as one that involves repeatedly overwriting the old file with random characters.

How Are Computer Disks Discarded?

From time to time, the news media report what has become a standard story: Someone sells or discards a computer on which confidential information is discovered. A few examples were cited earlier in this chapter. If a computer disk or other electronic storage medium stored confidential information, it should be completely degaussed or physically destroyed.

How Do You Guard Against Human Error in Handling Confidential Information?

Most people who have been online for a while are familiar with the sudden surprise that comes with the realization: I just sent that message to the wrong person! When we communicate over the Internet about confidential patient information, the price of human error can be steep. What procedures do you have in place to make sure that confidential information is not misaddressed?

How Do You Make Sure That Only the Intended Recipient Receives Your Confidential Information?

Even when we have made sure that an e-mail containing confidential information is addressed to the right person, the right person's e-mail address may be used by more than one person. Sometimes partners or family members share an e-mail address. Even if the sharing is not routine, a friend or family member may monitor someone's e-mails while the person is temporarily disabled, ill, or on vacation.

Do Your Clients Clearly Understand the Ways in Which They Can or Can't Communicate With You via E-Mail, Text Message, or Other Digital Means?

Each of us has our own way of approaching — or staying away from — digital technology in our work with patients. As the examples at the beginning of the chapter illustrated, e-mail, videoconferencing, and other digital formats are wonderful resources. But they also have risks. What is important is that patients understand how a specific clinician uses e-mail or other methods of digital communication. Clear understanding can prevent problems like these:

- A therapist giving a patient her e-mail address for anything important that the patient needs to communicate before the next session, which is 2 weeks later, and the patient begins sending 30 to 50 messages each day.
- A patient searching the web to find an e-mail address for the therapist, finding it, and sending messages to that address, when in fact it is the address of another person with the same name.
- A patient finding an e-mail address for the therapist and using it to send messages between therapy sessions about material that is too difficult for the patient to say face-to-face, when the e-mail address is an old one that the therapist does not use anymore.
- A patient finding a therapist's e-mail address and using it to tell the therapist that the patient will be taking an overdose of sleeping pills to commit

suicide later that night but that the therapist should respond only if the therapist thinks the patient is worth saving, and the e-mail account is one that the therapist checks only once a week.

Is Your Professional Website or the Website of the Clinic, Hospital, or Group Practice at Which You Work Accessible to People With Disabilities?

For additional resources in this area, please see "Seven Easy Steps Toward Web Site Accessibility" at http://kpope.com/seven/index.php; "Web Accessibility Verifiers" at http://kpope.com/verify/index.php; and the section titled "Accessibility for People With Disabilities" in Chapter 18.

If Your Website Includes a Function That Enables Patients to Communicate With You (e.g., by Signing on With a User Name and Password), Has It Been Adequately Secured?

Many of the security measures you take will be versions of the steps you take to secure your personal computer and network, guarding against hackers, hijackers, malware, unintentional viewing of confidential material, and so on.

If You Use Social Networking Media, Such as Facebook, Twitter, and So On, Does the Medium Form a Link Between You and Any of Your Patients or Your Patients' Family Members? If So, How, if at All, Does It Affect the Therapy or Your Relationships With Your Patients?

Introducing new forms of relationships with patients should be done with thoughtfulness and care. Countless problems — and sometimes catastrophes — can be avoided if we ourselves avoid entering new domains in a thoughtless and careless way. Thinking through new forms of relationships in terms of our own theoretical orientation and approach, the individual patient, the available research, the practicalities involved, informed consent issues, documentation, and so on, can help us meet the highest ethical and clinical standards.

Are You Competent to Provide Services Through Digital Media?

If, for example, you provide services in which you do not meet the patient face-to-face but provide therapy and communicate with the patient solely via e-mail, through a website, or using a web camera and microphone, have you received adequate training in this kind of therapy?

Are You Aware of the Relevant Laws and Regulations Governing the Use of Digital Media in Providing Clinical Services?

This area can be particularly complicated if you are in one state or province and the patient is in another state or province. Cross-jurisdictional provision of services may be limited to a certain period of time or may not be allowed at all. One good step to take is to check with the licensing boards in both jurisdictions. The provider of your professional liability policy may also provide helpful information and guidance. The company insuring your work has an obvious interest in helping you avoid problems. The Association of State and Provincial Psychology Boards (ASPPB) announced the introduction of the Psychology Interjurisdictional Compact (PSYPACT), which creates a legal and defensible yet practical system for regulating and facilitating the use of telecommunications and temporary face-to-face practice across jurisdictional boundaries. A resource kit is being developed by the Council of State Governments for the new interstate compact (ASPPB, 2015).

Are You Aware of Emerging Research on Clinical Services Offered Through Digital Media?

Research in these areas continues to evolve, using increasingly sophisticated methodologies. Helpful articles presenting or reviewing research into teletherapy and Internet-based therapy include Andersson, Cuijpers, Carlbring, Riper, & Hedman (2014); Clough and Casey (2015); Rooksby, Elouafkaoui, Humphris, Clarkson, and Freeman (2015); Ivarsson et al. (2014); Kok, van Straten, Beekman, & Cuijpers, (2014); Lindner et al. (2014); Mahoney, Mackenzie, Smith, & Andrews (2014); and Ye et al. (2014).

Are You Aware of the Professional Guidelines for Teletherapy, Internet Therapy, and Other Clinical Services Provided Through Digital Media?

As 2011 president of APA, one of the authors (Melba Vasquez) appointed a Joint Task Force on the Development of Guidelines for the Practice of Telepsychology (APA, 2013b) comprised of representatives from APA, ASPPB, and APA Insurance Trust (now The Trust). This was the first time APA had jointly developed professional practice guidelines with other organizations. Those and related guidelines give practitioners useful information and guidance for providing clinical services using telecommunication technologies (APA, 2013b).

These documents made available by professional organizations may be useful in deciding whether and how to use different kinds of digital technology to provide clinical services. Links to each of them (State Psychology Board

Telepsychology Laws/Regulations/Policies/Opinions) are available at http://kspope.com/telepsychology.php

- American Academy of Child and Adolescent Psychiatry: Practice Parameter for Telepsychiatry With Children and Adolescents
- American Medical Association: Guidelines for Patient–Physician Electronic Mail
- American Medical Informatics Association: Guidelines for the Clinical Use of Electronic Mail With Patients
- American Psychological Association: Guidelines for the Practice of Telepsychology
- American Telemedicine Association: Clinical Guidelines for Telepathology
- American Telemedicine Association: Core Operational Guidelines for Telehealth Services Involving Provider–Patient Interactions
- American Telemedicine Association: Evidence-Based Practice for Telemental Health
- American Telemedicine Association: Guidelines for TeleICU Operations
- American Telemedicine Association: Home Telehealth Clinical Guidelines
- American Telemedicine Association: Practice Guidelines for Video-Based Online Mental Health Services
- American Telemedicine Association: Practice Guidelines for Videoconferencing-Based Telemental Health
- Association for Counselling and Therapy Online: Professional Conduct and Code of Ethics
- Association of Psychology Postdoctoral and Internship Centers: Guidelines for the Practice of Telepsychology
- Association of Social Work Boards: Standards for Technology and Social Work Practice
- Canadian Psychological Association: Providing Psychological Services via Electronic Media
- Centers for Medicare & Medicaid Services, U.S. Department of Health and Human Services: Final Rule for Telemedicine Credentialing and Privileging
- Federation of State Medical Boards of the United States: Model Guidelines for the Appropriate Use of the Internet in Medical Practice
- Federation of State Medical Boards of the United States and American College of Physicians: Online Medical Professionalism: Patient and Public Relationships: Policy Statement
- National Association of Social Workers: Standards for Technology and Social Work Practice

- National Board for Certified Counselors and Center for Credentialing and Education, Inc.: The Practice of Internet Counseling
- New Zealand Psychologists Board: Draft Guidelines: Psychology Services Delivered via the Internet and Other Electronic Media
- Ohio Psychological Association (2010): Telepsychology Guidelines
- Online Therapy Institute: Ethical Framework for the Use of Social Media by Mental Health Professionals
- Royal Australian and New Zealand College of Psychiatrists: Professional Practice Standards and Guides for Telepsychiatry

We are in a time of very fast, significant change in the development of and in the requirements of handling protected health information. Psychotherapists are thus required to keep abreast of changes related to risks to privacy (The Trust, 2014).

Chapter 12

COMPETENCE AND THE HUMAN THERAPIST

When patients come to us for help, they trust us to be competent. Ethical practice hinges on competence. Society holds us accountable for competence through courts and licensing boards.

Cynthia Belar (2009; see also Fouad et al., 2009; Fouad & Grus, 2014; Hatcher et al., 2013; N. J. Kaslow et al., 2009; McDaniel et al., 2014; Shen-Miller et al., 2014) discusses our ethical responsibility to train competent psychologists and to maintain our own competence as our "social contract." She emphasizes that a central question for our training programs

> is whether we are producing what we say we are producing—a psychologist competent for entry to practice. This question comes from prospective students, prospective employers, and the public. Indeed our social contract with the public as an independent profession requires that we self-regulate in these matters. (Belar, 2009, p. S63)

Of course, some patients expect magic. For them, competence means we guarantee results, act flawlessly, and meet all needs. Many of us tend to find it tempting to play this imaginary superhero role. Unfortunately, a few give in to the temptation and start to suffer from these delusions.

This chapter is a reminder that as therapists, we are all human and imperfect. We all have weaknesses and blind spots along with our strengths and insights. Failures of competence often spring from our human vulnerabilities. We face temptations, pressures, distractions, demands, and countless other forces that can distort our sense of the limits of our competence or can block our ability to be competent in certain situations. Consider, for example, the ways in which we react to members of different groups. Few, if any of us, are free of all attitudes, beliefs, and preconceptions that could affect our competence to provide therapy or counseling to members of certain groups. Each of us seems to have our own array of group-based reactions that can stunt our competence. See if the following self-assessment turns up any challenges to competence for you. Imagine you are in your office and a new patient walks in. Set aside for the moment whether you have training to work with a member of the group; focus solely on whether the patient's group membership evokes any reactions in you that might weaken your competence to welcome, listen openly to, empathize with, and create a positive working relationship with.

The array of patients you meet in this exercise is as follows:

- A rich, young White man dressed in preppy clothes and speaking in a condescending tone
- An extremely aggressive malpractice attorney who has rarely lost a case, specializes in suing clinicians, and tends to win large judgments
- A heavily tattooed gang member
- A Black woman who is richer, more professionally successful, and personally happier that you've ever hoped you could be and whose minor problem, which brought her to seek therapy, is one you also have and have been unable to overcome
- A leader of the antichoice movement
- Someone who uses racial slurs
- A gay-rights activist
- A migrant worker who speaks English with a thick accent that you can barely understand
- An animal-rights activist who breaks into research labs to free the animals
- A physician whose specialty is performing abortions
- A gun-rights activist who carries a gun where open-carry laws allow but who also has a permit to carry a concealed weapon
- A therapist who specializes in conversion or reparative therapy
- An orthodox Jew
- A Catholic priest
- A devout Muslim
- A medical researcher whose experiments on dogs involve inducing disabling pathologies, painful surgeries, and death within a matter of months
- Someone who believes in the intellectual and moral superiority of their race

How did you do? Turn up any potential challenges to competence? Achieving awareness of these challenges puts us in a better position to handle them carefully, knowledgeably, and ethically.

Keeping in mind that all of us have blind spots, we can acknowledge that despite our best efforts to spot problem areas, some may stay hidden from our awareness for quite a while. We may pride ourselves on our lack of bias toward a certain group and yet our behavior may sometimes (or more often) seem "off" somehow. Others may view what we say or do in regard to members of that group as avoidant, passive-aggressive, subtly hostile (words and behaviors sometimes termed *microaggressions*), or more openly biased — all of which may escape our attention.

The theme of these ethical challenges arising among us on the individual level runs throughout this book and is the focus of the chapter on "Culture, Context, and Individual Differences," but a parallel theme is the way they appear in organizations. For example, think of the different clinics, hospitals, and other agencies with which you're familiar. Imagine each of the patients listed earlier entering that agency, walking to the reception desk, and asking about getting help there. To what extent do you think each person would actually *feel* welcomed and be provided access to help?

The opening chapters of this book rejected views of ethics as rigid rule following and presented an approach in which professional codes, administrative directives, legislative requirements, and other givens mark the start of a process of creative questioning and critical thinking. We search for the most ethical and positive way to respond to each unique patient with unique needs and resources in a unique context.

We carry on this creative questioning and critical thinking as fallible human beings, vulnerable to fatigue, discouragement, frustration, anger, fear, and feeling overwhelmed. Our work depends on not just intellectual competence (knowing about and knowing how) but also what might be called *emotional competence for therapy* (Pope & Brown, 1996).

COMPETENCE AS AN ETHICAL AND LEGAL RESPONSIBILITY

Competence is hard to define. Licensing boards and civil courts sometimes specify defining criteria for areas of practice. More often they require only that in whatever area of therapy and counseling the clinician is practicing, he or she should possess demonstrable competence. Demonstrable competence requires clinicians to produce evidence of the competence. Usually this evidence comes from formal education, professional training, and carefully supervised experience, followed by continuing education.

A competence requirement often appears in ethical, legal, and professional standards. Here are some examples:

- Article 8 (Rules of Professional Conduct), Section 1396, of California Title 16 declares: "The psychologist shall not function outside his or her particular field or fields of competence as established by his or her education, training and experience" (State of California, Department of Consumer Affairs, 2015, p. 61).

- Ethical Standard 2.01a of APA's "Ethical Principles of Psychologists and Code of Conduct" (2010a) states: "Psychologists provide services, teach, and conduct research with populations and only within the boundaries of their competence, based on their education, training, supervised experience, or appropriate professional experience."
- The February 2015 draft of the fourth edition of the Canadian Code of Ethics for Psychologists (CPA, 2015) states that in adhering to the Principle of Responsible Caring, psychologists would "offer or carry out (without supervision) only those activities for which they have established their competence to carry them out to the benefit of others."

The ethical requirement of competence recognizes that the therapist's power and influence (see Chapter 9) should not be handled in a careless, ignorant, thoughtless manner. The complex, hard-to-define nature of therapy tends to cloud why this requirement makes sense. It becomes clearer by analogy to other fields. A physician who is an internist or general practitioner may do excellent work, but would any of us want that physician to perform coronary surgery or neurosurgery on us if he or she does not have adequate education, training, and supervised experience in these forms of surgery? A skilled professor of linguistics may have a solid grasp of a variety of Indo-European languages and dialects but be completely unable to translate a Swahili text.

COMPETENCE AND CONFLICT

Pulled by patients holding exaggerated beliefs about our abilities and pushed by our own impulse to step in and help, we may resist admitting to ourselves and our patients that we lack competence for a particular situation. We may need new clients to pay the bills and fear shutting off a valued referral source. Managed care may require us to take the patient. Nevertheless, extensive education, training, and supervised experience in working with adults do not qualify us to work with children, solid competence in providing individual therapy does not qualify us to lead a therapy group, and expertise in working with people who are profoundly depressed does not qualify us to work with people who have developmental disabilities.

At times, complex situations require great care to determine how to respond to a client's needs while staying within our areas of competence.

For example, a counselor begins working with a client on issues related to depression, an area in which the counselor has had considerable education, training, and supervised experience. Much later the therapeutic journey leads into a problem area — bulimia — for which the counselor has no competence.

Or a client starts meeting with a counselor to deal with problems concentrating at work. Soon the client says she suffers from agoraphobia. Can the counselor ethically assume that the course on anxieties and phobias that she took 10 years ago in graduate school makes her competent? The counselor must decide whether she has the time, energy, and desire to gain competence through continuing education, study, or consultation (APA, 2010a) to provide up-to-date treatment for agoraphobia or whether she needs to refer the client or find some other way for the client to get competent help for agoraphobia.

Clinicians who work in isolated or small communities often face this dilemma. They often take workshops, consult long distance with experts, and come up with creative strategies to make sure that their clients receive competent care.

Despite the clear ethical and legal mandates to practice only with competence, some of us suffer lapses. A national survey of psychologists, for example, found that almost one fourth of the respondents indicated that they had practiced outside their area of competence either rarely or occasionally (Pope, Tabachnick, & Keith-Spiegel, 1987).

INTELLECTUAL COMPETENCE: KNOWING ABOUT AND KNOWING HOW

Intellectual competence involves "knowing about." In our graduate training, internships, supervised experience, continuing education, and other contexts, we learn about the empirical research, theories, interventions, and other topics that we need to do our work. We learn to question the information and assess its validity and relevance for different situations and populations. We learn to create and test hypotheses about assessment and interventions. We find ways to keep up with the latest therapy research.

Part of intellectual competence is learning which clinical approaches, strategies, or techniques show evidence or promise of effectiveness. If clinical methods are to avoid charlatanism, hucksterism, and well-meaning ineffectiveness, they must work (at least some of the time). The practitioner's supposed competence means little if his or her methods lack competence. In his provocative article "The Scientific Basis of Psychotherapeutic Practice: A Question of Values and Ethics," Jerry Singer (1980) emphasized the importance of clinicians remaining knowledgeable concerning the emerging research basis of the methods they use.

Intellectual competence also means learning what approaches have been shown to be invalid or perhaps even harmful. George Stricker (1992) wrote:

> Although it may not be unethical to practice in the absence of knowledge, it is unethical to practice in the face of knowledge. We all must labor with the absence of affirmative data, but there is no excuse for ignoring contradictory data. (p. 544)

Intellectual competence is not frozen in time. David Barlow showed how quickly well-designed research can change our views of which interventions are effective, worthless, or even detrimental. "Stunning developments in health care have occurred during the last several years. Widely accepted health-care strategies have been brought into question by research evidence as not only lacking benefit but also, perhaps, as inducing harm" (Barlow, 2004, p. 869; see also Barlow, 2005a, 2005b, 2010; Courtois, 2015; Huppert, Fabbro, & Barlow, 2006; Linden, 2013; McHugh, Murray, & Barlow, 2009; Sue, 2015b).

Intellectual competence also means admitting what we do not know. We may know about depression in adults but not depression in kids. We may be familiar with the culture of one Asian population but not others. We may understand the degree to which the Minnesota Multiphasic Personality Inventory-2 can assess malingering among criminal defendants but not whether it can identify leadership strengths among job candidates in the tech industry.

Intellectual competence also involves knowing how to do certain clinical tasks. We gain this kind of competence, the development of skills, through carefully supervised experience. We can't learn how to do therapy just by reading a book or sitting in a classroom. The APA Ethics Code Standard 2.01c (APA, 2010a) encourages properly trained psychologists planning to provide services new to them to achieve competence in those new services through relevant education, training, supervised experience, consultation, or study. Both the APA Ethics Code (Standard 2.03) and the CPA's Ethics Code (CAP, 2015, Standards IV.3 and IV.4) recognize that knowledge becomes obsolete and that psychologists don't stop developing and maintaining competence when they become licensed.

EMOTIONAL COMPETENCE FOR THERAPY: KNOWING YOURSELF

Emotional competence for therapy, as described by Pope and Brown (1996), reflects our awareness and respect for ourselves as unique, fallible human beings. It includes self-knowledge, self-acceptance, and self-monitoring. We must know our own emotional strengths and weaknesses, our needs and resources, our abilities and limits for doing clinical work.

Therapy can stir strong emotions in both therapist and client. Some clinical work places great emotional demands on us. For example, working with people who survive torture can evoke a variety of intense reactions that can lead to secondary trauma, despair, helplessness, and burnout (Allden & Murakami, 2015; Pope, 2012; Pope & Garcia-Peltoniemi, 1991).

To the degree that we are unprepared for the emotional stresses and strains of therapy, our attempts to help may be futile and perhaps even harmful.

Table 12.1 presents research findings about intense emotions experienced in therapy. The numbers indicate the percentage of therapists in each study who reported at least one instance of each behavior. Readers who have had

Table 12.1. Intense Emotion and Other Reactions in Therapy (in percentages).

Behavior	Study 1[a]	Study 2[b]	Study 3[c]
Crying in the presence of a client	56.5		
Telling a client that you are angry at him or her	89.7	77.9	
Raising your voice at a client because you are angry at him or her			57.2
Having fantasies that reflect your anger at a client			63.4
Feeling hatred toward a client			31.2
Telling clients of your disappointment in them	51.9		
Feeling afraid that a client may commit suicide			97.2
Feeling afraid that a client may need clinical resources that are unavailable			86.0
Feeling afraid because a client's condition gets suddenly or seriously worse			90.9
Feeling afraid that your colleagues may be critical of your work with a client			88.1
Feeling afraid that a client may file a formal complaint against you			66.0
Using self-disclosure as a therapy technique	93.3		
Lying on top of or underneath a client			0.4
Cradling or otherwise holding a client in your lap		8.8	
Telling a sexual fantasy to a client			6.0
Engaging in sexual fantasy about a client	71.8		
Feeling sexually attracted to a client	89.5		87.3
A client tells you that he or she is sexually attracted to you			73.3
Feeling sexually aroused while in the presence of a client			57.9
A client seems to become sexually aroused in your presence		48.4	
A client seems to have an orgasm in your presence			3.2

[a]A national survey of 1,000 psychologists with a 46% return rate.
[b]A national survey of 4,800 psychologists, psychiatrists, and social workers with a 49% return rate.
[c]A national survey of 600 psychologists with a 48% return rate.

Source: Study 1 adapted from "Ethics of Practice: The Beliefs and Behaviors of Psychologists as Therapists," by K. S. Pope, B. G. Tabachnick, and P. Keith-Spiegel, 1987, *American Psychologist, 42,* pp. 993–1006. Study 2 adapted from "Dual Relationships Between Therapist and Client: A National Study of Psychologists, Psychiatrists, and Social Workers," by D. S. Borys and K. S. Pope, 1989, *Professional Psychology: Research and Practice, 20,* pp. 283–293. Study 3 is adapted from "Therapists' Anger, Hate, Fear, and Sexual Feelings: National Survey of Therapists' Responses, Client Characteristics, Critical Events, Formal Complaints, and Training," by K. S. Pope and G. B. Tabachnick, 1993, *Professional Psychology: Research and Practice, 24,* pp. 142–152. Copyright 1987, 1993, by the American Psychological Association. Adapted with permission.

experience as therapists or patients may wish to compare their own experience to these findings.

Therapists, of course, bring something to the work they do. Each of us has a unique personal history. Table 12.2 presents national survey results showing therapists' self-reports of their experiences of various kinds of abuse during childhood, adolescence, and adulthood (Pope & Feldman-Summers, 1992). These results suggest that almost one third of male therapists and over two thirds of female therapists experience at least one of these forms of abuse over their lifetimes.

Table 12.2. Percentages of Male and Female Therapists Reporting Having Been Abused.

Type of Abuse	Men	Women
Abuse during childhood or adolescence		
Sexual abuse by relative	5.84	21.05
Sexual abuse by teacher	0.73	1.96
Sexual abuse by physician	0.0	1.96
Sexual abuse by therapist	0.0	0.0
Sexual abuse by nonrelative (other than those previously listed)	9.49	16.34
Nonsexual physical abuse	13.14	9.15
At least one of the above	26.28	39.22
Abuse during adulthood		
Sexual harassment	1.46	37.91
Attempted rape	0.73	13.07
Acquaintance rape	0.0	6.54
Stranger rape	0.73	1.31
Nonsexual physical abuse by a spouse or partner	6.57	12.42
Nonsexual physical abuse by an acquaintance	0.0	2.61
Nonsexual physical abuse by a stranger	4.38	7.19
Sexual involvement with a therapist	2.19	4.58
Sexual involvement with a physician	0.0	1.96
At least one of the above	13.87	56.86
Abuse during childhood, adolescence, or adulthood	32.85	69.93

Source: From "National Survey of Psychologists' Sexual and Physical Abuse History and Their Evaluation of Training and Competence in These Areas," by K. S. Pope and S. Feldman-Summers, 1992, *Professional Psychology: Research and Practice, 23*, pp. 353–361. Copyright 1992 by the American Psychological Association. Adapted with permission.

These experiences *may — or may not —* affect emotional competence for any of us as individuals. It is important not to assume a one-size-fits-all theory about how any form of abuse (or any other experience) affects an individual therapist. No research supports the notion that all those who have a history of abuse are more competent or less competent as therapists, or that those who have no history of abuse are more or less competent as therapists. Each instance must be evaluated on an individual basis, with the full range of available information and without stereotypes. What is key is for us to be aware of how such events affect us and what role, if any, they play in our emotional competence.

Ethical intelligence requires continuous awareness to prevent compromised performance, especially when we go through hard or challenging times. Chapter 13 discusses common consequences when the therapist is distressed, drained, or demoralized. Common consequences include disrespecting clients; disrespecting work; making more mistakes; lacking energy; using work to block out unhappiness, pain, and discontent; and losing interest.

Emotional competence includes the process of constant questioning of the self: Do the demands of the work or other factors suggest that the therapist needs therapy in order to maintain or restore emotional competence? For many of us, creating self-care strategies that fit us as unique individuals and that sustain, replenish, and give meaning are an essential part of our work to maintain competence (see chapter 13), particularly to maintain "emotional competence for therapy" (Pope & Brown, 1996; Pope, Sonne, & Greene, 2006).

The psychology profession emphasizes the ethical aspects of self-care. General Principle A, Beneficence and Nonmaleficence, and Standard 2.06 of the APA Ethics Code (APA, 2010a) encourage psychologists to be aware of the possible effects of their own physical and mental health on their ability to help those with whom they work. The Canadian Code of Ethics for Psychologists, Standard II.11 (CPA, February 2015 Draft), states that psychologists "seek appropriate help and/or discontinue scientific, teaching, or practice activity for an appropriate period of time, if a physical or psychological condition reduces their ability to benefit and not harm others." Standard II.12 states that psychologists "engage in self-care activities that help to avoid conditions (e.g., burnout, addictions) that could result in impaired judgment and interfere with their ability to benefit and not harm others."

The National Association of Social Workers (2008) and the American Counseling Association (2005) are among the other major mental health professions whose ethics codes highlight the role of self-care in supporting competence and preventing impairment.

Table 12.3 presents the results of a national study of therapists as therapy patients (Pope & Tabachnick, 1994). Eighty-four percent of the therapists in this study reported that they had been in personal therapy. Only two respondents indicated that the therapy was not helpful, but 22% reported that their

Table 12.3. Therapists' Experiences as Therapy Patients.

Item	Never	Once	Rarely	Sometimes	Often
In your own personal therapy, how often (if at all) did your therapist (N = 400):					
Cradle or hold you in a nonsexual way	73.2	2.7	8.0	8.8	6.0
Touch you in a sexual way	93.7	2.5	1.8	0.3	1.0
Talk about sexual issues in a way that you believe to be inappropriate	91.2	2.7	3.2	0.5	1.3
Seem to be sexually attracted to you	84.5	6.2	3.5	3.0	1.5
Disclose that he or she was sexually attracted to you	92.2	3.7	1.0	1.3	0.8
Seem to be sexually aroused in your presence	91.2	3.7	2.2	0.8	1.3
Express anger at you	60.7	14.3	16.8	5.7	1.8
Express disappointment in you	67.0	11.3	14.8	4.7	1.3
Give you encouragement and support	2.5	0.8	6.2	21.8	67.5
Tell you that he or she cared about you	33.7	6.7	19.5	21.8	16.3
Make what you consider to be a clinical or therapeutic error	19.8	18.0	36.2	19.0	5.5
Pressure you to talk about something you didn't want to talk about	57.5	7.5	21.3	8.8	4.0
Use humor in an appropriate way	76.7	8.8	10.0	2.2	1.5
Use humor in an inappropriate way	5.2	2.5	12.5	35.0	43.5
Act in a rude or insensitive manner toward you	68.7	13.0	12.0	4.0	1.5
Violate your rights to confidentiality	89.7	4.5	2.7	1.3	1.8
Violate your rights to informed consent	93.2	3.2	1.3	0.3	0.3
Use hospitalization as part of your treatment	96.2	1.8	0.5	0.5	1.0

(continued)

Table 12.3. (continued)

Item	Never	Once	Rarely	Sometimes	Often
In your own personal therapy, how often (if at all) did you (N = 400):					
Feel sexually attracted to your therapist	63.0	8.0	14.0	7.5	6.5
Tell your therapist that you were sexually attracted to him or her	81.5	6.2	5.5	3.0	2.7
Have sexual fantasies about your therapist	65.5	8.0	12.8	7.0	5.2
Feel angry at your therapist	13.3	9.5	32.7	28.5	15.0
Feel that your therapist did not care about you	49.5	13.0	19.0	12.3	5.5
Feel suicidal	70.0	8.5	9.5	8.3	3.0
Make a suicide attempt	95.5	2.5	1.0	0.0	0.0
Feel what you would characterize as clinical depression	38.5	15.8	16.0	16.5	12.5

Note: Rarely = two to four times; sometimes = five to ten times; often = over ten times.

Source: From "Therapists as Patients: A National Survey of Psychologists' Experiences, Problems, and Beliefs," by K. S. Pope and B. G. Tabachnik, 1994, *Professional Psychology: Research and Practice, 25,* pp. 247–258. Copyright 1994 by the American Psychological Association. Reprinted with Permission.

own therapy included what they believed to be harmful aspects (regardless of whether it also included positive aspects).

This research suggests that most therapists experience, at least once, deep distress. For example, 61% reported experiencing clinical depression, 29% reported suicidal feelings, and 3.5% reported attempting suicide. About 4% reported having been hospitalized. Readers may wish to consider their own experiences in the light of these findings.

Emotional competence in therapy is no less important than intellectual competence, and it is for that reason that we have included, beginning with Chapter 18, clinical scenarios at the end of each chapter. These scenarios describe hypothetical situations that this book's readers might encounter. Each is followed by a handful of questions designed to provide practice in the processes of the critical thinking explored in detail in Chapters 4–8. The first question in each sequence is a variant of "What do you feel?" Emotional competence leaves little room for denying, discounting, or distorting how we respond emotionally to the challenges of clinical work.

To the extent that these scenarios and questions form the basis of class or group discussion in graduate school courses, internships, in-service training, continuing education workshops, or other group settings, their value may be in direct proportion to the class's or group's ability to establish a genuinely safe environment in which participants are free to disclose responses that may be politically incorrect or "psychologically incorrect" (Pope, Sonne, et al., 2006) or otherwise at odds with group norms or with what some might consider the "right" response. Only if participants are able to speak honestly with each other about responses that they might be reluctant to speak aloud in other settings and to discuss these responses with mutual respect will the task of confronting these questions likely prove helpful in developing emotional competence (Pope, Sonne, et al., 2006).

Learning to discuss these sensitive topics and our personal responses with others helps us only to strengthen our emotional competence but also to develop resources for maintaining competence throughout our careers (see Pope, Sonne, et al., 2006, for a more thorough discussion of understanding taboos that hurt therapists and clients). Our colleagues constitute an invaluable source of help to avoid or correct mistakes, identify stress or personal dilemmas that threaten to overwhelm us, and provide fresh ideas, new perspectives, and second and third opinions. A national survey of psychologists, in fact, found that therapists rated informal networks of colleagues as the most effective resource for prompting effective, appropriate, and ethical practice (Pope et al., 1987). Informal networks were seen as more valuable in promoting ethical practice than laws, ethics committees, research, continuing education programs, or formal ethical principles. Our colleagues can help sustain us, replenish us, enrich our lives, and play an important role in our self-care, the focus of the next chapter.

Chapter 13

CREATING – AND USING – STRATEGIES FOR SELF-CARE

The theme of personal responsibility runs through this book. We cannot escape responsibility for what we choose to say and do or for those times we choose to remain silent and do nothing. We cannot hand over responsibility for our actions or failure to act to an ethics code, our colleagues, our government, our employer, an insurance company, a managed care organization, a professional association, or any other source outside ourselves. Strengthening and *using* our ethical intelligence is an active process that involves increasing awareness and constant questioning. Few of us can engage in this process effectively if we are personally drained, overwhelmed, or demoralized.

We recommend creating strategies for self-care as early as possible in your education, training, and practice. "Promoting self-care during training is likely to provide a foundation for career sustaining self-care practices that prevent burnout in later professional life" (Pakenham, 2015, p. 145). Neglecting an ethic of self-care early on can drain the enthusiasm, joy, resilience, and meaning out of a career. It can undermine our competence and hurt our ability to practice ethically. It can sink us in discouragement, compassion fatigue, and burnout.

PAYING ATTENTION TO THE SELF

Psychotherapy is demanding work. It can leave us physically and emotionally drained. Even what we have to do when we are not doing psychotherapy — writing chart notes, requesting authorizations from managed care companies, billing insurance companies, returning phone calls between sessions, sending a second bill to insurance companies after receiving notification that they never received the first bill we sent, filling out disability claim forms, sitting on hold while waiting to ask the insurance company why it is now saying that we used the wrong code on the second bill we sent when that is exactly the code it told us to use when we called before sending in the first bill, and trying to find time in our schedule to consult about a suicidal patient who does not seem to be responding to therapy — can run us ragged.

In the midst of these demands, paying attention to the self is crucial. An occupational hazard that trips up too many of us is failing to stop and pay attention when we become too exhausted, too discouraged, too frustrated, too sad, too angry, too disillusioned, or too cynical. We try to plow ahead, pushing aside the awareness that we are hurting. Instead of taking steps to acknowledge the problem and do something about it, we try to ignore it. Or explain it away. Or assume there is nothing we can do.

Good strategies for self-care include reminders to stop and ask ourselves if we are hurting and, if we are, to ask ourselves why and what we can do about it. Actively looking for red flags — common signs that we may not be taking good care of ourselves — can be helpful. The next section discusses a few of these red flags.

WHAT HAPPENS WHEN SELF-CARE IS NEGLECTED

Neglecting self-care can have corrosive consequences for the therapist and the work. Every psychologist is unique in important ways, does work that is unique in important ways, and experiences the effects of neglecting self-care in a personal way. Yet some themes appear often. Each of the following may be a consequence of, intensified by, or a reflection of neglecting self-care, though each, of course, can have other causes.

Disrespecting Clients

When work is overwhelming, therapists may start disrespecting their clients, talking about them in ways that are demeaning and lack fundamental respect. They may complain about how unmotivated, ungrateful, selfish, insensitive, dishonest, lazy, and generally undesirable their clients are. They may grow harsh, judgmental, and rejecting. They may lose empathy, kindness, and connection. They may distance and dehumanize their clients, referring to them only by labels (e.g., "that borderline"). They may tell jokes about their clients and ridicule them in other ways.

Disrespecting Work

Depleted and discouraged through lack of self-care, therapists may trivialize or ridicule their work. They may speak of therapy as a charade, a fraud, or a joke. They may view their work as empty, ineffective, and meaningless. They may repeatedly show up late for sessions, decide to skip some scheduled sessions altogether, or fail to return clients' telephone calls.

Making More Mistakes

Despite our best efforts, we all make mistakes. Acknowledging, accepting responsibility for, and attempting to address the consequences of our mistakes is one of our fundamental responsibilities as therapists. But self-neglect can hurt our ability to attend to work. We may begin making more and more mistakes. We find ourselves scheduling two clients at the same time, forgetting to show up for an appointment, calling a client by the wrong name, misplacing a client's chart, or locking ourselves out of our own office.

Lacking Energy

If we do not take care of ourselves, we can run out of energy and find ourselves without sources of rest and renewal. We wake up tired, barely find the will to drag ourselves out of bed and to work, fight to stay awake during a session, wonder how we will ever make it through the rest of the day, leave work — *finally!* — too exhausted to socialize or do anything fun, and face the prospect of going to bed only to start the grueling routine all over again.

Becoming Anxious and Afraid

If we fail to care for ourselves, we may fall victim to exaggerated fear and anxiety. We begin to feel that we are no longer up to dealing with the uncertainties, challenges, demands, and stresses of practice. What if our referral sources all dry up and our current clients terminate? Did we bungle that last assessment, wind up with the wrong diagnosis, and miss crucial aspects? Did we say the wrong thing when responding to a suicidal crisis, and will that person commit suicide before the next session? What if that agitated client becomes violent during a session? What if someone files a malpractice suit?

Using Work to Block Out Unhappiness, Pain, and Discontent

If our self-care has been neglected and work no longer brings meaning or satisfaction to our lives, one self-defeating response is to try to lose ourselves and our uncomfortable feelings in work — wall-to-wall work. More and more clients, projects, and responsibilities crowd our lives until we lack free time to reflect on our lives, spend time alone apart from work, or face how lost, empty, or miserable we are. Some therapists work long hours and revel in it, finding great joy and fulfillment, but the pattern here is different: Filling the time with work brings little to nourish the self — it only distracts us from an unfulfilling life. Excessive work is only one of the destructive coping strategies (others are abusing food, alcohol, and drugs) that we use to block out what happens when self-care is neglected.

Losing Interest

Neglecting self-care can lead to an empty professional life that no longer brings excitement, joy, growth, meaning, and fulfillment; as a result, we may lose interest in it. We no longer feel committed to the work or connected to our clients. We go numb and try to get by on automatic pilot. We go through the motions, forcing ourselves to do as good a job as we can. Our heart is no longer in it.

MAKING SURE THE STRATEGIES FIT

Goodness of fit is as important in self-care strategies as it is in clothes. Making or buying clothes that fit our friends, or that fit the average person, or that match the most popular sizes won't help most of us find clothes that fit well. Using self-care strategies that are lifesavers for our colleagues may make us miserable. What sustains, replenishes, and gives meaning may flow far from the mainstream. Few of us would tell someone who has found happiness, significance, and contentment in choosing a solitary monastic life with vows of silence and poverty, "You know, you really ought to get out and socialize more and find ways to earn some money so that you'll have a nest egg you could rely on. I know you'd feel better about yourself and have a better life! It's worked for me and so many others!"

Listening to ourselves, experimenting, being honest with ourselves about what does and does not work are part of creating self-care strategies that fit us as individuals. Although there is no one-size-fits-all to any self-care strategy, here are a few of the challenging areas that many therapists contend with in making sure that they are taking good care of themselves.

Isolation Versus Connection

Solo practice can isolate us by its very nature. We spend our days in our office, seeing client after client. Especially if we work long hours, we can lose touch with our friends, colleagues, and the world beyond our office. Even during free time when no patient is scheduled, there are always charts to update, bills to prepare, work-related telephone calls to make, and so on. Some therapists find it helpful to place strict limits on the time they spend in the office and schedule activities that bring them out of isolation. Creating ways to stay connected to others seems a basic self-care strategy for many therapists.

Monotony Versus Variety

Even when we limit our time with clients to, say, 30 to 35 hours a week, spending so much time seeing clients can be too much for some therapists. Some find work to break up their days and provide variety: teaching a course; consulting; leading a supervision group; getting active in local, state, regional, or national professional organizations.

Fatigue Versus Limits, Rest, and Renewal

How much time do you need between clients: 5, 10, or 15 minutes? How many clients can you see in a row without needing a longer break of at least an hour or more? How many clients can you see in the course of a day without feeling so tired that the quality of your work falls toward the end of the day? Therapists differ greatly in these areas. Some work four consecutive 50-minute sessions with a 10-minute break between each, take an hour off for lunch, and return for another four consecutive sessions without any lapse in enthusiasm or competence. Others can do their best work with no more than five clients each day. Knowing and respecting our personal limits is a key aspect of self-care. Some consider 25 to 30 client-hours a week to be full time because of the additional hours needed to keep clinical records, return telephone calls, and so on.

Part of self-care in this area is learning what workload we can handle well and creating a schedule that matches that workload. The focus must remain on the amount of work that we can do well, not the amount that we feel we should do, or used to be able to do, or that some of our colleagues do. Sometimes the number of hours we can do good work with clients conflicts with the number of hours we believe we must spend with clients in order to pay the bills, develop our practice, or please our employer.

Effective self-care strategies not only influence our patterns of breaks — everything from the breaks we take between sessions to our vacations — but also emphasize activities, attitudes, and approaches that help us recover from fatigue, that replenish and renew us on a daily basis.

The Sedentary Life Versus Physical Activity and Exercise

Psychological assessment and therapy are usually — not always — done while the client is sitting (or lying down) and the psychologist is sitting, neither of them moving around much. For many therapists, self-care includes creating opportunities during the day for moving, stretching, and physical exercise. Physical exercise is a major self-care strategy for many therapists, not only for its physical benefits and the break it provides from work, but also for its psychological benefits (see, e.g., Gaitan-Sierra & Hyland, 2014; K. Hays, 2002; McMorris & Hale, 2012; Rebar et al., 2015; Wang et al., 2014).

The Dispirited Life Versus Nurturing the Spirit

If a psychology practice does not provide enough physical movement and exercise for many therapists, it may also fail for many to nurture the life of the spirit adequately. Setting aside time and opportunity for meditation, prayer, and other spiritual or religious practices can be an important aspect of self-care for some therapists. Some find that such diverse activities as reading or writing poetry, hiking through the woods, playing or listening to music, sitting on a riverbank, acting in or viewing a play, or watching a sunset helps nourish their spiritual lives. For many, these experiences often bring a sense of awe, peace, joy, and transcendence.

The Unsupported Life Versus Support Networks

Graduate schools and internships place us in a network of professors, supervisors, administrators, and other students. Facing a challenge, we can talk it over with teachers and classmates. Our clinical work is closely monitored, and we receive positive and negative feedback, ideas, suggestions, and guidance. When we start an independent practice or begin work in an agency that tends to be unsupportive and isolating, the responsibility to create that network of support falls to us. What are some important components of a support network? This is not an exhaustive list but the following are 10 important components.

Supervision, Consultation, and Additional Training

Identify or create resources for talking over your work, expanding your knowledge and skills, and continuing to grow as a psychologist. Is there someone you would like to hire to provide you with supervision or consultation? (Understanding how *supervision* and *consultation* are defined under state laws and regulations is crucial. They tend to differ in such areas as who is primarily responsible for clinical care and decision making.) Would you like to create a peer-consultation group that meets on a regular basis? What continuing education courses, workshops, and other activities would you find helpful in updating your knowledge, improving your skills, and expanding your areas of competence? What organizations at the local, state, national, or international level will provide you with information and support? Consider what other sources of support you'll need to practice effectively.

Accountant

We recommend that you find and work with an accountant you trust, reviewing your business plans, looking at your current financial resources, and advising you on tax matters. The accountant will be able to discuss issues such as the pros and cons of incorporation, what expenses will be deductible, procedures for keeping records and receipts for tax purposes, and comparing the relative financial merits of a home office compared to a separate office.

Billing/Bookkeeper

Many practitioners do their own billing and bookkeeping. If you choose this route, you might look into software programs that can help with these tasks. Other clinicians prefer not to take on this additional administrative task. Instead, they hire an individual or company to do their bookkeeping and billing. Some communities have services that specialize in this area for psychotherapists or for health-care providers more generally. Check with colleagues in your community for recommendations.

Psychopharmacology Resources

Unless you are able to prescribe medications, find someone skilled in psychopharmacology who will work collaboratively with you and your patients. Some patients, of course, do not need psychotropic medications, and others may come to you already taking medications prescribed by someone else. You may wish to refer some patients to a psychopharmacologist with prescription authority for an evaluation to see if medications might be helpful.

Emergency and Hospitalization Resources

What are the emergency, inpatient, day treatment, and similar mental health services available in your community? How much do they cost, and what are their admission criteria? Visit them, and introduce yourself to the staff and administration. Find out about their policies and procedures and whether you are eligible for staff privileges. If one of your clients needs hospitalization or other crisis services, you will be familiar with available options and the necessary steps for each. Some clinicians include a telephone number for emergency services on their answering machine's outgoing message; others include it on their informed consent form.

Mandatory and Discretionary Reporting Resources

Find the contact information for the agencies to which you would file mandatory or discretionary reports of such matters as suspected child abuse or elder abuse. There may be times when you are unsure of whether you are obligated to file a report. One source of consultation you can draw on at such times is the agency to which you would file the report. You can call and, without disclosing any identifying information about the actual people involved, provide the agency with a hypothetical situation and ask if such a fact pattern falls under the duty to report. Be sure to document that consultation as one of the steps you took to decide whether to report. You may also call your attorney, your licensing board, or your professional liability carrier for guidance.

Attorney

We recommend finding an attorney experienced in mental health issues in your jurisdiction as early as possible in your career. He or she can review your forms, policies, and procedures; answer your questions about legal requirements and pitfalls; and be a telephone call away if you are in the midst of responding to an urgent situation and need legal advice. Some state or provincial psychological associations offer an attorney consultant as part of the membership services.

Personal Relationships

Good relationships can be key to our sense of well-being. An absence of good friends (and the time to spend with them) or spending too much time in toxic relationships can lead to burnout. Feminist Jean Baker Miller (1988, 1991) described the qualities and dynamics of relationships that make us feel understood, valued, and more alive. Judy Jordan (1997) emphasized the importance of a sense of connection. "Ruptures" in our important personal or work relationships can be devastating. Seymour Sarason (1974) looked at the social environment that we find or create for ourselves and emphasized the "psychological sense of community," that feeling that one is part of a larger dependable and stable structure (p. 157; see also Clark, Murdock, & Koetting, 2009; Love, 2007; Nistor, Daxecker, Stanciu, & Diekamp, 2015; Obst & White, 2007; Pozzi, Marta, Marzana, Gozzoli, & Ruggieri, 2014; Vora & Kinney, 2014).

Maintaining Health

Moving from a graduate school environment that often includes a student health service and health coverage to suddenly being out on our own in independent practice or into organizational employment that offers little or no health coverage makes it easy to neglect our health and medical needs. It becomes our responsibility to find affordable health-care coverage well matched to our individual needs and a competent physician whom we trust. Medical insurance can be obtained from a variety of sources, including professional organizations; self-employment associations, such as the National Association for the Self-Employed; and some local associations, such as the local chamber of commerce. Colleagues and local insurance brokers may be good sources of information.

Managing Stress

Therapists may experience periods of extreme unhappiness and distress. Some of the themes in Chapter 3 on the human therapist are worth reviewing here.

In one national study of therapists' accounts of their own experiences as therapy patients (Pope & Tabachnick, 1994), of the 84% of the therapists who had been in therapy, 61% reported experiencing at least one episode of what they termed clinical depression, 29% reported having felt suicidal, and 4% reported having attempted suicide.

Practice itself may be stressful. In another national study of practicing therapists (Pope & Tabachnick, 1993), 97% reported fearing that a client would commit suicide, 91% reported fearing that a client would get worse, 89% reported fearing that client would attack a third party, 88% reported fearing that colleagues would be critical of their work with a patient, 86% reported fearing that a client would need clinical resources that are unavailable, 83% reported fearing being attacked by a patient, and 18% reported having been attacked by a patient. Over half reported having been so afraid about a client that it affected their eating, sleeping, or concentration. About 12% reported that a client had filed a formal complaint (e.g., about malpractice or licensing) against them. Over 3% had obtained a weapon to protect themselves from a patient.

Anger was another major theme of the study. For example, 83% reported anger at a client because of unpaid bills, 81% reported anger at a client who was verbally abusive to them, and 46% reported having become so angry at a patient that they did something that they later regretted.

Effective self-care strategies take realistic account of both how stressful doing therapy can be and how distressed we can become. What resources can we develop for coping with the stresses of our work? How can we address our own distress, seek professional help if we need it, and become aware if we reach a point of being too distressed or impaired to work effectively?

THE NEED FOR CHANGE

Self-care strategies that support, strengthen, deepen, replenish, and enliven may, less than a year later, become a senseless obligation, distraction, and waste of time. Therapists who focus on the subtle, sweeping, and profound changes in their clients' lives can overlook changes in their own lives and how these changes can affect self-care needs and strategies. Effective self-care includes paying attention to the ways in which our needs for self-care can change over time, calling us to change course and create new strategies.

Chapter 14

CREATING A PROFESSIONAL WILL

If you are one of those lucky psychologists who is invincible and immortal, don't bother to create a professional will. But it's a good idea for the rest of us. Otherwise we risk stranding our patients and colleagues, leaving them without access to vital records, schedules, contact information, and resources when our unexpected incapacity or death has stunned them with its suddenness.

The theme of therapists as vulnerable runs throughout this book. We therapists share many vulnerabilities. We can't wall ourselves off from the unexpected. A drunk driver, stroke, mugger, heart attack, fire, plane crash, and countless others jolts can strike us down without warning. We bear an ethic to take these possibilities into account in our planning.

A professional will is a plan for what happens if we die suddenly or become incapacitated without warning. It helps those whom we designate to respond to our clients' needs and to the unfinished business of our practice. It spells out decisive details that can be hard or impossible to come by at a time of shock and mourning.

The best time to create a professional will is now rather than later. Even with the best of planning and consultation, we cannot schedule our catastrophes that suddenly take us out of action for a while or longer so that they will happen only at the end of our careers or — better — after retirement. We must prepare for the possibility that something can happen to us — robbing us of our ability to function — at any time, without warning. And if we decide "not now," making a professional will take its place at the end of that list of things we'll take care of when we get a little free time, it may spend its whole life (and ours) growing old on that well-meaning list.

No standardized approach to creating a professional will works with every therapist or situation. Here are some steps you may find helpful in thinking through a professional will that fits your individual needs, setting, practice, values, and resources.

WHO TAKES CHARGE?

Who would respond effectively in the event that you suddenly die or become incapacitated? Who can take care of things in a time of great stress? Who would do it with sensitivity and understanding? Who would take care of the details, making sure nothing is overlooked? Who is the best person to talk to your clients?

A good professional will name a qualified executor to carry out the will's tasks.

How can the executor be reached if your professional will suddenly becomes active? What are the best telephone, fax, and pager numbers? What are your office and e-mail addresses? Can you list other people likely to know where the executor is if he or she proves hard to reach?

WHO SERVES AS BACKUP?

Life loves surprises and sometimes hesitates to cooperate with our plans. When it's time to step in and take charge, the executor may be presenting a paper at a conference half a world away, struggling to handle a family emergency, recovering from a stroke, or otherwise unavailable. Second and third designees need to be ready to step in if needed.

COORDINATED PLANNING

Coordinated planning allows executors to carry out each step much more efficiently. You can meet with your primary designee and both backups to go over what needs to be done and provide the needed information. Someone may think of something that the others have overlooked.

What you may think goes without saying ("You all know that bookshelf where I keep my appointment book, don't you?") may actually need to be said. If designees don't understand where something is, you can show them. You can introduce them to the people they will need to work with (e.g., your secretary, the executor of your personal will, your accountant, your attorney, your office landlord). They can exchange contact information with each other.

When the time comes to carry out the professional will, the executor will understand what to do, the key people to contact, where your records are, and so on.

YOUR OFFICE, ITS KEY, AND ITS SECURITY

The will should provide the *specific* location of each key to your office — for example, "There are four copies of the key to my office. One is on the key ring that I always carry with me. It is the key with the blue plastic on it. My partner, whose contact information is. . . , also has a key to the office. My secretary, whose contact information is. . . , has a key. The building manager, who can be contacted in an emergency at. . . , has a key."

Don't forget any separate keys for each of the consulting room doors, the storage room, the filing cabinets, the desks, the computer, and the door to the building itself. Some of these may be easy to overlook but essential. If your office security systems require a code, be sure to supply the necessary codes, the instructions, and the system's location.

YOUR SCHEDULE

Where is your schedule kept: in a daily planner you keep with you, an appointment book at the office, on your computer or personal digital assistant? Once the record of your scheduled appointments is located, is additional information needed to access it? For example, if you keep your schedule on your computer, what passwords are used to log on and access the schedule, where on the drive is the schedule kept, what are the names of the relevant files, and is there a backup somewhere if the copy on your computer has become corrupted or if the computer itself is unavailable (e.g., destroyed in an office fire or earthquake or stolen)?

CLIENT RECORDS AND CONTACT INFORMATION

A useful professional will include clear instructions about how to locate and access client records and contact information. The ability to locate treatment records promptly may become exceptionally important because the sudden death of a therapist may trigger a crisis for some clients. The executor (or someone appointed by the executor) may need to contact your clients quickly. Because some clients may not have told their family members that they are seeking care, the process of notification may be complicated. Make clear in your professional will if you have a place in your files indicating how clients prefer to be contacted The professional will should also designate whether the executor or someone else will maintain the client records of the incapacitated or deceased therapist. This information can be announced via local newspapers, your voicemail or answering service, your website, a notice at your office, information filed with the state psychology licensing board and state psychological association, or all these methods.

AVENUES OF COMMUNICATION FOR CLIENTS AND COLLEAGUES

How do clients and colleagues contact you: answering machine, e-mail, other methods? Clearly describe each and how the person carrying out your professional will can access the messages. What codes are used to retrieve messages from your answering machine? What are the names of any relevant e-mail accounts along with the user name, password, server address for receiving and sending mail, and so on?

NEW MESSAGES FOR YOUR ANSWERING MACHINE, E-MAIL ACCOUNT, AND SO ON

The prior step made sure the executor can retrieve messages from your answering machine, e-mail account, and so on. But what kinds of outgoing messages, if any, are appropriate for these different channels of communication? What recorded message should callers hear when they reach your answering machine? Should an auto-response be set up for your e-mail account? There are no easy answers to these questions, but you will likely know best what is most appropriate for your particular practice.

INFORMED CONSENT

Clients have a right to give or withhold informed consent for release of information. Documentation of consent for providing the executor with client contact information and access to client charts can be kept with the client charts and a note of it made in the professional will. One option is to include the name(s) of the executor in the original description of services that patients read and sign as part of informed consent. In other words, it would be helpful to include a statement indicating that you have designated a colleague as your professional executor in the case of death or disability to have access to the client's records, to provide psychological services if needed, or to refer to another qualified professional if needed.

CLIENT NOTIFICATION

Therapists may choose one or more methods to notify clients of a therapist's incapacitation or death, such as calling each client, placing a notice in the local newspaper, changing the outgoing message on the answering machine to include the announcement, changing the answering machine message to ask clients to call the clinician who is implementing the deceased therapist's professional will, and sending letters. It is worth spending some time considering the potential impact of each method and considering it in terms of the Golden Rule — Would any of us want to learn of our own therapist's or clinical supervisor's death by reading about it in the newspaper or hearing a recorded announcement on an answering machine? — and of how each of our current and former clients might respond.

Are there resources that clients might find helpful in these circumstances (e.g., designated colleagues who will make appointments available to your clients to help them deal with the immediate consequences and, if the clients choose, to locate subsequent therapists)? You will have a good sense of which approaches will work best for your individual practice and the relationship you have with your clients. Some long-term patients may require special consideration.

The notification method must respect each client's right to privacy. Letters and phone messages that are not carefully handled can lead unintentionally to the disclosure to third parties that a person is seeing a therapist. Family members and others may not always respect the privacy of someone's mail and may, perhaps accidentally, open and read mail that is not addressed to them. A telephone message left on an answering machine sometimes can be heard by those for whom it was not intended. In some cases, such unintentional disclosures can place a client at great risk. The abusive partner, for example, of a client who sought therapy because she is a battered woman may become enraged at finding out, through an intercepted letter or telephone message, that the client has sought help and may react violently, perhaps lethally.

COLLEAGUE NOTIFICATION

What colleagues should be notified immediately? Are you a member of a group practice, or do you share a suite of offices? Are there clinicians who provide consultation or supervision to you on a regular basis or who receive those services from you? Do you co-lead a therapy group or family sessions with anyone? Are there conferences or workshops where you are regularly present? It can be helpful to check the listings in your scheduling book for a few months to make sure that you do not overlook any colleagues who should be listed (along with contact information) in your professional will for immediate notification.

PROFESSIONAL LIABILITY COVERAGE

Make sure your executor knows the name of the company providing professional liability coverage, contact information, the policy number, and instructions for the company to be notified immediately on the therapist's death or incapacitation.

ATTORNEY FOR PROFESSIONAL ISSUES

Many therapists consult an attorney for professional issues. You may have arranged for an attorney to review your office forms (informed consent, release of information, etc.) to ensure that they conform to state legislation and case law requirements. You may have discussed with your attorney your policies and procedures, format for keeping records, or particularly troublesome cases that raised puzzling legal questions. You may have sought legal consultation about how to respond to a subpoena or legal representation in a malpractice suit. Your executor is likely to find it helpful to know the name and contact information for any attorney you've consulted. The attorney you consult for professional issues may also help you in creating a professional will.

BILLING RECORDS, PROCEDURES, AND INSTRUCTIONS

Your executor will need to know where the billing records are, how to access them (e.g., if they are maintained by computer software), who prepares and processes the bills (e.g., a billing service, accountant, or office clerical worker), and how pending charges are to be handled.

Some therapists may wish to forgive part or all of any remaining unpaid bills that were to be paid out of their clients' own pockets. Some may wish to provide a session — at the deceased therapist's expense — for each client, during which the clinician serving as executor of the professional will would work with the client to discuss the situation, assess current needs, and explore options for future therapy. The professional will should include explicit instructions about any such wishes.

EXPENSES

How have you and your designated executor and backup executors decided on the executor's compensation? Perhaps the easiest arrangement is at the executor's customary hourly rate, but other approaches can be used — for example, a flat fee, a token payment, the executor declining any compensation for rendering this service to a friend, or a contribution to a charity chosen by the executor.

A professional will needs to include clear instructions about how all business-related expenses are to be paid.

YOUR PERSONAL WILL

Reviewing both your professional will and your personal will side by side to spot any inconsistencies can head off unintended problems and conflicts. If a personal will, for example, directs all assets to be disbursed in a certain way but makes no mention of funds to be used to pay the executor of your professional will, problems can arise. It is useful if each will makes explicit reference to the other.

LEGAL REVIEW

Review of the professional will by an attorney skilled and experienced in mental health law can prevent numerous problems. The executor of the professional will can consult with the attorney about any legal questions arising in the days, weeks, and months after the therapist's death.

The attorney can advise on whether, in the light of state legislation and case law, the professional will is best authenticated simply by the signatures of disinterested witnesses, the seal of a notary, or other means.

COPIES OF THE PROFESSIONAL WILL

Give copies of your professional will to those designated as potential executors and to your attorney. Some therapists may consider making special arrangements to ensure the executor gains access to information such as their passwords for retrieving e-mail and answering machine messages only after their death. These arrangements avoid having confidential information in multiple copies of the will distributed to others.

REVIEW AND UPDATE

People, practices, situations, and times change. The passage of a year or two may turn a professional will that is perfectly suited to use when we draw it up into a storehouse of out-of-date instructions and information. It is helpful to review a professional will on a regular basis — say, once a year — and make an immediate update whenever there is a significant change in our circumstances.

Chapter 15

CODES AND COMPLAINTS IN CONTEXT

Historical, Empirical, and Actuarial Foundations*

A s therapists, we are members of the mental health profession. Exactly what we profess has been subject to debate from the beginning. We have a hard time defining what we do.

The 1949 Boulder Conference tried to define psychotherapy so it could be taught to clinical and counseling psychologists. Carl Rogers, president of the American Psychological Association (APA) in 1947, appointed David Shakow to chair a committee on defining and teaching psychotherapy. The Shakow report, adopted at the 1947 APA convention, resulted in the Boulder Conference two years later.

On August 28, 1949, the recorder for the Boulder task force for defining psychotherapy and setting forth criteria for adequate training provided this summary: "We have left therapy as an undefined technique which is applied to unspecified problems with a nonpredictable outcome. For this technique we recommend rigorous training" (Lehner, 1952, p. 547).

* We greatly appreciate the extraordinary help we received from these people, who provided the actuarial data that are key to this chapter and who reviewed early drafts: Stephen Behnke and Lindsay Childress-Beatty, American Psychological Association Ethics Office staff; Steve DeMers, chief executive director and Janet Orwig, staff, Association of State and Provincial Psychology Boards; Jana Martin, CEO, The Trust; Karen Cohen, Chief Executive Officer, Canadian Psychological Association; and Carole Sinclair, CPA Committee on Ethics Chair.

Since the Boulder Conference, other conferences and various groups have tried to define psychotherapy and the practice of psychology. The "2002 Competencies Conference: Future Directions in Education and Credentialing in Professional Psychology" (Kaslow et al., 2004), for example, identified competencies in professional psychology and discussed effective strategies for teaching and assessing these competencies (Kaslow, 2004; see also Belar, 2009; Fouad et al., 2009; Kaslow et al., 2009). Chapter 12 presents a more detailed discussion of competence.

Forces outside the profession also influence practice. For example, managed care companies can require a diagnosis from a specific manual, can limit or deny assessment and therapy sessions, can require therapists to document that therapy is a matter of medical necessity, can require specific interventions for particular disorders, and can require that outcome be measured using a limited number of criteria defined by the company.

Not surprisingly, these measures — often described as cost cutting — can create conflict between company administrators and therapists (Reed & Eisman, 2006). They also spark critiques of methodology. Beehler and Trickett (in press), for example, discuss problems with current methodologies that produce the "evidence" in "evidence-based practice," and the unintended consequences of using this model. The requirement that only certain interventions be used for a particular diagnosis highlights a controversy within the profession: Should the definition and practice of psychotherapy be limited to interventions supported by research and, if so, what kind of research? Must the research use random assignment in a double-blind model, be published in peer-reviewed journals, be independently replicated by other researchers, and meet other standards?

The answers to these questions will profoundly affect what therapies are seen as legitimate and reimbursable by third parties. Kazdin (2008b; see also Duncan, Miller, Wampold, & Hubble, 2010; Kazdin, 2008a) points out that there are over 550 psychological interventions designed for children and adolescents but that only a relatively small percentage have been researched.

Littell (2010) describes the tensions between the work of therapists and researchers:

> Clinicians and social scientists have distinct imperatives and sensibilities. Therapy requires action and faith in the process, whereas science demands observation and skepticism. Most scientific knowledge is tentative and nomothetic, not directly applicable to individual cases. Experts have stepped into this breach by packaging empirical evidence for use in practice. Sometimes this is little more than a ruse to promote favorite theories and therapies. Yet, wrapped in scientific rhetoric, some authoritative pronouncements have become orthodoxy. (pp. 167–168)

Westen and Bradley (2005) note that

> evidence-based practice is a construct (i.e., an idea, abstraction, or theoretical entity) and thus must be operationalized (i.e., turned into some concrete form that comes to define it). The way it is operationalized is not incidental to whether its net effects turn out to be positive, negative, or mixed. (p. 226; see also Westen, Novotny, & Thompson-Brenner, 2004)

Psychotherapy researchers Crits-Christoph, Wilson, and Hollon (2005) believe that "randomized controlled trials remain the most powerful way to test notions of causal agency" (p. 412). Yet Kazdin (2006), previous editor of the Association for Psychological Science's journal *Current Directions in Psychological Science*, wrote: "Psychotherapy outcome research has been dominated by randomized controlled trials.... However, pivotal features of these trials make them not very relevant for clinical practice" (p. 170; see also Goodheart, 2006; Sternberg, 2006).

APA's (2006) Presidential Task Force on Evidence-Based Practice noted both the limits of clinical hypothesis testing and need for clinical expertise:

> Yet clinical hypothesis testing has its limits, hence the need to integrate clinical expertise with the best available research. Perhaps the central message of this task force report — and one of the most heartening aspects of the process that led to it — is the consensus achieved among a diverse group of scientists, clinicians, and scientist-clinicians from multiple perspectives that EBPP [evidence-based psychology practice] requires an appreciation of the value of multiple sources of scientific evidence. In a given clinical circumstance, psychologists of good faith and good judgment may disagree about how best to weigh different forms of evidence; over time, we presume that systematic and broad empirical inquiry — in the laboratory and in the clinic — will point the way toward best practice in integrating best evidence. What this document [*Report of the APA Presidential Task Force on Evidence-Based Practice*] reflects, however, is a reassertion of what psychologists have known for a century: The scientific method is a way of thinking and observing systematically, and it is the best tool we have for learning about what works for whom. (p. 282)

There is more evidence now than ever before for the effectiveness of psychotherapy (APA, 2012e; Wampold & Imel, 2015), so much so that APA developed a resolution on the effectiveness of psychotherapy. The resolution supports the position that psychotherapy should be included in the health care system as an evidence-based practice. The empirical evidence on the outcomes of psychotherapy informs us that generally, treatment is highly effective. Most effects of psychological treatments are caused by common factors, including: the therapeutic alliance between therapist and client; the belief in the treatment; and the client's belief in the therapist's rationale about why the therapist has developed the problems (APA, 2012e; Lambert, 2004; Norcross, 2011).

However, the complexity of many variables leaves room for the development of broad clinical guidelines. APA has initiated a process for the development of clinical treatment guidelines that address practice with particular patients or with particular problems without focusing on specific disorders or treatments (APA, Practice Organization, 2015).

MECHANISMS OF ACCOUNTABILITY

Difficulties in defining psychotherapy and psychological practice with precision do not free the profession from the basic responsibility of setting forth its ethics. The hallmark of a profession is the recognition that the work its members carry out affects the lives of their clients, sometimes in direct, profound, and immediate ways. The powerful nature of this influence makes the customary rules of the marketplace (often resting on variations of the principle "Let the buyer beware") inadequate (see Chapter 9).

Society asks that the profession set forth a code to which the members of the profession agree to be held accountable. At its heart, this code calls for the professional to protect and promote the welfare of clients and avoid letting the professional's self-interests place the client at risk for harm. In addition to the fundamental code of ethics, there may be codes or statements of the rights of patients (e.g., APA, 1997) or of the ethics as applicable in a specific setting, such as managed care organizations (e.g., National Academies of Practice, 1997).

Perhaps because society never completely trusts professions to enforce their own standards and perhaps because the professions have demonstrated that they, at least occasionally, are less than effective in governing their own behavior, society has established its own means for making sure that professions meet minimal standards in their work and that those whom professionals serve are protected from incompetent, negligent, and dishonest practitioners.

Four major mechanisms hold therapists and counselors accountable to explicit standards: professional ethics committees, state licensing boards, civil (e.g., malpractice) courts, and criminal courts. Each of these four mechanisms uses different standards, though they may overlap. Behavior may be clearly unethical and yet not form the basis for criminal charges.

In some cases, therapists and counselors may feel that these different standards clash. They may, for example, feel that the law compels them to act in a way that violates the welfare of the client and the clinician's own sense of what is ethical. A national survey of psychologists found that a majority (57%) of the respondents had intentionally violated the law or a similar formal standard because, in their opinion, not to do so would have injured the client or violated some deeper value (Pope & Bajt, 1988). The actions reported by two or more respondents included refusing to report child abuse (21%), illegally divulging confidential information (21%), engaging in sex with a patient (9%), engaging in nonsexual dual relationships (6%), and refusing to make legally required warnings regarding dangerous patients (6%).

That almost 1 out of 10 of the respondents reported engaging in sex with a client (see Chapter 21) using the rationale of patient welfare or deeper moral value highlights the risks, ambiguities, and difficulties of evaluating the degree to which our own individual behavior is ethical.

Pope and Bajt (1988) reviewed the attempts of philosophers and the courts to judge those times when a person decides to go against the law (e.g., engage in civil disobedience). On one hand, for example, the U.S. Supreme Court emphasized that in the United States, no one could be considered higher than the law: "In the fair administration of justice no man can be judge in his own case, however exalted his station, however righteous his motives, and irrespective of his race, color, politics, or religion" (*Walker v. City of Birmingham*, 1967, pp. 1219–1220).

On the other hand, courts endorsed Henry David Thoreau's (1849/1960) injunction that if a law "requires you to be the agent of injustice to another, then . . . break the law" (p. 242). The California Supreme Court, for example, tacitly condoned violation of the law only when the principles of civil disobedience are followed:

> If we were to deny to every person who has engaged in . . . nonviolent civil disobedience . . . the right to enter a licensed profession, we would deprive the community of the services of many highly qualified persons of the highest moral courage (*Hallinan v. Committee of Bar Examiners of State Bar*, 1966, p. 239)

As Pope and Bajt note, civil disobedience (Gandhi, 1948; M. L. King, 1958, 1964; Plato, 1956a, 1956b; Thoreau, 1849/1960; Tolstoy, 1894/1951) is useful in many contexts for resolving this dilemma. The individual breaks a law considered to be unjust and harmful but does so openly, inviting the legal penalty both to demonstrate respect for the system of law and to call society's attention to the supposedly unjust law. Counselors and therapists, however, often find this avenue of openness unavailable because of confidentiality requirements (see Chapter 24).

If we as individuals and a profession are to address the possible conflicts between the law and the welfare of our clients, one of the initial steps is to engage in frequent, open, and honest discussion of the issue. The topic needs open and active discussion in graduate courses, internship programs, case conferences, professional conventions, and informal meetings with colleagues.

Clients may understandably wind up confused about how therapists are held accountable for their actions. They may mistakenly believe that a professional ethics committee can revoke a license or that a licensing board can expel a practitioner from a professional organization like APA. The next sections describe the four major mechanisms of accountability.

ETHICS COMMITTEES, CODES, AND COMPLAINTS

Professional associations of therapists and counselors are voluntary organizations; membership is not a state or federal requirement for the practice of the profession. A psychologist can, for example, be licensed (by the state) and practice as a psychologist without being a member of APA or any other association. Each psychological organization describes the benefits of membership. One benefit is to provide direction and guidance about the standards in psychology. An association, through its ethics committee, holds its members accountable to the ethical principles it sets forth in the code it has developed. To illustrate how such a code is developed, we will describe how two organizations approached the challenge.

The American Psychological Association, in 2015, had 122,500 members, including researchers, educators, clinicians, consultants, and students.

The 2014 membership count for the Canadian Psychological Association cites 7,037 members including members, fellows, student and international affiliates, retired and honorary members, and those who are joint APA/CPA members (Stacey-Holmes, personal communication, May 5, 2015).

American Psychological Association Approach to an Ethics Code

Founded in 1892 and incorporated in 1925, APA first formed the Committee on Scientific and Professional Ethics in 1938. As complaints were brought to its attention, this committee improvised solutions on a private, informal basis. There was no formal or explicit set of ethical standards, so all of the committee's work was, of necessity, done on the basis of consensus and persuasion.

A year later, the committee was charged with determining whether a formal code of ethics would be useful for the organization. In 1947, it decided that a formal code of ethics would indeed be useful, stating, "The present unwritten code is tenuous, elusive, and unsatisfactory" ("A Little Recent History," 1952, p. 425). The board of directors established the Committee on Ethical Standards for Psychology to determine what methods to use in drafting the code. Chaired by Edward Tolman, the committee members were John Flanagan, Edwin Ghiselli, Nicholas Hobbs, Helen Sargent, and Lloyd Yepsen (Hobbs, 1948).

Some members strongly opposed the development of an explicit set of ethical standards, and many of their arguments appeared in *American Psychologist*. Calvin S. Hall (1952), for example, wrote that any code, no matter how well formulated,

> plays into the hands of crooks.... The crooked operator reads the code to see how much he can get away with, and since any code is bound to be filled with ambiguities and omissions, he can rationalize his unethical conduct by

pointing to the code and saying, "See, it doesn't tell me I can't do this," or "I can interpret this to mean what I want it to mean." (p. 430; see the discussion of the Enron code and the studies of effects of ethics codes in Chapter 26)

Hall endorsed accountability, but he believed that it could be enforced without an elaborate code. He recommended that the application form for APA membership contain this statement:

> As a psychologist, I agree to conduct myself professionally according to the common rules of decency, with the understanding that if a jury of my peers decides that I have violated these rules, I may be expelled from the association. (pp. 430–431)

Hall placed most of the responsibility on graduate schools. He recommended that "graduate departments of psychology, who have the power to decide who shall become psychologists, should exercise this power in such a manner as to preclude the necessity for a code of ethics" (p. 431).

The APA Committee on Ethical Standards (APA Committee) determined that because empirical research was a primary method of psychology, the code itself should be based on such research and should draw on the experience of APA members. As Hobbs (1948, p. 84) wrote, the method would produce "a code of ethics truly indigenous to psychology, a code that could be lived." The board of directors accepted this recommendation, and a new committee was appointed to conduct the research and draft the code. Chaired by Nicholas Hobbs, the new committee members were Stuart Cook, Harold Edgerton, Leonard Ferguson, Morris Krugman, Helen Sargent, Donald Super, and Lloyd Yepsen (APA Committee, 1949).

In 1948, all 7,500 members of APA were sent a letter asking each member "to share his experiences in solving ethical problems by describing the specific circumstances in which someone made a decision that was ethically critical" (APA Committee, 1949, p. 17). The committee received reports of over 1,000 critical incidents. During the next years, the incidents, with their accompanying comments, were carefully analyzed, categorized, and developed into a draft code.

The emerging standards, along with the illustrative critical incidents, were published in *American Psychologist* (APA Committee, 1951a, 1951b, 1951c). The standards were grouped into six major sections:

1. Ethical standards and public responsibility
2. Ethical standards in professional relationships
3. Ethical standards in client relationships
4. Ethical standards in research
5. Ethical standards in writing and publishing
6. Ethical standards in teaching

The draft generated considerable discussion and was revised several times. Finally, in 1952, it was formally adopted as the Ethical Standards of Psychologists, and it was published in 1953.

In 1954, information on the complaints that the committee had handled for the past 12 years (during most of which there had been no formal code of ethics) was published in *American Psychologist* ("Cases and Inquiries," 1954). During this period, the ethical principles most frequently violated were

- Invalid presentation of professional qualifications (cited 44 times).
- Immature and inconsiderate professional relations (23).
- Unprofessional advertisement or announcement (22).
- Unwarranted claims for tests or service offered usually by mail (22).
- Irresponsible public communication (6).

The Empirical Approach to a Code Half a Century Later

Many of the early APA pioneers provided reasons that an empirical approach would be useful in constructing an ethics code. But a critical incident survey of APA members could also serve another purpose. While the actuarial data of ethics committees, licensing boards, and civil and criminal courts can reveal trends in ethical or legal violations as they are established by review agencies, empirical critical incident studies can reveal ethical dilemmas and concerns as they are encountered in day-to-day practice by the broad range of psychologists (i.e., not just those who are subject to formal complaint).

The APA critical incident study undertaken in the 1940s was replicated in the 1990s and published in the *American Psychologist* (Pope & Vetter, 1992). In this study, 1,319 randomly sampled APA members were asked to describe incidents that they found ethically challenging or troubling: 679 psychologists described 703 incidents in 23 categories, as shown in Table 15.1.

The following is a sample of the ethical concerns that the psychologists described in this anonymous survey.

Confidentiality
- "The executive director of the mental health clinic with which I'm employed used his position to obtain and review clinical patient files of clients who were members of his church. He was [clerical title] in a . . . church and indicated his knowledge of this clinical (confidential) information would be of help to him in his role as [clerical title]."
- "Having a psychologist as a client who tells me she has committed an ethical violation and because of confidentiality I can't report it."
- "One of my clients claimed she was raped; the police did not believe her and refused to follow up (because of her mental history). Another of my clients described how he raped a woman (the same woman)."

Table 15.1. Ethical Problems Reported by a National Sample of APA Members.

Category	Number	Percentage
Confidentiality	128	18
Blurred, dual, or conflictual relationships	116	17
Payment sources, plans, settings, and methods	97	14
Academic settings, teaching dilemmas, and concerns about training	57	8
Forensic psychology	35	5
Research	29	4
Conduct of colleagues	29	4
Sexual issues	28	4
Assessment	25	4
Questionable or harmful interventions	20	3
Competence	20	3
Ethics and related codes and committees	17	2
School psychology	15	2
Publishing	14	2
Helping the financially stricken	13	2
Supervision	13	2
Advertising and (mis)representation	13	2
Industrial-organizational psychology	9	1
Medical issues	5	1
Termination	5	1
Ethnicity	4	1
Treatment records	4	1
Miscellaneous	7	1

Source: Adapted with permission from "Ethical Dilemmas Encountered by Members of the American Psychological Association: A National Survey," by K. S. Pope and V. A. Vetter, 1992, *American Psychologist, 47,* 397–411, p. 399. Available at http://kspope.com. Copyright 1992 by the American Psychological Association.

Blurred, Dual, or Conflictual Relationships

- "I live and maintain a . . . private practice in a rural area. I am also a member of a spiritual community based here. There are very few other therapists in the immediate vicinity who work with transformational, holistic, and feminist principles in the context of good clinical training that 'conventional' people can also feel confidence in. Clients often come to me because they know me already, because they are not satisfied with the other services available, or because they want to work with someone who understands their spiritual practice and can incorporate its principles and practices into the process of transformation, healing, and change. The stricture against dual relationships helps me to maintain a high degree of sensitivity to the ethics (and potentials for abuse or confusion) of such situations, but doesn't give me any help in working with the actual circumstances of my practice. I hope revised principles will address these concerns!"

- "Six months ago, a patient I had been working with for three years became romantically involved with my best and longest friend. I could write no less than a book on the complications of this fact! I have been getting legal and therapeutic consultations all along and continue to do so. Currently they are living together, and I referred the patient (who was furious that I did this and felt abandoned). I worked with the other psychologist for several months to provide a bridge for the patient. I told my friend soon after I found out that I would have to suspend our contact. I'm currently trying to figure out if we can ever resume our friendship and under what conditions." [This latter example is one of many that demonstrate the extreme lengths to which most psychologists are willing to go to ensure the welfare of their patients.]

Payment Sources, Plans, Settings, and Methods

- "A 7-year-old boy was severely sexually abused and severely depressed. I evaluated the case and recommended 6 months' treatment. My recommendation was evaluated by a managed health care agency and approved for 10 sessions by a nonprofessional in spite of the fact that there is no known treatment program that can be performed in 10 sessions on a 7-year-old that has demonstrated efficacy."
- "Much of my practice is in a private hospital that is in general very good clinically. However, its profit motivation is so very intense that decisions are often made for $ reasons that actively hurt the patients. When patients complain, this is often interpreted as being part of their psychopathology, thus reenacting the dysfunctional families they came from. I don't do this myself and don't permit others to do so in my presence — I try to mitigate the problem — but I can't speak perfectly frankly to my patients and I'm constantly colluding with something that feels marginally unethical."
- "A managed care company discontinued a benefit and told my patient to stop seeing me, then referred her to a therapist they had a lower fee contract with."

Academic Settings, Teaching Dilemmas, and Concerns About Training

- "I employ over 600 psychologists. I am disturbed by the fact that those psychologists with marginal ethics and competence were so identified in graduate school and no one did anything about it."

Forensic Psychology

- "A psychologist in my area is widely known to clients, psychologists, and the legal community to give whatever testimony is requested in court. He has a very commanding presence, and it works. He will say anything, adamantly, for pay. Clients/lawyers continue to use him because if the other side uses him, that side will probably win the case (because he's so persuasive, though lying)."
- "Another psychologist's report or testimony in a court case goes way beyond what psychology knows or his own data supports. How or whether I should respond."
- "I find it difficult to have to testify in court or by way of deposition and to provide sensitive information about a client. Although the client has given permission to provide this information, there are times when there is much discomfort in so doing."

Research

- "I am co-investigator on a grant. While walking past the secretary's desk, I saw an interim report completed by the PI [principal investigator] to the funding source. The interim report claimed double the number of subjects who had actually entered the protocol."
- "I have consulted to research projects at a major university medical school where 'random selection' of subjects for drug studies was flagrantly disregarded. I resigned after the first phase."
- "Deception that was not disclosed, use of a data videotape in a public presentation without the subject's consent (the subject was in the audience), using a class homework assignment as an experimental manipulation without informing students."

Conduct of Colleagues

- "As a faculty member, it was difficult dealing with a colleague about whom I received numerous complaints from students."
- "At what point does 'direct knowledge' of purportedly unethical practices become direct knowledge which I must report — is reporting through a client 'direct' knowledge?"
- "I referred a child to be hospitalized at a nearby facility. The mother wanted to use a particular psychiatrist.... When I called the psychiatrist to discuss the case, he advised me that, since he was the admitting professional, he'd assume full responsibility for the case.... He advised how he had a psychologist affiliated with his office whom he preferred to use."
- "I see foster children who have little control over their lives and case workers who have little time/interest in case management. How can I maintain good professional relationships with those who don't function up to their duties?"

- "A director of the mental health center where I worked was obviously emotionally disturbed, and it impacted on the whole center — quality of service to clients, staff morale, etc. He would not get professional help or staff development assistance."
- "The toughest situations I and my colleague seem to keep running into (in our small town) are ones involving obvious (to us) ethical infractions by other psychologists or professionals in the area. On three or more occasions he and I have personally confronted and taken to local boards . . . issues which others would rather avoid, deal with lightly, ignore, deny, etc., because of peer pressure in a small community. This has had the combined effect of making me doubt my reality (or experience), making me wonder why I have such moral compunctions, making me feel isolated and untrusting of professional peers, etc."

Sexual Issues

- "A student after seeing a client for therapy for a semester terminated the therapy as was planned at the end of the semester, then began a sexual relationship with the client. . . . I think APA should take a stronger stance on this issue."
- "I currently have in treatment a psychiatrist who is still in the midst of a 6-year affair with a patient. He wishes to end the affair but is afraid to face the consequences."
- "My psychological assistant was sexually exploited by her former supervisor and threatened her with not validating her hours for licensure if she didn't service his needs."

The Current APA Ethics Code

The most recent version of the ethical principles (APA, 2010a), the *Ethical Principles of Psychologists and Code of Conduct With the 2010 Amendments*, is the eleventh version. APA published versions of the code in these years: 1953, 1959, 1963, 1968, 1977, 1979, 1981, 1990, 1992, 2002, and 2010. The 2010 version consists of an introduction, a preamble, five general principles, and specific ethical standards. The preamble and general principles, which include beneficence and nonmaleficence, fidelity and responsibility, integrity, justice, and respect for people's rights and dignity, are aspirational goals to guide psychologists toward the highest ideals of psychology. The specific ethical standards are enforceable rules for conduct.

Canadian Psychological Association's Approach to an Ethics Code

The CPA was organized in 1939, incorporated under Part II of the Canada Corporations Act in 1950, and received its Certificate of Continuance under

Canada's Not-for-Profit Corporations Act in 2013. In the mid-20th century, Canada was a geographically large country with relatively few psychologists. Because it would have been hard to bring these psychologists together to create an ethics code, "the Canadian Psychological Association...decided to adopt the 1959...APA code for a three-year trial. This was followed by adoptions (with minor wording changes) of the 1963 and 1977 APA revised codes" (Sinclair & Pettifor, 2001, p. i).

Discontent with the APA code and the perception that it was not a good fit for Canadian psychologists led the CPA to create its own code. Prior to developing its own code, there was evidence of periodic discontent by CPA members with the APA code. For example, in a 1976 document titled "Alternative Strategies for Revising CPA's Code of Ethics," the statement was made that the 10 APA ethical principles were "clearly designed for the current American social and moral climate and geared to American traditions and law." However, it was not until the 1977 revision of the APA code that the discontent became serious. Of particular concern was the fact that, in response to U.S. court applications of antitrust law to professional activities, APA had removed some of its restrictions on advertising. Many Canadian psychologists believed such application of antitrust laws ran the risk of changing the nature of the professional relationship from a primarily fiduciary contract to a commercial one (Sinclair, Simon, & Pettifor, 1996, p. 7).

To create an ethics code, CPA began with a critical analysis of the international and interdisciplinary literature to determine the primary purposes of codes of ethics and their perceived strengths and weaknesses. This was followed by sending out 37 ethical dilemmas (Sinclair, Poizner, Gilmour-Barrett, & Randall, 1987). Psychologists were asked how they would act in these situations and, equally important, to describe their reasoning. The responses yielded four basic ethical principles (CPA, 1986):

1. Respect for the Dignity of Persons
2. Responsible Caring
3. Integrity in Relationships
4. Responsibility to Society

The original CPA ethics code began with a Preamble, which included a model of ethical decision making (see Chapter 17; see also Pope, 2011b; Sinclair & Pettifor, 2001; Sinclair et al., 1987; Truscott & Crook, 2013), in which the four ethical principles are to be considered and balanced. The Preamble was followed by four sections, one for each of the ethical principles, in which statements of values that give definition to the ethical principle are followed by a list of standards that illustrate the application of the principle to the activities of psychologists. Although the code was revised in 1991 and 2000, its original structure and emphases on the four ethical principles and ethical decision making has remained (Sinclair, 1998, 2011).

A third revision of the Canadian Code of Ethics for Psychologists is underway and a draft has been widely disseminated. The draft maintains the structure and emphases of previous editions of the Code, but with clarification, updates, and additions related primarily to the following themes: (1) the role of "the personal" (e.g., virtue, character, self-knowledge) in ethical decision making; (2) more examples on the application of the principles and values to the use of technologies; (3) more attention to collaborative/interdisciplinary practice; and (4) more attention to the impact of diversity and globalization on both society and psychology. CPA expects that this fourth edition of the Code will be finalized in 2016 (K. Cohen & C. Sinclair, personal communication, May 14, 2015; http://www.cpa.ca/aboutcpa/committees/ethics/codeofethics).

PATTERNS OF ETHICS COMPLAINTS FOR CPA AND APA

In 1985, the CPA Board approved a framework for redirecting to a regulatory body any complaint against a CPA member who is registered with that regulatory body. Although CPA would review the outcome of adjudication of the complaint, this review is to determine whether the individual's CPA membership should be terminated or whether any conditions should be placed on the membership. The complaint is not readjudicated. This practice has remained in effect to the present. However, CPA does accept and adjudicate complaints about CPA members who are not registered, as well as complaints that regulatory bodies believe do not come under their jurisdiction.

In the 1980s and 1990s, the CPA Committee on Ethics fully adjudicated one or two complaints a year. However, from 2001 to mid-2015, only five complaints were fully adjudicated. One possible reason for the change in the number of adjudicated complaints over this time period is the increased development in Canadian society of formal structures for addressing some types of complaints that had been brought to CPA in the past (e.g., Research Ethics Boards [REBs] for complaints regarding research; wider acceptance of sexual harassment complaints by various employers). Another possible reason is the broadening by regulatory bodies of what they consider to come under their jurisdiction (e.g., increased acceptance of complaints from students regarding the behavior of their professors or supervisors). CPA's Ethics Officer provides ethics consultation to members.

Processing complaints and notices from licensing boards continues to be a focus of the APA Ethics Committee. There are two programs: a complaint program in which the committee considers formal complaints that have been submitted to the committee, and a show cause/*sua sponte* program in which the committee decides whether to act when licensing boards take disciplinary action against APA members.

In addition, the Ethics Committee and the Ethics Office have continued to expand their ethics education (including presentations to state psychological associations, to state licensing boards, at APA conventions, at international programs, in articles in *Monitor on Psychology* and other publications) and consultation activities. Special projects such as diversity initiatives, awards programs, international programs, and convention programming were activities of the Ethics Committee (APA Ethics Committee, 2010, 2011, 2012, 2013, 2014).

Since 2000, the Ethics Committee and the American Psychological Association of Graduate Students (APAGS) present an award to the graduate student who submits the best paper on psychology and ethics. The graduate student prize includes both a $1,000 cash prize and funding to attend and present the paper at the APA annual convention. The Ethics Committee also collaborates with APAGS and Division 44 (Society for the Psychological Study of Lesbian, Gay, Bisexual, and Transgender Issues) to award LGBTQ graduate students of color on the basis of essays about the intersection of ethics and diversity issues. The students are awarded $1,000 to fund travel to attend the National Multicultural Conference and Summit, held every 2 years. The Ethics Educator Award is presented annually to an APA member who demonstrates significant and outstanding contributions to the profession of psychology through ethics education. It alternates from year to year between a local and international focus.

Examples of complex topics that the Ethics Committee reviewed and responded to in 2013 include exceptions to confidentiality and mandatory reporting for suspected child abuse, disclosures of confidential information to protect third parties, executive coaching, forensic and child custody matters, gifts from clients, maintaining test security in didactic presentations and scholarly publications, multiple relationships in training programs, negotiating potential tensions between aspects of diversity such as sexual orientation and religious beliefs, providing psychological services through electronic media, psychologists' consulting to reality TV programs, psychologists' use of social networking sites, the relationship between state law and the Ethical Principles of Psychologists and Code of Conduct (APA, 2002, 2010a), and appropriate termination of psychotherapy (APA Ethics Committee, 2014).

In conjunction with the APA Education Directorate, the Ethics Office offers a four-credit web-based continuing education (CE) course, "APA Ethics Code: An Introduction and Overview," offered at the APA Online Academy, http://www.apa.org/education/ce/index.aspx.

APA bylaws require that the Ethics Committee report the number and types of ethics complaints and the major programs undertaken. In the most recent year reported (APA Ethics Committee, 2014), conducting investigations continued to be a central activity of the Ethics Office on behalf of the Ethics

Committee. The total number of active matters at all stages (complaint or notice, preliminary investigation, etc.) was 383 for the year 2013. Active matters for each year 2009 through 2012 were reported as 624, 607, 619, and 607, respectively, because they included inquires that were active at some point during those years.

The Ethics Office decided to discontinue an investigation of each inquiry made to the office. The discontinuation of the inquiry process was made because (1) the complainants are now able to access directly whether the psychologist is a member of APA by calling the membership office; (2) this results in a significant reduction in the amount of staff time spent. Previously, opening a complaint for each inquiry involved sending out complaint forms many of which were never completed (APA Ethics Committee, 2014).

Show cause cases are generally based on loss of licensure as decided by state licensing boards and/or conviction of a felony, the basis for the most frequent type of case to be opened by the Ethics Committee. For 2013, all seven cases opened (100%) were such matters. For 2009 through 2013, the average percentage of such show cause cases was 88%. Of the seven cases opened up in 2013, sexual misconduct was the behavior in four cases (57%).

Of the five cases involving dual relationships, 20% were nonsexual in 2013 compared to 38%, 36%, 29%, and 29% from 2009 to 2012, respectively. In 2013, two cases were opened involving sexual relationships involving male psychologists with female clients, one case of a female psychologist with male and female clients in couples therapy, and one case resulted from a male supervisor's sexual involvement with two interns. One case of nonsexual dual relationship involved a male psychologist with male adolescent clients (APA Ethics Committee, 2014).

THE HOFFMAN REPORT

On November 14, 2014, APA (2014c) issued a press release that began:

> The American Psychological Association (APA) Board of Directors has reviewed the allegation in James Risen's book, *Pay Any Price: Greed, Power and Endless War*, that APA colluded with the Bush administration to support torture during the war on terror. Specifically, Risen alleges that APA supported the development and implementation of "enhanced" interrogation techniques that constituted torture, and was complicit with the CIA and U.S. military to this end.
>
> We believe that APA's October 16th statement refuting Risen's assertion was a fair and accurate response. However, the allegation made by Mr. Risen is highly charged and very serious. His book has created confusion for the public and APA members. This confusion, coupled with the seriousness of the allegation, requires a definitive, independent and objective review of the allegation and all relevant evidence.

Toward that end, and to fulfill its values of transparency and integrity, the APA Board has authorized the engagement of David Hoffman of the law firm Sidley Austin to conduct an independent review of whether there is any factual support for the assertion that APA engaged in activity that would constitute collusion with the Bush administration to promote, support or facilitate the use of "enhanced" interrogation techniques by the United States in the war on terror.

On July 10, 2015, the Hoffman report (Hoffman, Carter, Lopez, et al, 2015), which was exceptionally critical of APA, was released to the public. Our book was already at the publishers at the time; however, we have each provided a brief discussion of the report and its implication in the appendix.

LICENSING BOARDS

Each of the United States and Canadian jurisdictions (e.g., states, provinces) has its own requirements and standards for practicing as (or, in some states and jurisdictions, identifying oneself as) a therapist or counselor. Some, but not all, administrative standards embody ethical principles (e.g., some may set forth the relatively mundane obligation to pay an annual licensing fee). Formal licensing actions are how therapists and counselors are held accountable to these standards of practice. Violation of these standards can lead to the suspension or revocation of the practitioner's license or certification.

The data reviewed in Tables 15.2 to 15.4 concerning licensing disciplinary actions of psychologists were collected by the Association of State and Provincial Psychology Boards (ASPPB) from actions reported to the ASPPB disciplinary data system by member licensing boards in the United States and Canada (J. Pippin Orwig, Association of State and Provincial Psychology Boards, personal communication, April 5, 2015). Table 15.2 demonstrates the types of disciplinary actions (revocations, suspensions, probations, and reprimands) taken per year for years 2010–2014.

The data for Table 15.3 are abstracted from the ASPPB Disciplinary Data System (DDS) Reports from 1974 to 2014. ASPPB reports its codes to match the Healthcare Integrity and Protection Data Bank coding system, the national reporting data bank. The total number of reported actions in the system is 5,582. The top reasons for disciplinary action for all the DDS entries reported by ASPPB member boards include unprofessional conduct, sexual misconduct, negligence, nonsexual dual relationships, conviction of crime, failure to maintain adequate or accurate records, failure to comply with continuing education or competency requirements, incompetence, improper or inadequate supervision or delegation, and substandard or inadequate care. Table 15.4 demonstrates the variations of reasons for disciplinary action year to year from 2010 to 2014.

Table 15.2. ASPPB Disciplinary Data System: Historical Discipline Report. *Reported Disciplinary Actions for Psychologists: 1974–2014*

Total Number of Reported Actions in the ASPPB Disciplinary Data System:					5,582
Disciplinary Actions Taken Per Year (Past 5 Years)					
Type of Sanction	2014	2013	2012	2011	2010
Total Reported Actions	153	234	216	222	254
Revocations	7	18	13	13	15
Suspensions	28	35	32	33	43
Probations	25	34	39	39	58
Reprimands	54	32	54	53	56

Note. Each disciplinary action could contain multiple sanctions including other sanctions not listed such as supervision, mandatory continuing education, and so on. Therefore, the total number of sanctions reported here does not equal the total number of disciplinary actions reported.

Source: Compiled by the Association of State and Provincial Psychology Boards from actions reported to the ASPPB Disciplinary Data System by member boards. Obtained through personal communication with ASPPB staff member Janet Orwig, April 5, 2015.

Table 15.3. Top 10 Reasons for Disciplinary Action. *Historical Information: Data Compiled From All DDS Entries*

Reason for Disciplinary Action	Number Disciplined
Unprofessional Conduct	919
Sexual Misconduct	893
Negligence	586
Nonsexual Dual Relationship	585
Conviction of Crime	466
Failure to Maintain Adequate or Accurate Records	395
Failure to Comply With Continuing Education or Competency Requirements	346
Incompetence	307
Improper or Inadequate Supervision or Delegation	285
Substandard or Inadequate Care	282
Other (the combined total of the 76 remaining reasons)	4,205

Note. Based on the 5,582 total reports of disciplinary action submitted to the ASPPB Disciplinary Data System. Each action could contain multiple reasons for discipline such that the total number of reasons reported far exceeds the total number of actions.

Source: Compiled by the Association of State and Provincial Psychology Boards from actions reported to the ASPPB Disciplinary Data System by member boards. Obtained through personal communication with ASPPB staff member Janet Orwig, April 5, 2015.

Table 15.4. Top 10 Disciplinary Reasons by Year

Reason for Disciplinary Action	Number Disciplined
2014	
Negligence	21
Nonsexual Dual Relationship	16
Conviction of Crime	12
Practicing Without a License	12
Unable to Practice Safely by Reason of Alcohol or Other Substance Abuse	12
Failure to Meet Licensing Board Reporting Requirements	11
Failure to Comply With Continuing Education or Competency Requirements	9
Sexual Misconduct	9
Violation of Federal or State Statutes, Regulations, or Rules	8
Unprofessional Conduct	8
2013	
Failure to Comply With Continuing Education or Competency Requirements	56
Negligence	29
Unprofessional Conduct	22
Sexual Misconduct	15
Incompetence	15
Practicing With an Expired License/Certification/Registration	15
Violation of Federal or State Statutes, Regulations, or Rules	14
Conviction of Crime	13
Nonsexual Dual Relationship	12
Failure to Meet Licensing Board Reporting Requirements	11
2012	
Unprofessional Conduct	27
Nonsexual Dual Relationship	27
Negligence	20
Incompetence	17
Professional Opinion/Testimony Without Adequate Foundation	17
Failure to Maintain Adequate or Accurate Records	17
Failure to Obtain Informed Consent	14
Failure to Meet Licensing Board Reporting Requirements	13
Substandard Testing/Assessment Procedures	13
Conviction of Crime	13

Table 15.4. *(continued)*

Reason for Disciplinary Action	Number Disciplined
2011	
Failure to Comply With Continuing Education or Competency Requirements	43
Unprofessional Conduct	26
Conviction of Crime	24
Sexual Misconduct	24
Negligence	17
Substandard or Inadequate Care	14
Professional Opinion/Testimony Without Adequate Foundation	14
Nonsexual Dual Relationship	13
Incompetence	13
Failure to Maintain Adequate or Accurate Records	13
2010	
Unprofessional Conduct	31
Sexual Misconduct	31
Nonsexual Dual Relationship	28
Conviction of Crime	21
Failure to Maintain Adequate or Accurate Records	21
Professional Opinion/Testimony Without Adequate Foundation	18
Failure to Comply With Continuing Education or Competency Requirements	17
Negligence	15
Incompetence	15
Improper or Inadequate Supervision or Delegation	12

Source: Compiled by the Association of State and Provincial Psychology Boards from actions reported to the ASPPB Disciplinary Data System by member boards. Obtained through personal communication with ASPPB staff member Janet Orwig, April 5, 2015.

Van Horne (2004) reviewed data about licensing complaints against psychologists. She found that "few complaints are filed, many of those complaints are not investigated, informal actions taken that are not reported to the ASPPB Disciplinary Data System are few, and even fewer formal actions are taken against psychologists' licenses" (p. 175). She noted:

> The perception of disciplinary actions taken by licensing boards is dependent on the vantage point of the observer. If one is the subject of a licensing board

action, there is no doubt the board is vigilant, if not downright victimizing, in the pursuit of discipline. If one is the consumer/complainant seeking action by the licensing board, there is no doubt the board is cautious, if not downright distrustful of the complainant, in the investigative process. If one is a board member, there is no doubt the board is fair, if not downright obsessive, in its efforts to consider the rights of all concerned. If one is a journalist, there is no doubt the licensing board is protective of the psychologist, if not downright negligent in its failure to hold colleagues accountable. There is little doubt that one can find evidence for each of these perspectives. However, the larger picture of psychology licensing board complaints and both informal and formal disciplinary actions reflects a much more balanced outcome of the board mandate to protect consumers of psychological services. It is no surprise that fears abound in light of the high stakes involved for both complainants and licensees, but the facts should ease those fears. (p. 170)

Stephen T. DeMers, chief executive officer of ASPPB, described several projects that ASPPB has developed. The Certificate of Professional Qualification allows psychologists to avoid mobility problems and facilitates obtaining a license in a new jurisdiction. In addition, an interjurisdictional practice credential has been designed to help industrial organizational and forensic psychologists to engage in short-term practice in a jurisdiction in a sanctioned and regulated way (S. T. DeMers, personal communication, November 11, 2005; J. Orwig, personal communication, February 16, 2010). ASPPB announced the introduction of the Psychology Interjurisdictional Compact, which creates a legal and defensible yet practical system for regulating and facilitating the use of telecommunications and temporary face-to-face practice across jurisdictional boundaries. A resource kit is being developed by the Council of State Governments as an informational document in support of the new interstate compact (ASPPB, 2015). ASPPB has also recently launched a universal application for psychology license, Psychology Licensure Universal System, where ASPPB collects and verifies all information that any of its members boards would need for licensure. This information is stored electronically for later transmission to a board should the psychologist seek an additional license in another jurisdiction (J. Orwig, personal communication, May 17, 2015).

CIVIL STATUTES AND CASE LAW

Each state and province has its own legislation and accumulated case law that can serve as the basis of malpractice suits against therapists and counselors. Because the states and provinces differ in their legal standards, an act that one jurisdiction may require can violate the legal standards in another jurisdiction.

The United States and Canada provide a stark contrast in lawsuits against psychologists. Unlike their colleagues south of the border, Canadian psychologists apparently get sued very rarely (J. Service, personal communication, May 26, 2006).

Jana N. Martin, PhD, chief executive officer of The Trust, provided us with some interesting information about trends in lawsuits against psychologists (personal correspondence, March 19, 2015), prefacing them with the following comments about context:

- The data were collected and assigned to the respective categories by staff at the insurance company following a cursory review of the initial claim filed against the defendant.
- It is assumed that assignment of claims to a specific category is based on the primary allegation listed in the lawsuit; however, this is only an assumption.
- Most lawsuits contain a number of counts against the defendant. As a malpractice suit proceeds through the judicial system, the lawsuit is frequently amended to add new counts or remove certain counts. These data do not reflect any such amendments, subsequent filings, or final dispositions.
- Many lawsuits against psychologists are based on the shotgun approach, where the defendant is accused of multiple misdeeds, even though some of the allegations of wrongdoing may be dropped during the settlement discussions or prior to or during trial. Regardless of the underlying alleged misconduct, it is highly likely that the lawsuit will assert ineffective treatment, failure to consult, failure to refer, failure to diagnose, and/or improper diagnosis. This would be especially true when the underlying primary issue may be something like improper financial transactions or sexual misconduct.
- Psychologists tend to place heavy reliance on data such as provided here. In many cases, numbers tend to garner more significance than is appropriate.

With these caveats in mind, Martin pointed out some interesting trends when comparing data from 2010/2011 to 2013/2014:

- Since 2011, the percentage of claims for custody disputes has increased from 9% to 11%.
- The percentage of claims for sexual misconduct has increased from 3% to 5%.
- The percentage of claims involving suicide has been stable at about 5%.
- Forensic work (custody evaluations and evaluations affecting hiring, promotion, or retention in the workplace, etc.) represent an emerging high-risk area of practice.
- Suits filed in retaliation for fee collection appear to have decreased from 7.5% to 3%, probably because psychologists, knowing the dangers

associated with fee collection actions, are less likely to bring such suits against current or former patients.
- Other major areas of professional liability claims against psychologists include credentialing/billing improperly and dual relationships/boundary violations.
- The number of licensing board complaints has been relatively flat from 54% in 2010/2011to 52% in 2013/2014. (J. Martin, personal correspondence, March 2015)

CRIMINAL STATUTES

Each state and province has its own set of criminal laws, generally set forth in the penal code. Although we were unable to find reliable actuarial data concerning therapists convicted of crimes, one of the most frequently mentioned areas involves fraud, particularly related to third-party billings. Donald Bersoff, then attorney representing APA, emphasized the importance of conforming to all rules and regulations regarding billing practices for third-party coverage, both public and private, and noted that therapists currently serving time in prison could attest to the significance of violating those rules and regulations (see APA Ethics Committee, 1988).

Another of the areas in which therapists may face criminal prosecution is sexual involvement with patients (see Chapter 21). While many of the laws are civil reporting laws and injunctive relief statutes, as of October 2005, at least 25 states had enacted criminal statues regarding therapist–patient sexual contact (see Pope, 1994; Pope, Sonne, & Greene, 2006).

CONCLUSION

Exceptional caution is appropriate in attempts to generalize, compare, or interpret this chapter's actuarial data from ethics committees, licensing boards, and malpractice courts. Various types of actual violations, as the research indicates, may lead only rarely to a formal complaint with a criminal court, civil court, licensing board, or ethics committee. Certain types of violation can be hard to prove. Formal complaints may be informally resolved and not appear in archival data. And, as noted, there are significantly different ways of classifying complaints.

Nevertheless, the general trends in the archival data and critical incident studies can be useful to us. They call attention to aspects of our own practice where there is room for improvement. They suggest possible topics for which we might want to take continuing education courses. They provide a resource for us as individuals and as a helping profession seeking to maintain the high standards and integrity of our work and to minimize possible harm to those we serve.

These mechanisms of accountability and their relationship to ethical behavior warrant caution. It is so easy to confuse ethical behavior with what keeps us out of trouble with these review agencies (see Chapter 8). Our sense of what is ethical runs through a reductionistic mill and becomes, in the worst-case scenarios, "avoiding detection," "eliminating risk," or "escaping accountability." Much that we may do that is unethical may never come to the light and may never trigger inquiry by one of these mechanisms of accountability.

As noted in Chapter 1, the standards, principles, and guidelines articulated by our profession, the licensing boards, and the civil and criminal courts should never serve to inhibit careful ethical deliberation or serve as a substitute for thoughtful decision making and personal responsibility. They provide a framework that broadens our awareness and informs our thinking. They support us in the process of ethical struggle and constant questioning that an inescapable part of what we do as therapists and counselors.

Chapter 16

RESPONDING TO ETHICS, LICENSING, OR MALPRACTICE COMPLAINTS

Malpractice suits can strike like earthquakes. Confidence can shake and shatter. Reputation can rattle and crumble into ruin. Interrogatories, depositions, planning, meetings with attorneys, worry, and what-ifs rob from us the time we once spent with patients, friends, and family. Complaints to licensing boards and ethics committees can wreak the same havoc.

Stunned, the unprepared therapist can rush to respond, turning a bad situation into a catastrophe. Preparation helps us take informed, thoughtful, effective steps.

Preparation also helps us to view the possibility of a formal complaint realistically. Anxiety about being sued can grow into terror or obsession. A single-minded, intense, fearful struggle to avoid any possibility of a lawsuit can blot out the reasons we got into this line of work to begin with: helping people; earning money to support ourselves and our loved ones; doing meaningful, fulfilling work that we enjoy and are good at. We change our primary occupation from therapist to risk manager.

Intelligent risk management is part of ethical intelligence and good practice, but that is all it is: a *part*. Once we start living and working in fear of a complaint and allow that fear to dominate all decisions, something vital goes missing.

We recommend preparing for these possibilities early, as part of thinking through an approach to ethics and therapy, which is why we do not tack on this chapter at the end of the book.

Here are some considerations you may find helpful in responding to a formal complaint.

DON'T PANIC

Okay, go ahead and panic if you can't help it or believe that if you don't show some panic then your psychologist friends will accuse you of being in denial. Then take deep breaths, pull yourself together, and do whatever you need to do to think clearly. Avoid letting panic drive your decisions.

CONSULT YOUR ATTORNEY FIRST — AND MAKE SURE YOU HAVE A GOOD ONE!

Many therapists forget this step or try to save time and money by ignoring it. Opening an envelope to discover a licensing complaint, some psychologists figure that this minor misunderstanding can be resolved quickly by sending an explanation along with supporting documents. Receiving notice of a malpractice suit, other therapists hope that inviting the client to come in for a free session to discuss it "without all these lawyers" is the best way to reach a positive resolution and convince the client that there really was no reason to file a suit.

Responding to formal complaints before consulting an attorney can lead to disasters. The psychologist is moving into a different realm. An attorney can help guide us through the minefields of formal complaints. Good malpractice attorneys work in the world of complex legislation, case law, and court customs governing malpractice actions and some specialize in defending mental health professionals against licensing board complaints. Attorneys experienced in licensing and ethics hearings know the norms and customs. They can interpret the rules and procedures.

Good attorneys bring not only specialized knowledge and experience. They also bring another perspective: The attorney is not the object of the complaint. As the old aphorism has it, the person who represents him- or herself has a fool for a client.

Attorneys point out the pitfalls of strategies that otherwise seem to make perfect sense. A psychologist who has not consulted an attorney may talk to colleagues about the case, talk to the opposing attorney, write letters to various people mentioning the case, or blow off steam about the case within earshot of others and discover only later that these spoken and written statements and outpourings, which are not privileged, become key evidence.

Attorneys may give strong advice — sometimes a stern list of dos and don'ts. But a good part of what an attorney does is lay out options. For example, attorneys can tell us whether we can discuss the case with a supervisor, a consultant, a colleague, a friend, a family member, or anyone else and have what we say remain confidential and privileged. Attorneys can explain the effects and implications of turning down a settlement offer from the plaintiff in a malpractice suit.

Since so much can depend on your attorney's knowledge, skill, experience, trustworthiness, and dedication, make sure you have a good one. It is stunning how many therapists spend much more time researching a new computer, car, or refrigerator than they do for a new attorney. They may talk with several carpenters or contractors before hiring one to do work on their home but hire an attorney without considering alternatives. Ask colleagues about their experiences and recommendations. How many cases like yours has the attorney handled? What were the outcomes? How available is he or she? Will the attorney you are considering handle the case personally, or will a junior associate take over once you commit?

NOTIFY YOUR PROFESSIONAL LIABILITY CARRIER

A professional liability policy may include a requirement to notify the company immediately not only if you are sued but also if you have reason to believe that you will or may be sued. But requirements aside, it makes sense to let the carrier know if you become aware of a possible or actual formal complaint. The carrier may give you helpful guidance and provide you with an attorney. Some liability insurance companies offer financial coverage of legal representation for licensing complaints.

WHO IS YOUR ATTORNEY'S CLIENT?

The answer seems obvious: You are! But if the insurance company pays the attorney, are the insurance carrier's interests and your interests the same? What if the insurance company approves only a very limited discovery, hoping to hold down expenses? What if the carrier believes it makes sense financially (i.e., it is in the carrier's financial interests) to settle a case that you believe is bogus and would be decided in your favor were it vigorously defended? Settling the case, which would likely become a matter of public record, could devastate your career, particularly if you often testify as an expert witness.

In some rare circumstances, if you (or you and the attorney) are unable to persuade the carrier to litigate rather than settle the case or to provide an adequate discovery and vigorous defense, you might consider hiring your own attorney with your own funds. In some cases, however, you may not have to pick up the tab for this attorney. Some states, such as Alaska and California, have statutes providing what is called a Cumis counsel, an attorney you hire when you have a conflict of interest with your professional liability insurance company but whose fees are paid for by the insurance company. Some other states, such as Maryland and Texas, lack Cumis statutes but have established the right to Cumis council, at least under certain conditions, through case law.

IS THE COMPLAINT VALID?

When someone files a formal complaint against us, it is natural to feel hurt and attacked. Malpractice trials can fan the fires of anger on both sides. Before that process goes too far, ask yourself: Did you actually do what someone has accused you of doing? Setting aside defensiveness, rationalization, counter-attacks, and the fact that the charges may be overstated and wrong in the details, is there any truth to the claim that you did something you should not have done or that you failed to do something that you should have done?

Being relentlessly honest under these circumstances is anything but easy. Acknowledging that you may have done something wrong may seem self-destructive, indulging a tendency to beat yourself up when you need all your survival skills to rescue your reputation and career. But holding tight to the reality of what happened — avoiding memory's revisionism — can help you to respond effectively to the complaint and survive the ordeal in a way that is the very opposite of self-destructive.

DID YOU MAKE A FORMAL COMPLAINT MORE LIKELY?

It is worth asking: Regardless of whether you did or did not do what you are accused of doing, did you somehow make the complaint more likely? Did you, for example, make a normal, run-of-the-mill human error — not something illegal or unethical but just a mistake — and, when given a chance, refuse to acknowledge it or say you were sorry? Was there a misunderstanding — perhaps a client mistakenly thought you had done something wrong — that you refused to clarify? In other words, as you think through what happened with the benefit of hindsight, did your attitude or behavior increase the chances that this complaint would be filed?

In our experience, many (but by no means all) formal complaints seem to have less to do with a therapist doing something unethical than with the therapist–client relationship. The therapist has come across to the client as lacking respect, caring, and a reasonable ability to listen. Therapists who communicate these positive qualities to clients often seem to make all sorts of mistakes, misjudgments, and violations of standards without triggering a complaint, while therapists who fail to communicate these qualities must endure complaints even when they have otherwise seemed to adhere to the highest standards. (This, of course, does not imply that it is somehow okay to bumble our way into careless mistakes, misjudgments, and violations or that we can use what we communicate to the client to justify, discount, trivialize, or rationalize what we've done wrong and the consequences of our behavior, a process described in Chapter 8, "Ethics Placebos, Cons, and Creative Cheating: A User's Guide.") Formal complaints sometimes seem to represent a client's last desperate attempt to catch the attention of an unresponsive therapist.

APOLOGIZE AND ACCEPT RESPONSIBILITY?

If the complaint is valid, we must choose whether to acknowledge what we did, accept responsibility, and apologize. It seems to be part of the human condition that it is hard for many of us to admit mistakes, especially when those mistakes have hurt someone, and to say we're sorry. It can be much harder when it will go on the record, may be influential in sustaining the validity of the complaint, and is given to someone who is angry — perhaps enraged — at us. Some friends and colleagues may loyally take our side and advise us to despise the person who filed the complaint and to fight the complaint no matter what.

When facing a valid complaint, therapists may carefully consider, in consultation with their attorney, apologizing, accepting responsibility, and — if possible and appropriate — trying to make things right. Discussion with an attorney is an important part of this consideration. Attorneys may advise that a therapist should not speak to a complainant once a formal complaint has been filed. The attorney can explain the legal consequences (e.g., possible effects on the resolution of the complaint) and possible formats (e.g., in some situations it may be prohibited for the therapist to contact the complainant directly).

There can be strong reasons favoring and opposing a direct apology at this stage, depending on the circumstances, and it is impossible to foresee all the consequences and implications of taking or not taking this path. Each psychologist must choose what is right for his or her own values and situation.

WHAT ARE YOU WILLING TO HAVE DONE?

If you contest the charges, consider — before the adversarial process heats up — what you are willing to allow in defending your case. As an extreme hypothetical, imagine that an extremely fragile single mother sues you for malpractice. You believe her to be a basically good and competent person who has mistakenly but in good faith filed suit against you. Whatever your view of her, the claim she has filed threatens your reputation, career, and income. If the verdict goes against you, referral sources may dry up, the licensing board may launch an investigation, and your work as an expert witness on the standard of care may fall apart.

With all that at stake, would you be willing for your attorney to depose her and cross-examine her at trial in a way that misleadingly raises questions about her honesty? Would you be willing for the attorney to use your chart notes to create through innuendo the false impression that she is not an adequate mother and that perhaps she even neglected or abused her child? Would you be willing to testify (falsely) that she suffers from borderline personality disorder and threatened to sue you and ruin your reputation if you did go along with her attempts at seducing you?

Or would you be tempted to clarify your chart notes, a euphemism for changing your notes after the fact but submitting them as if they were contemporaneous? The potential self-serving justifications for submitting fraudulent records — a practice that is never ethical — are endless. Those notes may have been done hurriedly, may not have mentioned everything that was done, and may be misleading because of the way they were written. Wouldn't it be better to copy over those notes so that they include the material that you had neglected to put in the first time around on what are, really, if you come to think of it, your draft notes? Wouldn't it actually be a service to the court to remove the unintentional ambiguities along with the parts that are relatively unimportant, that clutter up your account of the treatment? In other words, stripped of its rationalization, would you be willing to hide your actual notes and submit a bogus chart more favorable to your defense?

Feeling attacked and facing the loss of reputation, career, and income can stir our most basic instincts to fight, to do anything to survive. It may tempt us toward unethical extremes, such as lying while testifying or committing a fraud on the court by submitting bogus chart notes that we've secretly doctored. It may draw us toward pretending our hands are clean by letting our attorney use unethical or unfair tactics on our behalf. A question worth asking before the process builds up too much steam is: Am I willing to win at any cost? If not, where do I draw the line? What, if anything, am I unwilling to do — or to have done by others in my defense — to win?

RECOGNIZE HOW THE COMPLAINT IS AFFECTING YOU

Formal complaints can devastate us. They can hit us with all of these feelings and more:

- Numbing shock that suddenly reputation and career may be at stake.
- A sense of betrayal that someone we tried to help has turned against us.
- Fear of uncertainty and the unknown horrors in store for us.
- Reflexive self-blame, assuming that we must have done something terrible or else we would not be in this fix.
- Embarrassment, imagining that our colleagues now think the worst about us.

- Self-doubt; if we did so poorly with this patient that we wound up in court, what if our other patients sue us?
- Depression.
- Suspicion of our other patients (are they going to sue us?) and colleagues (is there anyone we trust to talk this over with?).
- Anxiety about what lies ahead — being deposed and cross-examined, who will be in the courtroom during the trial (the media?), and on and on and on.
- Obsessive and intrusive thoughts, finding it hard to think about anything else.
- Insomnia, tossing and turning, thinking endlessly about what has happened and what may happen.
- Catastrophizing.
- Loss of appetite, eating or drinking too much, or abusing prescription or illegal drugs as a response to the stress.

We believe that for some therapists, being sued can bring on reactions akin to posttraumatic stress disorder. If we can be honest about our reactions, we are in a better position to respond to those reactions constructively.

GET THE HELP AND SUPPORT YOU NEED

What help, if any, do you need in dealing with these reactions? Some clinicians return to therapy or start therapy for the first time. Some reach out to friends, colleagues, and family. An attorney's guidance can be invaluable in keeping what you say to others from becoming part of the case against you. For example, consultation (with friends, with colleagues) tends to be discoverable while what you disclose to your therapist or attorney tends (with exceptions) to be covered by therapist–patient or attorney–client privilege. As another example, a military judge may, in certain instances, rule therapy notes both relevant and admissible.

WHAT CAN THE ORDEAL TEACH?

For understatement it is hard to beat: No one ever wishes a formal complaint or lawsuit. But this unwelcome process brings opportunity.

We may find flaws and weaknesses in our policies, procedures, and approach to clinical work. We may learn to spot red flags in our practice and to do something about them. We may learn about our colleagues — who can we count on for support and who abandons and avoids us. We may learn how our own work and the complaints against us are evaluated during adversarial procedures. And in our reactions and decisions, we may learn about ourselves.

Chapter 17

STEPS IN ETHICAL DECISION MAKING

It's easy to miss an ethical dilemma's vital details or possible solutions. Competing values, conflicting regulations, scarce resources, misinformation, deadlines, fear of making a catastrophic mistake, and a stampede of other pressures and complications can make it hard to think clearly, carefully, and creatively.

This chapter provides useful steps for understanding, thinking through, and responding effectively to ethical dilemmas, especially when faced with complex ethical gray zones. The steps help identify key aspects of a situation, consider benefits and drawbacks of our options, and discover better approaches.

The Canadian Psychological Association (CPA) emphasized the importance of such steps by including seven in its original ethics code (1986) and increasing the number to 10 in subsequent editions (1991, 2000, February 2015 draft). The asterisks in the following list mark steps that are versions of those that appear in the CPA code.

Seventeen steps appear here, but not every step fits every situation, and some steps may need to be adapted.

STEP 1: STATE THE QUESTION, DILEMMA, OR CONCERN AS CLEARLY AS POSSIBLE

Does the statement do the situation justice? Does it make clear what the problem is and why it is a problem? Does it miss anything important to thinking through possible courses of action? Does any part of it get lost in the mists of vagueness, ambiguity, or professional jargon? Are some of the words misleading or not quite right? Is there anything questionable about the statement's scope, perspective, or assumptions? Are there other valid ways to define the problem?

Tight schedules, urgent situations, and an eagerness to solve the problem can rush us past this step, but coming up with the best approach depends on clearly understanding the ethical challenge.

STEP 2: *ANTICIPATE WHO WILL BE AFFECTED BY THE DECISION

No one lives in a vacuum. How often do our ethical decisions affect only a single person and no one else? A client shows up for a session drunk. Whether the client drives home drunk and kills a pedestrian can depend on how we define our responsibility. A colleague begins to show signs of Alzheimer's. Our choices can affect the safety and well-being of the colleague and his or her patients. A therapy client tells us about embezzling pension funds. Confidentiality laws may direct us to tell no one else, and the client may refuse to discuss the issue. How we respond can determine whether hundreds of families retain the pensions they earned or are thrown into poverty. An insurance claims manager refuses to authorize additional sessions for a client we believe is at risk for killing his wife and children and then committing suicide. Our supervisor may agree with the manager that no more sessions are needed. Whether the family lives or dies may depend on what we do.

STEP 3: FIGURE OUT WHO, IF ANYONE, IS THE CLIENT

Is there any ambiguity, confusion, or conflict about who the client is (if it is a situation that involves a psychotherapist–client relationship)? If one person is the client and someone else pays our fee, do we feel any divided loyalty, any conflict that might shade our judgment?

STEP 4: ASSESS WHETHER OUR AREAS OF COMPETENCE – AND OF MISSING KNOWLEDGE, SKILLS, EXPERIENCE, OR EXPERTISE – FIT THE SITUATION

Are we well prepared to handle this situation? What steps, if any, could we take to make ourselves more effective? In the light of all relevant factors, is there anyone available to step in and do a better job? If so, what reasons weigh against referring the client?

STEP 5: REVIEW RELEVANT FORMAL ETHICAL STANDARDS

Do the ethical standards speak directly or indirectly to this situation? Does this situation involve conflicts within the ethical standards or between the ethical standards and other (e.g., legal) requirements or values? In what ways, if any, do the ethical standards seem helpful, irrelevant, confusing, outdated, or misdirected when applied to this situation? Would it be helpful to talk with an ethicist, a member of a national, state, or provincial ethics committee?

STEP 6: REVIEW RELEVANT LEGAL STANDARDS

What legislation and case law speak to this situation? Does a legal standard conflict with other standards, requirements, or values? Do the relevant laws support — or at least allow — the most ethical response to the situation, or do they seem to work against or even block the most ethical response? Would it be helpful to consult an attorney who has experience and expertise in these issues?

STEP 7: REVIEW THE RELEVANT RESEARCH AND THEORY

Have we kept up with the emerging theory, research, and practice that might help us think through this situation? An occupational hazard of a field with such diverse approaches — cognitive, psychodynamic, pharmacological, behavioral, feminist, psychobiosocial, family, multicultural, and existential, to name but a few — is that we often lose touch with new ideas, findings, and approaches arising outside the walls of our own theoretical orientation.

STEP 8: *CONSIDER WHETHER PERSONAL FEELINGS, BIASES, OR SELF-INTEREST MIGHT SHADE OUR ETHICAL JUDGMENT

Does the dilemma make us angry, sad, or afraid? Do we want to please someone? Do we desperately need to avoid conflict? Do we fear that choosing the most ethical path will get us into trouble, make someone mad at us, be second-guessed by colleagues, or be hard to square with the law or the ethics code? Will doing the right thing cost us time, money, friends, referrals, prestige, a promotion, our job, or our license? Being relentlessly honest with ourselves as we feel our way through as well as think our way through ethical challenges can help us avoid rationalizing our way off the path toward the most ethical response for this specific situation.

STEP 9: CONSIDER WHETHER SOCIAL, CULTURAL, RELIGIOUS, OR SIMILAR FACTORS AFFECT THE SITUATION AND THE SEARCH FOR THE BEST RESPONSE

An act can take on sharply different meanings in different societies, cultures, or religions. The most ethical response in one context may violate sacred values in another society, culture, or spiritual tradition. What contexts — or conflicts between contexts — may have escaped our notice? Does our own social identity in relation to the client's social identity enter into the process? Could our own limited or biased view of other cultures, religions, and so on, throw off how we think through this ethical dilemma?

STEP 10: CONSIDER CONSULTATION

Is there anyone who could help us think through the issues and possible responses? Who has expertise in the relevant areas? Is there someone who has faced a similar situation and handled it well — or who might tell us what does not work and what pitfalls to avoid? Is there a colleague whose perspective might be helpful? Is there someone whose judgment we trust? When drawing a blank in the face of these questions, sometimes it is useful when a question takes this form: If what we decide to do were to end in disaster, is there some particular person we wish we had consulted?

As noted in earlier chapters, consultation — unlike communications protected by therapist–patient or attorney–client privilege — is usually discoverable in legal proceedings. This may be an important consideration in some situations.

STEP 11: *DEVELOP ALTERNATIVE COURSES OF ACTION

What possible ways of responding to this situation can you imagine? What alternative approaches can you create? At first we may come up with possibilities that seem not bad or good enough. The challenge is not to quit too soon but to keep searching for our best possible response.

STEP 12: *THINK THROUGH THE ALTERNATIVE COURSES OF ACTION

What impact is each action likely to have — and what impact could each have under the best possible and worst possible outcome that you can imagine — for each person who will be affected by your decision? What are the immediate and longer-term consequences and implications for each individual, including yourself, and for any relevant organization, discipline, or society? What are the risks and benefits? Almost any significant action has unintended consequences — what could they be for each possible course of action? As with so many aspects of thinking through ethical dilemmas, one of the best strategies is to imagine that you decided upon the option, tried it out, and it ended in disaster — What flaws do you spot? What do you wish you would've considered before you acted on it? How could that option have been strengthened? Or should it have been discarded in favor of a better option?

STEP 13: TRY TO ADOPT THE PERSPECTIVE OF EACH PERSON WHO WILL BE AFFECTED

Putting ourselves in the shoes of those affected by our decisions can change our understanding. What would each person consider the most ethical response? This approach can compensate for the distortion that often comes from seeing things only from our own perspective. One example is *correspondence bias* (Bauman & Skitka, 2010; Blanchard-Fields et al., 2007; Ross, 1977; Ross & Nisbett, 2011; Stockus & Walter, 2015; see Chapter 5, "Ethical Judgment Under Uncertainty and Pressure: Critical Thinking About Heuristics, Authorities, and Groups"). Although we often explain our own behavior in specific situations as due to external factors, we tend to attribute the behavior of others to their dispositions.

Another example is what Meehl (1977) called a "double-standard of morals" (p. 232): We hold other people's explanations to much higher scientific standards of logic, plausibility, persuasiveness, and proof than we use for our own explanations.

STEP 14: *DECIDE WHAT TO DO, REVIEW OR RECONSIDER IT, AND TAKE ACTION

Once we decide on a course of action, we can — if time permits — rethink it. Sometimes simply making a decision to choose one option and exclude all others makes us suddenly aware of flaws in that option that had gone unnoticed up to that point. Rethinking gives us one last chance to make sure we have come up with the best possible response to a challenging situation.

STEP 15: *DOCUMENT THE PROCESS AND ASSESS THE RESULTS

Keeping track of the process through documentation helps us remain clear about what went into our decision: the elements of the problem; the options and potential consequences; the guidance provided by others; the perspective of the client, including the relevant rights, responsibilities, risks, and possible unintended consequences. Careful record keeping involves tracking not only what led up to our decision but also what happened afterward. What happened when we acted? Did we accomplish what we'd hoped and intended? Did unseen factors and unforeseen consequences spring up? Knowing what we know now, would we have taken the same path or tried a different response?

STEP 16: *ASSUME PERSONAL RESPONSIBILITY FOR THE CONSEQUENCES

If what we did seems clumsy, misguided, or downright wrong in hindsight, if it brought about needless trouble, pain, loss, or problems, how do we respond to the fallout of what we did or failed to do? Can we openly and honestly admit and own our mistakes and shortcomings and take clear steps both to set things right, if possible, and to avoid these missteps in the future?

STEP 17: *CONSIDER IMPLICATIONS FOR PREPARATION, PLANNING, AND PREVENTION

Does this situation, how we responded to it, and the effects of our response suggest useful possibilities in the areas of preparation, planning, and prevention? What could we do to head off future problems or strengthen our responses? Would making changes in our policies, procedures, or practices help?

Chapter 18

BEGINNINGS AND ENDINGS, ABSENCE AND ACCESS

You return a phone call from a middle-aged man who is looking to begin therapy. He finds himself worrying that the company he works for has been struggling and may lay him off. He can't find any other openings in the area and can't stand the thought that he might not be able to support his family. You talk with him about 10 or 15 minutes getting basic information, including his insurance, and set up an appointment 10 days later, your first opening. Four days later a public defender calls you. The company fired the man, who returned with a gun and shot his supervisor. The public defender is calling you to ask if you would send him your records and talk with her a little about your assessment of the man, who has named you as his therapist. But wait! Did one phone call mean you're the man's therapist? Did your professional responsibilities start when you talked with him, heard why he wanted therapy, asked him for basic information, and decided to schedule a session with him?

Your client stops coming to therapy. You don't know why. She does not return the phone messages or respond to the letter you sent her. Five weeks have passed. Does this meet the clinical, ethical, and legal standards of "termination" in your jurisdiction? What additional steps, if any, would your take?

A fragile client has been making gradual progress in therapy when his partner dies unexpectedly and he becomes suicidal. The same week the managed care company sends you notice that the client has reached the coverage limits and the company will approve no additional sessions.

Ethical intelligence includes thinking clearly about the boundaries of our relationships with our clients. Where is the boundary marking the start of therapy? What marks the end? Discussing information about the beginning and ending of therapy, as well as about availability of services during therapy, helps enable a client to provide consent that is truly informed. (Chapter 19 provides a more detailed discussion of informed consent.)

People who come to us for help have a right to know when they become our client as well as when the professional relationship ends. They need to know how available we are, including when and how can they get in touch with us. This chapter discusses some of those issues of beginnings, access, absences, and endings.

ACCESSIBILITY FOR PEOPLE WITH DISABILITIES

Our decisions about how accessible we make our services to people with disabilities reflect our ethical values (Pope, 2005). They also affect many people in Canada and the United States. Statistics Canada (2014) reported that around 11% of Canadian citizens aged 25–64 reported being limited in their activities because of one or more disabilities. Psychologist Martha Banks wrote:

> Approximately one-fifth of U.S. citizens have disabilities. The percentage is slightly higher among woman and girls (21.3%) than among men and boys (19.8%). Among women, Native American women and African American women have the highest percentages of disabilities.... As a result of limited access to funds, more than one-third of women with work disabilities and more than 40% of those with severe work disabilities are living in poverty. (2003, p. xxiii)

What barriers, if any, do people who use wheelchairs encounter when they come to the building in which you do therapy and enter your office (Pope & Vasquez, 2005)? Would a client who is deaf face needless challenge reaching you? Would a person who is blind find it easy to navigate your building and find the right room? If you have a website, is it accessible to those who are disabled and use assistive technologies? (For articles and other resources to address these issues, go to *Accessibility and Disability Information and Resources in Psychology Training and Practice* at http://kpope.com.)

CLARIFICATION

Therapists must be alert to possible complications and confusions. Someone may call for an initial appointment. The therapist may assume that the session is one of initial evaluation regarding possible courses of action (e.g., if therapy makes sense for the individual, or what modality of therapy under what conditions implemented by what clinician seems most promising). The individual, however, may assume that the clinician, by virtue of accepting that request for an initial appointment, has become his or her therapist. Another client, several months into treatment, may boil over with rage at the therapist but be unable to give voice to the anger, bolt from the room halfway through a session, and stay out of touch for the next 5 weeks, missing the weekly appointment time. Is that client still a client, or has termination occurred?

Acting to prevent unnecessary misunderstandings about the beginning and ending of therapy is part of our more ethical responsibility to clarify the availability of and access to therapeutic resources. One of the more immediate aspects of this responsibility is for both therapist and client to understand clearly when and under what circumstances the therapist will be available for sessions or for telephone or other communication, and what resources will be available for the client when the therapist is not available.

Clarification is important for at least five reasons:

1. It forces the therapist to consider carefully this client's needs for telephone, e-mail, or other access during the course of therapy (see Chapter 11). For example, is this an impulsive, depressed client with few friends who might need contact with the therapist or some other professional in the middle of the night to avert a suicide? Clarification enables the therapist to plan for such contingencies.

2. By leading the therapist to specify backup availability — for example, what clients can do if they are unable to reach the therapist in an emergency — the efforts to clarify availability enable the therapist to prepare for therapeutic needs that are difficult or impossible to anticipate. For example, a client with moderate coping resources may attend appointments regularly over the course of a year or two, never contacting the therapist between sessions. However, during a period when the therapist is seriously ill and unavailable, the client may receive numerous shocks, such as the loss of a job or the death of a child. The client may become acutely suicidal and need fast access to therapeutic resources. Careful planning by the therapist may meet such needs that are virtually impossible to anticipate with a specific client.

3. Clarifying access to the therapist or to other therapeutic resources encourages the therapist to think carefully about how times of access and lack of access may affect clients and the course of treatment. For example, some clients are likely to experience overwhelming feelings of sadness, anger, or abandonment when the therapist goes on vacation. Other clients may find the clear boundaries that the therapist has established so uncomfortable and infuriating that they are constantly testing both the therapist and the boundaries. Such clients may frequently show up at the therapist's office at the wrong time for their appointment, may

leave urgently cryptic messages ("Am quitting therapy; no hope; life too painful; can't go on") for the therapist without leaving a number where they can be reached, and may persistently try to discover the therapist's home or e-mail address, home or cell phone telephone numbers (if the therapist customarily keeps these private).

4. When therapist and client work together to develop a plan for emergencies during which the therapist might not be immediately available, the process can help the patient to assess his or her dependence and needs for help and to assume — to the extent that he or she is able — realistic responsibility for self-care during crises. For example, the therapist may ask the client to locate the nearest hospital providing 24-hour services and develop ways of reaching the hospital in an emergency. As the client assumes responsibility for this phase of crisis planning, he or she increases the sense of self-efficacy and self-reliance (within a realistic context), becomes less inclined to view therapy as a passive process (in which the therapist does all the work), and may feel less panicky and helpless when facing an impending crisis or the therapist's future absences. In this sense, planning becomes an empowering process for the client.

5. The process of clarification encourages the therapist to consider carefully his or her own needs for time off, away from the immediate responsibilities of work. Such planning helps ensure that the therapist does not become overwhelmed by the demands of work and does not experience burnout. The drawing of such boundaries also encourages the therapist to attend explicitly to other sources of meaning, joy, fulfillment, and support so that he or she does not begin looking to clients to fill personal needs (see Chapter 22). This is a crucial aspect of the therapist's maintaining emotional competence (see Chapter 12).

Setting the boundaries availability involves balancing our own personal needs, theoretical orientation, and style of practice with each client's clinical needs. Some therapists maintain flexible boundaries in several areas, including time limits. Others hold to exact time boundaries. With virtually no exceptions, they begin and end the session on the dot. Even if the client has just experienced a painful breakthrough and is in obvious distress, they do not extend the therapy session. In some situations, ending promptly is a practical necessity: The therapist may have another client scheduled to begin a session immediately. In other situations, observing strict time boundaries is required by the theoretical orientation: Running over the time boundary might be considered by the therapist to constitute a breaking of the frame of therapy or represent the therapist and client colluding in acting out.

When we arrive at an approach to time boundaries that best fit our personal needs, our approach to therapy, and the client's clinical needs, we must make sure that the client understands our policy.

THERAPIST AVAILABILITY BETWEEN SESSIONS

When and under what conditions do we make ourselves available to clients between sessions? Some therapists receive nonemergency calls from clients whenever they are free during reasonable weekday hours (e.g., 9:00 a.m. to 6:00 p.m.). A very few therapists take nonemergency calls when they are conducting therapy. We recommend against this practice, which seems disrespectful of the client who is in session and seems to have many potentially harmful effects on the course of therapy of the client whose session is interrupted (or is aware that any session might be interrupted at any time by nonemergency calls to the therapist).

The therapist needs to be clear about the times between sessions when he or she can be contacted on a nonemergency basis. For example, are weekend calls or calls on holidays such as Labor Day, Memorial Day, or Martin Luther King Day acceptable?

An extremely important point to clarify is whether the therapist will speak with the client more than briefly by telephone when there is no emergency. Some clients like to use telephone calls or e-mail communication to address unresolved issues from the previous therapy session, share a dream while it is still fresh in their mind, or talk over how to handle a situation at work. Some therapists may see such extra communications as therapeutically useful for some clients. The telephone sessions may, for example, help particularly fragile and needy clients, who might otherwise require day treatment or periodic hospitalizations, to function under the constraints of once- or twice-weekly outpatient therapy. They may help some clients learn how to use and generalize the adaptive skills they are acquiring in office sessions; the extra communications serve as a bridge between office therapy sessions and independent functioning by the client.

Other therapists may prefer to keep the work in the frame of the therapy session. They believe that telephone or e-mail communications during which therapy is conducted are — except under rare emergency conditions — countertherapeutic. For example, they might view extended telephone contacts between sessions as similar in nature and effect to going beyond the temporal boundary at the end of a session. Other therapists may, as part of their own self-care (see Chapter 13), limit out-of-office contacts to emergencies. Some therapists may suggest that clients journal their thoughts and feelings between sessions and bring those to the next session for possible discussion. Communication of therapeutic content via e-mail should be considered carefully and used only with adequate safeguards to protect confidentiality.

Again, whether the therapist uses an approach that includes or prohibits discussions with clients between regularly scheduled in-person therapy sessions matters less than that (a) the therapist thinks through the issues carefully in terms of consistency with his or her theoretical orientation and personal approach, (b) the therapist considers carefully the implications of the policy for the individual client, and (c) both therapist and client clearly understand the ground rules, including any charges for these sessions.

It can also be important to clarify under what circumstances, if any, the therapist will be available for e-mail communication and how privacy issues will be addressed; for example, do any third parties have access to the therapist's or the client's e-mail accounts? Some therapists have been surprised to receive unexpected e-mail from a client who has searched the Internet and discovered the therapist's supposedly personal e-mail address. Both therapist and client must clearly understand whether e-mail can be used to schedule and cancel sessions, check in between regularly scheduled office sessions, or provide therapy or counseling over the Internet. Informed consent should be provided given the limitations of e-mail privacy (see Chapter 11).

Many standards, guidelines, and codes address communication with clients using telephone, e-mail, or other electronic means. Links to 24 sets of professional guidelines focusing on telepsychology and Internet-based therapy, citations for 51 recent articles on that topic, and links to state psychology board telepsychology laws/regulations/policies/opinions are provided on the following web page: http://kspope.com/telepsychology.php. Chapter 11 of this book provides a discussion of the benefits and risks of the digital world.

An excellent resource is a survey of ethical dilemmas that psychologists encountered in telephone counseling (Dalen, 2006). Dilemmas involving "confidentiality and professional secrecy" were the most frequently reported (p. 240). Dilemmas involving integrity were also frequently reported, although dilemmas involving competence were rarely mentioned.

VACATIONS AND OTHER ANTICIPATED ABSENCES

Extended and sometimes even brief interruptions in the schedule of appointments can stir puzzling, strong, or even overwhelming reactions from a client. What is important is that therapists give the client adequate notice of the anticipated absence. If therapists take a 2-week vacation at the same time each year or travel frequently for various reasons, there may be no reason to omit this information from the customary orientation provided to a new client. Therapists who find that they will be taking a 6-week sea cruise during the coming year should consider carefully if there is any compelling clinical or practical reason to withhold this information from a client as soon as reservations are made. While most clients may take such absences in stride, others may have intense reactions. Prompt notification of anticipated therapist absences minimizes the likelihood that a client will experience a psychologically paralyzing traumatic shock, gives the client maximal time to mobilize the resources to cope with a therapist's absence in a way that promotes independence and growth, and enables the client to become aware of reactions and work with them during the sessions before and after the absence.

SERIOUS ILLNESS AND OTHER UNANTICIPATED ABSENCES

Both therapists and clients tend to find comforting the myth that the therapist is immortal and invulnerable (Pope, Sonne, & Greene, 2006). Therapists may relish the feeling of strength and of being a perfect caregiver that such a fantasy, which sometimes occurs on an unconscious level, provides. Clients may soothe themselves (and avoid confronting some personal issues) with the fantasy that they are being cared for by an omnipotent, immortal parental figure.

Although we have not completed our careful study of every therapist who has ever lived — for which we wildly underbudgeted only 6 weeks to conduct the interviews — our preliminary results suggest that there has yet to appear a therapist who is immortal and invulnerable. For all of us who are mortal and vulnerable, it is important to prepare for those unexpected times when we are suddenly unavailable to our clients (see Chapter 14).

STEPS FOR MAKING HELP AVAILABLE IN A CRISIS

Once clients clearly understand how to contact the therapist between regularly scheduled appointments, therapist and clients can discuss how to prepare for times when these plans aren't enough. A client, for example, may experience an unanticipated crisis and be unable to reach the therapist promptly by telephone because the therapist's line is busy for an extended time, the therapist's answering service mishandles the client's call, the therapist is in session with another client who is in crisis, or any number of other typical or once-in-a-lifetime delays, glitches, or human errors. For the reasons cited earlier, planning for such unanticipated breakdowns can enable access to prompt clinical services in time of crisis.

If the client's need for help is urgent and the therapist can't be reached, is there a colleague who is providing coverage for the therapist? Some settings, such as health maintenance organizations and community mental health centers, assign clinicians to serve on-call rotations so that someone is always available in a crisis. However, many therapists, particularly those in solo independent practice, may need to create and implement their own plans to ensure coverage in an emergency, should they be unavailable.

The decision of whether to arrange for coverage for a specific client is complex. Perhaps the first question is what sort of information the covering clinician will be provided about the client. Will the covering therapist receive a complete review and periodic update of the client's clinical status, treatment plan, and therapeutic progress? Will the covering therapist have access to the client's chart? Will the covering therapist keep a separate set of notes regarding information supplied by the primary therapist? To what extent will the covering therapist need to secure independent informed consent for treatment by the client? The more foreseeable or the greater the risk is that the client will experience a serious crisis demanding prompt intervention, the more compelling the reason is for the primary therapist to brief the covering therapist in a careful, thorough manner.

Once the therapist has determined what degree of coverage seems appropriate for a specific client, a second question is how to introduce the possibility of or actually implement such coverage affecting the client's status or treatment. Some clients might feel greatly reassured to know that the therapist is taking his or her responsibilities seriously and is carefully thinking through possible, even if unlikely, treatment needs. Other clients may become alarmed and feel as if the therapist is predicting that a crisis will occur. Still other clients may stall in their progress; the strict privacy and confidentiality of therapy is essential for them, and the knowledge that the therapist will be sharing the contents of sessions with the covering therapist inhibit their ability to explore certain issues or feelings. In many cases, discussion between the therapist and client of the question of whether specific coverage will be provided is useful therapeutically.

If it is decided that specific coverage will be provided, a third question for the therapist is what will best serve the client's right to adequate informed consent for sharing information with the covering therapist and otherwise making arrangements for the coverage.

A fourth question addresses the selection of a clinician to provide the coverage. The primary therapist may incur legal (i.e., malpractice) liability for negligence in selecting the coverage. If, for example, the clinician providing the coverage mishandles a crisis situation or otherwise harms the client through inappropriate acts or failures to act, the primary therapist may be held accountable for failure to screen and select an appropriate clinician.

However, the ethical and clinical issues are much more subtle. It is important to select a clinician who is well trained to provide the type of care that the client may need. The primary therapist may be tempted to select a clinician solely (and perhaps inappropriately) on grounds of expedience. The primary therapist may know that the clinician is not a very good one and is perhaps less than scrupulous in professional attitudes and actions. Furthermore, the primary therapist may be aware that the clinician does not tend to work effectively with the general client population that the therapist treats. Nevertheless, the therapist may push such uncomfortable knowledge out of awareness because this particular clinician is handy, and it might take considerable effort to locate an appropriate and trustworthy covering therapist. As in so many other situations discussed in this book, the Golden Rule seems salient. If we were the client, or if it were our parent, spouse, or child who desperately needed help in a crisis when the primary therapist is unavailable, if the careful handling of the crisis were potentially a matter of life and death, what level of care would we believe adequate in selecting a clinician to provide the coverage? If, for example, our parent became suddenly despondent, received a totally inadequate response from the clinician providing the coverage, and committed suicide, would convenience seem sufficient rationale for the primary therapist's selection of that clinician to provide the coverage?

If no clinician has been identified to provide coverage or if the identified clinician is for some reason unavailable, to whom does the client in crisis turn when the primary therapist is unavailable? It may be useful for the client to locate a psychiatric hospital, a general hospital with psychiatric services, or other facility providing emergency psychiatric services. There are at least five crucial questions:

1. Is the facility nearby?
2. Are the services available on a 24-hour basis? (If the crisis occurs in the middle of the night, on a weekend, or on a holiday, will the client find help available?)
3. Can the client afford to use the facility? Some facilities charge exceptionally high prices and may offer services only to those who can provide proof of ability to pay — for example, an insurance policy currently in effect.
4. Does the client know where the facility is located and what its telephone number is? Especially during a crisis, even basic information (such as the name of a hospital) may be hard to remember. In some instances — for example, both the therapist and client believe that there is a high risk for a crisis — it may be useful for the client to write down the name of the hospital, the address, and the telephone number to carry with him or her and to leave by the telephone at home. Sometimes close friends or family play a vital role in supporting a client in times of crisis. If the circumstances are appropriate, the client may also wish to give this information to a close friend or relative.
5. Do both therapist and client have justifiable confidence that the facility provides adequate care? Substandard care may make a crisis worse. Sometimes no care from certain facilities may be better than an inappropriate response.

If the primary therapist, secondary therapist, and designated facility are all unavailable — for whatever reason — in time of crisis, is there a hotline or other 24-hour telephone service that can provide at least an immediate first-aid response to the crisis and attempt to help the client locate a currently available source of professional help? Some areas have 24-hour suicide hotlines. There may be a 24-hour crisis line providing help for individuals with certain kinds of problems. At a minimum, such a telephone service may help a client survive a crisis. For some clients (e.g., those who cannot afford a telephone or access to secure e-mail at their residence), identifying channels of communication that will be accessible in times of crisis will be an important part of the planning.

If all of the resources noted are inaccessible to the client, the client may nevertheless be able to dial 911, the operator, or a similar general call for emergency response. The client may then be guided to sources of help, or, if appropriate, an ambulance or other emergency response may be dispatched.

Whenever a therapist is assessing a client's resources for coping with a crisis that threatens to endanger or overwhelm the client, it is important to assess not only the professional resources but also the client's social resources. Individual friends and family members may play key roles in helping a client to avert or survive a crisis (although a friend or family member can also initiate, intensify, or prolong a crisis). In some instances, nonprofessional groups, such as Alcoholics Anonymous, may provide access to support. The presence of such social supports gains in relative importance when the client's access to professional help is difficult. For example, some clients (especially those who cannot afford a telephone) cannot access a telephone, particularly if they are experiencing a crisis in the middle of the night. For many clients, the awareness of such social supports helps them to feel less isolated and thus less vulnerable to becoming overwhelmed by a crisis.

Sometimes therapy begins with the client in crisis and that the client's access to a team of clinicians or caregivers may be useful. *American Psychologist* presented the next case study illustrating a situation in which the immediate creation of a crisis team proved helpful when a person without funds or coverage needed help:

> In an instance in which a woman required daily sessions during a critical time in her life, colleagues accepted [the therapist's] request that they serve pro bono as an interdisciplinary team, offering detailed daily consultation to him and providing periodic psychological assessment and clinical interviews for the woman. Her meetings with diverse professionals let her know that many people cared about her. These colleagues mobilized to help a battered woman, a victim of multiple sexual assaults, now penniless and homeless, living in her car and hiding from a stalker. She and [the therapist] began meeting daily (later gradually reduced to weekly) for crisis intervention. They agreed that the first priority was her safety. [The therapist] gave her the number of an old college friend in another state. The friend immediately wired her $500 for food and housing and an airline ticket with an open date for use any time she felt in danger from the stalker. The friend asked her not to repay this loan directly to him but rather to give the money to someone else for whom it would make a difference as it did for her now. Within a year, the woman had taken legal action against the stalker and recovered enough to support herself. (K. S. Pope Biography, 1995, p. 242)

ENDINGS

Therapists are ethically required to end the therapeutic relationship under certain conditions. The APA Ethics Code (APA, 2010a) Standard 10.10a clarifies responsibilities to end the therapeutic relationship when appropriate by indicating that "psychologists terminate therapy when it becomes reasonably clear that the client no longer needs the service, is not likely to benefit, or is being harmed by continued service." The Canadian Psychological Association Code of Ethics (CPA, February 2015 draft) Standard II.37 requires that psychologists "terminate an activity when it is clear that the activity carries more than minimal risk of harm and is found to be more harmful than beneficial, or when the activity is no longer needed" (p. 22).

One way to view termination is as an intentional process that happens over time when a client has achieved most of the goals of treatment or when therapy must end for other reasons. The process of termination typically allows clients an opportunity to review their goals, describe the changes they've made, and work through feelings in bringing the therapy process to an end (Vasquez, Bingham, & Barnett, 2008).

In an ideal world, therapists provide continuing service as long as it is needed and beneficial. But few of us live in that particular world. Insurance companies may refuse to approve additional sessions, despite the therapist's professional judgment that terminating services would be harmful — and perhaps fatal — for a client judged to be at risk for suicide. Insurance companies may provide only a limited number of sessions annually for clients without the diagnosis of serious mental illness. Some clients who do not meet the relevant criteria may suffer crises that cannot be safely or effectively addressed in the limited number of sessions. For some such patients, interrupting treatment, even though in accordance with the insurance company's policies and procedures, may constitute abandonment.

How do therapists and clients know when to terminate therapy? One strategy is for therapist and client to review from time to time the presenting concerns, goals, and progress. This discussion helps clarify how much has been accomplished, as well as what still needs to be addressed, and whether the client and therapist wish to continue. Some clients are able to easily announce that they are ready to stop coming or that their employer has switched insurance therapists and that they would like your help to choose their next therapist from their new therapist list. Others may panic at the notion of stopping without more lead time and preparation.

The issue becomes more complex if the therapist believes therapy is going well, but the client either is wavering about continuing or wants to stop but finds it hard to say so. Sometimes these clients just stop coming. They say they'll call to schedule the next appointment or else cancel a scheduled appointment, but in either case you don't hear from them again. In addition, many people use therapy in short installments and drop out for a while, later returning to the same clinician or starting with a new therapist. When clients who seemed successfully engaged in therapy stop coming, a note or call to provide them with options can be helpful and provide useful information. Examples of options may include coming in for a review and termination session, terminating by telephone or note, or returning to therapy.

In some instances, the therapist may determine that it is both too dangerous and counterproductive to continue working with a patient in therapy. For example, Kivisto, Berman, Watson, Grube, and Paul (2015) found that "nearly three in four psychologists . . . were harassed at some point in their career, over one in five threatened, and about one in seven stalked" (see also Carr, Goranson, & Drummond, 2014; Gadit, Mugford, Callanan, & Aslanov, 2014; Mastronardi, Pomilla, Ricci, & D'Argenio, 2013; Nelsen, Johnson, Ostermeyer, Sikes, & Coverdale, 2015). Clinicians need to be knowledgeable about the potential threats they face and prepare themselves *in advance* to address them as safely, competently, and effectively as possible. "59 Resources for Therapists & Therapists-in-Training Who Are Stalked, Threatened, or Attacked by Patients," at http://kspope.com/stalking.php, provides relevant information.

When approaching termination, therapists bear an ethical responsibility to address questions that tend to arise around termination. The American Psychological Association's Ethical Principles and Code of Conduct (2010a) Standard 10.10c states the responsibilities of a therapist to engage in a termination process: "Except where precluded by the actions of clients or third-party payers, prior to termination psychologists provide pre-termination counseling and suggest alternative service therapists as appropriate." The Ethics Code notes that we have the right to terminate therapy when we are threatened by the client or patient or another person with whom the client or patient has a relationship (Standard 10.10b). This is an attempt to balance the importance of therapist self-care with the responsibilities to the client. It is probably not appropriate to terminate when a client is in crisis.

Vasquez et al. (2008, pp. 661–662) provide 12 recommendations to help to make sure that termination goes as well as possible and meets the highest ethical and clinical standards:

1. Provide patients with a complete description of the therapeutic process, including termination; obtain informed consent for this process at the beginning of treatment; and provide reminders throughout treatment.
2. Ensure that the therapist and client collaboratively agree on the goals for therapy and the ending of therapy.
3. Provide periodic progress updates that include discussions of termination and, toward the end of therapy, provide pretermination counseling.
4. Offer a contract that provides patients with a plan in case the therapist is suddenly unavailable (including death, or financial, employment, or insurance complications).

5. Help clients develop health and referral plans for posttermination life.
6. Make sure you understand termination and abandonment, and their potential effects on patients.
7. Consider developing (and updating) your professional will to proactively address unexpected termination and abandonment, including the name(s) of colleagues who will contact current patients in the case of your sudden disability or death.
8. Contact clients who prematurely terminate via telephone or letters to express your concern and offer to assist them.
9. Use the APA Ethics Code (2002), your state practice regulations, and consultation with knowledgeable colleagues to help guide your understanding and behavior in regard to therapy termination.
10. Review other ethics codes for discussions of abandonment. The American Counseling Association . . . and the American Mental Health Counselors Association . . . contain prohibitions against abandonment.
11. Make the topic of termination a part of your regular continuing education or professional development.
12. Be vigilant in monitoring your clinical effectiveness and personal distress (e.g., Baker, 2003; Norcross & Guy, 2007). Therapists who self-monitor and practice effective self-care are less likely to have inappropriate terminations or clients who feel abandoned.

For those looking for a more detailed discussion of the practical issues of termination and how they can be addressed in ethically and clinically sound ways, we highly recommend two books: *Terminating Therapy: A Professional Guide to Ending on a Positive Note* (Davis, 2008), and *Termination That Works With At-Risk Children and Adolescents: Four Steps That Build Resilience and Give Hope to Challenging Populations* (21st Century Seminars, 2014).

CONCLUSION

Constant awareness — particularly a careful, imaginative awareness — and a sense of personal responsibility play a fundamental role in making sure that clients have adequate access to the help they need, particularly in times of crisis when the therapist can't be reached. In hospital and similar settings, the apparent abundance of staff may lead to a diffusion of responsibility in which no one is available to help a patient in crisis. Levenson and Pope (1981), for example, present a case study in which a psychology intern was assigned responsibility to promptly contact a suicidal individual who had been referred to the outpatient unit by the crisis service and arrange for conducting an intake assessment. The intern, however, was absent from the staff meeting at which the assignment was made. His supervisor, also absent from the meeting, had sent him to attend a two-day training session at another institution. During the next few days, the individual committed suicide.

> The hospital's thanatology committee concluded that the crisis service had handled the situation appropriately in referring to the outpatient unit. The outpatient unit itself was not involved in the postmortem investigation because, according to the hospital's procedures, outpatient cases are not opened until the potential patient is contacted by the outpatient unit for an intake screening. The intern himself struggled with his reactions to these events. Among his conclusions was that he had "at some level internalized the organizational view that no one is really responsible." (Levenson & Pope, 1981, p. 485)

Imagination is useful in creating an awareness of the types of crises a client might experience and what difficulties he or she might experience in trying to gain timely access to needed resources. The scenarios for discussion presented at the end of this chapter provide examples.

Thinking things through in advance on a worst-possible-case basis can help the therapist to anticipate the devious ways in which Murphy's Law pays surprise visits in our work. If we look back from that imaginative perspective, we can ask ourselves: If any of the worst possible case outcomes had happened, what, if anything, do we wish we would have done to prevent them, lessen their impact, or prepare for addressing these events?

No therapist is infallible. The most careful and confident assessment of a client's potential for crisis can go awry for any number of reasons. But the therapist should take into account his or her own fallibility and plan for the unexpected.

Similarly, imaginative approaches can create accessibility to needed resources. For example, a therapist was treating an extremely isolated, anxious, and troubled young woman pro bono because of the client's lack of money. From time to time, the client became overwhelmed by anxiety and was acutely suicidal. However, she had no practical access to hospitalization because of her financial status and the absence in the community of sufficient beds for those who lacked adequate funds or insurance coverage. In similar cases, the therapist had encouraged clients to make arrangements to have a trusted friend come by to stay with them during periods of extreme dysfunction and suicidal risk. However, this client was so socially isolated that she had no friends, and the therapist was unable to locate an individual — from local church and synagogue groups or from hospital volunteer organizations — who could stay with her in times of crisis. Determined to come up with some arrangement that would help ensure the client's safety and welfare should she experience a crisis and the therapist be unavailable, the therapist and client finally hit on the possibility of her going to the local hospital's waiting room. (The waiting room adjacent to the emergency room was open around the clock.) The therapist contacted hospital personnel to make sure that they would not object to the client showing up at odd hours to sit for long periods of time in the waiting room.

The arrangement worked well during the remaining course of therapy. According to the client, simply knowing that there was someplace for her to go helped her to avoid becoming completely overwhelmed by external events or by her own feelings. On those occasions when she did feel that she was in crisis and at risk for taking her own life, she found that going to the hospital waiting room seemed helpful; it made her feel more active and aware that she was doing something for herself. Being out of her rather depressing and claustrophobic apartment, sitting in a "clean, well-lighted place," and being around other people (who, because they were strangers, would be unlikely to make, in her words, "demands" on her) were all factors that helped her feel better. Knowing that there were health-care professionals nearby (even though she had no contact with them) who could intervene should her impulses to take her own life become too much for her, and aware that she was carrying out a "treatment plan" that she and her therapist had developed together, helped her to feel calmer, less isolated, and comforted in crisis. The waiting room strategy enabled this highly suicidal client to be treated safely, although hospitalization was not feasible, during the initial period of therapy when outpatient treatment alone seemed, in the judgment of both the therapist and an independent consultant, inadequate and when the client could not afford additional resources. It made imaginative use of resources that were readily available in the community and were accessible to the client.

Understanding the degree to which individual clinicians and mental health organizations will be accessible and will make help available is a crucial aspect of the client's informed consent, the focus of Chapter 19.

SCENARIOS FOR DISCUSSION

Chapters 18 through 27 in this book end with scenarios, each accompanied with a set of questions for discussion. This approach had been used in *Sexual Feelings in Therapy: Explorations for Therapists and Therapists-in-Training* (Pope, Sonne, & Holroyd, 1993). Although we have created original vignettes for the other chapters in this book, the following scenarios and questions come from *Sexual Feelings in Therapy* and *What Therapists Don't Talk About and Why: Understanding Taboos That Hurt Us and Our Clients* (Pope, Sonne, et al., 2006).

You notice that it is exactly 2:00 p.m., the time you are scheduled to meet a new client, and your waiting room is still empty.

(continued)

(*continued*)

The telephone rings. It is your new client. She asks if you would mind coming out to the front steps. You're puzzled but say "I'll be right there." When you go to the front steps, you see your new client in her wheelchair at the bottom of the steps.

- How do you feel?
- What thoughts go through you mind?
- What do you think is the first thing you would say?
- What would you like to do?
- What do you think you would do?

■ ■ ■

You are late getting to the airport, in danger of missing your plane (during a holiday season, so it would be very hard to get space on a later flight), when you receive an emergency call from a local hospital. One of your therapy patients has tried to commit suicide and has been hospitalized. The client is desperate to talk with you in person — refusing to talk over the telephone — immediately about having just discovered a horrifying secret. You have no idea what the "secret" is.

- How do you feel?
- Are there any feelings about the patient, the emergency room staff person who called you, or the situation that are particularly difficult to acknowledge?
- What are your immediate options?
- What do you think you would do?
- To what extent, if at all, do any concerns about a malpractice suit influence your judgment?

■ ■ ■

A new client begins the first session by saying, "I need therapy because I lost my job, and my partner, whom I lived with for 3 years, left me for someone else. I don't know whether to kill myself, kill my boss, kill everyone else, or just try to hang on since now I'm all my little baby has left."

- How do you feel?
- Assuming that you cannot rule out that the person's threats are serious, what steps do you take in clarifying access to

you and others before the client leaves this first appointment?

- What concerns, if any, do you have about this person's adequate access to prompt and adequate help?
- Is there anything you wish you would have told the person about your availability or anything else before the person made these statements?

■ ■ ■

You work for a large Employee Assistance Program providing individual and family therapy full time. You meet with your manager late Friday afternoon and are told that the company has been taken over by a new owner, who is merging several companies. There are now too many therapists, and it is with the greatest regret that your manager tells you that reorganization has led to your no longer being retained by the company. This is your last day. Your clients are being reassigned. You will be allowed to return to your office only with a security guard, you will be able to stay only 30 minutes to clean out your desk, and you will not be allowed to copy any telephone numbers or other information or to take any charts with you.

- How do you feel?
- What are your options?
- What steps do you think you would take?
- Would you make any effort to contact the clients you had been seeing? If so, how and what would you tell them?

■ ■ ■

A former client, whom you had seen in therapy for three years, called in crisis. She said that she had started therapy with someone else, given a change of jobs and a new insurance plan. You were not listed on the new insurance provider list. However, she cannot reach that new therapist during her crisis. Besides, she feels more comfortable with you.

- What do you feel?
- Do you have any legal or ethical obligations to this former client, and, if so, what are they?

(*continued*)

(continued)

- If you agree to talk with this client on the telephone for a while or meet with her for one or more crisis sessions, what legal, ethical, or clinical responsibilities, if any, do you have in regard to coordinating your work with her current managed care therapist?
- Do you chart this telephone call?
- Do you have a clear policy regarding contacts with former clients? If so, are clients made aware of this policy prior to termination?

Chapter 19

INFORMED CONSENT AND INFORMED REFUSAL

E thical therapy shows due respect for each patient's freedom, autonomy, and dignity. Informed consent — perhaps the most extensively recognized of the ethical safeguards in clinical work (Amer, 2013) — reflects that respect. Ethics codes highlight consent as a key value. Truscott and Crook (2013) note that "informed consent is the most represented value in the Canadian Code of Ethics for Psychologists" (p. 55). The American Psychological Association (APA) ethics code sets forth specific standards for informed consent (Sections 3.10, 10.01, 10.02, 10.03, and 10.04).

Strengthening our ethical intelligence in this area helps us avoid the common pitfalls. For example, nothing blocks a patient's access to help with such cruel efficiency as a bungled attempt at informed consent. We've made our offices warm and inviting, welcoming and accessible to all. But not even the hardiest patients can make their way past intimidating forms (which clerks may shove at them when they first arrive), our set speeches full of noninformative information, and our nervous attempts to meet externally imposed legalistic requirements such as the U.S. Health Insurance Portability and Accountability Act (HIPAA) or the Canadian Personal Information Protection and Electronic Documents Act (PIPEDA).

One trap we can fall into is resenting consent as a formality to be gotten out of the way. Daniel Sokol (2009) wrote:

> [W]hat is the most redoubtable obstacle to valid consent? It is the still prevalent attitude that obtaining consent is a necessary chore, a . . . hurdle to jump over. Too often "consenting" a patient is reduced to the mechanistic imparting of information from clinician to patient or, worse still, the mere signing of a consent form, rather than the two way, meaningful conversation between

clinician and patient it should be. If we can change this mindset [*sic*] and view obtaining consent as an ethical duty first and foremost, one that is central to respecting the autonomy and dignity of patients, then we will have taken a major step towards first class consent and uninterrupted lunches. (p. 3224)

Viewing consent as an obligation and burden makes it hard to meet the needs of patients. Discussing their questionnaire study of patients' perceptions of written consent, Andrea Akkad and her colleagues (2006) wrote:

> Our findings add to evidence showing that even when the consent process satisfies administrative and legal requirements, patients' needs may not be met.... Though patients did identify several important advantages of the consent process, there was substantial uncertainty about the implications of signing or not signing the consent form.... Many patients did not see written consent as functioning primarily in their interests nor as a way of making their wishes known.... Although there is no straightforward relation between knowledge of rights and ability to exercise those rights, a lack of awareness of the limits and scope of consent is clearly undesirable, potentially causing patients to feel disempowered and lacking in control. (p. 529)

A first step in remedying the situation is to recognize that informed consent is not a static ritual but a *useful* process.

PROCESS OF INFORMED CONSENT

The Canadian Psychological Association (CPA, February 2015 draft) Ethics Code Section 1.17 notes that psychologists "Recognize that informed consent is not simply a matter of having a consent form signed; rather, it is a process and may need to be obtained more than once (e.g., if significant new information becomes available), and involves taking time to establish an appropriate trusting relationship and to reach an agreement to work collaboratively." The process of informed consent provides both the patient and us an opportunity to make sure that we adequately understand our shared venture. It is a process of communication and clarification. Do we understand why the patient is seeking our help? Do we know what the patient expects, hopes, or fears from therapy? Does the patient understand the approach we will be using to assess and address the problem? Does the patient know the common effects of using such an approach and alternative approaches to his or her problem?

The U.K. Supreme Court (2015) described the process that creates an agreement to work together. It includes dialogue, the aim of which is to ensure that the patient understands the seriousness of her condition, and the anticipated benefits and risks of the proposed treatment and any reasonable alternatives, so that she is then in a position to make an informed decision. This role will only be performed effectively if the information provided is comprehensible. The doctor's duty is not therefore fulfilled by bombarding the patient with technical information, which she cannot reasonably be expected to grasp, let alone by routinely demanding her signature on a consent form (*Montgomery v Lanarkshire Health Board*, 2015).

Culture can affect this process of communication and clarification. For example, the therapist might be from the majority culture while the patient might be a recent immigrant who is currently in the process of adapting to the majority culture. Chong Wang (2009) points out that the level of acculturation can influence the desire for independent decision making; ways of relating within cultural contexts; and the ways in which psychological disorders, authority, and so on are perceived.

Wang suggests 11 steps as helpful in assessing the level of acculturation:

1. In general, what language(s) do you read and speak?
2. What was the language(s) you used as a child?
3. What language(s) do you usually speak at home?
4. In which language(s) do you usually think or dream?
5. What language(s) do you usually speak with your friends?
6. In what language(s) are your preferred TV/radio programs?
7. In general, what language(s) are the movies, TV, and radio programs you prefer to watch and listen to?
8. Your close friends are . . . ?
9. You prefer going to social gatherings/parties at which people are . . . ?
10. The persons you visit or who visit you are . . . ?
11. If you could choose your children's friends you would want them to be . . . ?

Informed consent also involves making decisions. The patient must decide whether to undertake this course of assessment and treatment, whether to start now or later, and whether to try a different approach or a different therapist.

We therapists must decide whether the patient is competent to exercise informed consent. For example, young children, adults who have been declared legally incompetent, and those who have significant intellectual impairment may not be capable of providing fully informed consent.

The presence of a severe psychological disorder requiring hospitalization does not by itself mean that the patient lacks the ability to give or refuse meaningful consent to therapy. Debra Pinals (2009) wrote:

> Adult patients with psychotic disorders are not automatically or always incompetent. Research has shown that most inpatients with mental illness have capacities to make treatment decisions similar to persons with medical illness. Patients with schizophrenia, however, have deficits relevant to capacity to

make treatment decisions more often than patients with medical illnesses and depressive disorders. Patients with depressive disorders also are more likely to have some decision-making impairment compared with persons with medical illnesses. (p. 35)

If informed consent is not possible, we therapists must decide whether the situation justifies an intervention in the absence of fully informed consent. We must also consider whether a fully competent patient has the information to make an informed decision, adequately understands that information, and is providing consent voluntarily.

Patrick O'Neill, a former president of the CPA, suggests that the process of informed consent take the form of negotiation:

> While most therapists recognize that negotiation can clear up clients' misconceptions, fewer recognize that negotiation is also a vehicle for clearing up the *therapist's* misconceptions. An open dialogue can make the therapist aware of features of the case that depart from both the therapist's model and his or her previous experience, and thus it serves as a corrective to the representativeness and availability biases. (1998, p. 176)

Finally, informed consent is a continuing process. Williams (2008) wrote: "Obtaining consent is not a discrete event; rather, it is a process that should occur throughout the relationship between clinician and patient" (p. 11). The patient may consent to an initial psychological, neuropsychological, and medical assessment as well as to a course of individual therapy based on an initial, very provisional treatment plan. Later the assessment results, the patient's response to treatment, and changing circumstances may lead to a radical revision in the treatment plan. The patient needs to understand these revisions and agree to them.

THE FOUNDATION OF INFORMED CONSENT

Informed consent is one way we try to make sure that the patient's trust is justified, we do not abuse our power, and we express our caring in ways that the patient understands and agrees to. But for many decades, health-care ethics overlooked the concept. How did informed consent move from invisibility to center stage? Several key court cases gave strong shoves to the professions, insisting that they recognize patients' fundamental right to informed consent. These decisions often involved medical practice, but much of the reasoning applies to assessment and psychotherapy.

Traditionally, the health-care professions took an arrogant, authoritarian approach: The physician alone decided what treatment the patient received. The Hippocratic Oath lacked the principle of informed consent. During the centuries leading up to the modern era, physicians tended to share the belief that doctors' decisions should not be questioned and that patients obviously lacked the training, knowledge, and objectivity to know what was good for them. This approach violated "the value of respect for persons' autonomy and their right to define their own goals and make choices designed to achieve those goals" (Grady, 2015, p. 855; see also Campbell, Vasquez, Behnke, & Kinscherff, 2010; Robeson & King, 2014).

A legal case involving a hospital in New York marked a landmark in the shift away from this authoritarian approach. In 1914, Judge Benjamin Cardozo, who later became a justice of the U.S. Supreme Court, wrote that "every human being of adult years and sound mind has a right to determine what shall be done with his own body" (*Schloendorf v. Society of New York Hospital*, 1914, p. 93).

It was not so much that this case changed the customary procedures by which doctors went about their work; it was more that Judge Cardozo articulated clearly the principle that it was the *patient*, rather than the doctor, who had the right to decide whether to undertake a specific treatment approach. The implications of this principle lay dormant for decades.

The Nuremberg trials and subsequent Nuremberg Code on Medical Intervention and Experimentation focused attention on the importance of informed consent. The trials revealed the horrific and inhumane practices of many health-care professionals during World War II under the guise of "treatment" and "research" (Adam, 2007; Beauchamp 2014; Cocks, 1985; Gallagher, 1990; Geuter, 1992; Koenig, 2000; Lifton, 1986; Lopez-Munoz et al., 2007; Muller-Hill, 1988; Pope, 1991; Proctor, 1988; Spitz, 2005; Thieren & Mauron, 2007). The Nuremberg trials and code emphasized the individual's fundamental right to informed consent to or informed refusal of participation in treatment or research. O'Neill (1998) wrote:

> The two main ways of protecting the public from the healer are oversight and consent. Throughout most of the history of healing, the emphasis was on oversight: monitoring of professional activity by professional associations, regulatory bodies, or the courts. The Nuremberg Declaration gave a new, privileged position to consent, putting control into the hands of the client. (pp. 13–14)

Shuster (1998) noted how easy it could be, when the right to consent or refusal is ignored, to allow purportedly good ends to justify inflicting terrible — sometimes fatal — "treatments" on human beings without their knowledge or consent:

> This was the case of ionising radiation research motivated by the cold war and sponsored by the US government for national security. Patients in hospital, children, mentally ill and impaired persons, pregnant women, workers,

soldiers, and others were used as experimental subjects often without their knowledge, or that of their families; many believed they were being treated for their medical conditions. (p. 976; see also Advisory Committee on Human Radiation Experiments, 1995)

The landmark 1960 Kansas case of *Natanson v. Kline* focused on community standards for fulfilling the patient's right to informed consent. The court reaffirmed the Cardozo principle: "Anglo-American law starts with the premise of thorough-going self-determination. It follows that each man is considered to be master of his own body" (p. 1104). The court stated that to make this determination, the patient obviously needed the relevant information. But what information was relevant was left entirely to the community of doctors to decide:

> The duty . . . to disclose . . . is limited to those disclosures which a reasonable . . . practitioner would make under the same or similar circumstances. . . . So long as the disclosure is sufficient to assure an informed consent, the physician's choice of plausible courses should not be called into question if it appears, all circumstances considered, that the physician was motivated only by the patient's best therapeutic interests and he proceeded as competent medical men would have done in a similar situation. (p. 1106)

This case exemplifies the "community standard" rule: Informed consent procedures must adhere only to what the general community of doctors customarily do. It also reflects the strong value of autonomy and self-determination that underlies western law, policy, and ethical decision making.

In 1972, with decisions handed down by the Federal District Court in Washington, DC, and the California Supreme Court, the full implications of Judge Cardozo's principle were realized. The reasoning began with the reaffirmation of *Schloendorf v. Society of New York Hospital* and an emphasis that the patient must have relevant information that only the doctor can provide:

> The root premise is the concept, fundamental in American jurisprudence, that "every human being of adult years and sound mind has a right to determine what shall be done with his own body. . . ." True consent to what happens to one's self is the informed exercise of a choice, and that entails an opportunity to evaluate knowledgeably the options available and the risks attendant upon each. The average patient has little or no understanding of the medical arts, and ordinarily has only his physician to whom he can look for enlightenment with which to reach an intelligent decision. From these almost axiomatic considerations springs the need, and in turn the requirement, of a reasonable divulgence by physician to patient to make such a decision possible. (*Canterbury v. Spence*, 1972, p. 780)

It is the *patient*, and not the doctor, who must make the final decision, and this decision, to be meaningful, must be based on an adequate range of information provided by the doctor:

> It is the prerogative of the patient, not the physician, to determine for himself the direction in which he believes his interests lie. To enable the patient to chart his course knowledgeably, reasonable familiarity with the therapeutic alternatives and their hazards becomes essential. (*Cobbs v. Grant*, 1972, p. 514)

This line of reasoning emphasized the exceptional trust and dependence inherent in health care, differentiating them from the milder versions of trust and dependence, often dealt with using a caveat emptor principle, characteristic of less intense, less intimate transactions in the marketplace:

> A reasonable revelation in these aspects is not only a necessity but, as we see it, is as much a matter of the physician's duty. It is a duty to warn of the dangers lurking in the proposed treatment, and that is surely a facet of due care. It is, too, a duty to impart information which the patient has every right to expect. The patient's reliance upon the physician is a trust of the kind which traditionally has exacted obligations beyond those associated with arms-length transactions. His dependence upon the physician for information affecting his well-being, in terms of contemplated treatment, is well-nigh abject. (*Canterbury v. Spence*, 1972, p. 782)

This landmark case law specifically rejected the idea that doctors, through their "community standards," could determine what degree of information the patient should or should not have. It was not up to doctors, individually or collectively, to decide what rights a patient should have with regard to informed consent or to determine those rights indirectly by establishing customary standards regarding what information was and was not to be provided. Patients were held to have a right to make an informed decision, and the courts were to guarantee that they had the relevant information for making the decision. The court observed in *Canterbury v. Spence*:

> We do not agree that the patient's cause of action is dependent upon the existence and nonperformance of a relevant professional tradition . . . . Respect for the patient's right of self-determination on particular therapy demands a standard set by law for physicians rather than one which physicians may or may not impose upon themselves. (1972, pp. 783–784)

The case law clearly states the need for doctors to provide adequate relevant information regardless of whether the patient actively asked the "right" questions in each area. As a result, doctors were prevented from withholding or neglecting to provide relevant information because a patient did not inquire. The doctors were seen as having an affirmative duty to make an adequately full disclosure:

> We discard the thought that the patient should ask for information before the physician is required to disclose. Caveat emptor is not the norm for the consumer of medical services. Duty to disclose is more than a call to speak merely on the patient's request, or merely to answer the patient's questions: it is a duty to volunteer, if necessary, the information the patient needs for intelligent decision. The patient may be ignorant, confused, overawed by the physician or frightened by the hospital, or even ashamed to inquire.... Perhaps relatively few patients could in any event identify the relevant questions in the absence of prior explanation by the physician. Physicians and hospitals have patients of widely divergent socio-economic backgrounds, and a rule which presumes a degree of sophistication which many members of society lack is likely to breed gross inequalities. (*Canterbury v. Spence*, 1972, p. 783; see also *Montgomery v. Lanarkshire Health Board*, 2015, which emphasized this principle)

Realizing that some patients would certainly choose not to undertake specific assessment or treatment procedures, the courts emphasized that understanding what might happen as a result of not getting adequate assessment or treatment was as relevant to making an informed decision as understanding the assessment and treatment procedures themselves. Thus, the California Supreme Court in 1980 not only reaffirmed the principles previously set forth in *Canterbury v. Spence* and *Cobbs v. Grant* but also affirmed that patients have a right to informed refusal of treatment as well as a right to informed consent to treatment:

> The rule applies whether the procedure involves treatment or a diagnostic test.... If a patient indicates that he or she is going to *decline* a risk-free test or treatment, then the doctor has the additional duty of advising of all the material risks of which a reasonable person would want to be informed before deciding not to undergo the procedure. On the other hand, if the recommended test or treatment is itself risky, then the physician should always explain the potential consequences of declining to follow the recommended course of action. (*Truman v. Thomas*, 1980, p. 312)

Recognizing that some doctors might be intimidated by the daunting thought of presenting to patients essentially all they had learned during their training and that patients might be ill-suited recipients of jargon-filled lectures, the court emphasized that the patient needed only the relevant information to make an informed decision but needed it in clear, straightforward language: "The patient's interest in information does not extend to a lengthy polysyllabic discourse on all possible complications. A mini-course in medical science is not required" (*Cobbs v. Grant,* 1972, p. 515).

In summary, in 1970, the courts gave to patients the right to make decisions to accept or reject treatment and gave to doctors the responsibility for making sure that patients had adequate information for making that decision. The California Supreme Court attempted to articulate the basis of this concept of informed consent:

> We employ several postulates. The first is that patients are generally persons unlearned in the medical sciences and therefore, except in rare cases, courts may safely assume the knowledge of patient and physician are not in parity. The second is that a person of adult years and in sound mind has the right, in the exercise of control over his own body, to determine whether or not to submit to lawful medical treatment. The third is that the patient's consent to treatment, to be effective, must be an informed consent. And the fourth is that the patient, being unlearned in medical sciences, has an abject dependence upon and trust in his physician for the information upon which he relies during the decisional process, thus raising an obligation in the physician that transcends arm-length transactions. From the foregoing axiomatic ingredients emerges a necessity, and a resultant requirement, for divulgence by the physician to his patient of all information relevant to a meaningful decisional process. (*Cobbs v. Grant,* 1972, p. 513)

These principles began to pass from case law into legislation. Section F of Indiana's House Enrolled Act of 1984, for example, stated:

> All patients or clients are entitled to be informed of the nature of treatment or habilitation program proposed, the known effects of receiving and of not receiving such treatment or habilitation, and alternative treatment or habilitation programs, if any. An adult voluntary patient or client, if not adjudicated incompetent, is entitled to refuse to submit to treatment or to a habilitation program and is entitled to be informed of this right.

The American Psychological Association's Ethics Code reflects the increasing emphasis on the importance of informed consent. Celia Fisher, director of the Fordham University Center for Ethics Education and Marie Doty University Chair in Psychology, wrote:

> Informed consent is seen by many as the primary means of protecting the self-governing and privacy rights of those with whom psychologists work. In the 1992 Ethics Code, the obligation to obtain informed consent was limited to research and therapy. In the 2002 Ethics Code, the broader informed consent requirement for most psychological activities reflects the societal sea change from a paternalistic to an autonomy based view of professional and scientific ethics. (2003, p. 77)

ADEQUATE INFORMATION

The information provided during the consent process will differ according to the professional service (e.g., assessment, therapy) and other factors. However, any consent process can be evaluated in terms of whether it adequately addresses the next questions. This list may be useful in planning and in concurrent review of consent procedures in any setting:

- Does the patient understand who is providing the service and the clinician's qualifications (e.g., license status)? If more than one person is involved (e.g., a therapist and clinical supervisor; see Chapter 27), does the patient understand the nature and implications of this arrangement?
- Does the patient understand the reason for the initial session? Although in many instances patients will have scheduled an initial appointment on their own initiative and for relatively clear reasons, in other instances they may have been referred by others (perhaps an internist or a court) and not clearly understand the reason for the session.
- Does the patient understand the nature, extent, and possible consequences of the services the clinician is offering? Does the patient understand the degree to which there may be alternatives to the services provided by the clinician?
- Does the patient understand actual or potential limitations to the services (e.g., a managed care plan's limitation of eight therapy sessions; an insurance policy's limitation of coverage to a specific dollar amount) or to the clinician (e.g., the therapist is an intern whose rotation will conclude in 3 months, after which he or she will no longer be available to the patient)? Does the patient understand the ways in which the services may be terminated?
- Does the patient understand fee policies and procedures, including information about missed or canceled appointments?
- Does the patient understand policies and procedures concerning access to the clinician, to those providing coverage for the clinician, or to emergency services? For example, under what conditions, if any, will a therapist (or someone else providing coverage) be available by telephone between sessions during business hours, at night, or on weekends? (Chapter 18 discusses these issues.)
- Does the patient understand exceptions to confidentiality, privilege, or privacy? For example, does the patient understand the conditions, if any, under which the clinician might disclose information about the patient to an insurance company, the police, or the courts? Does the person understand under what conditions other people in the setting (such as clerical workers, clinical supervisors or consultants, administrative supervisors or other administrative staff, quality control personnel, utilization review committees, auditors, researchers) may learn about the patient

and the services provided to him or her, whether through discussion (case conferences, supervision, consultation) or writings (clinical chart notes, treatment summaries, administrative records)? Chapter 24 provides a discussion of these issues and exceptions.

CONSIDERATIONS IN PROVIDING INFORMED CONSENT

No rigid method can do the work of fulfilling a patient's right to informed consent. No set method can relieve us of a thoughtful response to the unique individual patient.

Informed consent is a recurring process, not a static set of pro forma gestures, that develops out of the relationship between clinician and patient. It must fit the situation and the setting. It must respond not only to the standards of the clinician's professional associations, such as the APA or the CPA, but also to the relevant state and federal laws. It must be sensitive to the client's ability to understand the relevant information (Is the client a young child, developmentally disabled, suffering from severe thought disorder?) and the patient's situation (Is the patient in the midst of a crisis, referred for mandatory treatment by the courts, being held against his or her will in a mental hospital?). We can never do away with human sensitivity and professional judgment.

The following considerations can help us create and nurture the process of informed consent.

FAILING TO PROVIDE INFORMED CONSENT

In considering how to ensure the patient's right to informed consent, we must remain aware that the right is violated, perhaps often. We can take those instances to justify our own decisions not to accord patients informed consent, or we can use those instances as an opportunity to strengthen our ethical intelligence and consider the matter from the patient's perspective. How would we feel if we were the patients who had been kept in the dark and had not been given the chance to make a decision on an informed basis?

An example of the withholding of informed consent involved the provision of free medical care to hundreds of U.S. citizens (J. H. Jones, 1981; see also Rivers, Schuman, Simpson, & Olansky, 1953; U.S. Public Health Service, 1973). The program began in 1932 and continued to 1972. If all we were told was that the government, through what eventually became the U.S. Public Health Service, was giving us comprehensive medical care, how would we likely feel? Grateful? Relieved that we would be spared financial burdens? Excited that we would have access to state-of-the-science medical interventions provided by the federal government? Who among us would turn down this rare opportunity?

What the participants were not told is that they were being used to research the effects of syphilis when it goes untreated. Treatment for syphilis was in fact withheld from all the individuals. Research procedures were presented as treatment; for example, painful spinal taps were described to the subjects as a special medical treatment. Although Public Health Service officials denied that there were any racist aspects to this research, admission to the program was limited to male African Americans. The 40-year Tuskegee syphilis experiment is one of the most infamous in United States history and stands as one of the worst violations of ethical standards of biomedical research. It led to the institution of federal Institutional Review Boards for protection of human subjects (U.S. Centers for Disease Control and Prevention, n.d.).

Other examples are numerous. Hospitals, for example, perform AIDS tests on virtually all patients without patients' knowledge or permission, sometimes in direct violation of state law (Pope & Morin, 1990). As another example, Stevens (1990) described a testing center that administered the Stanford-Binet Intelligence Scale so that students could be placed in the appropriate classes at school. The information schools received contradicted that given to the child's parents. In one case, for example, the report sent to the school "recommended that David be placed in a class for average students"; the report sent to the parents recommended that "David should be placed in a class for superior students" (p. 15). Here is how the testing center explained the policy: "The [report] we send to the school is accurate. The report for the parents is more soothing and positive" (p. 15).

How would we feel if we relied on the government and health-care professions to provide us with free medical care when in fact they were observing the untreated consequences of a painful, virulent, usually fatal disease? How would we feel if we went to a hospital for help and were given an AIDS test without our knowledge or permission? How would we feel if we were given completely inaccurate information about the results of an intelligence assessment because someone else thought it would be "more soothing"?

BENEFITS OF INFORMED CONSENT

Approaching the issue of informed consent, we may, as clinicians, fear that providing adequate information to patients and explicitly obtaining their consent will somehow derail therapy and may in fact have detrimental consequences for our patients. The research has not supported these fears. The process of informed consent tends to be beneficial. A variety of studies have indicated that the use of informed consent procedures makes it more likely that patients will become less anxious, follow the treatment plan, recover more quickly, and be more alert to unintended negative consequences of the treatment (Handler, 1990). Debra Pinals (2009) wrote that "informed consent can enhance the therapeutic alliance and help improve treatment adherence" (p. 33).

LIMITS OF CONSENT

Informed consent is not a strategy to insulate a clinician from responsibility when performing unethical or illegal acts:

> At least one case has suggested that there are limits to what a patient can validly consent to. In that case, several adults were treated with a form of therapy that involved physically beating them. The defendants argued they could not be sued because the plaintiffs had consented to the treatment; however, the Court of Appeals refused to accept the consents as a defense. This decision implies that a patient's consent will not be deemed valid if acts consented to would otherwise be illegal or contrary to public policy (such as a sexual relationship between therapist and patient). An earlier case held that whether touching is therapeutic or nontherapeutic goes to the essence of the act and may vitiate a consent. (Caudill & Pope, 1995, pp. 553–554)

CONSENT FOR FAMILIES AND OTHER MULTIPLE CLIENTS

When we provide therapy to couples, families, or groups, we have a special responsibility to provide adequate informed consent and informed refusal to each person and to address issues specific to therapies involving more than one patient. For example, what are the limits of confidentiality and privilege for material disclosed by one of the patients involved in couples, family, or group services? Will the therapist hold confidential from one family member material disclosed by another family member? What effect would that have on the trust of the other family member if that other family member discovers the secret and that you kept it from him or her? If one client receiving couples therapy waives privilege, does the privilege still apply to the other member of the couple? APA Ethics Code (APA, 2010) standards 10.02 (a) and (b), Therapy Involving Couples or Families, describes the importance of clarifying who the patient is and the relationship the psychologist will have with each person involved. The standard also provides guidance in addressing conflicting roles, should they arise.

These issues are best clarified at the outset of the treatment, and on a continuing basis to clarify conflicts or potential conflicts that might arise during the therapy process. The 2002 APA Ethics Code included a new standard 10.03, Group Therapy, that requires that "when psychologists provide services to several persons in a group setting, they describe at the outset the roles and responsibilities of all parties and the limits of confidentiality" (p. 1073). Thus, psychologists must describe at the outset of group therapy the unique roles and responsibilities of both therapist and patients in the group therapy, including the fact that while group members are advised to maintain confidentiality about other group members, they are not held to legal liability or ethical codes of conduct. It may be helpful, although not required, to have group members sign an informed consent document, including the group rules and guidelines.

UNEQUAL OPPORTUNITY FOR INFORMED CONSENT

It is crucial that we do not accord unequal opportunities to our clients for informed consent based on prejudice and stereotypes (see Chapter 23). Research suggests that this unfortunately happens, at least occasionally, depriving some clients of their right to informed consent. For example, in an examination of informed consent practices, Benson (1984) found that whether important information was disclosed by a sample of physicians was systematically related to such factors as the patient's race and socioeconomic status.

COGNITIVE PROCESSES

Clinicians must maintain up-to-date knowledge of the evolving research and theory regarding the cognitive processes by which people arrive at decisions (see, e.g., Arbuthnott, Arbuthnott, & Thompson, 2006; Bruine de Bruin, Parker, & Fischoff, 2015; Hess, Lipner, Thompson, Holmboe, & Graber, 2015; Hess, Strough, & Lockenhoff, 2015; Kahneman, 2011; Kleespies, 2014; Taleb, 2010; Zsambok & Klein, 2014). This research and theory can help clinicians understand the factors that influence clients who are choosing whether to participate in assessment or treatment procedures.

At a Harvard University hospital, McNeil, Pauker, Sox, and Tversky (1982) presented individuals with two options based on actuarial data concerning patients suffering from lung cancer. The data indicated whether patients had chosen a surgical or a radiological treatment for their cancer and what the outcome had been. Of those who chose surgery, 10% died during the operation itself, an additional 22% died within the first year after the surgery, and another 34% died within 5 years. Of those who chose radiation therapy, none died during the radiation treatments, 23% died within the first year, and an additional 55% died by the end of 5 years.

If you were given those actuarial data, which intervention would you choose? When these data were presented, 42% of the participants in the study indicated that they would choose radiation. Note that the data were presented in terms of mortality — the percentages of patients who died. When the same actuarial information was presented in terms of percentages of patients who survived at each stage — for radiation, 100% survived the treatment, 73% survived the first year, and 22% survived 5 years — only 25% chose radiation. The change from a mortality to a survivability presentation caused a change in the way individuals cognitively processed the information and arrived at a decision.

Because our interventions may have profound effects for our patients and the decisions they may make regarding whether to begin therapy and what sort of therapeutic approaches to try are significant, we have an important ethical responsibility to attend carefully to the form in which we present information relevant to those decisions.

PROBLEMS WITH FORMS

Many of us may be so eager to start doing therapy that we try to avoid talking with our clients about consent issues. We try to push all the responsibility off onto a set form and let the form do the work. Those of us who work in clinics or hospitals may not even handle such forms. The client who shows up for an initial appointment may be handed an imposing-looking form by the receptionist, asked to read it, sign it, and return it before seeing the therapist. The form itself may have been crafted by the clinic's or hospital's attorney and may not even have been reviewed by a clinician. The wording may be in intimidating legalese and bureaucratic jargon. Such forms may be intended more to protect the organization against successful lawsuits than to help the client understand the options and make reasonable decisions. Bemister and Dobson warn against putting all our trust in forms: "The extent to which these consent forms are true indicators of consent is debatable" (2011, p. 303; see also Pope, 2015).

Providing information in written form can be vital in ensuring that clients have the information they need. But the form cannot serve as a substitute for an adequate process of informed consent. At a minimum, the clinician must discuss the information with the client and arrive at a professional judgment that the client has adequate understanding of the relevant information.

Clinicians using consent forms must ensure that their clients have the requisite reading skills. Illiteracy is a major problem in the United States; clinicians cannot simply assume that all of their clients can read. Moreover, some clients may not be well versed in English, perhaps having only rudimentary skills in spoken English as a second or third language.

Not only must the client be able to read, but the form itself must be readable. Grundner (1980) noted that great effort has been made to ensure that "consent forms have valid content, but little effort has been made to ensure that the average person can read and understand them" (p. 900). He analyzed five forms with two standardized readability tests and found that "the readability of all five was approximately equivalent to that of material intended for upper division undergraduates or graduate students. Four of the five forms were written at the level of a scientific journal, and the fifth at the level of a specialized academic magazine."

Reading a form does not ensure that the client understands the material or can remember it even a short time later. Robinson and Merav (1976) reinterviewed 20 patients 4 to 6 months after they had read and signed a form for informed consent and had undergone treatment. They found that all patients showed poor recall regarding all aspects of the information covered by the form, including the diagnosis, potential complications, and alternate methods of management. Cassileth, Zupkis, Sutton-Smith, and March (1980) found that only one day after reading and signing a form for informed consent, only 60% of the patients understood the purpose and nature of the procedures. A perfunctory indication from clients that they understand can be unreliable (Irwin et al., 1985). The clinician bears the responsibility for ensuring that the client understands the information.

It would be comforting to believe that the identification of problems in these early studies led to effective solutions. Unfortunately, the problems continue to emerge in contemporary research. For example, research by Akkad et al. (2006; see also Armstrong, Dixon-Woods, Thomas, Rusk, & Tarrant, 2012; Commons et al., 2006; Dixon-Woods et al., 2006; Wallace, et al., 2008) found that

> As suggested in previous work, . . . many thought the primary function of the form was to protect the hospital. . . . These findings are disconcerting for healthcare professionals and patients alike and raise questions about how far current consent processes genuinely fulfil their aim of safeguarding autonomy and protecting patients' rights. (p. 529)

Ozhan et al. (2014) found that over half the patients surveyed in the study reported that they had not even read the form, citing a variety of reasons such as they found the form hard to understand, they did not have enough time, or they didn't have their glasses with them.

ADDITIONAL RESOURCES

A web page (*Informed Consent in Therapy & Counseling: Forms, Standards & Guidelines, & References*) at http://kspope.com/consent/index.php provides resources that may be helpful in thinking through the process of informed consent. The web page's resources fall into three categories:

1. Links to a variety of forms for informed consent from the Trust (formerly APA Insurance Trust); the University of Rochester Counseling Center; Laura Brown, PhD, ABPP; Keely Kolmes, PsyD; Bruce Borskosky, PsyD; and the Center for Ethical Practice
2. Excerpts addressing informed consent from the standards and guidelines of professional associations (with links to the original documents) including: American Association for Marriage & Family Therapy; American Association of Christian Counselors; American Association of Spinal Cord Injury Psychologists & Social Workers; American Group Therapy Association; American Mental Health Counselors Association; American Psychoanalytic Association; American Psychological Association; Association for Specialists in Group Work; British Association

for Counseling & Therapy; British Columbia Association of Clinical Counselors; California Board of Behavioral Sciences; Canadian Counseling Association; Canadian Psychiatric Association; Canadian Psychological Association; European Federation of Psychologists' Associations; Irish Association for Counseling & Therapy; National Association of Social Workers; National Board for Certified Counselors; and Psychological Society of Ireland.

3. Quotes and information about informed consent from articles, books, and studies.

SCENARIOS FOR DISCUSSION

You work full time for a health maintenance organization (HMO) that requires the clinician to obtain written informed consent from all patients before providing therapy. One of the HMO physicians refers a patient to you for therapy. When the patient shows up for the initial session, you discover that the patient has recently been permanently blinded by an explosion and wants help in making the transition to living without reliance on this particular sense.

- How do you feel?
- What are the initial consent issues that you consider?
- In what ways, if at all, should the consent process explicitly address therapeutic approaches specifically developed for those without sight?
- If you were not fluent in Braille, the HMO provided no consent forms in Braille, and no HMO employee could write in Braille, how would you approach the HMO's requirement that written consent be obtained before clinical services were provided?
- If the patient asked if any of the interventions you planned to use had been validated as effective for those without sight, how would you respond?
- If the patient asked if your graduate training and supervised experience included adequate work with sightless patients so that you were competent to provide services to this population, how would you respond?

You work for a managed care facility that allows no more than eight sessions of outpatient therapy in any given year. A new

(continued)

(*continued*)

client tells you during the first session that surprising and intrusive memories have started to occur about experiences of incest as a child. The client thinks that the parent who perpetrated the incest may now be sexually abusing several grandchildren.

- How do you feel?
- What are the informed consent and informed refusal issues, if any, that you consider during this initial session regarding a formal assessment of this client?
- What are the informed consent and informed refusal issues, if any, that you consider during this initial session regarding potential clinical interventions for this person?

You have just begun working as a counselor at a university counseling center. At your first meeting with the counseling center director, you ask if the center has consent forms. The director replies, "I'm so glad you brought that up. We've been leaving that up to individual counselors, but we need one that everyone can use. I've been looking at your curriculum vitae, and I think you're the perfect person to design the form. Please have it on my desk by next Thursday."

- How do you feel?
- Assuming that there is no way you can get out of this task, what process would you use for designing the form?
- What issues or elements are you sure the informed consent form should address?

You have agreed to provide therapy to an adolescent who had gotten in trouble for drinking. The parents have agreed to allow the sessions to be confidential, given your ethical responsibilities. However, they now request to see the records because they have reason to believe that their adolescent is smoking pot.

- How do you feel?
- What are the legal and ethical factors you consider?
- What do you think you might say to the parents?
- What do you think you might say to your client?
- To what extent does your form for informed consent adequately address the issues that this scenario raises?

You are a provider of services for a managed care company. Utilization reviews are required before additional sessions are provided. You realize, during the review, that although you believe sexual orientation is a critical issue and focus for your gay client, you did not inform your client that the information would be revealed to the reviewer.

- How do you feel?
- What consent issues does this situation involve?
- What possible approaches do you consider in deciding how to handle this situation?
- What information concerning utilization review, peer review, and similar review processes should an adequate form for informed consent and informed refusal contain?

Chapter 20

ASSESSMENT, TESTING, AND DIAGNOSIS

Assessment, testing, and diagnosis can change the course of clients' lives. A psychological evaluation can determine whether someone gets a job, custody, security clearance, declaration of disability, or release from involuntary hospitalization. It can shape a jury's verdict or a judge's sentence. Evaluations for jobs, custody, security, disability, hospitalization release, and criminal trials require different sets of competencies (Campbell, Vasquez, Behnke, & Kinscherff, 2010; Ready & Veague, 2014; Rust & Golombok, 2014; Wygant & Lareau, 2015). The once-popular all-purpose "general psychological evaluation" has largely given way to assessments based on tests and other methods validated to answer specific questions. Conducting these assessments can present a range of ethical challenges.

The settings we work in can make meeting these challenges more complex. In organizational settings, we can face limits on the time and resources we devote to each assessment. In solo practice, we can face challenges in conducting evaluations that are ethical, accurate, useful, and consistent with current research and theory. We often lack the ready-made professional support, educational resources, and peer review that many clinics and hospitals provide through in-service training programs, grand rounds, case conferences, and program evaluation. We may need to work harder to update, improve, and monitor our practice.

The increasing diversity of racial ethnic minority populations has led to increased need for tests normed, validated, and otherwise useful for the relevant population, as well as the increased need for clinicians trained and competent in the use of these tests (American Psychological Association [APA], 2002; Vasquez, 2015; see also Chapter 23 on culture, context, and individual differences).

This chapter suggests ways to strengthen ethical intelligence, helping us to spot and avoid pitfalls and make sure that diagnosis, testing, and assessment are as valid and useful as possible.

AWARENESS OF STANDARDS AND GUIDELINES

The American Psychological Association (APA) and the Canadian Psychological Association (CPA) publish standards and guidelines for testing, assessment, and diagnosis. Reviewing them often helps us make sure that our work meets the highest standards. For example, APA's (2010) Ethical Principles and Code of Conduct includes sections relevant to assessment, including "Evaluation, Diagnosis, and Interventions in Professional Context," "Competence and Appropriate Use of Assessments and Interventions," "Test Construction," "Use of Assessment in General and with Special Populations," "Interpreting Assessment Results," "Unqualified Persons," "Obsolete Tests and Outdated Test Results," "Test Scoring and Interpretation Services," "Explaining Assessment Results," "Maintaining Test Security," "Forensic Assessments," and "Describing the Nature and Results of Psychological Services."

The draft of the fourth edition of the Canadian Code of Ethics for Psychologists (CPA, 2015) includes relevant statements such as that psychologists "establish procedures for reasonably ready access to confidential information about an individual or group in a psychological record to that individual or group when requested, unless non-access is required or justified by law (e.g., potential serious harm to a third party; potential serious harm to the physical, emotional, or mental health of the individual or group)" (Section III.15i) and that psychologists "protect the skills, knowledge, and interpretations of psychology from being misused, used incompetently, or made useless (e.g., loss of security of assessment techniques by others)" (Section IV.11).

APA and CPA publish other documents helpful in this area, including:

- *Guidelines for Psychological Practice with Older Adults* (APA, 2014b)
- *Guidelines for Assessment of and Intervention with Persons with Disabilities* (APA, 2011a)
- *Guidelines on Multicultural Education, Training, Research, Practice, and Organizational Change for Psychologists* (APA, 2003a) (Under review/revision)
- *Guidelines for Psychological Practice with Girls and Women* (APA, 2007).
- *Guidelines for Ethical Psychological Practice with Women* (CPA, 2007).
- *Guidelines for Psychological Practice with Lesbian, Gay, and Bisexual Clients* (APA, 2012d)
- *Guidelines for Child Custody Evaluations in Family Law Proceedings* (APA, 2010b)

- *Guidelines for Psychological Evaluations in Child Protection Matters* (APA, 2013a)
- *Guidelines for Test User Qualifications* (APA, 2001, under review/revision)
- *Guidelines for the Evaluation of Dementia and Age-Related Cognitive Change* (APA, 2012c)
- *General Guidelines for Providers of Psychological Services* (APA, 1987b)
- *Practice Guidelines for Providers of Psychological Services* (CPA, 2001a)
- *Professional practice guidelines for school psychologists in Canada* (CPA, 2007)
- *Rights and Responsibilities of Test Takers: Guidelines and Expectations* (APA, 1998)
- *Specialty Guidelines for Forensic Psychology* (APA, 2013c)
- *Standards for Educational and Psychological Testing* (American Educational Research Association, APA, and National Council on Measurement in Education, 2014). (There are links to the full text of these documents at http://kspope.com/ethcodes/index.php.)
- *The pre-employment clinical assessment of police candidates: Principles and guidelines for Canadian psychologists* (CPA, 2013).

Many of these are updated every few years or so.

STAYING WITHIN AREAS OF COMPETENCE

A psychology degree, internship, and license do not by themselves qualify a professional to administer, score, or interpret psychological tests.

Over three decades ago, Hall and Hare-Mustin (1983) reported an APA ethics case that shows how long psychologists have recognized that testing requires specific training:

> One psychologist charged another with incompetence, especially in testing.... CSPEC (Committee on Scientific and Professional Ethics and Conduct [the former name of the APA Ethics Committee]) reviewed the report of the state committee, which had carried out the investigation, and found that the person had no training or education in principles of psychological testing but was routinely engaged in evaluations of children in child custody battles. The committee found violation of Principle 2a, competence in testing, and stipulated that the member should work under the supervision of a clinical psychologist for one year. (p. 718)

Psychological testing requires competence based on formal education, training, and supervised experience. This point applies to diagnosis, evaluation, and assessment more generally even if testing is not involved.

MAKING SURE THAT OUR TESTS AND ASSESSMENT METHODS STAY WITHIN THEIR AREAS OF COMPETENCE

Competence is specific to the task and method. We may be competent to assess a child's intellectual strengths and weaknesses but not an adult's neuropsychological functioning. Our competence in one area does not necessarily generalize to another area. The tests and other assessment methods we use face the same limitation. A particular standardized test, for example, might help us determine whether clients are malingering but not whether they will respond better to group than individual therapy.

When we consider a particular psychological test, we must ask whether it is both valid and reliable for the use to which we want to put it and has been normed and validated for the relevant groups (e.g., age) to which our client belongs. For example, the APA Ethics Code (2010) urges psychologists to "use assessment instruments whose validity and reliability have been established for use with members of the population test. When such validity or reliability has not been established, psychologists describe the strengths and limitations of test results and interpretation."

Perlin and McClain (2009) provide an example of important issues of equivalence to consider when taking culture into account:

> Technical equivalence refers to the method of data collection. For example, in some cultures unfamiliar with formal testing, results may not lead to valid outcomes due to reluctance to disclose or confusion regarding testing.... Metric equivalence refers to analysis of the same concepts across cultures and the notion that the construct can be measured through the same scale after proper translation. Statistical behavior of the items in each culture must be the same. Validity of the measurement itself is the most critical issue in the cross-cultural application of testing. In other words, do the results really represent the issues being measured? Validity for the threshold or cutoff point refers to the point at which results should be considered impaired or psychopathological. Decisions about the criteria for threshold should be determined based upon sociocultural considerations and will likely affect various cultural groups differently. (p. 265)

UNDERSTANDING MEASUREMENT, VALIDATION, AND RESEARCH

Being able to document substantial course work, supervised training, and extensive experience in a given area like neuropsychological assessment of geriatric populations, intelligence testing of young children, or personality testing of adults helps a professional establish competence in that area of testing in an ethics committee hearing, licensing hearing, or malpractice suit. But a basic understanding of measurement, validation, and research is another key component of competence.

Sanders and Keith-Spiegel (1980) described an APA ethics case in which a psychologist evaluated a person using a Minnesota Multiphasic Personality Inventory (MMPI), among other resources. The person who was evaluated felt that the test report, particularly the part based on the MMPI results, was not accurate. All materials, including the test report and raw data, were submitted to the APA Ethics Committee, which in turn submitted the materials for evaluation to two independent diplomates with expertise in testing.

The committee concluded that the psychologist did not demonstrate adequate understanding of measurement, validation, and inference in his report:

> The only test used by the complainee that has any established validity in identifying personality disorders is the MMPI, and none of the conclusions allegedly based on the MMPI are accurate. We suspect that the complainee's conclusions are based upon knowledge of a previous psychotic episode and information from the psychiatric consultant, whose conclusions seem to have been accepted uncritically. The complainee's report is a thoroughly unprofessional performance, in our opinion. Most graduate students would do much better. (Sanders & Keith-Spiegel, 1980, p. 1098)

ENSURING THAT PATIENTS UNDERSTAND AND CONSENT TO TESTING

Making sure that a patient understands the nature, purposes, and techniques of a given instrument helps to fulfill the client's right to give or withhold informed consent to assessment or treatment (see Chapter 19). Determining that the patient understands the testing differs from just presenting the information. Some patients may be anxious, distracted, preoccupied, or so eager to please that they nod their heads as if to acknowledge that they understand an explanation when, in fact, they have understood none of it. Some patients are unfamiliar with technical terms and concepts that we take for granted. Often this lack of communication combines with our own eagerness to get on with the testing and the client's fear of appearing ignorant.

The clinician is responsible for both explaining the assessment process and for forming a professional opinion about whether the patient understands and consents. For a patient to be adequately informed, the consent must be given or withheld in the light of adequate knowledge about who will or may receive the results, which in turn may be affected by the Health Insurance Portability and Accountability Act (HIPAA), the Personal Information Protection and Electronic Documents Act (PIPEDA), and other legislation. Although these issues concern the variety of people who may eventually receive copies of the report and the associated raw data once the assessment has been completed, they must be addressed with the patient *before* starting the assessment, so that the client's decision to give or withhold consent is adequately informed. The next section discusses clarifying these issues.

CLARIFYING ACCESS TO THE TEST REPORT AND RAW DATA

We work within a complex framework of legal and ethical standards governing the discretionary and mandatory release of test information. The U.S. Privacy Act of 1974, the California truth-in-testing statute, *Detroit Edison v. National Labor Relations Board*, the 1996 HIPAA, and the Canadian 2000 Personal Information Protection and Electronic Documents Act (PIPEDA) are examples of legislation and case law that affect access to assessment documents. The APA Ethics Code (APA, 2010) Standard 9.04, Release of Test Data, (a) and (b) provides a definition of *test data* and guidance about the release of test data:

> (a) The term *test data* refers to raw and scaled scores, patient responses to test questions or stimuli, and psychologists' notes and recordings concerning patient statements and behavior during an examination. Those portions of test materials that include patient responses are included in the definition of *test data*. Pursuant to a patient release, psychologists provide test data to the patient or other persons identified in the release. Psychologists may refrain from releasing test data to protect a patient or others from substantial harm or misuse or misrepresentation of the data or the test, recognizing that in many instances release of confidential information under these circumstances is regulated by law. (See also Standard 9.11, Maintaining Test Security.)
>
> (b) In the absence of a patient release, psychologists provide test data only as required by law or court order.

The next fictional vignette shows the complex judgments therapists must make about withholding or disclosing assessment information:

A 17-year-old boy comes to your office and asks for a comprehensive psychological evaluation. He has been experiencing some headaches, anxiety, and depression. A high school dropout, he has been married for a year and has a 1-year-old baby but has left his wife and child and returned to live with his parents. He works full time as an auto mechanic and has insurance that covers the testing procedures. You complete the testing. During the following year, you receive requests for information about the testing from a number of people:

- The boy's physician, an internist.
- The boy's parents, who are concerned about his depression.
- The boy's employer, in connection with a worker's compensation claim filed by the boy.
- The attorney for the insurance company that is contesting the worker's compensation claim.

- The attorney for the boy's wife, who is suing for divorce and for custody of the baby.
- The attorney for the boy, who is considering suing you for malpractice because he does not like the results of the tests.

Each request asks for the full formal report, the original test data, and copies of each test (e.g., instructions and all items for the MMPI-2).

To which of these people are you ethically or legally obligated to supply all information requested, partial information, a summary of the report, or no information at all? Which requests require the boy's written informed consent for release of information?

There is no set of answers to these complex questions that would fit all or even most readers. Each state, province, and other jurisdiction has its own evolving legislation and case law that address, sometimes in an incomplete or confusing manner, clinician responsibilities. Such questions can, however, provide a basis for discussion in ethics courses, clinical supervision and consultation, staff meetings, or workshops. Answers can be sought for a specific jurisdiction.

Practitioners can work through their local professional associations to develop clear guidelines to the current legal requirements. If the legal requirements in this or any other area of practice seem unethical, unreasonable, unclear, or potentially damaging to clients, practitioners can propose and support remedial legislation.

FOLLOWING STANDARD PROCEDURES FOR ADMINISTERING TESTS

When we are reciting the instructions to the Wechsler Intelligence Scale for Children-Revised (WISC-R) or the Halstead Category Test for the 500th time, we may experience the urge to break the monotony, liven things up, and let our originality show through. And particularly when we are in a hurry, we may want to shorten the instructions. After all, the client will catch on as we go along.

The assumption underlying standardized tests is that the test-taking situation and procedures are as similar as possible for everyone. If we change the procedures on which the norms are based, the standardized norms lose their direct applicability and the "standard" inferences drawn from those norms fall into question.

Reasonable accommodations for assessing people with disabilities may sometimes include changing the method of test administration. Lee, Reynolds, and Willson (2003) wrote:

> The 1999 Standards for Educational and Psychological Testing adopted by AERA [American Educational Research Association], APA, and NCME

[National Council on Measurement in Education] requires examiners to make reasonable accommodations for individuals with disabilities when administering psychological tests to such persons. Changes in test administration may be required, but the Standards also require the examiner to provide evidence associated with the validity of test score interpretation in the face of such changes in administration. Departures from standard procedures during test administration may change the meaning of test scores, because scores based on norms derived from standardized procedures may not be appropriate; error terms and rates may also be affected. (p. 55)

APA's Committee on Professional Standards (1984) published a finding that allowing a client to take home a test such as the MMPI departs from the "standard procedure." The "Casebook for Providers of Psychological Services" (APA Committee on Professional Standards, 1984) describes a case in which a psychologist permitted his client to take the MMPI home to complete. When the complaint was filed with APA, the Committee on Professional Standards stated that whenever a psychologist

Does not have direct, first-hand information as to the condition under which the test is taken, he or she is forced (in the above instance, unnecessarily) to assume that the test responses were not distorted by the general situation in which the test was taken (e.g., whether the client consulted others about test responses). Indeed the psychologist could have no assurance that this test was in fact completed by the client. In the instance where the test might be introduced as data in a court proceeding, it would be summarily dismissed as hearsay evidence. (p. 664)

Unless the assessment is carefully monitored, there is no way to know the conditions under which the person filled out response sheets and completed other aspects of the testing. Psychologist Jack Graham, an expert in the MMPI, described an interesting test administration in an inpatient setting (Pope, Butcher, & Seelen, 2006). He noticed a large gathering of patients. Several times a minute, some of the patients would raise their hands. Graham became intrigued and asked one of the patients to tell him what was going on. The patient explained that a psychologist had given an MMPI to one of the patients, asking him to complete it and then return it to the psychologist's office. The patient had asked for help from the other patients. The patient was reading each MMPI item aloud, and the patients raised their hands to vote on whether that item should be answered true or false.

Psychologist Jim Butcher, another expert in the MMPI, observed a patient sitting with his spouse outside a psychologist's office while filling out an MMPI. From time to time as the patient marked an answer, his wife, reading along, would tell him he was wrong and should change his answer, which the patient dutifully did (Pope et al., 2006).

KNOWING THE LITERATURE ON RECORDINGS AND THIRD-PARTY OBSERVERS

In some cases we may want to audiotape or videotape an assessment, or allow a third party to be present. In other cases, a judge may allow the presence of a recording device or third party regardless of our objections. Whenever third parties or recording devices are present, we need to know how this can affect the assessment. For example, Constantinou, Ashendorf, and McCaffrey (2002) found that "in the presence of an audio-recorder the performance of the participants on memory tests declined. Performance on motor tests, on the other hand, was not affected by the presence of an audio-recorder" (p. 407). Gavett, Lynch, and McCaffrey (2005) found that "third party observers have been found to significantly impair neuropsychological test performance on measures of attention, verbal memory, verbal fluency, and cognitive symptom validity" (p. 49; see also Constantinou, Ashendorf, & McCaffrey, 2005; Eastvold, Belanger, & Vanderploeg, 2012; Lynch, 2005; Yantz & McCaffrey, 2005).

We also need to be aware of the policy statements and similar articles in this area. For example, the documents that address third-party presence in neuropsychological assessments include:

- American Academy of Clinical Neuropsychology's "Policy Statement on the Presence of Third Party Observers in Neuropsychological Assessment" (2001)
- Axelrod and colleagues' "Presence of Third Party Observers During Neuropsychological Testing: Official Statement of the National Academy of Neuropsychology" (2000)
- Duff and Fisher's "Ethical Dilemmas with Third Party Observers" (2005)
- Lynch and McCaffrey's "Neuropsychological Assessments in the Presence of Third Parties: Ethical Issues and Literature Review" (2004)
- McSweeny and colleagues' "Ethical Issues Related to the Presence of Third Party Observers in Clinical Neuropsychological Evaluations" (1998)

The Canadian Psychological Association (2009a) issued the following policy statement:

> It is not permissible for involved third parties to be physically or electronically present during the course of neuropsychological or similar psychological evaluations of a patient or plaintiff. Exceptions to this policy are only permissible when in the sole professional opinion of the assessing psychologist, based on their clinical judgment and expertise, that a third party would allow more useful assessment data to be obtained. Typical examples may include the inclusion of a parent or caregiver until a full rapport is gained. The presence of these observers should be cited as a limitation to the validity of the assessment.

APA's Committee on Psychological Tests and Assessment (2007) summarizes complex issues involving third parties:

> Inclusion of a third party in the assessment and testing process may affect validity of an evaluation or threaten test security and copyright. However, a third party may facilitate validity and fairness of the evaluation or be required by law. Options to address the request for external observation include, but are not limited to (1) conducting the evaluation in the presence of an observer, (2) minimizing the intrusion afforded by observation, (3) utilizing assessment measures that are less affected by observation, (4) recommending that the request for a third party be withdrawn, and (5) declining to perform the assessment under observation. (p. 5)

AWARENESS OF BASIC ASSUMPTIONS

Fundamental assumptions and theoretical frameworks often affect our assessments. Langer and Abelson's classic study (1974), "A Patient by Any Other Name," for example, shows one way in which behavior therapists and psychoanalytically oriented therapists can differ when viewing the same individual:

> Clinicians representing two different schools of thought, behavioral and analytic, viewed a single videotaped interview between a man who had recently applied for a new job and one of the authors. Half of each group was told that the interviewee was a "job applicant" while the remaining half was told that he was a "patient." At the end of the videotape, all clinicians were asked to complete a questionnaire evaluating the interviewee.
>
> The interviewee was described as fairly well adjusted by the behavioral therapists regardless of the label supplied. This was not the case, however, for the more traditional analytic therapists. When the interviewee was labeled "patient," he was described as significantly more disturbed than he was when he was labeled "job applicant." (p. 4)

The point here is not whether either of these two orientations is more valid, reliable, respectable, empirically based, or useful but rather to underscore the obvious: Different theoretical orientations can lead to different assessments. Clinicians conducting assessments and assigning diagnoses need to be continually aware of their own theoretical orientation and how that orientation will affect the evaluation. Langer and Abelson (1974) wrote:

> Despite the questionable light in which the analytic therapist group was cast in the present study, one strongly suspects that conditions might be arranged wherein the behavior therapists would fall into some kind of error, as much as the traditionalists. No single type of orientation toward clinical training is likely to avoid all types of biases or blind spots. (p. 9)

Woodward, Taft, Gordon, and Meis (2009) conducted a similar study and wrote:

> The finding that psychodynamic therapists were more likely to diagnose BPD [borderline personality disorder] than PTSD [posttraumatic stress disorder] is consistent with previous research which has found that psychodynamic clinicians tend to apply the BPD diagnosis when BPD criteria are not met more frequently than clinicians of other orientations . . . . It is also of note that in the current study, CBT [cognitive behavioral therapy] clinicians were more likely to diagnose PTSD than BPD. That theoretical orientation significantly affects a clinician's diagnosis raises concerns because it suggests that clinicians may be applying their own theories to the atheoretical diagnostic criteria of *DSM-IV* [*Diagnostic and Statistical Manual of Mental Disorders*, 4th ed.; American Psychiatric Association, 1994]. How clinicians conceptualize their clients' distress will impact those clients' treatment plans and possibly the effectiveness of the intervention. We encourage clinicians to reflect upon their own theoretical biases when assessing new clients and to form comprehensive treatment plans to address those difficulties most relevant for each patient. (p. 287)

AWARENESS OF PERSONAL FACTORS LEADING TO MISUSING DIAGNOSIS

In addition to a lack of awareness of our basic assumptions and our assumptions in specific areas, insufficient attention to our own personal reactions and dynamics makes us vulnerable to faulty evaluations. Reiser and Levenson's excellent article, "Abuses of the Borderline Diagnosis" (1984), focuses on six ways in which the diagnosis of borderline personality disorder is commonly abused "to express countertransference hate, mask imprecise thinking, excuse treatment failures, justify the therapist's acting out, defend against sexual clinical material, and avoid pharmacologic and medical treatment interventions" (p. 1528). Openness to such issues within ourselves and frequent consultations with colleagues can help prevent abuses of this kind and help our assessments meet the highest ethical standards.

AWARENESS OF FINANCIAL FACTORS LEADING TO MISUSING DIAGNOSIS

Therapists who depend on third-party coverage learn quickly which diagnostic categories are "covered" and which are not. Insurance companies, health maintenance organizations (HMOs), and managed care companies may authorize services for only a very restricted range of diagnoses. For example, the personality or character disorders are rarely covered. Unfortunately, the temptation to substitute a fraudulent but covered diagnosis for an honest but unreimbursable one can influence even senior and well-respected practitioners, as shown in a national study (Pope & Bajt, 1988). Kovacs (1987), in his strongly worded article on insurance billing, issued a stern warning that those

> Who are naive about insurance billing or who play a little fast and loose with carriers are beginning to play Russian Roulette. The carriers are now prepared to spend the necessary funds for investigators and for lawyers which will be required to sue in civil court and/or to bring criminal charges against colleagues who do not understand their ethical and legal responsibility in completing claim forms on behalf of their patients. (p. 24)

"Advice on Ethics of Billing Clients" (1987), an article in the APA *Monitor*, lists among "billing practices that should be avoided": "Changing the diagnosis to fit reimbursement criteria" (p. 42).

The APA's Ethical Principles of Psychologists and Code of Conduct (2010), Standard 6.06, Accuracy in Reports to Payors and Funding Sources, states:

> In their reports to payors for services or sources of research funding, psychologists take reasonable steps to ensure the accurate reporting of the nature of the service provided or research conducted, the fees, charges, or payments, and where applicable, the identity of the provider, the findings, and the diagnosis. (See also Standards 4.01, Maintaining Confidentiality; 4.04, minimizing Intrusions on Privacy; and 4.05, Disclosures.)

Unfortunately, many managed care companies and other third-party payers limit reimbursement for assessment to 1 hour. Often a full evaluation to determine accurate diagnoses requires several hours of testing and report preparation. Either the provider of services must provide rationale for further reimbursement or provide services pro bono. (Note: Finn [2007] describes an assessment process that has therapeutic impact and also describes how to bill third-party payers for therapeutic assessment sessions.)

The problem of financial factors leading to false diagnosis appears to be significant. Gross (2004) wrote that

> The abuse of insurance is one of the most common ethical and legal violations committed by practicing therapists, resulting in imposed sanctions by licensing agencies and criminal convictions.... Unfortunately for the profession, abuse of insurance has become so commonplace that many practitioners have deceived themselves into believing it is normal or acceptable behavior. (p. 36)

ACKNOWLEDGING LOW BASE RATES[1]

If an assessment involves an attribute — for example, a condition, ability, aptitude, or quality — rarely found in the population, overlooking the low base rate

---

[1] Reprinted with permission from "Fallacies and Pitfalls in Psychological Assessment," by K. S. Pope. Copyright © 2003 by K. S. Pope. Available at http://kspope.com/fallacies/index.php

causes problems. Even when psychological tests are accurate, low base rates can cause big mistakes.

Imagine you have been commissioned to develop an assessment procedure that will identify crooked judges so that candidates for judicial appointment can be screened. It is a difficult challenge, in part because only 1 out of 500 judges is (hypothetically speaking) dishonest.

You pull together all the actuarial data you can find and develop a screening test for crookedness based on personality characteristics, personal history, and test results. Your method is 90% accurate.

When your method is used to screen the next 5,000 judicial candidates, there might be 10 candidates who are crooked (because about 1 out of 500 is crooked). A 90% accurate screening method will identify 9 of these 10 crooked candidates as crooked and 1 as honest.

So far, so good.

The problem is the 4,990 honest candidates. Because the screening is wrong 10% of the time and the only way for the screening to be wrong about honest candidates is to identify them as crooked, it will falsely classify 10% of the honest candidates as crooked. The test will incorrectly classify 499 of these 4,990 honest candidates as crooked.

So out of the 5,000 candidates who were screened, the 90% accurate test classified 508 of them as crooked: Nine who actually were crooked and 499 who were honest. Every 508 times the screening method indicates crookedness, it tends to be right only nine times. And it has falsely branded 499 honest people as crooked.

ACKNOWLEDGING DUAL HIGH BASE RATES[2]

The following example shows why it is crucial to recognize dual high base rates.

As part of a disaster response team, you are flown in to work at a community mental health center in a city that has experienced a severe earthquake. Taking a quick look at the records the center has compiled, you note that of the 200 people who have come for services since the earthquake, there are 162 who are of a particular religious faith and are diagnosed with posttraumatic stress disorder (PTSD) related to the earthquake and 18 of that faith who came for services unrelated to the earthquake. Of those who are not of that faith, 18 have been diagnosed with PTSD related to the earthquake, and 2 have come for services unrelated to the earthquake.

It looks like there is a strong link between that particular religious faith and developing PTSD related to the earthquake: 81% of the people who came for services were of that religious faith and had developed PTSD. Perhaps this faith

[2] Reprinted with permission from "Fallacies and Pitfalls in Psychological Assessment," by K. S. Pope. Copyright © 2003 by K. S. Pope. Available at http://kspope.com/fallacies/index.php

makes people vulnerable to PTSD. Or perhaps it is a more subtle association: This faith might make it easier for people with PTSD to seek mental heath services.

But the inference of an association is a fallacy: Religious faith and the development of PTSD in this community are independent factors. Ninety percent of all people who seek services at this center happen to be of that specific religious faith (90% of those who had developed PTSD and 90% who had come for other reasons) and 90% of all people who seek services after the earthquake (90% of those with that particular religious faith and 90% of those who are not of that faith) have developed PTSD. The two factors appear to be linked because both have high base rates, but they are statistically unrelated.

AVOIDING CONFUSION BETWEEN RETROSPECTIVE AND PREDICTIVE ACCURACY

The *predictive accuracy* of an assessment instrument focuses first on the test results and asks: What are the chances, expressed as a conditional probability, that a person with these results has a particular condition, ability, aptitude, or quality? The *retrospective accuracy* of an assessment instrument focuses first on the particular condition, ability, aptitude, or quality and asks: What are the chances, expressed as a conditional probability, that a person who has this particular condition or ability will show these test results? Many problems spring from this common mistake of confusing the directionality of the inference.

This mistake of confusing retrospective with predictive accuracy often resembles the *affirming the consequent* logical fallacy (see Chapter 6):

People with condition X are overwhelmingly likely to have these specific test results.

Person Y has these specific test results.

Therefore, Person Y is overwhelmingly likely to have condition X.

AWARENESS OF FORENSIC ISSUES

As our society becomes more litigious, we find ourselves appearing in court more frequently as fact witnesses (if we are testifying about our therapy client) or expert witnesses, and preparing documents that will become part of legal proceedings. Forensic settings are a baffling brave new world for many therapists and we need to become aware of ground rules. For example, financial factors can, under certain circumstances, create a bias — or at least the appearance of bias — in carrying out and reporting assessments. For this reason, forensic texts have long mandated that no psychologist accept a contingency fee. Blau (1984) wrote: "The psychologist should never accept a fee contingent upon the outcome of a case" (p. 336). Shapiro (1990) stated: "The expert witness should never, under any circumstances, accept a referral on a contingent fee basis" (p. 230). Only about 15% of the respondents in a national survey reported engaging in this practice (Pope, Tabachnick, & Keith-Spiegel, 1987), and about the same percentage (14%) believe it to be good practice or good under most circumstances (Pope, Tabachnick, & Keith-Spiegel, 1988). Kesselhelm and Studdert (2007) note that "many codes . . . reject witness fees that are contingent on the litigation outcome" (p. 2907). The Committee on Medical Liability and Risk Management of the American Academy of Pediatrics (2009) emphasizes that "the medical profession has deemed it unethical for expert witnesses to base their fees for testifying contingent on the outcome of the case" (p. 433). The APA *Specialty Guidelines for Forensic Psychology* states: "Because of the threat to impartiality presented by the acceptance of contingent fees and associated legal prohibitions, forensic practitioners strive to avoid providing professional services on the basis of contingent fees" (APA, 2013, p. 12).

Another potentially troublesome area in forensic practice involves conducting child custody assessments. Shapiro (1990), for example, states that "under no circumstances should a report on child custody be rendered to the court, based on the evaluation of only one party to the conflict" (p. 99). The "Guidelines for Child Custody Evaluations in Family Law Practice" (APA, 2010) provides guidance for psychologists in this area. According to this document, the best interest of the child is the primary purpose of the evaluation and is considered paramount. Other useful sources of information on potential problems in this area include: Ackerman and Pritzl (2011); Benuto, Leany, and Garrick (2015); Chiu (2014); Haney-Caron and Heilbrun (2014); Pepiton, Zelgowski, Geffner, and Pegolo de Albuquerque (2014); Pickar and Kaufman (2015); R. A. Simon (2014); and Zelechoski, Fuhrmann, Zibbell, and Cavallero (2012).

Clinicians face a particularly difficult dilemma when asked to provide copies of copyrighted psychological assessment instruments such as the MMPI-2 to attorneys, who may submit the instrument, including all its questions or other test items, into evidence and as a result seemingly violate test security. Awareness of the ethical and legal standards is key as is awareness of possible approaches to this dilemma. The appellate court in *Carpenter v. Superior Court* (2006) affirmed the psychologist's obligation, in that particular case, to provide plaintiff's counsel with the test items. However, it also quoted test publishers' recommendation for protecting test security:

Both Pearson and Harcourt also suggest a satisfactory means by which the tests can be provided after the mental examination. In essence, the publishers propose, the test questions and answers may be given to plaintiff's counsel or a designated psychologist, subject to a protective order strictly limiting the use and further disclosure of the material, and providing for other safeguards against access that would compromise the integrity and validity of the tests.

HIGH-STAKES TESTING

Intelligence and other forms of testing are "high stakes" and may be used for admission to educational programs, special education, employment selection, and even death penalty cases. Translation and adaptation of various tests can be challenging in use with various subcultures and languages. Overlooking factors like language, acculturative learning, education, and socioeconomic status can lead to invalid results, with disastrous consequences, when assessing intelligence, competence, disability, neuropsychological status, and so on (Benuto et al., 2015; Brown, Vinson, & Abdulah, 2015; Harry & Klingner, 2014; Ortiz & Melo, 2015; Puente, Ojeda, Zink, & Portillo Reyes, 2015; Vasquez, 2015).

ATTENTION TO POTENTIAL MEDICAL CAUSES

Whenever the patient's symptoms hit all of the diagnostic criteria for a psychological disorder, it is tempting to ignore possible medical causes for distress or disability. A comprehensive evaluation, however, needs to rule out (or identify) possible medical causes.

Rick Imbert, when he was president of the American Professional Agency, a company that provides professional liability coverage, stressed that "if there is any indication of a physical problem, then have a full medical screening; for example, symptoms which appear to be part of a schizophrenic process can actually be caused by a brain tumor" (personal communication, April 18, 1988). The case of Mr. Alvarez in Chapter 2 reminds us of what can happen when we reflexively dismiss possible physical causes for symptoms that appear to have psychological causes.

CRITICALLY EXAMINING PRIOR RECORDS AND HISTORY

Prior records of assessment and treatment can provide invaluable information and context to a comprehensive psychological evaluation. The courts have held that neglecting to make any effort to recognize, obtain, and use this resource violates, in some instances, the standard of care. In the federal case of *Jablonski v. United States* (1983), for example, the U.S. Ninth Circuit Court of Appeals upheld a "district court judge's findings of malpractice . . . for failure to obtain the past medical records."

Critical examination is crucial. Some records may contain information that is wrong, biased, misleading, or out of date. Test scores may be based on tests that have been revised or shown to produce questionable results for the purpose at hand. Prior intelligence testing may have used inappropriate norms in light of the Flynn Effect (the general population's performance on intelligence tests improves over time). Pietschnig and Voracek's (2015) meta-analysis of the Flynn Effect from 1909 to 2010 found

> . . . a Flynn effect of about 3 IQ points per decade. However, this estimate reflects global linear gains by assuming uniform gains over a period of more than 100 years. The data suggest that this assumption may well not be justified, as the strength of gains could be shown to vary according to country, intelligence domains, and the investigated time span. (p. 296)

Regardless of whether prior records exist or are obtainable, obtaining an adequate history can be crucial to an adequate assessment. Psychologist Laura Brown (1994b), for instance, discussed the pioneering work of independent practitioner Lynne Rosewater and George Washington University professor Mary Anne Dutton in demonstrating how overlooked history could lead to misdiagnosis when relying on standardized tests:

> Their work has involved collecting data on large numbers of battered women and identifying common patterns of response on the testing. In effect, they have noted that the standard mainstream texts and computerized scoring systems for the MMPI do not take into account the possibility that the person taking the test is a woman who currently is, or recently has been, beaten by her spouse or partner . . . .
>
> As Rosewater first pointed out, without the context, specifically the identification of the presence of violence, battered women look like schizophrenics or borderline personalities on the MMPI. With the context of violence explicitly framing the interpretation of the test findings, however, it is possible to note that the sort of distress indicated on the testing is a reasonable response to events in the test-taker's life. That is to say, when a woman's partner is beating her, it makes sense that she is depressed, confused, scattered, and feeling overwhelmed. It is not necessarily the case that this state of response to life-threatening violence is either usual for the woman in question or a sign of psychopathology. (p. 187)

CLEARLY STATE ALL RESERVATIONS ABOUT RELIABILITY AND VALIDITY

If any circumstances might have affected the results of psychological testing, such as dim lighting, frequent interruptions, a noisy environment, or medication, or if there is doubt that the person being tested shares all relevant characteristics with the reference groups on which the norms are based, these factors and their possible implications need to appear clearly in the formal report.

This means we must remain alert to the diverse array of factors that may affect validity and reliability. For example, if we test someone whose first language is not English, we must decide whether the testing in English is appropriate. Often, referral of the client to a mental health professional who is competent in the client's language is the best course. If translation is necessary, we avoid if at all possible relying on a translator who has the kind of dual role with the client (e.g., a family member) that may jeopardize the validity of the client's responses. Clients may feel ashamed, embarrassed, or afraid to say certain things in front of a family member. They may be reluctant to say something that might irritate, anger, sadden, embarrass, or shock a mother, father, son, daughter, or other family member. They may fear that their relative will share what they are saying with other relatives or friends. They may be concerned that the relative will want to talk with them about topics that they are mentioning only as part of the assessment and do not wish to discuss with anyone.

A wide variety of clinical, intellectual, and other tests have been translated, normed, and validated with a variety of ethnic minority populations (Vasquez, 2015). A competent examiner will review resources that provide reviews of various assessment instruments and methods in terms of cultural equivalence of measures, validity and reliability, and psychometric support of the instruments (for example, see Geisinger, 2015).

PROVIDING ADEQUATE FEEDBACK

Feedback is a dynamic, interactive process in which the results and implications of testing or other forms of assessment are shared with the person who is being assessed, and providing feedback is, with certain exceptions, a basic responsibility (Pope, 1992). APA (2010; see also Curry & Hanson, 2010; Jacobson, 2014) Ethics Code Standard 9.10, Explaining Assessment Results, states:

> Regardless of whether the scoring and interpretation are done by psychologists, by employees or assistants, or by automated or other outside services, psychologists take reasonable steps to ensure that explanations of results are given to the individual or designated representative unless the nature of the relationship precludes provision of an explanation of results (such as in some organizational consulting, preemployment or security screenings, and forensic evaluations), and this fact has been clearly explained to the person being assessed in advance.

Three major factors can block this process.

1. HMOs and other managed care organizations can inflict harsh, sometimes unrealistic, demands on clinicians' time. The rationing of time may allow too little opportunity to sit with a client to discuss an assessment and attend carefully to the client's questions and concerns. Similarly, federal, state, and private mental health insurance may disallow coverage for all but the most minimal feedback session. For example,

there may be a standard fixed payment for administrating a specific psychological test; the payment may barely (sometimes inadequately) cover the time necessary to administer the test and prepare a brief write-up of the results. The clinician may have to donate pro bono the time required to provide adequate feedback.

2. Advertisements and marketing literature may promote individual tests, versions of tests, or test batteries by stressing how little time they take. One continually reads of quick, brief, short, and abbreviated tests. Such promotion may unintentionally nurture the notion that a complex assessment can be carried out in just a few minutes with no real demands on the clinician's time, skills, judgment, or even attention. This rush to judgment may encourage clinicians to match their quick, brief, short, and abbreviated testing with quick, brief, short, and abbreviated feedback.

3. On a personal level, therapists and counselors may be uncomfortable discussing assessment results with a client. Some may be reluctant to be the bearer of what they fear the client will receive as bad news. Others may be uncomfortable trying to translate for the client the technical jargon that clogs so many test interpretation texts, computer interpretation printouts, volumes on diagnosis, and so forth. Still others may be uneasy facing a client's expectations of clear results with test results that may necessarily leave many important questions unanswered.

These and other factors may encourage clinicians to forget that feedback is a dynamic, interactive process that is an aspect of the larger process of assessment and that the assessment often continues during what is called the feedback session or phase. Consequently, feedback may come to be viewed as simply a pro forma, static method of closure or an obligatory technicality in which the "results" are dumped in the client's lap (or referral source or someone else). This view of feedback seems so aversive and unproductive that some clinicians may decide — wrongly — to withhold feedback altogether. No rote, by-the-numbers approach to feedback can replace a thoughtful discussion with the client of what the results are, what they mean, and what they do not mean.

SCENARIOS FOR DISCUSSION

You are attending your first rounds at the community mental health center where you began working last week. Your supervisor discusses a recent intake who will be assigned to you for therapy. The supervisor, who assessed the new client using the MMPI-2 and a clinical interview, says that the assessment shows that the client's claims about being raped are clearly false.

The treatment plan, which you will be implementing, will be to help the new client realize that this confabulation is not real.

- How do you feel?
- What options do you have?
- What would you like to say to the supervisor?
- What do you think that you would say to the supervisor?

You work for an HMO. A new patient shows up at your office for an initial session. The person says: "I have felt so incredibly edgy all week. I don't know what's wrong with me. But I feel like I want to smash someone in the mouth, like I want to get my gun and blow someone's brains out. I don't even know who, but it's like something's building up and it just won't be stopped."

- How do you feel?
- When the person stopped talking, what would be the first things you would say?
- How do you go about creating an assessment plan in this situation? What phases of the assessment would you make sure to complete before the person left your office, and how would you go about completing them? What phases of the assessment would you schedule for later? Who else, if anyone, would you involve in the assessment?

You are responsible for all intakes on Mondays, Wednesdays, and Fridays. After discussing recent intakes with you, your supervisor tells you: "From now on, I want to obtain standardized testing data on all intakes. I want you to administer the [names a test] to all intakes. I think we need to base our decisions on test data." You believe that this test lacks adequate validity and reliability for clinical work and is therefore not useful. You diplomatically say that you are not sure about giving the test, but your supervisor says, "I can understand that. No method is endorsed by everyone. But I'm responsible for intakes, and I'll take responsibility for this. All you need to do is administer, score, and interpret them."

- How do you feel?
- What would you like to say to the supervisor?
- What do you think you'd end up saying to the supervisor?

(continued)

(continued)

- What are your options?
- What would you do?

A parent schedules an appointment with you. The parent shows up with a child and says, "The people at school say that my Jesse here cheats at school. Can you talk with Jesse and give some tests to find out if that's true?"

- How do you feel?
- What are your options?
- What ethical concerns do you have? How would you address them?

A former client, whom you liked very much, calls and reports that she and her spouse are getting divorced. The client asks to return for an evaluation, as requested by her attorney, regarding a child custody dispute. She expresses her assumption that you will testify in court on her behalf.

- How do you feel?
- What are your options?
- What issues do you consider?
- How do you think you would respond?

An attorney calls to ask you to provide a basic evaluation for a patient who will be deported unless proof can be provided that the attorney's client is under severe duress as a refugee. The hearing is in 1 week, and the attorney says that no other resources for obtaining an evaluation are available and that there are waiting lists at the clinics providing such evaluations. The hearing judge has refused to grant an extension. The client does not speak English but has a family member who can interpret. You do not speak the client's language. You have attended multicultural diversity workshops and classes.

- How do you feel?
- What issues do you consider in deciding whether to schedule the assessment?
- What assessment approaches, including any standardized tests, would you consider in planning such an evaluation?
- Assume you agreed to conduct the assessment and when you began you found that the family member had minimal skills in speaking English. What would you do?

Chapter 21

SEXUAL ATTRACTION TO PATIENTS, THERAPIST VULNERABILITIES, AND SEXUAL RELATIONSHIPS WITH PATIENTS

The prohibition against engaging in sex with a patient stands as one of our oldest ethical standards. Annette Brodsky (1989) noted that this rule is even older than the 2,500-year-old Hippocratic Oath. The ancient code of the Nigerian healing arts contained this prohibition.

Despite centuries of teaching and efforts at prevention, violations persist. Hollwicha, Frankeb, Riecher-Rösslerc, and Reiter-Theila (2015) note that "a substantial proportion of psychotherapists engage in sexual interactions with their clients . . . . Such behaviour contrasts significantly with the unanimous disapproval of TCS expressed in the literature . . . as well as in professional ethical guidelines, codes and laws . . . " (2015; see also Fasasi & Olowu 2013; Herlihy & Corey, 2014; Sonne & Jochai, 2014).

The common experience of *feeling* sexually attracted toward a patient seems to have gained a guilt by association with *acting* on those feelings by engaging in sex with the patient. Research reviewed in this chapter suggests that simply feeling attracted to patient makes most of us uncomfortable. Sexual feelings may lead to fantasies that can stir up complex and conflicting responses. Andrea Celenza (2007) wrote: "The fantasy that one might desire another person profoundly enough to risk one's entire professional career is at once horrifying and intriguing" (p. 27).

Even fantasizing about becoming sexually involved with a patient after termination is a fantasy about an act that can involve considerable risk. Gorman (2009) pointed out that in "nearly two dozen states, a psychologist risks losing his license to practice if he has sex with a former client within one, two, or even five years of the end of treatment" (p. 983; see also Feeny, 2009; Sarkar, 2009; Vasquez, 1991). Some ethics codes prohibit sexual relationships between therapists and their former patients in perpetuity. Principle 2.6 of the Code of Ethics of the Royal Australian and New Zealand College of Psychiatrists (2004), for example, states: "Sexual relationships between psychiatrists and their former patients are always unethical" (p. 6).

Our field continues to have a hard time facing honestly and realistically both attraction to patients and the temptation to act on that attraction. This chapter takes a look at different facets of this complex and emotionally charged area, including:

- How Modern Ethics Codes Address Therapist–Client Sex
- How Therapist–Client Sex Can Injure Clients
- Gender and Other Patterns of Perpetrators and Victim
- Common Scenarios of Therapist–Client Sex
- Therapist Risk Factors
- Why Do Therapists Refrain When They Are Tempted?
- Confronting Daily Issues
- Physical Contact With Clients
- Sexual Attraction to Clients
- When the Therapist Is Unsure What to Do
- Working With Clients Who Have Been Sexually Involved With a Therapist
- Ethical Aspects of Rehabilitation
- Hiring, Screening, and Supervising
- Scenarios for Discussion

HOW MODERN ETHICS CODES ADDRESS THERAPIST–CLIENT SEX

Modern ethics codes contained no explicit mention of this topic until research began revealing that many therapists were violating the prohibition. Although the codes had not highlighted this particular form of patient exploitation by name, therapist–patient sex violated ethics codes sections prior to the 1970s. Rachel Hare-Mustin (1974), former chair of the American Psychological Association's (APA) Ethics Committee, noted that the 1963 Ethical Standards of Psychologists of APA contained standards that would prohibit therapist–patient sexual involvement. She wrote that in the light of "a review of principles relating to competency, community standards and the client relationship that genital contact with patients is ethically unacceptable" (p. 310).

Jean Holroyd, professor at the University of California-Los Angeles and senior author of the first national study of therapist–patient sex, explained that the 1977 code did not represent a change in the standards regarding sexual activities with patients:

> Administrative law judge: Was it [the 1977 ethics code] a codification of what was already the standard of practice?
>
> Holroyd: Yes, it was making it very explicit in the ethics code.
>
> Administrative law judge: What I am asking is whether or not the standard of practice prior to the inclusion of that specific section in the [1977] ethics code, whether or not that changed the standard of practice.
>
> Holroyd: No, it did not change the standard of practice. The standard of practice always precluded a sexual relationship between therapist and patient.
>
> Administrative law judge: Even though it was not expressed in the ethics codes?
>
> Holroyd: From the beginning of the term psychotherapy with Sigmund Freud, he was very clear to prohibit it in his early publications. (*In the Matter of the Accusation Against: Myron E. Howland*, 1980, pp. 49–50)

The courts recognized the long history of prohibition against therapist–patient sexual involvement. In the mid-1970s, New York Supreme Court Presiding Justice Markowitz noted the long history of professional agreement that therapist–patient sex harms patients: "Thus from [Freud] to the modern practitioner we have common agreement of the harmful effects of sensual intimacies between patient and therapist" (*Roy v. Hartogs*, 1976, p. 590).

That this prohibition has remained constant over so long a time and throughout so many diverse cultures reflects to some extent the recognition that sex involvement places the patient at risk for serious harm.

The longstanding ethical prohibition, however, failed to prevent a significant number of therapists from sexual exploitation. Feminist psychologists were among the first to point out that psychotherapy with women was plagued with what would today be considered unethical sexual interactions between therapist and client (Brown, 2010; Chesler, 1972; Holroyd, 1983; Holroyd & Brodsky, 1977; Pope & Bouhoutsos, 1986; Vasquez & Vasquez, 2016).

Up until the mid-1960s, the understanding of therapist–client sexual involvement was informed mainly by theory, common sense, and individual case studies. Only after that period of awakening has a considerable body of diverse systematic investigations informed our understanding with empirical data. Some subsequent sections of this chapter summarize some of the findings. (For more detailed presentations of that groundbreaking research, see Gabbard, 1989; and Pope, 1992, 1993, 1994.)

HOW THERAPIST–CLIENT SEX CAN INJURE CLIENTS

Beginning with Masters and Johnson (1966, 1970, 1975), investigators examined how therapist–client sexual involvement affects clients (Ben-Ari & Somer, 2004; Bouhoutsos, Holroyd, Lerman, Forer, & Greenberg, 1983; Brown, 1988; Butler & Zelen, 1977; Feldman-Summers & Jones, 1984; Herman, Gartrell, Olarte, Feldstein, & Localio, 1987; Nachmani & Somer, 2007; Pope & Vetter, 1991; Somer & Saadon, 1999; Sonne & Jochai, 2014; Sonne, Meyer, Borys, & Marshall, 1985; Vinson, 1987). Approaches to learning about effects included studies of clients who have returned to therapy with a subsequent therapist as well as those who undertook no further therapy after their sexual involvement with a therapist.

The consequences for clients who have been sexually involved with a therapist have been compared to those for matched groups of therapy clients who have not been sexually involved with a therapist and of patients who have been sexually involved with a (nontherapist) physician. Subsequent treating therapists (of those clients who undertook a subsequent therapy), independent clinicians, and the clients themselves have evaluated the effects. Standardized psychological assessment instruments supplemented clinical interviews and behavioral observation. These diverse approaches to systematic study have supplemented individual patients' firsthand accounts (Bates & Brodsky, 1989; Freeman & Roy, 1976; Noel & Waterson, 1992; Plaisil, 1985; Walker & Young, 1986).

The consequences for the clients tend to cluster into 10 very general categories:

1. Ambivalence
2. Guilt
3. Emptiness and isolation
4. Sexual confusion
5. Impaired ability to trust
6. Confused roles and boundaries
7. Emotional lability
8. Suppressed rage
9. Increased suicide risk
10. Cognitive dysfunction, frequently in the areas of concentration and memory and often involving flashbacks, intrusive thoughts, unbidden images, and nightmares (Pope, 1988b, 1989a, 1989b).

GENDER AND OTHER PATTERNS OF PERPETRATORS AND VICTIMS

Significant numbers of therapists have reported on anonymous surveys that they have become sexually involved with at least one client. When the data from the first eight national self-report surveys published in peer-reviewed journals are pooled, 5,148 participants provided anonymous self-reports (Akamatsu, 1988; Bernsen, Tabachnick, & Pope, 1994; Borys & Pope, 1989; Holroyd & Brodsky, 1977; Pope, Keith-Spiegel, & Tabachnick, 1986; Pope, Levenson, & Schover, 1979; Pope, Tabachnick, & Keith-Spiegel, 1987). Each of the three professions — psychiatry, psychology, and social work — is represented by at least two studies conducted in different years.

According to these pooled data, about 4.4% of the therapists reported becoming sexually involved with a client. The gender differences are significant: 6.8% of the male therapists and 1.6% of the female therapists reported engaging in sex with a client.

Data from these studies as well as others (e.g., reports by therapists working with patients who have been sexually involved with a prior therapist) suggest that therapist–patient sex resembles other forms of abuse such as rape and incest in that the perpetrators are overwhelmingly (though not exclusively) male and the victims are overwhelmingly (though not exclusively) female (Pope, 1989b). For example, Bouhoutsos et al. (1983) reported a study in which 92% of the cases of therapist–patient sex involved a male therapist and female patient. Gartrell, Herman, Olarte, Feldstein, and Localio (1986), who reported the first national self-report study of sexual involvement between psychiatrists and their patients, found that 88% of the "contacts for which both the psychiatrist's and the patient's gender were specified occurred between male psychiatrists and female patients" (p. 1128).

Data based on therapists' reports of engaging in sex with patients or on therapists' work with patients who have been sexually exploited by a prior therapist have been supplemented with national survey data from patients who have been sexually involved with a therapist. In one study, about 2.19% of the men and about 4.58% of the women reported having become sexually involved with their own therapists (Pope & Feldman-Summers, 1992).

Yet another source of data (supplementing those provided through reports by subsequent therapists, therapists' anonymous self-reports, and patients' anonymous self-reports) is consistent with the significant gender differences. Data obtained from licensing disciplinary actions suggested that about 86% the therapist–patient cases are those in which the therapist is male and the patient is female (Pope, 1993).

This significant gender difference has long been a focus of scholarship in the area of therapist–patient sex but is still not well understood. Holroyd and Brodsky's report (1977) of the first national study of therapist–patient sex concluded with a statement of major issues that had yet to be resolved: "Three professional issues remain to be addressed: (a) that male therapists are most often involved, (b) that female patients are most often the objects, and (c) that therapists who disregard the sexual boundary once are likely to repeat" (p. 849). Holroyd (1983) suggested that the significant gender differences reflected sex role stereotyping and bias: "Sexual contact between therapist and patient is perhaps the quintessence of sex-biased therapeutic practice" (p. 285).

Holroyd and Brodsky's landmark research (1977) was followed by a second national study focusing on not only therapist–patient but also professor-student sexual relationships (Pope et al., 1979):

> When sexual contact occurs in the context of psychology training or psychotherapy, the predominant pattern is quite clear and simple: An older, higher-status man becomes sexually active with a younger, subordinate woman. In each of the higher-status professional roles (teacher, supervisor, administrator, therapist), a much higher percentage of men than women engage in sex with those students or clients for whom they have assumed professional responsibility. In the lower-status role of student, a far greater proportion of women than men are sexually active with their teachers, administrators, and clinical supervisors. (p. 687; see also Pope, 1989a, 1994)

Although statistical analyses of the first eight national self-report studies published in peer-reviewed journals reveal significant gender effects and also significant effects related to the year of the study (the pooled data suggest that each year, there are about 10% fewer self-reports of therapist–patient sex than the year before), there is no significant effect due to profession. According to these data, psychologists, psychiatrists, and social workers report engaging in sex with their patients at about the same rates. Apparent differences are actually due to differing years in which the studies were conducted (there was a confounding correlation between the professions and the years they were studied). The statistical analysis tested the predictive power of each variable (profession and year) once the variance accounted for by the other variable had been subtracted. Year had significantly more predictive power once effects due to profession had been accounted for than the predictive power of profession once effects due to year had been accounted for. Once year of study is taken into account, significant differences between professions disappear.

Bates and Brodsky (1989) examined the various risk factors that have been hypothesized at one time or another to make certain clients more vulnerable to sexual exploitation by a therapist. Their analysis led them not to the personal history or characteristics of the client but rather to prior behavior of the therapist: The most effective predictor of whether a client will become sexually involved with a therapist is whether that therapist has previously engaged in sex with a client.

With access to a considerable set of historical and actuarial data, the APA Insurance Trust (1990) revealed that "the recidivism rate for sexual misconduct is substantial" (p. 3). Holroyd and Brodsky's landmark survey (1977) found that 80% of the therapists who reported engaging in therapist–patient sexual intimacies indicated that they became involved with more than one patient. In 1997 the California Department of Consumer Affairs (1997) reported that according to their review of the available data "80% of the sexually exploiting therapists have exploited more than one client. In other words, if a therapist is sexually exploiting a client, chances are he or she has done so before" (p. 14). In a 2011 update, the department noted: "In recent years, aggressive prosecution of offending therapists — and passage of laws that facilitate the enforcement work of licensing boards — have helped to significantly reduce the number of such cases reported to the licensing boards" (California Department of Consumer Affairs, 2011).

Table 21.1 presents additional information, based on a national survey, of 958 patients who had been sexually involved with a therapist. In this study, 80% of the patients who had become sexually involved with a therapist only after termination of the therapy were found to have been harmed.

Five percent of the patients described in Table 21.1 were minors at the time that they were sexually involved with a therapist. This finding underscores an important aspect of therapist–patient sex: Although much of the literature on this topic seems to assume that the patient is an adult, this is not always the case. In a national study focusing exclusively on minor patients who were sexually involved with a therapist, most (56%) were female (Bajt & Pope, 1989).

Table 21.1. Characteristics of 958 Patients Who Had Been Sexually Involved With a Therapist

Characteristics	Number	Percentage
Patient was a minor at the time of the involvement	47	5
Patient married the therapist	37	3
Patient had experienced incest or other child sex abuse	309	32
Patient had experienced rape prior to sexual involvement with therapist	92	10
Patient required hospitalization considered to be at least partially a result of the sexual involvement	105	11
Patient attempted suicide	134	14
Patient committed suicide	7	1
Patient achieved complete recovery from any harmful effects of sexual involvement	143	17[a]
Patient seen pro bono or for reduced fee	187	20
Patient filed formal (for example, licensing, malpractice) complaint	112	12

[a]Refers to 17% of the 866 patients who experienced harm.

Source: Adapted from "Prior Therapist–Patient Sexual Involvement among Patients Seen by Psychologists," by K. S. Pope and V. A. Vetter, 1991, *Psychotherapy, 28*, pp. 429–438. Available at http://kspope.com. Copyright 1991 by Division of Psychotherapy (22) of the American Psychological Association. Reprinted with permission.

The average age of these girls who were sexually involved with a therapist was 13, and the range was from age 17 down to age 3. The average age of the male minor patients was 12, ranging from 16 down to 7.

COMMON SCENARIOS OF THERAPIST-CLIENT SEX

It is useful for therapists to be aware of the common scenarios in which therapists sexually exploit their patients. Pope and Bouhoutsos (1986, p. 4) presented 10 of the most common scenarios:

1. *Role Trading.* Therapist becomes the "patient" and the wants and needs of the therapist become the focus.
2. *Sex Therapy.* Therapist fraudulently presents therapist–patient sex as valid treatment for sexual or related difficulties.
3. *As If. . . .* Therapist treats positive transference as if it were not the result of the therapeutic situation.
4. *Svengali.* Therapist creates and exploits an exaggerated dependence on the part of the patient.
5. *Drugs.* Therapist uses cocaine, alcohol, or other drugs as part of the seduction.
6. *Rape.* Therapist uses physical force, threats, and/or intimidation.
7. *True Love.* Therapist uses rationalizations that attempt to discount the clinical/professional nature of the professional relationship and its duties.
8. *It Just Got Out of Hand.* Therapist fails to treat the emotional closeness that develops in therapy with sufficient attention, care, and respect.
9. *Time Out.* Therapist fails to acknowledge and take account of the fact that the therapeutic relationship does not cease to exist between scheduled sessions or outside the therapist's office.
10. *Hold Me.* Therapist exploits patient's desire for nonerotic physical contact and possible confusion between erotic and nonerotic contact.

It is important to emphasize, however, that these are only general descriptions of some of the most common patterns, and many instances of therapist–patient sexual involvement will not fall into these categories.

THERAPIST RISK FACTORS

While emphasizing that therapist risk factors do not release therapists from the ethical responsibility to ensure that therapist–patient sex does not occur and that it is the *therapist* (never the patient) who "always bears the professional burden in this regard" (p. 518), Norris, Gutheil, and Strasburger (2007; see also

Pope, 1994; Pope & Bouhoutsos, 1986; Subotsky, Bewley, & Crowe, 2010) call our attention to some of the major therapist risk factors for the therapist engaging in sex with the client. Here are a few:

- Life crises
- Employment transition (retirement, transfer, promotion, termination)
- Illness
- Loneliness and the impulse to confide
- Idealizing the client
- Self-esteem issues (pride, shame, and envy)
- Problems setting limits
- Denial (e.g., "This couldn't happen to me")

Ethical intelligence includes remaining alert to these and other factors that may make it more likely that we will act on our sexual feelings about clients — *and taking steps to address them* promptly and effectively. When we spot both our own sexual attraction to a client and our risk factors early, we can head off potential ethical violations before we begin using the common rationalization that therapist–client sex will not harm and may actually benefit the client (Dahlberg, 2014).

WHY DO THERAPISTS REFRAIN WHEN THEY ARE TEMPTED?

Although our apparent insights into our own motives as therapists may be questionable at best, it is worth asking: Why do the overwhelming majority of therapists avoid sexually exploiting patients? Table 21.2 presents the answers to this question as provided by therapists in two national studies: one of psychologists and the other of social workers.

CONFRONTING DAILY ISSUES

The issue of therapist–client sexual involvement reflects some major themes of this book. The great vulnerability of the client highlights the power of the therapist and the trust that must characterize the client's relationship with the therapist (see Chapter 4). The therapist's caring may be crucial in protecting against the temptation to exploit the client.

The issue of therapist–client sexual involvement illustrates another fundamental theme of this book: Ethics is not mindlessly following a list of dos and don'ts but always involves active awareness, thinking, and questioning. There is, of course, a clear prohibition: Avoid any sexual involvement with clients. No cause, situation, or condition could ever legitimize such intimacies with

Table 21.2. Reasons Therapists Offer for Refraining from Sexual Involvement With Clients

Reasons	Social Workers	Psychologists
Unethical	210	289
Countertherapeutic/exploitative	130	251
Unprofessional practice	80	134
Against therapist's personal values	119	133
Therapist already in a committed relationship	33	67
Feared censure/loss of reputation	7	48
Damaging to therapist	39	43
Disrupts handling transference/countertransference	10	28
Fear of retaliation by client	2	19
Attraction too weak/short-lived	16	18
Illegal	14	13
Self-control	8	8
Common sense	7	8
Miscellaneous	13	3

Source: Adapted from "Prior Therapist–Patient Sexual Involvement among Patients Seen by Psychologists," by K. S. Pope and V. A. Vetter, 1991, *Psychotherapy, 28,* pp. 429–438. Available at http://kspope.com. Copyright 1991 by Division of Psychotherapy (22) of the American Psychological Association. Reprinted with permission.

any client (see, e.g., Gabbard & Pope, 1989). "Context is important for understanding the transgression of sexual boundaries in therapy, but this behavior is unethical in any context" (Gutheil & Brodsky, 2008, p. 175). The prohibition stands as a fundamental ethical mandate no matter what the rationalizations. Taking this prohibition seriously, however, marks the initial rather than the final steps in meeting our ethical responsibilities in this area. Several associated issues that we must confront and struggle with follow.

PHYSICAL CONTACT WITH CLIENTS

The very topic of therapist–client sexual involvement as well as concern that we may be subject to an ethics complaint or malpractice suit may make many of us very nervous. We may go to great lengths to ensure that we maintain physical distance from our clients and under no circumstances touch them for fear that this might be misconstrued. A similar phenomenon seems to be occurring in regard to increasing public acknowledgment of child sexual abuse: Adults may be reluctant to hold children and engage in nonsexual touch that is a normal part of life.

Is there any evidence that nonsexual touching of patients is actually associated with therapist–client sexual involvement? Holroyd and Brodsky (1980) examined this question and found no indications that physical contact with patients made sexual contact more likely. They did find evidence that differential touching of male and female clients (i.e., touching clients of one gender significantly more than clients of the other gender) was associated with sexual intimacies:

> Erotic contact not leading to intercourse is associated with older, more experienced therapists who do not otherwise typically touch their patients at a rate different from other therapists (except when mutually initiated). Sexual intercourse with patients is associated with the touching of opposite-sex patients but not same-sex patients. It is the differential application of touching — rather than touching per se — that is related to intercourse. (p. 810)

If the therapist is personally comfortable engaging in physical contact with a client, maintains a theoretical orientation for which therapist–client contact is not antithetical, and has competence (education, training, and supervised experience) in the use of touch, then the decision of whether to make physical contact with a particular client must be based on a careful evaluation of the clinical needs of the client at that moment in the context of any relevant cultural and other contextual factors. When solidly based on clinical needs and a clinical rationale, touch can be exceptionally caring, comforting, reassuring, or healing. When not justified by clinical need and therapeutic rationale, nonsexual touch can also be experienced as intrusive, frightening, or demeaning. The decision must always be made carefully and in full awareness of the power of the therapist and the trust (and vulnerability) of the client. For discussions of various approaches to nonerotic touch in psychotherapy, please see Asheri (2009); Bonitz (2008); Downey (2001); Fuller (2006); Kepner (2001); McNeil-Haber (2004); Phelan (2009); Pope, Sonne, and Greene (2006); Stenzel and Rupert (2004); and Young (2007).

Our responsibility to be sensitive to the issues of nonsexual touch and explore them carefully extends to other therapeutic issues conceptually related to the issue of therapist–client sexual involvement. Our unresolved concerns with therapist–client sexual intimacies may prompt us to respond to the prospect of nonsexual touching either phobically — avoiding in an exaggerated manner any contact or even physical closeness with a client — or counterphobically — engaging in apparently nonsexual touching such as handshakes and hugs as if to demonstrate that we are very comfortable with physical intimacy and experience no sexual impulses. These unresolved concerns can also elicit phobic or counterphobic behavior in other areas, such as the clinician's initiating discussion or focusing on sexual issues to an extent that is not based on the client's clinical needs. To respond ethically, authentically, and therapeutically to such issues, we must come to terms with our own unresolved feelings of sexual attraction to our clients.

SEXUAL ATTRACTION TO CLIENTS

Sexual attraction to clients seems to be a prevalent experience that evokes negative reactions. National survey research suggests that over 4 out of 5 psychologists (87%) and social workers (81%) report experiencing sexual attraction to at least 1 client (Bernsen et al., 1994; Pope et al., 1986). As Table 21.3

Table 21.3. Characteristics of Clients to Whom Therapists Are Attracted

Characteristics	Social Workers	Psychologists
Physical attractiveness	175	296
Positive mental/cognitive traits or abilities	84	124
Sexual	40	88
Vulnerabilities	52	85
Positive overall character/personality	58	84
Kindness	6	66
Fills therapist's needs	8	46
Successful	6	33
"Good patient"	21	31
Client's attraction	3	30
Independence	5	23
Other specific personality characteristics	27	14
Resemblance to someone in therapist's life	14	12
Availability (client unattached)	0	9
Pathological characteristics	13	8
Long-term client	7	7
Sociability (sociable, extroverted)	0	6
Miscellaneous	23	15
Same interests/philosophy/background as therapist	10	0

Sources: Social work data are from "National Survey of Social Workers' Sexual Attraction to Their Clients: Results, Implications, and Comparison to Psychologist," by A. Bernsen, B. C. Tabachnick, and K. S. Pope, 1994, *Ethics and Behavior, 4*, pp. 369–388. Available at http://kspope.com. Copyright 1994 by Lawrence Erlbaum Associates, Inc. Adapted with permission. Psychology data are from "Sexual Attraction to Patients: The Human Therapist and the (Sometimes) Inhuman Training System," by K. S. Pope, P. Keith-Spiegel, and B. G. Tabachnick, 1986, *American Psychologist, 41*, pp. 147–158. Available at http://kspope.com. Copyright 1986 by American Psychological Association. Adapted with permission.

illustrates, therapists identify many aspects of patients that, according to the therapists, are the source or focus of the attraction. Yet simply experiencing the attraction (without necessarily even feeling tempted to act on it) causes most of the therapists who report such attraction (63% of the psychologists and 51% of the social workers) to feel guilty, anxious, or confused about the attraction.

That sexual attraction causes such discomfort among so many psychologists and social workers may be a significant reason that graduate training programs and internships tend to neglect training in this area. Only 9% of psychologists and 10% of social workers surveyed in these national studies reported that their formal training on the topic in graduate school and internships had been adequate. A majority of psychologists and social workers reported receiving no training about attraction.

This discomfort may also be a significant reason that scientific and professional books seem to neglect this topic:

> In light of the multitude of books on human sexuality, sexual dynamics, sex therapies, unethical therapist–patient sexual contact, management of the therapist's or patient's sexual behaviors, and so on, it is curious that sexual attraction to clients per se has not served as the primary focus of a wide range of texts. The professor, supervisor, or librarian seeking books that turn their *primary* attention to exploring the therapist's *feelings* in this regard would be hard pressed to assemble a selection from which to choose an appropriate course text. If someone unfamiliar with psychotherapy were to judge the prevalence and significance of therapists' sexual feelings on the basis of the books that focus exclusively on that topic, he or she might conclude that the phenomenon is neither widespread nor important. (Pope, Sonne, & Holroyd, 1993, p. 23)

These and similar factors may form a vicious circle: Discomfort with sexual attraction may have fostered an absence of relevant textbooks and graduate training; in turn, an absence of relevant textbooks and programs providing training in this area may sustain or intensify discomfort with the topic (Pope et al., 1993). The avoidance of the topic may produce a real impact. Koocher (1994) wrote, "How can the extant population of therapists be expected to adequately address [these issues] if we pay so little attention to training in these matters?" (p. viii).

These studies reveal significant gender effects in reported rates of experiencing sexual attraction to a patient. About 95% of the male psychologists and 92% of the male social workers compared with 76% of the female psychologists and 70% of the female social workers reported experiencing sexual attraction to a patient. The research suggests that just as male therapists are significantly more likely to become sexually involved with their patients, male therapists are also more likely to experience sexual attraction to their patients.

These national surveys suggest that a sizable minority of therapists carry with them — in the physical absence of the client — sexualized images of the client and that a significantly greater percentage of male than of female therapists experience such cognitions. About 27% of male psychologists and 30% of male social workers, compared with 14% of female psychologists and 13% of female social workers, reported engaging in sexual fantasies about a patient while engaging in sexual activity with another person (not the patient). National survey research has found that 46% of psychologists reported engaging in sexual fantasizing (regardless of the occasion) about a patient on a rare basis and that an additional 26% reported more frequent fantasies of this kind (Pope et al., 1987), and 6% have reported telling sexual fantasies to their patients (Pope & Tabachnick, 1993). Such data may be helpful in understanding not only how therapists experience and respond to sexual feelings but also how therapists and clients represent (e.g., remember, anticipate, think about, fantasize about) each other when they are apart and how this affects the psychotherapeutic process and outcome (see Geller, Cooley, & Hartley, 1981; Orlinsky & Geller, 1993; Pope & Brown, 1996; Pope & Singer, 1978; Pope, Sonne, & Greene, 2006).

For any of us who experience sexual attraction to a client, it is important to recognize that the research suggests that this is a common experience (Sonne & Jochai, 2014). To feel attraction to a client is not unethical; to acknowledge and address the attraction promptly, carefully, and adequately is an important ethical responsibility. Understanding the phenomenon of attraction has implications for training, supervision and consultation (Giovazolias & Davis, 2001; Pope et al., 1993; Pope et al., 2006). For some of us, consultation with respected colleagues will be useful. For others, obtaining formal consultation (if licensed; supervision if not) for our work with that client may be necessary. For still others, entering or reentering psychotherapy can be helpful.

WHEN THE THERAPIST IS UNSURE WHAT TO DO

What can the therapist do when he or she does not know what to do? The book *Sexual Feelings in Psychotherapy* (Pope et al., 1993) suggests a 10-step approach to such daunting situations, which are summarized here. A repeated theme of that book is that therapists lack easy, one-size-fits-all answers to what sexual feelings about patients mean or their implications for the therapy. Different theoretical orientations provide different, sometimes opposing ways of approaching such questions. Each person and situation is unique. Therapists must explore and achieve a working understanding of their own unfolding, evolving feelings and the ways in which these feelings may play a helpful role in deciding what to say or do next. Cookbook approaches can block rather than foster this process.

The approach outlined here places fundamental trust in the individual therapist, adequately trained and consulting with others, to draw his or her own conclusions. Almost without exception, therapists learn at the outset the fundamental resources for helping themselves explore problematic situations. Depending on the situation, they may introspect, study the available research and clinical literature, consult, seek supervision, or begin or resume personal therapy. But sometimes, even after the most sustained exploration, the course is not clear. The therapist's best understanding of the situation suggests a course of action that seems productive yet questionable and perhaps potentially harmful. To refrain from a contemplated action may cut the therapist off from legitimately helpful spontaneity, creativity, intuition, and ability to respond effectively to the patient's needs. But engaging in the contemplated action may lead to disaster. When reaching such an impasse, therapists may find it useful to consider the potential intervention in the light of these 10 considerations.

Fundamental Prohibition

Is the contemplated action consistent with the fundamental prohibition against therapist–client sexual intimacy? Therapists must never violate this special trust. If the considered course of action includes any form of sexual involvement with a patient, it must be rejected.

Slippery Slope

The second consideration may demand deeper self-knowledge and self-exploration. Is the contemplated course of action likely to lead to or create a risk for sexual involvement with the patient? The contemplated action may seem unrelated to any question of sexual exploitation of a patient. Yet depending on the personality, strengths, and weaknesses of the therapist, the considered action may constitute a subtle first step on a slippery slope. In most cases, the therapist alone can honestly address this consideration.

Consistency of Communication

The third consideration invites the clinician to review the course of therapy from the start to the present: Has the therapist consistently and unambiguously communicated to the client that sexual intimacies cannot and will not occur, and is the contemplated action consistent with that communication? Does the contemplated action needlessly cloud the clarity of that communication? The human therapist may be intensely tempted to act in ways that stir the patient's sexual interest or respond in a self-gratifying way to the client's sexuality. Does the contemplated action represent, however subtly, a turning away from the legitimate goals of therapy?

Clarification

The fourth consideration invites therapists to ask if the contemplated action would be better postponed until sexual and related issues have been clarified. Assume, for example, that a therapist's theoretical orientation does not preclude physical contact with clients and that a client has asked that each session conclude with a reassuring hug between therapist and client. Such ritualized hugs could raise complex questions about their meaning for the client, their impact on the relationship, and how they might influence the course and effectiveness of therapy. It may be important to clarify such issues with the client before making a decision to conclude each session with a hug.

Client's Welfare

The fifth consideration is one of the most fundamental touchstones of all therapy: Is the contemplated action consistent with the client's welfare? The therapist's feelings may become so intensely powerful that they may create a context in which the client's clinical needs may blur or fade out altogether. The client may express wants or feelings with great force. The legal context — with the litigiousness that seems so prevalent in current society — may threaten the therapist in a way that makes it difficult to keep a clear focus on the client's welfare. Despite such competing factors and complexities, it is crucial to assess the degree to which any contemplated action supports, is consistent with, is irrelevant to, or is contrary to the patient's welfare.

Consent

The sixth consideration is yet another fundamental touchstone of therapy: Is the contemplated action consistent with the basic informed consent of the client?

Adopting the Client's View

The seventh consideration urges the therapist to empathize imaginatively with the client: How is the client likely to understand and respond to the contemplated action?

Therapy is one of many endeavors in which exclusive attention to theory, intention, and technique may distract from other sources of information, ideas, and guidance. Therapists in training may cling to theory, intention, and technique as a way of coping with the anxieties and overwhelming responsibilities of the therapeutic venture. Seasoned therapists may rely almost exclusively on theory, intention, and technique out of learned reflex, habit, and the sheer weariness that approaches burnout. There is always risk that the therapist will fall back on repetitive and reflexive responses that verge on stereotype. Without much thought or feeling, the anxious or tired therapist may, if analytically minded, answer a client's question by asking why the client asked the question; if holding a client-centered orientation, may simply reflect or restate what the client has just said; if gestalt-trained, may ask the client to say something to an empty chair; and so on.

One way to help avoid responses that are driven more by anxiety, fatigue, or other similar factors is to consider carefully how the therapist would think, feel, and react if he or she were the client. Regardless of the theoretical soundness, intended outcome, or technical sophistication of a contemplated intervention, how will it likely be experienced and understood by the client? Can the therapist anticipate at all what the client might feel and think? The therapist's attempts to try out, in his or her imagination, the contemplated action and to view it from the perspective of the client may help prevent, correct, or at least identify possible sources of misunderstanding, miscommunication, and failures of empathy (Pope et al., 1993, pp. 185–186).

Competence

The eighth consideration is one of competence: Is the therapist competent to carry out the contemplated intervention? Ensuring that a therapist's education, training, and supervised experiences are adequate and appropriate for his or her work is a fundamental responsibility.

Uncharacteristic Behaviors

The ninth consideration involves becoming alert to unusual actions: Does the contemplated action fall substantially outside the range of the therapist's usual behaviors? That an action is unusual does not, of course, mean that something is necessarily wrong with it. Creative therapists occasionally try creative interventions, and it is unlikely that even the most conservative and tradition-bound therapist conducts therapy the same way all the time. However, possible actions that are considerably outside the therapist's general approaches likely warrant special consideration.

Consultation

The tenth consideration concerns secrecy: Is there a compelling reason for not discussing the contemplated action with a colleague, consultant, or supervisor? Therapists' reluctance to disclose an action to others is a red flag to possibly inappropriate action. Therapists may consider any possible action in the light of this question: If they took this action, would they have any reluctance for all of their professional colleagues to know that they had taken it? If the response is yes, the reasons for the reluctance warrant examination. If the response is no, it is worth considering if one has adequately taken advantage of the opportunities to discuss the matter with a trusted colleague. If discussion with a colleague has not helped to clarify the issues, consultation with additional professionals, each of whom may provide different perspectives and suggestions, may be useful.

WORKING WITH CLIENTS WHO HAVE BEEN SEXUALLY INVOLVED WITH A THERAPIST

It is likely that any therapist, counselor, or trainee reading this book will encounter clients who have been sexually victimized by a prior therapist. A national study of 1,320 psychologists found that 50% reported working with at least one client who, in the therapist's professional opinion, had been a victim of therapist–client sexual intimacies (Pope & Vetter, 1991). About 4% reported working with at least one client who, in the therapist's opinion, had made false allegations about sex with a prior therapist.

It is crucial that clinicians working with such clients be genuinely knowledgeable about this area. Clients who have been sexually exploited tend to be exceptionally vulnerable to revictimization when their clinical needs are not recognized. Special methods and considerations for providing therapeutic services to victims of therapist–patient sexual intimacies have been developed and continue to evolve (Pope, 1994). One of the first steps toward gaining competence in this area is recognition of the diverse and sometimes extremely intense reactions that encountering a client who reports sexual involvement with a former therapist can evoke in the subsequent therapist. Table 21.4 identifies some of the most common reactions.

Awareness of these reactions can prevent them from blocking the therapist from rendering effective services to the patient. The therapist can be alert for such reactions and sort through them should they occur. In some instances, the therapist may seek consultation to help gain perspective and understanding.

ETHICAL ASPECTS OF REHABILITATION

Unfortunately, therapists and counselors may act in ways that discount the harm done by perpetrators of therapist–patient sex, obscure the responsibilities of perpetrators, and enable perpetrators to continue — sometimes after a period of suspension — victimizing clients (Bates & Brodsky, 1989; Gabbard, 1989). The rehabilitation methods by which perpetrators are returned to practice focus many of this book's themes and pose difficult ethical dilemmas. Pope (1990c, 1990d, 1991) reviewed some of the crucial but difficult ethical questions facing therapists and counselors considering rehabilitation efforts; they are summarized next.

Table 21.4. Common Therapists' Reactions to Victims of Therapist–Patient Sexual Involvement

1. **Disbelief and denial:** The tendency to reject reflexively — without adequate data gathering — allegations about therapist–patient sex (because, for example, the activities described seem outlandish and improbable)

2. **Minimization of harm:** The tendency to assume reflexively — without adequate data gathering — that harm did not occur or that, if it did, the consequences were minimally, if at all, harmful

3. **Making the patient fit the textbook:** The tendency to assume reflexively — without adequate data gathering and examination — that the patient must inevitably fit a particular schema

4. **Blaming the victim:** The tendency to attempt to make the patient responsible for enforcing the therapist's professional responsibility to refrain from engaging in sex with a patient and holding the patient responsible for the therapist's offense

5. **Sexual reaction to the victim:** The clinician's sexual attraction to or feelings about the patient; such feelings are normal but must not become a source of distortion in the assessment process

6. **Discomfort at the lack of privacy:** The clinician's (and sometimes patient's) emotional response to the possibility that under certain conditions (for example, malpractice, licensing, or similar formal actions against the offending therapist; a formal review of assessment and other services by the insurance company providing coverage for the services) the raw data and the results of the assessment may not remain private

7. **Difficulty "keeping the secret":** The clinician's possible discomfort (and other emotional reactions) when he or she has knowledge that an offender continues to practice and to victimize other patients but cannot, in the light of confidentiality or other constraints, take steps to intervene

8. **Intrusive advocacy:** The tendency to want to guide, direct, or determine a patient's decisions about what steps to take or what steps not to take in regard to a perpetrator

9. **Vicarious helplessness:** The clinician's discomfort when a patient who has filed a formal complaint seems to encounter unjustifiable obstacles, indifference, lack of a fair hearing, and other responses that seem to ignore or trivialize the complaint and fail to protect the public from offenders

10. **Discomfort with strong feelings:** The clinician's discomfort when experiencing strong feelings (for example, rage, neediness, or ambivalence) expressed by the patient and focused on the clinician

Source: From *Sexual Feelings in Psychotherapy: Explorations for Therapists and Therapists-in-Training* (pp. 241–261), by K. S. Pope, J. L. Sonne, and J. Holroyd, 1993, Washington, DC: American Psychological Association. Copyright 1993 American Psychological Association. Adapted with permission.

Competence

Does the clinician who is implementing the rehabilitation plan possess demonstrable competence in the areas of rehabilitation and therapist–patient sexual intimacies?

Has the rehabilitation method the clinician uses been adequately validated through independent studies? Obviously, a clinician who was claiming an effective "cure" for pedophilia, kleptomania, dyslexia, panic attacks, or a related disorder would need to present the scientific evidence for the intervention's effectiveness. Ethical standards for claims based on evidence in this area — particularly given the risks for abuse to which future patients may be exposed — should not be waived. Such evidence must meet the customary requirement of publication in peer-reviewed scientific or professional journals.

> Research results that survive and benefit from this painstaking process of systematic review created to help ensure the scientific integrity, merit, and trustworthiness of new findings may be less likely (than data communicated *solely* through press conferences, popular lectures, books, workshops, and television appearances) to contribute to . . . "social-science fiction." (Pope, 1990d, p. 482)

We have been unable to locate any independently conducted, replicated research published in peer-reviewed scientific or professional journals that supports the effectiveness of rehabilitation efforts in this area.

Informed Consent

Whether the rehabilitation technique is viewed as an intervention of proven effectiveness (through independently conducted research trials) or an experimental research trial for a promising approach, have those who are put at risk for harm been adequately informed and been given the option of not assuming the risk, should the rehabilitation fail to be 100% effective?

Assessment

Do the research trials investigating the potential effectiveness of the rehabilitation method meet at least minimal professional standards? For example, is the research conducted independently? (We are rarely disinterested judges of the profundity, effectiveness, and near perfection of our own work.)

A more complex requirement concerns whether the base rate of discovery of abuse is adequately taken into account in conducting and reporting the results of experimental trials of rehabilitation efforts. Perpetrators may continue to engage in sexual intimacies with clients during (or after) rehabilitation efforts, even when they are supervised (see, e.g., Bates & Brodsky, 1989). The abuse may come to the light only if the client reports it. Yet the base rate of such reports by clients is quite low. Surveys of victims suggest that only about 5% report the behavior to a licensing board (see Pope & Vetter, 1991). The percentage appears to be significantly lower when the number of instances of abuse estimated from anonymous surveys of clinicians (who report instances in which they have engaged in abuse) is compared with complaints filed with licensing boards, ethics committees, and the civil and criminal courts. Using the higher 5% reporting estimate, assume that you conduct research in which a licensing board refers 10 offenders to you for rehabilitation. You work with the offenders for several years and are convinced that you have completely rehabilitated all 10. You assure the licensing board of your complete confidence that none of the 10 will pose any risk to future clients. But also assume that your rehabilitation effort fails miserably: All 10 offenders will engage in sex with a future client. What are the probabilities that any of the 10 future abuse victims will file a complaint? If each client has only a 5% probability of reporting the abuse, there is a 59.9% probability that none of the 10 will file a complaint. Thus, there is close to a 60% chance that these research trials, even if independently evaluated, will appear to validate your approach as 100% effective when in fact it was 100% ineffective. If ignored in conducting and reporting research, the low base rate can make a worthless intervention appear completely reliable.

Power and Trust

The ethics of psychotherapy and counseling are inherently related to power and trust. How are these factors relevant to the dilemmas of rehabilitation?

If a judge were convicted of abusing the power and trust inherent in the position of judgeship by allowing bribes to determine the outcome of cases, numerous sanctions, both criminal and civil, might follow. However, even after the judge paid the debt due to society by the abuse of power and trust, the judge would not be allowed to resume the bench, regardless of any "rehabilitation."

Similarly, if a preschool director were discovered to have sexually abused students, he or she would likely face both civil and criminal penalties. The director might undergo extensive rehabilitation efforts to help reduce the risk that he or she would engage in further abuse of children. However, regardless of the effectiveness of the rehabilitation efforts, the state would not issue the individual a new license to found and direct another preschool.

Neither of these two offenders would necessarily be precluded from practicing their professions. The former judge and preschool director, once rehabilitated, might conduct research, consult, publish, lecture, or pursue other careers within the legal and educational fields. However, serving as judge or as preschool director are positions that involve such trust by both society and the individuals subject to their immediate power that the violation of such an important and clearly understood prohibition against abuse of trust (and power) precludes the opportunity to hold such special positions within the fields of law and education.

The helping professions must consider the ethical, practical, and policy implications of allowing and enabling offenders to resume the positions of special trust that they abused. Do psychotherapy and counseling involve or require a comparable degree of inviolable trust, from individual clients and from the society more generally, and ethical integrity as the positions of judge and preschool director within the legal and educational fields?

HIRING, SCREENING, AND SUPERVISING

Those who work within health maintenance organizations, hospitals, and other structures hiring clinicians have a responsibility to attend carefully to the risks that staff may sexually exploit clients. Carefully structured and adequately comprehensive forms and procedures (verifying education, supervision, licensure, employment, history of licensing or ethics complaints, etc.) for screening potential personnel, establishing and monitoring policies prohibiting sex with clients, and so on have long been advocated as important in minimizing the risk that organizational personnel will sexually exploit clients (see Pope, 1994; Pope & Bouhoutsos, 1986). More recently, however, the usefulness of such forms and procedures that operationally define screening procedures and policy implementation has been recognized as an important component of malpractice risk management not only in hospitals but also in clinics, group practices, and similar settings. As defense attorney Brandt Caudill (1993) stated:

> Given the current state of the law, it seems clear that psychologists must assume that they may be sued if a partner, employee, or supervisee engages in a sexual relationship with a patient, because it appears that the courts are moving to the position that a sexual relationship between a therapist and a patient is a recognizable risk of employment which would be within the scope of the employer-employee relationship. (pp. 4–5)

It may be very difficult for employers and those with administrative or clinical supervisory responsibilities to argue successfully that the sexual relationship involving a supervisee or employee was not within the scope of employment. As one court held:

> We believe that the nature of the work performed by a therapist is substantially different than that of a day-care teacher as in Randi F. or a security guard as in Webb or a medical doctor as in Hoover so that a therapist who engages in sexual relations with a patient could not be said, as a matter of law, to have acted outside the scope of his employment. (St. Paul Fire & Marine Insurance Company v. Downs, 1993, p. 344)

Illinois is an example of a state that enacted legislation making an employer liable when it knows or should reasonably know that a therapist–employee engaged in sexual contact with a patient (Ill. Rev. Stat. 1991, chap. 70, para. 803).

Here are some steps that have been suggested previously as useful in addressing these issues when screening job applicants (Pope, 1994; Pope & Bouhoutsos, 1986):

- Discuss with the applicant any formal or informal training experiences in such areas as identifying and addressing both the clinician's and the client's sexual feelings. Are there classroom teachers, practicum supervisors, or previous employers who have provided such training and could be contacted to obtain information?

- Use an employment application form that traces back in sufficient detail from the present to college graduation. Ensure that there are no gaps in education or employment that are not clearly explained in writing.
- Provide a form for release of information that will enable the prospective employer to check with each setting of previous training, employment, or experience.
- Check with supervisors at any institutions at which the applicant obtained graduate training.
- Verify that the applicant was awarded all degrees claimed on the application form.
- Verify that any internships, practica, or postdocs were successfully completed. Check with a supervisor at each site.
- Check for information with each state that has issued the applicant a clinical license. Verify that no license has been revoked or subject to disciplinary procedures in which the applicant was found to have engaged in prohibited activities.
- Obtain a copy of all significant certifications.
- Obtain a copy of the applicant's resume or curriculum vitae. Ensure that it is consistent with the responses to the application form described in the second bullet point.
- Ensure that the applicant fully understands the explicit policies of the organization in regard to prohibited activities with clients and that he or she signs an agreement to that effect.

If entering into a sexual relationship with a client must be avoided, what about entering into a nonsexual relationship? The next chapter focuses on these nonsexual dual and multiple relationships.

SCENARIOS FOR DISCUSSION

It has been an extremely demanding week, and you are looking forward to going to the new movie with your life partner. The theater is packed, but you find two seats on the aisle not too close to the screen. You feel great to have left work behind you at the office and to be with your lover for an evening on the town. As the lights go down, you lean over to give your partner a passionate kiss. For some reason, while kissing, you open your eyes and notice that, sitting in the seat on the other side of your partner

(continued)

(continued)

and watching you, is a therapy client who just that afternoon had revealed an intense sexual attraction to you.

- What feelings does this scenario evoke in you?
- If you were the therapist, what, if anything, would you say to the client at the time of this event? What would you say during the next therapy session?
- How would the client's presence affect your subsequent behavior at the theater?
- How might this event affect the therapy and your relationship with the client?
- What, if anything, would you say to your partner — either at the theater or later — about what had happened? Are there any circumstances under which you would call the client before the next scheduled appointment to discuss the matter?
- Imagine that during a subsequent therapy session, the client begins asking about whom you were with at the theater. How would you feel? What would you say?
- What if the client were a business client of your partner (or knew your partner in another context) and they begin talking before the movie? What feelings would this discovery evoke in you? What would you consider in deciding how to handle this matter?
- To what extent do you believe that therapists should be free to be themselves? To what extent should they behave in public as if a client might be observing them?

During your first session with a new client, he tells you that he has always been concerned that his penis was too small. Suddenly he pulls down his pants and asks you if you think it is too small. [Consider the same scenario with a new patient who is concerned about the size of her breasts.]

- What are you feelings?
- What are you thinking?
- What are your fantasies about this scenario?
- What would you, as therapist, want to say first? Why?
- What do you think you would say first? Why?
- What difference would it make if this were a client you had been treating for a year rather than a new client?

- How, if at all, would your feelings and actions be different according to whether treatment was conducted on an inpatient or an outpatient basis?
- How, if at all, would your feelings and actions differ according to the gender of the client?
- Imagine that the client in the scenario is 15 years old. What feelings does the scenario evoke in you? What do you do? What fantasies occur to you about what might happen after the event described in the scenario?

Your client describes to you her troubled marriage. Her husband used to get mad and hit her — "not too hard," she says — but he has pretty much gotten over that. Their sex life is not good. Her husband enjoys anal intercourse, but she finds it frightening and painful. She tells you that she would like to explore her resistance to this form of sexual behavior in her therapy. Her goal is to become comfortable engaging in the behavior so that she can please her husband, enjoy sex with him, and have a happy marriage.

- What are you feeling when the client says that her husband used to "get mad and hit her"?
- What are you thinking?
- What are you feeling when she says that she finds anal intercourse frightening and painful?
- What are you thinking?
- What do you feel when she describes her goals in therapy?
- What are you thinking?
- In what ways do you believe that your feelings may influence how you proceed with this client?

The therapy group you are leading is into its eighth month of weekly meetings. One of the members of the group begins sobbing, describes terrible feelings of depression, and ends by pleading "I need someone to hold me!"

Bob, another member of the group, spontaneously jumps up and goes over to the other member, who stands up. As they embrace, it becomes obvious that Bob is getting an erection. He continues the hugging, which the other group member seems to find comforting, and seems to be stimulating himself by rubbing up against the other person.

(continued)

(*continued*)

- When you imagine this scenario, what do you feel?
- Would you, as therapist, call attention to what is happening? If so, how?
- If you were the therapist, could you imagine that such an event might make you feel aroused? frightened? upset? angry? confused?
- Do any of the following considerations change the feelings that this scenario evokes in you:
  - Whether your supervisor is watching this scene through a one-way mirror
  - Whether Bob and the client are the same gender
  - Whether Bob is suffering from schizophrenia
  - Whether Bob is a pedophile
  - Whether the client receiving the hug seems to be aroused
  - Whether Bob had been sexually abused during childhood
  - Whether this is an inpatient group
  - Whether all members of this group are suffering from terminal illnesses
  - Whether the client receiving the hug had been sexually abused during childhood
  - Whether the client receiving the hug has sued a prior therapist for malpractice in regard to sexual issues

You are working in a busy mental health center in which the doors to the consulting rooms, while offering some privacy, are not completely soundproof. As long as therapist and client are talking at a normal level, nothing can be heard from outside the door. But words spoken loudly can be heard and understood in the reception area.

A client, Sal, sits in silence during the first 5 minutes of the session, finally saying "It's been hard to concentrate today. I keep hearing these sounds, like they're ringing in my ear, and they're frightening to me. I want to tell you what they're like, but I'm afraid to."

After offering considerable reassurance that describing the sounds would be okay and that you and Sal can work together to try to understand what is causing the sounds, what they mean, and what you might do about them, you notice that Sal seems to be gathering the courage to reveal them to you.

Finally, Sal leans back in the chair and imitates the sounds. They build quickly to a very high pitch and loud volume. They sound exactly like someone becoming more and more sexually aroused and then experiencing an intense orgasm.

You are reasonably certain that these sounds have been heard by the receptionist, some of your colleagues, the patients sitting in the waiting room, and a site visitor from the Joint Commission for the Accreditation of Hospitals who is deciding whether the hospital in which your clinic is based should have its accreditation renewed.

- What feelings does this scenario evoke in you?
- As you imagined the scene, was the client male (Salvador) or female (Sally)? Does the client's gender make any difference in the way you feel?
- If Sal began to make the sounds again, would you make any effort to interrupt or ask the client to be a little quieter? Why?
- If none of the people who might have heard the sounds mentioned this event to you, would you make any effort to explain what had happened?
- Imagine that just as Sal finishes making these sounds, someone knocks loudly on the door and asks, "What's going on in there?" What do you say or do?
- Would your feelings or behavior be any different if the sounds were of a person being beaten rather than having an orgasm?
- How would you describe this session in your chart notes?
- If you were being supervised, would you feel at all apprehensive about discussing this session with your supervisor?
- What approach do you usually take toward your clients' making loud noises that might be heard outside the consulting room?

Chapter 22

NONSEXUAL MULTIPLE RELATIONSHIPS AND OTHER BOUNDARY CROSSINGS

The Therapeutic, the Harmful, the Risky, and the Inevitable

Crossing a boundary can be powerfully therapeutic. It can reshape how the patient views the therapist. It can make the working relationship stronger and deeper. It can heal rifts, stir growth, and break through an impasse. It can make a patient feel less alone, less hopeless, less like committing suicide.

In some cases, a refusal to cross a boundary can be more than a lost opportunity, it can be harmful. For example, one of this book's authors (Pope), as one of the descriptions over the decades of his own nonsexual boundary crossings with patients and how they turned out, described in *American Psychologist* in 1995 (K. S. Pope Biography, 1995) his daily therapy sessions with a patient that included such boundary crossings as having a friend send $500 and an open airline ticket to the patient. He believed that not to cross these boundaries would have been harmful to this patient in these circumstances.[1]

Vasquez (2009) describes how failure to cross boundaries with multicultural clients can sometimes risk damage to the basic working alliance (Vasquez, 2009), which in turn can lead clients to abandon therapy.

---

[1] Martin Williams's discussion of this case appears later in this chapter.

Like many powerful resources, crossing a boundary involves risk. Done in the wrong situation, at the wrong time, or with the wrong person, it can knock the therapy off track, sabotage the treatment plan, and offend, exploit, or even harm the patient.

The question "Do I cross this particular boundary with this particular patient now?" confronts us every day.

- My client has just told me that his mother died unexpectedly and he's asked me to attend the funeral. What should I tell him?
- My favorite musician who never tours in this part of the country has scheduled a one-night-only concert here. It was sold out before I could buy a ticket but a client has brought me a ticket and backstage pass as a gift. Is there any reason I should turn her down?
- My reading group meets every month to discuss a new novel and how it relates to our lives. On the way to our cars at the end of the meeting, one member asked to make an appointment with me. He wants to begin therapy. It caught me off guard — I didn't know what to say.
- My client asked me if I believe in God. I'm not sure how I should handle that question. She has been talking about how her synagogue views her sexuality and I believe she will also ask me my sexual orientation. I wish I knew how to handle personal questions.
- My client has just lost her wife and two young children in a fire and has just started sobbing — Should I end the session on time — which is now — or extend it another 5-10-15 minutes longer? But I have just enough time to make it to the court to testify as an expert witness.
- Just as I was ending the last session of the day, a thunderstorm erupted. My client usually walks home — it's about a quarter of a mile. Is there any reason I shouldn't offer a ride?
- My client will lose her home if she can't come up with a payment by tomorrow. She starts her new job in two weeks. If she has nowhere else to turn, should I lend her the money to tide her over until she starts receiving her salary?

The following sections explore this rich array of complex issues:

- How the Field Changed Its View of Boundary Issues
- What Makes This Area So Hard for Us?
- Research Leading to a Call for a Change in the Ethics Code
- Multiple Relationships as Defined by the APA and CPA Ethics Codes
- Three Interesting Examples of Multiple Relationships
- Research Review
- Self-Disclosure
- Bartering
- Multiple Relationships and Boundary Issues in Small Communities

- Seven Common Therapist Errors and Mending Fences
- Sources of Guidance
- Additional Resources
- Scenarios for Discussion

HOW THE FIELD CHANGED ITS VIEW OF BOUNDARY ISSUES

The way that the profession approached these questions changed radically in the period that began in 1980 and ran into the mid-1990s. During that period of intense questioning, thoughtful articles, books, and chapters explored and argued about boundaries from virtually every possible point of view. This healthy storm of controversy blew away the dust that had settled over all the old ideas about dual relationships and other boundary issues, and in many cases blew away the ideas themselves. New ideas were argued. New perspectives were tried on for size. Authors explored key factors that had been relatively neglected. Every suggested standard, guideline, and approach was examined carefully for possible benefits, drawbacks, and unintended consequences.

In 1981 Samuel Roll and Leverett Millen, for example, presented "A Guide to Violating an Injunction in Psychotherapy: On Seeing Acquaintances as Patients." Patricia Keith-Spiegel and Gerald Koocher's 1985 edition of their influential textbook, *Ethics in Psychology: Professional Standards and Cases*, examined ways in which boundary crossings in ethical therapy and counseling may be unavoidable. They provided an approach to examining the ethical aspects of various dual relationships and other boundary issues.

Karen Kitchener's influential 1988 article, "Dual Role Relationships," helped readers sort out "counselor-client relationships that are likely to lead to harm and those that are not likely to be harmful" (p. 217). Kitchener suggested that dual relationships are more likely to cause problems if they involve "(1) incompatibility of expectations between roles; (2) diverging obligations associated with different roles, which increases the potential for loss of objectivity and divided loyalties; and (3) increased power and prestige between professionals and consumers, which increases the potential for exploitation" (p. 217).

Robert Ryder and Jeri Hepworth (1990) argued thoughtfully that the AAMFT should not prohibit dual relationships in its ethics code. Janet Sonne (1994) examined the ways in which the then-current APA ethics code addressed multiple relationships and argued that some segments represented "steps backward" (p. 343). Vincent Rinella and Alvin Gerstein wrote that "the underlying moral and ethical rationale for prohibiting dual relationships (DRs) is no longer tenable" (1994, p. 225). Tom Gutheil and Glen Gabbard (1993) maintained that "boundary crossings may be benign or harmful" (p. 195) and explored factors that influence the impact.

Elisabeth Horst (1989), Amy Stockman (1990), and Floyd Jennings (1992) helped raise our awareness and appreciation of the special challenges that rural settings present for dual relationships and other boundary issues. Laura Brown (1989; see also 1994b) was among those who thoughtfully argued against a simple prohibition when considering dual relationships and other boundary issues in the lesbian therapy community in "Beyond Thou Shalt Not: Thinking About Ethics in the Lesbian Therapy Community."

Melanie Geyer (1994) proposed adopting some of the special guidelines for considering multiple relationships and other boundary issues in rural settings and adapting them for difficult dilemmas faced by Christian counselors (and counselors for whom other religious faiths are a primary foundation and concern of practice). Bruce Sharkin and Ian Birky (1992) focused attention on the unplanned, unexpected encounters between therapists and clients and on the difficulties of maintaining boundaries during incidental encounters.

Jeanne Adleman and Susan Barrett (1990) were among those who pioneered considering multiple relationships and other boundary issues afresh using feminist principles. Patruska Clarkson's "In Recognition of Dual Relationships" explored the implications of believing in a "mythical, single relationship" and cautioned therapists and counselors against "an unrealistic attempt to avoid all dual relationships" (1994, p. 32). Ellen Bader (1994) maintained that we should stop focusing on whether there are dual roles and consider instead whether each instance represents exploitation.

In 1994, the journal *Ethics and Behavior* invited some of the major voices in the area to debate the topic of boundaries in therapy (Borys, 1994; Bennett, Bricklin, & VandeCreek, 1994; Brown, 1994a; Gabbard, 1994; Gottlieb, 1994; Gutheil, 1994; Lazarus, 1994a, 1994b).

Smith and Fitzpatrick summarized a review of the research that had occurred during this period of rethinking nonsexual boundaries in the years leading up to 1995:

> The effects of crossing commonly recognized boundaries range from significant therapeutic progress to serious, indelible harm.... Although setting appropriate boundaries is a professional imperative, flexibility in their maintenance is equally important. Clinicians should avoid setting simplistic standards that may create barriers to therapeutic progress. In the final analysis, ethical practice is governed less by proscriptions than by sound clinical judgment bearing on the therapeutic interventions that will advance the client's welfare. (1995, p. 505)

The care with which this and other work from the 1980s into the mid-1990s called attention to the many factors (for example, setting, culture, expectations, theoretical orientation) to be taken into account when considering whether a specific multiple relationship or other boundary crossing with a specific client in a specific situation is likely to be helpful or hurtful has encouraged therapists and counselors to appreciate the complexity of these decisions and engage in careful questioning rather than unthinking rule following. It is a process that also often involves the therapist's or counselor's feelings, as Jeffrey Kottler's frank exploration discloses:

> Sorting out dual relationships has become the most prevalent ethical issue of our time.... Our family members and friends constantly ask us for advice. Although we may do our best to beg off, the truth of the matter is that we may well enjoy being needed. I love it when people ask me what to do.... I feel so self-important that someone else thinks I know something that they do not. I pretend I am a little annoyed by those who ask me how to handle their children, confront their bosses, or straighten out their lives, but I appreciate the fact that they thought enough of me to ask. (2003, p. 4)

WHAT MAKES THIS AREA SO HARD FOR US?

Sabine Wingenfeld-Hammond (2010) notes that "one of the most challenging ethical issues for professional psychologists involves maintaining and managing professional boundaries" (p. 135). Why is this area so challenging for almost all of us as individuals and as a profession? Here are five potential causes that may be at work.

First, boundary dilemmas can catch us off-guard and unprepared. They can sweep us into unfamiliar territory and call for quick decisions that can have lasting impacts. In Chapter 25 on responding to suicidal risk, we provide an example of how a sudden decision about a boundary crossing can have a profoundly transformative and healing effect. In this example, Stone (1982) describes a young woman, hospitalized during a psychotic episode, who continuously vilified her therapist for not caring about her. Without warning, she escaped from the hospital:

> The therapist, upon hearing the news, got into her car and canvassed all the bars and social clubs in Greenwich Village which her patient was known to frequent. At about midnight, she found her patient and drove her back to the hospital. From that day forward, the patient grew calmer, less impulsive, and made great progress in treatment. Later, after making substantial recovery, she told her therapist that all the interpretations during the first few weeks in the hospital meant very little to her. But after the "midnight rescue mission" it was clear, even to her, how concerned and sincere her therapist had been from the beginning. (p. 271)

Interestingly, from the time that this example and related accounts of the positive and healing potential of boundary crossings appeared in the first edition of this book in 1991, they have been one of the most frequent topics of reader comments.

Second, opportunities to cross boundaries can — as Jeffrey Kottler's courageous statement shows — tap into some of our most basic needs and strongest desires. It is possible to fall vulnerable to fallacies in reasoning and judgment (see Chapters 4 through 8) and mistake our own self-interest as if it were the client's needs. Our own needs and desires prompt us to see crossing the boundaries that we want to cross in the way that we want to cross them as the only meaningful clinical intervention, the only humane approach, the only prospect for helping the client. We become convinced that what we want to do is an ethical imperative. Glen Gabbard wrote:

> Harry Stack Sullivan (1954) once observed that psychotherapy is a unique profession in that it requires therapists to set aside their own needs in the service of addressing the patient's needs. He further noted that this demand is an extraordinary challenge for most people, and he concluded that few persons are really suited for the psychotherapeutic role. Because the needs of the psychotherapist often get in the way of the therapy, the mental health professions have established guidelines, often referred to as boundaries, that are designed to minimize the opportunity for therapists to use their patients for their own gratification. (1994, p. 283)

Third, the need for clarity about boundaries can be misunderstood as the need for inflexible boundaries reflexively applied. Clearly thinking through boundary issues for each patient is essential. Reflexively applying a rigid set of rules about inflexible boundaries can never be an acceptable substitute for thinking through boundary issues for an individual client as clearly and carefully as possible. Decisions about boundaries must reflect strong ethical intelligence about the potential benefits and harm, the patient's needs and well-being, informed consent and informed refusal, the psychotherapist's motives, and the psychotherapist's knowledge and competence. A subsequent section in this chapter lists resources that can help therapists as they think through dilemmas in this area.

Fourth, boundary decisions can evoke anxiety and even fear. For example, clinical and forensic psychologist Martin Williams points out that some may try to avoid the area entirely to minimize the risk of being sued. He describes how the fear of lawsuits and ethics complaints can lead clinicians to avoid even justifiable boundary crossings. He uses the work of one of this book's authors as an example. This example, originally published in *American Psychologist* ("Biography," 1995), was mentioned at the opening of this chapter. The example involved providing psychological services to a homeless woman who had survived an assault, who was being stalked, and whose life was at risk. Williams noted how the author's work with the client included instances of what Gutheil and Gabbard (1993) might term boundary crossings (although not boundary violations)

> [This] treatment carried out by Pope had included daily meetings without fee and his arranging for a personal friend of his to lend the patient money and to provide her with an airline ticket and a place to stay. In the context of the particular case, these boundary excursions appeared to be both humane and sensible. However, some practitioners might, in the interest of risk management, avoid making similar modifications. (1997, p. 248)

Fifth, we find relatively little guidance in making real-world decisions about boundary crossings in our classrooms and treatment guides. Moreover, many boundary crossings are subject to misinterpretation. Former American Psychological Association president Gerry Koocher's account of his own boundary crossings frequently, as he writes, makes some of his students gasp:

> On occasion I tell my students and professional audiences that I once spent an entire psychotherapy session holding hands with a 26-year-old woman together in a quiet darkened room. That disclosure usually elicits more than a few gasps and grimaces. When I add that I could not bring myself to end the session after 50 minutes and stayed with the young woman holding hands for another half hour, and when I add the fact that I never billed for the extra time, eyes roll.
>
> Then, I explain that the young woman had cystic fibrosis with severe pulmonary disease and panic-inducing air hunger. She had to struggle through three breaths on an oxygen line before she could speak a sentence. I had come into her room, sat down by her bedside, and I asked how I might help her. She grabbed my hand and said, "Don't let go." When the time came for another appointment, I called a nurse to take my place. By this point in my story most listeners, who had felt critical of or offended by the "hand holding," have moved from an assumption of sexualized impropriety to one of empathy and compassion. The real message of the anecdote, however, lies in the fact that I never learned this behavior in a classroom. No description of such an intervention exists in any treatment manual or tome on empirically-based psychotherapy. (2006, p. xxii)

RESEARCH LEADING TO A CALL FOR CHANGES IN THE ETHICS CODE

Chapter 15 noted that the original APA ethics code was empirically based, the result of a survey of the membership, asking them what ethical dilemmas they encountered. It also described a replication of that critical incident study a half-century later. This 1992 replication, published in *American Psychologist*, found that the second most often reported ethical dilemmas were in the area of "blurred, dual, or conflictual relationships" (Pope & Vetter, 1992).

On the basis of their findings, Pope and Vetter called for changes to the APA ethical principles in the areas of dual relationships, multiple relationships, and boundary issues so that the ethics code would, for example:

> Define dual relationships more carefully and specify clearly conditions under which they might be therapeutically indicated or acceptable.
>
> Address clearly and realistically the situations of those who practice in small towns, rural communities, remote locales, and similar contexts (emphasizing that neither the current code in place at the time nor the draft revision under consideration at that time fully acknowledged or adequately addressed such contexts).
>
> Distinguish between dual relationships and accidental or incidental extratherapeutic contacts (for example, running into a patient at the grocery market or unexpectedly seeing a client at a party) and to address realistically the awkward entanglements into which even the most careful therapist can fall. (p. 401)

The following excerpt from that article ("Ethical Dilemmas Encountered by Members of the American Psychological Association: A National Survey," Pope & Vetter, 1992) presents those findings and recommendations in detail, including examples provided by the survey participants:

> Blurred, Dual, or Conflictual Relationships
>
> The second most frequently described incidents involved maintaining clear, reasonable, and therapeutic boundaries around the professional relationship with a client. In some cases, respondents were troubled by such instances as serving as both "therapist and supervisor for hours for [patient/supervisee's] MFCC [marriage, family, and child counselor] license" or when "an agency hires one of its own clients." In other cases, respondents found dual relationships to be useful "to provide role modeling, nurturing and a giving quality to therapy"; one respondent, for example, believed that providing therapy to couples with whom he has social relationships and who are members of his small church makes sense because he is "able to see how these people interact in group context." In still other cases, respondents reported that it was sometimes difficult to know what constitutes a dual relationship or conflict of interest; for example, "I have employees/supervisees who were former clients and wonder if this is a dual relationship."
>
> . . .
>
> Taken as a whole, the incidents suggest, first, that the ethical principles need to define dual relationships more carefully and to note with clarity if and when they are ever therapeutically indicated or acceptable. For example, a statement such as "Minimal or remote relationships are unlikely to violate this standard" ("Draft," 1991, p. 32) may be too vague and ambiguous. A psychologist's relationship to a very casual acquaintance whom she or he meets for lunch a few times a year, to an accountant who only does very routine work in filling out her or his tax forms once a year (all such business being

conducted by mail), to her or his employer's husband (who has no involvement in the business and with whom the psychologist never socializes), and to a travel agent (who books perhaps one or two flights a year for the psychologist) may constitute relatively minimal or remote relationships. However, will a formal code's assurance that minimal or remote relationships are unlikely to violate the standard provide a clear, practical, valid, and useful basis for ethical deliberation to the psychologist who serves as therapist to all four individuals? Research and the professional literature focusing on nonsexual dual relationships underscores the importance and implications of decisions to enter into or refrain from such activities (e.g., Borys & Pope, 1989; APA Ethics Committee, 1988; Keith-Spiegel & Koocher, 1985; Pope & Vasquez, 1991; Stromberg et al., 1988).

Second, the principles must address clearly and realistically the situations of those who practice in small towns, rural communities, and other remote locales. Neither the current code nor the current draft revision explicitly acknowledges and adequately addresses such geographic contexts. Forty-one of the dual relationship incidents involved such locales. Many respondents implicitly or explicitly complained that the principles seem to ignore the special conditions in small, self-contained communities. For example,

> I live and maintain a . . . private practice in a rural area. I am also a member of a spiritual community based here. There are very few other therapists in the immediate vicinity who work with transformational, holistic, and feminist principles in the context of good clinical training that "conventional" people can also feel confidence in. Clients often come to me because they know me already, because they are not satisfied with the other services available, or because they want to work with someone who understands their spiritual practice and can incorporate its principles and practices into the process of transformation, healing, and change. The stricture against dual relationships helps me to maintain a high degree of sensitivity to the ethics (and potentials for abuse or confusion) of such situations, but doesn't give me any help in working with the actual circumstances of my practice. I hope revised principles will address these concerns!

Third, the principles need to distinguish between dual relationships and accidental or incidental extratherapeutic contacts (e.g., running into a patient at the grocery market or unexpectedly seeing a client at a party) and to address realistically the awkward entanglements into which even the most careful therapist can fall. For example, a therapist sought to file a formal complaint against some very noisy tenants of a neighboring house. When he did so, he was surprised to discover "that his patient was the owner-landlord." As another example, a respondent reported,

> Six months ago a patient I had been working with for three years became romantically involved with my best and longest friend. I could write no less than a book on the complications of this fact! I have been getting legal and therapeutic consultations all along, and continue to do so.

Currently they are living together and I referred the patient (who was furious that I did this and felt abandoned). I worked with the other psychologist for several months to provide a bridge for the patient. I told my friend soon after I found out that I would have to suspend our contact. I'm currently trying to figure out if we can ever resume our friendship and under what conditions.

The latter example is one of many that demonstrate the extreme lengths to which most psychologists are willing to go to ensure the welfare of their patients. Although it is impossible to anticipate every pattern of multiple relationship or to account for all the vicissitudes and complexities of life, psychologists need and deserve formal principles that provide lucid, useful, and practical guidance as an aid to professional judgment (Pope & Vetter, 1992, pp. 400–401).

Since the publication of these findings, both the APA and CPA Ethics Codes have developed clearer, more flexible guidance regarding multiple relationships.

MULTIPLE RELATIONSHIPS AS DEFINED BY THE APA AND CPA ETHICS CODES

Janet Sonne has noted how concerns about multiple relationships may not be founded on an accurate understanding of multiple relationships or the ethical standards:

You may have heard in workshops or read in books or journals that hugging a client, giving a gift to a client, or meeting a client outside of the office constitutes a multiple relationship and is prohibited by our ethics code or by the standard of care sustained by professional licensing boards.

Not accurate.

You may also have heard or read that telling a client something personal about yourself or unexpectedly encountering a client at a social event are examples of unprofessional multiple relationships.

Again, not accurate.

The inaccuracies, or errors, in our thinking about nonsexual multiple relationships, mire us in confusion and controversy. (2005)

It is worth taking a look at the APA and CPA codes to see how they define this concept. The APA Ethics Code defined multiple relationships for the first time in the 2002 revision (APA, 2002). According to Standard 3.05a,

A multiple relationship occurs when a psychologist is in a professional role with a person and (1) at the same time is in another role with the same person, (2) at the same time is in a relationship with a person closely associated with or related to the person with whom the psychologist has the professional

relationship, or (3) promises to enter into another relationship in the future
with the person or a person closely associated with or related to the person.
(p. 1065)

Most commonly, the second role is social, financial, business, or
professional.

Standard 3.05a notes that *not all* (emphasis added) multiple relationships
are problematic and provides guidance as to when to avoid inappropriate multiple relationships:

> A psychologist refrains from entering into a multiple relationship if the mul-
> tiple relationship could reasonably be expected to impair the psychologist's
> objectivity, competence, or effectiveness in performing his or her functions
> as a psychologist, or otherwise risks exploitation or harm to the person with
> whom the professional relationship exists. (p. 1065)

Thus, psychologists avoid dual or multiple roles with clients unless there
is no reasonable likelihood that a secondary role would interfere with one's
objectivity, competence, or effectiveness in therapy.

The draft of the fourth edition of the Canadian Ethics Code (CPA, 2015)
provides a similar caution. Section III.33 states, "Avoid dual or multiple relationships (e.g. with primary clients, client examinees, research participants,
employees, supervisees, students, trainees) that are not justified by the nature
of the activity, by cultural or geographic factors, or where there is a lack of
reasonably accessible alternatives."

Standard III.34 also acknowledges that some multiple relationships are
unavoidable and suggests ways to avoid risk of harm:

> Manage dual or multiple relationships or any other conflict-of-interest situ-
> ation entered into in such a way that bias, lack of objectivity, and risk of
> exploitation or harm are minimized. This might include involving the affected
> party(ies) in clarification of boundaries and expectations, limiting the dura-
> tion of the relationship, obtaining ongoing supervision or consultation for
> the duration of the dual or multiple relationship, or involving a third party
> in obtaining consent (e.g., approaching a primary client or employee about
> becoming a research participant). (CPA, 2015)

THREE INTERESTING EXAMPLES OF MULTIPLE RELATIONSHIPS

The abstract, generalized term "multiple relationships" lulls many of us into
ignoring the diverse, subtle ways that therapists can enter into these multiple
relationships with our clients. Specific examples may strengthen our ethical
intelligence in this area. Here are three:

Opportunity

Bill just opened his private practice office and has exactly two patients. One of them, Mr. Lightfoot, is an extremely successful investment analyst who is grateful to Bill for all the benefits he is getting from psychotherapy. The worst of Mr. Lightfoot's depression seems to be in remission, and he is now focusing on his relationships with those whose financial matters he handles. Bill, who genuinely likes Mr. Lightfoot, finds himself especially attentive when his patient talks about new investment opportunities. Unexpectedly, Mr. Lightfoot says that Bill might make a great deal of money if he invests in a certain project that is now being planned. The more Bill thinks about it, the more this seems like a terrific opportunity. It will help Mr. Lightfoot's sense of self-esteem because he will be in the position of helping Bill rather than always receiving help from him. It will not cost Mr. Lightfoot anything. Finally, it may allow Bill to survive in private practice and thus enable him to continue to help others. (Bill's overhead was greater than expected, the anticipated referrals were not materializing, and he was down to his last ten thousand dollars in savings, which would not last long given his office rent and other expenses.) He decides to give his savings to Mr. Lightfoot to invest for him.

Employee Benefits

Dr. Ali is a successful psychotherapist who now owns and manages his own mental health clinic. Lately he has noticed that his normally outstanding secretary, Mr. Miller, has been making numerous mistakes, some of them resulting in considerable financial losses for the clinic. Dr. Ali's customary toleration, encouragement, and nonjudgmental pointing out of the errors have not improved his secretary's performance. He decides that a serious and frank discussion of the situation is necessary. When he begins talking with his secretary about the deteriorating performance, Mr. Miller reveals some personal and financial stresses that he has been encountering that make it difficult for him to attend to his work. Dr. Ali is aware that his secretary cannot afford therapy and that the chances of hiring a new secretary with anywhere near Mr. Miller's previous level of skills is at best a long shot. Even if a good secretary could be found in what is a cutthroat job market, there would be a long period of orientation and training during which Dr. Ali anticipates he would continue to lose revenue. He decides that the only course of action that makes sense, that creatively solves all problems, is to take on Mr. Miller as a patient for 2 or 3 hours each week until Mr. Miller has a chance to work through his problems. Mr. Miller could continue to work as secretary and would not be charged for the therapy sessions. Dr. Ali would provide them without charge as part of a creative and generous "employee benefit."

Helping as a Friend

Rosa, an attorney, is going through one of the worst times in her life. For several weeks, she had been experiencing mild abdominal discomfort and had dismissed it as a muscle strained while jogging or nervousness about the case she was preparing to argue in her first appearance before the state supreme court. The pains become worse, and she manages to drive herself to the emergency room. A medical resident tells her that she has a large lump on her ovary and that she should make an appointment for tests to see if the lump is cancerous. Before she can say anything, he checks his watch and breezes out of the room

Rosa is terrified. The tests are scheduled for 2 days from now. She has to cope not only with the pain but also with the uncertainty of what the physicians will discover. She goes immediately to the house of her best friend, June, a psychotherapist. June suggests showing Rosa some self-hypnotic and imagery techniques that might help her cope with her pain and anxiety. As June leads her through the exercises, Rosa begins to feel relieved and comforted. However, when she tries to use the techniques by herself, she experiences no effects at all. June agrees to lead her through the hypnotic and imagery exercises two or three times a day until the medical crisis is resolved. During the fourth meeting, spontaneous images that are quite troubling begin occurring. Rosa starts talking about them and feels they are related to things that happened to her as a small child. She discusses them in detail with June, and by the end of the sixth session, June recognizes that an intense transference has developed. She encourages Rosa to consult another therapist but Rosa refuses, saying that there is no one else she could trust with these matters and that terminating the sessions would make her feel so betrayed and abandoned that she fears she would take her own life.

RESEARCH REVIEW

There has been considerable research regarding sexual multiple relationships (see Chapter 21). Research concerning the prevalence of nonsexual multiple relationships, however, has been rarer. Tallman (1981) conducted perhaps the earliest study on nonsexual multiple relationships. Of the 38 psychotherapists participating, about 33% indicated that they had formed social relationships with at least some of their patients. An intriguing aspect of the findings was that although only half of the participants were male, all of the therapists who developed these social relationships with patients were male. This significant gender difference is remarkably consistent not only in terms of both sexual and nonsexual multiple relationships in psychotherapy but also in terms of multiple relationships involving teaching and supervision.

Borys and Pope summarized the initial decade or so of research in this area:

First, the significant difference (i.e., a greater proportion of male than of female psychologists) that characterizes sexualized multiple relationships conducted by both therapists and educators (teachers, clinical supervisors, and administrators) also characterizes nonsexual multiple relationships conducted by therapists in the areas of social/financial involvements and multiple professional roles. Male respondents tended to rate social/financial involvements and multiple professional roles as more ethical and reported engaging in these involvements with more clients than did female respondents. Second, the data suggest that male therapists tend to engage in nonsexual multiple relationships more with female clients than with male clients.... Third, these trends hold for psychologists, psychiatrists, and clinical social workers. Note that these statistical analyses take into account the fact that most therapists are male and most patients are female. (1989, p. 290)

Pope, Tabachnick, and Keith-Spiegel (1987) included several items regarding nonsexual multiple relationships — "accepting services from a client in lieu of fee," "providing therapy to one of your friends," "going into business with a former client" — in their survey of the ethical beliefs and practices of a thousand clinical psychologists (the return rate was 46%). Their findings were consistent with a larger-scale multidisciplinary study focusing on multiple relationships.

This survey of 1,600 psychiatrists, 1,600 psychologists, and 1,600 social workers (with a 49% return rate) examined beliefs and behaviors regarding a range of multiple relationships (Borys & Pope, 1989). The survey's findings included these three points:

1. There was no significant difference among the professions in terms of sexual intimacies with clients before or after termination (see Chapter 12) or in terms of nonsexual multiple professional roles, social involvements, or financial involvements with patients.
2. The percentage of therapists who rated each multiple relationship behavior as ethical under most or all conditions was invariably less than the percentage of therapists viewing it as never ethical or ethical under only some or rare conditions.
3. Psychiatrists tend, as a whole, to view such relationships as less ethical than do psychologists or social workers.

The study found that various beliefs and behaviors in regard to these boundary issues tended to be significantly related to

- Therapist's gender
- Profession (psychiatrist, psychologist, social worker)
- Therapist's age

- Therapist's experience
- Therapist's marital status
- Therapist's region of residence
- Client gender
- Practice setting (such as solo or group private practice and outpatient clinics)
- Practice locale (size of the community)
- Therapist's theoretical orientation

Baer and Murdock (1995) conducted a national survey using a slightly modified version of the Therapeutic Practices Survey reported by Borys and Pope (1989). Their findings suggested

> Therapists judged social and/or financial involvements with their clients as the least ethical of the three classes of nonerotic dual relationships.... That psychologists appear clear about the importance of meeting their own social and financial needs (other than payment for therapy) through people who are not their clients is important and can be viewed as promising. (p. 143)

Lamb and Catanzaro (1998) interviewed therapists, supervisors, and instructors in an academic setting and found that those who admitted to engaging in sexual relationships with clients, supervisees, or students also reported being more likely to engage in nonsexual multiple relationships. They also rated nonsexual multiple relationships as less negative than participants who did not engage in sexual boundary violations. The authors provided helpful guidelines cited later in this chapter.

Lamb, Catanzaro, and Moorman (2004) found that

> a new relationship involving social interactions and events appears to be the type of new relationship that psychologists face most often and about which the greatest clarification may be needed, but psychologists need to be aware of other new relationships as well (e.g., new collegial or professional relationships). Discussing new relationships was reported as occurring most frequently with former (as opposed to current) clients, supervisees, or students, particularly former supervisees. (p. 252)

These studies of nonsexual multiple relationships in psychotherapy provide some initial empirical data on which to develop an understanding of the phenomenon and provide some intriguing hypotheses. What is striking, however, is the scarcity of such studies. We need critical self-study, including the systematic collection of data, regarding the occurrence and effects of multiple relationships.

SELF-DISCLOSURE

In contrast to multiple relationships, therapist self-disclosure is one of the most extensively researched boundary issues. Jourard's pioneering book, *The Transparent Self*, sparked widespread interest in the topic when it was published in 1964. His subsequent book, *Self Disclosure: Experimental Analysis of the Transparent Self* (1971) fostered diverse studies. In 1978, Weiner's landmark *Therapist Disclosure: The Use of Self in Psychotherapy*, followed by an updated second edition in 1983, reviewed theory, research, and practice in this area. More recent works that review this area include those by Farber, 2006; Henretty and Levitt (2010), Holmqvist, R. (2015); Kuchuck (2009); Tsai, Plummer, Kanter, Newring, and Kohlenberg (2010); and Ziv-Beiman (2013).

A meta-analysis found that self-disclosure "may be beneficial for building rapport, strengthening alliance, and eliciting client disclosure, with similar [counselor self-disclosure] being especially beneficial" (Henretty, Currier, Berman, & Levitt, 2014).

Gutheil and Brodsky (2008) suggest four ideas for therapists to consider when making self-disclosure decisions:

1. Some degree of self-disclosure by a therapist is inevitable, but such disclosures can become boundary violations when they are not made for the benefit of the patient.
2. Different schools of therapy involve different levels of disclosure, which in turn serve the needs of different patients.
3. Self-disclosures of a personal nature that do not have a clinical purpose . . . may [not be helpful and may violate boundaries].
4. Decisions about the therapeutic use of self-disclosure need to be made on a case-by-case basis in the context of the type of therapy offered. (p. 128)

BARTERING

Hill (1999) noted that although bartering carried risks, "it is one way of increasing the availability of therapy, respecting class differences, and avoiding the problems associated with using insurance for payment" (p. 81).

APA allows bartering under some conditions and states that "barter is the acceptance of goods, services, or other nonmonetary remuneration from clients/patients in return for psychological services. Psychologists may barter only if (1) it is not clinically contraindicated, and (2) the resulting arrangement is not exploitative (see also Standards 3.05, Multiple Relationships, and 6.04, Fees and Financial Arrangements)" (APA, 2010; see also Sonne, 1994).

Different disciplines have tended to take different views of boundary issues — for example, a national survey found that psychiatrists viewed a variety of boundary-crossing behaviors as less ethical than did psychologists or social workers (Borys & Pope, 1989) — and this is true for bartering as well. A national survey of the beliefs and behaviors of psychologists who were therapists found that most participants viewed bartering with a client as either unethical or unethical under most circumstances (Pope, Tabachnick, & Keith-Spiegel, 1987; see also Baer & Murdock, 1995). A similar survey of certified counselors, however, found that 63% viewed bartering for a client's goods and 53% viewed bartering for a client's services as ethical (Gibson & Pope, 1993).

The APA *Ethics Code Commentary and Case Illustrations* (Campbell, Vasquez, Behnke, & Kinscherff, 2010) describes why the APA Ethics Code allows bartering as a means of payment. Psychologists may consider bartering primarily in the light of the client's financial limitations or the values of the community or culture in which the therapist works. Pro bono services, although sometimes a good option, may not always be possible because of therapeutic issues, the discomfort or unwillingness of the patient to accept free services, or financial pressures on the therapist. However, the therapeutic impact of financial agreements may affect the quality of the relationship.

A number of factors can affect decision making about bartering:

- The client's strengths, weaknesses, needs, and expectations
- The cultural and other relevant context and history
- The nature, duration, and intensity of the psychological services
- Possible benefits and possible harm
- Informed consent and informed refusal
- The therapist's theoretical approach, competence, and motives
- The nature of possible bartering arrangements

The draft of the fourth edition of the Canadian Ethics Code (CPA, 2015) does not directly address bartering, but many of the standards would apply in decision making; for example, Standard I.15 requires that fees be fair, and Standard IV.12 encourages psychologists to contribute to the welfare of society by providing work for little or no financial return.

A number of therapists oppose bartering. Robert Woody (1998), for example, provides a thoughtful review of the ethical and legal issues and wrote that his "foremost conclusion is that bartering is a bad idea and should be avoided" (p. 177). However, for those who choose to barter with a client, Woody suggests the following guidelines:

1. Unique financial arrangements should be minimized; that is, terms and conditions for any compensation, including the use of bartering, should be as close to established practices as possible and be consonant with the prevailing standards of the profession.
2. The rationale for any compensation decision, including the use of bartering, should be documented in the case records.

3. Discussions about any financial matters should be detailed in writing, giving equal emphasis to what is said by the psychologist and the client.

4. If bartering is used, there should be a preference for goods instead of services; this will minimize (but not eliminate) the possibility of inappropriate personal interactions.

5. The value of the goods (or services) should be verified by an objective source; this may, however, involve additional cost.

6. To guard against any semblance of undue influence, both parties should reach a written agreement for the compensation by bartering.

7. Any new, potentially relevant observations or comments about compensation by bartering should be entered into the client's records, even though a previous agreement exists.

8. The agreement should contain a provision for how valuations were determined and how any subsequent conflicts will be resolved (e.g., a mediator); this may, however, involve additional cost (and a concern about confidentiality), which will have to be accommodated by the psychologist (i.e., the added expense should not elevate the cost to the client beyond the established service fee).

9. If a misunderstanding or disagreement begins to develop, the matter should be dealt with by the designated conflict resolution source (e.g., a mediator), not the psychologist and client; again, recall the issues of added cost and concern for confidentiality stated in the preceding guideline.

10. If monitoring by the individualized treatment plan reveals a possible negative effect potentially attributable to the compensation arrangement, it should be remedied or appropriate termination of the treatment relationship should occur (p. 177).

MULTIPLE RELATIONSHIPS AND BOUNDARY ISSUES IN SMALL COMMUNITIES

A community's size and nature provide important context for boundary issues. A varied and helpful literature explores boundary questions for therapists working in closely knit communities. Examples include some lesbian, gay, bisexual, and transgender communities (Brown, 1984, 1988, 1989; Dworkin, 1992; Gartrell, 1992; Greene, 1997a, 1997b; Greene & Croom, 1999; Kessler & Waehler, 2005; Smith, 1990), some ethnic minority communities (Comas-Diaz & Greene, 1994; Landrine, 1995; Pack-Brown & Williams, 2003; Ridley, Liddle, Hill, and Li, 2001; D. W. Sue & Sue, 2003; Vasquez, 2005; Velasquez, Arellano, & McNeill, 2004), and some rural communities (Barnett & Yutrzenka, 1995; Brownlee, 1996; Campbell & Gordon, 2003; K. K. Faulkner & Faulkner, 1997; Gripton & Valentich, 2004; Harowski,

Turner, LeVine, Schank, & Leichter, 2006; Horst, 1989; Jennings, 1992; Pugh, 2007; Schank & Skovholt, 1997, 2006; R. I. Simon & Williams, 1999).

A central theme of this book is that we cannot shift responsibility to a set of rules, reflexively applied. Every client is unique in some ways, as is every therapist. Each situation is unique in some ways, and situations continue to change. Nothing can spare us the personal responsibility of making the best effort we can to assess the potential effects of boundary crossings, which tend to occur more often in small communities, and to act in the most ethical, informed, aware, and creative way possible.

The Feminist Therapy Institute's feminist code of ethics (2000) and the APA Multicultural Guidelines (APA, 2003b) encourage advocacy efforts, community involvement, and activism (see also Arredondo et al., 1996; Constantine & Sue, 2005; Harper & McFadden, 2003; Moodley & Palmer, 2006; Pack-Brown & Williams, 2003; Roysircar, Sandu, & Bibbins, 2003; Sue, 1995). These activities may create overlapping relationships among therapists and clients, which require careful attention to informed consent, privacy and confidentiality issues, power differentials, and potential pitfalls.

Vasquez (2005) described how small communities and other contexts brought awareness that it is often useful to think of boundaries as continuous rather than dichotomous features of our work. In some small communities, for example, therapists encounter clients and clients' families and friends almost any time they set foot outside. Vasquez addresses decision making in areas like self-disclosure, nonsexual touch (see also the section on nonsexual touch in Chapter 21), giving and receiving gifts, attending an important event for a client (for example, a wedding or funeral), and others. Culture can be critical (see Chapter 23). For example, refusing to accept a gift can create a shaming experience for clients from some cultures.

SEVEN COMMON THERAPIST ERRORS AND MENDING FENCES

The article "A Practical Approach to Boundaries in Psychotherapy: Making Decisions, Bypassing Blunders, and Mending Fences" (Pope & Keith-Spiegel, 2008) discusses common cognitive errors when making boundary decisions. The errors fall into the following seven categories:

Error #1: What happens outside the psychotherapy session has nothing to do with the therapy.

Error #2: Crossing a boundary with a therapy client has the same meaning as doing the same thing with someone who is not a client.

Error #3: Our understanding of a boundary crossing is also the client's understanding of the boundary crossing.

Error #4: A boundary crossing that is therapeutic for one client will also be therapeutic for another client.

Error #5: A boundary crossing is a static, isolated event.

Error #6: If we ourselves don't see any self-interest, problems, conflicts of interest, unintended consequences, major risks, or potential downsides to crossing a particular boundary, then there aren't any.

Error #7: Self-disclosure is, per se, always therapeutic because it shows authenticity, transparency, and trust.

The article also suggests nine steps that may be helpful when boundary crossings cause or seem headed toward serious problems.

SOURCES OF GUIDANCE

Although Chapter 12 provides steps useful in thinking through ethical issues and making ethical decisions, there are decision-making guides that focus specifically on multiple relationships. Here are seven decision-making guides that readers may find helpful when considering multiple relationships and other boundary issues:

1. Gottlieb's "Avoiding Exploitive Dual Relationships: A Decision-Making Model" (1993, available at http://kspope.com/dual/index.php)
2. Faulkner and Faulkner's guide for practice in rural settings: "Managing Multiple Relationships in Rural Communities: Neutrality and Boundary Violations" (1997)
3. Lamb and Catanzaro's model in "Sexual and Nonsexual Boundary Violations Involving Psychologists, Clients, Supervisees, and Students: Implications for Professional Practice" (1998)
4. Younggren's model in "Ethical Decision-Making and Dual Relationships" (2002, available at http://kspope.com/dual/index.php)
5. Campbell and Gordon's five-step approach for considering multiple relationships in rural communities: "Acknowledging the Inevitable: Understanding Multiple Relationships in Rural Practice" (2003)
6. Sonne's "Nonsexual Multiple Relationships: A Practical Decision-Making Model for Clinicians" (2005, available at http://kspope.com)
7. Pope and Keith-Spiegel's "A Practical Approach to Boundaries in Psychotherapy: Making Decisions, Bypassing Blunders, and Mending Fences" (2008, available at http://kspope.com)

In addition, Pope, Sonne, and Greene (2006) provide a decision-making model for when we are stuck and have no idea what to do. It was created for those times when "our best understanding of the situation may suggest a course of action that seems productive yet questionable and potentially harmful. To refrain from a contemplated action may shut the door to our spontaneity, creativity, intuition, and ability to help; to refrain may stunt the patient's progress or impede recovery. To engage in the contemplated action, however, may lead to disaster." They suggest eight steps that can help therapists and counselors find their ways through such impasses.

For internship settings, Burian and Slimp provide a thoughtful approach to making decisions in "Social Dual-Role Relationships During Internship: A Decision-Making Model" (2000; see also Slimp & Burian, 1994).

ADDITIONAL RESOURCES

A web page ("Dual Relationships, Multiple Relationships, & Boundary Decisions") at http://kspope.com/dual/index.php provides resources that may be helpful in thinking through possible dual relationships, multiple relationships, and other boundary issues. The web page's resources fall into four categories:

1. **Widely used decision-making guides** (Sonne's "Nonsexual Multiple Relationships: A Practical Decision-Making Model for Clinicians"; Younggren's "Ethical Decision-making and Dual Relationships"; and Gottlieb's "Avoiding Exploitive Dual Relationships: A Decision-making Model")

2. **Excerpts addressing dual relationships and multiple relationships from the standards and guidelines of professional associations** (with links to the original documents) including American Association for Marriage and Family Therapy (AAMFT); American Association of Christian Counselors; American Association of Pastoral Counselors; American Association of Sex Educators, Counselors and Therapists; American Board of Examiners in Clinical Social Work; American Counseling Association; American Mental Health Counselors Association; American Music Therapy Association; American Psychoanalytic Association; American Psychological Association; American School Counselor Association; Association of State and Provincial Psychology Boards; Australian Association of Social Workers; Australian Psychological Society; British Association for Counselling and Psychotherapy; British Association of Social Workers; British Columbia Association of Clinical Counsellors; California Association for Counseling and Development; California Association of Marriage and Family Therapists; Canadian Counselling Association; Canadian Psychological Association; Canadian Traumatic Stress Network [Reseau Canadien du Stress Traumatique]; European Association for Body-Psychotherapy; European Federation of Psychologists' Associations; Feminist Therapy Institute; Irish Association for Counseling and Therapy; National Association of Social Workers; National Council for Hypnotherapy; and Psychological Society of Ireland

3. Quotes and information about boundaries in therapy and counseling from articles, books, and studies

4. Articles on dual relationships, multiple relationships, and other boundary topics from *American Psychologist*, *Professional Psychology*, *American Journal of Psychiatry*, etc. ("A Practical Approach to Boundaries in Psychotherapy: Making Decisions, Bypassing Blunders, and Mending Fences"; "Misuses and Misunderstandings of Boundary Theory in Clinical and Regulatory Settings"; "The Concept of Boundaries in Clinical Practice: Theoretical and Risk-Management Dimensions"; "A Study Calling for Changes in the APA Ethics Code Regarding Dual Relationships, Multiple Relationships, and Boundary Decisions"; "Dual Relationships Between Therapist and Client: A National Study of Psychologists, Psychiatrists, and Social Workers"; "Dual Relationships: Trends, Stats, Guides, and Resources"; "Nonsexual Multiple Relationships and Boundaries in Psychotherapy")

SCENARIOS FOR DISCUSSION

You decide to teach a course in basic psychopathology as part of the local community college's associate of arts degree program. You show up on the first day of class and see that there are ten students who have signed up. Two of them are current psychotherapy clients in your practice.

- How do you feel?
- Does their presence change how you teach your first class session?
- What options do you have for addressing this issue?
- What do you think you would do?
- How, if at all, would you address this issue in the chart notes for these two clients?

You live in a very small community. You are the only psychotherapist providing services through the local managed care plan. One day one of your closest friends, someone you have known for several decades, shows up at your office, seeking therapy.

- How do you feel?
- Do you share any of your feelings or concerns with the client during this session? If so, what do you say?

(continued)

(continued)

- Assume that you do not believe that you can serve as therapist in the light of your close friendship with this person. However, the client points out that not only are you the only one designated to provide therapy under the managed care plan, but that since you are also virtually the only one anywhere near this small community who matches the client in terms of characteristics that the client feels are important (this person believes that only someone who matches the patient's gender, race, and sexual orientation will understand the issues and be able to help), the client cannot really get help from anyone but you. How do you address this? What are your options? What steps would you take?

You have been suffering some financial losses and are close to bankruptcy. You will likely lose everything if you are unable to sell your house. You have been trying to sell your house for close to two years and have not received a serious offer. You hold yet another open house. The only person to show up is one of your psychotherapy clients/patients who says, "This is a great house! I'd love to buy it. And although I'd be buying it anyway, it's nice that it'll end up helping you."

- How do you feel?
- What do you think you would say?
- What options do you consider?
- What do you think you'd end up doing?

A couple, who are your close friends, is aware that you will likely be spending Thanksgiving alone. They invite you to share Thanksgiving day with them, preparing the meal during the morning, feasting at lunch, going for a leisurely walk in the woods during the afternoon, then returning for a light dinner. You show up to discover that they have, without letting you know, invited another unattached person who is presumably your blind date for the day. That person is currently a client/patient to whom you have been providing psychotherapy for two years.

- How do you feel?
- What are your options?
- What do you think you would do?

- How, if at all, would your feelings, options, or probable course change were the person a former client?
- What if the other guest were your therapy supervisor rather than your client?
- What if the other guest were your own therapist?

During a session, a patient mentions that because of her job, she receives many free tickets to concerts, plays, and other events. She loves giving them to her various doctors because she greatly appreciates their hard work and because it costs her nothing. She tells you that the day before she mailed you a pair of tickets to an upcoming concert because you had happened to mention that you are a fan of the performer, who has never held a concert in your part of the country before. You have tried to find tickets to take your daughter, who very much wants to attend, but tickets were immediately sold out and no source seems to have them available at any price.

- What do you feel?
- What issues do you consider?
- Is there any more information that you would want before deciding what to do? If so, what information would you seek?
- Under what conditions, if any, would you accept the tickets?
- After the session is over, how, if at all, would you describe this situation in your chart notes?

You are very involved in your community, and you have been appointed to a new board that is engaged in the kind of activism that you value. When you attend your first board meeting, you discover that one of your new clients is also on the board. Your client comes over at a break to tell you how pleased she is that you share similar values and will be working together.

- How do you feel?
- What feelings do you imagine that your client might be experiencing?
- What issues do you consider?
- What do you think you would say to your client?
- Would you remain on the board? What reasoning leads you to this decision?
- How, if at all, would you chart this interaction?

Chapter 23

CULTURE, CONTEXT, AND INDIVIDUAL DIFFERENCES

W e live and work in countries rich in diversity. Different groups develop in different contexts, often creating surprising patterns. Ethical assessment and intervention depend on our competence in recognizing what this diversity — diversity of groups, diversity within groups, diversity of development, and diversity of contexts — means for each of us and our profession. As Guthrie's classic book *Even the Rat Was White: A Historical View of Psychology* (2004; see also Graham, 1992; Hall, 1997; Ridley, 2005; Sue, 1999, 2010) carefully documents, psychology was slow to recognize these varied forms of diversity and their scientific, clinical, and ethical significance. Our ethical intelligence helps us understand how these diverse groups, contexts, and patterns influence us, our clients, our clinical work, and our ethical responsibilities. Our understanding in turn helps us speak up and ask questions when we have reached the limits of that understanding, even when social taboos, what we think is "political correctness," and our own nervousness press us to remain silent (Sue, 2015a).

This chapter looks at varied forms of diversity, their implications for our work, and steps to recognize and overcome barriers to ethical practice in the context of diversity. We begin by highlighting how diversity can create complex patterns. Jeanne Miranda (2006) described one striking example:

> Rates of depression and substance abuse disorders are low among Mexican Americans born in Mexico . . . , and immigrant Mexican American women have a lifetime rate of depression of 8%, similar to the rates of nonimmigrant Mexicans . . . . However, after 13 years in the United States, rates of depression

for those women who immigrated to the U.S. rise precipitously. U.S.-born women of Mexican heritage experience lifetime rates of depression similar to those of the White population in the United States, nearly twice the rate of immigrants. These findings are mirrored in other indicators of health.... Despite high rates of poverty, Mexican American immigrant women have low rates of physical and mental health problems (Vega et al., 1998), Chinese American immigrant women have a lifetime rate of major depression near 7%, approximately half that of White women.... These results suggest that some aspects of culture may protect against depression (pp. 115–116; see also Gonzales, Jensen, Montano, & Wynne, 2015; Heckert, 2012; Yeh, Liao, Ma, et al., 2014).

Catharine Costigan, Tina Su, and Josephine Hua (2009) give us another example, focusing on how a country's policies may support and encourage diversity:

> Canada has an official policy of multiculturalism, which promotes the mainte-nance of one's cultural heritage alongside full participation and acceptance in the larger society.... Consistently, Canadians, on average, support the bicul-tural integration of new immigrants into Canadian society over assimilation or separation modes of integration.... Therefore, immigrant and ethnic minor-ity youth in Canada live in a national context that encourages and values the retention of a strong sense of ethnic identity. (pp. 261–262)

Jennifer Glick, Littisha Bates, and Scott Yabiku (2009) provide yet another example. They explored patterns of relationship between the cognitive devel-opment of young children from diverse cultures and their mother's age when their mother arrived in the United States. They found that "parenting practices and home environment are associated with cognitive development and act as partial mediators between cognitive scores and mother's age at arrival" (p. 367).

We also live amid a diverse array of languages. The 2010 U.S. Census Bureau Report showed a big jump in the number of people who speak a language other than English at home. The report revealed that

> The number of people 5 and older who spoke a language other than English at home has more than doubled in the last three decades and at a pace four times greater than the nation's population growth, according to a new U.S. Census Bureau report analyzing data from the 2007 American Community Survey and over a time period from 1980 to 2007. In that time frame, the percentage of speakers of non-English languages grew by 140 percent while the nation's overall population grew by 34 percent. Spanish speakers accounted for the largest numeric increase — nationwide, there were 23.4 million more speakers in 2007 than in 1980 representing a 211 percent increase. The Vietnamese-speaking population accounted for the largest percentage increase of 511 percent (1.0 million speakers) over the same timeframe.

One in five people in the United States is a first- or second-generation immigrant, and nearly one in four of the people under the age of 18 has an immigrant parent (APA, 2012a). Therapists are and increasingly will be providing services to immigrant adults and their children in varied settings including schools, community centers, clinics, hospitals, and their practices. An APA Presidential Task Force report, *Crossroads: The Psychology of Immigration in the New Century* (APA, 2012a), is a valuable resource for learning about the current state of our scientific and professional knowledge about immigration.

Similarly, Statistics Canada (2011; see also Dheer, Lenartowicz, Peterson, & Petrescu, 2014) reports a foreign-born population of about 20.6%, the highest proportion among the G8 Countries. About one in four people under 18 living in Toronto and Vancouver were recent immigrants or born in Canada to parents who were recent immigrants. Most of these young people live in homes where the main language spoken by the parents is neither English nor French.

The United States population reveals remarkable and ever-shifting racial and ethnic patterns. The U.S. Census Bureau reports that over one third of the U.S. population identifies as racial or ethnic minority, including Black (13%), American Indian or Alaska Native (.9%), Asian (5%), Native Hawaiian or Other Pacific Islander (.2%), and Hispanic or Latino (16.3%) (U.S. Census Bureau, 2011; see also Dheer et al., 2014).

We live also in the midst of an amazing religious diversity. Melton's (2009) *Encyclopedia of American Religions* describes over 2,800 religious groups in the U.S. and Canada. Just a few of the many religions in these two countries include Baptist, Buddhist, Catholic, Christian Science, Church of Jesus Christ of Latter-day Saints (Mormon), Eastern Orthodox, Episcopal, Greek Orthodox, Hindu, Islam, Jehovah's Witnesses, Judaism, Methodist, Muslim, Native American, Pentecostalism, Russian Orthodox, Sikhism, and Unitarian Universalist. An important aspect of the religious diversity, of course, many are atheist or agnostic. We are also home to diverse spiritual traditions not based on religion (see, e.g., Comas-Díaz, 2008).

The Pew Forum on Religion & Public Life (2015) conducted interviews with more than 35,000 adults and found that religious affiliation in the United States is exceptionally diverse and extremely fluid. Twenty-eight percent of U.S. adults left the faith in which they were raised and the number of people unaffiliated with any particular faith has grown to 16.1%. The United States is on the verge of becoming a minority Protestant population (51%), characterized by significant internal diversity and fragmentation, encompassing hundreds of different denominations (Pew Forum on Religion & Public Life, 2015).

This diversity of cultures, languages, religion, and other factors has ethical implications for therapists and counselors. Both the American Psychological Association (2010) and the Canadian Psychological Association (2015) offer helpful guidance in their ethics codes for situations in which there are significant social class, cultural, or other group differences. Therapists can also find useful resources in CPA's (2001c) *Guidelines for Nondiscriminatory Practice*; APA's *Guidelines on Multicultural Education, Training, Research, Practice, and Organizational Change for Psychologists* (2003a); APA's *Guidelines for Psychological Practice with Older Adults* (2003b); APA's *Guidelines for Psychotherapy with Lesbian, Gay, and Bisexual Clients* (2011b); APA's *Guidelines for Psychological Practice with Girls and Women* (2007); and APA's *Guidelines for Assessment of and Intervention with Persons with Disabilities* (2011a).

Our cultural diversity provides a rich context for becoming more aware of how culture can influence our own ethical views and reasoning. Ronald Francis (2009) wrote:

> One of the singular merits of ethical considerations in a cross-cultural context is the way in which it forces us to confront our own values, to develop them, and to defend them. Cross-cultural comparisons afford a marvelous opportunity to examine the bases of our ethical codes in a manner which does not invite the heat more commonly attending intercultural value debates.
>
> Ethics is essentially about human values. Since not all values are shared we are compelled to consider the issues we have in common; and those on which we divide. For instance, what may seem self-evident in one culture may be ethically repugnant to another. Ethics affords an opportunity to discuss and resolve these human values in a non-threatening frame of reference. (pp. 182–193)

CONTEXT, COMPETENCE, AND PERSONAL RESPONSIBILITY

Our personal responsibility in this area begins with a realistic appraisal of our own competence in a specific situation. The CPA Code of Ethics Standard II.10 encourages psychologists to "evaluate how their own experiences, attitudes, culture, beliefs, values, social context, individual differences, specific training, and stresses influence their interactions with and perceptions of others, and integrate this awareness into their efforts to benefit and not harm others" (2015, p. 19). Standard IV.15 requires that psychologists "acquire an adequate knowledge of the culture, social structure, customs and laws or policies of organizations, communities and peoples before beginning any major work there, obtaining guidance from appropriate members of the organization, community, or people as needed" (p. 33).

APA Ethics Code Standard 2.01b, Boundaries of Competence, states:

> Where scientific or professional knowledge in the discipline of psychology establishes that an understanding of factors associated with age, gender, gender identity, race, ethnicity, culture, national origin, religion, sexual orientation, disability, language, or socioeconomic status is essential for effective implementation of their services or research, psychologists have or

obtain the training, experience, consultation, or supervision necessary to ensure the competence of their services, or they make appropriate referrals, except as provided in Standard 2.02, Providing Services in Emergencies. (2010, pp. 1063–1064)

Competence includes knowledge of both individual and group differences. On the one hand, the clinician must become adequately knowledgeable and respectful of the client's relevant cultural or socioeconomic contexts. Therapists who ignore cultural values, attitudes, and behaviors different from their own deprive themselves of crucial information and may tend to impose their own worldview and assumptions on clients in a misguided and harmful approach. On the other hand, the clinician must avoid making simplistic, unfounded assumptions on the basis of cultural or other identity factors and contexts such as sex and gender, race and ethnicity, socioeconomic status, sexual orientation, heritage, immigration experience, disabilities, religion and spirituality. Knowledge of how those strands of identity combine to influence problems, life challenges, and ways of coping becomes the basis for informed inquiry rather than the illusion of uniform group characteristics with which to stereotype the client. Neither variation between groups nor within groups can be discounted or ignored (Vasquez, in press).

Some readers may object to the apparent restriction of this two-fold ethical responsibility to clinical situations in which the clinician and client are of different cultural identities. They might argue that the need to understand any client's background or context and avoid assuming that the individual can somehow be summarized by certain group characteristics are essential ethical responsibilities in any clinical endeavor. We generally agree with that view. As Pedersen, Draguns, Lonner, and Trimble (1989, p. 1) emphasize in *Counseling Across Cultures*, "Multicultural counseling is not an exotic topic that applies to remote regions, but is the heart and core of good counseling with any client."

However, historically, many training programs have fallen short in showing us why cultural diversity matters and how we can put our cultural knowledge to use so that our assessments and therapy truly fit the individual, effectively addressing clinical needs in full context. When we fail to reach beyond the context, values, and views of the majority culture and traditional therapy, our work may stray from the appropriate to the useless or even to the oppressive (Burkard & Knox, 2004; Gómez, 2015; Sue, 1978, 2015b). Psychological theories may attempt universal generalization without any scientific evidence, valid explanation, or critical thinking. Greene (1997a), for example, noted that sometimes the empirical literature does not take account of cultural and other differences:

A preponderance of the empirical research on or with lesbians and gay men has been conducted with overwhelmingly white, middle-class respondents

(Chan, 1989, 1992; Gamets & Kimmel, 1991; Gock, 1985; Greene, 1994, 1996; Greene & Boyd-Franklin, 1996; Mays & Cochran, 1988; Morales, 1992). Similarly, research on members of ethnic minority groups rarely acknowledges differences in sexual orientation among group members. Hence there has been little exploration of the complex interaction between sexual orientation and ethnic identity development, nor have the realistic social tasks and stressors that are a component of gay and lesbian identity formation in conjunction with ethnic identity formation been taken into account. Discussion of the vicissitudes of racism and ethnic identity in intra- and interracial couples of the same gender and their effects on these couples' relationships has also been neglected in the narrow focus on heterosexual relationships found in the literature on ethnic minority clients. There has been an equally narrow focus on predominantly white couples in the gay and lesbian literature. (pp. 216–217)

Yet even within such a complex framework of cultural and other forms of difference, it may be deceptively tempting to view each person as a fixed set of characteristics or descriptors:

Although identity is a fluid concept in psychological and sociological terms, we tend to speak of identities in fixed terms. In particular, those aspects of identity that characterize observable physical characteristics, such as race or gender, are perceived as unchanging ascribed identities. Examples of these would include identifications such as *Chinese woman*, or *Korean American woman*, or even broader terms such as *woman of color*, which are ways of grouping together individuals who are not of the hegemonic "white" race in the United States. We base these constructions of identity upon physical appearance and an individual's declaration of identity. However, even these seemingly clear distinctions are not definitive. For example, I, as a woman of Asian racial background, may declare myself a woman of color because I see myself as belonging to a group of ethnic/racial minorities. However, my (bio-logical) sister could insist that she is not a woman of color because she does not feel an affiliation with our group goals, even though she is a person of Chi-nese ancestry. Does her nonaffiliation take her out of the group of people of color? Or does she remain in regardless of her own self-identification because of her obvious physical characteristics? Generally, in the context of identities based upon racial and physical characteristics, ascribed identities will, rightly or wrongly, continue to be attributed to individuals by others. It is left up to individuals themselves to assert their identities and demonstrate to others that they are or are not what they might appear to be upon first notice. (Chan, 1997, pp. 240–241; see also Wyatt, 1997)

BRINGING IT ALL BACK HOME

We meet the diversity of cultures, races, religions, and so many other forms of difference as we go about our lives, we learn about it in our studies, we work on developing ethical intelligence in approaching it in our clinical work, but we also carry our own private — and sometimes not so private — views and feelings about specific cultures, races, religions, and so on. Most readers would have no trouble naming areas in the world in which people are fighting each other in part because of religion, culture, ethnicity, and similar factors. Most could name groups in their own countries that view members of another group with suspicion, unease, resentment, disdain, or hostility.

It would be remarkable if we therapists were completely free of the prejudices that afflict the rest of humanity. Life is remarkable in so many ways, but not that one. For any of us, various cultural, racial, ethnic, political, religious, and other groups — or topics related to these groups — may evoke an intense emotional response. The response may be subtle or powerful. We may be ashamed of it or embrace it as important. We may be reluctant to mention it to certain people. We may view it as not politically correct or — a more forbidding barrier for many of us — as not emotionally correct (Pope, Sonne, & Greene, 2006).

These psychological reactions may block or diminish our competence to work with certain issues or certain groups. It is important to assess not only our intellectual competence but also what Pope and Brown (1996) termed *emotional competence for therapy*. We invite each of us to take a moment now to ask ourselves privately:

- Do you have positive or negative feelings toward most or virtually all members of any particular groups based on race, ethnicity, religion, culture, ability and disability status (e.g., possessing or lacking the ability to see, hear, walk), gender, age, sexual orientation or identity, or other such factors?
- If so, how if at all do you think it affects your clinical work?
- Would you feel comfortable hiring, supervising, or accepting as a client, or working for a member of that group?
- Would you feel comfortable sharing these feelings with your graduate school faculty, internship supervisors, employer, or colleagues?
- Have you shared these feelings with your graduate school faculty, internship supervisors, employer, or colleagues?
- How well do you believe your graduate program, internship, and continuing education courses have dealt with these issues?
- How well do you believe the profession has dealt with these issues?
- Do you believe it is paying too much, too little, or just about the right amount of attention to them?

Becoming aware of the ways we may fail to recognize and respect a group that is different from us challenges all of us. Easy to recognize in theory, the influence of our own culture and context often escapes our notice in practice. A remarkable book, *The Spirit Catches You and You Fall Down: A Hmong*

Child, Her American Doctors, and the Collision of Two Cultures (Fadiman, 1997), illustrates the potential costs of overlooking the influence of culture and context on everyone involved. The book describes the efforts of a California hospital staff and a Laotian refugee family to help a Hmong child whose American doctors had diagnosed with epilepsy. Everyone involved had the best of intentions and worked hard to help the girl, but a lack of awareness of cultural differences had tragic effects. The book quotes medical anthropologist Arthur Kleinman:

> As powerful an influence as the culture of the Hmong patient and her family is on this case, the culture of biomedicine is equally powerful. If you can't see that your own culture has its own set of interests, emotions, and biases, how can you expect to deal successfully with someone else's culture? (p. 261)

CONTEXT OF OPPRESSION, EXCLUSION, DISCRIMINATION, AND INEQUITY

Canetto, Timpson, Borrayo & Vang (2003) show how addressing diversity — with its variability in individual and group identities and characteristics, including social and cultural identities — must include recognizing the ever-present influences of unequal social status, acceptance, power, privilege, and wealth. Groups with significantly less social status, acceptance, power, privilege, wealth, and access to fair hearings before the courts often share experiences of oppression, exclusion, discrimination, and lack of both human and civil rights that differ sharply from the experiences of the mainstream or dominant group. Ethical intelligence and cultural competence include recognizing that in whatever country or region we live, some groups in our society confront clearly different conditions from those of the mainstream. What does this mean for our clinical work?

A positive sense of self worth and self-respect are essential ingredients of healthy identity and humanness. Both open and covert discrimination attack the self-worth of the person serving as its target. People subjected to dehumanizing treatment often become anxious, depressed, ashamed, and lonely. Dignity is as essential to psychological well-being as water, food and oxygen are to human life. Lewis, Cogburn, & Williams (2015) reviewed studies showing consistent associations between exposure to discrimination and a wide range of diagnosed mental disorders as well as objective physical health outcomes. Clinically and ethically competent therapy depends on our understanding how such experiences have affected our clients as well as our own potential for responding — however unintentionally — with our own biases, prejudices, unjustified assumptions, or microaggressions.

In "Do We Practice What We Preach? An Exploratory Survey of Multicultural Psychotherapy Competencies," Nancy Hansen and her colleagues presented the results of a study that found that "overall and for 86% of the individual items, participants did not practice what they preached" (Hansen et al., 2006, p. 66) in terms of what they endorsed as the need for multicultural competencies. They concluded that

> psychotherapists need to recognize their vulnerability to not following through with what they know to be competent practice, and they need, in advance, to problem solve creative solutions. It would be helpful to identify your personal barriers in this regard: Are you anxious about raising certain issues with racially/ethnically different clients? Are you uncertain about how best to intervene? Do you fear you will 'get in over your head' exploring these issues? What will it take to work through (or around) these barriers to become more racially/ethnically responsive in your psychotherapy work? (p. 72)

The next section focuses on recognizing those barriers and overcoming them.

OVERCOMING BARRIERS TO ETHICAL SERVICES

Keeping our eyes open to the following issues can help us recognize and overcome barriers to ethical services.

One good place to start is to look at how our graduate training programs are experienced by some students. To what degree is diversity respected, valued, welcomed, its potential approached in positive, creative ways? To what extent is it approached in ways that divide, isolate, set people against each other? Franklin (2009), for example, wrote:

> Ethnic minority students often felt trapped between, if not victimized by, the roles of cultural educator and student. However, students as cultural brokers in class are often educators without a portfolio in the eyes of professors and fellow classmates. Challenging psychological information being presented that did not accurately represent our experiences could bring...a label as an impudent student. Parenthetically, it was not uncommon to have our personal insights as members of the community also challenged or dismissed by professors or researchers who had no experience with our communities other than their readings in psychology. This was infuriating to many colleagues and students, given their lived experiences.... These in class and work experiences were frustrating, intimidating, humiliating, and discouraging to students and subsequently early career professionals in particular. This circumstance continues to contribute to the attrition of students of color in training programs and later becomes a deterrent to participation in organized psychology. (p. 419; see also Kaduvettoor, O'Shaughnessy, Mori, et al., 2009)

Socioeconomic Differences

We've mentioned several identity factors and contexts as important to consider, such as race and ethnicity, sex and gender, sexual orientation, heritage, immigration experience, disabilities, religion, and spirituality. Another critical aspect of ethical intelligence is maintaining active awareness of the socioeconomic differences that exist in our society. It is exceptionally easy for us to create a cognitive map of the world in which over 90% of the area is represented by our own immediate environment. We lose active awareness that many people live in significantly different contexts. We minimize the differences and forget the contrasts and their implications.

An epidemiological study of New York City published in the *New England Journal of Medicine* (McCord & Freeman, 1990; see also Geronimus, Bound, Waidmann, Hillemeier, & Burns, 1996; Lee, Marotta, Blay-Tofey, Wang, & de Bourmont, 2014) provides an example of the extreme conditions for some U.S. citizens. The analysis showed that 54 of the 353 health areas in New York City had at least double the anticipated mortality rate for people under 65 years old.

With only one exception, all of these 54 areas were predominantly African American or Hispanic. "Survival analysis showed that black men in Harlem were less likely to reach the age of 65 than men in Bangladesh" (p. 173). The authors pointed out that their findings were similar to those for natural disaster areas.

What does it mean to us as psychotherapists and counselors that our fellow citizens live in such conditions? At a minimum, it requires that we acknowledge the reality of such conditions and inform ourselves adequately when we provide services to those from such lethal conditions or from other distinct contexts that differ from our own.

Providing services also entails awareness of how the conditions themselves may affect treatment choices in ways that may be questionable. Research suggests, for example, poor children are 4 times more likely than children who are not poor to receive anti-psychotic medications, and also to receive them for less severe conditions (Wilson, 2009).

Research also suggests that people of low socioeconomic status are more likely to become depressed and experience persistent depressive symptoms (Lorant et al., 2003). Lack of access to critical economic and social resources is stressful and depression often develops in the context of psychosocial stress. Stress arises not only from material deprivation but also from perceptions and experiences of relative inequality. Stress-based theories of health suggest that lack of access to economic and social resources and other sources of stress exposure due to social disadvantage, such as racism and discrimination, may increase risk for poor physical and mental health.

But such conditions also confront us with inescapable ethical questions regarding the degree to which we as individuals and as a profession view ourselves as responsible in some part for addressing these conditions, regardless of whether circumstances bring clients from those conditions to our offices. There is an extensive literature exploring these questions from diverse perspectives (APA, 2003b; Arredondo et al., 1996; Brown, 1994b, 1996; Casas, Cabrera & Vasquez, 2014; Constantine & Sue, 2005; Feminist Therapy Institute, 1987; Goodyear & Sinnett, 1984; Harper & McFadden, 2003; Lott & Bullock, 2001, 2007; Moodley & Palmer, 2006; Pack-Brown & Williams, 2003; Pope, 1990b; Roysircar, Sandhu, & Bibbins, 2003; Sue, 1995).

Potential Problems With Assessment Instruments

Another useful step in addressing the issue of difference is to remain alert to the possibility that standardized tests and other assessment instruments may manifest bias. APA Ethics Code Standard 9.06, Interpreting Assessment Results, speaks to competency in assessment in reminding psychologists that when interpreting assessment results they take into account various factors, including situational, personal, linguistic, and cultural differences that might affect psychologists' judgments or reduce the accuracy of their interpretations (APA, 2010). A culturally competent assessment implies the importance of the consideration of the many aspects of human difference. The social construction of race and ethnicity, gender, social class, and other variables affects the various strands of identities, and is important to consider in the assessment process and reporting of reports (Vasquez, 2015).

LaFromboise and Foster (1989), for example, discuss the case of *Larry P. v. Riles* in which the intelligence testing that led to the placement of an African American student into a special education class was unlawful because of the bias of the tests used. They describe two instruments that were specifically developed to avoid racial or cultural bias in assessment of abilities: the Adaptive Behavior Scale (American Association on Mental Deficiency, 1974) and the System of Multicultural Pluralistic Assessment (Mercer, 1979).

An example of a standardized personality test that has been called into question in regard to potential bias is the original Minnesota Multiphasic Personality Inventory (MMPI; not the revised MMPI-2). African Americans, Native Americans, Hispanics, and Asian Americans were among the groups omitted from the sample from which the original MMPI norms were developed. What implications does this exclusion have for the ethical use of the test? Faschingbauer (1979) vividly described his reservations:

> The original Minnesota group seems to be an inappropriate reference group for the 1980s. The median individual in that group had an eighth-grade education, was married, lived in a small town or on a farm, and was employed as a lower level clerk or skilled tradesman. None was under 16 or over 65 years of age, and all were white. As a clinician I find it difficult to justify comparing

anyone to such a dated group. When the person is 14 years old, Chicano, and lives in Houston's poor fifth ward, use of original norms seems sinful. (p. 385)

A former president of the APA Division of the Society for Personality Assessment, Phil Erdberg (1988), reported that in one research study, a single item from the original MMPI discriminated perfectly on the basis of race, that is, it differentiated all African American test takers from all Caucasian test takers in this rural community. These problems were carefully considered in the revision process leading to the MMPI-2 and MMPI-A (Pope, Butcher, & Seelen, 2006).

Cultural competence must include recognizing these challenges in appropriate development, selection, and use of tests especially given the incredible diversity of groups (Vasquez, 2015). Language and acculturative learning, for example, have been identified as two of the most critical variables related to test performance in evaluation of intelligence and learning disability (Ortiz & Melo, 2015). In addition, educational level and socioeconomic status affect neuropsychological testing of Spanish speakers (Puente, Ojeda, Zink, & Portillo Reyes, 2015).

Fallacies of Difference

Another useful step in addressing issues of difference effectively is to remain mindfully aware of common fallacies in the interpretation of group and individual differences. Pat O'Neill (2005), a former president of the Canadian Psychological Association, discusses the common fallacy of misinterpreting correlation between a particular difference and a problem as the difference causing the problem:

> In those days (the early 1970s), we early community psychology graduate students were reading William Ryan's (1971) *Blaming the Victim*. Ryan presented example after example of social problems being reduced to individual differences. The strategy, Ryan said, was to find out how the afflicted person differed from others, then treat that difference as the cause of the problem. He called this "the art of savage discovery." (p. 13)

Potential Problems in the Clinical Relationship

Maintaining active awareness of the subtle ways that issues of difference affect our relationship with clients can be an essential step to avoiding pitfalls. Whether we are conducting an assessment or conducting therapy or counseling, our interaction with the client is of great significance. J. M. Jones (1990) reviewed a variety of research studies demonstrating the degree to which such factors as race could, if not addressed carefully, undermine the process. For example, failing to take such factors into account can contribute to a high premature dropout rate for minorities seeking mental health services.

One set of studies conducted by Word, Zanna, and Cooper (1974) demonstrates the degree to which subtle, unintentional discrimination by the individual conducting the assessment can lead to impaired performance by the person being assessed. In the first part of the study, White interviewers asked questions of both White and African American individuals. There were significant differences in interviewer behavior. Those conducting the assessment spent more time with the White interviewees, looked directly at White interviewees a greater portion of the time, maintained less physical distance from White interviewees, and made fewer speech errors with White interviewees.

For the second part of the study, White interviewers were trained to become aware of and use both styles of interview. They were then asked to interview a number of White people. With half of the White interviewees, the interviewer conducted the interview in a style consistent for White interviewees (for example, a longer interview at less distance). With the other half of the White interviewees, the interviewer followed a style consistent for Black interviewees (shorter interview, more distance). The latter interviewees performed much less well on a series of objective measures during the assessment interview. Thus, even if the tests or assessment instruments themselves are relatively free of bias, the behavior of the interviewer can influence those who are being assessed in a discriminatory way that impairs performance.

In "Why Can't We Just Get Along? Interpersonal Biases and Interracial Distrust," Dovidio, Gaertner, Kawakami, and Hodson (2002; see also Sue, 2015a) reviewed a series of studies showing that contemporary racism can be subtle, unintentional, and below the level of awareness. The ways that racial bias — operating outside awareness — can influence interactions between two people (for example, a therapist and client) may create or nurture race-based self-fulfilling processes. Taking into consideration research findings by Dovidio and his colleagues and others who study this area may help enable us to acknowledge and address these issues more directly.

Perhaps one of the greatest challenges is how to reconcile the trend toward using interventions that have been supported by research — a trend that in practice has led toward uniform therapies provided to broad ranges of clients — with the exceptional diversity of clients. In "Cultural Adaptation of Treatments: A Resource for Considering Culture in Evidence-Based Practice," Bernal, Jiménez-Chafey, and Rodríguez (2009) wrote that

> with the increased focus on empirical information regarding treatment development, efficacy, or effectiveness, the past two decades have been marked by efforts to achieve uniformity in providing care to a broad base of clients. Promoting a systematic approach to treatment is a double-edged sword; on one hand, greater structure for researchers and practitioners and a call for

accountability for treatment and research procedures are attractive features for those who espouse a scientist-practitioner model to psychological practice or training. On the other hand, such systematization can potentially increase the risk of adopting a one-size-fits-all approach to interventions and intervention research that is contrary in practice to what the movement intended to promote in spirit (i.e., competent practice). (p. 361)

Creative methods being developed to meet this challenge are provided or reviewed by Bernal and Domenech Rodriguez (2012); Bernal, Jiménez-Chafey, and Rodríguez (2009); Hays (2008, 2009); Huey, Tilley, Jones and Smith, 2014; Horrell (2008); Hwang (2009); Kendall and Beidas (2007); Kim, Yang, and Hwang (2006); Matos, Torres, and Santiago (2006); Nicolas, Arntz, and Hirsch (2009); Pederson et al. (2008); D. W. Sue and Sue (2008); Vasquez (2007; in press); Weisner and Hay, 2015; and Whaley and Davis (2007).

Appreciating Cultural Specifics and Their Effects

Addressing the issue of difference involves more than acknowledging important differences and avoiding prejudice and stereotyping; it involves an active appreciation of the context in which clients live and understand their lives. Westermeyer (1987, pp. 471–472) provides an example of this appreciation:

A 48-year-old ethnic Chinese woman had been receiving antipsychotic and antidepressant medication for psychotic depression. On this regimen, the patient had lost even more weight and more hope and had become more immobilized. A critical element in this diagnosis of psychosis was the woman's belief that her deceased mother, who had been appearing in her dreams, had traveled from the place of the dead to induce the patient's own death and to bring her to the next world. We interpreted this symptom not as a delusional belief but as a culturally consistent belief in a depressed woman who had recently begun to see her deceased mother in her dreams (a common harbinger of death in the dreams of some Asian patients). This patient responded well after the antipsychotic medication was discontinued, the antidepressant medication was reduced in dosage, and weekly psychotherapy was instituted.

Similarly, the research of Amaro, Russo, and Johnson (1987) demonstrates the importance of an attentive and informed appreciation of different contexts. In comparing sources of strength and stress for Hispanic and Anglo female professionals, they found similar family and work characteristics to be associated with positive mental health. Income was the most consistently related demographic factor across all measures of psychological well-being. In addition, Hispanic women's psychological well-being was related to the experience of discrimination, which was reported by more than 82% of the sample. Those of us who are not subject to discrimination in our day-to-day lives may find it easy to misinterpret and mistreat the distress and dysfunction that can result from prejudice.

Future research will hopefully shed light on the strengths and survivorship of various ethnic groups in the face of systematic and persistent challenges. Cultural factors may provide powerful sources of emotional resilience. Various reports, for example, indicated that despite enduring poverty-level income, many Latinos exhibit values and behaviors reflective of significant resilience. The CDC reports that Hispanics living in the United States enjoy significantly better health, though not in all areas, than Whites who are not Hispanic (Bernstein & Nutt, 2015). Latinas have the highest life expectancy rate of any other group in the United States! Latinas, who were age 25 in 2008, can expect to live 84 years, or 4.3 years longer than their male Hispanic counterparts, 2.7 and 5.8 years longer than White and African American women, respectively. Life expectancy for Hispanic males, who were 25-years old in 2008, is 79.7 years. They will outlast their non-Hispanic White agemates by 2.4 years and their Black cohorts by 7.3 years (Arias, 2010). How do we explain this finding? Among the possibilities are that because extended families provide emotional support, Hispanic women are less likely to live alone and less likely to be smokers or drinkers, they may have a better diet, and their infant mortality rate is lower than that of other groups. Research may uncover keys to sources of resilience for specific groups facing specific challenges, and these keys may help guide therapy, social interventions, and policy.

Context of Language

In some cases, cultural and other forms of difference are relevant to therapists and counselors in assessing their fundamental competence to render services:

> When approached by people in need, therapists need to evaluate whether the anticipated issues fall within their realm of competence or expertise. To use an extreme example, an Anglo therapist who speaks only English and has never learned about or conducted clinical work with abuse victims should evaluate carefully whether he or she is the best person to work with a Hispanic patient who speaks very little English and who has recently recovered memories of childhood sexual abuse. Even when therapist and client speak the same basic language, it can be important to attend carefully to possible regional cultural or language differences that could lead to potentially problematic confusions of meaning. In one instance, a woman born in Puerto Rico walked into her office and found someone rifling through her purse. The potential thief ran off in the midst of an emotional confrontation, although no one was touched. Later, the woman described this event in Spanish to a social worker who had been born in Cuba. She used the word *asalto* to mean a "confrontation." The social worker, however, understood this term to refer to

a physical assault . . . because the term was used differently in Cuban Spanish than in Puerto Rican Spanish. (Pope & Brown, 1996, pp. 179–180)

Perlin and McClain (2009) describe another example of the problems that can occur when cultural factors are not considered in translations:

> Semantic or translation equivalence refers specifically to whether concepts can be appropriately conveyed from one culture to another when translated. Discrepancies can lead to nonequivalence. For example, a Chinese man living in the United States was charged with [the] homicide of his work supervisor. At the trial, interpreters were used by both prosecution and defense. However, the (female) defense interpreter modified the words to avoid using disrespectful curse words . . . spoken by the victim instead of his actual words . . . . Similarly, the prosecution interpreter used the word "killed" the boss more than ten times with a knife instead of "stabbed." Thus, instead of interpreting the defendant's words to say he used a knife to try to defend himself when his boss pulled a knife, his words were interpreted to say that he "killed" the boss . . . . (p. 265)

H. R. Searight and Searight (2009) provide recommendations for clinicians working with foreign language interpreters. Centeno (2009) discusses practical issues in providing clinical services to minority bilingual patients whose ability to communicate has been impaired by strokes and other medical causes.

Creativity

Yet another step involves a creative and thorough approach to human diversity. In a careful series of studies at Harvard University, Langer, Bashner, and Chanowitz (1985) asked children to consider individuals who were different from the mainstream in that they were physically disabled. In one study, the experimental group of children were asked to think of as many ways as possible that a disabled person might meet a particular challenge, and the control group children were simply asked if the disabled person could meet the challenge. For example, children were shown a picture of a woman in a wheelchair and were asked either *how* the woman could drive a car or *whether* the woman could drive a car. In another study, children in the experimental group were asked to give numerous reasons not only that a disabled individual — a blind person, for example — might be bad at a particular profession but also why he or she might be good at it.

In these and other studies, Langer (2014) found that creativity in responding to forms of human difference can indeed be taught and that it can lead to more realistic, less prejudiced reactions to individuals who differ in some way from the mainstream. The research showed that children can be taught that handicaps are function-specific and not person-specific. Those given training in making mindful distinctions learned to be discriminating without prejudice. This group was also less likely than the control group to avoid a handicapped person. In essence, the children were taught that attributes are relative and not absolute, that whether or not something is a disability depends on context. (p. 168)

Whether we practice in private offices, HMOs, hospitals, clinics, community mental health centers, university settings, or elsewhere, we must remain alert and creative in regard to the contexts in which we work and the characteristics of those who need our help. Is our setting responsive to the needs of those who use wheelchairs, those for whom English is a new language, those who use American Sign Language to communicate, or those who are blind? For whom is our setting open, inviting, accessible, and genuinely helpful? Who is shut out or discouraged from approaching? To what degree do we acknowledge or assume responsibility for the nature of the settings in which we practice?

Beware Barnum

In 1949, Bert Forer published a landmark experiment. He gave his students the results of a personality test they had taken. The students tended to be surprised at how well the test had captured their own unique personality. He then revealed that each student had received the same description: a list of statements that tended to apply to almost everyone. Paul Meehl (1956) named Forer's finding the "Barnum Effect" in honor of P. T. Barnum's idea that the circus should have something for everybody.

Research continues to find the "Barnum Effect" popping up in diverse environments. Henley-Einion and Blagrove (2014), Lawson and Crane (2014), Mason and Budge (2011), Pant, McCabe, Deskovitz, Weed, and Williams (2014), and Weinstein (2015) provide a few recent examples.

Levy (2010) discusses how easy such fits-almost-everyone statements can play into stereotypes. Here are a few of his "Sociocultural Barnum Statements" (p. 255):

- Caucasians favor members of their own group.
- Latinos can be very passionate.
- Italians enjoy food.
- African Americans are sensitive to certain words.
- Christians try to forgive.
- Jewish people yearn to survive.
- Europeans have had their share of troubles.
- Americans are a diverse group of individuals.
- Minorities just want their rights.
- Senior citizens don't want to be ignored.

- Infants seek pleasure.
- Teenagers want to be seen for who they are.
- Men care about success.
- Women resent being taken for granted.
- The physically disabled resent being seen as inferior.
- Artists want the freedom to express themselves.
- Schizophrenics view the world in a unique way.

Speaking Openly, Honestly, and Respectfully

Racial, cultural, and other group differences can make us uncomfortable. Pope, Sonne, and Greene (2006) discussed the ways in which certain topics have become taboo, the myths that flourish in the absence of frank discussion, and the harm that often follows. It is important that relevant issues be addressed openly and frankly. This process obviously does not mean replacing silence and avoidance with politically correct (or psychologically correct) clichés but rather approaching the issues honestly. Discussing how race, religion, and culture influenced clinical work with older people, Hinrichsen (2006) wrote:

> How are ethnic or minority service providers perceived by White older clients? An African American psychology intern in her mid-20s whom I supervised began to conduct psychotherapy with a man in his 70s for the treatment of depression triggered by an increasing number of health problems. The intern mentioned that the older client persisted with telling stories about "Negro fellas" in the army during World War II. The emphasis of the stories was usually on how much he liked his Black comrades and the contributions that they made to the army. When asked how she handled this issue, the intern reported she said to the older client, "I guess you noticed I'm Black." This statement led to a productive discussion of a variety of concerns that included worry that he might say something racially related that would offend the intern and concern about whether a Black service provider could understand his experience. At times, during intakes into our geriatric clinic, a prospective client will frankly state, "I'd like a White doctor" or "I want a Jewish doctor." Clinical geropsychologists sometimes have noted that some older adults will make disparaging racial or ethnic remarks rarely made by younger adults. In part, open expression of these remarks reflects the reality that the current generation of older adults grew into adulthood during a time when racial and ethnic segregation were government and institution sanctioned and that it was socially acceptable in some circles to publicly and unfavorably caricature racial or ethnic minorities. (p. 32)

Ethical intelligence helps us to navigate the conflicts and difficulties that diversity can sometimes bring as well as to appreciate the strengths, new perspectives, opportunities for growth, untapped potential that it can bring to our work. Taking the risk of being open and honest with ourselves, our professors, our supervisors, our students, and our colleagues about our discomforts can, as discussed earlier in this chapter, help us develop ethical competence in dealing with diversity and difference. It can feel like an even greater risk to listen respectfully with an open mind and heart when a professor, supervisor, student, or colleague challenges our most firmly held beliefs in these areas. It is so much easier to dismiss, discount, or disparage those who disagree sharply with us. We might take a page from the clinical literature. Qualities that can contribute to working effectively with culturally different individuals include being flexible, honest, respectful, trustworthy, confident, warm, interested and open (Ackerman & Hilsenroth, 2003; see also Decker, Nich, Carroll, & Martino, 2014; Fife, Whiting, Bradford, & Davis, 2014; Heinonen, Lindfors, Härkänen, Virtal, Jääskeläinen, & Knekt, 2014; Holdsworth, Bowen, Brown, & Howat, 2014; Zeeck, Orlinsky, Hermann, et al., 2012).

Being flexible, honest, respectful, trustworthy, confidant, warm, interested and open — not a bad way for us to be with our professors, supervisors, students, and colleagues, as well as with our clients.

SCENARIOS FOR DISCUSSION

You are conducting an intake examination at an HMO. The client's first words to you are, "I'm having some problems with my sexual identity, but I think I can only work with someone who understands where I'm coming from, who has faced these same issues, and who knows what its like. What's your sexual orientation?"

- How do you feel?
- What goals would you have in mind in responding to the client?
- Under what conditions, if any, would you disclose your sexual identity to the client?
- To what extent has your training included research and theory relevant to sexual identity?

You share a suite of offices with several other therapists. The name of each therapist is on the door to that therapist's office. One morning you find that the door to one of the offices has been broken in and the office vandalized. The name on the door was Jewish. Swastikas along with epithets have been spray-painted on the walls, desk, floor, and bookshelves. You have no evidence but believe the vandal may have been one of your patients — someone who has expressed strong anti-Semitic views during therapy sessions, embraces the view that the

Holocaust is fiction, and has described fantasies of vandalizing synagogues. But if you were to ask him during the next therapy session whether he had anything to do with vandalizing your colleague's office, he would deny it.

- How do you feel?
- What would you like to do?
- What do you think you would actually do?
- Would you mention your suspicion that your client may have vandalized your colleague's office to the colleague, the police, or anyone else? If so, how do you address issues of client privacy and confidentiality?
- Would you mention your suspicion to your client? If so, how?
- How, if at all, would you address your client's anti-Semitism in therapy?

You are a Latino psychotherapist who speaks Spanish only moderately well. Your policy is to try to refer all those who speak only Spanish to fluent Spanish speakers, but you will see Spanish speakers who also speak English if they wish. A South American client who speaks fluent English and Spanish sees you because you are the only Latino available on her HMO list. At the first session, she insists that you should be ashamed for not speaking better Spanish and that you therefore have no culture.

- How do you feel?
- What are your thoughts and feelings about this client?
- How would you respond to this client?
- Under what conditions would you continue to see or decline to see this client?

You have been leading a therapy group at a large mental health facility. As one of the sessions begins, a group member interrupts you and says, "I want to ask you about something. Have you noticed how none of the doctors here are Black, Latino, or Latina but almost all the cleaning crew are? Why do you work in a system like that? Don't you think that has any effects on us patients?"

- How do you feel?
- What are the possible replies you consider?

(*continued*)

(continued)

- What do you think you would say?
- What effects, if any, might such a system have on clients?

You work in a large office building. As your therapy client, a Sikh, is getting ready to leave your office, the police show up at the door, handcuff him, and say they are taking him to the station for questioning. When they leave, the accountant across the hall comes over and says that someone saw your client in the lobby, thought he was acting suspiciously, and called the police to report someone who seemed to be an Arab terrorist.

- How do you feel?
- What do you consider doing?
- What would you like to do?
- What do you think you would do?
- How, if at all, might this affect the therapy?
- How, if at all, would you chart this?

You are working with a client who is of a different race and sexual orientation from you and your supervisor. One day the client is 15 minutes late for a session, and you spend some of the session discussing the reasons for the client not being on time. When you bring up the topic to your supervisor, the response is, "Oh, that lateness doesn't mean anything psychological. That's just the way those people are."

- How do you feel?
- What possible responses to your supervisor's comments do you consider?
- What do you think that you'd actually say to your supervisor?
- When you imagined this scenario, what race and sexual orientation did you imagine the client was? Why?

A married couple come to you for counseling. Both believe that men are the natural leaders in a marriage and that a woman's rightful place is to be obedient to her husband. However, they often have what they describe as "slips," when he seems to look to her for guidance or when she finds it hard to accept his decisions. They are seeking marital counseling to help them eliminate these "slips."

- How do you feel?
- What are your thoughts and feelings about the wife?
- What are your thoughts and feelings about the husband?
- What are your thoughts and feelings about the marital relationship that they value and have chosen for themselves?
- How do you think you would respond?

You are a therapist at an agency with a policy that says that if a client misses two appointments without calling, the therapy automatically terminates. A client who is a single mother, uses public transportation, has no telephone, and is often distressed by a babysitter who does not show up, misses her appointment for the second time. Your supervisor insists that you terminate by letter, given the long waiting list of potential clients.

- What feelings do you experience?
- What are your assumptions about the client's not showing up? In what way, if any, might her diagnosis be relevant?
- What do you think and feel about the relevance of the policy for clients such as this one?
- What are your options in responding to your supervisor? To the agency policy? To the client?

Chapter 24

CONFIDENTIALITY

Clients trust us to guard their confidences. They trust that digital records of their diagnosis, treatment plan, home address, and billing information will not spill out onto the Internet, finding their way to social media, curious eyes, and identity thieves. They trust that we will lock up paper charts. They trust us not to discuss their treatment with colleagues as we walk down hospital halls, eat in the clinic cafeteria, or chat on a cell phone at the train station.

Leaks of all kinds can cause all kinds of problems. A hurried response to a subpoena may allow a law firm to get their hands on documents they

Note to Readers

Confidentiality has emerged as a major, persistent ethical challenge for psychologists. Over half (62%) of the therapists in one national study reported unintentionally violating their patients' confidences (Pope, Tabachnick, & Keith-Spiegel, 1987). Another national study found that the most frequently reported intentional violation of the law or ethical standards by senior, prominent psychologists involved confidentiality (Pope & Bajt, 1988). In 21% of the cases, therapists violated confidentiality in transgression of law. In another 21% of the cases, therapists refused to breach confidentiality to make legally required reports of child abuse. Therapists may have experienced violations of confidentiality when they themselves were patients. In one national survey, about 10% of the therapists who had been in therapy reported that their own therapist had violated their rights to confidentiality (Pope & Tabachnick, 1994).

have no right to. A phone message asking a client to return a call may let a battered woman's partner discover that against his wishes she has reached out to a therapist.

The consequences of seemingly confidential information passed along without the client's awareness can hit clients without warning. According to a CBC News report,

> More than a dozen Canadians have told the Psychiatric Patient Advocate Office in Toronto within the past year that they were blocked from entering the United States after their records of mental illness were shared with the U.S. Department of Homeland Security.... According to diplomatic cables released earlier this year by WikiLeaks, any information entered into the national Canadian Police Information Centre (CPIC) database is accessible to American authorities. Local police officers take notes whenever they apprehend an individual or respond to a 911 call, and some of this information is then entered into the CPIC database, says Stylianos.... [RCMP Insp. Denis St. Pierre says the CPIC] 'also can contain individuals' history of mental illness, including suicide attempts.' (Bridge, 2011; see also "Canadians' Mental-Health Info Routinely Shared With FBI, U.S. Customs," 2014)

Clinicians may communicate, with the client's consent, confidential clinical information to insurance companies, managed care companies, and other agencies as a condition of coverage. With increasing frequency, these arrays of confidential information are subsequently aggregated into large research databases in ways intended to make it impossible to identify individual clients. But can sophisticated strategies reidentify individuals and put the information into the hands of advertisers, loan officers, employment screeners, law enforcement, credit monitoring agencies, and others willing to pay for the data or extract it on their own?

Latanya Sweeney, Director of Harvard's Data Privacy Lab, reported in a *Scientific American* interview that she had reidentified people with Huntington's disease although all identifying information had been removed in creating a large database. She described how a banker followed a cross-referencing strategy when looking at publicly available de-identified data "to see if any of his clients had cancer. If they did, he called in their loans" (Walter, 2007, p. 92; see also Benitez & Malin, 2010; El Emam, Jonker, Arbuckle, & Malin, 2011; Gymrek, McGuire, Golan, Halperin, & Erlich, 2013; Loukides, Denny, & Malin, 2010; Rothstein, 2010).

Ohm (2010) wrote that

> scientists have demonstrated they can often 'reidentify' or 'deanonymize' individuals hidden in anonymized data with astonishing ease. By understanding this research, we will realize we have made a mistake, labored beneath a fundamental misunderstanding, which has assured us much less privacy than we

have assumed. This mistake pervades nearly every information privacy law, regulation, and debate . . . ' (p. 1701).

The U.S. President's Council of Advisors on Science and Technology reported: "Long used in health-care research and other research areas involving human subjects, anonymization (also termed deidentification) applies when the data, standing alone and without an association to a specific person, do not violate privacy norms . . . . Unfortunately, it is increasingly easy to defeat." (2014, p. 38; see also Daries et al., 2014)

Confidentiality helps clients talk freely but tends to trip up us therapists from time to time and calls for us to strengthen our ethical intelligence. We're all human and none of us can catch and counter all potential threats to confidentiality. Fatigue, stress, and routine dull our awareness, lull us into ethical sleep, put us on automatic when we need to wake up to what we are missing. Threats to confidentiality can disappear into the demands and distractions of our work.

As with driving, even a brief lapse of attention can cause disaster. We do the hard work of sorting through the legislation and case law that govern confidentiality and privilege in our local jurisdiction, study the relevant ethics codes and professional guidelines, consult with an attorney, and keep up with the evolving standards of care. But somehow our mind wanders, our ethical intelligence falters, and we stumble into trouble.

Bemister and Dobson provide a thoughtful analysis of how "maintaining and protecting the confidentiality of client records has become far more complex in recent years" (2011, p. 302; see also Bemister & Dobson, 2012; Pope, 2015a). Allen (2009) discusses additional layers of complexity and potential confusion — resulting in additional pitfalls — that variations in the nature of confidential material and the number of people entitled to receive it can cause. She emphasizes that confidential material includes more than facts alone. "Facts, impressions, events, and data of all sorts can be deemed confidential" (p. 127). Similarly, she notes the great range of people to whom the therapist may — or may not — be allowed or obligated to disclose confidential information. "[T]he community authorized to receive confidential information can be smaller than a family or as large as a workforce" (p. 127; see also Jain & Roberts, 2009).

This chapter highlights some of those easy-to-overlook pitfalls that can lead to violations of confidentiality.

REFERRAL SOURCES

We appreciate referrals. But should we tell the referral source whether someone scheduled an appointment with us, whether the person showed up for the appointment, or what might have been discussed or decided if the patient has not authorized the disclosure? Unfortunately, therapists may unintentionally violate confidentiality by sending referral sources a thank-you note mentioning a specific patient and providing a detail or two about what happened without the patient's knowledge or consent.

PUBLIC CONSULTATION

Consultation provides an invaluable resource for meeting the highest ethical, legal, and clinical standards. It gives us easy access to new information, support, informal peer review, and a different perspective. Psychologists in a national study rated "consultation with colleagues" as the most effective source of guidance for practice (Pope, Tabachnick, & Keith-Spiegel, 1987). They judged such consultation to be more effective than 14 other possible sources, such as graduate programs, internships, state licensing boards, and continuing education programs.

Consultation about patients deserves the same confidentiality as the psychotherapy it focuses on. We lead busy lives and want to make the most of our time. Often the most convenient way to catch a colleague for a quick consult is while we are walking through the halls of a clinic, or sitting together at a large table while waiting for the last arrivals so that a meeting can begin, or at a restaurant during a lunch break, or in other public places. The problem with such on-the-run consultations is that confidential information is often discussed within earshot of people who are not authorized to receive the information. Many of us have probably overheard such talk in clinic hallways or elevators. Perhaps we heard the patient's name, someone we recognized as a friend, neighbor, or colleague. In one case, a therapist consulted a colleague on a crowded elevator about a particularly "difficult" patient, unaware that the patient was standing only a few feet behind her, listening carefully.

Guarding confidentiality includes making sure that we keep private consultations private.

GOSSIP

Few would argue that therapy is easy work. Sometimes it involves considerable stress, and we need to blow off steam. Talking about our work with others — at lunch, in the staff lounge, on the racquetball court, at parties — may make us feel better. Those settings make it easy to let slip the identity of one of our patients or betray what a patient has told us in confidence.

Some patients may be in the news or tell us fascinating information. The urge to tell others that we know them can be almost overwhelming. Many of us may know through the grapevine who is in treatment with whom and even what led them to seek therapy. This kind of insider trading of confidences is unethical.

CASE NOTES AND PATIENT FILES

Have you ever seen a patient's chart you were not authorized to see? It is likely that at least some — if not most — of this book's readers have happened to see unsecured documents containing patient names and other confidential information. Some clinics and individuals may have difficulty meeting their responsibility to keep confidential records confidential. During a visit to a prestigious university-affiliated teaching hospital, one of the authors noticed, while walking down a public hallway, that the mental health clinic's patient charts were stacked along the walls. The hallway was unattended. The names of the patients were clearly visible, and had the author opened any of the charts, he could have read a wealth of confidential information. When he asked later about charts being left in the hall, he was assured that this was temporary: Due to insufficient funds, additional storage space was not yet available, and this manner of "filing" was most convenient for the business office personnel.

Some of us may have visited colleagues who leave charts and other patient information lying on top of their desks. Patients' names and other information may be hard to miss.

There are at least two important issues here. One is keeping information about patients out of sight of people who are not authorized to see that information. Making sure that documents are inside the chart (or some other protective covering), the chart folder is closed, and the patient's name does not appear on the outside of the chart (a coding system can provide for convenient filing and retrieval) are useful steps to take when charts are visible in a well-attended area open to the public or other patients. Guarding even the patient's name may seem excessive to some, yet the fact that a person is consulting a therapist is a fact worth treating confidentially.

The second issue concerns the security of charts left in an unattended area. There should be a lock between the charts and anyone not authorized to see them. Regarding the security of charts, as in so many other aspects of maintaining appropriate confidentiality, the Golden Rule can be a useful guide. What steps would we want a therapist to take if it were our chart, containing our deepest secrets, our personal and family history, our conflicts, our diagnosis, the medications we were taking, and our prognosis? What steps would we want our therapist to take to make sure that no part of this confidential information was carelessly left visible or available to whomever — other patients, our employer or employees, neighbors, relatives, colleagues — might, for any reason, pass by? How much care would we want our own therapist to use in handling these documents?

PHONES, FAXES, AND MESSAGES

Some of this book's readers may have visited clinics in which phone messages mentioning a patient's name, telephone number, and reason for calling were left out where they could be seen by those who should not see it. Some may have visited a colleague's office just as a fax about a patient was coming in and . . . well, just could not help seeing who it was from and what it was about. Some readers may have overheard a therapist take a phone call from a patient and heard both sides of the conversation (and may have been surprised to recognize the patient's voice).

Answering machines and voice mails with speakerphones create special pitfalls for confidentiality. It is tempting, if our time for lunch is limited, to play back accumulated messages — some from patients — while a friend is waiting to accompany us to the nearest restaurant. If our answering machine is at home, we need to make sure that our family, friends, and others do not overhear messages as they are recorded or played back. Again, the Golden Rule can provide a useful guide to anticipating potential problems and recognizing the need to remain constantly mindful, aware, and alert.

HOME OFFICE

As discussed in prior editions of this book and in *How to Survive and Thrive as a Therapist* (Pope & Vasquez, 2005), home offices pose special challenges to confidentiality and privacy. Is it likely that patients — some of whom may not want anyone else to know that they are in psychotherapy — will encounter family members or friends when arriving, waiting for the appointment, or leaving? Any chance that kids will interrupt therapy sessions? Will files, appointment books, message slips, and other documents stay out of sight when family members enter the office? Will family members be able to overhear phone or Skype sessions with patients? Is confidential information about patients stored on a computer that other family members use? If so, how is it secured against accidental discovery? Is the telephone answering machine that receives calls from or about patients shared with other family members? If so, how can those calls be protected against accidental playback for other family members? Are answering machine messages from or about clients ever played back in the presence of family members?

SHARING WITH LOVED ONES

Some therapists may hold back no secrets from a spouse, partner, or other loved ones. For some, sharing what happened during the day with a loved one may be a crucial act of intimacy. The ethical challenge is to do this without violating patient confidentiality.

COMMUNICATIONS IN GROUP OR FAMILY THERAPY

When therapy includes more than one individual, as in group and family therapy, patients have a right to know in advance, as part of the informed consent process, any limitations of privacy, confidentiality, or privilege affected by the presence of more than one patient. For example, if a clinician is providing family therapy, will he or she keep confidential from other family members information conveyed in a telephone call from a minor son that he is using drugs, from a minor daughter that she is pregnant, from the father that he is engaging in an extramarital affair and plans to leave his wife, or from the mother that she has secretly withdrawn the family's savings and is using it to gamble? What does a psychotherapist need to tell prospective patients about how "secrets" will be handled so that the clients' consent can be informed (see, e.g., Kuo, 2009)?

Psychotherapy involving more than one patient emphasizes a major theme of this book: trust. The therapist and members of a therapy group may assume that everyone involved is trustworthy. But what if that is wrong? What if a group member is a newspaper or magazine reporter gathering information for an exposé of what the reporter considers bogus therapy groups, or of the therapist, or of what the reporter considers a "culture of dependency"? Or what if a group member later decides to write a memoir to be published in a magazine or book about what the experience of group therapy was like? Or what if some of the group members simply pass along what they learn about other group members to their family and friends and that information ripples outward to those who recognize and know members of the group? Group and family therapists must struggle with these issues in a way that respects the patients' legitimate rights to privacy, confidentiality, and privilege and their right to know the limits — both legal and practical — of their privacy, confidentiality, and privilege.

Therapy involving more than one person also presents challenges to documentation. If, for example, the therapist keeps one set of therapy records for "the family" or "the group," what happens if one member of the family or group requests or subpoenas a copy of those records? How can a therapy record that mentions more than one patient by name be turned over without the informed consent or legal waiver of each patient? One approach that some therapists use is to keep a separate chart for each patient in a family or group.

WRITTEN CONSENT

A common problem is failing to obtain written informed consent to release confidential information.

As discussed in Chapter 19, both the APA Ethics Code and the CPA Ethics Code address documenting a patient's consent with either a signed consent form or a note in the record about obtaining consent orally.

Obtaining written consent can help promote clarity of communication between therapist and patient in situations when misunderstandings can be disastrous. Both need to understand exactly what information the therapist will release. Is the therapist free to discuss any aspect of the client's history, situation, and treatment? Is the therapist authorized to provide a written summary or all clinical files? When exactly does the client's authorization end? If the person who is to receive the confidential information contacts the therapist with additional questions next month, next year, or several years from now, does the written consent need to be renewed, or does it explicitly cover such future requests?

Patients may not understand the type of information that insurance companies require to authorize coverage and the degree to which information will or will not be sufficiently safeguarded by the insurance company. Keith-Spiegel and Koocher (1985) describe a hypothetical example of a therapist's routine statement to patients regarding insurance coverage:

> If you choose to use your coverage, I shall have to file a form with the company telling them when our appointments were and what services I performed (i.e., psychotherapy, consultation, or evaluation). I will also have to formulate a diagnosis and advise the company of that. The company claims to keep this information confidential, although I have no control over the information once it leaves this office. If you have questions about this you may wish to check with the company providing the coverage. You may certainly choose to pay for my services out-of-pocket and avoid the use of insurance altogether, if you wish. (p. 76)

MANAGED CARE ORGANIZATIONS

How widely do your therapy reports circulate within health maintenance organizations and other managed care facilities. Many patients feel betrayed when records of their psychotherapy sessions become part of their general medical or health record in an HMO and may in turn find their way into other hands. One woman was shocked to find her treatment mentioned on the employee relations bulletin board where she worked. Management and the union, eager to cut both sick leave and the costs for their health-care plan, had decided to post all utilizations of the health-care plan by employees. Under the terms of the contract that had been negotiated by labor and management, the date and reason for each utilization was provided by the health-care organization to officials for both union and management.

From the creation of the first managed care organizations, challenges to confidentiality have grown:

> Managed care companies generally ask for much more information than third parties have traditionally requested from clinicians. The ethical

explanations given for such requests generally have fallen into two categories. One is based on the known history of some clinicians to distort information on forms.... Then managed care companies began to discover that some clinicians charged for sessions not provided or approved. A more general reason applicable to all clinicians is to make sure that the intended treatment meets criteria of medical necessity as designated in the third-party benefits. In addition to treatment plans, managed care companies will often ask for copies of any notes kept on patients; they sometimes do on-site reviews of charts in hospitals, and on occasion they even talk directly to the patient to try to verify information. (Moffic, 1997, p. 97)

The National Academies of Practice (including dentistry, medicine, nursing, optometry, osteopathic medicine, podiatric medicine, psychology, social work, veterinary medicine, audiology, occupational therapy, physical therapy, and speech and language pathology) adopted Ethical Guidelines for Professional Care and Services in a Managed Care Environment (1996). Confidentiality is one of five guidelines listed as a primary concern. While the National Academies of Practice acknowledges that utilization and quality assurance reviews are appropriate functions in a health-care system, they emphasize the importance of safeguards to protect the privacy and confidentiality of patient data and the practitioner's clinical materials. They state,

The rationale for this position is founded on the patient's autonomous right to control sensitive personal information. It is further based upon an historical recognition in the oath of Hippocrates and corroborated throughout the centuries, of the enduring value of preserving confidentiality in order to enhance mutual trust and respect in the patient-provider relationship. (p. 5)

Anne Slowther and Irwin Kleinman (2008) wrote:

The increasing capacity to generate and disseminate information in health care, together with the increasing complexity of healthcare provision, has implications for our understanding of the nature and limits of confidentiality. Development of multidisciplinary healthcare teams raises questions of how much information can be shared within the team, and who is recognized as a team member for this purpose. (p. 43)

Health-care organizations may not always monitor who attends case conferences, and discussions of a patient's condition may be overheard inadvertently by an inappropriate audience.

Similarly, Anne Ward (2010) discusses "how difficult it can be for teams to keep the psychotherapeutic aspects of confidentiality in mind and how, in the current electronic age, fears can arise that patient records may be circulated more widely than is appropriate" (p. 113).

Electronic medical records (EMRs) post difficult challenges to confidentiality. In "Electronic Medical Records: Confidentiality Issues in the Time of HIPAA," Margaret Richards (2009) wrote:

> For a psychologist in a major academic or medical institution, the EMR provides unique ethical conflicts of which the psychologist may be unaware. By documenting within the EMR, the psychologist is potentially informing all members of that patient's medical team that this patient is involved in psychological care. While most informed consents discuss the limits of confidentiality, patients may not always realize the information that is being shared and with whom. At a minimum, the psychologist using an EMR is providing information regarding the patient's participation in therapy, dates of appointments, types of services offered, and diagnoses, even if the content of the session is not revealed. Typically, this is the same information that is being provided to insurance companies as a natural part of the billing process since the advent of HIPAA (Freeny, 2007). Yet, this may not be information that a client wants his primary care physician to have. (p. 553; see also Chapter 11 on working in the digital world)

Updates from HIPPA (2013) explained key changes affecting psychologists, who store and/or transmit client information electronically, including enforcement and penalties, breach notification, notice of privacy practices, and business associates. The first two changes heighten the risks for those practitioners who should be, but are not, complying with the HIPAA Security Rule (APA Practice Organization, 2013). If psychologists store or transmit Protected Health Information (PHI) electronically, we must comply with the HIPAA Security Rule. PHI includes electronically stored client contact information, even if unaccompanied by clinical information. The Security Rule compliance requires a comprehensive review of security risks, in addition to a few steps like encryption. Encryption is an advantage in that it protects client information by making it very difficult for a breacher to crack your encryption, if, for example, your laptop or smart phone is lost or stolen. Encryption is thus a necessary, but not sufficient step in the process of protecting PHI. A Security Rule Online Compliance Workbook can be obtained from the APA Practice Organization http://www.apapracticecentral.org/ce/courses/1370027 .aspx. For Privacy Rule Compliance, a product developed by the APA Practice Organization and Insurance Trust is available at http://www.apapracticecentral .org/ce/courses/1370022.aspx.

Who participates in treatment planning, implementation, and review can be a challenging issue in small towns. In one instance, the chief health-care administrator proposed a periodic case review of current patients to be conducted by staff psychologists. In this town of fewer than 10,000 people, the psychologists would have known many of the patients in a variety of social and business roles. The patients had not given informed consent for this review.

This confidentiality issue is not easily addressed. One solution would be for the administrator to agree to hire a psychologist from another community who did not know the population served by the hospital to visit the hospital once a month to review the cases and make sure that patients understood the review process.

DISCLOSING CONFIDENTIAL INFORMATION FOR MANDATED REPORTS ONLY TO THE EXTENT REQUIRED BY LAW

Evolving legislation and case law in each jurisdiction define the limits of information to reveal in making legally mandated reports. For example, a psychologist was contacted by a mother who wished to arrange appointments for her daughter and her daughter's stepfather to see the therapist regarding allegations that the stepfather engaged in sexual intimacies with his stepdaughter. The psychologist agreed to meet with him and immediately filed a formal report of suspected child abuse.

The next day, a deputy sheriff contacted the psychologist for information. The psychologist furnished information about his meeting with the daughter. He would meet with the stepfather later in the day. The deputy called later and asked for information concerning the session with the stepfather and, reading from the Child Abuse Reporting Law, emphasized that the psychologist was obligated to supply additional information, which the psychologist reluctantly provided.

The stepfather claimed in court that the psychologist, after making the initial formal report, should not have disclosed any additional information. The Supreme Court of California agreed with the stepfather:

> The psychologist was under no statutory obligation to make a second report concerning the same activity.... We have recognized the contemporary value of the psychiatric [sic] profession, and its potential for the relief of emotional disturbances and of the inevitable tensions produced in our modern, complex society.... That value is bottomed on a confidential relationship; but the doctor can be of assistance only if the patient may freely relate his thoughts and actions, his fears and fantasies, his strengths and weaknesses, in a completely uninhibited manner. (*People v. Stritzinger*, 1983, p. 437)

Psychotherapists who disclose confidential information even in court settings may be subject to suit by the client. California, for example, has general legislation protecting individuals from lawsuits for any statements made as part of court proceedings. Nevertheless, a district court of appeal ruled that a psychologist "can be sued for disclosing privileged information in a court proceeding when it violates the patient's constitutional right of privacy" (Chiang, 1986, p. 1).

PUBLISHING CASE STUDIES

Publishing case studies or other confidential information about patients requires exceptional care. Merely changing the patient's name and a few other details may not be sufficient. Pope, Simpson, and Weiner (1978) discussed a case in New York in which a therapist was successfully sued for publishing a book in which he described his treatment of a patient. The patient asserted that the therapist had not obtained her consent to write about her treatment and had not adequately disguised the presentation of her history.

APA's *Casebook on Ethical Principles of Psychologists* (1987a, p. 72) presents a situation in which a psychologist wished to write a book about an assessment:

> Psychologist G conducted a professional evaluation of the accused murderer in a sensational and well-publicized case in which six teenage girls, who vanished over a period of 18 months, were later found stabbed to death in an abandoned waterfront area of the city. The lurid nature of the crimes attracted nationwide publicity, which only increased as allegations of negligence were pressed against the city administration and the police force. In order to construct a psychological diagnostic profile, Psychologist G spent several days with the accused, conducting interviews and psychometric tests. He presented his findings in court with the full consent of the accused.
>
> Six months later, following the sentencing of the now convicted murderer, Psychologist G determined that he would like to write a book about the murderer and the psychology behind the crimes, which he anticipated would be a lucrative undertaking.
>
> Psychologist G wrote to the Ethics Committee to inquire whether it would be ethical for him to do so. The convicted murderer had refused permission to publish in a book the results of the psychological evaluation, despite the fact that the information was now considered part of the public domain because it had been admitted in court as evidence.
>
> Opinion: The Ethics Committee responded to Psychologist G that to write the proposed book would be a legal but unethical undertaking. The fact that material has entered the public domain or that there may have been an implied waiver of consent does not free the psychologist from the obligation under Principle 5.b of the Ethical Principles to obtain prior consent before presenting in a public forum personal information acquired through the course of professional work. In this case, the ethics code sets a higher standard than the law would require. Psychologist G thanked the Committee for its advice and dropped the idea of writing the book.

DISTRACTION

Momentary distractions can cause lasting problems. No matter how senior our status, how extensive our training, or how naturally skilled any of us may be, none of us is perfect. All of us have moments when we are tired, overwhelmed, rushing, or careless. James F. Masterson, a prominent therapist who has written extensively concerning borderline personality disorders, showed courage in writing about an instance in which he betrayed a patient's confidence because of something that had happened in his own life:

> One morning I was late and dented my car as I parked in the office garage. A bit frazzled from the experience, I rushed into my office and admitted my first patient who asked me how another patient of mine was doing, calling her by name. I was startled because their appointments were at very different times. I wondered if they had met socially, or if he was dating her. Then I realized what had happened. Worried about my dented fender, I had inadvertently picked her file out of the drawer instead of his, and he had read her name on the folder. My distraction represented a countertransferential failure to pay proper attention to my patient. I apologized for taking out the wrong chart and told him I was distracted by the accident. (Masterson, 1989, p. 26)

FOCUSING ON LEGAL RESPONSIBILITIES TO THE EXCLUSION OF ETHICAL RESPONSIBILITIES

Mary Alice Fisher (2008) discussed ways in which confidentiality workshops often focus on laws and risk management while spending relatively little time on ethical responsibilities. Noting that HIPAA brought forth the growth of attorney-led HIPAA-compliance training that further overshadowed ethics training in confidentiality, Fisher wrote:

> Such legally based training creates several ethical problems for psychologists. First, it fosters the impression that attorneys — not clinicians — have become the only "real" experts about this aspect of practice. Second, it creates a legal language about confidentiality that threatens to usurp psychologists' own clinical or ethical language about it: Laws take center stage, when what is needed is a language for placing them into ethical context. Third, it exacerbates the figure-ground confusion (by substituting legal rules for ethical rules) and often takes a risk-management perspective that raises anxiety: It encourages psychologists to focus on obeying laws in order to avoid risks to themselves, when what they need is a clearer focus on their ethical obligations and the potential risks to clients. Finally, the legal emphasis obscures an important fact about risk management: Understanding and following the relevant ethical principles is an essential ingredient in avoiding a malpractice suit. . . . (p. 6; see also Fisher, 2013)

SCENARIOS FOR DISCUSSION

You have been working for 2 years with a patient who has multiple problems and has disclosed extremely sensitive information to you. The insurance company sends you a letter requesting the entire file, including all of your chart notes and all raw data from the psychological assessment, in order to determine whether further therapy is warranted and, if so, in what form. When you call the insurance company to discuss the matter, the head of claims review (not a mental health professional and whose previous job was quality control officer in a paper clip company) tells you that they must have all these materials within five business days or else therapy will be discontinued.

- How do you feel?
- What options do you consider?
- If the patient refuses to provide consent for you to send the materials, even though it means there are no longer resources to pay for the therapy, and decides to terminate therapy rather than allow the information to go to third parties, what do you do?

You have been working with a 14-year-old patient for several months. During one session, the patient suddenly discloses having sex with a parent for the past four years. The patient, who has been chronically depressed, threatens, "If you tell anyone about this, I will find a way to kill myself." You believe that this is not an idle threat.

- How do you feel?
- Under what circumstances, if any, do you believe you might disclose information about the client's claim of having been sexually involved with a parent to any of the following: (a) child protective services or other governmental agency authorized to receive reports of suspected child abuse, (b) your clinical supervisor, (c) any family member, or (d) anyone else?
- What objectives or priorities would shape your interventions?
- To what extent, if at all, would your own potential legal liability affect your emotional responses to this situation and your course of action?

(continued)

(*continued*)

You are working with a patient who engages in unprotected sex with a variety of partners. Two months ago, the client became infected with HIV. Recent sessions have focused on many topics, one of which is the patient's decision not to begin using protection during sex and not to disclose the HIV status to any partners. The client shows no likelihood of changing this decision.

- How do you feel?
- Does the patient's decision affect your ability to empathize in any way?
- Under what conditions, if any, would you act against the patient's wishes and communicate information about the client's HIV status and sexual activity to third parties?
- What information would you disclose, to whom would you disclose it, and what are the likely or possible outcomes?

You work for an HMO, spending 4 hours a day, 3 days a week providing outpatient therapy at its facility. Four other clinicians provide therapy in the same office. According to HMO policy, all patient charts of all clinicians using that room must remain locked in a single filing cabinet in the corner of the room. Each clinician has a key to the filing cabinet. You become aware that several of your patients have social relationships with the other therapists. You are also aware that their charts contain extremely sensitive information about them. You also notice the names of two of your friends on the charts of the other clinicians. The HMO refuses to change this policy.

- How do you feel?
- What courses of action do you consider?
- Are the clients entitled to know about this arrangement? If so, at what point should they be made aware of it?
- If you were the client in such a situation, do you believe that you would be entitled to know about this arrangement?

You have reached a therapeutic impasse with a patient. For weeks, the therapy has seemed stalled, but you have not understood what is wrong. During the past few supervision sessions, you discovered that this client has stirred up some intense emotions in you. You've mentioned to your supervisor some painful events in your own history about which you have felt ashamed and confused. You have yet to discuss these events with anyone else, even your own therapist. One afternoon you head to the staff lounge but pause just before entering the room. Through the door, you hear your supervisor talking with others about the painful events you had discussed in supervision.

- How do you feel?
- Which of the following do you think you'd do and why: (a) leave immediately, hoping no one saw you; (b) linger at the door, hoping to hear more; (c) enter the room, pretending that you hadn't heard anything; (d) enter the room and indicate that you had heard what they had said; or (e) something else?
- Under what circumstances, if any, do you believe that clinical supervisors should discuss what their supervisees tell them? In your experience, have these boundaries of confidentiality been explicit and well understood by supervisees and supervisors? In your experience, have supervisors respected these boundaries?
- Have the clinical supervisors you have known or known of kept notes or otherwise documented the supervision sessions? What ethical, legal, or other considerations affect the privacy and confidentiality of supervision notes (for example, are they legally privileged communications)?

Chapter 25

RECOGNIZING, ASSESSING, AND RESPONDING TO SUICIDAL RISK

Clinicians may find the following 22 factors useful in assessing suicidal risk. Four qualifications are key. First, the factors are general, and exceptions are frequent. In many instances, two or more factors may interact. For example, being married and being younger, taken as individual factors, tend to be associated with lower risk for suicide. However, married teenagers have historically shown an extremely high suicide rate (Peck & Seiden, 1975; Solotaroff & Pande, 2014). Second, these factors are not static. New research enriches our understanding as well as reflects changes. The suicide rate for women, for example, has been increasing, bringing it closer to that for men. Third, the list is far from comprehensive. Fourth, these factors may be useful as guidelines but cannot be applied in an unthinking, mechanical, conclusive manner. Someone may rank in the lowest-risk category of each factor and still commit suicide. These factors can help us think through a situation but never replace a comprehensive, humane, and personal evaluation of a unique patient's suicidal risk. Again it is worth returning to a central theme of this book's approach to ethics: perhaps the most frequent threat to ethical behavior is the therapist's inattention. Making certain that we consider such factors with each patient can help us prevent the ethical lapses that come from neglect.

1. *Direct verbal warning.* A direct statement of intention to commit suicide serves as one of the most useful single predictors. Take any such statement seriously. Resist the temptation to reflexively dismiss

such warnings as "a hysterical bid for attention," "a borderline manipulation," "a clear expression of negative transference," "an attempt to provoke the therapist," or "yet another grab for power in the interpersonal struggle with the therapist." It may be any or all of those and yet still foreshadow suicide.

2. *Plan.* The presence of a plan increases the risk (see, e.g., Stack, 2014). The more specific, detailed, lethal, and feasible the plan is, the greater the risk.

3. *Past attempts.* Most, and perhaps 80% of, completed suicides follow a prior attempt. Schneidman (1975; see also Mackelprang, Bombardier, Fann, et al., 2014; Wong et al., 2008) found that the client group with the greatest suicidal rate were those who had entered into treatment with a history of at least one attempt.

4. *Indirect statements and behavioral signs.* People planning to end their lives may communicate their intent indirectly through their words and actions — for example, talking about "going away," speculating on what death would be like, giving away their most valued possessions, or acquiring lethal instruments.

5. *Depression.* The suicide rate for those with clinical depression is about 20 times greater than for the general population. Guze and Robins (1970; see also Stack, 2014; Taliaferro & Muehlenkamp, 2014; Vuorilehto, Melartin, & Isometsa, 2006), in a review of 17 studies concerning death in primary affective disorder, found that 15% of the individuals suffering from this disorder killed themselves. Effectively treating depression may lower the risk of suicide (Gibbons, Hur, Bhaumik, & Mann, 2005; Mann, 2005).

6. *Hopelessness.* The sense of hopelessness appears to be an aspect of depression closely associated with suicidal intent (Beck & Weishaar, 1990; Beck, Kovaks, & Weissman, 1975; Maris, 2002; Martin, Dorken, Simpson, McKenzie, & Colman, 2014; Petrie & Chamberlain, 1983; Taliaferro & Muehlenkamp, 2014; Violanti et al., 2015; Wetzel, 1976).

7. *Intoxication.* Between one fourth and one third of all suicides are linked to alcohol as a contributing factor; a much higher percentage may be associated with the presence of alcohol (without clear indication of its contribution to the suicidal process and lethal outcome). Moscicki (2001; see also Buri, Von Bonin, Strik, & Moggi, 2009; Crosby, Espitia-Hardeman, Hill, Ortega, & Clavel-Arcas, 2009; Kõlves, Värnik, Tooding, & Wasserman, 2006; Sher, 2006; Sher et al., 2009) notes that perhaps as many as half of those who kill themselves are intoxicated at the time. Darke, Duflou, and Torok (2009) found that

alcohol was more common where a suicide note was left and where relationship problems were involved. Pharmaceuticals were more common where a previous attempt was noted. Licit and illicit substances are strongly associated with suicide, even when the method does not involve drug overdose. (p. 490)

Hendin, Haas, Maltsberger, Koestner, and Szanto's study, "Problems in Psychotherapy with Suicidal Patients" (2006), emphasized that "addressing and treating suicidal patients' substance abuse, particularly alcohol abuse, is critical in effective treatment of other problems, including lack of response to antidepressant medication" (p. 71; see also Zhang, Conner, & Phillips, 2010).

8. *Marital separation (distinct from divorce)*. Wyder, Ward, and De Leo (2009) found that "for both males and females separation created a risk of suicide at least 4 times higher than any other marital status. The risk was particularly high for males aged 15 to 24..." (p. 208).

9. *Clinical syndromes*. People suffering from depression or alcoholism are at much higher risk for suicide. Other clinical syndromes may also be linked to an increased risk. Perhaps as many as 90% of those who take their own lives have a formal diagnosis (Moscicki, 2001). Kramer, Pollack, Redick, and Locke (1972) found that the highest suicide rates exist among clients diagnosed as having primary mood disorders and psychoneuroses, with high rates also among those having organic brain syndrome and schizophrenia (see also Draper, Peisah, Snowdon, & Brokaty, 2010; Novick, Swartz, & Frank, 2010). Palmer, Pankratz, and Bostwick (2005; see also Brenner, Homaifar, Adler, Wolfman, & Kemp, 2009; Loas, Azi, Noisette, Legrand, & Yon, 2009; Preti, Meneghelli, & Cocchi, 2009) found that the lifetime risk for suicide among people with schizophrenia was around 5%. Drake, Gates, Cotton, and Whitaker (1984) discovered that those suffering from schizophrenia who had very high internalized standards were at particularly high risk. In a long-term study, Tsuang (1983) found that the suicide rate among the first-degree relatives of schizophrenic and manic-depressive clients was significantly higher than that for a control group of relatives of surgery patients; furthermore, relatives of clients who had committed suicide showed a higher rate than relatives of clients who did not take their lives. Using meta-analytic techniques, Harris and Barraclough (1997) obtained results suggesting that "virtually all mental disorders have an increased risk of suicide excepting mental retardation and dementia. The suicide risk is highest for functional and lowest for organic disorders" (p. 205; see also Chan et al., 2009).

10. *Sex*. The suicide rate for men is more than 3 times that for women (CDC, 2010; see also Joiner, 2005, 2010). For youths, the rate is closer to 5 to 1 (see Safer, 1997). The rate of suicide attempts for women is about 3 times that for men.

11. *Age.* A significant change occurred in this category. The earlier editions of this book had noted that the risk for suicide tended to increase over the adult life cycle. However, more recently suicide has peaked in middle age: "The highest rates of suicide by age group occurred among persons aged 45–54 years, 75–84 years, and 35–44 years (17.6, 16.4, and 16.3 per 100,000 population, respectively" (CDC, 2010, p. 9). As noted earlier in this chapter, Hempstead and Phillips (2015) report that 1991 marked the start of a significant rise in middle-age suicide rates, a rise that speeded up beginning in 2007. Suicide risk assessment differs also according to whether the client is an adult or a minor. The assessment of suicidal risk among minors presents special challenges. Safer's review of the literature indicated that the "frequent practice of combining adult and adolescent suicide and suicide behavior findings can result in misleading conclusions" (1997, p. 61). Zametkin, Alter, and Yemini (2001) note that the

> rate of suicide among adolescents has significantly increased in the past 30 years. In 1998, 4153 young people aged 15 to 24 years committed suicide in the United States, an average of 11.3 deaths per day. Suicide is the third leading cause of death in this age group and accounts for 13.5% of all deaths.... Children younger than 10 years are less likely to complete suicide, and the risk appears to increase gradually in children between 10 and 12 years of age. However, on average, 170 children 10 years or younger commit suicide each year. (p. 3122)

12. *Race.* Generally in the United States, Caucasians tend to have one of the highest suicide rates (CDC, 2010). Gibbs (1997) discusses the apparent cultural paradox: "African-American suicide rates have traditionally been lower than White rates despite a legacy of racial discrimination, persistent poverty, social isolation, and lack of community resources" (p. 68). EchoHawk (1997) notes that the suicide rate for Native Americans is "greater than that of any other ethnic group in the United States, especially in the age range of 15–24 years" (p. 60). In Canada, the Nunavut Inuit suicide rate is 13 times higher than the rate in the rest of Canada ("Suicide Numbers in Nunavut in 2013 a Record High; Nunavut Youth Decry Lack of Help for Those Thinking About Suicide," 2014).

13. *Religion.* The suicide rates among Protestants tend to be higher than those among Jews and Catholics.

14. *Living alone.* The risk of suicide tends to be reduced if someone is not living alone, reduced even more if he or she is living with a spouse, and reduced even further if there are children.

15. *Bereavement.* Bereavement tends to place survivors at increased risk of taking their own lives (Hollingshaus & Smith, 2015; Pitman, Osborn, King, & Erlangsen, 2014). Brunch, Barraclough, Nelson, and Sainsbury (1971) found that 50% of those in their sample who had committed suicide had lost their mothers within the past 3 years (compared with a 20% rate among controls matched for age, sex, marital status, and geographical location). Furthermore, 22% of the suicides, compared with only 9% of the controls, had experienced the loss of their father within the past 5 years. Krupnick's review of studies (1984) revealed "a link between childhood bereavement and suicide attempts in adult life," perhaps doubling the risk for depressives who had lost a parent compared to depressives who had not experienced the death of a parent. Klerman and Clayton (1984; see also Beutler, 1985) found that suicide rates are higher among the widowed than the married (especially among elderly men) and that among women the suicide rate is not as high for widows as for the divorced or separated. The suicide risk tends to rise around the anniversary of the loss (Rostila, Saarela, Kawachi, & Hjern, 2015).

16. *Unemployment.* Unemployment tends to increase the risk for suicide.

17. *Health status.* Illness and somatic complaints are associated with increased suicidal risk, as are disturbances in patterns of sleeping and eating. Clinicians who are helping people with AIDS, for example, need to be sensitive to this risk (Pope & Morin, 1990).

18. *Impulsivity.* Those with poor impulse control are at increased risk for taking their own lives (Rimkeviciene & De Leo, 2015; see also Maloney, Degenhardt, Darke, & Nelson, 2009; Patsiokas, Clum, & Luscumb, 1979; Wu et al., 2009).

19. *Rigid thinking.* Suicidal individuals often display a rigid, all-or-none way of thinking (Maris, 2002; Neuringer, 1964). A typical statement might be, "If I can't find a job by the end of the month, the only real alternative is suicide."

20. *Stressful events.* Excessive numbers of undesirable events with negative outcomes have been associated with increased suicidal risk (Cohen-Sandler, Berman, & King, 1982; Isherwood, Adam, & Homblow, 1982). Bagley, Bolitho, and Bertrand (1997), in a study of 1,025 adolescent women in grades 7 to 12, found that "15% of 38 women who experienced frequent, unwanted sexual touching had 'often' made suicidal gestures or attempts in the previous 6 months, compared with 2% of 824 women with no experience of sexual assault" (p. 341; see also McCauley, Kern, Kolodner, Dill, & Schroeder, 1997). Some types of recent events may place clients at extremely high risk. For example, Ellis, Atkeson, and Calhoun (1982) found that 52% of their sample of multiple-incident victims of sexual assault had attempted suicide.

21. *Release from hospitalization.* Beck (1967, p. 57) has noted that "the available figures clearly indicate that the suicidal risk is greatest during weekend leaves from the hospital and shortly after discharge." Hunt and colleagues' study of "Suicide in Recently Discharged Psychiatric Patients: A Case-Control Study" (Hunt et al., 2009) found that the

> weeks after discharge . . . represent a critical period for suicide risk. Measures that could reduce risk include intensive and early community follow-up. Assessment of risk should include established risk factors as well as current mental state and there should be clear follow-up procedures for those who have self-discharged. (p. 443)

Francis (2009) points out the relationship between suicidal risk and release from hospitalization may be complex when borderline personality disorder is at issue:

> People with borderline personality disorder (BPD) are sometimes admitted to inpatient wards due to risk to themselves. However, recent research indicates inpatient settings are detrimental to BPD and can worsen symptoms (unless they are planned short stays). Staff are often too fearful . . . to release them if they are still expressing suicidal thoughts. If the presentation is not different (no major crises have occurred, no major losses made) then clinically indicated risk-taking is the recommended course of action. (p. 253)

22. *Lack of a sense of belonging.* Joiner's review of the research and his own studies led him to conclude that

> an unmet need to belong is a contributor to suicidal desire: suicidal individuals may experience interactions that do not satisfy their need to belong (e.g., relationships that are unpleasant, unstable, infrequent, or without proximity) or may not feel connected to others and cared about. (2005, p. 97; see also Joiner, 2010)

Appelbaum and Gutheil (2007) focus on the risk factor of

> personal isolation, which can derive from a number of sources (for example, immigrants who have not found a local community, those who are retired or unemployed, those living alone, even those living in transient or disorganized areas such as resort towns whose populations fluctuate wildly on a seasonal basis). (p. 52)

SPECIAL CONSIDERATIONS

Knowing and understanding the risks of patient suicide creates a special set of responsibilities. The way we handle those responsibilities can have life or death consequences. The following steps may be helpful in handling those responsibilities:

- *Screen all patients for suicidal risk during initial contact, and remain alert to this issue throughout the therapy.* Even patients who are seriously thinking of taking their own life may not present the classic picture of agitated depression or the stereotype of grim determination. Some suicidal patients seem, during initial sessions, calm, composed, and concerned with a seemingly minor presenting problem. Patients who are not suicidal during initial sessions and who started therapy for a minor problem may become suicidal. The rise in suicidal risk may be caused by external events, such as the loss of a job or a loved one, or internal events, such as setting aside psychological defenses or the start of Alzheimer's disease. What is crucial is an assessment of the patient's suicidal potential at adequate intervals. In some cases, comprehensive psychological testing or the use of standardized scales developed to evaluate suicidal risk may be useful (see, for example, Beck, Resnick, & Lettieri, 1974; Butcher, Graham, Williams, & Ben-Porath, 1990; Lettieri, 1982; Neuringer, 1974; Nugent, 2006; Ostergaard et al., 2015; Weisman & Worden, 1972). Range and Knott (1997) evaluated 20 suicide assessment instruments for validity and reliability. On the basis of their analysis, they recommended three most highly: Beck's Scale for Suicide Ideation series, Linehan's Reasons for Living Inventory, and Cole's self-administered adaptation of Linehan's structured interview called the Suicidal Behaviors Questionnaire.
- *Check the literature or consult with an expert in this area to see if current research and practice offer any approaches that might be particularly effective with a particular situation or population.* For example, randomized research suggests dialectical behavior therapy seems effective and well-suited for people with borderline personality disorder who are suicidal (Linehan et al. 2006).
- *Work with the client to arrange an environment that will not offer easy access to whatever the patient might use to commit suicide.* Suicidal clients who have purchased a gun may agree to place it where they will not have access to it until the crisis is over. Suicidal clients who are currently taking psychotropic or other medication may be planning an overdose. The use of materials prescribed by and associated with mental health professionals may have great symbolic meaning for the patient. Arrange that the patient does not have access to enough medication at one time to carry out a suicidal plan. In a study of the relationship between diagnosis and means in completed suicide, Huisman, van Houwelingen, and Kerkhof (2009) found:

Possible means of suicide prevention suggested by this study include limiting access to tall buildings or structures to patients with psychotic disorders; careful prescription of medication to female patients and particularly to patients with substance-related disorders; and limiting easy access to railways near clinical settings to patients with bipolar and psychotic disorders. Limiting access to means of suicide may be less effective for suicidal patients with depressive disorders who may switch to other available methods.

- *Work with the patient to create an actively supportive environment.* To what extent can family, friends, and other resources such as community agencies and group or family therapy help a suicidal person through a crisis?
- *While not denying or minimizing the patient's problems and desire to die, also recognize and work with the patient's strengths and desire to live.* Patients' awareness of their strengths, resilience, and reasons to live can often help them regain perspective, often lost during despair.
- *Make every effort to communicate realistic hope.* Discuss practical approaches to the patient's problems.
- *Explore any fantasies the client may have regarding suicide.* Reevaluating unrealistic beliefs about what suicide will and will not accomplish can be an important step for clients attempting to remain alive.
- *Make sure communications are clear, and assess the probable impact of any interventions.* Ambiguous or confusing messages are unlikely to be helpful and can cause considerable harm. The literature documents the hazards of using such techniques as paradoxical intention with suicidal clients. Even well-meant and apparently clear messages may go awry in the stress of crisis. Beck (1967, p. 53) provides an example:

> One woman, who was convinced by her therapist that her children needed her even though she believed herself worthless, decided to kill them as well as herself to 'spare them the agony of growing up without a mother.' She subsequently followed through with her plan.

- *When considering hospitalization as an option, explore the drawbacks as fully as the benefits, the probable long-term and the immediate effects of this intervention.* Norman Farberow (see Colt, 1983, p. 58), cofounder and former codirector and chief of research at the Los Angeles Suicide Prevention Center, warns: "We tend to think we've solved the problem by getting the person into the hospital, but psychiatric hospitals have a suicide rate more than 35 percent greater than in the community."
- *Be sensitive to negative reactions to the patient's behavior.* James Chu (quoted by Colt, 1983, p. 56), a psychiatrist in charge of Codman House at McLean Hospital, a psychiatric hospital near Boston, comments:

When you deal with suicidal people day after day after day, you just get plain tired. You get to the point of feeling, "All right, get it over with." The potential for fatigue, boredom, and negative transference is so great that we must remain constantly alert for signs that we are beginning to experience them. Maltsberger and Buie discuss therapists' repression of such feelings. A therapist may glance often at his watch, feel drowsy, or daydream — or rationalize referral, premature termination, or hospitalization just to be rid of the patient. (Many studies have detailed the unintentional abandonment of suicidal patients; in a 1967 review of 32 suicides. . . Bloom found "each. . . was preceded by rejecting behavior by the therapist.") Sometimes, in frustration, a therapist will issue an ultimatum. Maltsberger recalls one who, treating a chronic wrist-cutter, just couldn't stand it, and finally she said, "If you don't stop that I'll stop treatment." The patient did it again. She stopped treatment and the patient killed herself. (Colt, 1983, p. 57)

- *Perhaps most important, communicate caring.* Therapists differ in how they attempt to express this caring. A therapist (cited by Colt, 1983, p. 60) recounts an influential event early in her career:

> I had a slasher my first year in the hospital. She kept cutting herself to ribbons — with glass, wire, anything she could get her hands on. Nobody could stop her. The nurses were getting very angry. . . . I didn't know what to do, but I was getting very upset. So I went to the director, and in my best Harvard Medical School manner began in a very intellectual way to describe the case. To my horror, I couldn't go on, and I began to weep. I couldn't stop. He said, "I think if you showed the patient what you showed me, I think she'd know you cared." So I did. I told her that I cared, and that it was distressing to me. She stopped. It was an important lesson.

Relatively unusual and rare interventions such as home visits, long and frequent sessions, therapist's late-night search for a runaway patient, and other special measures already noted are ways some therapists have found useful to communicate this caring, although such approaches obviously do not fit all therapists, all patients, all theoretical orientations, or all situations. Some ethics committee and licensing board members may be concerned about these strategies. However, these strategies may be options on occasion. One of the most basic aspects of this communication of caring is the therapist's willingness to listen, to take seriously what the patient has to say. Farberow (1985, p. C9) puts it well:

> If the person is really trying to communicate how unhappy he is, or his particular problems, then you can recognize that one of the most important things is to be able to hear his message. You'd want to say, "Yes, I hear you. Yes, I recognize that this is a really tough situation. I'll be glad to listen. If I can't do anything, then we'll find someone who can."

AVOIDING PITFALLS: ADVICE FROM EXPERTS

A central theme of this book is that inattention or a lack of awareness is a frequent cause violating clinical responsibilities and patient trust. We asked prominent therapists with expertise in identifying and responding to suicidal risk to discuss factors that contribute to therapists' inattention or lack of awareness when working with potentially suicidal patients. Their advice can help us save lives.

The late *Norman Farberow*, PhD, a great friend who died while this 5th edition was in production, was cofounder and former codirector and chief of research at the first suicide prevention center in the U.S., the Los Angeles Suicide Prevention Center. He believed that there are four main problem areas. First, therapists tend to feel uncomfortable with the subject; they find it difficult to explore and investigate suicidal risk: "We don't want to hear about it. We discount it. But any indication of risk or intention must be addressed." Second, we must appreciate that each client is a unique person: "Each person becomes suicidal in his or her own framework. The person's point of view is crucial." Third, we tend to forget the preventive factors: "Clinicians run scared at the thought of suicide. They fail to recognize the true resources." Fourth, we fail to consult: "Outside opinion is invaluable."

Marsha Linehan, PhD, ABPP, is a professor of psychology, adjunct professor of psychiatry and behavioral sciences at the University of Washington, and director of the Behavioral Research and Therapy Clinic. Her primary research is the development of effective treatments for suicidal behaviors, drug abuse, and borderline personality disorder. She believes that

> the single biggest problem in treating suicidal clients is that most therapists have inadequate training and experience in the assessment and treatment of suicidal behaviors. More distressing than that is that there does not appear to be a hue and cry from practicing therapists demanding such training. Deciding to limit one's practice to non-suicidal clients is not a solution because individuals can and do become suicidal after entering treatment. Secondary problems are as follows. (1) Therapists treating clients with disorders that make them high risk for suicide (e.g., depression, borderline personality disorder, bipolar disorder) do not ask about suicide ideation and planning in a routine, frequent way: depending on clients who have decided to kill themselves to first communicate risk directly or indirectly can be a fatal mistake. (2) Fears of legal liability often cloud therapists' abilities to focus on the welfare of the client: fear interferes with good clinical judgment. Many outpatient therapists simply "dump" their suicidal clients onto emergency and inpatient facilities believing that this will absolve them of risk. There is no empirical data that emergency department and/or inpatient treatment reduces suicide risk in the slightest and the available literature could support a hypothesis that it may instead increase

suicide risk. (3) Therapists often do not realize that when treating a highly suicidal client they must be available by phone and otherwise after hours: treating a highly suicidal client requires personally involved clinical care.

Nadine J. Kaslow, PhD, ABPP, professor and chief psychologist at Emory School of Medicine, a well-funded researcher on the assessment and treatment of abused and suicidal African American women, the recipient of the American Psychological Association's 2004 award for Distinguished Contributions to Education and Training, and a former American Psychological Association president told us that

assessment and intervention of suicidal persons need to be culturally competent, gender sensitive, and developmentally informed. Our approach to suicidal individuals needs to consider both the relevant evidence base and sensitive attention to the person's unique struggles, strengths, and sociocultural context. We need to interact with suicidal people with compassion and a desire to understand why their pain feels so intolerable that they believe that suicide will offer the only form of relief. It is always important to take suicidal concerns seriously, convey an appreciation for the person's plight, and engage in a collaborative process. Since suicidal people often feel socially isolated and social support is a buffer against suicidal behavior, it is imperative that we assist suicidal men and women in mobilizing their social support networks. We must build on people's strengths, help them find meaning and hope, and empower them to overcome the trials and tribulations that lead them to feel and think that life is not worth living. As therapists, we will find our own countertransference reactions to be a very useful guide with regard to risk assessment, disposition planning, and the implementation of therapeutic strategies. Our own histories with suicide, whether that be our own suicidality, the loss of a loved one to suicide, or the death of a former patient to suicide, will greatly impact how we approach and respond to people who think actively about suicide, take steps to end their own life, or actually kill themselves. Our histories and reactions can also be instrumental in our efforts to help suicidal people heal from their pain so that they find life worth living. This in turn, enriches our own lives.

Ricardo F. Muñoz, PhD, is Distinguished Professor of Clinical Psychology at Palo Alto University; Professor of Psychology, Emeritus at the University of California, San Francisco Department of Psychiatry at San Francisco General Hospital; and served as principal investigator on the Depression Prevention Research Project involving English-, Spanish-, and Chinese-speaking populations, funded by the National Institute of Mental Health. Here are his thoughts:

First, clinicians often fail to identify what suicidal clients have that they care about, that they are responsible for, that they can live for. Include animals, campaigns, projects, religious values. Second, inexperienced liberal therapists in particular may fall into the trap of attempting to work out their philosophy regarding the right to die and the rationality or reasonableness of suicide while they are working with a client who is at critical risk. These issues demand careful consideration, but postponing them until the heat of crisis benefits no one. In the same way that we try to convince clients that the darkest hour of a severe depressive episode is not a good time to decide whether to live or die, clinicians must accept that while attempting to keep a seriously suicidal person alive is not a good time to decide complex philosophical questions. Third, don't overestimate your ability to speak someone else's language. Recently, a Spanish-speaking woman, suicidal, came to the emergency room talking of pills. The physician, who spoke limited Spanish, obtained what he thought was her promise not to attempt suicide and sent her back to her halfway house. It was later discovered that she'd been saying that she'd already taken a lethal dose of pills and was trying to get help.

Jessica Henderson Daniel, PhD, ABPP, director of training in psychology in the Department of Psychiatry and associate director of the Leadership Education in Adolescent Health Training Program in the Division of Adolescent Medicine at Boston's Children's Hospital, told us:

As some adolescents can be prone to be dramatic, i.e. using exaggerated language and gestures, and consequently their comments about suicide may not be taken seriously. The adolescent may make several statements before actually engaging in suicidal behavior. The adolescent needs to know that some caring and responsible persons may take the following actions: follow-up with an urgent appointment with their therapist, evaluation in the emergency room, and/or in-patient hospitalization. Also, adolescents can become very upset about matters that may seem trivial to adults. Providers are reminded that the perspective of the patient trumps their views. When adolescents are in the midst of despair, minimizing the worry, hurt, and hopelessness can be problematic. Some providers may feel that life really cannot be that bad. Talking with and, more importantly, listening carefully to the adolescent will help providers make a more informed decision. Also, parents matter. State regulations can determine the legal role of parents when their adolescents are in the need of care. It is important to know this information. Should parents be legally responsible for their adolescent, providers may be reluctant to override the decision of parents who cannot bear to think that their child may be suicidal and who insist on taking them home. When the patient is a child or an adolescent, the parents are a critical part of the management of the case and may need their own providers as well. Finally, consultation is critical in thinking through how to best provide under the particular circumstances.

Danny Brom, PhD, is Director of the Israel Center for the Treatment of Psychotrauma of Herzog Hospital in Jerusalem (www.traumweb.org) and

Professor at the Paul Baerwald School of Social Work and Social Welfare of Hebrew University. The mission of his community-based trauma center is to develop and test new methods of intervention for mitigating the effects of trauma on children and adults. His latest book, with Pat-Horenczyk and Vogel, is *Helping Children Cope with Trauma: Individual, Family and Community Perspectives* (Pat-Horenczyk, Brom, & Vogel, 2014). He told us:

> The client that taught me this lesson had been abused in ways that I had not heard about before and have rarely heard about after. Tortured, abused, made totally dependent and helpless. She suffered from DID. During the course of a long therapy she would become suicidal. When we discussed suicidality, I wanted to have a clear understanding with her that she would call me first if she would feel that she was going commit suicide. She then made it very clear to me that suicide for her had been and still was her only access to real freedom. If I would take that away from her or block that way by insisting on a contract, she felt that then she really would have to commit suicide. The freedom to commit suicide gave her the freedom to live.

M. David Rudd, PhD, ABPP, is Provost and Distinguished University Professor at the University of Memphis. He served as president of the American Association of Suicidology and as consultant to the U.S. Army, the U.S. Air Force, the Beijing Suicide Prevention and Research Center, and other organizations. He told us:

> One of the all-too-frequently neglected areas in suicide risk assessment is recognizing, discussing, and implementing a distinction between acute and chronic risk. Assessment of acute risk alone is how the overwhelming majority of clinicians approach the task. Over the past decade, converging scientific evidence suggests it is important to address enduring or "chronic" suicidality in patients. More specifically, those who have made two or more suicide attempts likely have a "chronic" aspect to their presentation. Although acute risk may well resolve, it is important for the clinician to make a note about the individual's enduring vulnerabilities and continuing suicide risk. It's as straightforward as making a note such as: "Although acute risk has resolved, the patient has made three previous suicide attempts and there are aspects of the clinical scenario that suggest chronic risk for suicide. More specifically, the patient's history of previous sexual abuse, episodic alcohol and cannabis abuse, along with two previous major depressive episodes, all indicate the need for longer-term and continuing care in order to more effectively treat these chronic markers of risk."

David H. Barlow, PhD, is a diplomate in clinical psychology and founding director of the Center for Anxiety and Related Disorders at Boston University. He is former president of the Society of Clinical Psychology of APA and maintains a private practice. He believes that there are two common problems often encountered in working with young or inexperienced therapists confronting a possible suicidal patient:

> First, after forming an alliance with a new patient, some therapists begin to spin away from a professional, objective clinical stance and treat seemingly off-hand comments about not wanting to live as casual conversation that might be occurring after work over a drink with a friend or in a college dormitory. Thus, they may respond sympathetically but not professionally by downplaying the report: "Sometimes I feel that way too — I can understand how you'd get to that place." Of course, one must always step back if this comes up and conduct the proper exam for intent, means, etc., and take appropriate action. Second, some therapists undervalue the power of a contract, since patients sometimes say something like, "Well . . . I'll say that if you want me to, but I don't know if my word is worth anything." The fact is, in the context of a good therapeutic relationship, the contract is very powerful, the occasional report to the contrary notwithstanding.

Rosa E. Garcia-Peltoniemi, PhD, is Staff Clinical Psychologist and Senior Consulting Clinician at the Center for Victims of Torture. Since 1987, she has been at the forefront of developing clinical services for refugees and asylum seekers who have suffered torture at the hands of foreign governments both in the United States and internationally. Here is what she states regarding specific issues in treating survivors of torture in this country:

> For torture survivor clients trying to obtain asylum in the U.S., adverse decisions carrying the risk of deportation to the very countries in which they were tortured are frequently times of increased suicidal risk. The prospect of being sent back becomes not only very frightening but also an intolerable repetition of a past that was already extremely costly to escape. It is not unusual for torture survivors in these situations to say that they would rather die by their own means than return to their countries and be tortured again. Even less drastic immigration outcomes such as being put on an ankle brace electronic monitor, a practice that has become increasingly common, can carry an increased risk of suicide for torture survivors. Diagnoses of illnesses perceived as terminal or to bring shame (e.g., HIV/AIDS) are also triggers for suicidal ideation in torture survivors; chronic, debilitating illnesses preventing the survivor from taking care of important obligations such as providing or caring for family members often lead to suicidal thinking based on the belief that loved ones would not be burdened, would be better off, happy, etc., following their deaths. Interpersonal losses, particularly the death of parents and children left behind in the country of origin, but also through divorce or abandonment, also tend to be triggers for suicidal risk among torture survivors. Many survivors from various different cultures have stated that they don't talk about problems unless they are asked; to talk about suicide carries an even higher burden due to cultural proscriptions for some or simply because of the belief that the rest of the community is also suffering in various

different ways. Finding ways to give survivors permission to say how they are feeling then becomes extremely important for clinicians and includes knowing culturally sensitive ways to ask about suicidal ideation. Consultation with knowledgeable cultural providers is a must. Finally, it is important to keep in mind that many torture survivors have suffered traumatic brain injury which may lead to less predictable responses to psychiatric medications, increased risk for adverse outcomes, and an overall requirement of close collaboration across disciplines.

The late *Erika Fromm,* PhD, a diplomate in both clinical psychology and clinical hypnosis, was professor emeritus of psychology at the University of Chicago, clinical editor of the Journal of Clinical and Experimental Hypnosis, and recipient of the American Psychological Association Division 39 (Psychoanalysis) 1985 Award for Distinguished Contributions to the Field. She stated:

> Perhaps it's the countertransference or the highly stressful nature of this work, but some clinicians seem reluctant to provide suicidal patients anything more than minimal reassurance. We need to realize that the people who are about to take their own lives are crying out, are communicating their feelings that no one really cares about them. They are crying, in the only way they know how: "Show me that you really care!" It is so important for us to communicate that we care about them. When my patients are suicidal, I tell them that I care deeply about them and am fond of them. I do everything I can to let them know this.

Gary Schoener, clinical psychologist and executive director emeritus of the Walk-In Counseling Center in Minneapolis, consults, trains, and testifies around North America concerning professional boundaries and clinical supervision. He told us:

> Four most common deadly failures are (1) the failure to screen for the possession of firearms (it's not enough to ask about "weapons") with all distressed clients; (2) when acute suicidality becomes chronic, failure to appropriately refer to a DBT [dialectic behavior therapy] program or qualified provider for cases of chronic suicidality; (3) reliance on the QPR [question, persuade, refer] method with refugees and others, especially Muslims, for whom suicide is a serious sin and who should not be asked directly about suicidal thinking; and (4) overreliance on "no-suicide agreements" despite the fact that they do not work. (No problem in using them clinically, but don't count on them.)

Marla C. Craig, PhD, is psychologist and clinical director at the University of Texas Counseling and Mental Health Center in Austin, Texas. She has previously worked as instructor and coordinator of a campus-wide suicide prevention program at St. Edward's University. She reported:

> Most clinicians may not know that suicide is the second leading cause of death among college students. This information is important since there may be

a tendency for clinicians not to take college students' presenting concerns seriously enough. Presenting concerns such as academic and relationship difficulties may mask the underlying condition of depression. Also, stereotypes of college students' being overly dramatic and emotional with fluctuating moods and situations can interfere with a clinician's judgment to thoroughly assess for suicide. It also may be easy for clinicians to forget that traditional college students are still adolescents transitioning into young adulthood, and they may or may not be able to verbally identify what is going on internally/ emotionally. Hence, it is important to assess for suicide even if the college student does not present as depressed. Finally, due to confidentiality and college students being eighteen years of age and older, clinicians may be reluctant to get parents involved. If the parents are a source of support, do not hesitate to work with the college student to get them involved.

Jesse Geller, PhD, formerly director of the Yale University Psychological Services Clinic and director of the Psychotherapy Division of the Connecticut Mental Health Center, currently maintains an independent practice. He told us:

> One of the two main problems in treating suicidal patients is our own anger and defensiveness when confronted by someone who does not respond positively — and perhaps appreciatively — to our therapeutic efforts. It can stir up very primitive and childish feelings in us — we can start to feel vengeful, withholding, and spiteful. The key is to become aware of these potential reactions and not to act them out in our relationship with the patient. The other main problem seems to be more prevalent among beginning therapists. When we are inexperienced, we may be very cowardly regarding the mention of suicide in our initial interviews. We passively wait for the patient to raise the subject and we may unconsciously communicate that the subject is "taboo." If the subject does come up, we avoid using "hot" language such as "murder yourself" or "blow your brains out." Our avoidance of clear and direct communication, our clinging to euphemisms implies to the patient that we are unable to cope with his or her destructive impulses.

Danny Wedding, PhD, MPH, is Chair of Behavioral Sciences, College of Medicine, American University of Antigua. Danny has completed Fulbright Fellowships in Thailand and Korea, and he has lectured widely on suicide prevention. He is especially concerned about the growing problem of adolescent suicide in Asian countries. He notes

> Suicide is a serious public health problem, and about a million people die by suicide each year — more than are lost to either homicide or war. Prevalence, methods, and risk factors vary widely across cultures and ethnic groups, and clinicians need to be sensitive to these cultural differences. For example, suicide by pesticide poisoning is common in China and Sri Lanka but rare in

Thailand, and suicide rates among American Indian/Alaskan Native adolescents and young adults in the United States are about twice the national average. However, there are also commonalities across cultures — e.g., we know that glamorized media portrayal of suicide can lead to a contagion effect in almost every country. The growing access to the Internet found in almost all developing countries poses special challenges (especially cyber bullying) for those of us interested in suicide prevention. Some of the techniques that have been shown to be effective in preventing youth suicide in other countries include screening, gatekeeper training, crisis hotlines, media education, and skills training.

Don Hiroto, PhD, has maintained an independent practice for over 35 years while also teaching and supervising future psychologists at UCLA. He was chief of the Depression Research Laboratory at the Brentwood Veterans Administration Medical Center, and is a former president of the Los Angeles Society of Clinical Psychologists. He believes that a major area of difficulty involves alcohol use:

Alcoholics may constitute the highest-risk group for violent death. The potential for suicide among alcoholics is extraordinarily high. At least 85% of completed suicides show the presence of at least some level of alcohol in their blood. There are two aspects to the problem for the clinician. First, there is the tendency for us to deny or minimize alcohol consumption as an issue when we assess all of our clients. Second, we are not sufficiently alert to the suicidal risk factors that are especially associated with alcoholics: episodic drinking, impulsivity, increased stress in relationships (especially separation), alienation, and the sense of helplessness.

The late **Helen Block Lewis**, PhD, was a diplomate in clinical psychology who maintained a private practice in New York and Connecticut; she also was professor emeritus at Yale University, president of the American Psychological Association Division of Psychoanalysis, and editor of *Psychoanalytic Psychology*. She believed that therapists tend to pay insufficient attention to the shame and guilt their clients experience. For example, clients may experience a sense of shame for needing psychotherapy and for being "needy" in regard to the therapist. The shame often leads to rage, which in turn leads to guilt because the client is not sure if the rage is justified. According to Lewis, the resultant "shame/rage" or "humiliated fury" can be a major factor in client suicides:

Clients may experience this progression of shame-rage-guilt in many aspects of their lives. It is important for the therapist to help the client understand the sequence not only as it might be related to a current incident "out there" but also as it occurs in the session. Furthermore, it is helpful for clients who are in a frenzied suicidal state to understand that the experience of shame and guilt may represent their attempt to maintain attachments to important people in their lives. Understanding these sequences is important not only for the client but also for the therapist. It is essential that we maintain good feelings for our clients. Sometimes this is difficult when the client is furious, suicidal, and acting out. Our understanding that such feelings and behaviors by a client represent desperate attempts to maintain a connection can help us as therapists to function effectively and remain in touch with our genuine caring for the client.

Michael Peck, PhD, a diplomate in clinical psychology, maintains a private practice and was a consultant to the Los Angeles Suicide Prevention Center. He observes,

> Many therapists fail to consult. Call an experienced clinician or an organization like the L.A. Suicide Prevention Center. Review the situation and get an outside opinion. Therapists may also let a client's improvement (for example, returning to school or work) lull them to sleep. Don't assume that if the mood is brighter, then the suicidal risk is gone.

He stresses the importance of keeping adequate notes, including at least the symptoms, the clinician's response, and consultations and inquiries.

> There are special issues in treating adolescents," Peck adds. "When they're under 16, keep the parents informed. If they are 17 (when the client, rather than the parents, possesses the privilege) or older but still living with the parents, tell the client that you will breach confidentiality only to save his or her life. In almost every case, the family's cooperation in treatment is of great importance.

The late *Hans Strupp*, PhD, a diplomate in clinical psychology, was distinguished professor of psychology and director of clinical training at Vanderbilt University. He believed that one of the greatest pitfalls is the failure to assess suicidal potential comprehensively during initial sessions. Another frequent error, he told us, is that there too often is a failure to have in place a network of services appropriate for suicidal clients in crisis:

> Whether it is an individual private practitioner, a training program run by a university, a small clinic, or [therapists] associated in group practice — there needs to be close and effective collaboration with other mental health professions . . . and with facilities equipped to deal with suicidal emergencies. I'm not talking about pro forma arrangements but a genuine and effective working relationship. In all cases involving suicidal risk, there should be frequent consultation and ready access to appropriate hospitals.

SCENARIOS FOR DISCUSSION

You have been working with a moderately depressed client for four months. You feel that you have a good rapport, but the treatment plan does not seem to be doing much good. Between sessions, you check your answering machine and find this message from the patient: "I want to thank you for trying to help me, but now I realize that nothing will do me any good. I won't be seeing you or anyone else ever again. I've left home and won't be returning. I didn't leave any notes because there really isn't anything to say. Thank you again for trying to help. Good-bye." Your next patient is scheduled to see you in two minutes, and you have patients scheduled for the next 4 hours.

- What feelings do you experience?
- What do you want to do?
- What are your options?
- What do you think you would do?
- If there are things that you want to do but don't do, why do you reject these options?
- What do you believe that your ethical and legal obligations are? Are there any contradictions between your legal responsibilities and constraints and what you believe is ethical?
- To what extent do you believe that your education and training have prepared you to deal with this situation?

You have been working with a patient within a managed care framework. You believe that the patient is at considerable risk for suicide. The case reviewer disagrees and, noting that the approved number of sessions have been provided, declines, despite your persistent protests, to approve any additional sessions.

- How do you feel?
- What are your options?
- What do you believe your legal obligations to client are?
- What do you believe your ethical responsibilities to the client are?
- What would you do?

You have been providing family therapy to a mother and father and their three adolescents for four sessions. After the fourth session, you find that one of the adolescents has left a note on your desk. Here is what the note says: "My father has molested me for the past 2 years. He has threatened to kill my mother and me if anyone else finds out. I could not take it if you told anyone else. If you do, I will find a way to kill myself." Your clinical judgment, based on what you have learned during the course of the four sessions, is that the adolescent is extremely likely to commit suicide under those circumstances.

- How do you feel?
- More specifically, what are your feelings about the patient who left you the note? What are your feelings about the father? What are your feelings about the mother? What are your feelings about the other two adolescents?
- What do you believe that your legal obligations are?
- What do you believe that your ethical responsibilities are?
- What, if any, conflicts do you experience? How do you go about considering and deciding what to do about these conflicts?
- What do you believe that you would do?

A patient you have been seeing in outpatient psychotherapy for two years does not show up for an appointment. The patient has been depressed and has recently experienced some personal and occupational disappointments, but the risk of suicide as you have assessed it has remained at a very low level. You call the patient at home to see if this person has forgotten the appointment or if there has been a mixup in scheduling. You reach a family member, who tells you that the patient has committed suicide.

- What do you feel?
- Are there any feelings that are difficult to identify or put into words?
- What options do you consider?
- Do you tell the family member that you were the person's therapist? Why or why not? What, if anything, do you volunteer to tell the family?
- Do you send flowers? Why or why not? Do you attend the funeral? Why or why not?
- If a family member says that the suicide must have been your fault, what do you feel? What would you do?

(continued)

(continued)

- Do you tell any of your friends or colleagues? Why? What concerns, if any, do you have?
- Do your case notes and documentation show your failure to assess accurately the patient's suicidal risk? Why or why not? Do you have any concerns about your documentation?

You have been discussing a new HMO patient, whom you have seen for three outpatient sessions, with your clinical supervisor and the chief of outpatient services. The chief of services strongly believes that the patient is at substantial risk for suicide, but the clinical supervisor believes just as strongly that there is no real risk. You are caught in the middle, trying to create a treatment plan that makes sense in the light of the conflicting views of the two people to whom you report. One morning you arrive at work and are informed that your clinical supervisor has committed suicide.

- What do you feel?
- Are there any feelings that are particularly difficult to identify, acknowledge, or articulate?
- How, if at all, do you believe that this might influence your work with any of your patients?
- Assume that at the first session, you obtained the patient's written informed consent for the work to be discussed with this particular clinical supervisor who has been countersigning the patient's chart notes. What, if anything, do you tell the patient about the supervisor's suicide or the fact that the clinical work will now be discussed with a new supervisor?
- To what extent has your graduate training and internship addressed issues of clinicians' own suicidal ideation, impulses, or behaviors?

Chapter 26

STEPS TO STRENGTHEN ETHICS IN ORGANIZATIONS

Research Findings, Ethics Placebos, and What Works*

Our work brings us into contact with a remarkable array of organizations. We may work for clinics or hospitals; collect fees from insurance companies or managed care organizations; join professional associations; provide forensic services at prisons; or provide EAP services to large corporations. Throughout this book we've highlighted the ethical issues that can arrive in organizational settings, and in the chapter "Moral Distress and Moral Courage," we focused on the intense ethical challenges that arise when organizations and other forces violate our professional or personal ethical values. This chapter suggests steps to strengthen ethics in organizations.

We live in an age rich with opportunities to make organizational ethics stronger. Striking betrayals of ethics and trust grab headlines:

- In 2014, General Motors (GM) admitted that since 2001 it had hidden a potentially fatal design defect. GM engineers, investigators, and lawyers knew, but the company decided that recalling cars would cost too much. Instead, they kept the flaw secret for more than a decade. They kept selling risky cars while the deaths and injuries piled up (Bennett, 2014a,

---

* This chapter is adapted from and used with permission from "Steps to Strengthen Ethics in Organizations: Research Findings, Ethics Placebos, and What Works," by K. S. Pope, 2015, *Journal of Trauma & Dissociation, 16,* 139–152. © Taylor & Francis.

2014b, 2014c; *Consumer Reports*, 2014; Ivory & Abrams, 2014; Plungis & Higgins, 2014; Viscusi, 2015; Young, 2014).

- Famous for its football program's integrity, Penn State covered up child abuse for years, allowing the abuser to continue committing crimes. The university-commissioned report stressed "the total and consistent disregard by the most senior leaders at Penn State for the safety and welfare of Sandusky's child victims" (Freeh, Sporken, & Sullivan, LLP, 2012, p. 14).

- California had repealed its "compulsory sterilization laws [that] targeted minorities, the poor, the disabled, the mentally ill and criminals" (Johnson, 2014) that allowed the state to force sterilization on more than 20,000 citizens in state-run institutions (Stern, 2005; Wellerstein, 2011), but the California State Auditor (2014) reported that between 2005 and 2013 the state prison system had continued to sterilize some female prisoners, violating both the law and women's right to informed consent.

- Many Veterans Administration (VA) executives pocketed hefty bonuses for making sure that sick veterans got prompt care, but it was a con. Hospitals reported that they were giving all veterans prompt care when needed but were shunting tens of thousands of veterans to secret waiting lists where they languished without care for months and some died without care (Bronstein & Griffin, 2014; Daly & Tang, 2014; Hoyer & Zoroya, 2014; Oppel & Shear, 2014; VA Office of the Inspector General, 2014; Wagner, 2014a, 2014b).

Studies suggest that many organizations violate basic ethical standards and betray our trust:

- Huberts (2014) noted that almost half of U.S. workers reported seeing one or more acts of wrongdoing (e.g., accepting kickbacks or bribes, offering bribes to public officials, lying to outside stakeholders, environmental violations) on the job within the past year.

- A study of full-time U.S. workers found that almost three fourths reported encountering ethical lapses at work, with one tenth believing that the lapse could create a scandal or business disruption (LRN, 2007).

- According to Stevens (2013), "Confidence in the ethics of the U.S. business executive remains fairly low on the Gallup Poll surveys and the U.S. has declined on the CPI (Consumer Price Index) and Edelman Trust Barometer" (p. 361).

- In the introduction to a special issue of the *Journal of Law, Medicine & Ethics*, Rodwin (2013) wrote that "today, the goals of pharmaceutical policy and medical practice are often undermined due to institutional corruption — that is, widespread or systemic practices, usually legal, that undermine an institution's objectives or integrity" (p. 544). Elliott (2014) noted that in 2010 the pharmaceutical industry eclipsed the defense industry as the biggest defrauder of the U.S. government.

- A study found that campus judicial systems tend to give light sentences (e.g., writing an essay) for serious violations such as sexual assaults, physical attacks causing serious injuries, robberies, and other violent felonies, leaving many students reporting that "the system is unfair" and that the campus "has betrayed them" (Binkley, Wagner, Riepenhoff, & Gregory, 2014).

- Twenge, Campbell, and Carter (2014) reported that "confidence in institutions . . . reached historic lows among Americans" (p. 1920). They emphasized that the loss of trust and confidence extends across a wide array of institutions: "The trend is not limited to distrust in government; the declines also appear in Americans' confidence in institutions unconnected to the government, such as medicine, religion, the news media, and TV" (p. 1921).

This chapter suggests three steps to strengthen ethics in organizations.

KEEP CODES IN CONTEXT

Organizations often point with pride to their ethics codes, highlighting high ideals and clear prohibitions of questionable conduct. Codes can communicate basic standards and admirable aspirations. (For discussion of the American Psychological Association and Canadian Psychological Association ethics codes, see Chapter 15, "Codes and Complaints in Context: Historical, Empirical, and Actuarial Foundations"; see also Pope 1991, 2011). But ethics codes — including those backed by good-faith enforcement — often fall short of fostering an ethically strong organization. Unethical acts may go unnoticed, noticed acts may go unreported, reported acts may not be fully and fairly investigated, and investigation findings may not be adequately acted on.

Enron's famous 84-page organizational code illustrates the illusions that codes out of context can create. Enron required every employee to read and sign the code, which was widely praised for years as a model for other groups wishing to achieve Enron's reputation for integrity, innovation, and profitability. Years later, Enron's code of ethics shifted from fame to notoriety as prosecutors used it to cross-examine employees in trials that convicted 21 felons after the company collapsed into bankruptcy and caused investors to lose $74 billion, with losses due to fraud up to $45 billion (Arbogast, 2013; Axtman, 2005; McLean & Elkind, 2013; Pasha, 2006; Watkins, 2013). Lease (2006) wrote that "the literature supports . . . the contention that an ethical organizational culture cannot be created through the imposition of a code"

(p. 29) but that a code can play a key role if those at the top provide ethical leadership by modeling ethical behavior and creating a culture of commitment to ethics throughout the organization.

Kish-Gephart, Harrison, and Treviño's (2010) meta-analysis found that the "mere existence of a code of conduct has no detectable impact on unethical choices, despite the considerable amount of statistical power that comes from doing a meta-analytic summary" (p. 21). However, the study also found "a strong, negative link . . . between code enforcement and unethical choice" (p. 13).

Weaver (2014) noted that "empirical research has been clear" that organizational codes per se have "limited, if any, influence on ethical behavior" (p. 293) but must be part of an organization climate in which ethical issues are discussed on an everyday basis and become an ordinary aspect of decision making and behavior (see also Nicholson, 2008; Weiss, 2014). The organization's ethical culture becomes internalized as part of each individual's personal values (Hill, Jones, & Schilling, 2014).

These and other studies suggest that many ethics codes may be little more than an ethics placebo. Codes work to prompt ethical thinking and action when rooted in an ecology of strong ethical leadership, effective enforcement, and a culture of ethical concern. Ethics questions can rise for everyone to the level of daily concern often devoted to questions of profits, promotions, and will this meeting ever end? To make ethics stronger in any organization, a reasonable first step is surveying all employees, members, and other stakeholders about current leadership, enforcement, and culture; asking them about needed changes; and opening up discussions.

RESPECT THE TRUE COSTS OF BETRAYING ETHICS

When it comes to ethics, none of us is perfect. We all fall short, miss red flags, face risky moments of weakness and temptation. How do we mask, reinterpret, or justify our unethical acts to ourselves and, when needed, to others? Each of us likely has our own set of go-to strategies when we find it hard to pass up temptation. Chapters 4 through 8 discuss ways to strengthen our ethical intelligence and critical thinking so that we can spot and avoid some of the most common means — logical fallacies, flawed judgments, tricks of language, and cognitive strategies of justification — of spinning ethically questionable or objectionable options into seemingly acceptable choices.

These ethical spins deny or downplay the true costs of our unethical acts. The costs of betraying ethics range from seemingly minor wrongs to people dying, as in the GM example. In betraying ethics, GM betrayed its customers, who trusted and relied on the company's honesty, integrity, and good faith. As a result, some GM customers died. Others suffered needless catastrophic injuries. Families suddenly lost a mother, a father, a child, or another loved one. These are the true costs of deciding that fixing a design flaw is "not worth the cost" (Viscusi, 2015, p. 7).

Research supports the idea that betrayal per se can cause harm and may deepen the response to other bad acts. Rachman (2010) noted that betrayal's effects may include "shock, loss and grief, morbid pre-occupation, damaged self-esteem, self-doubting, anger" and sometimes "life-altering changes" (p. 304). Koehler and Gershoff's (2003) set of experiments "found that people reacted more strongly... to acts of betrayal than to identical bad acts that do not violate a duty or promise to protect" (p. 244; see also Beamish, 2001).

Research also supports the idea that when betrayal happens within organizational dynamics, it may cause institutional betrayal trauma (Freyd, Klest, & Allard, 2005; Smith & Freyd, 2013). Organizations often betray customers, students, parishioners, prisoners, and others who are not employees, but organizations can also betray their own employees. Kirschman, Kamena, and Fay (2013), for example, described organizational betrayal that many police officers experience. They wrote that when this betrayal occurs, it "complicates traumatic reactions by creating huge doubts about the future" (p. 73) and "makes everything else worse" (p. 57). Surís, Lind, Kashner, and Borman (2007, p. 179; see also Surís, Lind, Kashner, Borman, & Petty, 2004) found that when female soldiers were sexually assaulted within the context of the military organization (i.e., by officers or other military personnel), there were "additional negative consequences above and beyond the effects of [civilian sexual assault]." Ethically strong organizations work to avoid the logical fallacies, judgment errors, tricks of language, and cognitive strategies of justification — discussed in chapters 4 through 8 — that hide betrayals and their true costs.

To appreciate the ability of such a common event as betrayal to stay out of sight, it may be helpful to remember that psychology itself was slow to recognize it as a topic of study. The PsycNET database includes millions of articles in psychology journals dating back to 1900, but a study — or article of any kind — with the term *betrayal* in the title did not appear in a psychology journal until a single article was published during the 1960s, followed by an average of less than one each year for the next two decades. It was not until 1992, when a special double issue (Volume 8, Issues 3–4) of *Psychotherapy Patient* published seven articles focusing on betrayal, and 1994, when Freyd published "Betrayal Trauma: Traumatic Amnesia as an Adaptive Response to Childhood Abuse," which was followed by *Betrayal Trauma: The Logic of Forgetting Childhood Abuse* in 1996, that a significant body of published research, theory, and thoughtful discussions began to appear.

The anonymous survey and open discussion recommended previously might include the following questions:

* How has the organization betrayed — or seemed at risk for betraying — ethical standards or aspirations, the organization's employees or members, and others affected by the organization's behavior?

- How has the organization denied or downplayed betrayals and their consequences?
- How has the organization failed to assume responsibility for its betrayals?
- What changes would be helpful, and who should make them?

ENCOURAGE SPEAKING UP, LISTENING CAREFULLY, AND ACTING WITH FAIRNESS

Prior sections suggest an anonymous survey as a starting point. Why? Because organizational culture often silences concerns that the organization's leadership, culture, code enforcement, or behavior are questionable, somewhat flawed, or worse. Kish-Gephart, Detert, Treviño, and Edmondson (2009) wrote, "In every organization, individual members have the potential to speak up about important issues, but a growing body of research suggests that they often remain silent instead, out of fear of negative personal and professional consequences" (p. 163; see also Mayer, Milliken, Morrison, & Hewlin, 2003). Detert and Treviño (2010) noted that many employees believe from the time they set foot in the door that part of their organizational role is to "'tread lightly around those in power'" (p. 264).

Sometimes the belief that speaking up achieves nothing compels those concerned to keep their mouths shut. In some organizations, people in power turn a deaf ear to unwelcome questions, concerns, or reports (see, e.g., Peirce, Rosen, & Smolinski, 1998; Pinder & Harlos, 2001). Does the organization welcome and appreciate critics as providing an opportunity to rethink issues, try out new perspectives, and perhaps correct course? Does leadership model for its employees, members, clients, and other stakeholders openly acknowledging, taking responsibility for, and apologizing for ethical lapses or mistakes, however unintentional? In any organization, it is worth evaluating how many, if any, of the leaders have publicly acknowledged, taken responsibility for, and apologized for their own or the organization's ethical missteps. If there have been few instances in the history of the organization, perhaps it is a red flag. One aspect of organizational climate is the degree to which the organization is open to discussing such questions, issues, and concerns.

Stakeholders may also lack confidence that ethics concerns or complaints will be met with fairness and justice (Cropanzana, Bowen, & Gilliland, 2007; Dunford, Jackson, Boss, Tay, & Boss, 2014; Qin, Ren, Zhang, & Johnson, 2014). Does the history of the organization show that formal complaints against leadership and others with power, status, and connections are investigated and adjudicated with the same attention, diligence, care, and level of scrutiny as complaints against others? If members of any organization believe that there is one system of ethical accountability and discipline for those with power, status, and connections and a different system for everyone else, it may create a climate in which the privileged can act with impunity and others learn that voicing ethical questions or concerns about those at the top will at best come to nothing.

Research suggests that those who choose to act as whistleblowers must overcome concerns that they will face retaliation or that the risks they take will be in vain (Mayer, Nurmohamed, Treviño, Shapiro, & Schminke, 2013; Mesmer-Magnus & Viswesvaran, 2005; Miceli, Near, & Dworkin, 2013). These concerns are often well placed. Dyer (2014), for example, reported that "more than half the whistleblowers who contacted the UK charity Public Concern at Work for advice in 2012 were sacked or resigned after raising concerns about wrongdoing, risk, or malpractice" (p. 6285). An additional 22% were disciplined or punished in other ways. Only 6% reported that their speaking up led to improvements in the workplace.

Rothschild and Miethe (1999) found that whistleblowers tend to "suffer severe retaliation from management, especially when their information proves significant" (p. 107). McDonald and Ahern (2000) found that nurse whistleblowers tended to suffer severe consequences, whereas those who kept silent experienced few negative effects. The official reprisals included demotion (4%), reprimand (11%), and referral to a psychiatrist (9%). Whistleblowers also reported that they received professional reprisals in the form of threats (16%), rejection by peers (14%), pressure to resign (7%), and being treated as a traitor (14%). Ten percent reported that they felt their career had been halted (McDonald & Ahern, 2000, p. 313).

Sherron Watkins (2013), formerly of Enron, described how blowing the whistle on questionable activities can derail a career. The media provided positive coverage of her insider disclosures of Enron's wrongdoing and her testifying as a key prosecution witness in the criminal and civil trials. She shared the cover of *Time* with two other whistleblowers from other organizations as *Time*'s "Person of the Year." The corporate world, however, took a dimmer view. A decade later she wrote that "the label Enron whistleblower means I will not work in Corporate America again" (p. ix).

Jackall (1988) gathered the rules of organizational silence into a series of five warnings:

> (1) You never go around your boss. (2) You tell your boss what he wants to hear, even when your boss claims that he wants dissenting views. (3) If your boss wants something dropped, you drop it. (4) You are sensitive to your boss's wishes so that you anticipate what he wants; you don't force him, in other words, to act as boss. (5) Your job is not to report something that your boss does not want reported, but rather to cover it up. You do what your job requires, and you keep your mouth shut. (p. 115)

A culture of silence and silencing can close off many routes to better organizational ethics. An anonymous survey might begin by asking the following: If you were to raise concerns about ethics or blow the whistle on unethical behavior, how do you think your colleagues and those higher up in the organization would respond, what would happen to your concerns, and what would happen to you? But if the organization's culture lacks trust, those asked to fill out the survey may wonder: Will they recognize my identity in some way? Are the forms coded? If I go to all the trouble of filling it out, will anyone even read it? Take it seriously? Treat it fairly? Use it to make things better?

In some cases, it may make more sense to simply start looking for ways to change the culture and dynamics of silencing. What immediate steps would encourage and support speaking up and show that valid criticism is heard, valued, and acted on with fairness and justice? Can the costs of speaking up be eliminated or at least minimized?

CONCLUSION: ONLY IF WE ACT

Any steps to make organizational ethics stronger can succeed only if we actually take the steps. Taking action requires us to leave our role as passive bystanders (aka enablers) when we learn of questionable or unacceptable behavior, especially when the welfare of others is at stake.

We must often teach ourselves how to leave the comfort and safety of "it's not my problem," "someone else will take care of this," "it's probably not as bad as it looks," or "speaking up won't make any difference." However, formal programs show promise in teaching and encouraging bystanders to take action in a range of situations such as theft, sexual harassment, interpersonal or systemic racism, bullying, or sexual assault (Chiose, 2014; Guerette, Flexon, & Marquez, 2013; Kleinsasser, Jouriles, McDonald, & Rosenfield, 2014; Nelson, Dunn, & Paradies, 2011; Nickerson, Aloe, Livingston, & Feeley, 2014; Palm Reed, Hines, Armstrong, & Cameron, 2014; Salmivalli, 2014; van Bommel, van Prooijen, Elffers, & van Lange, 2014; Wonderling, 2013).

Serrat (2010) described the ways in which moral courage (see the chapter, "Moral Distress and Moral Courage") can strengthen organizational ethics: "At its most basic, moral courage helps cultivate mindful organizational environments that, among others, offset groupthink; mitigate hypocrisy and 'nod-and-wink' cultures; educate mechanical conformity and compliance; bridge organizational silos; and check irregularities, misconduct, injustice, and corruption" (p. 2; see also Hannah, Avolio, & Walumbwa, 2011; Osswald, Greitemeyer, Fischer, & Frey, 2010; Simola, 2015). It often takes moral courage to take action — whether action means using a survey to find out what changes might make organizational ethics stronger, trying to help bring about those changes, or blowing the whistle inside or outside the organization.

Finally, even if we are concerned about, committed to, and focused on taking steps to prevent questionable or objectionable practices on an individual and organizational level, our lives may be so textured with tight schedules, heavy responsibilities, and constant distractions that we miss chances to make a difference. Darley and Batson (1973) conducted an experiment showing how a lack of attention to our immediate surroundings — the here and now — can lead to missed opportunities. Princeton Theological Seminary students participated in an experiment in which they were given time to prepare a brief talk in one locale and then had to give the talk in another building. As the students walked through an alley between the buildings, each found someone pretending to be a victim in need of help — slumped over in a doorway, eyes shut, head down, unmoving. The victim coughed and groaned. Half of the students prepared a talk on the parable of the Good Samaritan, and yet many did not stop to help the victim. Those who were about to talk about the importance of acting like the Good Samaritan were no more likely to stop to help than those who were assigned to talk about another topic. To save time, some stepped over the victim rather than going around.

As we go about taking steps to make ethics stronger in organizations, this study reminds us that a chance to make a difference can come at an inconvenient time and catch us off guard by appearing in forms we did not expect, that we can pass by it without noticing, and that we need to pay attention to what shows up unannounced at every step.

Chapter 27

SUPERVISION

Supervision draws together many themes running through this book. We began our clinical careers as supervisees. It is not hard to think of ways our supervisors shaped our growth. Some spoke words of comfort, warning, wisdom, or support at just the right time. Some opened our eyes and hearts by who they were as people and how they were with people. One or two may have given us a gift both unexpected and invaluable: Their arrogance, rudeness, corner-cutting, or dogmatism inspired us to look inward, see how we were like them, and work on our own less charming traits.

Supervision involves considerable power, trust, and caring, although they take different forms than in therapy (see Chapter 9).

CLEAR TASKS, ROLES, AND RESPONSIBILITIES

Supervision includes at least three people: client, supervisee, and supervisor. Relationships and agendas can easily blur into confusion. A basic ethical responsibility for supervisors is to clarify the tasks, roles, and responsibilities. For example, they avoid drifting into the role of the supervisee's therapist. Some forms of supervision may share common aspects with some forms of therapy. If supervisees become aware of psychological problems and decide to seek therapy, they should consult a therapist in addition to continuing to work with their supervisor on how their issues affect their psychotherapy with clients.

Working in some organizations can create challenges for clarifying tasks, roles, and responsibilities. Norton and Solosky (2015), for example, discuss the challenges of clinical supervision with U.S. Army chaplains who are trained as marriage and family therapists: "The unique challenges presented in this clinical supervision setting include: issues specific to chaplains' rank as military officers, countertransference, confidentiality, use of military language, and the struggle to integrate three professional role identities" (p. 21). Brown, Murdock, and Abels (2014) studied the challenges in another organizational setting: university counseling centers (UCCs). They noted difficult issues regarding potential multiple relationships:

> Some of these multiple relationships are unavoidable in UCCs, such as ... the situation when a staff member of a shared university committee discovers that a current or former client (or that of a supervisee) is also a member. Similarly because trainees and their clinical supervisors represent a limited pool of counseling professionals providing service, staff counselors, trainees, and university student-clients may know each other prior to beginning counseling. (p. 274)

Clarifying the tasks, roles, and responsibilities includes discussing these issues with the supervisee. Kozlowski, Pruitt, DeWalt, and Knox (2014) note that discussions with supervisees "allow clarification of boundaries, show respect for the supervisee, and possibly allow supervisors to avoid crossing boundaries they might not be aware of."

Although the supervisor has responsibilities for the client's care and the supervisee's professional growth, the client's welfare must be primary. The supervisor must make sure that no aspect of training puts the client at undue risk. Supervision often takes place in a hospital or clinic, and the therapist-trainees may have predetermined internships or rotations (for example, 6 months or an academic calendar year). Such time sequences and boundaries must be taken into account when considering the client's welfare. Frequent terminations and transfers can cause significant problems for some clients. The informed consent process should include letting the client know if a therapist will be available for only a few months.

When a therapist-trainee becomes licensed and leaves a setting, do the clients remain at the setting or follow the newly licensed therapist? Who decides? Can agency policies prevent the therapist from opening an office too close to the original setting or from inviting clients to follow to the new office? These issues are best addressed *before* training begins and should be clarified in a written agreement. Otherwise disagreements can grow into formal complaints and lawsuits (see, e.g., Pope, 1990a). A supervision contract can head off countless potential problems (Falender, Shafranske, & Ofek, 2014).

The supervisor is ultimately responsible, ethically and legally, for the clinical services that the supervisee provides. Supervisor and supervisee must address any conflicts about treatment approaches when they first arise (Canadian Psychological Association, 2009). Both may avoid addressing — or even acknowledging — conflicts that make them uncomfortable, and some of the conflicts may involve ideas that are "politically incorrect" and perhaps even "psychologically incorrect" (Pope, Sonne, & Greene, (2006).

Unaddressed conflicts between supervisor and supervisee almost always interfere with therapy and supervision. These conflicts are often acted out or mirrored in the supervisee-client relationship. Similarly, the dynamics of the relationship between supervisee and client are often recreated or echoed in the supervisor-supervisee relationship. The ways that unaddressed conflicts affect the therapy and supervision are a normal part of training. They are not a sign that the therapy is terribly misguided, the supervisee needs to withdraw from graduate training and seek a line of work that does not involve being around other people, or the supervisor is a monster suffering from delusions of adequacy. What they do signal is that important dynamics of the supervisor-supervisee-client triad need to be addressed

Nonsexual dual relationships can complicate the supervisor's ethical responsibility to clarify roles. Should a supervisor enter into various social relationships with a supervisee? The answer, as it so often is in our work, is: It depends. The general principles in the chapter on multiple relationships and boundaries in therapy apply here: Clarifying where the boundaries are enables us to decide when crossing them would be helpful and when it would undermine good supervision. Crossing the boundaries of supervision by, for example, entering into a nonsexual dual relationship, can enrich the working relationship and the supervisee's development. Sometimes a supervisor's decision not to cross a boundary can represent a lost opportunity. But the supervisor bears the responsibility to avoid boundary violations, which can undermine the work of supervision and demean, exploit, or abuse the supervisee.

A fundamental theme running through this book is that codes, laws, and standards are the beginning — not the end — of our ethical considerations. Nothing can spare us the struggle with complex questions involving unique people in unique situations. The codes, laws, and standards inform — but do not replace — our efforts to think through issues. Burian and Slimp (2000; see also Gottlieb, Robinson, & Younggren, 2007; Slimp & Burian, 1994) provide a thoughtful model for thinking through social dual-role relationships during internships that can be adapted to many supervision settings. Their decision-making model helps supervisors to consider a variety of useful issues like the reasons for the relationship, the power difference between supervisor and supervisee, the nature of the social activities, and the effects on other supervisees.

Kitchener (2000) also addresses multiple-role relationships in supervision and uses social role theory to reveal the ambiguity inherent in role conflicts. Supervision involves many responsibilities, such as helping trainees develop, evaluating supervisees, protecting the public from incompetent or inept therapists, and making sure that clients receive a decent standard of care. Kitchener (2000) points out that the supervisee may be involved with the supervisor in a variety of other roles, including consulting, coauthoring papers or presentations, and attending social functions together. These multiple roles are complicated because supervisees may be much more personally vulnerable than those who are in a teacher-student relationship, given the revelation of personal secrets that may be blocking work with clients. Yet supervision differs from therapy, partly because of the evaluative component in supervision and partly because confidentiality and privilege do not have the same status in supervision as they do in therapy.

The confidentiality of what the supervisee does disclose to the supervisor deserves explicit discussion at the start. The Canadian Psychological Association (2009b) emphasizes that supervisor and supervisee should "clearly define the parameters of supervisee and supervisor confidentiality of personal information shared during supervision, including stated limitations relevant to reasonable curricular and educational planning for the enhancement of learning, evaluations of competency for independent practice as required by regulatory bodies, and legal requirements to prevent serious and imminent harm" (p. 6).

COMPETENCE

Like therapy, supervision requires demonstrable competence. "It is vital that the supervisor be well trained, knowledgeable, and skilled in the practice of clinical supervision" (Stoltenberg & Delworth, 1987, p. 175). It would be no more ethical to improvise supervision if one lacked education, training, and supervised experience than if one were to improvise hypnotherapy, systematic desensitization, or a neuropsychological assessment without adequate preparation. Carol Falender and Edward Shafranske (2004; see also 2008, 2010; Falender, Shafranske, & Falicov, 2014; Falender, Shafranske, & Ofek, 2014) emphasize supervision as a distinct professional activity when they define the term:

> Supervision is a distinct professional activity in which education and training aimed at developing science-informed practice are facilitated through a collaborative interpersonal process. It involves observation, evaluation, feedback, the facilitation of supervisee self-assessment, and the acquisition of knowledge and skills by instruction, modeling, and mutual problem solving. In addition, by building on the recognition of the strengths and talents of the supervisee, supervision encourages self-efficacy. Supervision ensures that clinical consultation is conducted in a competent manner in which ethical standards, legal prescriptions, and professional practices are used to promote and protect the welfare of the client, the profession, and society at large. (p. 3)

Despite the importance of supervision and its key role in professional development, training *in* supervision was often overlooked. Kathleen Malloy and her colleagues (Malloy, Dobbins, Ducheny, & Winfrey, 2010) pointed out that supervision has not "been well represented in graduate education or in the accreditation process" and that "supervision has only recently received attention as a core domain for clinical training" (p. 161).

The field still struggles with how competence in supervision can best be achieved. There is some evidence that — not surprisingly — how we as individuals were trained to supervise shapes what we view as the best training. Jeffrey Rings and his colleagues (2009) surveyed predoctoral internship training directors about their views of competence in supervision. The survey revealed

> patterns of disagreement on the importance of both supervision coursework and supervision of supervision. On the surface, the degree of importance placed in one's completing supervision coursework seemed to reflect the amount of supervision training one might have had, as indicated by the type of supervision training received. Those who completed supervision coursework were significantly more likely to agree with its importance than were those who attended a supervision workshop, who in turn agreed with its importance significantly more so than those who had no supervision training whatsoever. (p. 145)

The state of the art and science of supervision does not stand still any more than other areas of our work. Only if we keep up with the literature can we make sure that the evolving research and theory informs our work as supervisors. The supervision literature itself is of course diverse, spanning diverse theoretical orientations (see, e.g., Boswell, Nelson, Nordberg, McAleavey, & Castonguay, 2010; Celano, Smith, & Kaslow, 2010; Farber, 2010; Farber & Kaslow, (2010); Guiffrida, 2015; Mcaleavey, Castonguay, & Xiao, 2014; Watkins, 2014; Wolff & Aukenthaler, 2014).

As emphasized throughout this book, our work often requires multicultural competence, especially as multicultural issues become key in a given supervisory situation (see, e.g., Falender, Shafranske, & Falicov, 2014; Falender, Burnes & Ellis, 2013; Soheilian, Inman, Klinger, Isenberg, & Kulp, 2014; Tsong & Goodyear, 2014). Kissil, Davey, and Davey (2015), for example, discuss the implications of their research, noting that it is

> especially important for clinical supervisors to openly discuss and actively explore cross-cultural interactions with foreign-born supervisees, including all parts of the training triad and the sociopolitical context (supervisor/supervisee, therapist/client, therapist/larger community where therapist works). Supervisors can become more aware of their own worldviews and gain more knowledge about acculturation experiences and their possible effects on foreign-born therapists' clinical self-efficacy. Supervisors can also encourage foreign-born supervisees to more deeply examine their experiences of acculturation and any perceived prejudice in the United States to identify

how these experiences might emerge during therapeutic encounters with U.S. clients. (p. 57; see also Kissil, Davey, & Davey, 2013)

Discussing multicultural competence as essential to supervisor competence, Falender and Shafranske (2014) note:

Although greater attention is being directed to diversity, still data are emerging that supervisors often are not initiating consideration of multiple diversity factors in supervision, nor are factors of privilege, historical trauma, and oppression being addressed .... Specific competence is needed to address the multiple identities (e.g., race, socioeconomic status, sexual orientation, gender identity, ethnicity, religion, disability, age) among client, supervisee/psychotherapist, and supervisor to consider the multiple worldviews and the effects of these upon the assessment and treatment of the client. (p. 1034)

Beyond maintaining competence in supervision, supervisors must also maintain competence in the approaches used to assess and treat the client and make sure that supervisees are at least minimally competent to provide services to the client. A temptation for some supervisors is to form a relationship with a promising supervisee who has had course work in clinical techniques for which the supervisor may have only superficial or outdated knowledge. These supervisors may, if they are not scrupulously careful, find themselves supervising interventions for which they have no demonstrable competence. For example, supervisors whose practice is exclusively psychoanalytical and who have no training in cognitive-behavioral techniques may find themselves supervising students who are using covert conditioning; supervisors who have worked only with adults may find themselves supervising child therapy; supervisors who take an existential-humanistic approach and do not use standardized tests may find themselves trying to help a supervisee interpret an MMPI-2.

Constant questioning has been a theme throughout this book. Supervisors can ask themselves, "Even though I have solid competence in supervision and the approaches used to assess and help the client, are there other relevant issues for which I lack competence? For example, are there any issues of background, culture, language, religion, or values among the client, the supervisee, and me that make it hard for us to understand each other and work together? If so, is that issue related to competence and how is it best addressed?" Some resources that may be helpful include the Canadian Psychological Association's "Guidelines for Ethical Practice with Diverse Populations" (part of the Canadian Psychological Association's *Guidelines for Non-Discriminatory Practice*, 2001b) and the American Psychological Association's "Guidelines on Multicultural Education, Training, Research, Practice and Organizational Change for Psychologists" (2003b).

ASSESSMENT AND EVALUATION

The supervisor must assess continually both the clinical services provided to the client and the supervisee's professional development. This responsibility can make many of us supervisors uncomfortable.

The evaluation component of supervision may make supervisees uncomfortable. In graduate training programs, internships, arrangements in which supervised hours are accumulated as a prerequisite to licensure, and many institutional settings, the supervisor must report to third parties an assessment of the supervisee's strengths, weaknesses, and progress. These reports may profoundly influence the supervisee's opportunities for continuing in the training program or for future employment.

Supervisors must clearly, frankly, and promptly communicate to supervisees their assessment of strengths, weaknesses, and development. In some cases, supervisors may determine that the supervisee is unable, either temporarily or more permanently, to do clinical work. Those supervisors must try to determine *why* the supervisee is unable to work. Some supervisees suffer from the strain of the workload, a personal loss, financial problems, aging and infirm parents, or marital conflicts. Others find that doing therapy brings up personal conflicts or unresolved issues from the past. Others experience thought disorders, depression, or anxiety so severe that it blocks their ability to function effectively. And still others may suffer from developmental or personality disorders.

The supervisor's responsibility is clear and unavoidable in such circumstances. The APA's policy for training programs more generally is also relevant for individual supervisors. The Commission on Accreditation for the American Psychological Association (2013) stated that all programs have special responsibility to assess continually the progress of each student and that trainees receive timely written notification of all problems that have been noted, the opportunity to discuss them, and guidance regarding steps to remedy them if remediable. Trainees should also receive written feedback about whether corrective actions have been successful (APA, 2013). Supervisors must be prepared to protect the public and well-being of the clients, while simultaneously supporting the professional development of the supervisee (APA, 2014).

The Americans With Disabilities Act sets forth special responsibilities in this area. Carol Falender, Christopher Collins, and Edward Shafranske (2009) provide a helpful discussion of these issues in their article "'Impairment' and performance issues in clinical supervision: After the 2008 ADA Amendments Act." They emphasize:

> After ensuring client care (their first responsibility), supervisors enter into processes in which they must articulate specific areas of problematic professional behavior and develop with their supervisees plans to enhance clinical competence. When evaluating, communicating, and documenting

performance problems, supervisors must be mindful to avoid the misuse of the term impairment as well as to understand their legal obligations, when impairment contributes to performance difficulties. (p. 247)

The warning to avoid misuse of the word "impairment" can head off countless problems. Rebecca Schwartz-Mette (2011) summarized some central problems:

> Impairment typically is utilized as an umbrella term to describe both performance and behavioral problems with myriad etiological factors including underlying disability, personal problems, and inadequate training. However, use of the term in this general or global way is rife with problems, as it confounds descriptions with causes of problem behavior and fails to distinguish between competence that was lost and that which was never attained (Elman & Forrest, 2007). Further, as Collins and colleagues discuss here and elsewhere (Calender et al., 2005, 2009), imprecise use of impairment contributes to confusion and legal risk in the identification, assessment, and remediation of trainees' problematic performance, as impairment connotes disability under the Americans with Disabilities Act (ADA; 1990). (p. 431)

While supervisors must, when circumstances warrant, ensure that unsuitable and unqualified individuals do not become therapists or counselors — a responsibility we owe to future clients who might be harmed by incompetent or unscrupulous practice — we must do so in a way that spares the supervisee any unnecessary pain and that is scrupulously fair. Koocher and Keith-Spiegel (2008) wrote: "Only when sensitive attempts to resolve the problems have failed, when no biases or unfair discrimination exists, and when institutional policies regarding termination from the program have been scrupulously followed should the trainee be dismissed" (p. 361).

INFORMED CONSENT

Supervisors have an ethical responsibility to provide appropriate informed consent to both supervisee and client. Supervisees have a right to know how they will be evaluated — what sorts of information the supervisor will use for forming an opinion and what criteria will be used for evaluating that information. They must understand clearly what is expected of them and what resources are available to them. They need to know to what degree or under what conditions what they reveal to the supervisor will be kept confidential. For example, supervisees may disclose in supervision that they are in therapy, are members of a 12-step program, or were abused as children. They must understand clearly whether such information will be shared with others, and for what purposes.

Clients whose therapists are being supervised also have an ethical right to informed consent to the supervisory arrangements. The first step, of course, is simply to make sure that they know that the clinical services they are receiving are being formally supervised. On January 30, 1984, the APA's Committee on Scientific and Professional Ethics and Conduct (currently termed the Ethics Committee) issued a formal statement about supervision:

> During the onset of a professional relationship with a client, a client should be informed of the psychologist's intended use of supervisors/consultants, and the general nature of the information regarding the case which will be disclosed to the supervisor/consultant. This permits the client to make an informed decision regarding the psychological services with an understanding of the limits of confidentiality attendant to the relationship. Failure to inform the client of such limits violates the patient's confidentiality when the psychologist, without the patient's awareness, discusses the patient/client and his/her diagnosis and treatment or consultation with a supervisor/consultant. The Committee feels that during the onset of a professional relationship with a client, the client should be clearly informed of the limits of confidentiality in that relationship.

The 2010 Ethical Principles of Psychologists and Code of Conduct (APA) Standard 10.01c states:

> When the therapist is a trainee and the legal responsibility for the treatment provided resides with the supervisor, the client, as part of the informed consent procedure, is informed that the therapist is in training and is being supervised and is given the name of the supervisor.

The February 2015 draft of the 4th Edition of the Canadian Code of Ethics for Psychologists (CPA, 2015), Standard III.22, requires that psychologists "make no attempt to conceal the status of a trainee, and if a trainee is providing direct service, ensure that the client or contract examinee is informed of that fact" (p. 25).

In some cases, state laws or regulations may specify the obligation of supervisees to disclose their status. Section 1396.4 of California's Rules of Professional Conduct (Title 16) states,

> A psychological assistant shall at all times and under all circumstances identify himself or herself to patients or clients as a psychological assistant to his or her employer or responsible supervisor when engaged in any psychological activity in connection with that employment. (State of California, Department of Consumer Affairs, 2015, p. 121)

Both supervisor and supervisee have an ethical responsibility to make sure that the client understands the supervisee's qualifications and credentials (Pope, 1990a). Clinicians may engage in extensive rationalizations regarding fraudulently presenting supervisees as possessing a level of training that they have not achieved. For example, in many hospital settings, psychological interns may be presented to patients as "Dr." even though they have not yet received the doctorate. Clients have a fundamental right to know whether their therapist possesses the doctorate and a license to practice independently.

SEXUAL ISSUES

Sexual attraction to clients is a common occurrence for therapists. Supervisors have an important ethical responsibility to ensure that the supervisory relationship provides a safe and supportive opportunity to learn to recognize and handle appropriately such feelings.

Supervisors also have an ethical responsibility to ensure that a sexual relationship between supervisor and supervisee does not occur. The ethics code of the American Psychological Association (2010), for example, states in Section 7.07 ("Sexual Relationships with Students and Supervisees"), "Psychologists do not engage in sexual relationships with students or supervisees who are in their department, agency, or training center or over whom psychologists have or are likely to have evaluative authority. (See also Standard 3.05, Multiple Relationships.)" The ethics code of the Canadian Psychological Association (February 2015 draft) states in Section 11.28 that psychologists should "not encourage or engage in sexual intimacy with students, trainees or others with whom the psychologist has an evaluative or other relationship of direct authority. (Also see Standard III.31.)"

Anonymous surveys have gathered information about sexual involvements between psychologists and their trainees (Glaser & Thorpe, 1986; Harding, Shearn, & Kitchener, 1989; Pope, Levenson, & Schover, 1979; Robinson & Reid, 1985). The evidence strongly suggests that female trainees, much more than male trainees, are involved in such sexual relationships, even when data are adjusted for the relative numbers of male and female supervisors and of male and female supervisees. One study found that one of every four women who had received her doctorate in psychology within the past 6 years had engaged in sexual intimacies with at least one of her psychology educators (Pope et al., 1979; see also Pope, 1989b). Glaser and Thorpe (1986) found that in most cases (62%), the intimacy occurred either before or during the student's working relationship with the educator.

Supervisors bear the responsibility not only of seeing that such involvements do not occur but also of making sure that sexual issues arising in the therapy are addressed frankly, sensitively, and respectfully:

> Students need to feel that discussion of their sexual feelings will not be taken as seductive or provocative or as inviting or legitimizing a sexualized relationship with their educators .... Educators must display the same frankness, honesty,

and integrity regarding sexual attraction that they expect their students to emulate. Psychologists need to acknowledge that they may feel sexual attraction to their students as well as their clients. They need to establish with clarity and maintain with consistency unambiguous ethical and professional standards and boundaries regarding appropriate and inappropriate handling of these feelings. (Pope, Keith-Spiegel, & Tabachnick, 1986, p. 157; see also Pope, Sonne, & Greene, 2006)

SUPERVISEE PERCEPTIONS OF SUPERVISOR'S UNETHICAL BEHAVIOR

Supervisors serve as ethics mentors and models for supervisees. In some unfortunate cases, they model unethical behavior. Susan Neufeldt (2003) reviewed research suggesting that most supervisees believe that their supervisors have committed at least one ethical violation. She wrote:

As a supervisor, you should particularly watch the most frequently violated guidelines noted by supervisees: adequate performance evaluation, confidentiality of supervision sessions, and ability to work with and at least respect alternative perspectives. You cannot count on your supervisees' letting you know about their dissatisfactions. If you can create a safe environment where your supervisees can comfortably reveal their feelings and ideas, and especially their negative feelings about you as the supervisor, you will likely have a successful supervisory relationship. (p. 215)

Jennifer Crall (2011) reported research whose findings revealed that one third of supervisors continued to violate ethical standards. The most frequent ethical violations include failure to evaluate and monitor supervisees, inadequate session boundaries, unwillingness to consider alternative perspectives and failure to model ethical behavior. (p. 48)

BEGINNINGS AND ENDINGS, ABSENCE AND AVAILABILITY

At the start of supervision, supervisees must clearly understand when the supervisor will and will not be available. If the client has an emergency, does the supervisee know how to reach the supervisor quickly? Will the supervisor be available for telephone supervision between scheduled sessions? Can the supervisor be reached during late-night hours, on weekends, or on holidays? Are there adequate preparations for supervisor absences, both planned and unanticipated? If the supervisor is unavailable during a crisis, does the supervisee have several back-up options for getting help?

Issues regarding the beginning and ending of the supervision process must be adequately addressed. The termination is likely to elicit a variety of feelings. Both supervisor and supervisee may feel tempted to collude in avoiding issues related to the termination of clients. They may also find it easy to avoid issues related to the termination of supervision. If the process has not gone as well as expected, both supervisor and supervisee may feel frustration, regret, anger, and relief at the prospect that it is all — *finally* — over. Open and honest discussion of how the problems arose and why they were not resolved more effectively may be hard. If the process has gone well, both may feel joy, pride, and exhilaration, but they may also experience a sense of loss and sorrow that the time spent together and the shared, intense, productive work are ending.

Such responses should not be denied or neglected. An important part of supervision involves supervisor and supervisee honestly confronting their reactions to each other and to their collaborative work together. What has each gained from the other? In what ways has each surprised, disappointed, angered, or hurt the other? In what ways has the relationship been characterized by interest, attentiveness, support, and creativity? In what ways has it been characterized by dishonesty, betrayal, avoidance, and stubbornness? How has the setting influenced the relationship? How have power, trust, and caring manifested themselves in the relationship between supervisor and supervisee and during supervision?

The integrity of the supervision depends on the degree to which we acknowledge and confront such issues. We begin our clinical work as supervisees, and unless we are exceptionally afraid or uncaring, our growth and development as therapists and counselors continue during our career. As we complete our supervision requirements, we must find alternate ways to nurture this process through consultation, study groups, continuing education, and other means.

We have chosen work that involves intense and intimate relationships with other people. It is work with great influence and great vulnerability. Whether our relationships with our clients and supervisees are helpful or hurtful depends to a great extent on fulfilling our ethical responsibilities in regard to power, trust, and caring.

SCENARIOS FOR DISCUSSION

After receiving your doctorate in psychology, you decide you want to live in an area of the country you have never visited before. After a long search, you secure a job at the only clinic in a small town. You'll be able to secure the year's worth of postdoc supervised hours required for licensing. You pack up and move and find you love the new town and your job at the clinic. Ten months into the year, your supervisor says, "I have some bad

(continued)

(continued)

news. The clinic has decided to get rid of us psychologists, so we're both losing our jobs as of the end of this week. I've decided to retire and travel for the next year or so. I know that there's no other job for you here in town, and that leaves you without the supervised hours you need for licensure. But you've been a great supervisee and I'm willing to give you credit for the last two months. I'll just put down on the form that you worked under my supervision for a year."

- How do you feel?
- How do you weigh the possibilities?
- What would you like to say to your supervisor?
- What do you think you would say to your supervisor?

You are conducting family therapy with a family of five. The mother, age 31, is Caucasian. The mother's partner, age 54, is Hispanic. The three children are preteens. You discuss with your supervisor the tensions that the family members are experiencing and your beliefs about the causes of those tensions. Your supervisor says: "I think maybe you're seeing it that way because you are [your own race or ethnicity]."

- How do you feel?
- What do you think you might say to your supervisor?
- What would you like to say to your supervisor?
- Would your supervisor's race or ethnicity make any difference in how you feel or how you react to this situation? If so, what difference would it make, and why?
- Did you imagine the mother's partner as male or female? What do you believe influenced whether you imagined the person as a man or a woman?

You have just completed an intake session with a person who is extremely fearful, hears voices, and seems to have a thought disorder. Your provisional diagnosis is some form of schizophrenia, although there are other possibilities you plan to explore during the next session. You meet with your supervisor, review your notes for the intake, state your opinion that the difficulty likely involves a schizophrenic process, and list the questions that you plan to address in your next session. Your supervisor's first comment is, "Boy, those schizos really are interesting, aren't they!"

- How do you feel?
- What responses do you consider giving to this comment?
- How do you think you actually would respond to this comment?
- If this supervisor had a reputation as extremely thin-skinned and averse to criticism and if this supervisor were also someone with considerable power over your training, how, if at all, might this affect your decision about responding?

You are a supervisor who has had a very challenging supervisee. The supervisee has, for example, made demeaning and passive-aggressive comments to clients and often jokes about them in a cruel and disrespectful way. You have attempted to provide feedback throughout supervision, documenting these attempts and their (lack of) effect. The supervisee schedules an additional session with you and says, "I've been looking at my evaluation forms, and I think you've been very unfair with me. I've talked to some other people, and they agree with me. It is important that you change some of these ratings so that they reflect a fair and unbiased evaluation. If you don't, it will continue to hurt my career. My attorney believes that I have a legal right to a fair evaluation that does not defame me."

- How do you feel?
- How, if at all, would your feelings differ depending on the supervisee's gender, race, age, or other demographics?
- What are your options for responding?
- How would you like to respond? How do you think you would respond? If there is any difference between your answers to these two questions, what causes the difference?
- How, if at all, would the way you responded be affected by the supervisee's gender, race, age, or other demographics?

You have been working with a client who is in desperate need of treatment for multiple serious problems. Without treatment, the client, a single parent, is likely to decompensate and perhaps place the children at risk. Suicide is a possibility. Unfortunately, the client does not qualify for therapy in the light of the current symptoms and the terms of insurance coverage. Your supervisor

(continued)

(continued)

and you discuss all the alternatives, none of which seems acceptable. Finally, your supervisor says, "Look, the only way to get this client the help that is absolutely necessary is to come up with a diagnosis that will meet the terms of the insurance coverage." The supervisor then suggests a diagnosis that will ensure coverage but clearly does not fit the client in any way.

- How do you feel? Are there any feelings that are difficult to acknowledge, disclose, or consider? Aside from your feelings, what thoughts do you have about your supervisor's suggestion? What courses of action do you consider in the light of your supervisor's suggestion? What are your feelings in regard to each one?
- What do you think you would end up doing?
- How, if at all, would your chart notes be affected by your supervisor's suggestion?

You are working with a client who describes graphic sexual fantasies that make you somewhat uncomfortable. At your next supervision session, you tell the supervisor about the counseling session and also about your discomfort with the fantasies. Your supervisor says, "So you are uncomfortable with that kind of sexual fantasizing. What kind of sexual fantasies are you comfortable with?"

- How do you feel?
- What would you like to say to your supervisor?
- What do you think you would end up saying to your supervisor?
- If there is any difference between your answers to questions 2 and 3, why is there a difference?
- Does the gender, sexual orientation, age, or race of your supervisor make any difference in terms of the feelings you experience or the responses you would make or would like to make?

You and your supervisor have had substantial disagreements about clients'/patients' diagnoses and treatment planning. You discuss your differences extensively, but neither convinces the other. During one supervision session, your supervisor says, "I've been concerned about the difficulties you seem to have in conceptualizing these cases and in formulating effective treatment plans. I believe that there are some personal factors interfering with your clinical judgment. I've discussed these issues with the director of clinical training and senior staff, and we think that you need to enter therapy to address these problems."

- How do you feel? Are there any feelings that are particularly hard to acknowledge, disclose, or discuss?
- What are the possible ways you might respond to the supervisor's comments?
- How would you like to respond to the comments?
- How do you think you would end up responding to the comments?
- If there is any difference between your response to questions 3 and 4, what is the difference, and what is the reason for the difference?
- If you were the supervisor and you believed that the supervisee was experiencing personal problems that interfered with clinical judgment, how would you address it? What feelings would you experience as you addressed this situation? How, if at all, would your feelings affect your ability to address this situation effectively and humanely?
- If you ever experienced problems that interfered with your clinical judgment or competence and you were unaware of the situation, how would you like others to respond? What would you find helpful and what would you find hurtful?

INTRODUCTION TO APPENDICES

The fourth edition of this book included a chapter, "Different Conclusions: Example from the Interrogation Controversy." We believe that thoughtful psychologists who have kept up to date with the theory, research, and practice relevant to ethics and carefully consider the full range of differing views may — and often will — disagree on a variety of important issues. That chapter on "Different Conclusions" presented an example of our own disagreement over APA's ethics policies in regard to detainee interrogations. Each of us presented our own position, supported by evidence and reasoning. The chapter also presented an example of two colleagues who are friends and respect each other listening carefully to what the other has to say and agreeing to disagree on an issue of great importance to both.

The following two appendices replace that chapter, which focused on APA's ethics policies relevant to detainee interrogation at the time that the fourth edition was published. Here's the background: When the Hoffman Report was released on July 10, 2015, and we read the 72-page executive summary, we realized immediately that a discussion of the Report belonged in our ethics book. We decided that we would read the entire report and add two appendices — Melba writing one; Ken writing the other — to the fifth edition, which we had just completed. We would write about our responses to the report, which seemed especially important in light of our new Chapter 26, "Steps to Strengthen Ethics in Organizations: Research Findings, Ethics Placebos, and What Works." We have also added a very brief description of how the Hoffman report came about to Chapter 15.

In this appendix, we present our individual responses to the Hoffman Report as of September 15, 2015, when we turned in these appendices. In the fourth edition Melba presented first, followed by Ken. This time we reverse the order and Ken presents first. Regardless of whether you agree or disagree, we hope you find reading these two perspectives helpful as you think through the complete and difficult issues raised by the Hoffman Report.

THE HOFFMAN REPORT AND THE AMERICAN PSYCHOLOGICAL ASSOCIATION

Meeting the Challenge of Change

Kenneth S. Pope, PhD, ABPP

If I value transparency, it is a good idea for me to practice it, so in the interest of transparency and self-disclosure of my perspective (or potential bias), it is important that readers know upfront that I resigned from APA in 2008 over changes APA had been making in its approach to ethics. The Hoffman Report discusses these changes. I wrote that "I respectfully disagree with these changes; I am skeptical that they will work as intended; and I believe that they may lead to far-reaching unintended consequences." Both my letter of resignation online at http://kspope.com/apa/index.php and my articles and chapters (Pope, 2011a, 2011c, 2014, in press; Pope & Gutheil, 2009) present my beliefs along with the evidence and reasoning that in my opinion support them.

In 2014, the American Psychological Association (APA) made a monumental move toward more transparency. The organization took a courageous step unthinkable at any time in its 121-year history: Having denied for years reports of evidence that APA had covertly supported, enabled, and provided cover for torture during the war on terror — including the recent evidence revealed by Pulitzer Prize winning investigative reporter James Risen (2014) – the organization opened up to a former federal prosecutor, giving him access to all documents and personnel. They announced this striking step in a press release that began:

> The American Psychological Association (APA) Board of Directors has reviewed the allegation in James Risen's book, *Pay Any Price: Greed, Power and Endless War*, that APA colluded with the Bush administration to support torture during the war on terror. Specifically, Risen alleges that APA supported the development and implementation of "enhanced" interrogation techniques that constituted torture, and was complicit with the CIA and U.S. military to this end. We believe that APA's October 16th statement refuting Risen's assertion was a fair and accurate response. However, the allegation made by Mr. Risen is highly charged and very serious. His book has created confusion for the public and APA members. This confusion, coupled with the seriousness of the allegation, requires a definitive, independent and objective review of the allegation and all relevant evidence. Toward that end, and to fulfill its values of transparency and integrity, the APA Board has authorized the engagement of David Hoffman of the law firm Sidley Austin to conduct an independent review of whether there is any factual support for the assertion that APA engaged in activity that would constitute collusion with the Bush administration to promote, support or facilitate the use of "enhanced" interrogation techniques by the United States in the war on terror. (APA, 2014c)

This Independent Review Report, commonly known as the Hoffman Report (Hoffman, Carter, Lopez, et al., 2015a & b) set off an ethical earthquake. It revealed evidence that validated Risen's disclosures. It also supported other books, articles in newspapers and professional journals, books, and reports from human rights and humanitarian organizations that had been published over the years exploring APA's role in the war on terror and the stark contrast between APA's ethics policies and public statements and its behavior (for a review, see Pope (2011a , 2011c, in press).

The investigation uncovered e-mails and other documents containing linguistic tricks that mislead and manipulate, logical fallacies in ethical reasoning, biased ethical judgment, hypocrisy, and creative cheating that this book's five chapters (chapters 4–8) focusing on critical thinking in ethics prepare us to notice and avoid. These uncovered documents confront us with the challenge of change. The challenge brings questions. What changes need to occur in ourselves as individuals, in APA as an organization, and in the larger professional community? What internal and external forces will block, weaken, delay, or divert needed change? How can we respond effectively to these forces? Can we avoid mistaking quick changes in policy and personnel for meaningful changes in the organization's ethical culture, character, and dynamics?

None of these questions comes with a simple answer that will please everyone. All come wrapped in complex puzzles of politics, practicality, and conflicting values. None of the questions allows us easy escape. How we answer them — or fail to answer them — will determine whether we bring about needed change. This appendix looks at the questions and challenges that the Hoffman Report has brought to our doorstep.

WHAT DOES THE HOFFMAN REPORT HAVE TO DO WITH EACH OF US AS AN INDIVIDUAL APA LEADER, MEMBER, OR OUTSIDER?

What does the Report have to do with us? When scandal explodes, our shared human tendency is to blame bad apples: "It's their fault! Maybe we made some well-intentioned mistakes, which we regret, but if you're looking for the real cause of this mess, it's them, not us." Bad apples come in three varieties: personnel, policies, and procedures. We toss the bad apples, find shiny new replacements, and think we've fixed the problem. Countless organizations make personnel moves that affect only a handful of people who are seen as "bad apples," vote to replace "bad apple" policies, and create committees to cancel some "bad apple" procedures and issue new guidelines. They find out only long after that they've gained little beyond better public relations and the illusion of reform. Both the external forces and the organizational culture, character, and dynamics that gave rise to the problem remain unchanged.

Or we can head into discrediting mode as a tactic to avoid change: "We chose the person we thought best suited to give us the definitive account of what happened, but he failed us. He gave us a report that, whatever new facts it brought out, is full of flaws and wild conjecture. A psychologist would have understood our profession, our organization, our history, our culture, and the way we do things. But he's a prosecutor and he was out to prosecute us in public and make us look bad. He started with a biased view, did sloppy work, and got key things wrong. And after all, it's just one outsider's opinion."

Answering the question "What does this have to do with us?" requires us to move beyond our human habit to deny, discredit, or dismiss what we do not want to know or be known. We may find that harder than usual in this case. The Hoffman Report documents years of improper behavior. But it also documents that for years APA as an organization and some APA defenders denied, discredited, or dismissed revelations of this improper behavior as they appeared in newspapers, professional journals, books, reports from human rights organizations, and other media. Changing habitual behavior that has settled into a familiar routine is rarely easy for any of us. Changing habitual behavior that is part of organizational culture, character, and dynamics can be even harder.

Moving beyond our shared tendency to shield ourselves from unwanted information and personal responsibility allows each of us to learn what the report has to do with each of us *as an individual*: If we can summon the courage and resolve to look without squinting or flinching away, the Hoffman Report and particularly the emails and other documentary evidence that accompanied it can serve as an ethical mirror. The evidence collected during the investigation was organized into 6 pdf binders (available at http://www .apa.org/independent-review/index.aspx). I strongly recommend reading all 6 binders for two major reasons. First, reading the primary source data allows us to judge for ourselves the emails and other documentary evidence instead of simply viewing it through the perspective of someone else. Second, the full arrays of evidence fills in what the Hoffman Report only summarizes. What may seem unclear, unjustified, or incomplete when reading the report may come across in a different way in view of the full range of evidence in the binders.

Taking the time to read the report and the full range of evidence on which it is based can teach us something about ourselves and help us take a personal ethics inventory. Reading the entire report and all the evidence, we can begin to see the complex relationship between what we did or failed to do and the events that the report describes and documents. When we take time to read these documents, they point the way to effective change, in ourselves and in our profession. If we set them aside unread or settle for second-hand summaries, we turn the ethics mirror to the wall and imagine a more personally flattering picture.

WHAT COULD EACH OF US HAVE DONE DIFFERENTLY?

Reading the Hoffman Report and the binders of documents that accompany it prepares us to struggle with one of the hardest challenges: Answering the questions: As an APA leader, member, or outsider, what could I have done differently? How does my answer to that question help me decide what to do from this point forward? No matter what our position or circumstance, each of us can think of things we might have done, or done better. Only the delusional can gaze into the Report's mirror and see ethical perfection. Only those needing an ethics ophthalmologist will notice merely a handful of things they could and should have done or done differently over the days, weeks, months, and years covered in the Hoffman Report.

Struggling with this challenge is hard, often painful work. It takes time — not a sprint and perhaps not so much a marathon as a continuing daily run. And aren't we all tempted to cheat, sleep in, or go easy on ourselves? We all know how to put denial, discrediting, and dismissing to work when searching for our own ethical disconnects, flaws, weaknesses, and violations. Politicians master this art of pseudo-self-examination.

We can use the Hoffman Report and its binders of evidence to hold our-selves personally accountable for all the things we might have done, or done differently. This puts us in a better position to join with others in our diverse communities from our small informal groups and networks to large national and international professional organizations to bring about needed, meaningful change in our profession in all its diversity.

WHAT DO WE WANT OUR ETHICS AND OUR ETHICS ENFORCEMENT TO BE?

The Hoffman Report challenges us to decide what kind of ethics each of us believes in and whether we are willing to be held accountable. A fundamen-tal question is: Do we choose professional ethics or guild ethics? Professional ethics protect the values that its members affirm as greater than self-interest and protect the public against misuse of professional power, expertise, and practice. Guild ethics place the interests of the guild and its members above the public interest, edge away from actual enforcement and accountability, and draw on skilled public relation to resemble professional ethics.

The Hoffman Report documents that for over 15 years APA had turned its ethics policies and enforcement procedures toward protecting its members from public accountability. In the words of the report, APA "prioritized the protection of psychologists — even those who might have engaged in uneth-ical behavior — above the protection of the public" (p. 63). The Association made this switch to "a highly permissive APA ethics policy based on strategy and PR, not ethics analysis" (p. 16) well before the detainee controversy, all the way back to the 1990s. The Report provides accounts of extraordinary interven-tions to undermine the process of adjudicating ethics complaints and protect high-profile or well-connected members dating back to the mid-1990s. Depriv-ing people who file formal complaints of a fair hearing and a just resolution can serve guild interests but it can also encourage members and nonmembers alike to believe that voicing ethical questions or concerns that might reflect badly on individual members or damage the organization's interests "will at best come to nothing" (Pope, 2015b, p. 144).

APA had turned away from its responsibility to protect the public. The Hoff-man Report quotes the APA's Ethics Director's statement that the role of APA Ethics "is not protection of the public and that protection of the public is a func-tion for state licensing boards" (p. 475). APA embraced this model of ethics and modeled it for students, trainees, its members, state psychological associations, and the national and international community for 15 years.

APA's initial move away from protecting the public sparked great controversy with publication of the 1992 ethics code. As Carolyn Payton, who had served on both the APA Policy and Planning Board and the Public Policy Committee, wrote in 1994 in *Professional Psychology: Research and Practice*:

> All previous codes seemed to have been formulated from a perspective of protecting consumers. The new code appears to be driven by a need to protect psychologists.... It reads as though the final draft was edited by lawyers in the employment of the APA. (p. 317)

She critiqued the "many instances of exceptions to the rule" that protect members against enforcement of the ethical standards:

> The forcefulness of the proscriptions on harassment, e.g., is diminished in the Other Harassment standard, Standard 1.12, which brings up the qualifier "knowingly" (APA, 1992, p. 1601), as in psychologists do not knowingly engage in harassment. Try using the argument of ignorance with the Internal Revenue Service to explain your failure to withhold appropriate taxes for the housekeeper or baby-sitter. (p. 320)

She wrote that "removal of the many instances of exceptions to the rule would make the code more enforceable and more reflective of our discipline, which at one time was dedicated to the promotion of human welfare" (p. 320).

Don Bersoff used a colorful term to describe these exceptions and qualifiers that characterized the 1992 code: "weasel words." Bersoff, who had served as APA's general counsel and would later serve as its president, emphasized that "as almost all the reviewers pointed out, the code is full of such lawyer-driven 'weasel words' as reasonable and feasible." (1994, p. 383). He summed up a dominant theme emerging from the reviewers: "it is a document designed more to protect psychologists than to protect the public" (1994, p. 383).

APA's new ethics, based on "First, do no harm to psychologists," created a public relations problem. How could the Association explain to the public that protecting them from the harm that can result from unethical assessment, therapy, counseling, forensic practice, research, publication, teaching, and so on, was not its concern? Could it honestly announce that the function of APA ethics "is not protection of the public and that protection of the public is a function for state licensing boards"? The answer had the simplicity of Orwell's double-speak: War is peace, ignorance is strength, freedom is slavery — "To advance its PR strategy, APA issued numerous misleading statements that hid its true motives, in an attempt to explain and justify its ethics policy" (Hoffman et al., 2015, p. 15).

But what are *our* true motives — yours and mine? What do each of us see when we look in the mirror? What are our own personal ethics? To what extent are they public relations, more appearance than practice? How much time do we spend searching for ways to strengthen them and eliminate gaps, flaws, and contradictions? How rigorous are we in holding ourselves accountable to these ethics? What would we do if we knew we could get away with it and no one would find out?

When we struggle with these questions, we put ourselves in a better position to join with others to think through how to use the Hoffman Report to strengthen the ethical culture and practices of psychologists and our diverse groups, networks, and organizations.

WHAT DO WE DO TO DISCOVER OR SCREEN OUT WHAT HAPPENS?

Reading the Hoffman Report provides each of us with an opportunity to take a look at how we personally respond to critical information and criticism. The 6 binders of emails and other documents that accompany the Report show the fascinating but dismaying ways that "based on strategic goals, APA intentionally decided not to make inquires . . . thus effectively hiding its head in the sand" and "remained deliberately ignorant" (p. 11). This very human process of protecting ourselves from what we don't want to see or hear rings a familiar bell throughout history. When scandals or atrocities, especially those involving human rights, rattle a business, organization, or country, shocked looks of innocence spring to face after face, accompanied by the refrain: "I saw nothing! I knew nothing! We never suspected!"

But what about both the documented information and criticism published year after year in newspapers, professional journals, books, human rights reports, and other sources? Critical information that ran contrary to APA's strategic goals met with vigorous denial, discounting, and discrediting. The Hoffman Report describes how those who defended the PENS ethics policy and APA's actions dismissed the criticism as "baseless" and the critics' statements "as false and defamatory." They made claims about the critics' "political and financial motivation" (p. 2).

The Hoffman Report invites each of us to consider our personal strategies to avoid finding out what we don't want to know. How do we screen out or distract ourselves from troubling information? How do we snuggle into the warm, protective blanket of denial? How do we discount, discredit, and dismiss the bearers of bad news? The hard work of looking deep into the mirror to answer these questions prepares us to communicate more clearly, openly, and honestly within our own groups, networks, and organizations, especially with those who express different views. It readies us to work with a wider array to create real and lasting change.

WHERE DO WE GO FROM HERE?

The Hoffman Report challenges us do some critical thinking about:

- What each of us might have done or what might we have done better
- What our own ethics are and whether we are willing to hold ourselves accountable through a realistic method of enforcement

- What we do to deny, discredit, or dismiss what we don't want to see or believe

When complicity with torture, violations of human rights, misleading the public, and other vital matters are at stake, organizations must address not only personnel, policies, and procedures but also the powerful incentives from inside and outside the organization, sources of institutional resistance to change, conflicting ethical and political values within the organization, and issues of institutional character, culture, and dynamics that allowed the problems to metastasize for years, protected by APA's denials.

Organizations facing ethical scandals often publicly commit to admirable values such as accountability, transparency, openness to criticism, strict enforcement of ethical standards, and so on. These institutional commitments often meet the same fate as our own promises to stick with a program of personal change. We make a firm New Year's resolution to lead a healthier life. We pour time, energy, and sometimes money into making sure the change happens. We buy jogging shoes and a cookbook of healthy meals. We take out a gym membership. We discuss endlessly what approaches yield the best results. We commit to eating only healthy foods and to getting up 5 days a week at 5 a.m. for an hour of stretching, aerobics, and resistance exercises. But 1, 2, and 3 months later, the commitment to change that had taken such a fierce hold of us and promised such wanted, needed, and carefully planned improvement has somehow loosened or lost its grip.

Decades of research and case studies in organizational and individual psychology show that major change is hard to make and maintain over the long haul. Distractions grab attention and drain our will. Old habits return. Temptations hit at unguarded moments. Memories of the need for change fade. Imaginary change starts to look like the real thing. We find that the more things change, the more they remain the same.

How can we hope to tell if what we are creating meaningful change? Pseudo-change often appears *only* in public statements, pledges of improvement, personnel turnover, the formation of committees, new organizational charts, and discussions. Meaningful change is reflected in measurable progress. We can look to see if all our discussions, statements, and activities are creating meaningful, measurable progress.

The enforcement of the ethics code itself gives us a possible measure of meaningful change. The 6 binders of emails and other documents that accompanied the Hoffman Report show a wide range of improper behaviors involving conflicts of interest, improper handling of ethics complaints to protect psychologists, issuing misleading statements that hid true motives, to name but a few, as well as activities related to torture and violations of human rights. If none of these diverse improper behaviors violates any ethical standard in APA's Code that may tell us something about the code itself. If any of the diverse improper behaviors violates any standard in APA's code, and neither the APA Ethics Committee, nor any state psychological association or state psychology licensing board that has adopted APA's code as enforceable, takes action sua sponte (on its own initiative) or in response to a formal complaint, that may also tell us something.

Enforcement of APA's policies on interrogation and torture provide a second possible measure of meaningful change. For many years, APA has countered criticism by citing its various policies prohibiting torture and a 2008 policy governing interrogation of detainees. Critics, however, have discussed not only the seeming lack of enforcement in this area — see, for example, "U.S. Psychology Body Declines to Rebuke Member in Guantánamo Torture Case" in the *Guardian* (Ackerman, 2014) — but the question of whether these policies are enforceable per se (see Pope, 2011a & b, in press for a review). The most recent policy (23B), which the APA Council of Representatives passed after the Hoffman report was released and which bans psychologists' participation in detainee interrogations, raises similar complex questions of enforceability. For example APA's Associate General Counsel wrote:

> A policy passed by COR [Council of Representatives] does not become part of the Ethics Code no matter what the policy says. Only the Ethics Committee can make changes to the Ethics code under the Bylaws and Rules. So when CoR acts to pass a policy that says that psychologists cannot do X, there is no enforcement mechanism through the Ethics Committee and an enforcement mechanism cannot be built in to it unilaterally as this violates the bylaws. With regards to 23B (and therefore with the 2008 resolution) while this new Council resolution invokes Ethical Principle A to "take care to do no harm," it does not amend the Ethics Code and is not enforceable as a result. (J. Raben, personal communication, August 17, 2015; see also Grohol, 2015)

Evidence that these publically promoted policies are not just enforceable but are enforced when APA members are involved would be a clear measure of meaningful change.

These and other observable signs of meaningful change (e.g., whether APA and its elected officers representing the membership publish formal corrections or retractions of factually incorrect statements appearing in journals or press releases that denied, discounted, or dismissed reports of improper behavior, just as researchers fulfill their ethical responsibility to correct the formal record) allow us to hold a mirror up to both our own individual and our psychological community's ability and willingness to meet the challenge of change.

THE HOFFMAN REPORT

Resetting APA's Moral Compass

Melba Vasquez

In November 2014, the American Psychological Association Board of Directors hired an independent reviewer, former Inspector General and former federal prosecutor David H. Hoffman, JD, of the Chicago-based Sidley Austin Law firm, to conduct a thorough and independent review to investigate the relationship between various activities of the APA and Bush Administration policies on interrogation techniques used on foreign detainees. On July 10, 2015, the report ("Hoffman Report"; see http://www.apa.org/independent-review/APA-FINAL-Report-7.2.15.pdf) was released to the public. It described previously unknown and very troubling facts that led Mr. Hoffman to conclude that collusion among some APA staff and members with the Department of Defense (DOD) led to a weakening of the expressed ethical values and principles of the association, and may have enabled the government's use of abusive interrogation techniques of foreign detainees.

Mr. Hoffman and his staff investigated the process of development of a specific policy paper, the 2005 Psychological Ethics and National Security (PENS) report, a document developed with the intention to provide guidance to military psychologists who asked for support in providing ethical processes in their involvement in interrogations. That report became a very controversial one over an 8-year period among members in the association, and was ultimately rescinded in 2013, after a series of resolutions and policy statements that more accurately reflected the values of the association and its members.

The Hoffman Report found that during the production of the 2005 PENS report, the usual internal checks and balances in regard to the production of policy failed to detect the collusion and significant conflicts of interest in the development of the PENS report resulting in what he determined was a lack of meaningful field guidance for military psychologists.

One of the key points of debate and controversy has involved whether psychologists should participate in the interrogation of persons held in custody by military and intelligence authorities. One side suggested that psychologists should never be present for those, and even not present at all at such sites as Guantanamo and Abu Ghraib, especially given that abuses were endorsed as "legal" by the Bush Administration. Others believed that our behavioral science informed us that the most ethical and effective methods of interrogation included effectively building rapport, and that the presence of psychologists with that expertise and knowledge to facilitate this goal would help to protect detainees from abusive interrogations. Other diverse views addressed what types of involvement in what locations under what rules and oversight and for what purposes. Although the controversy continues, at the point of this writing, before the August 2015 APA convention in Toronto, where the Council of Representatives meets, the Board of Directors has recommended to the Council of Representatives that they adopt a variety of policies in response to the Hoffman Report (see http://www.apa.org/independent-review/index.aspx)

The report *did not* conclude that APA supports torture; however, the report *did* conclude that there was collusion between APA and the DOD to allow psychologists to be present at interrogations where torture may have existed. The report did not take a position on whether psychologists should be present in interrogations but noted that there was an inherent tension when psychologists are present even when designed as safety monitors.

The findings of the Hoffman Report are deeply disturbing; its impact has been a bombshell of seismic proportions for APA and for psychology. The Director of the APA Ethics Office has been apparently fired from his job, the Chief Executive Officer (CEO) and the Deputy CEO have announced early retirements, the APA Executive Director for public and member communications has resigned, and certain members have been asked to step down from their governance activities. In addition, several APA members are reporting experiencing repercussions either in their work places, in APA, or both.

The Hoffman Report is a wake-up call for APA. It highlights areas of needed reform, action, and self-reflection. However, I agree with a variety of views that sees that the Report is not without its problems (e.g., numerous statements of assumption; failure to interview key participants in APA's anti-torture efforts; omissions of testimony; the selectivity of information requested, etc.). I recommend that everyone with interest in the issue read the entire Report carefully, as there is much to learn from it. Where does it identify facts that are of concern? Where does it provide interpretations that lack evidence?

Regardless of its imperfections, the Hoffman Report underlines the loss of an ethical focus on supporting fundamental human rights. Zimbardo (2007) made the point that the PENS report made several important contributions to the complex ethical issue of psychologists serving in working arrangements within the national security framework. Many of us were concerned about appropriate treatment of detainees who were not White (thus, vulnerable to racism), who were not Christian (and vulnerable to further bias), who were designated as "foreign combatants" (e.g., did not have rights to due process under the law as U.S. citizens), and who were feared for having potential information about future terrorism. This alerted us to be extra vigilant for this vulnerable population. The majority of those of us in governance believed that supporting the PENS report (not being aware of the behind-the-scenes collaboration with the Department of Defense personnel on wording in this report), including allowing for trained military psychologists to be present at interrogations, would have protected detainees from torture and abusive interrogations. Many others believed that we needed to go further, and over the 8 years following the release of the PENS guidelines, a number of individuals worked tirelessly to strengthen APA's position against torture both inside and outside of national security settings. Progress was made over time (see the Conclusion for a summary).

It will take a long time to sort out the problems identified in the Hoffman Report, and many groups, including the APA Council of Representatives, APA's policy-making body, will examine what happened, why it happened, what went wrong, and what is best for the organization in the future. In the meantime, there are many lessons to be learned that reflect the ethical principles we have tried to impart in this book. I use the structure described in Chapter 26, "Steps to Strengthen Ethics in Organization," to describe lessons to be learned.

LESSONS LEARNED
Keep Codes in Context

We described in Chapter 26 the risk that ethics codes can fall short of fostering an ethically strong organization. What dynamics in organizations contribute to violating a culture of ethical concern, ethical leadership, and ethical enforcement?

The Dangers of Dichotomous Us/Them Thinking

One of the problems has been the tendency to engage in our propensity to categorize, and join with one group or another. Opotow (1990) described how we form groups in a we/they dichotomy. This leads to a subconscious and automatic categorization of people into our "in-groups," those with whom we identify, and our "out-groups," those whom we see as being outside our realm of identification. People in our in-groups are more highly valued, are more trusted, and engender greater cooperation as opposed to competition. We have more compassion and empathy for those in our in-group than for those in our out-group and are more likely to endorse and support those in this category.

On the other hand, people in our out-groups are implicitly conceptualized as "they," or the "other," and these categorizations affect behavior. We tend to treat out-group members as objects, in insensitive ways. At minimum, people in our out-groups are ignored or neglected; we tend to stop listening.

In the days following the release of the Hoffman Report, I became alarmed that this unfortunate process was activated in the wake of the crisis. I agree with Woolf's (July 21, 2015, with permission) email message to colleagues where she pointed out her concern about this tendency characterizing some of the current conversation post Hoffman Report. She urges us to consider that there are many complex issues being discussed and, without clear knowledge of all, it becomes easy to view problems in dichotomous frames of good versus evil. Frank Worrell (personal communication, July 15, 2015, with permission) indicated that although he was dismayed and saddened by the Hoffman Report, he was equally dismayed by many of the disrespectful and inflammatory comments on the APA listservs following its release. He called upon all of us to be leaders in restoring trust in the Association, and to put governance processes in place to try to ensure that breeches do not re-occur. Indeed, the commitment to engage in mutual respect and to listen carefully and openly to the "other" voice are important strategies that counteract the we/they dichotomies. We must not betray our ethics in our rush to punish the "others" (see Chapter 26).

Other Problematic Dynamics That Undermine Ethical Organizations

Maureen O'Hara (personal communication, July 15, 2015) described more about how dynamics in organizations can undermine ethical commitments:

> In our research on how organizations that aspire to be virtuous end up doing evil . . . , my colleague Aftab Omer and I found what we termed "the myth of innocence" as a key factor that makes it more likely that good people end up doing evil deeds. We found that when accusations of behavior surface that call into question their identity as good guys they will protect their sense of collective innocence by a whole range of defensive strategies. These processes operate below the level of perception so are not recognized as defenses in the service of (false) innocence. Group think, denial, cover ups, silencing victims and whistle blowers, gag orders, executive sessions, confidentiality policies, strategic communications techniques, blaming the victim, scapegoating, revisionism, smoke screens, discrediting evidence by discrediting the credentials of those who bring them figure prominently [in] cases of collective evil doing. There are healthy practices that make such conduct less likely and can help organizations recover from scandalous conduct but at times of crisis, when they are needed more, people often default to blaming rather than understanding, to sacrificing a few scapegoats, and to "moving on" before lessons are really learned.

O'Hara goes on to describe the elements that will allow for a more ethical, conscious association.

What happens from here, in my view, will depend on whether there is a collective will to engage in some compassionate, serious, and redemptive self-reflection and take the necessary steps (not just in the case of the Hoffman Report but in APA governance in general) to learn how to rebuild a more conscious organization.

Encourage Speaking Up, Listening Carefully, and Acting With Fairness

The Influence of Context

We must remember to be hypervigilant especially when the context is one of crisis. Our chapter on ethics in organizations reminds us that unethical acts may go unnoticed or unreported, and we may be particularly vulnerable to this at times of crisis. In this context, the emotional and political atmosphere following the 9/11 terrorist acts resulted in fear, grief, and anger that eventually led the country to war and to the government's "legalized" use of torture and abusive interrogations at Guantanamo and Abu Ghraib. That context perhaps led many of us in the APA to fail to listen, engage in open communication, critically and thoughtfully analyze situations, to pause and reflect, and to fail to treat each other with respect.

Take Care to Not Move Too Swiftly in Those Crises

The governance processes and procedures typically serve as a way to ensure that policies and reports are vetted, and that all voices are heard, as much as possible. Guidelines, resolutions, and reports are typically reviewed by APA Boards and Committees, key experts, divisions and state and provincial psychological associations, the Council of Representatives, and other interested parties for one or more rounds of comments. The process is long and tedious, but it works to allow concerns to be addressed, compromises to be made, and corrections to be incorporated. This process makes room for as many voices to be heard, respected, and included so that usually a collective wisdom can be reached. Because information and knowledge evolves over time, some documents such as guidelines are required to be reviewed and updated every 10 years.

The system also allows for a bypassing of the process in cases of emergency, such as when funds and other supports are offered after natural disasters, such as the 2004 Indian Ocean earthquake and tsunami, and the 2005 Hurricane Katrina in New Orleans.

Because of the perceived urgency of the need for guidance for military psychologists, in 2005, the movers of the PENS report bypassed the usual process and it was treated as an emergency event. The lesson learned here is that when the nature of the product contains many controversial and complex issues, we should not bypass the longer vetting process. Presumptive actions can lead to a derailing of the processes and procedures to ensure diversity of voice through Machiavellian maneuverings. A reactionary zeitgeist can derail important reviews, procedures, due processes and other judicious policies.

Communicate to Increase Understanding

The nature of organizations is political. Competing interests within them have to be balanced through communication, debate, negotiation, and compromise. Sometimes debates take the form of win/lose, and in that context, debates can take a negative, destructive tone. Attempts are made to silence people by treating them with disrespect; at times, it seems that there is competition for individuals on all sides to be the meanest person in the debate. We must never lose sight that the primary goal of communication is to increase understanding. In any situation with competing interests, it is optimal if consensus is reached; if not, it comes to a democratic vote. However, destructive communications are never acceptable or appropriate. All voices should be heard; participants should listen carefully; and the process should promote respect and fairness.

APA as an Association for All Psychologists

One of the wonderful things about the APA is that it is a broad tent that tries to provide a home for all psychologists. It is also a challenge in that many subspecialties and disciplines in psychology are varied and at times at odds. Did we try to bend over too far to consider the guidance needed by military psychologists? I tend to think not. What is more possible is that the perceived urgency leading to a suspension of usual processes allowed for secretive behind-the-scenes communications to have undue power. This does not mean that we should stop listening to the needs of the wide variety of psychologists; it means we must continue to consider how to work through the conflicts to produce good work, even when this takes time.

Respect the True Costs of Betraying Ethics

How do we prevent masking, reinterpreting, or justifying risky acts that may be unethical, or that represent flawed judgments, logical fallacies, and cognitive strategies of justification?

Engage in Self-Examination

Many of us as individuals, and the APA as an organization, are in the process of engaging in self-examination. I am looking at my own actions while serving on the Council of Representatives (2004–2006), Board of Directors (2007–2009), and as president-elect, president, and past president (2010–2012). I have talked to several colleagues and friends who were also in leadership during this period, and we are examining what we did, what we didn't do, what we wished we had done, and to reconsider all of it in light of what has been described in the Hoffman Report. How can we train ourselves to do so on a regular, ongoing basis in regard to any controversial issues that we address?

Seriously and Carefully Attend to Conflicts of Interest

Because of the importance of trust, standards that apply to public governmental officials should also apply to APA members and staff. They should be stringent, and require not only avoidance of conflict of interest, but also the appearance of conflict of interest.

Make Amends and Apologize

An important part of finding our moral compass to "right the ship" is to acknowledge our errors, neglect, missteps, and harm done. We have to stop and truly understand who and how we harmed others and offer specific apologies because that is the beginning of the healing process. Many of us, me included, experience regret, sadness, shame, and heartbreak. APA provided an apology in the first public announcement, "APA Apologizes for 'Deeply Disturbing' Findings and Organizational Failures; Announces Initial Policy and Procedural Actions to Correct Shortcomings" (July 10, 2015; see http://www.apa.org/news/press/releases/2015/07/independent-review-release.aspx

In an early release of his September 2015 *Monitor on Psychology* column, CEO Norman Anderson also apologized: "As your CEO, I want to express my deepest regrets for the events described in the report, which hurt all of us tremendously" (Anderson, September, 2015, p. 11).

CONCLUSION

On many listservs, I have seen messages that convey beliefs to which I resonate. The American Psychological Association has extraordinary power to do good, and has a solid history of having done so. We are truly committed to meaningful change. The fact that APA leadership commissioned the Hoffman Report and publicly disclosed it in its entirety was an act of transparency and courage. In addition, Linda Woolf reminded us of the strides that were taken in the 8 years post PENS report (that were not addressed in the Hoffman Report). She states (personal communication, July 15, 2015, with permission):

> One of my primary concerns with recent dialogue as well as the Hoffman Report is that it fails to take into account the changes post-PENS to bring about stronger anti-torture policy. There were individuals working within APA and many Divisions (e.g., the Divisions for Social Justice) who worked tirelessly to strengthen APA's position against torture both inside and outside of

national security settings. Some of these efforts were successful, some were largely successful, and some failed. However, regular progress was made over time. It is an error to paint APA as a whole with a broad brush as being supportive of torture, "enhanced interrogations," or abusive conditions of confinement. Some efforts post-PENS include:

2006 Resolution Against Torture and Other Cruel, Inhuman, and Degrading Treatment or Punishment–http://www.apa.org/about/policy/torture-2006.aspx. This policy is a broad-based policy condemning torture in all contexts and against all persons. There was only one concern about the policy presented after its passage. The definition of "cruel, inhuman, and degrading" if taken from a highly legalistic perspective (certainly, not the intent of the authors and most likely not the intent of those who voted to accept the definition) could be perceived as a possible loophole. The definition was added at the CoR meeting as a friendly amendment due to concerns expressed by clinicians about the threat of spurious lawsuits, if no definition was added. The definition was taken from U.S. policy related to the UN Convention Against Torture. There is a NBI that should be coming before Council at this Convention to fix this wording issue.

2007 APA Reaffirmation of the American Psychological Association Position Against Torture and Other Cruel, Inhuman, or Degrading Treatment or Punishment and Its Application to Individuals Defined in the United States Code as "Enemy Combatants." Had some wording issues, which were corrected in 2008.

2007 Moratorium on Psychologist Involvement in Interrogations in National Security Settings. Failed at Council. It is my hope that a prohibition against psychologist involvement in national security settings will be revisited at this Council meeting.

2008 APA Amendment to the Reaffirmation of the American Psychological Association Position Against Torture and Other Cruel, Inhuman, or Degrading Treatment or Punishment and Its Application to Individuals Defined in the United States Code as "Enemy Combatants." Rectified the problematic wording from 2007.

2008 APA Petition Resolution Ballot–(http://www.apa.org/news/press/statements/work-settings.aspx). The membership voted to approve this policy. It still needs to be further developed for implementation. The 2008 Report of the APA Presidential Advisory Group on the Implementation of the Petition Resolution with recommendations for implementation can be found at https://www.apa.org/ethics/advisory-group-final.pdf. More work needs to be done in relation to full implementation.

2010 Ethics Code Change, which speaks to the inviolate nature of human rights. http://www.apa.org/news/press/releases/2010/02/ethics-code.aspx. This change is foundational.

2013 Policy Related to Psychologists' Work in National Security Settings and Reaffirmation of the APA Position Against Torture and Other Cruel, Inhuman, or Degrading Treatment or Punishment (http://www.apa.org/about/policy/national-security.aspx and Related Report – http://www.apa

.org/about/policy/psychologists-national-security.pdf). This policy represents the strongest, most comprehensive anti-torture policy and is directly related to psychologists' work in national security settings. The Hoffman Report has nothing negative to say about this policy that was voted on and approved by Council in 2013.

2013 PENS Rescinded - Council voted to rescind the PENS Report at the 2013 Council meeting at Convention.

Is there more work to do? Absolutely. However, it is false to say that APA as a whole or even majority was solely supportive of psychologists' involvement in destructive interrogation or confinement conditions or that no change has occurred since 2005.

In addition, it is helpful to note that the Hoffman Report concluded that some longstanding criticisms aimed at the APA regarding these matters were inaccurate. Most notably, Mr. Hoffman concluded that counter to critics' claims of APA collusion with the CIA there was "no evidence of significant CIA interactions regarding PENS."

Mr. Hoffman also said his inquiry "did not find evidence" that supporting the Justice Department's legal rationale for approving abusive interrogation techniques was "part of the thinking or motive of APA officials."

Additionally, the report confirmed that the organization's 2002 change in its Code of Ethics was not the product of collusion. Mr. Hoffman "did not see evidence" that the revisions "were a response to, motivated by, or in any way linked to the attacks of September 11th or the subsequent war on terror. Nor did we see evidence that they were the product of collusion with the government to support torture." As the organization has repeatedly stated, the ethics code was revised to provide a support for psychologists when their ethical obligations on client confidentiality conflicted with court-ordered directive ordering disclose of confidential patient information. When it was perceived that the change could inadvertently provide a "Nuremberg defense," the code was revised in 2010 (see Woolf citation above).

APA and its members have made tremendous strides in developing ways to treat human suffering. APA Executive Director of the Public Interest Directorate, Gwen Keita, stated:

> For all of the missteps APA took with regard to coercive interrogations and despite a pattern of cover-up over the years, in the end the organization took a positive and courageous step in hiring an independent investigator and made a prior commitment that his findings would be made public no matter what they showed. As courageous as that step was, it is clearly only the first step. Hoffman provided the data, now APA leadership must do something transformative as a result. (personal communication, July 25, 2015)

Many colleagues have expressed optimism that in this crisis, there exists an opportunity for APA to grow and to learn as an ethical organization. Sandy Shullman (personal communications, July 24, 2015) eloquently stated:

> . . . there are some great lessons here and also some great opportunities for many dedicated and talented people to break mindset about how you show up as a member of an organization and do your level and ethical best, which could ultimately lead our field to a much better place. I am not . . . minimizing the hurt and damage, but I know many great discoveries and moments of true progress followed on the heels of colossal mistakes. What we do with our recent knowledge and learning will ultimately determine the real impact of our current flaws and also the continued growth of our profession and discipline.

Ethical behavior is indeed both evolutionary and revolutionary.

There is strong commitment to learn from terrible mistakes and to do everything to strengthen our organization to demonstrate commitment to ethics and human rights. Working together, the Council of Representatives, Board of Directors, other members, and the APA staff will continue to benefit society and improve people's lives. APA will find the moral compass to right its ship.

REFERENCES

Abrahamson, M. (Ed.). (1967). *The professional in the organization*. Chicago, IL: Rand McNally.

Ackerman, M. J., & Pritzl, T. B. (2011). Child custody evaluation practices: A 20-year follow-up. *Family Court Review, 49*(3), 618–628.

Ackerman, S. (2014, January 22). U.S. Psychology Body Declines to Rebuke Member in Guantánamo Torture Case. *The Guardian*. Retrieved from http://www.theguardian .com/world/2014/jan/22/guantanamo-torture-mohammed-al-qahtani-suspected-9-11-hijacker

Ackerman, S., & Hilsenroth, M. (2003). A review of therapist characteristics and techniques positively impacting the therapeutic alliance. *Clinical Psychology Review, 23*, 1–33.

Adam, Y. G. (2007). Justice in Nuremberg: The doctors' trial — 60 years later. A reminder. *Israel Medical Association Journal, 9*(3), 194–195.

Adleman, J., & Barrett, S. E. (1990). Overlapping relationships: Importance of the feminist ethical perspective. In H. Lerman & N. Porter (Eds.), *Feminist ethics in psychotherapy* (pp. 87–91). New York, NY: Springer.

Advice on ethics of billing clients. (1987, November). *APA Monitor*, p. 42.

Advisory Committee on Human Radiation Experiments. (1995). *Final report*. Washington, DC: U.S. Government Printing Office.

Akamatsu, T. J. (1988). Intimate relationships with former clients: National survey of attitudes and behavior among practitioners. *Professional Psychology: Research and Practice, 19*, 454–458.

Akkad, A., Jackson, C., Kenyon, S., Dixon-Woods, M., Taub, N., & Habiba, M. (2006). Patients' perceptions of written consent: Questionnaire study. *British Medical Journal, 333*(7567), 528. doi:10.1136/bmj.38922.516204.55

Allden, K., & Murakami, N. C. S. W. (Eds.). (2015). *Trauma and recovery on war's border: A guide for global health workers*. Hanover, NH: Dartmouth College Press.

Allen, A. L. (2009). Confidentiality: An expectation in health care. In V. Ravitsky, A. Fiester, & A. L. Caplan (Eds.), *The Penn Center guide to bioethics* (pp. 127–135). New York, NY: Springer.

Alonso-Zaldivar, R. (2008, April 9). Effectiveness of medical privacy law is questioned. *Los Angeles Times*. Retrieved from http://8.12.42.31/2008/apr/09/nation/na-privacy9

Amaro, H., Russo, N. F., & Johnson, J. (1987). Family and work predictors of psychological well-being among Hispanic women professionals. *Psychology of Women Quarterly*, 11, 505–522.

Amer, A. B. (2013). Informed consent in adult psychiatry. *Oman Medical Journal*, 28(4), 228–231.

American Association of Critical-Care Nurses. (2012). *AACN position statement on moral distress*. Retrieved from http://www.aacn.org/WD/Practice/Docs/Moral_Distress.pdf

American Association on Mental Deficiency. (1974). *The Adaptive Behavior Scale: Manual*. Washington, DC: Author.

American Counseling Association. (2005). *ACA code of ethics*. Alexandria, VA: Author.

American Educational Research Association, American Psychological Association, & National Council on Measurement in Education. (2014). *The standards for educational and psychological testing*. http://www.apa.org/science/programs/testing/standards.aspx

American Psychiatric Association. (1994). *Diagnostic and statistical manual of mental disorders* (4th ed.). Washington, DC: Author.

American Psychological Association (1972a). *Ethical standards of psychologists*. Washington, DC: Author.

American Psychological Association (1972b). Guidelines for conditions of employment of psychologists. *American Psychologist*, 27, 331–334.

American Psychological Association. (1987a). *Casebook on ethical principles of psychologists*. Washington, DC: Author.

American Psychological Association. (1987b). General guidelines for providers of psychological services. *American Psychologist*, 42, 712–723.

American Psychological Association. (1992). Ethical Principles of Psychologists and Code of Conduct. *American Psychologist*, 47, 1597–1611.

American Psychological Association. (1997). *Your mental health rights: A joint initiative of mental health professional organizations*. Washington, DC: Author.

American Psychological Association. (1998). *Rights and responsibilities of test takers: Guidelines and expectations*. Washington, DC: Author.

American Psychological Association. (2001, under revision/review). Guidelines for test user qualifications: An executive summary. *American Psychologist*, 56, 1099–1113. doi:10.1037//OOO3-O66X.56.12.1O99

American Psychological Association. (2002). Ethical principles of psychologists and code of conduct. *American Psychologist*, 57, 1060–1073.

American Psychological Association. (2003a). Guidelines on multicultural education, training, research, practice, and organizational change for psychologists. *American Psychologist*, 58, 377–402. Retrieved from http://www.apa.org/pi/oema/resources/policy/multicultural-guideline.pdf

American Psychological Association. (2003b). *Guidelines for psychological practice with older adults*. Retrieved from http://www.apa.org/practice/Guidelines_for_Psychological_Practice_with_Older_Adults.pdf

American Psychological Association. (2007a). Guidelines for psychological practice with girls and women. *American Psychologist*, 62, 949–979. doi:10.1037/0003-066X.62.9.949. Also available at http://www.apa.org/practice/guidelines/girls-and-women.pdf

American Psychological Association. (2010a). *Ethical principles of psychologists and code of conduct with the 2010 amendments.* Retrieved from http://www.apa.org/ethics/code/index.aspx

American Psychological Association. (2010b). Guidelines for child custody evaluations in family law proceedings. *American Psychologist, 65,* 863–867. doi:10.1037/a0021250

American Psychological Association (2011a). *Guidelines for the assessment of and intervention with persons with disabilities.* Retrieved from http://www.apa.org/pi/disability/resources/assessment-disabilities.aspx

American Psychological Association. (2011b). *Guidelines for psychotherapy with lesbian, gay, and bisexual clients.* Retrieved from http://www.apa.org/pi/lgbt/resources/guidelines/aspx

American Psychological Association. (2012a). *Crossroads: The psychology of immigration in the new century.* Washington, DC: Author. Available at http://www.apa.org/topics/immigration/report.aspx

American Psychological Association. (2012b). *Dual pathways to a better America: Preventing discrimination and promoting diversity.* Washington, DC: Author. Available at http://www.apa.org/pubs/info/reports/promoting-diversity.aspx

American Psychological Association. (2012c). Guidelines for the evaluation of dementia and age-related cognitive change. *American Psychologist, 67,* 1–9. doi:10.1037/a0024643.

American Psychological Association. (2012d). Guidelines for psychological practice with lesbian, gay, and bisexual clients. *American Psychologist, 67,* 10–42. doi:10.1037/a0024659

American Psychological Association. (2012e). *Recognition of psychotherapy effectiveness.* Retrieved from http://www.apa.org/about/policy/resolution-psychotherapy.aspx

American Psychological Association. (2013a). Guidelines for psychological evaluations in child protection matters. *American Psychologist, 68,* 20–31. doi:10.1037/a0029891

American Psychological Association. (2013b). *Guidelines for the practice of telepsychology.* Washington, DC: Author. Available at http://www.apa.org/practice/guidelines/telepsychology.aspx?

American Psychological Association. (2013c). Specialty guidelines for forensic psychology. *American Psychologist, 68,* 719. doi:10.1037/a0029889

American Psychological Association. (2014a). *Guidelines for clinical supervision in health service psychology.* Retrieved from http://apa.org/about/policy/guidelines-supervision.pdf

American Psychological Association. (2014b). Guidelines for psychological practice with older adults. *American Psychologist, 69,* 34–65. doi:10.1037/a0035063.

American Psychological Association. (2014c, November 12). *Statement of APA Board of Directors: Outside counsel to conduct independent review of allegations of support for torture* [Press release]. Retrieved from http://www.apa.org/news/press/releases/2014/11/risen-allegations.aspx

American Psychological Association Commission on Accreditation. (2013). *Guidelines and principles for accreditation of programs in professional psychology.* Retrieved from http://www.apa.org/ed/accreditation/about/policies/guiding-principles.pdf

American Psychological Association, Committee on Ethical Standards for Psychology. (1949). Developing a code of ethics for psychologists. *American Psychologist, 4,* 17.

American Psychological Association, Committee on Ethical Standards for Psychology. (1951a). Ethical standards for psychology: Sections 1 and 6. *American Psychologist, 6*, 626–661.

American Psychological Association, Committee on Ethical Standards for Psychology. (1951b). Ethical standards for psychology: Sections 2, 4, and 5. *American Psychologist, 6*, 427–452.

American Psychological Association, Committee on Ethical Standards for Psychology. (1951c). Ethical standards for psychology: Section 3. *American Psychologist, 6*, 57–64.

American Psychological Association, Committee on Professional Standards. (1984). Casebook for providers of psychological services. *American Psychologist, 39*, 663–668.

American Psychological Association, Ethics Committee. (1988). Trends in ethics cases, common pitfalls, and published resources. *American Psychologist, 43*, 564–572.

American Psychological Association, Ethics Committee. (1997). Report of the Ethics Committee, 1996. *American Psychologist, 52*, 897–905.

American Psychological Association, Ethics Committee. (2009a). *No defense to torture under the APA Ethics Code.* Retrieved from http://www.apa.org/news/press/statements/interrogations.aspx

American Psychological Association, Ethics Committee. (2009b). Report of the Ethics Committee, 2008. *American Psychologist, 64*, 464–473.

American Psychological Association, Ethics Committee. (2010). Report of the Ethics Committee, 2009. *American Psychologist, 65*, 483–492. doi:10.1037/a0019515

American Psychological Association, Ethics Committee. (2011). Report of the Ethics Committee, 2010. *American Psychologist, 66*, 393–403. doi:10.1037/a0024003

American Psychological Association, Ethics Committee. (2012). Report of the Ethics Committee, 2011. *American Psychologist, 67*, 398–408. doi:10.1037/a0028356

American Psychological Association, Ethics Committee. (2013). Report of the Ethics Committee, 2013. *American Psychologist, 68*, 370–379. doi:10.1037/a0033032

American Psychological Association, Ethics Committee. (2014). Report of the Ethics Committee, 2014. *American Psychologist 69*, 520–529. doi:10.1037/a0036642

American Psychological Association, Insurance Trust. (1990). *Bulletin: Sexual misconduct and professional liability claims.* Washington, DC: Author.

American Psychological Association Practice Organization (2013). *The HIPAA Final Rule: What you need to do now. Guidance and privacy notice updates for psychologists.* Retrieved from http://store.apapractice.org/files/HIPAA_Final_Rule_July_2013.pdf

American Psychological Association, Practice Organization. (2015). *APA clinical practice guideline development.* Retrieved from http://www.apa.org/about/offices/directorates/guidelines/clinical-practice.aspx?

American Psychological Association, Presidential Task Force on Evidence-Based Practice. (2006). Evidence-based practice in psychology. *American Psychologist, 61*, 271–285. Doi:10.1037/0003-066X.61.4.271

Anderson, N. B. (September, 2015). A time of crisis, opportunity and growth. *Monitor on Psychology, 45*, p. 11.

Andersson, G., Cuijpers, P., Carlbring, P., Riper, H., & Hedman, E. (2014). Guided Internet-based vs. face-to-face cognitive behavior therapy for psychiatric and somatic disorders: A systematic review and metaanalysis. *World Psychiatry, 13*(3), 288–295.

Appelbaum, P. S., & Gutheil, T. G. (2007). *Clinical handbook of psychiatry & the law.* Philadelphia, PA: Lippincott Williams & Wilkins.

Appelbaum, P. S., & Kopelman, A. (2014). Social media's challenges for psychiatry. *World Psychiatry, 13*(1), 21–23.

Arbogast, S. V. (2013). *Resisting corporate corruption: Cases in practical ethics from Enron through the financial crisis.* Hoboken, NJ: Wiley.

Arbuthnott, K. D., Arbuthnott, D. W., & Thompson, V. A. (2006). *The mind in therapy: Cognitive science for practice.* Mahwah, NJ: Erlbaum.

Arias, E. (2010). *United States life tables by Hispanic origin. Vital Health Stat* 2(152). Retrieved from http://www.cdc.gov/nchs/data/series/sr_02/sr02_152.pdf

Arkes, H. R., Faust, D., Guilmette, T. J., & Hart, K. (1988). Eliminating the hindsight bias. *Journal of Applied Psychology, 73*(2), 305.

Armstrong, N., Dixon-Woods, M., Thomas, A., Rusk, G., & Tarrant, C. (2012). Do informed consent documents for cancer trials do what they should? A study of manifest and latent functions. *Sociology of Health & Illness, 34*(8), 1230–1245.

Arredondo, P., Toporek, R., Brown, S. P., Jones, J., Locke, D. C., Sanchez, J., & Stadler, H. (1996). Operationalization of the multicultural counseling competencies. *Journal of Multicultural Counseling and Development, 24*(1), 42–78.

Asheri, S. (2009). To touch or not to touch: A relational body psychotherapy perspective. In L. Hartley (Ed.), *Contemporary body psychotherapy: The Chiron approach* (pp. 106–120). New York, NY: Routledge/Taylor & Francis.

Association of State and Provincial Psychology Boards. (2015, February). *Psychology interjurisdiction compact (PSYPACT) announced.* Retrieved from www.asppb.net/resource/resmgr/Docs/PSYPACT_Press_Release_3.16.2.pdf

Attaran, A. (2015). Unanimity on death with dignity — Legalizing physician-assisted dying in Canada. *New England Journal of Medicine, 372*(22), 2080–2082.

Austin, W. J., Kagan, L., Rankel, M., & Bergum, V. (2008). The balancing act: Psychiatrists' experience of moral distress. *Medicine, Health Care and Philosophy, 11*(1), 89–97.

Austin, W., Rankel, M., Kagan, L., Bergum, V., & Lemermeyer, G. (2005). To stay or to go, to speak or stay silent, to act or not to act: Moral distress as experienced by psychologists. *Ethics & Behavior, 15*(3), 197–212.

Axtman, K. (2005, June 20). How Enron awards do, or don't, trickle down. *Christian Science Monitor.* Retrieved from http://www.csmonitor.com/2005/0620/p02s01-usju.html

B.C. privacy breach shows millions affected. (2013, January 15). *CBC News.* Retrieved from http://www.cbc.ca/news/canada/british-columbia/b-c-privacy-breach-shows-millions-affected-1.1342374

Bacon, F. (1955). The new organon. In *Selected writings of Francis Bacon* (pp. 455–540). New York, NY: Random House. (Original work published 1620)

Bader, E. (1994). Dual relationships: Legal and ethical trends. *Transactional Analysis Journal, 24*(1), 64–66.

Baer, B. E., & Murdock, N. L. (1995). Nonerotic dual relationships between therapists and clients: The effects of sex, theoretical orientation, and interpersonal boundaries. *Ethics and Behavior, 5*, 131–145.

Bagley, C., Bolitho, F., & Bertrand, L. (1997). Sexual assault in school, mental health and suicidal behaviors in adolescent women in Canada. *Adolescence, 32,* 341–366.

Bajt, T. R., & Pope, K. S. (1989). Therapist–patient sexual intimacy involving children and adolescents. *American Psychologist, 44,* 455. Available at http://kspope.com

Baker, E.K. (2003). *Caring for ourselves: A therapist's guide to personal and professional well-being.* Washington, DC: American Psychological Association.

Banks, M. E. (2003). Preface. In M. E. Banks & E. Kaschak (Eds.), *Women with visible and invisible disabilities: Multiple intersections, multiple issues, multiple therapists* (pp. xxi–xxxix). New York, NY: Haworth Press.

"Barbara McClintock — Banquet Speech." (1983). In W. Odelberg [Nobel Foundation], *The Nobel Prizes 1983.* Retrieved from http://www.nobelprize.org/nobel_prizes/medicine/laureates/1983/mcclintock-speech.html

Barlow, D. H. (2004). Psychological treatments. *American Psychologist, 59*(9), 869–878.

Barlow, D. H. (2005a). Clarification on psychological treatments and psychotherapy. *American Psychologist, 60*(7), 734–735.

Barlow, D. H. (2005b). What's new about evidence-based assessment? *Psychological Assessment, 17*(3), 308–311.

Barlow, D. H. (2010). Negative effects from psychological treatments: A perspective. *American Psychologist, 65,* 13–20.

Barnett, J. E., & Yutrzenka, B. A. (1995). Nonsexual dual relationships in professional practice, with special applications to rural and military communities. *Independent Practitioner, 14,* 243–248.

Bates, C. M., & Brodsky, A. M. (1989). *Sex in the therapy hour: A case of professional incest.* New York, NY: Guilford Press.

Bauer, L., & McCaffrey, R. J. (2006). Coverage of the Test of Memory Malingering, Victoria Symptom Validity Test, and Word Memory Test on the Internet: Is test security threatened? *Archives of Clinical Neuropsychology, 21,* 121–126. doi:10.1016/j.acn.2005.06.010

Bauman, C. W., & Skitka, L. J. (2010). Making attributions for behaviors: The prevalence of correspondence bias in the general population. *Basic and Applied Social Psychology, 32*(3), 269–277.

Beach, K., & Power, M. (1996). Transference: An empirical investigation across a range of cognitive-behavioural and psychoanalytic therapies. *Clinical Psychology and Psychotherapy, 3,* 1–14.

Beamish, T. D. (2001). Environmental hazard and institutional betrayal: Lay-public perceptions of risk in the San Luis Obispo County oil spill. *Organization & Environment, 14*(1), 5–33.

Beauchamp, T. L. (2014). In the shadow of Nuremberg: Unlearned lessons from the medical trial. In S. Rubenfeld & S. Benedict (Eds.), *Human subjects research after the Holocaust* (pp. 175–193). Cham, Switzerland: Springer.

Beck, A. T. (1967). *Depression.* Philadelphia: University of Pennsylvania Press.

Beck, A. T., Kovaks, M., & Weissman, A. (1975). Hopelessness and suicidal behavior: An overview. *Journal of the American Medical Association, 234,* 1146–1149.

Beck, A. T., Resnick, H. L. P., & Lettieri, D. (Eds.). (1974). *The prediction of suicide.* New York, NY: Charles Press.

Beck, A. T., & Weishaar, M. E. (1990). Suicide risk assessment and prediction. *Crisis: The Journal of Crisis Intervention and Suicide Prevention, 11*, 22–30.

Beehler, S., & Trickett, E. (in press). Community Psychology Misdirected? The case of evidence-based practice. In Bond, M., Serrano-Garcia, I., & Keys, C. (Eds.) *Handbook of Community Psychology*. Washington, DC: American Psychological Association.

Belar, C. D. (2009). Advancing the culture of competence. *Training and Education in Professional Psychology, 3*, S63–S65. doi:10.1037/a0017541

Bemister, T. B., & Dobson, K. S. (2011). An updated account of the ethical and legal considerations of record keeping. *Canadian Psychology/Psychologie canadienne, 52*(4), 296–309.

Bemister, T. B., & Dobson, K. S. (2012). A reply to Mills. Record keeping: Practical implications of ethical and legal issues. *Canadian Psychology/Psychologie canadienne, 53*(2), 143–145.

Ben-Ari, A., & Somer, E. (2004). The aftermath of therapist–client sex: Exploited women struggle with the consequences. *Clinical Psychology and Psychotherapy, 11*, 126–136.

Benitez, K., & Malin, B. (2010). Evaluating re-identification risks with respect to the HIPAA privacy rule. *Journal of the American Medical Informatics Association, 17*(2), 169–177.

Bennett, B. E., Bricklin, P. M., & VandeCreek, L. (1994). Response to Lazarus's "How certain boundaries and ethics diminish therapeutic effectiveness." *Ethics and Behavior, 4*(3), 263–266.

Bennett, D. (2014, January 22). Minister "outraged'" over stolen laptop holding 620,000 Albertans' health data. *Globe & Mail*. Retrieved from http://www.theglobeandmail .com/news/national/alberta-seeking-stolen-laptop-holding-620000-peoples-personal-health-data/article16459295/

Bennett, J. (2014a, March 12). GM now says it detected ignition switch problem back in 2001. *Wall Street Journal*. Retrieved from http://online.wsj.com/ articles/SB10001424052702304914904579435171004763740

Bennett, J. (2014b, June 30). GM to recall 8.45 million more vehicles in North America. *Wall Street Journal*. Retrieved from http://online.wsj.com/articles/gm-to-recall-7-6-million-more-vehicles-in-u-s-1404153705

Bennett, J. (2014c, November 9). GM ordered new switches long before recall: Emails show auto maker placed urgent order for 500,000 replacement switches in December 2013. *Wall Street Journal*. Retrieved from http://online. wsj.com/articles/gm-ordered-new-switches-long-before-recall-1415584224

Benson, P. R. (1984). Informed consent. *Journal of Nervous and Mental Disease, 172*, 642–653.

Benuto, L. T., Leany, B. D., & Garrick, J. (2015). Forensic assessment with the African American client. In L. Benuto & B. Leany (Eds.), *Guide to psychological assessment with African Americans* (pp. 313–329). New York, NY: Springer.

Bernal, G., & Domenech Rodriguez, M. M. (2012) (Eds.). *Cultural adaptations: Tools for evidence-based practice with diverse populations*. Washington, DC: American Psychological Association.

Bernal, G., Jiménez-Chafey, M. I., & Domenech Rodríguez, M. M. (2009). Cultural adaptation of treatments: A resource for considering culture in evidence-based practice. *Professional Psychology: Research and Practice, 40*, 361–368. doi:10.1037/a0016401

Bernsen, A., Tabachnick, B. G., & Pope, K. S. (1994). National survey of social workers' sexual attraction to their clients: Results, implications, and comparison to psychologist. *Ethics and Behavior, 4*, 369–388. Available at http://kspope.com

Bernstein, L., & Nutt, A.E. (2015, May 5). U.S. Hispanics are healthier than Whites, CDC says, despite many reasons that shouldn't be. *Washington Post*. Retrieved from http://www.washingtonpost.com/news/to-your-health/wp/2015/05/05/u-s-hispanics-are-healthier-than-whites-cdc-says-despite-many-reasons-that-shouldnt-be/?tid=hpModule_9d3add6c-8a79-11e2-98d9-3012c1cd8d1e&hpid=z11

Beutler, L. E. (1985). Loss and anticipated death: Risk factors in depression. In H. H. Goldman & S. E. Goldston (Eds.), *Preventing stress-related psychiatric disorders* (pp. 177–194). Rockville, MD: National Institute of Mental Health.

Bhandari, M., Busse, J. W., Jackowski, D., Montori, V. M., Schünemann, H., Sprague, S., & Devereaux, P. J. (2004). Association between industry funding and statistically significant pro-industry findings in medical and surgical randomized trials. *Canadian Medical Association Journal, 170*(4), 477480.

Binkley, C., Wagner, M., Riepenhoff, J., & Gregory, S. (2014, November 23). College disciplinary boards impose slight penalties for serious crimes. *Columbus Dispatch*. Retrieved from http://www.dispatch.com/content/stories/local/2014/11/23/campus‐injustice.html

Blanchard-Fields, F., Chen, Y., Horhota, M., & Wang, M. (2007). Cultural differences in the relationship between aging and the correspondence bias. *Journals of Gerontology: Series B: Psychological Sciences and Social Sciences, 62B*(6), P362–P365.

Blau, P., & Scott, W. (1962). *Formal organizations: A comparative approach*. San Francisco, CA: Chandler.

Blau, T. H. (1984). *The psychologist as expert witness*. New York, NY: Wiley.

Blumenthal, D., & McGraw, D. (2015). Keeping personal health information safe: The importance of good data hygiene. *JAMA, 313*(14), 1424.

Bonitz, V. (2008). Use of physical touch in the "talking cure": A journey to the outskirts of psychotherapy. *Psychotherapy: Theory, Research, Practice, Training, 45*, 391–404. doi:10.1037/a0013311

Borys, D. S. (1994). Maintaining therapeutic boundaries: The motive is therapeutic effectiveness, not defensive practice. *Ethics and Behavior, 4*(3), 267–273.

Borys, D. S., & Pope, K. S. (1989). Dual relationships between therapist and client: A national study of psychologists, psychiatrists, and social workers. *Professional Psychology: Research and Practice, 20*, 283–293. Available at http://kspope.com

Boswell, J. F., Nelson, D. L., Nordberg, S. S., McAleavey, A. A., & Castonguay, L. G. (2010). Competency in integrative psychotherapy: Perspectives on training and supervision. *Psychotherapy: Theory, Research, Practice, Training, 47*, 3–11. doi:10.1037/a0018848

Bouhoutsos, J. C., Holroyd, J., Lerman, H., Forer, B., & Greenberg, M. (1983). Sexual intimacy between psychotherapists and patients. *Professional Psychology: Research and Practice, 14*, 185–196.

Bower, B. (2013, May 16). Closed thinking: Without scientific competition and open debate, much psychology research goes nowhere. *Science News*. Retrieved from https://www.sciencenews.org/article/closed-thinking?mode=magazine & context= 4553

Boyatzis, R. E., Gaskin, J., & Wei, H. (2015). Emotional and social intelligence and behavior. In S. Goldstein, D. Princiotta, & J. Naglieri (Eds.) *Handbook of intelligence* (pp. 243–262). New York, NY: Springer.

Brenner, L. A., Homaifar, B. Y., Adler, L. E., Wolfman, J. H., & Kemp, J. (2009). Suicidality and veterans with a history of traumatic brain injury: Precipitating events, protective factors, and prevention strategies. *Rehabilitation Psychology*, *54*, 390–397. doi:10.1037/a0017802

Bridge, S. (2011, September 9). Canadians with mental illnesses denied U.S. entry. *CBC News*. Retrieved from http://bit.ly/DeniedEntry

Brodsky, A. M. (1989). Sex between patient and therapist: Psychology's data and response. In G. O. Gabbard (Ed.), *Sexual exploitation in professional relationships* (pp. 15–25). Washington, DC: American Psychiatric Press.

Bronstein, S., & Griffin, D. (2014, April 23). A *fatal wait: Veterans languish and die on a VA hospital's secret list*. CNN. Retrieved from http://www.cnn.com/2014/04/23/health/veterans-dying-health-care-delays/

Brown, C., Murdock, N. L., & Abels, A. (2014). Ethical issues associated with training in university counseling centers. *Training and Education in Professional Psychology*, *8*(4), 269–276.

Brown, L. S. (1984). The lesbian feminist therapist in private practice and her community. *Psychotherapy in Private Practice*, *2*, 9–16.

Brown, L. S. (1988). Harmful effects of posttermination sexual and romantic relationships between therapists and their former clients. *Psychotherapy*, *25*, 249–255.

Brown, L. S. (1989). Beyond thou shalt not: Thinking about ethics in the lesbian therapy community. *Women and Therapy*, *8*, 13–25.

Brown, L. S. (1994a). Concrete boundaries and the problem of literal-mindedness: A response to Lazarus. *Ethics and Behavior*, *4*(3), 275–281.

Brown, L. S. (1994b). *Subversive dialogues*. New York, NY: Basic Books.

Brown, L. S. (1996). Ethical concerns with sexual minority patients. In R. P. Cabaj & T. S. Stein (Eds.), *Textbook of homosexuality and mental health* (pp. 897–916). Washington, DC: American Psychiatric Press.

Brown, L. S. (2010). *Feminist therapy*. Washington, DC: American Psychological Association.

Brown, T. L., Vinson, E. S., & Abdullah, T. (2015). Cross-cultural considerations with African American clients: A perspective on psychological assessment. In L. T. Benuto & B. D. Leany (Eds.), *Guide to psychological assessment with African Americans* (pp. 9–18). New York, NY: Springer.

Brownlee, K. (1996). The ethics of non-sexual dual relationships: A dilemma for the rural mental health professional. *Community Mental Health Journal*, *32*, 497–503.

Bruine de Bruin, W., Parker, A. M., & Fischhoff, B. (2015). Individual differences in decision-making competence across the lifespan. In E. A. Wilhelms & V. F. Reyna (Eds.), *Frontiers of cognitive psychology. Neuroeconomics, judgment, and decision making* (pp. 219–236). New York, NY: Psychology Press.

Brunch, J., Barraclough, B., Nelson, M., & Sainsbury, P. (1971). Suicide following death of parents. *Social Psychiatry*, *6*, 193–199.

Buri, C., Von Bonin, B., Strik, W., & Moggi, F. (2009). Predictors of attempted suicide among Swiss patients with alcohol-use disorders. *Journal of Studies on Alcohol and Drugs, 70*, 668–674.

Burian, B. K., & Slimp, A. O. C. (2000). Social dual-role relationships during internship: A decision-making model. *Professional Psychology: Research and Practice, 31*(3), 332–338.

Burkard, A. W., & Knox, S. (2004). Effect of therapist color-blindness on empathy and attributions in cross-cultural counseling. *Journal of Counseling Psychology, 51*(4), 387.

Burke, J. (2014). Discretion to warn: Balancing privacy rights with the need to warn unaware partners of likely HIV/AIDS exposure. *Boston College Journal of Law & Social Justice, 35*, 89–153.

Bushyhead, J. B., & Christensen-Szalanski, J. J. (1980). Feedback and the illusion of validity in a medical clinic. *Medical decision making: An international journal of the Society for Medical Decision Making, 1*(2), 115–123.

Butcher, J. M., Graham, J. R., Williams, C. L., & Ben-Porath, Y. S. (1990). *Development and use of the MMPI-2 content scales*. Minneapolis: University of Minnesota Press.

Butler, S. E., & Zelen, S. L. (1977). Sexual intimacies between therapists and patients. *Psychotherapy, 14*, 139–145.

California Department of Consumer Affairs. (1997). *Professional therapy never includes sex* (2nd ed.). (Original work published 1990)

California Department of Consumer Affairs. (2011). *Professional therapy never includes sex* (Rev. ed.). Retrieved from http://www.dca.ca.gov/publications/proftherapy.shtm. (Original work published 1990)

California State Auditor. (2014, June). Sterilization of female inmates: Some inmates were sterilized unlawfully, and safeguards designed to limit occurrences of the procedure failed. Retrieved from https://www.auditor.ca.gov/pdfs/reports/ 2013-120.pdf

Campbell, C., & Gordon, M. (2003). Acknowledging the inevitable: Understanding multiple relationships in rural practice. *Professional Psychology: Research and Practice, 34*, 430–434.

Campbell, L., Vasquez, M., Behnke, S., & Kinscherff, R. (2010). *APA Ethics Code commentary and case illustrations*. Washington, DC: American Psychological Association.

Canadian Psychological Association. (1986). *Canadian Code of Ethics for psychologists*. Ottawa, Canada: Author.

Canadian Psychological Association. (1991). *Canadian Code of Ethics for psychologists*. Ottawa, Canada: Author.

Canadian Psychological Association. (2000). *Canadian Code of Ethics for psychologists*. Ottawa, Canada: Author.

Canadian Psychological Association. (2001a). *General guidelines for providers of psychological services*. Available at http://www.cpa.ca/cpasite/UserFiles/Documents/ publications/Practice%20Guidelines2001%282%29.pdf

Canadian Psychological Association. (2001b). *Practice guidelines for providers of psychological services*. Retrieved from http://www.acposb.on.ca/practice.htm

Canadian Psychological Association. (2001c). *Guidelines for nondiscriminatory practice*. Ottawa, Canada: Author.

Canadian Psychological Association. (2006). *Annual report, 2005–2006*. Retrieved from http://www.cpa.ca/aboutcpa/annualreports/

Canadian Psychological Association. (2007). *Guidelines for ethical psychological practice with women*. Ottawa, Ontario, Canada: Author.

Canadian Psychological Association (2007). *Professional practice guidelines for school psychologists in Canada*.Ottawa, Ontario, Canada: Author.

Canadian Psychological Association. (2009a). *Policy statement: The presence of involved third party observer in neuropsychological assessments*. Retrieved from http://www.cpa .ca/aboutcpa/policystatements/#policy1

Canadian Psychological Association. (2009b). *Ethical guidelines for supervision in psychology: Teaching, research, practice, and administration*. Ottawa, Ontario, Canada: Author.

Canadian Psychological Association. (2013). The pre-employment clinical assessment of police candidates: Principles and guidelines for Canadian psychologists. Ottawa, Ontario, Canada: Author.

Canadian Psychological Association. (2015). *Canadian Code of Ethics for Psychologists* (February 2015 draft of 4th ed.). Ottawa, Ontario, Canada: Author.

Canadians' mental-health info routinely shared with FBI, U.S. customs. (2014, April 14). *CBC News*. Retrieved from http://bit.ly/InfoCustomsFBI

Canetto, S. S., Timpson, W. M., Borrayo, E., & Yang, R. (2003). Teaching about human diversity: Lessons learned and recommendations. In W. M. Timpson, S. S. Canetto, E. Borrayo, & R. Yang (Eds.), *Teaching diversity: Challenges, complexities, identity and integrity* (pp. 275–294). Madison, WI: Atwood.

Canterbury v. Spence, 464 F.2d 772 (D.C. Cir. 1972).

Caplan, P. J. (1995). *They say you're crazy: The inside story of the DSM*. Reading, MA: Addison-Wesley.

Carpenter v. Superior Court (Yamaha Motor Corp., USA), 141 Cal.App.4th 249 (2006).

Carr, M. L., Goranson, A. C., & Drummond, D. J. (2014). Stalking of the mental health professional: Reducing risk and managing stalking behavior by patients. *Journal of Threat Assessment and Management, 1*, 4–22. 10.1037/tam0000003

Casas, J. M., Cabrera, A. P., & Vasquez, M. J. T. (2014). Adelante! Counseling the Latina/o from guiding theory to practice. In P. B. Pedersen, W. J. Lonner, J. G. Draguns, & J. E. Trimble (Eds.), *Counseling across cultures* (7th ed., pp. 163–184). Thousand Oaks, CA: Sage.

Cases and inquiries before the Committee on Scientific and Professional Ethics and Conduct. (1954). *American Psychologist, 9*, 806–807.

Cassileth, B. R., Zupkis, R. V., Sutton-Smith, K., & March, V. (1980). Informed consent—Why are its goals imperfectly realized? *New England Journal of Medicine, 323*, 896–900.

Caudill, O. B. (1993, Winter). Administrative injustice: Can psychologists be vicariously liable for sexual misconduct? AAP Advance Plan, Association for the Advancement of Psychology, 4–5.

Caudill, O. B., & Pope, K. S. (1995). *Law and mental health professionals: California*. Washington, DC: American Psychological Association.

Celano, M. P., Smith, C. O., & Kaslow, N. J. (2010). A competency-based approach to couple and family therapy supervision. *Psychotherapy: Theory, Research, Practice, Training, 47*, 35–44. doi:10.1037/a0018845

Celenza, A. (2007). *Sexual boundary violations: Therapeutic, academic, and supervisory contexts*. Lanham, MD: Jason Aronson.

Centeno, J. G. (2009). Issues and principles in service delivery to communicatively impaired minority bilingual adults in neurorehabilitation. *Seminars in Speech and Language, 30*, 139–152. doi: 10.1055/s-0029–1225951

Centers for Disease Control and Prevention. (n.d.). *U.S. Public Health Service Syphilis Study at Tuskegee*. Retrieved February 28, 2010, from http://www.cdc.gov/tuskegee

Chan, C. S. (1997). Don't ask, don't tell, don't know: The formation of a homosexual identity and sexual expression among Asian American lesbians. In B. Greene (Ed.), *Ethnic and cultural diversity among lesbians and gay men* (pp. 240–248). Thousand Oaks, CA: Sage.

Chan, S. S. M., Chiu, H. F. K., Chen, E. Y. H., Chan, W. S. C., Wong, P. W. C., Chan, C. L. W., . . . Yip, P. S. F. (2009). Population-attributable risk of suicide conferred by Axis I psychiatric diagnosis in a Hong Kong Chinese population. *Psychiatric Services, 60*, 1135–1138. doi:10.1176/appi.ps.60.8.1135

Chanowitz, B., & Langer, E. J. (1981). Premature cognitive commitment. *Journal of Personality and Social Psychology, 41*, 1051–1063.

Chesler, P. (1972). *Women and madness*. New York, NY: Doubleday.

Chiang, H. (1986, July 28). Psychotherapist is subject to suit for breaching privilege. *Los Angeles Daily Journal*, p. 1.

Chiose, S. (2014, October 31). Male bystander intervention can help end sexual assaults, experts say. Globe & Mail. Retrieved from http://www. theglobeandmail .com/news/national/male-bystander-intervention-is-key-to-ending-sexual-assault/ article21418259/?cmpid=rss1

Chiu, E. Y. (2014). Psychological testing in child custody evaluations with ethnically diverse families: Ethical concerns and practice recommendations. *Journal of Child Custody: Research, Issues, and Practices, 11*(2), 107–127.

Chung, E. (2014, April 25). Privacy Commissioner's office loses sensitive data. *CBC News*. Retrieved from www.cbc.ca/news/technology/privacy-commissioner-s-office-loses-sensitive-data-1.2622018

Chung, E. K., Kim, S. J., & Sohn, Y. W. (2014). Regulatory focus as a predictor of omission bias in moral judgment: Mediating role of anticipated regrets. *Asian Journal of Social Psychology, 17*, 302–311.

Cikara, M., Bruneau, E., Van Bavel, J. J., & Saxe, R. (2014). Their pain gives us pleasure: How intergroup dynamics shape empathic failures and counter-empathic responses. *Journal of Experimental Social Psychology, 55*, 110–125.

Clark, H. K., Murdock, N. L., & Koetting, K. (2009). Predicting burnout and career choice satisfaction in counseling psychology graduate students. *The Counseling Psychologist, 37*, 580–606.

Clarkson, P. (1994). In recognition of dual relationships. *Transactional Analysis Journal, 24*(1), 32–38.

Clough, B. A., & Casey, L. M. (2015). The smart therapist: A look to the future of smartphones and mhealth technologies in psychotherapy. *Professional Psychology: Research and Practice, 46*, 147–153. doi:10.1037/pro0000011

Cobbs v. Grant, 8 Cal.3d 229, 502 P.2d 1, 104 Cal. Rptr. 505 (Cal. 1972).

Cocks, G. (1985). *Psychotherapy in the Third Reich: The Göring Institute*. New York, NY: Oxford University Press.

Cohen, N. (2009, July 29). Has Wikipedia created a Rorschach cheat sheet? *New York Times*. Retrieved from http://bit.ly/4XgITf

Cohen-Sandler, R., Berman, A. L., & King, R. A. (1982). Life stress and symptomotology: Determinants of suicidal behavior in children. *Journal of the American Academy of Child Psychiatry, 21*, 178–186.

Colt, G. H. (1983). The enigma of suicide. *Harvard Magazine, 86*, 47–66.

Comas-Díaz, L. (2008). Latino psychospirituality. In K. J. Schneider (Ed.), *Existential-integrative psychotherapy: Guideposts to the core of practice* (pp. 100–109). New York, NY: Routledge/Taylor & Francis Group.

Comas-Díaz, L., & Greene, B. G. (1994). *Women of color: Integrating ethnic and gender identities in psychotherapy*. New York, NY: Guilford Press.

Committee on Medical Liability and Risk Management of the American Academy of Pediatrics. (2009). Policy statement — Expert witness participation in civil and criminal proceedings. *Pediatrics, 124*(1), 428–438. doi:124/1/428 [pii]10.1542/peds .2009-1132

Committee on Scientific Freedom and Responsibility.(1975). *Scientific freedom and responsibility*. Washington, DC: American Association for the Advancement of Science.

Commons, M. L., Rodriguez, J. A., Adams, K. M., Goodheart, E. A., Gutheil, T. G., & Cyr, E. D. (2006). Informed consent: Do you know it when you see it? Evaluating the adequacy of patient consent and the value of a lawsuit. *Psychiatric Annals, 36*(6), 430–435.

Compassion Resources for Therapists & Counselors. (2015). Retrieved February 8, 2015, from http://bit.ly/KenPopeCompassion

Connolly, T., Arkes, H. R., & Hammond, K. R. (Eds.). (2000). *Judgment and decision making: An interdisciplinary reader* (2nd ed.). New York, NY: Cambridge University Press.

Constantine, M. G., & Sue, D. W. (2005). *Strategies for building multicultural competence in mental health and educational settings*. Hoboken, NJ: Wiley.

Constantinou, M., Ashendorf, L., & McCaffrey, R. J. (2002). When the third party observer of a neuropsychological evaluation is an audiorecorder. *Clinical Neuropsychologist, 16*(3), 407–412.

Constantinou, M., Ashendorf, L., & McCaffrey, R. J. (2005). Effects of a third party observer during neuropsychological assessment: When the observer is a video camera. *Journal of Forensic Neuropsychology, 4*(2), 39–47.

Consumer Reports. (2014, March). GM recall raises concerns about warning systems for auto safety. *Consumer Reports*. Retrieved from http://consumerreports.org/cro/2014/03/gm-recall-raises-concerns-about-warning-systems-for-auto-safety/index .htm

Costigan, C., Su, T. F., & Hua, J. M. (2009). Ethnic identity among Chinese Canadian youth: A review of the Canadian literature. *Canadian Psychology/Psychologie canadienne, 50*, 261–272. doi:10.1037/a0016880

Courtois, C. A. (2015). First, do no more harm: Ethics of attending to spiritual issues in trauma treatment. In D. F. Walker, C. A. Courtois, & J. D. Aten (Eds.), *Spiritually oriented psychotherapy for trauma* (pp. 55–75). Washington, DC: American Psychological Association.

Crall, J. (2011). Ethical behavior of supervisors: Effects on supervisee experiences and behavior. *Theses and Dissertations. Paper 1182.* Lehigh University. Retrieved from http://preserve.lehigh.edu/etd

Crits-Christoph, P., Wilson, G. T., & Hollon, S. D. (2005). Empirically supported psychotherapies: Comment on Westen, Novotny, and Thompson-Brenner (2004). *Psychological Bulletin, 131*(3), 412–417.

Cropanzana, R., Bowen, D. E., & Gilliland, S. W. (2007). The management of organizational justice. *Academy of Management Perspectives, 21*(4), 34–48.

Crosby, A. E., Espitia-Hardeman, V., Hill, H. A., Ortega, L., & Clavel-Arcas, C. (2009). Alcohol and suicide among racial/ethnic populations — 17 states, 2005–2006. *Journal of the American Medical Association, 302,* 733–734.

Curry, K. T., & Hanson, W. E. (2010). National survey of psychologists' test feedback training, supervision, and practice: A mixed methods study. *Journal of Personality Assessment, 92*(4), 327–336.

Dahlberg, C. C. (2014). Sexual contact between patient and therapist. *Contemporary Psychoanalysis, 50*(1–2), 522.

Dalen, K. (2006). To tell or not to tell, that is the question: Ethical dilemmas presented by psychologists in telephone counseling. *European Psychologist, 11*(3), 236–243.

Daly, M., & Tang, T. (2014, June 6). *VA chief: 18 vets left off waiting list have died.* Retrieved from http://bigstory.ap.org/article/senate-moves-toward-vote-va-health-care

Daries, J. P., Reich, J., Waldo, J., Young, E. M., Whittinghill, J., Ho, A. D., . . . Chuang, I. (2014). Privacy, anonymity, and big data in the social sciences. *Communications of the ACM, 57,* 56–63.

Darke, S., Duflou, J., & Torok, M. (2009). Toxicology and circumstances of completed suicide by means other than overdose. *Journal of Forensic Sciences, 54,* 490–494. doi:10.1111/j.1556–4029.2008.00967.x

Darley, J. M. (1995). Constructive and destructive obedience: A taxonomy of principal-agent relationships. *Journal of Social Issues, 51,* 125–154.

Darley, J. M., & Batson, C. D. (1973). "From Jerusalem to Jericho": A study of situational and dispositional variables in helping behavior. *Journal of Personality and Social Psychology, 27*(1), 100–108.

Davis, D. (2008). *Terminating therapy: A professional guide to ending on a positive note.* Hoboken, NJ: Wiley.

de Vries, J., Byrne, M., & Kehoe, E. (2015). Cognitive dissonance induction in everyday life: An fMRI study. *Social Neuroscience, 10*(3), 268–281.

Decker, S. E., Nich, C., Carroll, K. M., & Martino, S. (2014). Development of the therapist empathy scale. *Behavioural and Cognitive Psychotherapy, 42*(03), 339–354.

Detert, J. R., & Treviño, L. K. (2010). Speaking up to higher-ups: How supervisors and skip-level leaders influence employee voice. *Organization Science, 21*(1), 249–270

Detroit Edison v. National Labor Relations Board. (1979). 440 U.S. 301, 313.

Dheer, R., Lenartowicz, T., Peterson, M. F., & Petrescu, M. (2014). Cultural regions of Canada and United States: Implications for international management research. *International Journal of Cross Cultural Management, 14*(3), 343–384.

Dixon-Woods, M., Williams, S. J., Jackson, C. J., Akkad, A., Kenyon, S., & Habiba, M. (2006). Why do women consent to surgery, even when they do not want to?

An interactionist and Bourdieusian analysis. *Social Science and Medicine*, 62(11), 2742–2753.

Dolan, P. L. (2009, October 12). Social media behavior could threaten your reputation, job prospects. *American Medical News*. Retrieved from http://www.ama-assn .org/amednews/2009/10/12/bil21012.htm

Dovidio, J. F., & Gaertner, S. L. (2010). Intergroup bias. In S. T. Fiske, D. T. Gilbert, & G. Lindzey (Eds.), *Handbook of social psychology* (5th ed., Vol. 2, pp. 1084–1121). Hoboken, NJ: Wiley.

Dovidio, J. F., Gaertner, S. L., Kawakami, K., & Hodson, G. (2002). Why can't we just get along? Interpersonal biases and interracial distrust. *Cultural Diversity and Ethnic Minority Psychology*, 8, 88–102.

Downey, D. L. (2001). Therapeutic touch in psychotherapy. *Psychotherapy Bulletin*, 36, 1, 35–39.

Downs, L. (2015). The duty to protect a patient's right to confidentiality: Tarasoff, HIV, and confusion. *Journal of Forensic Psychology Practice*, 15(2), 160–170.

Drake, R., Gates, C., Cotton, P., & Whitaker, A. (1984). Suicide among schizophrenics: Who is at risk? *Journal of Nervous and Mental Disease*, 172, 613–617.

Draper, B., Peisah, C., Snowdon, J., & Brodaty, H. (2010). Early dementia diagnosis and the risk of suicide and euthanasia. *Alzheimer's & Dementia*, 6, 75–82. doi:10.1016/j.jalz.2009.04.1229

Drum, K. B., & Littleton, H. L. (2014). Therapeutic boundaries in telepsychology: Unique issues and best practice recommendations. *Professional Psychology: Research and Practice*, 45(5), 309.

Dubin, S. S. (1972). Obsolescence or lifelong education: A choice for the professional. *American Psychologist*, 27(5), 486–498.

Duncan, B. L., Miller, S. D., Wampold, B. E., & Hubble, M. A. (Eds.). (2010). *The heart and soul of change: Delivering what works in therapy* (2nd ed.). Washington, DC: American Psychological Association. doi:10.1037/12075–000

Dunford, B. B., Jackson, C. L., Boss, A. D., Tay, L., & Boss, R. W. (2014). Be fair, your employees are watching: A relational response model of external third-party justice. *Personnel Psychology*, 68, 319–352. doi: 10.1111/peps.12081.

Dworkin, S. H. (1992). Some ethical considerations when counseling gay, lesbian, and bisexual clients. In S. H. Dworkin & F. J. Gutierrez (Eds.), *Counseling gay men and lesbians: Journey to the end of the rainbow* (pp. 325–334). Alexandria, VA: American Association for Counseling and Development.

Dyer, C. (2008, January 12). Whistleblower who was excluded from work for five years wins apology. *British Medical Journal*, 336(7635), 63. Retrieved from http://www .bmj.com/cgi/content/extract/336/7635/63-a. doi:10.1136/bmj.39454.502049.DB

Dyer, C. (2014). Half of whistleblowers who raised work concerns with charity were sacked or resigned. *BMJ*, 349, g6285.

Eastvold, A. D., Belanger, H. G., & Vanderploeg, R. D. (2012) Does a third party observer affect neuropsychological test performance? It depends. *Clinical Neuropsychologist*, 26, 520–541.

EchoHawk, M. (1997). Suicide: The scourge of Native American people. *Suicide and Life-Threatening Behavior*, 27, 60–67.

El Emam, K., Jonker, E., Arbuckle, L., & Malin, B. (2011). A systematic review of re-identification attacks on health data. *PloS One*, 6(12), e28071.

Elder, L. (2010, February 12). UTMB warns 1,200 of identity theft threat. *Galveston County Daily News*. Retrieved from http://www.galvnews.com/story.lasso?ewcd=710b7dd80a0d2263

Elliott, C. (2014). Relationships between physicians and Pharma: Why physicians should not accept money from the pharmaceutical industry. *Neurology: Clinical Practice, 4*(2), 164–167.

Ellis, E. M., Atkeson, B. M., & Calhoun, K. S. (1982). An examination of differences between multiple- and single-incident victims of multiple sexual assault. *Journal of Abnormal Psychology, 91*, 221–224.

Elman, N. S., & Forrest, L. (2007). From trainee impairment to professional competence problems: Seeking new terminology that facilitates effective action. *Professional Psychology: Research and Practice, 38*(5), 501.

Empathy Resources for Therapists & Counselors. (2015). Retrieved from http://bit.ly/KenPopeCompassion. Accessed February 8, 2015.

Endicott, W. (1972, January 19). Breakdown in mental health care charged. *Los Angeles Times*. P. 3.

Ent, M. R., & Baumeister, R. F. (2014), Obedience, self-control, and the voice of culture. *Journal of Social Issues, 70*, 574–586.

Ent, M. R., & Baumeister, R. F. (2015). Individual differences in guilt proneness affect how people respond to moral tradeoffs between harm avoidance and obedience to authority. *Personality and Individual Differences, 74*, 231–234.

Erdberg, P. (1988, August). *How clinicians can achieve competence in testing procedures*. Paper presented at the annual meeting of the American Psychological Association, Atlanta, GA.

Evans, J. (1989). *Bias in human reasoning: Causes and consequences*. Mahwah, NJ: Erlbaum.

Fadiman, A. (1997). *The spirit catches you and you fall down: A Hmong child, her American doctors, and the collision of two cultures*. New York, NY: Farrar, Straus and Giroux.

Falender, C.A., Burnes, T., & Ellis, M. (2013). Introduction to major contribution: Multicultural clinical supervision and benchmarks: Empirical support informing practice and supervisor training. The Counseling Psychologist, *41*, 8–27. doi:10.1177/0011000012438417.

Falender, C. A., Collins, C. J., & Shafranske, E. P. (2009, November). "Impairment" and performance issues in clinical supervision: After the 2008 ADA Amendments Act. *Training and Education in Professional Psychology, 3*(4), 240–249.

Falender, C. A., & Shafranske, E. P. (2004). *Clinical supervision: A competency-based approach*. Washington, DC: American Psychological Association.

Falender, C. A., & Shafranske, E. P. (2008). *Casebook for clinical supervision: A competency based approach*. Washington, DC: American Psychological Association.

Falender, C. A., & Shafranske, E. P. (2010). *Getting the most out of clinical supervision: A practical guide for interns and trainees*. Washington, DC: American Psychological Association.

Falender, C. A., & Shafranske, E. P. (2014). Clinical supervision: The state of the art. *Journal of Clinical Psychology, 70*(11), 1030–1041.

Falender, C. A., Shafranske, E. P., & Falicov, C. (Eds.). (2014). *Multiculturalism and diversity in clinical supervision: A competency-based approach*. Washington, DC: American Psychological Association.

Falender, C. A., Shafranske, E. P., & Ofek, A. (2014). Competent clinical supervision: Emerging effective practices. *Counselling Psychology Quarterly, 27*(4), 393–408.

Fan, V. Y., & Lin, S. C. (2013). It is time to include compassion in medical training. *Academic Medicine, 88*(1), 11.

Farber, B. A. (2006). *Self-disclosure in psychotherapy*. New York, NY: Guilford Press.

Farber, E. W. (2010). Humanistic-existential psychotherapy competencies and the supervisory process. *Psychotherapy: Theory, Research, Practice, Training, 47*, 28–34. doi:10.1037/a0018847

Farber, E. W., & Kaslow, N. J. (2010). Introduction to the special section: The role of supervision in ensuring the development of psychotherapy competencies across diverse theoretical perspectives. *Psychotherapy: Theory, Research, Practice, Training, 47*, 1–2. doi:10.1037/a0018850

Farberow, N. (1985, May 12). How to tell if someone is thinking of suicide. *Los Angeles Herald Examiner*, p. C9.

Faschingbauer, T. R. (1979). The future of the MMPI. In C. S. Newmark (Ed.), *MMPI: Clinical and research trends* (pp. 380–392). New York, NY: Praeger.

Fasasi, M. I., & Olowu, A. A. (2013). Boundary transgressions: An issue in psychotherapeutic encounter. *IFE Psychologia, 21*(3), 138–150.

Faulkner, K. K., & Faulkner, T. A. (1997). Managing multiple relationships in rural communities: Neutrality and boundary violations. *Clinical Psychology: Science and Practice, 4*(3), 225–234.

Feeny, L. J. (2009). There is more to post-termination boundary violations than sex. *Advances in Psychiatric Treatment, 15*, 318. doi:10.1192/apt.15.4.318

Feldman-Summers, S., & Jones, G. (1984). Psychological impacts of sexual contact between therapists or other health care professionals and their clients. *Journal of Consulting and Clinical Psychology, 52*, 1054–1061.

Feminist Therapy Institute. (1987). *Feminist therapy code of ethics*. Denver, CO: Author.

Feminist Therapy Institute. (2000). *Feminist Therapy Institute code of ethics*. Denver, CO: Author.

Festinger, L. (1964). *Conflict, decision, and dissonance*. Stanford, CA: Stanford University Press.

Fiedler, K., Kutzner, F., & Krueger, J. I. (2012). The long way from α-error control to validity proper problems with a short-sighted false-positive debate. *Perspectives on Psychological Science, 7*(6), 661–669.

Fife, S. T., Whiting, J. B., Bradford, K., & Davis, S. (2014). The therapeutic pyramid: A common factors synthesis of techniques, alliance, and way of being. *Journal of Marital and Family Therapy, 40*(1), 20–33.

Finn, S. E. (2007). *In our clients' shoes: Theory and techniques of therapeutic assessment*. Mahwah, NJ: Erlbaum.

Fischer, S., & Soyez, K. (2015). Trick or treat: Assessing Health 2.0 and its prospects for patients, providers and society. In S. Gurtner & K. Soyez (Eds.), *Challenges and opportunities in health care management* (pp. 197–208). Cham, Switzerland: Springer International.

Fischhoff, B. (1975). Hindsight is not equal to foresight: The effect of outcome knowledge on judgment under uncertainty. *Journal of Experimental Psychology: Human Perception and Performance, 1*(3), 288.

Fischhoff, B., & Beyth, R. (1975). I knew it would happen: Remembered probabilities of once — future things. *Organizational Behavior and Human Performance, 13*(1), 1–16.

Fisher, M. A. (2008). Clarifying confidentiality with the ethical practice model. *American Psychologist, 63*, 624–625. doi:10.1037/0003–066X.63.7.624

Fisher, M. A. (2013). *Ethics of conditional confidentiality: A practice model for mental health professionals.* New York, NY: Oxford University Press.

Flacco, M. E., Manzoli, L., Boccia, S., Capasso, L., Aleksovska, K., Rosso, A., . . . Ioannidis, J. P. (2015). Head-to-head randomized trials are mostly industry sponsored and almost always favor the industry sponsor. *Journal of Clinical Epidemiology, 68*(7), 811–820.

Fouad, N. A., & Grus, C. L. (2014). Competency-based education and training in professional psychology. In N. J. Kaslow & W. B. Johnson (Eds.), *Oxford handbook of education and training in professional psychology* (pp. 105–119). New York, NY: Oxford University Press.

Fouad, N. A., Grus, C. L., Hatcher, R. L., Kaslow, N. J., Hutchings, P. S., Madson, M. B., . . . Crossman, R. E. (2009). Competency benchmarks: A model for understanding and measuring competence in professional psychology across training levels. *Training and Education in Professional Psychology, 3*, S5–S26. doi:10.1037/a0015832

Fourie, C. (2015). Moral distress and moral conflict in clinical ethics. *Bioethics, 29*(2), 91–97.

Frances, A. (2013). *Saving normal: An insider's look at what caused the epidemic of mental illness and how to cure it.* New York, NY: Morrow.

Francis, R. D. (2009). *Ethics for psychologists* (2nd ed.). Chichester, UK: Blackwell-Wiley.

Franklin, A. J. (2009). Reflections on ethnic minority psychology: Learning from our past so the present informs our future. *Cultural Diversity and Ethnic Minority Psychology, 15*, 416–424. doi:10.1037/a0017560

Freeh, Sporken, & Sullivan, LLP. (2012, July 12). *Report of the Special Investigative Counsel regarding the actions of The Pennsylvania State University related to the child sexual abuse committed by Gerald A. Sandusky.* Retrieved from http://progress.psu.edu/assets/content/REPORT_FINAL_071212.pdf

Freeman, L., & Roy, J. (1976). *Betrayal.* New York, NY: Stein and Day.

Freeny, M. (2007). Whatever happened to clinical privacy? *Annals of the American Psychotherapy Association, 10*, 13–17.

Freud, S. (1952). *A general introduction to psychoanalysis.* [Authorized English translation of the revised edition by J. Riviere.] New York, NY: Washington Square Press. (Original work published 1924)

Freud, S. (1963). Further recommendations in the technique of psychoanalysis: Observations on transference-love. In P. Rieff (Ed.), *Freud: Therapy and technique* (pp. 167–179). [Authorized English translation of the revised edition by J. Riviere.] New York, NY: Collier Books. (Original work published 1915)

Frey, D., & Schulz-Hardt, S. (2001). Confirmation bias in group information seeking and its implications for decision making in administration, business and politics. In F. Butera & G. Mugny (Eds.), *Social influence in social reality: Promoting individual and social change* (pp. 53–73). Ashland, OH: Hogrefe & Huber.

Freyd, J. (1994). Betrayal trauma: Traumatic amnesia as an adaptive response to childhood abuse. *Ethics & Behavior, 4*(4), 307–329.

Freyd, J. J. (1996). *Betrayal trauma: The logic of forgetting childhood abuse.* Cambridge, MA: Harvard University Press.

Freyd, J. J., Klest, B., & Allard, C. B. (2005). Betrayal trauma: Relationship to physical health, psychological distress, and a written disclosure intervention. *Journal of Trauma & Dissociation, 6*(3), 83–104.

Fuller, K. (2006). Training students on the ethics of touch in psychotherapy. *Association of Directors of Psychology Training Clinics Newsletter, 8.* Retrieved from https://www .aptc.org/news/112006/article_one.html

Gabbard, G. O. (1994). Teetering on the precipice: A commentary on Lazarus's "How certain boundaries and ethics diminish therapeutic effectiveness." *Ethics and Behavior, 4*(3), 283–286.

Gabbard, G. O. (Ed.). (1989). *Sexual exploitation in professional relationships.* Washington, DC: American Psychiatric Press.

Gabbard, G. O., & Pope, K. (1989). Sexual involvements after termination: Clinical, ethical, and legal aspects. In G. O. Gabbard (Ed.), *Sexual exploitation in professional relationships* (pp. 115–127). Washington, DC: American Psychiatric Press.

Gadit, A. A. M., Mugford, G., Callanan, T., & Aslanov, R. (2014). Reported experiences of stalking behavior from patients towards psychiatrists from the Atlantic Provinces of Canada. *British Journal of Medicine and Medical Research, 4*(22), 3990–4003.

Gaitan-Sierra, C., & Hyland, M. E. (2014). Mood enhancement in health-promoting non-aerobic exercise: The role of non-specific mechanisms. *Journal of Health Psychology, 19*(7), 918–930.

Gallagher, H. G. (1990). *By trust betrayed: Patients, physicians, and the license to kill in the Third Reich.* New York, NY: Holt.

Gamondi, C., Borasio, G. D., Limoni, C., Preston, N., & Payne, S. (2014). Legalisation of assisted suicide: A safeguard to euthanasia?. *Lancet, 384*(9938), 127.

Gandhi, M. K. (1948). *Non-violence in peace and war.* Ahmedabad, India: Navajivan Publishing.

Ganske, K. M. (2010). Moral distress in academia. *The Online Journal of Issues in Nursing, 15*(3), 6.

Gartrell, N. K. (1992). Boundaries in lesbian therapy relationships. *Women & Therapy, 12*, 29–49.

Gartrell, N. K., Herman, J. L., Olarte, S., Feldstein, M., & Localio, R. (1986). Psychiatrist-patient sexual contact: Results of a national survey. I: Prevalence. *American Journal of Psychiatry, 143*, 1126–1131.

Gavett, B. E., Lynch, J. K., & McCaffrey, R. J. (2005). Third party observers: The effect size is greater than you might think. *Journal of Forensic Neuropsychology, 4*(2), 49–64.

Geisinger, K. F. (Ed.). (2015). *Psychological testing of Hispanics: Clinical, cultural, and intellectual issues* (2nd ed.). Washington, DC: American Psychological Association. doi:10.1037/14668-000

Geller, J. D., Cooley, R. S., & Hartley, D. (1981). Images of the psychotherapist: A theoretical and methodological perspective. *Imagination, Cognition, and Personality: Consciousness in Theory, Research, Clinical Practice, 3*, 123–146.

Gelso, C. J., & Bhatia, A. (2012). Crossing theoretical lines: The role and effect of transference in nonanalytic psychotherapies. *Psychotherapy, 49*(3), 384–390.

Geronimus, A. T., Bound, J., Waidmann, T. A., Hillemeier, M. M., & Burns, P. B. (1996). Excess mortality among blacks and whites in the United States. *New England Journal of Medicine, 335*(21), 1552–1558.

Geuter, U. (1992). *The professionalism of psychology in Nazi Germany*. New York, NY: Cambridge University Press.

Geyer, M. C. (1994). Dual role relationships and Christian counseling. *Journal of Psychology and Theology, 22*(3), 187–195.

Gibbons, R. D., Hur, K., Bhaumik, D. K., & Mann, J. J. (2005). The relationship between antidepressant medication use and rate of suicide. *Archives of General Psychiatry, 62*, 165–172.

Gibbs, J. T. (1997). African-American suicide: A cultural paradox. *Suicide and Life-Threatening Behavior, 27*, 68–79.

Gibson, W. T., & Pope, K. S. (1993). The ethics of counseling: A national survey of certified counselors. *Journal of Counseling and Development, 71*(3), 330–336.

Gilead, M., & Liberman, N. (2014). We take care of our own: Caregiving salience increases out-group bias in response to out-group threat. *Psychological Science, 25*(7), 1380–1387.

Gilovich, T., Griffin, D., & Kahneman, D. (Eds.). (2002). *Heuristics and biases: The psychology of intuitive judgment*. New York, NY: Cambridge University Press.

Giovazolias, T., & Davis, P. (2001). How common is sexual attraction towards clients? The experiences of sexual attraction toward their clients and its impact on the therapeutic process. *Counseling Psychology Quarterly, 14*, 281–286. doi:10.1080/09515070110100974

Glascock, A. (2009). Is killing necessarily murder? Moral questions surrounding assisted suicide and death. In J. Sokolovsky (Ed.), *The cultural context of aging: Worldwide perspectives* (3rd ed., pp. 77–92). Westport, CT: Praeger/Greenwood Publishing Group.

Glaser, R. D., & Thorpe, J. S. (1986). Unethical intimacy: A survey of sexual contact and advances between psychology educators and female graduate students. *American Psychologist, 41*, 43–51.

Glick, J. E., Bates, L., & Yabiku, S. T. (2009). Mother's age at arrival in the United States and early cognitive development. *Early Childhood Research Quarterly, 24*(4), 367–380.

Gold, M. (1999). *The complete social scientist: A Kurt Lewin reader*. Washington, DC: American Psychological Association.

Goleman, D. P. (1995). *Emotional intelligence: Why it can matter more than IQ for character, health and lifelong achievement*. New York, NY: Bantam.

Gómez, J. M. (2015). Microaggressions and the enduring mental health disparity: Black Americans at risk for institutional betrayal. *Journal of Black Psychology, 41*(2), 121–143.

Gonzales, N. A., Jensen, M., Montano, Z., & Wynne, H. (2015). The cultural adaptation and mental health of Mexican American adolescents. In Y. M. Caldera &

E. W. Lindsey (Eds.), *Mexican American children and families: Multidisciplinary perspectives* (pp. 182–196). New York, NY: Routledge/Taylor & Francis.

Goodheart, C. D. (2006). Evidence, endeavor, and expertise in psychology practice. In C. D. Goodheart, A. E. Kazdin, & R. J. Sternberg (Eds.), *Evidence-based psychotherapy: Where practice and research meet* (pp. 37–61). Washington, DC: American Psychological Association.

Goodman, M. (2015). *Future crimes: Everything is connected, everyone is vulnerable and what we can do about it.* New York, NY: Doubleday.

Goodyear, R. K., & Sinnett, E. R. (1984). Current and emerging ethical issues for counseling psychology. *Counseling Psychologist, 12,* 87–98.

Gorman, S. W. (2009, April). Comment: Sex outside of the therapy hour: Practical and constitutional limits on therapist sexual misconduct regulations. 56 *UCLA Law Review, 983.*

Gostin, L. (2006). Physician-assisted suicide: A legitimate medical practice? *Journal of the American Medical Association, 295*(16), 1941–1943.

Gottlieb, M. C. (1993). Avoiding exploitive dual relationships: A decision-making model. *Psychotherapy: Theory, Research, Practice, Training, 30*(1), 41–48. Available at http://kspope.com

Gottlieb, M. C. (1994). Ethical decision making, boundaries, and treatment effectiveness: A reprise. *Ethics and Behavior, 4*(3), 287–293.

Gottlieb, M. C., Robinson, K., & Younggren, J. N. (2007). Multiple relations in supervision: Guidance for administrators, supervisors, and students. *Professional Psychology: Research and Practice, 38*(3), 241.

Grady, C. (2015). Enduring and emerging challenges of informed consent. *New England Journal of Medicine, 372*(9), 855–862.

Graham, S. (1992). "Most of the subjects were White and middle class": Trends in published research on African Americans in selected APA journals, 1970–1989. *American Psychologist, 47*(5), 629.

Greenberg, G. (2013). *The book of woe: The DSM and the unmaking of psychiatry.* New York, NY: Penguin.

Greene, B. G. (1997a). Ethnic minority lesbians and gay men: Mental health and treatment issues. In B. Greene (Ed.), *Ethnic and cultural diversity among lesbians and gay men* (pp. 216–239). Thousand Oaks, CA: Sage.

Greene, B. G. (Ed.). (1997b). *Ethnic and cultural diversity among lesbians and gay men.* Thousand Oaks, CA: Sage.

Greene, B. G., & Croom, G. L. (1999). *Education, research, and practice in lesbian, gay, bisexual, and transgendered psychology: A resource manual.* Thousand Oaks, CA: Sage.

Gripton, J., & Valentich, M. (2004). Dealing with non-sexual professional-client dual/multiple relationships in rural communities. *Rural Social Work, 9*(2), 216–225.

Grohol, J. M. (2015, August 18). American Psychological Association's new torture policy is unenforceable. *PsychCentral.* Retrieved from http://bit.ly/1N7EUZl

Gross, B. (2004). Theft by deception. *Annals of the American Psychotherapy Association, 7*(1), 36–37.

Grundner, T. M. (1980). On the readability of surgical consent forms. *New England Journal of Medicine, 302,* 900–902.

Guazzini, A., Yoneki, E., & Gronchi, G. (2015). Cognitive dissonance and social influence effects on preference judgments: An eye tracking based system for their automatic assessment. *International Journal of Human-Computer Studies, 73*, 12–18.

Guerette, R. T., Flexon, J. L., & Marquez, C. (2013). Instigating bystander intervention in the prevention of alcohol-impaired driving: Analysis of data regarding mass media campaigns. *Journal of Studies on Alcohol and Drugs, 74*(2), 205–211.

Guiffrida, D. (2015). A constructive approach to counseling and psychotherapy supervision. *Journal of Constructivist Psychology, 28*(1), 40–52.

Gutheil, T. G. (1994). Discussion of Lazarus's "How certain boundaries and ethics diminish therapeutic effectiveness." *Ethics and Behavior, 4*(3), 295–298.

Gutheil, T. G., & Brodsky, A. (2008). *Preventing boundary violations in clinical practice.* New York, NY: Guilford Press.

Gutheil, T. G., & Gabbard, G. O. (1993). The concept of boundaries in clinical practice: Theoretical and risk-management dimensions. *American Journal of Psychiatry, 150*, 188–196.

Guthrie, R. V. (2004). *Even the rat was white: A historical view of psychology* (2nd ed.). Boston, MA: Pearson Education.

Guze, S. B., & Robins, E. (1970). Suicide and primary affective disorders. *British Journal of Psychiatry, 117*, 437–438.

Gymrek, M., McGuire, A. L., Golan, D., Halperin, E., & Erlich, Y. (2013). Identifying personal genomes by surname inference. *Science, 339*(6117), 321–324.

Hajdu, S. I. (2007). Persecution of noted physicians and medical scientists. *Annals of Clinical & Laboratory Science, 37*(3), 295297.

Hall, C. C. I. (1997). Cultural malpractice: The growing obsolescence of psychology with the changing US population. *American Psychologist, 52*(6), 642–651.

Hall, C. S. (1952). Crooks, codes, and cant. *American Psychologist, 7*, 430–431.

Hall, J. E., & Hare-Mustin, R. T. (1983). Sanctions and the diversity of complaints against psychologists. *American Psychologist, 38*, 714–729.

Hallinan v. Committee of Bar Examiners of State Bar, 55 Cal. Rptr. 228 (1966).

Hamric, A. B., & Blackhall, L. J. (2007). Nurse-physician perspectives on the care of dying patients in intensive care units: Collaboration, moral distress, and ethical climate. *Critical Care Medicine, 35*(2), 422–429.

Handler, J. F. (1990). *Law and the search for community.* Philadelphia: University of Pennsylvania Press.

Haney-Caron, E., & Heilbrun, K. (2014). Lesbian and gay parents and determination of child custody: The changing legal landscape and implications for policy and practice. *Psychology of Sexual Orientation and Gender Diversity, 1*(1), 19.

Hannah, S. T., Avolio, B. J., & Walumbwa, F. O. (2011). Relationships between authentic leadership, moral courage, and ethical and pro-social behaviors. *Business Ethics Quarterly, 21*, 555–578.

Hansen, N. D., Randazzo, K. V., Schwartz, A., Marshall, M., Kalis, D., Frazier, R., . . . Norvig, G. (2006). Do we practice what we preach? An exploratory survey of multicultural psychotherapy competencies. *Professional Psychology: Research and Practice, 37*(1), 66–74.

Harding, S. S., Shearn, M. L., & Kitchener, K. S. (1989, August). *Dual role dilemmas: Psychology educators and their students.* Paper presented at the annual meeting of the American Psychological Association, New Orleans, LA.

Hare-Mustin, R. T. (1974). Ethical considerations in the use of sexual contact in psychotherapy.*Psychotherapy: Theory, Research and Practice, 11*, 308–310.

Harowski, K., Turner, A. L., LeVine, E., Schank, J. A., & Leichter, J. (2006). From our community to yours: Rural best perspectives on psychology practice, training, and advocacy. *Professional Psychology: Research and Practice, 37*(2), 158–164.

Harper, F. D., & McFadden, J. (2003). *Culture and counseling: New approaches.* Needham Heights, MA: Allyn & Bacon.

Harris, E. C., & Barraclough, B. (1997). Suicide as an outcome for mental disorders: A meta-analysis. *British Journal of Psychiatry, 170*, 205–228.

Harry, B., & Klingner, J. K. (2014). Why are so many minority students in special education? Understanding race & disability in schools. New York, NY: Teachers College Press.

Hartmann, E., & Hartmann, T. (2014). The impact of exposure to Internet-based information about the Rorschach and the MMPI–2 on psychiatric outpatients' ability to simulate mentally healthy test performance. *Journal of Personality Assessment, 96*(4), 432–444.

Haslam, N., Loughnan, S., & Perry, G. (2014). Meta-Milgram: An empirical synthesis of the obedience experiments. *PloS One, 9*(4), e93927.

Hatcher, R. L., Fouad, N. A., Campbell, L. F., McCutcheon, S. R., Grus, C. L., & Leahy, K. L. (2013). Competency-based education for professional psychology: Moving from concept to practice. *Training and Education in Professional Psychology, 7*(4), 225234.

Hawn, C. (2009). Take two aspirin and tweet me in the morning: How Twitter, Facebook, and other social media are reshaping health care. *Health Affairs, 28*(2), 361–368.

Hays, K. (2002). *Move your body, tone your mood.* New York, NY: Harbinger.

Hays, P. A. (2008). *Addressing cultural complexities in practice: Assessment, diagnosis, and therapy* (2nd ed.). Washington, DC: American Psychological Association.

Hays, P. A. (2009). Integrating evidence-based practice, cognitive-behavior therapy, and multicultural therapy: Ten steps for culturally competent practice. *Professional Psychology: Research and Practice, 40*, 354–360. doi:10.1037/a0016250

Heckert, C. M. (2012). Latina immigrants in rural western Pennsylvania and use of mental health resources when coping with depression: Implications for practice. *International Journal of Culture and Mental Health, 5*(3), 182–189.

Hegazi, I., & Wilson, I. (2013). Maintaining empathy in medical school: It is possible. *Medical Teacher, 35*(12), 1002–1008.

Heingartner, D. (2009, November 30). The doctors were real, the patients undercover. *New York Times.* Retrieved from http://www.nytimes.com/2009/12/01/health/01dutch.html

Heinonen, E., Lindfors, O., Härkänen, T., Virtala, E., Jääskeläinen, T., & Knekt, P. (2014). Therapists' professional and personal characteristics as predictors of working alliance in short-term and long-term psychotherapies. *Clinical Psychology & Psychotherapy, 21*(6), 475–494.

Hempstead, K. A., & Phillips, J. A. (2015). Rising suicide among adults aged 40–64 years: The role of job and financial circumstances. *American Journal of Preventive Medicine, 48*(5), 491–500.

Hendin, H., Haas, A. P., Maltsberger, J. T., Koestner, B., & Szanto, K. (2006). Problems in psychotherapy with suicidal patients. *American Journal of Psychiatry, 163*(1), 67–72.

Henley-Einion, J. A., & Blagrove, M. T. (2014). Assessing the day-residue and dream-lag effects using the identification of multiple correspondences between dream reports and waking life diaries. *Dreaming, 24*(2), 71–88.

Henretty, J. R., Currier, J. M., Berman, J. S., & Levitt, H. M. (2014). The impact of counselor self-disclosure on clients: A meta-analytic review of experimental and quasi-experimental research. *Journal of Counseling Psychology, 61*(2), 191–207.

Henretty, J. R., & Levitt, H. M. (2010). The role of therapist self-disclosure in psychotherapy: A qualitative review. *Clinical Psychology Review, 30,* 63–77. doi:10.1016/j.cpr.2009.09.004

Herlihy, B., & Corey, G. (2014). *Boundary issues in counseling: Multiple roles and responsibilities.* Hoboken, NJ: Wiley.

Herman, J. L., Gartrell, N., Olarte, S., Feldstein, M., & Localio, R. (1987). Psychiatrist-patient sexual contact: Results of a national survey. II: Psychiatrists' attitudes. *American Journal of Psychiatry, 144,* 164–169.

Hess, B. J., Lipner, R. S., Thompson, V., Holmboe, E. S., & Graber, M. L. (2015). Blink or think: Can further reflection improve initial diagnostic impressions? *Academic Medicine, 90*(1), 112–118.

Hess, T. M., Strough, J., & Löckenhoff, C. E. (Eds.). (2015). *Aging and decision making: Empirical and applied perspectives.* San Diego, CA: Elsevier.

Hill, C. W., Jones, G. R., & Schilling, M. A. (2014). *Strategic management: Theory and cases: An integrated approach* (11th ed.). Boston, MA: Cengage.

Hill, C., Memon, A., & McGeorge, P. (2008). The role of confirmation bias in suspect interviews: A systematic evaluation. *Legal and Criminological Psychology, 13,* 357–371.

Hill, M. (1999). Barter: Ethical considerations in psychotherapy. *Women & Therapy, 22,* 81–91. doi:10.1300/J015v22n03_08

Hinrichsen, G. A. (2006). Why multicultural issues matter for practitioners working with older adults. *Professional Psychology: Research and Practice, 37*(1), 29–35.

Hobbs, N. (1948). The development of a code of ethical standards for psychology. *American Psychologist, 3,* 80–84.

Hoffman, D. H., Carter, D. J., Lopez, C. R.V., Benzmiller, H.L., Guo, A. X., Latifi, S. Y., & Craig, D. C. (2015a, July 2). *Report to the Special Committee of the Board of Directors of the American Psychological Association: Independent Review Relating to APA Ethics Guidelines, National Security Interrogations, and Torture.* Chicago: Sidley Austin LLP. Retrieved from http://www.apa.org/independent-review/APA-FINAL-Report-7.2.15.pdf

Hoffman, D. H., Carter, D. J., Lopez, C. R.V., Benzmiller, H.L., Guo, A. X., Latifi, S. Y., & Craig, D. C. (2015b, September 4). *Report to the Special Committee of the Board of Directors of the American Psychological Association: Independent Review Relating to APA Ethics Guidelines, National Security Interrogations, and Torture.* Chicago: Sidley Austin LLP. Retrieved from http://www.apa.org/independent-review/revised-report.pdf

Hoglend, P. (2014). Exploration of the patient-therapist relationship in psychotherapy. *American Journal of Psychiatry, 171*(10), 1056–1066.

Holdsworth, E., Bowen, E., Brown, S., & Howat, D. (2014). Client engagement in psychotherapeutic treatment and associations with client characteristics, therapist characteristics, and treatment factors. *Clinical Psychology Review, 34*(5), 428–450.

Hollingshaus, M. S., & Smith, K. R. (2015). Life and death in the family: Early parental death, parental remarriage, and offspring suicide risk in adulthood. *Social Science & Medicine, 131,* 181–189.

Hollwicha, S., Frankeb, I., Riecher-Rösslerc, A., & Reiter-Theila, S. (2015). Therapist-client sex in psychotherapy: Attitudes of professionals and students towards ethical arguments. *Swiss Medical Weekly, 145,* w14099. Retrieved from http://upkbs.ch/lehreforschung/erwachsene/publikationen/publikationen/Documents/Hollwich,Franke,Riecher,Reiter-Theil.%20SMW%202015.pdf

Holmqvist, R. (2015). The use of self-disclosure among Swedish psychotherapists. *European Journal of Psychotherapy & Counselling, 17*(1), 80–98.

Holroyd, J. (1983). Erotic contact as an instance of sex-biased therapy. In J. Murray & P. R. Abramson (Eds.), *Bias in psychotherapy* (pp. 285–308). New York, NY: Praeger.

Holroyd, J. C., & Brodsky, A. (1977). Psychologists' attitudes and practices regarding erotic and nonerotic physical contact with clients. *American Psychologist, 32,* 843–849.

Holroyd, J. C., & Brodsky, A. M. (1980). Does touching patients lead to sexual intercourse? *Professional Psychology, 11,* 807–811.

Horrell, S. C. V. (2008). Effectiveness of cognitive-behavioral therapy with adult ethnic minority clients: A review. *Professional Psychology: Research and Practice, 2,* 160–168.

Horst, E. A. (1989). Dual relationships between psychologists and clients in rural and urban areas. *Journal of Rural Community Psychology, 10*(2), 15–24.

Hoyer, M., & Zoroya, G. (2014, July 4). VA bonuses went to officials at delay-prone hospitals. *USA Today.* Retrieved from http://www.usatoday.com/story/news/nation/2014/07/03/va-care-delayed-bonuses-scandal/12159243/

Huberts, L. (2014). *Integrity of governance: What it is, what we know, what is done and where to go.* New York, NY: Palgrave Macmillan.

Huey Jr, S. J., Tilley, J. L., Jones, E. O., & Smith, C. A. (2014). The contribution of cultural competence to evidence-based care for ethnically diverse populations. *Annual Review of Clinical Psychology, 10,* 305–338.

Huisman, A., van Houwelingen, C. A. J., & Kerkhof, A. J. F. M. (2009). Psychopathology and suicide method in mental health care. *Journal of Affective Disorders.* doi:10.1016/j.jad.2009.05.024

Humphries, A., & Woods, M. (2015, January 6). A study of nurses' ethical climate perceptions: Compromising in an uncompromising environment. *Nursing Ethics,* 0969733014564101

Hunt, I. M., Kapur, N., Webb, R., Robinson, J., Burns, J., Shaw, J., & Appleby, L. (2009). Suicide in recently discharged psychiatric patients: A case-control study. *Psychological Medicine, 39,* 443–449. doi:10.1017/S0033291708003644.

Huppert, J. D., Fabbro, A., & Barlow, D. H. (2006). Evidence-based practice and psychological treatments. In C. D. Goodheart, A. E. Kazdin, & R. J. Sternberg (Eds.), *Evidence-based psychotherapy: Where practice and research meet* (pp. 131–152). Washington, DC: American Psychological Association.

Hwang, W. (2009). The formative method for adapting psychotherapy (FMAP): A community-based developmental approach to culturally adapting therapy. *Professional Psychology: Research and Practice, 40*, 369–377.

Illinois Revised Statutes of 1991. chap. 70, para. 803

Indiana General Assembly, House Enrolled Act #1830, Section F. (1984).

Insider tipped Eastern Health to latest privacy breach. (2014, May 14). *CBC News*. Retrieved from http://bit.ly/EasternHealthBreach

In the matter of the accusation against: Myron E. Howland. (1980). Before the Psychology Examining Committee, Board of Medical Quality Assurance, State of California, No. D-2212. Reporters' transcript. Vol. 3.

Irwin, M., Lovitz, A., Marder, S. R., Mintz, J., Winslade, W. J., Van Putten, T., & Mills, M. J. (1985). Psychotic patients' understanding of informed consent. *American Journal of Psychiatry, 142*, 1351–1354.

Isenberg-Grzeda, E., & Ellis, J. (2015). Editorial, supportive care and psychological issues around cancer. *Current Opinion in Supportive and Palliative Care, 9*, 38–39.

Isherwood, J., Adam, K. S., & Homblow, A. R. (1982). Life event stress, psychosocial factors, suicide attempt and auto-accident proclivity. *Journal of Psychosomatic Research, 26*, 371–383.

Ito, T. A. (Ed.). (2013). *Neuroscience of prejudice and intergroup relations*. New York, NY: Psychology Press.

Ivarsson, D., Blom, M., Hesser, H., Carlbring, P., Enderby, P., Nordberg, R., & Andersson, G. (2014). Guided internet-delivered cognitive behavior therapy for post-traumatic stress disorder: A randomized controlled trial. *Internet Interventions, 1*(1), 33–40.

Ivory, D., & Abrams, R. (2014, November 16). Deadline extended for G.M.A. accident claims. *New York Times*. Retrieved from http://www.nytimes.com/2014/11/17/business/deadline-extended-for-gm-accident-claims.html?ref=us

Jablonski v. United States, 712 F.2d 391 (1983).

Jackall, R. (1988). *Moral mazes: The world of corporate managers*. New York, NY: Oxford University Press.

Jacobson, R. M. (2014). *National survey of Canadian psychologists' test feedback training and practice: A mixed methods study* (Unpublished doctoral dissertation). University of Alberta, Edmonton, Canada.

Jain, S. H. (2009). Practicing medicine in the age of Facebook. *New England Journal of Medicine, 361*(7), 649–651. doi:10.1056/NEJMp0901277

Jain, S., & Roberts, L. (2009). Ethics in psychotherapy: A focus on professional boundaries and confidentiality practices. *Psychiatric Clinics of North America, 32*(2), 299–314.

Jameton, A. (1984). *Nursing practice: The ethical issues*. Englewood Cliffs, NJ: Prentice-Hall.

Jameton, A. (1992). Dilemmas of moral distress: Moral responsibility and nursing practice. *AWHONN's Clinical Issues in Perinatal and Women's Health Nursing, 4*(4), 542–551.

Janis, I. L. (1972). *Victims of groupthink*. Boston, MA: Houghton Mifflin.

Janis, I. L. (1982). *Stress, attitudes, and decisions*. New York, NY: Praeger.

Janis, I. L., & Mann, L. (1977). *Decision making: A psychological analysis of conflict, choice, and commitment*. New York, NY: Free Press.

Jennings, F. L. (1992). Ethics of rural practice. *Psychotherapy in Private Practice*, 10(3), 85–104.

Johnson, C. (2014, September 26). *California bans coerced sterilization of female inmates*. Retrieved from https://beta.cironline.org/reports/california-bans-coerced-sterilization-of-female-inmates/

Johnson, S. M., Cramer, R. J., Conroy, M. A., & Gardner, B. O. (2014). The role of and challenges for psychologists in physician assisted suicide. *Death Studies*, 38(9), 582–588.

Joiner, T. (2005). *Why people die by suicide*. Cambridge, MA: Harvard University Press.

Joiner, T. (2010). *Myths about suicide*. Cambridge, MA: Harvard University Press.

Jones, E. E. (1979). The rocky road from acts to dispositions. *American Psychologist*, 34(2), 107–117.

Jones, J. H. (1981). *Bad blood: The Tuskegee syphilis experiment — A tragedy of race and medicine*. New York, NY: Free Press.

Jones, J. M. (1990, September 14). Promoting diversity in an individualistic society. Keynote address at the Great Lakes College Association conference, Hope College, Holland, MI.

Jordan, J. V. (1997). A relational perspective for understanding women's development. In J. V. Jordan (Ed.), *Women's growth in diversity: More writings from the Stone Center* (pp. 9–24). New York, NY: Guilford Press.

Jordan, N. A., Russell, L., Afousi, E., Chemel, T., McVicker, M., Robertson, J., & Winek, J. (2014). The ethical use of social media in marriage and family therapy: Recommendations and future directions. *The Family Journal*, 22(1), 105112.

Jourard, S. M. (1964). *The transparent self*. Princeton, NJ: Van Nostrand.

Jourard, S. M. (1971). *Self disclosure: Experimental analysis of the transparent self*. New York, NY: Wiley.

Kaduvettoor, A., O'Shaughnessy, T., Mori, Y., Beverly, C., III, Weatherford, R. D., & Ladany, N. (2009). Helpful and hindering multicultural events in group supervision: Climate and multicultural competence. *Counseling Psychologist*, 37, 786–820. doi:10.1177/0011000009333984

Kahneman, D. (2011). *Thinking, fast and slow*. New York, NY: Farrar, Straus and Giroux.

Kahneman, D., & Klein, G. (2009). Conditions for intuitive expertise: A failure to disagree. *American Psychologist*, 64, 515–526. doi: 10.1037/a0016755.

Kahneman, D., Knetsch, J. L., & Thaler, R. H. (1991). Anomalies: The endowment effect, loss aversion, and status quo bias. *The Journal of Economic Perspectives*, 5(1), 193–206.

Kälvemark, S., Höglund, A. T., Hansson, M. G., Westerholm, P., & Arnetz, B. (2004). Living with conflicts — ethical dilemmas and moral distress in the health care system. *Social Science & Medicine*, 58(6), 10751084.

Kane, J. E., & Webster, G. D. (2013). Heuristics and biases that help and hinder scientists: Toward a psychology of scientific judgment and decision making. In G. J. Feist & M. E. Gorman (Eds.), *Handbook of the psychology of science* (pp. 437–459). New York, NY: Springer.

Kaslow, F. W., Patterson, T., & Gottlieb, M. (2011). Ethical dilemmas in psychologists accessing Internet data: Is it justified? *Professional Psychology: Research and Practice,* 42(2), 105.

Kaslow, N. J. (2004). Competencies in professional psychology. *American Psychologist,* 59, 774–781.

Kaslow, N. J., Borden, K. A., Collins, F. L., Forrest, L., Illfelder-Kaye, J., Nelson, P. D.,... Willmuth, M. W. (2004). Competencies conference: Future directions in education and credentialing in professional psychology. *Journal of Clinical Psychology,* 60(7), 699–712.

Kaslow, N. J., Grus, C. L., Campbell, L. F., Fouad, N. A., Hatcher, R. L., & Rodolfa, E. R. (2009). Competency assessment toolkit for professional psychology. *Training and Education in Professional Psychology,* 3, S27–S45. doi:10.1037/a0015833

Kazdin, A. E. (2006). Assessment and evaluation in clinical practice. In C. D. Goodheart, A. E. Kazdin, & R. J. Sternberg, *Evidence-based psychotherapy: Where practice and research meet* (pp. 153–178). Washington, DC: American Psychological Association.

Kazdin, A. E. (2008a). Evidence-based treatments and delivery of psychological services: Shifting our emphases to increase impact. *Psychological Services,* 5(3), 201–215.

Kazdin, A. E. (2008b). Evidence-based treatment and practice: New opportunities to bridge clinical research and practice, enhance the knowledge base, and improve patient patient care. *American Psychologist,* 63(3), 146–159.

Keith-Spiegel, P., & Koocher, G. P. (1985). *Ethics in psychology: Professional standards and cases.* New York, NY: Random House.

Kelly, R. E., Cohen, L. J., Semple, R. J., Bialer, P., Lau, A., Bodenheimer, A.,... Galynker, I. I. (2006). Relationship between drug company funding and outcomes of clinical psychiatric research. *Psychological Medicine,* 36(11), 1647–1656.

Kelm, Z., Womer, J., Walter, J. K., & Feudtner, C. (2014). Interventions to cultivate physician empathy: A systematic review. *BMC Medical Education,* 14(1), 219.

Kendall, P. C., & Beidas, R. S. (2007). Smoothing the trail for dissemination of evidence-based practices for youth: Flexibility within fidelity. *Professional Psychology: Research and Practice,* 38, 13–20.

Kepner, J. (2001). Touch in Gestalt body process psychotherapy: Purpose, practice, and ethics. *Gestalt Review,* 5, 97–114.

Kesselheim, A. S., & Studdert D. M. (2007). Role of professional organizations in regulating physician expert witness testimony. *Journal of the American Medical Association,* 298(24), 2907–2909.

Kesselheim, J. C., Batra, M., Belmonte, F., Boland, K. A., & McGregor, R. S. (2014). New professionalism challenges in medical training: An exploration of social networking. *Journal of Graduate Medical Education,* 6(1), 100–105.

Kessler, L. E., & Wachler, C. A. (2005). Addressing multiple relationships between clients and therapists in lesbian, gay, bisexual, and transgender communities. *Professional Psychology: Research and Practice,* 36(1), 66–72.

Kim, U., Yang, K, & Hwang, K. K. (Eds). (2006). *Indigenous and cultural psychology: Understanding people in context.* New York, NY: Springer SBM Publications.

King, M. L., Jr. (1958). *Stride toward freedom.* San Francisco, CA: HarperSanFrancisco.

King, M. L., Jr. (1964). *Why we can't wait*. New York, NY: Signet.

King, V. L., Stoller, K. B., Kidorf, M., Kindbom, K., Hursh, S., Brady, T., & Brooner, R. K. (2009). Assessing the effectiveness of an Internet-based videoconferencing platform for delivering intensified substance abuse counseling. *Journal of Substance Abuse Treatment, 36*, 331–338. doi:10.1016/j.jsat.2008.06.011

Kirschman, E., Kamena, M., & Fay, J. (2013). *Counseling cops: What clinicians need to know*. New York, NY: Guilford Press.

Kish-Gephart, J. J., Detert, J. R., Treviño, L. K., & Edmondson, A. C. (2009). Silenced by fear: The nature, sources, and consequences of fear at work. *Research in Organizational Behavior, 29*, 163–193.

Kish-Gephart, J. J., Harrison, D. A., & Treviño, L. K. (2010). Bad apples, bad cases, and bad barrels: Meta-analytic evidence about sources of unethical decisions at work. *Journal of Applied Psychology, 95*(1), 1–31.

Kissil, K., Davey, M., & Davey, A. (2013). Foreign-born therapists in the United States: Supervisors' multicultural competence, supervision satisfaction, and counseling self-efficacy. *Clinical Supervisor, 32*(2), 185–211.

Kissil, K., Davey, M., & Davey, A. (2015). Foreign-born therapists: How acculturation and supervisors' multicultural competence are associated with clinical self-efficacy. *Journal of Multicultural Counseling and Development, 43*(1), 38–57.

Kitchener, K.S. (1988). Dual role relationships: What makes them so problematic? *Journal of Counseling & Development, 67*, 217–221. doi:10.1002/j.1556-6676.1988.tb02586.x

Kitchener, K. S. (2000). *Foundations of ethical practice, research, and teaching in psychology*. Mahwah, NJ: Erlbaum.

Kivisto, A. J., Berman, A., Watson, M., Gruber, D., & Paul, H. (2015). North American psychologists' experiences of stalking, threatening, and harassing behavior: A survey of ABPP Diplomates. *Professional Psychology: Research and Practice, 46*, 277–286.

Kleespies, P. M. (Ed.). (2004). *Life and death decisions: Psychological and ethical considerations in end-of-life care*. Washington, DC: American Psychological Association.

Kleespies, P. M. (2014). Decision making under stress: Theoretical and empirical bases. In P. M. Kleespies, *Decision making in behavioral emergencies: Acquiring skill in evaluating and managing high-risk patients* (pp. 31–46). Washington, DC: American Psychological Association.

Kleinsasser, A., Jouriles, E. N., McDonald, R., & Rosenfield, D. (2014). An online bystander intervention program for the prevention of sexual violence. *Psychology of Violence, 5*, 227–235. doi:10.1037/a0037393

Klerman, G. L., & Clayton, P. (1984). Epidemiologic perspectives on the health consequences of bereavement. In M. Osterweis, F. Solomon, & M. Green (Eds.). *Bereavement: Reactions, consequences and care* (pp. 15–44). Washington, DC: National Academy Press.

Koehler, J. J., & Gershoff, A. D. (2003). Betrayal aversion: When agents of protection become agents of harm. *Organizational Behavior and Human Decision Processes, 90*(2), 244–261.

Koenig, R. (2000). Reopening the darkest chapter in German science. *Science, 288*(5471), 1576–1577.

Kohlstedt, S. G. (2004). Sustaining gains: Reflections on women in science and technology in 20th-century United States. *NWSA Journal, 16*(1), 1–26.

Kok, R. N., van Straten, A., Beekman, A. T., & Cuijpers, P. (2014). Short-term effectiveness of web-based guided self-help for phobic outpatients: randomized controlled trial. *Journal of Medical Internet Research, 16*(9), e226. doi: 10.2196/jmir.3429

Kõlves, K., Värnik, A., Tooding, L., & Wasserman, D. (2006). Role of alcohol in suicide: A case-control psychological autopsy study. *Psychological Medicine, 36*(7), 923–930.

Koocher, G. P. (1994). Foreword. In K. S. Pope (Ed.), *Sexual involvement with therapists: Patient assessment, subsequent therapy, forensics* (pp. vii–ix). Washington, DC: American Psychological Association.

Koocher, G. P. (2006). Foreword to the second edition: Things my teachers never mentioned. In K. S. Pope, J. L. Sonne, & B. Greene, *What therapists don't talk about and why: Understanding taboos that hurt us and our clients* (pp. xxi–xxiv). Washington, DC: American Psychological Association.

Koocher, G. P., & Keith-Spiegel, P. (2008). *Ethics in psychology and the mental health professions: Standards and cases* (3rd ed.). New York, NY: Oxford University Press.

Kooyman, L., & Barret, B. (2009). The duty to protect: Mental health practitioners and communicable diseases. In J. L. Werth, Jr., E. R. Welfel, & G. A. H. Benjamin (Eds.), *The duty to protect: Ethical, legal and professional considerations for mental health professionals.* Washington, DC: American Psychological Association.

Kottler, J. A. (2003). *On being a therapist* (3rd ed.). San Francisco, CA: Jossey-Bass.

Kovacs, A. L. (1987, May). Insurance billing: The growing risk of lawsuits against psychologists. *Independent Practitioner, 7*, 21–24.

Kozlowski, J. M., Pruitt, N. T., DeWalt, T. A., & Knox, S. (2014). Can boundary crossings in clinical supervision be beneficial? *Counselling Psychology Quarterly, 27*(2), 109–126.

Kramer, M., Pollack, E. S., Redick, R. W., & Locke, B. Z. (1972). *Mental disorders/suicide.* Cambridge, MA: Harvard University Press.

Krauth, D., Anglemyer, A., Philipps, R., & Bero, L. (2014). Nonindustry-sponsored preclinical studies on statins yield greater efficacy estimates than industry-sponsored studies: A meta-analysis. *PLoS Biology, 12*(1), e1001770.

Krupnick, J. L. (1984). Bereavement during childhood and adolescence. In M. Osterweis, F. Solomon, & M. Green (Eds.), *Bereavement: Reactions, consequences, and care* (pp. 99–141). Washington, DC: National Academy Press.

Kuchuck, S. (2009). Do ask, do tell? Narcissistic need as a determinant of analyst self-disclosure. *Psychoanalytic Review, 96*, 1007–1024. doi:10.1521/prev.2009.96.6.1007

Kuo, F. (2009). Secrets or no secrets: Confidentiality in couple therapy. *American Journal of Family Therapy, 37*, 351–354. doi:10.1080/01926180701862970

LaFromboise, T. D., & Foster, S. L. (1989). Ethics and multicultural counseling. In P. D. Pedersen, J. G. Draguns, W. J. Lonner, & E. J. Trimble (Eds.), *Counseling across cultures* (3rd ed., pp. 115–136). Honolulu: University of Hawaii Press.

Lamb, D. H., & Catanzaro, S. J. (1998). Sexual and nonsexual boundary violations involving psychologists, clients, supervisees, and students: Implications for professional practice. *Professional Psychology: Research and Practice, 29*, 498–503.

Lamb, D. H., Catanzaro, S. J., & Moorman, A. S. (2004). A preliminary look at how psychologists identify, evaluate, and proceed when faced with possible multiple relationship dilemmas. *Professional Psychology: Research and Practice, 35*(3), 248–254.

Lambert, M. J. (Ed.). (2004). *Bergin and Garfield's handbook of psychotherapy and behavior change* (4th ed.). New York, NY: Wiley.

Landrine, H. (Ed.). (1995). *Cultural diversity in feminist psychology: Theory, research, and practice.* Washington, DC: American Psychological Association.

Langer, E. (1989). *Mindfulness.* Reading, MA: Addison-Wesley.

Langer, E. J. (2014). *Mindfulness: 25th anniversary edition.* Philadelphia, PA: Da Capo Press.

Langer, E. J., & Abelson, R. P. (1974). A patient by any other name: Clinician group differences and labeling bias. *Journal of Consulting and Clinical Psychology, 42*, 4–9.

Langer, E. J., Bashner, R., & Chanowitz, B. (1985). Decreasing prejudice by increasing discrimination. *Journal of Personality and Social Psychology, 49*, 113–120.

Lawson, T. J., & Crane, L. L. (2014). Dowsing rods designed to sharpen critical thinking and understanding of ideomotor action. *Teaching of Psychology, 41*(1), 52–56.

Lazarus, A. A. (1994a). How certain boundaries and ethics diminish therapeutic effectiveness. *Ethics and Behavior, 4*(3), 255–261.

Lazarus, A. A. (1994b). The illusion of the therapist's power and the patient's fragility: My rejoinder. *Ethics and Behavior, 4*(3), 299–306.

Lazzarin, M., Biondi, A., & Di Mauro, S. (2012). Moral distress in nurses in oncology and haematology units. *Nursing Ethics, 19*(2), 183–195.

Lease, D. R. (2006). From great to ghastly: How toxic organizational cultures poison companies — The rise and fall of Enron, WorldCom, HealthSouth, and Tyco International. Retrieved from http://www.scribd.com/doc/74367362/David-Lease-Great-to-Ghastly

Lee, B. X., Marotta, P. L., Blay-Tofey, M., Wang, W., & de Bourmont, S. (2014). Economic correlates of violent death rates in forty countries, 1962–2008: A cross-typological analysis. *Aggression and Violent Behavior, 19*(6), 729–737.

Lee, D., Reynolds, C. R., & Willson, V. L. (2003). Standardized test administration: Why bother? *Journal of Forensic Neuropsychology, 3*(3), 55–81.

Lehner, G. F. J. (1952). Defining psychotherapy. *American Psychologist, 7*, 547.

Lettieri, D. J. (1982). Suicidal death prediction scales. In P. A. Keller & L. G. Ritt (Eds.), *Innovations in clinical practice* (Vol. 1, pp. 265–268). Sarasota, FL: Professional Resource Exchange.

Levenson, H., & Pope, K. S. (1981). First encounters: Effects of intake procedures on patients, staff, and the organization. *Hospital and Community Psychiatry, 32*, 482–485.

Levy, D. A. (2010). *Tools of critical thinking: Metathoughts for psychology* (2nd ed.). Long Grove, IL: Waveland Press.

Lewin, K. (1976). *Field theory in social science: Selected theoretical papers.* Chicago, IL: University of Chicago Press.

Lewis, T.T., Cogburn, C. D., & Williams, D. R. (2015). Self-reported experiences of discrimination and health: Scientific advances, ongoing controversies, and emerging issues. *Annual Review of Clinical Psychology, 11*, 407–440. doi:10.1146/annurev-clinpsy-032814-112728

Lexchin, J., Bero, L. A., Djulbegovic, B., & Clark, O. (2003). Pharmaceutical industry sponsorship and research outcome and quality: Systematic review. *BMJ*, *326*(7400), 1167–1170.

Lifton, R. J. (1986). *The Nazi doctors: Medical killing and the psychology of genocide.* New York, NY: Basic Books.

Lilienfeld, S. O., Marshall, J., Todd, J. T., & Shane, H. C. (2014). The persistence of fad interventions in the face of negative scientific evidence: Facilitated communication for autism as a case example. *Evidence-Based Communication Assessment and Intervention*, *8*(2), 62–101.

Lindblad, A., Löfmark, R., & Lynöe, N. (2008). Physician-assisted suicide: A survey of attitudes among Swedish physicians. *Scandinavian Journal of Public Health*, *36*, 720–727. doi:10.1177/1403494808090163

Linden, M. (2013). How to define, find and classify side effects in psychotherapy: From unwanted events to adverse treatment reactions. *Clinical Psychology & Psychotherapy*, *20*(4), 286–296.

Lindinger-Sternart, S., & Piazza, N. (2014). Major ethical considerations and technological challenges related to distance professional services. *International Journal of Social Science Studies*, *3*(1), 104–110.

Lindner, P., Olsson, E. L., Johnsson, A., Dahlin, M., Andersson, G., & Carlbring, P. (2014). The impact of telephone versus e-mail therapist guidance on treatment outcomes, therapeutic alliance and treatment engagement in Internet-delivered CBT for depression: A randomised pilot trial. *Internet Interventions*, *1*(4), 182–187.

Linehan, M. M., Comtois, K. A., Murray, A. M., Brown, M. Z., Gallop, R. J., Heard, H. L., & Lindenboim, N. (2006). Two-year randomized controlled trial and follow-up of dialectical behavior therapy vs therapy by experts for suicidal behaviors and borderline personality disorder. *Archives of General Psychiatry*, *63*(7), 757766.

Littell, J. H. (2010). Evidence-based practice: Evidence or orthodoxy? In B. L. Duncan, S. D. Miller, B. E. Wampold, & M. A. Hubble (Eds.), *The heart and soul of change: Delivering what works in therapy, Second edition* (pp. 167–198). Washington, DC: American Psychological Association. doi:10.1037/12075–006

A little recent history. (1952). *American Psychologist*, *7*, 425.

Litz, B. T., Stein, N., Delaney, E., Lebowitz, L., Nash, W. P., Silva, C., & Maguen, S. (2009). Moral injury and moral repair in war veterans: A preliminary model and intervention strategy. *Clinical Psychology Review*, *29*(8), 695706.

Liu, V., Musen, M. A., & Chou, T. (2015). Data breaches of protected health information in the United States. *JAMA*, *313*(14), 1471–1473.

Loas, G., Azi, A., Noisette, C., Legrand, A., & Yon, V. (2009). Fourteen-year prospective follow-up study of positive and negative symptoms in chronic schizophrenic patients dying from suicide compared to other causes of death. *Psychopathology*, *42*, 185–189. doi:10.1159/000209331

LoBello, S. G., & Zachar, P. (2007). Psychological test sales and internet auctions: Ethical considerations for dealing with obsolete or unwanted test materials. *Professional Psychology: Research and Practice*, *38*, 68–70. doi:10.1037/0735–7028.38.1.68

Lolak, S. (2013). Compassion cultivation: A missing piece in medical education. *Academic Psychiatry*, *37*(4), 285285.

Lopez-Munoz, F., Alamo, C., Dudley, M., Rubio, G., Garcia-Garcia, P., Molina, J. D., & Okasha, A. (2007). Psychiatry and political-institutional abuse from the historical perspective: The ethical lessons of the Nuremberg trial on their 60th anniversary. *Progress in Neuropsychopharmacology and Biological Psychiatry*, 31(4), 791–806. doi:S0278–5846(06)00442–8 [pii]10.1016/j.pnpbp.2006.12.007

Lorant, V., Deliege, D., Eaton, W., Robert, A., Phillppot, P., & Ansseau, M. (2003). Socioeconomic inequalities in depression: A meta-analysis. *American Journal of Epidemiology*, 157, 98–112.

Lott, B., & Bullock, H. E. (2001). Who are the poor? *Journal of Social Issues*, 57, 189–206.

Lott, B., & Bullock, H. E. (2007). *Psychology and economic injustice*. Washington, DC: American Psychological Association.

Loukides, G., Denny, J. C., & Malin, B. (2010). The disclosure of diagnosis codes can breach research participants' privacy. *Journal of the American Medical Informatics Association*, 17(3), 322–327.

Love, M. S. (2007). Security in an insecure world: An examination of individualism-collectivism and psychological sense of community at work. *Career Development International*, 12, 304–320.

LRN. (2007). *LRN ethics study: Workplace productivity: A report on how ethical lapses and questionable behaviors distract U.S. workers*. Los Angeles, CA: Author.

Lulé, D., Nonnenmacher, S., Sorg, S., Heimrath, J., Hautzinger, M., Meyer, T., . . . Ludolph, A. C. (2014). Live and let die: Existential decision processes in a fatal disease. *Journal of Neurology*, 261(3), 518–525.

Lundh, A., Sismondo, S., Lexchin, J., Busuioc, O. A., & Bero, L. (2012). Industry sponsorship and research outcome. *Cochrane Library*. Retrieved from http://onlinelibrary.wiley.com/doi/10.1002/14651858.MR000033.pub2/full

Lustgarten, S. D. (2015). Emerging ethical threats to client privacy in cloud communication and data storage. *Professional Psychology: Research and Practice*, 46, 154–160. doi:10.1037/pro0000018

Lyall, S. (2009, September 23). Guidelines in England for assisted suicide. *New York Times*. Retrieved from http://www.nytimes.com/2009/09/24/world/europe/24britain.html

Lynch, J. K. (2005). Effect of a third party observer on neuropsychological test performance following closed head injury. *Journal of Forensic Neuropsychology*, 4(2), 17–25.

Mackelprang, J. L., Bombardier, C. H., Fann, J. R., Temkin, N. R., Barber, J. K., & Dikmen, S. S. (2014). Rates and predictors of suicidal ideation during the first year after traumatic brain injury. *American Journal of Public Health*, 104(7), e100–e107.

Mahoney, A. E., Mackenzie, A., Williams, A. D., Smith, J., & Andrews, G. (2014). Internet cognitive behavioural treatment for obsessive compulsive disorder: A randomised controlled trial. *Behaviour Research and Therapy*, 63, 99–106.

Malloy, K. A., Dobbins, J. E., Ducheny, K., & Winfrey, L. L. (2010). The management and supervision competency: Current and future directions. In M. B. Kenkel & R. L. Peterson (Eds.), *Competency-based education for professional psychology* (pp. 161–178). Washington, DC: American Psychological Association.

Maloney, E., Degenhardt, L., Darke, S., & Nelson, E. C. (2009). Impulsivity and borderline personality as risk factors for suicide attempts among opioid-dependent individuals. *Psychiatry Research, 169*, 16–21. doi:10.1016/j.psychres.2008.06.026

Mann, C. K., & Winer, J. D. (1991). Psychotherapist's sexual contact with client. *American Jurisprudence Proof of Facts* (3rd ser., Vol. *14*, pp. 319–431). Rochester, NY: Lawyers Cooperative.

Mann, J. J. (2005, October 27). Drug therapy: The medical management of depression. *New England Journal of Medicine, 353*, 1819–1834.

Maris, R. W. (2002). Suicide. *Lancet, 360* (9329), 319–326.

Martin, M. S., Dorken, S. K., Simpson, A. I., McKenzie, K., & Colman, I. (2014). The predictive validity of the Depression Hopelessness Suicide screening form for self-harm among prisoners. *Journal of Forensic Psychiatry & Psychology, 25*(6), 733–747.

Martinez, A. G., Piff, P. K., Mendoza-Denton, R., & Hinshaw, S. P. (2011). The power of a label: Mental illness diagnoses, ascribed humanity, and social rejection. *Journal of Social and Clinical Psychology, 30*(1), 1–23.

Mason, O. J., & Budge, K. (2011). Schizotypy, self-referential thinking and the Barnum effect. *Journal of Behavior Therapy and Experimental Psychiatry, 42*(2), 145–148.

Masters, W. H., & Johnson, V. E. (1966). *Human sexual response.* New York, NY: Bantam.

Masters, W. H., & Johnson, V. E. (1970). *Human sexual inadequacy.* New York, NY: Bantam.

Masters, W. H., & Johnson, V. E. (1975, May). *Principles of the new sex therapy.* Paper presented at the annual meeting of the American Psychiatric Association, Anaheim, CA.

Masterson, J. F. (1989, May). Maintaining objectivity crucial in treating borderline patients. *Psychiatric Times, pp. 1*, 26–27.

Mastronardi, V. M., Pomilla, A., Ricci, S., & D'Argenio, A. (2013). Stalking of psychiatrists: Psychopathological characteristics and gender differences in an Italian sample. *International Journal of Offender Therapy & Comparative Criminology, 57*(5), 526–543.

Matos, M., Torres, R., Santiago, R., Jurado, M., & Rodríguez, I. (2006). Adaptation of parent-child interaction therapy for Puerto Rican families: A preliminary study. *Family Process, 45*, 205–222.

Matthews, A., & Yadron, D. (2015, February 4). Health insurer Anthem hit by hackers. *Wall Street Journal.* Retrieved from http://www.wsj.com/articles/health-insurer-anthem-hit-by-hackers-1423103720

Mayer, D. M., Nurmohamed, S., Treviño, L. K., Shapiro, D. L., & Schminke, M. (2013). Encouraging employees to report unethical conduct internally: It takes a village. *Organizational Behavior and Human Decision Processes, 121*(1), 89–103.

Mayer, J. D., Salovey, P., & Caruso, D. R. (2004). Emotional intelligence: Theory, findings, and implications. *Psychological Inquiry, 15*(3), 197–215.

Mcaleavey, A. A., Castonguay, L. G., & Xiao, H. (2014). Therapist orientation, supervisor match, and therapeutic interventions: Implications for session quality in a psychotherapy training PRN. *Counselling and Psychotherapy Research, 14*(3), 192–200.

McCarthy, E. (2014, August 18). Community Health Systems says it suffered criminal cyberattack. *Wall Street Journal*. Retrieved from http://www.wsj.com/articles/community-health-systems-says-its-suffered-criminal-cyberattack-1408365259

McCauley, J., Kern, D. E., Kolodner, K., Dill, L., & Schroeder, A. F. (1997). Clinical characteristics of women with a history of childhood abuse: Unhealed wounds. *Journal of the American Medical Association, 277*(17), 1362–1368.

McCord, C., & Freeman, H. P. (1990). Excess mortality in Harlem. *New England Journal of Medicine, 322*, 173–177.

McCoy, J. (2009, October 5). Outdated web policies expose hospitals to professional and legal trouble. HealthLeaders Media. Retrieved from http://bit.ly/Jypie

McDaniel, S. H., Grus, C. L., Cubic, B. A., Hunter, C. L., Kearney, L. K., Schuman, C. C., . . . Johnson, S. B. (2014). Competencies for psychology practice in primary care. *American Psychologist, 69*(4), 409.

McDonald, S., & Ahern, K. (2000). The professional consequences of whistleblowing by nurses. *Journal of Professional Nursing, 16*(6), 313–321.

McHugh, R. K., Murray, H. W., & Barlow, D. H. (2009). Balancing fidelity and adaptation in the dissemination of empirically-supported treatments: The promise of transdiagnostic interventions. *Behaviour Research and Therapy, 47*, 946–953. doi: 10.1016/j.brat.2009.07.005.

McLean, B., & Elkind, P. (2013). *The smartest guys in the room: The amazing rise and scandalous fall of Enron*. New York, NY: Penguin.

McMorris, T., & Hale, B. J. (2012). Differential effects of differing intensities of acute exercise on speed and accuracy of cognition: A meta-analytical investigation. *Brain and Cognition, 80*(3), 338–351.

McNeil, B., Pauker, S. G., Sox, H. C., & Tversky, A. (1982). On the elucidation of preferences for alternative therapies. *New England Journal of Medicine, 306*, 1259–1262.

McNeil-Haber, F. M. (2004). Ethical considerations in the use of nonerotic touch in psychotherapy with children. *Ethics & Behavior, 14*, 123–140. doi:10.1207/s15327019eb1402_3

Mednick, M. T. (1989). On the politics of psychological constructs: Stop the bandwagon, I want to get off. *American Psychologist, 44*(8), 1118–1123.

Meehl, P. (1977). Why I do not attend case conferences. In P. Meehl (Ed.), *Psychodiagnosis: Selected papers* (pp. 225–302). New York, NY: Norton. (Original work published 1973)

Meehl, P. E. (1956). Wanted — A good cookbook. *American Psychologist, 11*, 262–272.

Meeus, W. H. J., & Raaijmakers, Q. A. W. (1986), Administrative obedience: Carrying out orders to use psychological-administrative violence. *European Journal of Social Psychology, 16*, 311–324.

Meeus, W. H. J., & Raaijmakers, Q. A. W. (1995). Obedience in modern society: The Utrecht studies. *Journal of Social Issues, 51*(3), 155–175.

Melton, J. G. (2009). *Encyclopedia of American religions* (8th ed.). Detroit, MI: Gale Cengage Learning.

Mercer, J. R. (1979). *Technical manual: System of multicultural pluralistic assessment*. New York, NY: Psychological Corporation.

Mesmer-Magnus, J. R., & Viswesvaran, C. (2005). Whistleblowing in organizations: An examination of correlates of whistleblowing intentions, actions, and retaliation. *Journal of Business Ethics, 62*(3), 277–297.

Miceli, M. P., Near, J. P., & Dworkin, T. M. (2013). *Whistle-blowing in organizations.* New York, NY: Taylor & Francis.

Mischel, W. (2008, December 8). The toothbrush problem. *Observer.* Retrieved from http://www.psychologicalscience.org/index.php/publications/observer/2008/december-08/the-toothbrush-problem.html

Miller, J. (2014, December 24). Contractor security flaw puts data of 7,000 veterans at risk. *Federal News Radio.* Retrieved from http://www.federalnewsradio.com/1177/3769129/Contractor-security-flaw-puts-data-of-7000-veterans-at-risk

Miller, J. B. (1988). *Connections, disconnections and violations.* Retrieved from http://www.wcwonline.org/component/page,shop.product_details/flypage,shop.flypage/product_id,947/category_id,440

Miller, J. B. (1991). The development of women's sense of self. In J. V. Jordan, A. G. Kaplan, J. B. Miller, I. P. Stiver, & J. L. Surrey (Eds.), *Women's growth in connection: Writings from the Stone Center.* New York, NY: Guilford Press.

Milliken, F. J., Morrison, E. W., & Hewlin, P. F. (2003). An exploratory study of employee silence: Issues that employees don't communicate upward and why. *Journal of Management Studies, 40,* 1453–1476.

Miranda, J. (2006). Improving services and outreach for women with depression. In C. M. Mazure & G. P. Keita (Eds.), *Understanding depression in women: Applying empirical research to practice and policy* (pp. 113–135). Washington, DC: American Psychological Association.

Misra-Hebert, A. D., Isaacson, J. H., Kohn, M., Hull, A. L., Hojat, M., Papp, K. K., & Calabrese, L. (2012). Improving empathy of physicians through guided reflective writing. *International Journal of Medical Education, 3,* 71–77.

Mitton, C., Peacock, S., Storch, J., Smith, N., & Cornelissen, E. (2011). Moral distress among health system managers: Exploratory research in two British Columbia health authorities. *Health Care Analysis, 19*(2), 107–121.

Moffic, H. S. (1997). *The ethical way.* San Francisco, CA: Jossey-Bass.

Mohr, D. C. (2009). Telemental health: Reflections on how to move the field forward. *Clinical Psychology: Science and Practice, 16,* 343–347. doi:10.1111/j.1468-2850.2009.01172.x

Montgomery (Appellant) v Lanarkshire Health Board (Respondent) (Scotland), UKSC 11 (2015).

Moodley, R., & Palmer, S. (2006). *Race, culture and psychotherapy: Critical perspectives in multicultural practice.* Philadelphia, PA: Routledge/Taylor & Francis.

Moscicki, E. (2001). Epidemiology of suicide. In S. Goldsmith (Ed.), *Risk factors for suicide* (pp. 1–4). Washington, DC: National Academy Press.

Mullen, B., Atkins, J. L., Champion, D. S., Edwards, C., Hardy, D., Story, J. E., & Vanderklok, M. (1985). The false consensus effect: A meta-analysis of 115 hypothesis tests. *Journal of Experimental Social Psychology, 21*(3), 262–283.

Muller-Hill, B. (1988). *Murderous science: Elimination by scientific selection of Jews, Gypsies, and others, Germany 1933–1945.* (G. Fraser, Trans.). New York, NY: Oxford University Press.

Munro, G. D., & Stansbury, J. A. (2009). The dark side of self-affirmation: Confirmation bias and illusory correlation in response to threatening information. *Personality and Social Psychology Bulletin, 35,* 1143–1153. doi:10.1177/0146167209337163

Murphy, J. M. (1976). Psychiatric labeling in cross-cultural perspective. *Science, 191,* 1019–1028.

Nachmani, I., & Somer, E. (2007). Women sexually victimized in psychotherapy speak out: The dynamics and outcome of therapist–client sex. *Women & Therapy, 30,* 1–17. doi:10.1300/J015v30n01_01

Nader, R., Petkas, P., & Blackwell, K. (Eds.). (1972). *Whistle blowing: The report of the conference on professional responsibility.* New York, NY: Bantam Books.

Natanson v. Kline, 186 Kans. 393, 406, 350 P.2d 1093 (1960).

National Academies of Practice. (1996). *Ethical guidelines for professional care and services in a managed health care environment.* Washington, DC: Author. Retrieved from https://netforum.avectra.com/eWeb/DynamicPage.aspx?Site=NA P2&WebCode=PolicyPapers

National Academies of Practice. (1997). *Ethical guidelines for professional care in a managed care environment.* Washington, DC: Author.

National Association of Social Workers (2008). Code of Ethics of the National Association of Social Workers. Retrieved from http://www.socialworkers.org/pubs/Code/code.asp

Nebel, J. M. (2015). Status quo bias, rationality, and conservatism about value. *Ethics, 125*(2), 449–476.

Neimeyer, G. J., Taylor, J. M., & Rozensky, R. H. (2012). The diminishing durability of knowledge in professional psychology: A Delphi Poll of specialties and proficiencies. *Professional Psychology: Research and Practice, 43*(4), 364.

Neimeyer, G. J., Taylor, J. M., Rozensky, R. H., Cox, D.R. (2014). The diminishing durability of knowledge in professional psychology: A second look at specializations. *Professional Psychology: Research and Practice, 45*(2), 92–98.

Nelsen, A. J., Johnson, R. S., Ostermeyer, B., Sikes, K. A., & Coverdale, J. H. (2015). The prevalence of physicians who have been stalked: A systematic review. *Journal of the American Academy of Psychiatry and the Law Online, 43*(2), 177182.

Nelson, H. (1972, January 28). 'Man-made quake' hit by VA hospital doctor. *Los Angeles Times, Part II, p. 1.*

Nelson, J. K., Dunn, K. M., & Paradies, Y. (2011). Bystander anti-racism: A review of the literature. *Analyses of Social Issues and Public Policy, 11*(1), 263–284.

Neufeldt, S. A. (2003). Becoming a clinical supervisor. In M. J. Prinstein & M. D. Patterson (Eds.), *The portable mentor: Expert guide to a successful career in psychology* (pp. 209–218). New York, NY: Kluwer Academic/Plenum.

Neuringer, C. (1964). Rigid thinking in suicidal individuals. *Journal of Consulting Psychology, 28,* 54–58.

Neuringer, C. (1974). *Psychological assessment of suicidal risk.* New York, NY: Charles C. Thomas.

Nicholson, L. H. (2008). Culture is the key to employee adherence to corporate codes of ethics. *Journal of Business & Technology Law, 3,* 449–454.

Nickerson, A. B., Aloe, A. M., Livingston, J. A., & Feeley, T. H. (2014). Measurement of the bystander intervention model for bullying and sexual harassment. *Journal of Adolescence, 37,* 391–400.

Nicolas, G., Arntz, D. L., Hirsch, B., & Schmiedigen, A. (2009). Cultural adaptation of a group treatment for Haitian American adolescents. *Professional Psychology: Research and Practice, 40,* 378–384.

Nistor, N., Daxecker, I., Stanciu, D., & Diekamp, O. (2015). Sense of community in academic communities of practice: Predictors and effects. *Higher Education, 69*(2), 257–273.

Nock, M. K. (Ed.). (2014). *Oxford handbook of suicide and self-injury.* New York, NY: Oxford University Press.

Noel, B., & Watterson, K. (1992). *You must be dreaming.* New York, NY: Poseidon.

Norcross, J. (2011). *Psychotherapy relationships that work: Evidence-based responsiveness* (2nd ed.). New York, NY: Oxford University Press.

Norcross, J. C., & Guy, J. D. (2007). *Leaving it at the office: A guide to psychotherapist self-care.* New York, NY: Guilford.

Norris, D. M., Gutheil, T. G., & Strasburger, L. H. (2007). This couldn't happen to me: Boundary problems and sexual misconduct in the psychotherapy relationship. *Focus, 5*(4), 476–482.

Norton, A. M., & Soloski, K. L. (2015). Officer, chaplain, therapist: A feminist perspective on the challenges of supervising US Army chaplain-therapists. *Journal of Feminist Family Therapy, 27*(1), 21–39.

Novick, D. M., Swartz, H. A., & Frank, E. (2010). Suicide attempts in bipolar I and bipolar II disorder: A review and meta-analysis of the evidence. *Bipolar Disorders, 12*, 1–9. doi:10.1111/j.1399–5618.2009.00786.x

Nugent, W. R. (2006). A psychometric study of the MPSI Suicidal Thoughts subscale. *Stress, Trauma and Crisis: An International Journal, 9*(1), 1–15.

O'Neill, P. (1998). *Negotiating consent in psychotherapy.* New York, NY: New York University Press.

O'Neill, P. (2005). The ethics of problem definition. *Canadian Psychology, 46*(1), 13–20.

Obst, P. L., & White, K. M. (2007). Choosing to belong: The influence of choice on social identification and psychological sense of community. *Journal of Community Psychology, 35*, 77–90.

Ohio Psychological Association. (2010.) *Telepsychology guidelines, revised.* Retrieved from http://bit.ly/9jtzlK

Ohm, P. (2010). Broken promises of privacy: Responding to the surprising failure of anonymization. *UCLA Law Review, 57*, 1701–1778.

Olio, K. A., & Cornell, W. F. (1998). The facade of scientific documentation: A case study of Richard Ofshe's analysis of the Paul Ingram case. *Psychology, Public Policy, and Law, 4*(4), 1182–1197.

Opincar, J. T. (2013). Exploring ethical intelligence through ancient wisdom and the lived experiences of senior business leaders. *Dissertation Abstracts International Section A: Humanities and Social Sciences, 74*(3–A(E)). (UMI No. AAI3531372)

Opotow, S. (1990). Moral exclusion and injustice: An introduction. *Journal of Social Issues, 46*, 1–20.

Opotow, S. (1995). Drawing the line: Social categorization, moral exclusion, and the scope of justice. In B. B. Bunker & J. Z. Rubin (Eds.), *Conflict, cooperation, and justice* (pp. 347–369). San Francisco, CA: Jossey-Bass.

Opotow, S. (2005). Hate, conflict, and moral exclusion. In R. J. Sternberg (Ed.), *Psychology of hate* (pp. 121–153). Washington, DC: American Psychological Association.

Opotow, S. (2012). The scope of justice, intergroup conflict, and peace. In L. R. Tropp (Ed.), *Oxford handbook of intergroup conflict* (pp. 72–86). New York, NY: Oxford University Press.

Oppel, R. A., & Shear, M. D. (2014, May 29). Severe report finds V.A. hid waiting lists at hospitals. *New York Times*, p. A1.

Orlinsky, D. E., & Geller, J. D. (1993). Psychotherapy's internal theater of operation: Patients' representations of their therapists and therapy as a new focus of research. In N. E. Miller, J. Docherty, L. Luborsky, & J. Barber (Eds.), *Psychodynamic treatment research* (pp. 423–466). New York, NY: Basic Books.

Ortiz, S. O., & Melo, K. E. (2015). Evaluation of intelligence and learning disability with Hispanics. In K. F. Geisinger (Ed.), *Psychological testing of Hispanics: Clinical, cultural, and intellectual issues* (2nd ed., pp. 109–133). Washington, DC: American Psychological Association doi:10.1037/14668-007

Orwell, G. (1946). Politics and the English language. In G. Orwell (Ed.), *A collection of essays* (pp. 156–171). Orlando, FL: Harcourt.

Osswald, S., Greitemeyer, T., Fischer, P., & Frey, D. (2010). What is moral courage? Definition, explication, and classification of a complex construct. In C. L. S. Pury & S. J. Lopez (Eds.), *The psychology of courage: Modern research on an ancient virtue* (pp. 149–164). Washington, DC: American Psychological Association.

Ostergaard, S. D., Pedersen, C. H., Uggerby, P., Munk-Jorgensen, P., Rothschild, A. J., Larsen, J. I., & Bech, P. (2015). Clinical and psychometric validation of the psychotic depression assessment scale. *Journal of Affective Disorders, 173*, 261–268.

Ozcan, C. T., Oflaz, F., & Bakir, B. (2012). The effect of a structured empathy course on the students of a medical and a nursing school. *International Nursing Review, 59*(4), 532–538.

Özhan, M. Ö., Süzer, M. A., Çomak, İ., Çaparlar, C. Ö., Aydın, G. B., Eşkin, M. B., . . . Kurt, E. (2014). Do the patients read the informed consent?. *Balkan Medical Journal, 31*(2), 132–136,

Pack-Brown, S. P., & Williams, C. B. (2003). *Ethics in a multicultural context*. Thousand Oaks, CA: Sage.

Pakenham, K. I. (2015). Investigation of the utility of the acceptance and commitment therapy (ACT) framework for fostering self-care in clinical psychology trainees. *Training and Education in Professional Psychology, 9*(2), 144–152.

Palm Reed, K. M., Hines, D. A., Armstrong, J. L., & Cameron, A. Y. (2014). Experimental evaluation of a bystander prevention program for sexual assault and dating violence. *Psychology of Violence, 5*, 95–102. doi:10.1037/a0037557

Palmer, B. A., Pankratz, V. S., & Bostwick, J. M. (2005). The lifetime risk of suicide in schizophrenia: A reexamination. *Archives of General Psychiatry, 62*, 247–253.

Pant, H., McCabe, B. J., Deskovitz, M. A., Weed, N. C., & Williams, J. E. (2014). Diagnostic reliability of MMPI-2 computer-based test interpretations. *Psychological Assessment, 26*(3), 916.

Pasha, S. (2006, April 26). Lay, prosecutor clash at trial. *CNN News*. Retrieved from http://money.cnn.com/2006/04/26/news/newsmakers/enron_trial

Pat-Horenczyk, R., Brom, D., & Vogel, J. (Eds.) (2014). *Helping children cope with trauma: Individual, Family and Community perspectives*. New York, NY: Routledge.

Patsiokas, A. T., Clum, G. A., & Luscumb, R. L. (1979). Cognitive characteristics of suicidal attempters. *Journal of Consulting and Clinical Psychology, 47*, 478–484.

Payton, C. R. (1984). Who must do the hard things? *American Psychologist, 39*, 391–397. doi:10.1037/0003-066X.39.4.391

Peck, M., & Seiden, R. (1975, May). Youth suicide. *exChange, 3*(2), 17–20. Sacramento: California State Department of Health.

Pedersen, P. D., Draguns, J. G., Lonner, W. J., & Trimble, E. J. (1989). Introduction and overview. In P. D. Pedersen, J. G. Draguns, W. J. Lonner, & E. J. Trimble (Eds.), *Counseling across cultures* (3rd ed., pp. 1–2). Honolulu: University of Hawaii Press.

Peirce, P., Rosen, C. A., & Smolinski, B. (1998). Why sexual harassment complaints fall on deaf ears. *Academy of Management Executive, 12*(3), 41–57.

People v. Stritzinger, 194 Cal. Rptr. 431 (Cal. September 1, 1983).

Pepiton, M. B., Zelgowski, B. R., Geffner, R., & Pegolo de Albuquerque, P. (2014). Ethical violations: What can and does go wrong in child custody evaluations? *Journal of Child Custody, 11*(2), 81–100.

Perlin, M. L., & McClain, V. (2009). "Where souls are forgotten": Cultural competencies, forensic evaluations, and international human rights. *Psychology, Public Policy, and Law, 15*, 257–277. doi:10.1037/a0017233

Peters, C., & Branch, T. (1972). *Blowing the whistle: Dissent in the public interest.* New York, NY: Praeger.

Pew Forum on Religion & Public Life (2015). *U.S. religious landscape survey.* Washington, DC: Pew Research Center. Retrieved from http://religions.pewforum.org/reports#

Phelan, J. E. (2009). Exploring the use of touch in the psychotherapeutic setting: A phenomenological review. *Psychotherapy: Theory, Research, Practice, Training, 46*, 97–111. doi:10.1037/a0014751

Pickar, D. B., & Kaufman, R. L. (2015). Parenting plans for special needs children: Applying a risk-assessment model. *Family Court Review, 53*(1), 113–133.

Pietschnig, J., & Voracek, M. (2015). One century of global IQ gains: A formal meta-analysis of the Flynn effect (1909–2010). *Perspectives on Psychological Science, 10*(3), 282–306.

Pinals, D. (2009). Informed consent: Is your patient competent to refuse treatment? *Current Psychiatry, 8*(4), 33–43.

Pinder, C. C., & Harlos, K. P. (2001). Employee silence: Quiescence and acquiescence as responses to perceived injustice. *Research in Personnel and Human Resources Management, 20*, 331–369.

Pinker, S. (2006, December 31). Preface to dangerous ideas. *Edge.* Retrieved from https://edge.org/conversation/preface-to-dangerous-ideas

Pitman, A., Osborn, D., King, M., & Erlangsen, A. (2014). Effects of suicide bereavement on mental health and suicide risk. *Lancet Psychiatry, 1*(1), 86–94.

Plaisil, E. (1985). *Therapist.* New York, NY: St. Martin's Press.

Plato. (1956a). The apology. In E. H. Warmington & P. G. Rouse (Eds.), *Great dialogues of Plato* (W. H. D. Rouse, Trans., pp. 423–446). New York, NY: New American Library.

Plato. (1956b). Crito. In E. H. Warmington & P. G. Rouse (Eds.), *Great dialogues of Plato* (W. H. D. Rouse, Trans., pp. 447–459). New York, NY: New American Library.

Plungis, J., & Higgins, T. (2014, May 17). GM to pay record $35 million fine over handling of recall. *Bloomberg Businessweek*. Retrieved from http://www.bloomberg.com/news/2014-05-16/gm-said-to-agree-to-u-s-fine-over-ignition-switch-recall.html

Ponce, B. A., Determann, J. R., Boohaker, H. A., Sheppard, E., McGwin, G., & Theiss, S. (2013). Social networking profiles and professionalism issues in residency applicants: An original study-cohort study. *Journal of Surgical Education, 70*(4), 502–507.

Pope, K. S. (1988b). How clients are harmed by sexual contact with mental health professionals: The syndrome and its prevalence. *Journal of Counseling and Development, 67*, 222–226.

Pope, K. S. (1989a). Malpractice suits, licensing disciplinary actions, and ethics cases: Frequencies, causes, and costs. *Independent Practitioner, 9*(1), 22–26.

Pope, K. S. (1989b). Student-teacher sexual intimacy. In G. O. Gabbard (Ed.), *Sexual exploitation within professional relationships* (pp. 163–176). Washington, DC: American Psychiatric Press.

Pope, K. S. (1990a). Ethical and malpractice issues in hospital practice. *American Psychologist, 45*, 1066–1070. Also available at http://kspope.com

Pope, K. S. (1990b). Identifying and implementing ethical standards for primary prevention. In G. B. Levin, E. J. Trickett, & R. E. Hess (Eds.), *Ethical implications of primary prevention* (pp. 43–64). Binghamton, NY: Haworth Press.

Pope, K. S. (1990c). Therapist–patient sex as sex abuse: Six scientific, professional, and practical dilemmas in addressing victimization and rehabilitation. *Professional Psychology: Research and Practice, 21*, 227–239. Available at http://kspope.com

Pope, K. S. (1990d). Therapist–patient sexual involvement: A review of the research. *Clinical Psychology Review, 10*, 477–490. Available at http://kspope.com

Pope, K. S. (1991). Promoting ethical behaviour: The Canadian Psychological Association model. *Canadian Psychology/Psychologie canadienne, 32*(1), 74–76.

Pope, K. S. (1992). Responsibilities in providing psychological test feedback to clients. *Psychological Assessment, 4*, 268–271. Available at http://kspope.com

Pope, K. S. (1993). Licensing disciplinary actions for psychologists who have been sexually involved with a client: Some information about offenders. *Professional Psychology: Research and Practice, 24*, 374–377. Available at http://kspope.com

Pope, K. S. (1994). *Sexual involvement with therapists: Patient assessment, subsequent therapy, forensics.* Washington, DC: American Psychological Association.

Pope, K.S. (1996). *Memory, abuse, and science: Questioning claims about the false memory syndrome epidemic.* Invited address for the American Psychological Association's Award for Distinguished Contributions to Public Service delivered at the 103rd Annual Convention of the American Psychological Association. *American Psychologist, 51*, 957–974. Available at http://kspope.com

Pope, K.S. (1997). Science as careful questioning: Are claims of a false memory syndrome epidemic based on empirical evidence? *American Psychologist, 52*, 997–1006.

Pope, K. S. (1998). Pseudoscience, cross-examination, and scientific evidence in the recovered memory controversy. *Psychology, Public Policy, and Law, 4*(4), 1160.

Pope, K. S. (2005). Disability and accessibility in psychology: Three major barriers. *Ethics and Behavior, 15*(2), 103–106. Available at http://kspope.com

Pope, K. S. (2011a). Are the American Psychological Association's detainee interrogation policies ethical and effective? Key claims, documents, and results.

Zeitschrift fuer Psychologie/Journal of Psychology, 219(3), 150–158. Retrieved from http://bit.ly/APADetaineeInterrogationPolicies

Pope, K. S. (2011b). CPA's innovative work. *Canadian Psychology/Psychologie canadienne, 52*(3), 234.

Pope, K. S. (2011c). Psychologists and detainee interrogations: Key decisions, opportunities lost, and lessons learned. *Annual Review of Clinical Psychology, 7*, 459–481. Retrieved from http://bit.ly/dXpcIC

Pope, K. S. (2012). Psychological assessment of torture survivors: Essential steps, avoidable errors, and helpful resources. *International Journal of Law and Psychiatry, 35*(56), 418–426.

Pope, K. S. (2014). Ethics in clinical psychology. In D. H. Barlow (Ed.), *Oxford handbook of clinical psychology*: Updated edition (pp. 185–210). Oxford, UK: Oxford University Press.

Pope, K. S. (2015a). Record-keeping controversies: Ethical, legal, and clinical challenges. *Canadian Psychology, 56*(3), 348–356.

Pope, K. S. (2015b). Steps to strengthen ethics in organizations: Research findings, ethics placebos, and what works. *Journal of Trauma & Dissociation, 16*(2), 139–152. Retrieved from http://bit.ly/KenPopeStrengtheningEthicsInOrganizations

Pope, K. S. (in press). The Code Not Taken: The Path From Guild Ethics to Torture and Our Continuing Choices — Canadian Psychological Association Service Award Address. *Canadian Psychology/Psychologie canadienne.*

K. S. Pope biography. (1995). *American Psychologist, 50*(4), 242.

Pope, K. S., & Bajt, T. R. (1988). When laws and values conflict: A dilemma for psychologists. *American Psychologist, 43*, 828. Retrieved from http://kspope.com

Pope, K. S., & Bouhoutsos, J. C. (1986). *Sexual intimacies between therapists and patients.* Westport, CT: Praeger.

Pope, K. S., & Brown, L. (1996). *Recovered memories of abuse: Assessment, therapy, forensics.* Washington, DC: American Psychological Association.

Pope, K. S., Butcher, J. N., & Seelen, J. (2006). *The MMPI, MMPI-2 and MMPI-A in court: A practical guide for expert witnesses and attorneys* (3rd ed.). Washington, DC: American Psychological Association.

Pope, K. S., & Feldman-Summers, S. (1992). National survey of psychologists' sexual and physical abuse history and their evaluation of training and competence in these areas. *Professional Psychology: Research and Practice, 23*, 353–361. Available at http://kspope.com

Pope, K. S., & Garcia-Peltoniemi, R. E. (1991). Responding to victims of torture: Clinical issues, professional responsibilities, and useful resources. *Professional Psychology: Research and Practice, 22*, 269–276. Available at http://kspope.com

Pope, K. S., & Gutheil, T. G. (2009). Contrasting ethical policies of physicians and psychologists concerning interrogation of detainees. *British Medical Journal, 338*, 1178–1186.

Pope, K. S., & Keith-Spiegel, P. (2008). A practical approach to boundaries in psychotherapy: Making decisions, bypassing blunders, and mending fences. *Journal of Clinical Psychology, 64*, 638–652. Available at http://bit.ly/ksp777

Pope, K. S., Keith-Spiegel, P., & Tabachnick, B. G. (1986). Sexual attraction to patients: The human therapist and the (sometimes) inhuman training system. *American Psychologist, 41*, 147–158. Available at http://kspope.com

Pope, K. S., Levenson, H., & Schover, L. R. (1979). Sexual intimacy in psychology training: Results and implications of a national survey. *American Psychologist, 34,* 682–689. Available at http://kspope.com

Pope, K. S., & Morin, S. F. (1990). AIDS and HIV infection update: New research, ethical responsibilities, evolving legal frameworks, and published resources. *Independent Practitioner, 10,* 43–53.

Pope, K. S., Simpson, N. H., & Weiner, M. F. (1978). Malpractice in psychotherapy. *American Journal of Psychotherapy, 32,* 593–602.

Pope, K. S., & Singer, J. L. (Eds.). (1978). The stream of consciousness: Scientific investigations into the flow of human experience. New York, NY: Plenum Press.

Pope, K. S., Sonne, J. L., & Greene, B. (2006). *What therapists don't talk about and why: Understanding taboos that hurt us and our clients.* Washington, DC: American Psychological Association.

Pope, K. S., Sonne, J. L., & Holroyd, J. (1993). *Sexual feelings in psychotherapy: Explorations for therapists and therapists-in-training.* Washington, DC: American Psychological Association.

Pope, K. S., & Tabachnick, B. G. (1993). Therapists' anger, hate, fear and sexual feelings: National survey of therapists' responses, client characteristics, critical events, formal complaints and training. *Professional Psychology: Research and Practice, 24,* 142–152. Available at http://kspope.com

Pope, K. S., & Tabachnick, B. G. (1994). Therapists as patients: A national survey of psychologists' experiences, problems, and beliefs. *Professional Psychology: Research and Practice, 25,* 247–258. Available at http://kspope.com

Pope, K. S., Tabachnick, B. G., & Keith-Spiegel, P. (1987). Ethics of practice: The beliefs and behaviors of psychologists as therapists. *American Psychologist, 42,* 993–1006. Available at http://kspope.com

Pope, K. S., Tabachnick, B. G., & Keith-Spiegel, P. (1988). Good and poor practices in psychotherapy: National survey of beliefs of psychologists. *Professional Psychology: Research and Practice, 19,* 547–552. Available at http://kspope.com

Pope, K. S., & Vasquez, M. J. T. (1991). *Ethics in psychotherapy and counseling.* San Francisco, CA: Jossey-Bass.

Pope, K. S., & Vasquez, M. J. T. (2005). *How to survive and thrive as a therapist: Information, ideas, and resources for psychologist in practice.* Washington, DC: American Psychological Association.

Pope, K. S., & Vetter, V. A. (1991). Prior therapist–patient sexual involvement among patients seen by psychologists. *Psychotherapy, 28,* 429–438. Available at http://kspope.com

Pope, K. S., & Vetter, V. A. (1992). Ethical dilemmas encountered by members of the American Psychological Association: A national survey. *American Psychologist, 47,* 397–411. Available at http://kspope.com

Pozzi, M., Marta, E., Marzana, D., Gozzoli, C., & Ruggieri, R. (2014). The effect of the psychological sense of community on the psychological well-being in older volunteers. *Europe's Journal of Psychology, 10*(4), 598–612.

Preti, A., Meneghelli, A., Pisano, A., Cocchi, A., & the Programma 2000 Team. (2009). Risk of suicide and suicidal ideation in psychosis. *Schizophrenia Research, 113,* 145–150. doi:10.1016/j.schres.2009.06.007

Proctor, R. N. (1988). *Racial hygiene: Medicine under the Nazis*. Cambridge, MA: Harvard University Press.

Proudfoot, D., & Kay, A. C. (2014). System justification in organizational contexts: How a motivated preference for the status quo can affect organizational attitudes and behaviors. *Research in Organizational Behavior, 34*, 173–187.

Prozesky, M. (2007). *Conscience: Ethical intelligence for global well-being*. Scottsville, South Africa: University of KwaZulu-Natal Press.

Puente, A. E., Ojeda, C., Zink, D., & Portillo Reyes, V. (2015). Neuropsychological testing of Spanish speakers. In K. F. Geisinger (Ed.), *Psychological testing of Hispanics, second edition: Clinical, cultural, and intellectual issues* (pp. 135–152). Washington, DC: American Psychological Association. doi:10.1037/14668-008

Pugh, R. (2007). Dual relationships: Personal and professional boundaries in rural social work. *British Journal of Social Work, 37*, 1406–1423. doi:10.1093/bjsw/bcl088

Qin, X., Ren, R., Zhang, Z. X., & Johnson, R. E. (2014). Fairness heuristics and substitutability effects: Inferring the fairness of outcomes, procedures, and interpersonal treatment when employees lack clear information. *Journal of Applied Psychology, 100*, 749–766. doi: 10.1037/a0038084

Rachman, S. (2010). Betrayal: A psychological analysis. *Behaviour Research and Therapy, 48*(4), 304–311.

Range, L. M., & Knott, E. C. (1997). Twenty suicide assessment instruments: Evaluation and recommendations. *Death Studies, 21*, 25–58.

Ready, R. E., & Veague, H. B. (2014). Training in psychological assessment: Current practices of clinical psychology programs. *Professional Psychology: Research and Practice, 45*(4), 278.

Rebar, A. L., Stanton, R., Geard, D., Short, C., Duncan, M. J., & Vandelanotte, C. (2015). A meta-meta-analysis of the effect of physical activity on depression and anxiety in non-clinical adult populations. *Health Psychology Review., 9*(3), 366–378. doi:10.1080/17437199.2015.1022901

Reed, G. M., & Eisman, E. J. (2006). Uses and misuses of evidence: Managed care, treatment guidelines, and outcomes measurement in professional practice. In C. D. Goodheart, A. E. Kazdin, & R. J. Sternberg (Eds.), *Evidence-based psychotherapy: Where practice and research meet* (pp. 13–35). Washington, DC: American Psychological Association.

Reiser, D. E., & Levenson, H. (1984). Abuses of the borderline diagnosis: A clinical problem with teaching opportunities. *American Journal of Psychiatry, 141*, 1528–1532.

Rekdal, O. B. (2014). Academic urban legends. *Social Studies of Science, 44*(4), 638–654.

Reynolds, M. D. (2004). *American women scientists: 23 inspiring biographies, 1900–2000*. Jefferson, NC: McFarland.

Richards, M. M. (2009). Electronic medical records: Confidentiality issues in the time of HIPAA. *Professional Psychology: Research and Practice, 40*, 550–556. doi:10.1037/a0016853

Ridley, C. R. (2005). *Overcoming unintentional racism in counseling and therapy: A practitioner's guide to intentional intervention* (2nd ed.). Thousand Oaks, CA: Sage.

Ridley, C. R., Liddle, M. C., Hill, C. L., & Li, L. C. (2001). Ethical decision making in multicultural counseling. In J. G. Ponterotto, J. M. Casas, L. A. Suzuki, & C. M.

Alexander (Eds.), *Handbook of multicultural counseling* (2nd ed., pp. 165–188). Thousand Oaks, CA: Sage.

Rimkeviciene, J., & De Leo, D. (2015). Impulsive suicide attempts: A systematic literature review of definitions, characteristics and risk factors. *Journal of Affective Disorders, 171,* 93–104.

Rinella, V. J., & Gerstein, A. I. (1994). The development of dual relationships: Power and professional responsibility. *International Journal of Law and Psychiatry, 17*(3), 225–237.

Rings, J. A., Genuchi, M. C., Hall, M. D., Angelo, M.-A., Cornish, J. A., & Erickson, J. A. (2009). Is there consensus among predoctoral internship training directors regarding clinical supervision competencies? A descriptive analysis. *Training and Education in Professional Psychology, 3*(3), 140–147.

Risen, J. (2014). *Pay any price: Greed, power, and endless war* (Kindle ed.). New York, NY: Houghton Mifflin Harcourt.

Rittenmeyer, L., & Huffman, D. (2009). How professional nurses working in hospital environments experience moral distress: A systematic review. *International Journal of Evidence-Based Healthcare, 7*(3), 222–223.

Rivers, E., Schuman, S. H., Simpson, L., & Olansky, S. (1953). Twenty years of follow-up experience in a long-range medical study. *Public Health Reports, 68*(4), 391–395.

Robeson, R., & King, N. M. (2014). Loss of possession: Concussions, informed consent, and autonomy. *Journal of Law, Medicine & Ethics, 42*(3), 334–343.

Robinson, G., & Merav, A. (1976). Informed consent: Recall by patients tested postoperatively. *Annals of Thoracic Surgery, 22,* 209–212.

Robinson, W. L., & Reid, P. T. (1985). Sexual intimacies in psychology revisited. *Professional Psychology, 16,* 512–520.

Rodwin, M. A. (2013). Introduction: Institutional corruption and the pharmaceutical policy. *Journal of Law, Medicine & Ethics, 41,* 544–552.

Roll, S., & Millen, L. (1981). A guide to violating an injunction in psychotherapy: On seeing acquaintances as patients. *Psychotherapy: Theory, Research and Practice, 18*(2), 179–187.

Rooksby, M., Elouafkaoui, P., Humphris, G., Clarkson, J., & Freeman, R. (2015). Internet-assisted delivery of cognitive behavioural therapy (CBT) for childhood anxiety: Systematic review and meta-analysis. *Journal of Anxiety Disorders, 29,* 83–92.

Rosenhan, D. L. (1973). On being sane in insane places. *Science, 179,* 250–258.

Rosenzweig, P. (2014). *The halo effect: . . . and the eight other business delusions that deceive managers.* New York, NY: Simon & Schuster.

Ross, L. (1977). The intuitive psychologist and his shortcomings: Distortions in the attribution process. *Advances in Experimental Social Psychology, 10,* 173–220.

Ross, L., Greene, D., & House, P. (1977). The "false consensus effect": An egocentric bias in social perception and attribution processes. *Journal of Experimental Social Psychology, 13*(3), 279–301.

Ross, L., & Nisbett, R. E. (2011). *The person and the situation: Perspectives of social psychology* (2nd ed.). London, UK: Pinter & Martin.

Rostila, M., Saarela, J., Kawachi, I., & Hjern, A. (2015). Testing the anniversary reaction: Causal effects of bereavement in a nationwide follow-up study from

Sweden. *European Journal of Epidemiology*, 30, 239–247. doi: 10.1007/s10654 -015-9989-5.

Rothschild, J., & Miethe, T. D. (1999). Whistle-blower disclosures and management retaliation: The battle to control information about organization corruption. *Work and Occupations*, 26(1), 107–128.

Rothstein, M. A. (2010). Is deidentification sufficient to protect health privacy in research? *American Journal of Bioethics*, 10(9), 3–11.

Roysircar, G., Sandhu, D. S., & Bibbins, V. E. (2003). *Multicultural competencies: A guidebook of practices*. Alexandria, VA: Association for Multicultural Counseling and Development.

Rubenstein, S. (2008, September 22). Hospital employees fired for posting patient pics on MySpace. *Wall Street Journal*. Retrieved from http://bit.ly/4NfSUX

Rust, J., & Golombok, S. (2014). Modern psychometrics: The science of psychological assessment (3rd ed.). New York, NY: Routledge.

Ryder, R., & Hepworth, J. (1990). AAMFT ethical code: "Dual relationships." *Journal of Marital and Family Therapy*, 16(2), 127–132.

Safer, D. J. (1997). Adolescent/adult differences in suicidal behavior and outcome. *Annals of Clinical Psychiatry*, 9, 61–66.

Sagan, C. (1979). *Broca's brain*. New York, NY: Random House.

Sagan, C. (1991). The burden of skepticism. In K. Frazier (Ed.), *The hundredth monkey: And other paradigms of the paranormal* (pp. 1–9). New York, NY: Prometheus Books.

Salmivalli, C. (2014). Participant roles in bullying: How can peer bystanders be utilized in interventions? *Theory Into Practice*, 53, 286–292.

Salovey, P., & Mayer, J. D. (1990). Emotional intelligence. *Imagination, Cognition, and Personality*, 9, 185–211.

Saltzman, J. (2007, May 31). Blogger unmasked, court case upended. *Boston Globe*. Retrieved from http://bit.ly/8HiUUX

Sanders, J. R., & Keith-Spiegel, P. (1980). Formal and informal adjudication of ethics complaints against psychologists. *American Psychologist*, 35, 1096–1105.

Sarason, S. B. (1974). *The psychological sense of community*. San Francisco, CA: Jossey-Bass.

Sarason, S. B. (1985). *Caring and compassion in clinical practice*. San Francisco, CA: Jossey-Bass.

Sarkar, S. P. (2009) Life after therapy: Post-termination boundary violations in psychiatry and psychotherapy. *Advances in Psychiatric Treatment*, 15, 82–87. doi:10.1192/apt.bp.107.005108

Sauerland, J., Marotta, K., Peinemann, M. A., Berndt, A., & Robichaux, C. (2015). Assessing and addressing moral distress and ethical climate: Part II. Neonatal and pediatric perspectives. *Dimensions of Critical Care Nursing*, 34(1), 33–46.

Schank, J. A., & Skovholt, T. M. (1997). Dual-relationship dilemmas of rural and small-community psychologists. *Professional Psychology: Research and Practice*, 28(1), 44–49.

Schank, J. A., & Skovholt, T. M. (2006). *Ethical practice in small communities: Challenges and rewards for psychologists*. Washington, DC: American Psychological Association.

Schloendorf v. Society of New York Hospital, 211 N.Y. 125, 105 N.E. 92 (1914).

Schneidman, E. (1975). *Suicidology: Contemporary developments.* New York, NY: Grune & Stratton.

Schultz, D. S., & Loving, J. L. (2012). Challenges since Wikipedia: The availability of Rorschach information online and Internet users' reactions to online media coverage of the Rorschach–Wikipedia debate. *Journal of Personality Assessment, 94*(1), 73–81.

Schwartz-Mette, R. A. (2011). Out with impairment, in with professional competence problems: Response to commentary by Collins, Falender, and Shafranske. *Ethics & Behavior, 21*(5), 431–434.

Scott, W. (1969). Professional employees in a bureacratic structure: Social work. In A. Etzioni (Ed.), *The semi-professionals and their organization.* New York: Free Press, 1969.

Scribner, C. M. (2001). Rosenhan revisited. *Professional Psychology: Research and Practice, 32,* 215–216. doi:10.1037/0735–7028.32.2.215

Searight, H. R., & Searight, B. K. (2009). Working with foreign language interpreters: Recommendations for psychological practice. *Professional Psychology: Research and Practice, 40,* 444–451. doi:10.1037/a0016788

Serrat, O. (2010). *Moral courage in organizations.* Washington, DC: Asian Development Bank.

Shapiro, D. L. (1990). *Forensic psychological assessment: An integrative approach.* Needham Heights, MA: Allyn & Bacon.

Sharkin, B. S., & Birky, I. (1992). Incidental encounters between therapists and their clients. *Professional Psychology: Research and Practice, 23*(4), 326–328.

Shay, J. (2002). *Odysseus in America.* New York, NY: Scribner.

Shay, J. (2012). Moral injury. *Intertexts, 16*(1), 5766.

Shen-Miller, D. S., Schwartz-Mette, R., Van Sickle, K. S., Jacobs, S. C., Grus, C. L., Hunter, E. A., & Forrest, L. (2014). Professional competence problems in training: A qualitative investigation of trainee perspectives. *Training and Education in Professional Psychology, 9,* 161–169. doi:10.1037/tep0000072

Sher, L. (2006). Alcoholism and suicidal behavior: A clinical overview. *Acta Psychiatrica Scandinavica, 113*(1), 13–22.

Sher, L., Oquendo, M. A., Richardson-Vejlgaard, R., Makhija, N. M., Posner, K., Mann, J. J., & Stanley, B. H. (2009). Effect of acute alcohol use on the lethality of suicide attempts in patients with mood disorders. *Journal of Psychiatric Research, 43,* 901–905. doi:10.1016/j.jpsychires.2009.01.005

Shuster, E. (1998). The Nuremberg Code: Hippocratic ethics and human rights. *Lancet, 351,* 974–977.

Simola, S. (2015). Understanding moral courage through a feminist and developmental ethic of care. *Journal of Business Ethics, 130,* 29–44.

Simon, G. C. (1978). The psychologist as whistle blower: A case study. *Professional Psychology, 9*(2), 322–340.

Simon, R. A. (2014). Special considerations in conducting psychological custody evaluations with military families. *Family Court Review, 52*(3), 440–457.

Simon, R. I., & Williams, I. C. (1999). Maintaining treatment boundaries in small communities and rural areas. *Psychiatric Services, 50*(11), 1440–1446.

Sinclair, C. (2011). The evolution of the Canadian Code of Ethics over the years (1986–2011). *Canadian Psychology, 52,* 152–161.

Sinclair, C. M. (1998). Nine unique features of the Canadian Code of Ethics for Psychologists. *Canadian Psychology*, 39(3), 167–176.

Sinclair, C. M., & Pettifor, J. (2001). Introduction and acknowledgments. In C. Sinclair & J. Pettifor (Eds.), *Companion manual to the Canadian Code of Ethics for Psychologists* (3rd ed., pp. i–iv). Ottawa, Canada: Canadian Psychological Association.

Sinclair, C. M., Poizner, S., Gilmour-Barrett, K., & Randall, D. (1987). The development of a code of ethics for Canadian psychologists. *Canadian Psychology*, 28(1), 1–8.

Sinclair, C. M., Simon, N. P., & Pettifor, J. L. (1996). History of ethical codes and licensure. In L. J. Bass, S. T. DeMers, J. R. P. Ogloff, C. Peterson, J. L. Pettifor, J. R. P. Reeves, . . . R. M. Tipton (Eds.), *Professional conduct and discipline in psychology* (pp. 1–15). Washington, DC: American Psychological Association.

Singer, J. L. (1980). The scientific basis of psychotherapeutic practice: A question of values and ethics. *Psychotherapy: Theory, Research, and Practice*, 17, 373–383.

Slater, L. (2004). Opening Skinner's box: *Great psychological experiments of the twentieth century*. New York, NY: Norton.

Slimp, A. O. C., & Burian, B. K. (1994). Multiple role relationships during internship: Consequences and recommendations. *Professional Psychology: Research and Practice*, 25 (1), 39–45.

Slowther, A., & Kleinman, I. (2008). Confidentiality. In P. A. Singer & A. M. Viens (Eds.), *The Cambridge textbook of bioethics* (pp. 43–48). New York, NY: Cambridge University Press.

Smith, A. J. (1990). Working within the lesbian community: The dilemma of overlapping relationships. In H. Lerman & N. Porter (Eds.), *Feminist ethics in psychotherapy* (pp. 92–96). New York, NY: Springer.

Smith, C. P., & Freyd, J. J. (2013). Dangerous safe havens: Institutional betrayal exacerbates sexual trauma. *Journal of Traumatic Stress*, 26(1), 119–124.

Smith, D., & Fitzpatrick, M. (1995). Patient-therapist boundary issues: An integrative review of theory and research. *Professional Psychology: Research and Practice*, 26(5), 499–506.

Soheilian, S. S., Inman, A. G., Klinger, R. S., Isenberg, D. S., & Kulp, L. E. (2014). Multicultural supervision: Supervisees' reflections on culturally competent supervision. *Counselling Psychology Quarterly*, 27(4), 379–392.

Sokol, D. K. (2009). Informed consent is more than a patient's signature. *British Medical Journal*, 339, b3224. doi:10.1136/bmj.b3224

Solon, O. (2012, June 22). Galileo to Turing: The historical persecution of scientists. *Wired*. Retrieved http://www.wired.com/2012/06/famous-persecuted-scientists

Solotaroff, J. L., & Pande, R. P. (2014). *Violence against women and girls: Lessons from south Asia*. Washington, DC: World Bank Publications.

Somer, E., & Saadon, M. (1999). Therapist–client sex: Retrospective reports. *Professional Psychology: Research and Practice*, 30, 305–309.

Sonne, J. L. (1994). Multiple relationships: Does the new ethics code answer the right questions? *Professional Psychology: Research and Practice*, 25, 336–343.

Sonne, J. L. (2005). *Nonsexual multiple relationships: A practical decision-making model for clinicians*. Available at http://kspope.com.

Sonne, J. L., & Jochai, D. (2014). The "vicissitudes of love" between therapist and patient: A review of the research on romantic and sexual feelings, thoughts, and behaviors in psychotherapy. *Journal of Clinical Psychology, 70*(2), 182–195.

Sonne, J. L., Meyer, C. B., Borys, D., & Marshall, V. (1985). Clients' reaction to sexual intimacy in therapy. *American Journal of Orthopsychiatry, 55,* 183–189.

Spitz, V. (2005). *Doctors from hell: The horrific account of Nazi experiments on humans.* Boulder, CO: Sentient.

Spranca, M., Minsk, E., & Baron, J. (1991). Omission and commission in judgment and choice. *Journal of Experimental Social Psychology, 27*(1), 76–105.

Stack, S. (2014). Differentiating suicide ideators from attempters: Violence — A research note. *Suicide and Life-Threatening Behavior, 44*(1), 46–57.

State of California, Department of Consumer Affairs. (2015). *Laws and regulations relating to the practice of psychology.* Sacramento, CA: Author.

Statistics Canada (2011). *Immigration and ethnocultural diversity in Canada.* Retrieved from http://www12.statcan.gc.ca/nhs-enm/2011/as-sa/99-010-x/99-010-x2011001-eng.cfm

Statistics Canada. (2014, December 3). *Study: Persons with disabilities and employment.* Retrieved from http://www.statcan.gc.ca/daily-quotidien/141203/dq141203a-eng.htm

Staub, E. (2014). Obeying, joining, following, resisting, and other processes in the Milgram studies, and in the Holocaust and other genocides: Situations, personality, and bystanders. *Journal of Social Issues, 70*(3), 501–514.

Stenzel, C. L., & Rupert, P. A. (2004). Psychologists' use of touch in individual psychotherapy. *Psychotherapy: Theory, Research, Practice, Training, 41,* 332–345. doi:10.1037/0033–3204.41.3.332

Stern, A. M. (2005). Sterilized in the name of public health: Race, immigration, and reproductive control in modern California. *American Journal of Public Health, 95,* 1128–1138.

Sternberg, R. J. (2006). Evidence-based practice: Gold standard, gold plated, or fool's gold? In C. D. Goodheart, A. E. Kazdin, & R. J. Sternberg (Eds.), *Evidence-based psychotherapy: Where practice and research meet* (pp. 261–271). Washington, DC: American Psychological Association.

Sternberg, R. J. (2010). The Flynn effect: So what? *Journal of Psychoeducational Assessment, 28,* 434–440.

Stevens, B. (2013). How ethical are US business executives? A study of perceptions. *Journal of Business Ethics, 117*(2), 361–369.

Stevens, N. (1990, August 25). Did I say average? I meant superior. *New York Times,* p. 15.

Stice, E., Rohde, P., Butryn, M., Menke, K. S., & Marti, C. N. (2015). Randomized controlled pilot trial of a novel dissonance-based group treatment for eating disorders. *Behaviour Research and Therapy, 65,* 67–75.

Stockman, A. F. (1990). Dual relationships in rural mental health practice: An ethical dilemma. *Journal of Rural Community Psychology, 11*(2), 31–45.

Stockus, C. A., & Walter, M. I. (2015). I understand what you're saying, but I don't want to believe you: The interaction between social dominance orientation and the correspondence bias. *North American Journal of Psychology, 17*(1), 119–132.

Stoltenberg, C. D., & Delworth, U. (1987). *Supervising counselors and therapists.* San Francisco, CA: Jossey-Bass.

Stone, A. A. (1978, March 19). Mentally ill: To commit or not, that is the question. *New York Times*, p. 10E.

Stone, M. T. (1982). Turning points in psychotherapy. In S. Slipp (Ed.), *Curative factors in dynamic psychotherapy* (pp. 259–279). New York, NY: McGraw-Hill.

St. Paul Fire & Marine Insurance Company v. Downs, 617 N.E.2d 33g (Ill. App. 1 Dist) (1993).

Stricker, G. (1992). The relationship of research to clinical practice. *American Psychologist, 47*, 543–549.

Stromberg, C. D., Haggarty, R. F., McMillian, M. H., Mishkin, B., Rubin, B. L., & Trilling, H. R. (1988). *The psychologist's legal handbook.* Washington, DC: Council for the National Register of Health Service Providers in Psychology.

Subotsky, F., Bewley, S., & Crowe, M. (Eds.). (2010). *Abuse of the doctor-patient relationship.* London: RCPsych Publications.

Sue, D. W. (1978). Eliminating cultural oppression in counseling: Toward a general theory. *Journal of Counseling Psychology, 25*(5), 419.

Sue, D. W. (1995). Multicultural organizational development: Implications for the counseling profession. In J. G. Ponterotto, J. M. Casas, L. A. Suzuki, & C. M. Alexander (Eds.), *Handbook of multicultural counseling* (pp. 474–492). Thousand Oaks, CA: Sage.

Sue, D. W. (2015a). Race talk and the conspiracy of silence: Understanding and facilitating difficult dialogues on race. Hoboken, NJ: Wiley.

Sue, D. W. (2015b). Therapeutic harm and cultural oppression. *Counseling Psychologist, 43*, 393–403.

Sue, D. W., & Sue, D. (2003). *Counseling the culturally diverse: Theory and practice* (4th ed.). Boston, MA: Houghton Mifflin.

Sue, D. W., & Sue, D. (2008). *Counseling the culturally diverse: Theory and practice* (5th ed.). Hoboken, NJ: Wiley.

Sue, S. (1999). Science, ethnicity, and bias: Where have we gone wrong? *American Psychologist, 54*(12), 1070.

Sue, S. (2010, April 23). *Ethnic minority issues: Lessons learned from 40 years of research.* WPA Presidential Address at the 90th Annual Convention of the Western Psychological Association, Cancun, Mexico.

Suicide numbers in Nunavut in 2013 a record high; Nunavut youth decry lack of help for those thinking about suicide. (2014, January 10). *Canadian Broadcasting Corporation News.* Retrieved from http://www.cbc.ca/news/canada/north/suicide-numbers-in-nunavut-in-2013-a-record-high-1.2491117

Sunderland, N., Catalano, T., Kendall, E., McAuliffe, D., & Chenoweth, L. (2010). Exploring the concept of moral distress with community-based researchers: An Australian study. *Journal of Social Service Research, 37*(1), 73–85.

Sunderland, N., Harris, P., Johnstone, K., Del Fabbro, L., & Kendall, E. (2015). Exploring health promotion practitioners' experiences of moral distress in Canada and Australia. *Global Health Promotion, 22*, 32–45.

Surís, A., Lind, L., Kashner, T. M., & Borman, P. D. (2007). Mental health, quality of life, and health functioning in women veterans: Differential outcomes associated with military and civilian sexual assault. *Journal of Interpersonal Violence, 22*(2), 179–197.

Surís, A., Lind, L., Kashner, T. M., Borman, P. D., & Petty, F. (2004). Sexual assault in women veterans: An examination of PTSD risk, health care utilization, and cost of care. *Psychosomatic Medicine, 66,* 749–756.

Taleb, N. N. (2010). *The black swan: The impact of the highly improbable fragility* (2nd ed.). New York, NY: Random House.

Taleb, N. N., & Blyth, M. (2011). The black swan of Cairo: How suppressing volatility makes the world less predictable and more dangerous. *Foreign Affairs, 90,* 33–39.

Taliaferro, L. A., & Muehlenkamp, J. J. (2014). Risk and protective factors that distinguish adolescents who attempt suicide from those who only consider suicide in the past year. *Suicide and Life-Threatening Behavior, 44*(1), 6–22.

Tallman, G. (1981). *Therapist–client social relationships.* Unpublished manuscript, California State University, Northridge.

Tellides, C., Fitzpatrick, M., Drapeau, M., Bracewell, R., Janzen, J., & Jaouich, A. (2008). The manifestation of transference during early psychotherapy sessions. *Counselling & Psychotherapy Research, 8,* 85–92.

Thieren, M., & Mauron, A. (2007). Nuremberg code turns 60. *Bulletin of the World Health Organization, 85*(8), 573. doi:10.2471/BLT.07.045443

The Trust. (2014, September). *Choosing encryption software.* Retrieved from http://www.trustinsurance.com/resources/articles/choosing encryptionsoftware.aspx

Thoreau, H. D. (1960). *Walden and civil disobedience.* Boston, MA: Houghton Mifflin. (Original work published 1849)

Tolstoy, L. (1951). *The kingdom of God is within you* (L. Weiner, Trans.). Boston, MA: Page. (Original work published 1894)

Truscott, D., & Crook, K. H. (2013). *Ethics for the practice of psychology in Canada: Revised and expanded edition.* Edmonton, Canada: University of Alberta Press.

Tsai, M., Plummer, M. D., Kanter, J. W., Newring, R. W., & Kohlenberg, R. J. (2010). Therapist grief and functional analytic psychotherapy: Strategic self-disclosure of personal loss. *Journal of Contemporary Psychotherapy, 40,* 1–10. doi:10.1007/s10879-009-9116-6

Tschan, F., Semmer, N. K., Gurtner, A., Bizzari, L., Spychiger, M., Breuer, M., & Marsch, S. U. (2009). Explicit reasoning, confirmation bias, and illusory transactive memory: A simulation study of group medical decision making. *Small Group Research, 40,* 271–300.

Tsong, Y., & Goodyear, R. K. (2014). Assessing supervision's clinical and multicultural impacts: The Supervision Outcome Scale's psychometric properties. *Training and Education in Professional Psychology, 8*(3), 189–195.

Tsuang, M. T. (1983). Risk of suicide in relatives of schizophrenics, manics, depressives, and controls. *Journal of Clinical Psychiatry, 39,* 396–400.

Tversky, A., & Kahneman, D. (1974). Judgment under uncertainty: Heuristics and biases. *Science, 185*(4157), 1124–1131.

Twenge, J. M., Campbell, W. K., & Carter, N. T. (2014). Declines in trust in others and confidence in institutions among American adults and late adolescents, 1972–2012. *Psychological Science, 25,* 1914–1923.

21st Century Seminars. (2014). *Termination that works with at-risk children and adolescents: Four steps that build resilience and give hope to challenging populations.* Manhattan Beach, CA: 21st Century Seminars.

U.S. Bureau of the Census. (2010). New Census Bureau report analyzes nation's linguistic diversity. *Newsroom archive.* (Report No. CB10-CN.58). Retrieved from https://www.census.gov/newsroom/releases/archives/american_community_survey_acs/cb10-cn58.html

U.S. Bureau of the Census. (2011). 2010 Census shows America's diversity. *Newsroom Archive.* Washington, DC. Author. Retrieved from https://www.census.gov/newsroom/releases/archives/2010_census/cb11-cn125.html

U.S. Public Health Service. (1973). *Final report of the Tuskegee Syphilis Study Ad Hoc Advisory Panel.* Washington, DC: Author.

Unger, R. K. (1998). *Resisting gender: Twenty-five years of feminist psychology.* Thousand Oaks, CA: Sage.

VA Office of the Inspector General. (2014, May 28). Veterans Health Administration — Interim report — Review of patient wait times, scheduling practices, and alleged patient deaths at the Phoenix Health Care System. Retrieved from http://www.va.gov/oig/pubs/VAOIG-14-02603-178.pdf

van Bommel, M., van Prooijen, J.-W., Elffers, H., & van Lange, P. A. M. (2014). Intervene to be seen: The power of a camera in attenuating the bystander effect. *Social Psychological and Personality Science, 5,* 459–466.

Van Horne, B. A. (2004). Psychology licensing board disciplinary actions: The realities. *Professional Psychology: Research and Practice, 35,* 170–178. doi:10.1037/0735-7028.35.2.170

Vasquez, M. J. (1991). Sexual intimacies with clients after termination: Should a prohibition be explicit? *Ethics & Behavior, 1*(1), 45–61.

Vasquez, M. J. T. (2005). Independent practice settings and the multicultural guidelines. In M. G. Constantine & D. W. Sue (Eds.), *Strategies for building multicultural competence in mental health and educational settings* (pp. 91–108). Washington, DC: American Psychological Association.

Vasquez, M. J. T. (2007). Cultural difference and the therapeutic alliance: An evidence-based analysis. *American Psychologist, 62,* 878–885. doi:10.1037/0003-066X.62.8.878

Vasquez, M. J. T. (2009). Ethics in multicultural counseling practice. In J. G. Ponterotto, J. M. Casas, L. A. Suzuki, & C. M. Alexander (Eds.), *Handbook of multicultural counseling* (3rd ed., pp. 127–146). Thousand Oaks, CA: Sage.

Vasquez, M. J. T. (2015). Foreword. In K. F. Geisinger (Ed.), *Psychological testing of Hispanics: Clinical, cultural, and intellectual issues* (2nd ed., pp. xi–xvi). Washington, DC: American Psychological Association.

Vasquez, M. J. T. (in press). *Multicultural therapy.* Volume for Theories of Psychotherapy Series. Washington, DC: American Psychological Association.

Vasquez, M. J. T., Bingham, R. P., & Barnett, J. E. (2008). Psychotherapy termination: Clinical and ethical responsibilities. *Journal of Clinical Psychology, 64,* 653–665. doi:10.1002/jclp.20478

Vasquez, M. J. T., & Vasquez, E. (2016). Psychotherapy with women: Theory and practice. In L. E. Beutler, A. J. Consoli, & B. Bongar (Eds.), *Comprehensive textbook of psychotherapy: Theory and practice* (2nd ed.). New York, NY: Oxford University Press.

Vaughn, R. (1975). *The spoiled system.* New York, NY: McKay.

Velasquez, R. J., Arellano, L. M., & McNeill, B. W. (2004). *The handbook of Chicana/o psychology and mental health.* Mahwah, NJ: Erlbaum.

Vinson, J. S. (1987). Use of complaint procedures in cases of therapist–patient sexual contact. *Professional Psychology: Research and Practice, 18,* 159–164.

Violanti, J. M., Andrew, M. E., Mnatsakanova, A., Hartley, T. A., Fekedulegn, D., & Burchfiel, C. M. (2015). Correlates of hopelessness in the high suicide risk police occupation. *Police Practice and Research* (ahead-of-print).

Viscusi, W. K. (2015, May). Pricing lives for corporate risk decisions. *Vanderbilt Law Review,* 14–26.

Vora, R. S., & Kinney, M. N. (2014). Connectedness, sense of community, and academic satisfaction in a novel community campus medical education model. *Academic Medicine, 89*(1), 182–187.

Vuorilehto, M. S., Melartin, T. K., & Isometsa, E. T. (2006). Suicidal behaviour among primary-care patients with depressive disorders. *Psychological Medicine, 36*(2), 203–210.

Wagner, D. (2014a, June 9). VA scandal audit: 120,000 veterans experience long waits for care: Audit shows delayed care at VA facilities across U.S. *Arizona Republic.* Retrieved from http://www.azcentral.com/story/news/arizona/investigations/2014/06/09/va-scandal-audit-veterans-delayed-care/10234881/

Wagner, D. (2014b, November 24). VA fires Phoenix hospital director. *Arizona Republic.* Retrieved from http://www.azcentral.com/story/news/arizona/investigations/2014/11/24/va-fires-phoenix-hospital-director-helman/70056192/

Walker, E., & Young, T. D. (1986). *A killing cure.* New York, NY: Holt.

Walker v. City of Birmingham, 388 U.S. 307, 18 L.Ed.2d 1210 (1967).

Wallace, L. S., Keenum, A. J., Roskos, S. E., Blake, G. H., Colwell, S. T., & Weiss, B. D. (2008). Suitability and readability of consumer medical information accompanying prescription medication samples. *Patient Education and Counseling, 70* (3), 420–425.

Walter, C. (2007). A little privacy please. *Scientific American, 297*(8), 92–95.

Wampold, B. E., & Imel, Z. E. (2015). *The great psychotherapy debate: The evidence for what makes psychotherapy work.* New York, NY: Routledge.

Wang, C. (2009). *Managing informed consent and confidentiality in multicultural contexts.* Paper presented at the annual meeting of the American Psychological Association, Toronto, Canada.

Wang, C. W., Chan, C. H., Ho, R. T., Chan, J. S., Ng, S. M., & Chan, C. L. (2014). Managing stress and anxiety through qigong exercise in healthy adults: A systematic review and meta-analysis of randomized controlled trials. *BMC Complementary and Alternative Medicine, 14*(1), 8.

Ward, A. (2010). Confidentiality matters. In M. E. Heller & S. Pollet (Ed.), *The work of psychoanalysts in the public health sector* (pp. 113–123). New York, NY: Routledge/Taylor & Francis.

Watkins Jr, C. E. (2014, October). The competent psychoanalytic supervisor: Some thoughts about supervision competences for accountable practice and training. *International Forum of Psychoanalysis, 23*(4), 220–228.

Watkins, S. S. (2013). Foreword. In S. V. Arbogast, *Resisting corporate corruption: Cases in practical ethics from Enron through the financial crisis* (pp. ix–xii). Hoboken, NJ: Wiley.

Weaver, G. R. (2014). Encouraging ethics in organizations: A review of some key research findings. *American Criminal Law Review, 51*, 293–317.

Weiner, M. F. (1978). *Therapist disclosure: The use of self in psychotherapy*. Boston, MA: Butterworths.

Weiner, M. F. (1983). *Therapist disclosure: The use of self in psychotherapy* (2nd ed.). Baltimore, MD: University Park Press.

Weinstein, I. (2015). Learning and lawyering across personality types. *Clinical Law Review, 21*, 427.

Weisman, A. D., & Worden, J. W. (1972). Risk-rescue rating in suicide assessment. *Archives of General Psychiatry, 26*, 553–560.

Weisner, T. S., & Hay, M. C. (2015). Practice to research: Integrating evidence-based practices with culture and context. *Transcultural Psychiatry, 52*(2), 222–243.

Weiss, J. W. (2014). *Business ethics: A stakeholder and issues management approach* (6th ed.). San Francisco, CA: Berrett-Koehler.

Wellerstein, A. (2011). States of eugenics: Institutions and practices in compulsory sterilization in California. In S. Jasanoff (Ed.), *Reframing rights: Bioconstitutionalism in the genetic age* (pp. 29–58). Cambridge, MA: MIT Press.

Westen, D., & Bradley, R. (2005). Empirically supported complexity: Rethinking evidence-based practice in psychotherapy. *Current Directions in Psychological Science, 1*(10), 266–271.

Westen, D., Novotny, C. M., & Thompson-Brenner, H. (2004). The empirical status of empirically supported psychotherapies: Assumptions, findings, and reporting in controlled clinical trials. *Psychological Bulletin, 130*, 631–663.

Westermeyer, J. (1987). Cultural factors in clinical assessment. *Journal of Consulting and Clinical Psychology, 55*, 471–478.

Wetzel, R. (1976). Hopelessness, depression, and suicide intent. *Archives of General Psychiatry, 33*, 1069–1073.

Whaley, A. L., & Davis, K. E. (2007). Cultural competence and evidence-based practice in mental health services: A complementary perspective. *American Psychologist, 62*, 563–574.

Whitehead, P. B., Herbertson, R. K., Hamric, A. B., Epstein, E. G., & Fisher, J. M. (2014). Moral distress among healthcare professionals: Report of an institution-wide survey. *Journal of Nursing Scholarship, 47*(2), 117125.

Wickham, M., & O'Donohue, W. (2012). Developing an ethical organization: Exploring the role of ethical intelligence. *Organization Development Journal, 30*(2), 9–29.

Wike, K. (2014, June 19). HHS; Data breaches affect 1 in 10. *Health IT Outcomes*. Retrieved from http://www.healthitoutcomes.com/doc/hhs-data-breaches-affect-in-0001

Williams, J. R. (2008). Consent. In P. A. Singer & A. M. Viens (Eds.), *The Cambridge textbook of bioethics* (pp. 11–16). New York, NY: Cambridge University Press.

Williams, M. H. (1997). Boundary violations: Do some contended standards of care fail to encompass commonplace procedures of humanistic, behavioral, and eclectic psychotherapies? *Psychotherapy: Theory, Research, Practice, Training, 34*(3), 238–249.

Wilson, D. (2009, December 12). Poor children likelier to get antipsychotics. *New York Times*. Retrieved from http://www.nytimes.com/2009/12/12/health/12medicaid .html

Windschitl, P. D., Bruchmann, K., Scherer, A. M., & McEvoy, S. (2013). Egocentrism in judging the effectiveness of treatments. *Basic and Applied Social Psychology*, 35(4), 325–333.

Wingenfeld-Hammond, S. (2010). Boundaries and multiple relationships. In A. Allan & A. Love (Eds.), *Ethical practice in psychology: Reflections from the creators of the APS Code of Ethics* (pp. 135–147). Hoboken, NJ: Wiley-Blackwell.

Wolff, S., & Auckenthaler, A. (2014). Processes of theoretical orientation development in CBT trainees: What internal processes do psychotherapists in training undergo as they "integrate"? *Journal of Psychotherapy Integration*, 24(3), 223.

Wonderling, L. (2013). *Psychological first aid and the Good Samaritan.* Dewey, AZ: Cape Foundation Publications.

Wong, J. P. S., Stewart, S. M., Claassen, C., Lee, P. W. H., Rao, U., & Lam, T. H. (2008). Repeat suicide attempts in Hong Kong community adolescents. *Social Science & Medicine*, 66, 232–241. doi:10.1016/j.socscimed.2007.08.031

Wood, G. (1978). The knew-it-all-along effect. *Journal of Experimental Psychology: Human Perception and Performance*, 4, 345–353.

Woodward, H. E., Taft, C. T., Gordon, R. A., & Meis, L. A. (2009). Clinician bias in the diagnosis of posttraumatic stress disorder and borderline personality disorder. *Psychological Trauma: Theory, Research, Practice, and Policy*, 1, 282–290. doi:10.1037/a0017944

Woody, R. H. (1998). Bartering for psychological services. *Professional Psychology: Research and Practice*, 29(2), 174–178.

Word, C., Zanna, M. P., & Cooper, J. (1974). The nonverbal mediation of self-fulfilling prophecies in interracial interaction. *Journal of Experimental Social Psychology*, 10, 109–120.

Wu, C., Liao, S., Lin, K., Tseng, M. M., Wu, E. C., & Liu, S. (2009). Multidimensional assessments of impulsivity in subjects with history of suicidal attempts. *Comprehensive Psychiatry*, 50, 315–321. doi:10.1016/j.comppsych.2008.09.006

Wyatt, G. E. (1997). *Stolen women: Reclaiming our sexuality, taking back our lives.* New York, NY: Wiley.

Wyder, M., Ward, P., & De Leo, D. (2009). Separation as a suicide risk factor. *Journal of Affective Disorders*, 116, 208–213. doi:10.1016/j.jad.2008.11.007

Wygant, D. B., & Lareau, C. R. (2015). Civil and criminal forensic psychological assessment: Similarities and unique challenges. *Psychological Injury and Law*, 8(1), 11–26.

Yantz, C. L., & McCaffrey, R. J. (2005). Effects of a supervisor's observation on memory test performance of the examinee: Third party observer effect confirmed. *Journal of Forensic Neuropsychology*, 4 (2), 27–38.

Ye, X., Bapuji, S. B., Winters, S. E., Struthers, A., Raynard, M., Metge, C., & Sutherland, K. (2014). Effectiveness of Internet-based interventions for children, youth, and young adults with anxiety and/or depression: A systematic review and meta-analysis. *BMC Health Services Research*, 14(1), 313.

Yeh, C. J., Liao, H. Y., Ma, P. W. W., Shea, M., Okubo, Y., Kim, A. B., & Atkins, M. S. (2014). Ecological risk and protective factors of depressive and anxiety symptoms among low-income, Chinese immigrant youth. *Asian American Journal of Psychology, 5*(3), 190.

Young, A. (2014, June 2). GM ignition switch recall: What to expect from Valukas report. *International Business Times*. Retrieved from http://www.investing.com/news/stock-market-news/gm-ignition-switch-recall:-what-to-expect

Young, C. (2007). The power of touch in psychotherapy. *International Journal of Psychotherapy, 11*, 15–24.

Younggren, J. (2002). *Ethical decision-making and dual relationships*. Available at http://kspope.com.

Zametkin, A. J., Alter, M. R., & Yemini, T. (2001). Suicide in teenagers: Assessment, management, and prevention. *Journal of the American Medical Association, 286*(24), 3120–3125.

Zeeck, A., Orlinsky, D. E., Hermann, S., Joos, A., Wirsching, M., Weidmann, W., & Hartmann, A. (2012). Stressful involvement in psychotherapeutic work: Therapist, client and process correlates. *Psychotherapy Research, 22*(5), 543–555.

Zelechoski, A. D., Fuhrmann, G. S. W., Zibbell, R. A., & Cavallero, L. M. (2012). Evaluation for child custody: Using best practices in a worst case scenario. *Journal of Forensic Psychology Practice, 12*(5), 457470.

Zhang, Y., Conner, K. R., & Phillips, M. R. (2010). Alcohol use disorders and acute alcohol use preceding suicide in China. *Addictive Behaviors, 35*, 152–156. doi:10.1016/j.addbeh.2009.09.020

Zimbardo, P. G. (2007). Thoughts on psychologists, ethics, and the use of torture in interrogations: Don't ignore varying roles and complexities. In G. Mauryama & J. Peterson (Eds.), *Special Issue: Psychologists and the Use of Torture in Interrogations. Analyses of Social Issues and Public Policy (ASAP) Online SSPSI Journal, 7*, 65–73.

Ziv-Beiman, S. (2013). Therapist self-disclosure as an integrative intervention. *Journal of Psychotherapy Integration, 23*(1), 59–74.

Zsambok, C. E., & Klein, G. (Eds.). (2014). *Naturalistic decision making*. New York, NY: Psychology Press.

Zuckerman, L. (2014, June 24). Montana health record hackers compromise 1.3 million people. Reuters. Retrieved from http://www.reuters.com/article/2014/06/25/us-usa-hacker-montana-idUSKBN0F006I20140625

ABOUT THE AUTHORS

KEN POPE

Going to hear Dr. Martin Luther King, Jr., and the community organizer Saul Alinsky changed my life forever. Their words shook me awake and wouldn't let go.

By the time I graduated from college, their words had convinced me to delay a fellowship to study literature so that I could learn community organizing and try to make a difference. I worked in an inner-city area of severe poverty during the late 1960s and early 1970s. For the first time in my life, I lived where there were no neighbors of my own race.

Those years showed me how poverty, unmet basic needs, and injustice can assault individual lives. I also witnessed the power of people working together to bring about profound change.

A crucial lesson began one day in a corner cafe where the community gathered. A deacon in a church whose roots reached back to the days before the Civil War invited me to visit the church that Sunday.

I entered the church that weekend and found a seat at the back, looking forward to the minister's sermon. When the time came for the sermon, the minister walked up to the pulpit, looked out at us, and began, "We are most pleased that our neighbor, Mr. Ken Pope, agreed to visit us today, and we look forward to his sermon." This taught me not to assume that my understandings are always shared by others — and that life often calls us to do more than just show up.

After my years of living in that community, I began the delayed fellowship to study literature at Harvard. But the years between college and graduate school had changed me. When I received an M.A. at the end of the year, I did not want to continue studies in that field. I explained my change of heart, expecting to be shown the door. But they surprised me. They told me I could continue to study, taking whatever courses I found interesting in any fields. Some courses

I took the next year were in psychology and they felt like my home. I'll always be thankful to the university for their kindness in allowing me to delay my fellowship, in letting me take courses in diverse fields, and in the professors' generosity with their time, attention, and support. Because Harvard lacked a clinical psychology program, I transferred to Yale for my clinical psychology doctorate.

What happened in these early years has kept happening throughout my life: Fellow students, colleagues, patients, and others have made me realize that whatever beliefs I held at any given time could be rethought, that I needed to consider new perspectives, new possibilities, new ways of finding, creating, and making use of resources.

One example: Our faculty-intern discussions at San Francisco's Langley Porter Neuropsychiatric Institute followed a predictable pattern: Asked to present a case, each of us interns would choose to describe that week's version of "my toughest case," making clear not just how daunting the challenges we faced but how brilliant the insights and solutions we came up with. Midyear, an intern broke the pattern: "I feel awful this week. The situation was not that difficult but I made some bad mistakes, and ended up having to hospitalize the patient. I need help figuring out what's going on with this person, why I did what I did, and how I can do things differently." Her honesty, courage, integrity, and clear concern for the person she wanted to help woke us from our complacent habits of thinking and feeling. We confronted how we approached learning and how we treated each other. We talked about how our fear, envy, and competitiveness affected who we were, how we thought, what we did. One person had changed us and our community.

In my early years as a licensed psychologist, I served as clinical director of a nonprofit hospital and community mental health center. My earlier experiences led me to focus on the ability of the staff, the Board of Directors, and the surrounding community to work together identifying needs and creating ways to meet those needs. Working together, the diverse individuals in that array of groups created home-bound psychological services, a 24-hour crisis service, legal services for people who are poor or homeless, a program for people whose primary language is Spanish, and group homes allowing people who are mentally disabled to live independently. What the people in these groups accomplished showed again and again the decisive role that each can play in the lives of others, the ways we can awaken each other to new perspectives and possibilities, and how people working together can bring about change.

Teaching the occasional undergraduate course in the UCLA psychology department, supervising therapy in the UCLA Psychology Clinic, chairing the ethics committees of the American Psychological Association (APA) and the American Board of Professional Psychology (ABPP), becoming a charter member and later Fellow of what is now the Association of Psychological Science, and other experiences in those early years kept reminding me of the need to keep rethinking what I think I know and my ways of working, to ask "What if I'm wrong about this?," "Is there a better way to understand this?," "What else could I do that might be more effective?"

Since leaving institutional work in the mid-1980s, I've been an independent clinical and forensic psychologist, but the themes of my work, touched on above, continue, even as they continue to take on new forms.

One question I've struggled with is: How can psychologists find better access to the information they need without adding to the burdens on their time or pocketbooks? Over two decades ago, I started a Psychology News List via e-mail, free and open to all, to make it a little easier — especially for those in isolated areas or those who lack easy access to the relevant materials — to keep up with the new research, changing legal standards, controversial topics, and other trends that affect our work. Each day I send out 6 to 10 items, most of them excerpts from new and in-press articles from psychology and other scientific and professional journals, psychology-related articles from that day's newspapers, new court decisions affecting psychology, job announcements, and referral requests sent to me by list members. Although not a discussion list and now quite large, it has become a supportive community. From time to time members ask me to circulate a request for information or suggestions for dealing with an aging parent, a family emergency, a clinical or forensic issue, or a business-related problem with their practice. Almost all write me later to tell me how supported they felt to receive so many personal responses.

Every year I've sent two questions to the list: Early in spring I ask what sources of joy, meaning, or hope they have that particular year that sustain them in hard times; and between the Canadian and U.S. Thanksgivings, I ask what they are especially thankful for that year. When I circulate a compilation of all the responses, members tell me how much the process makes them feel less alone and more connected to others.

Another way we can make information more accessible is through websites that provide articles and other resources without making access contingent on subscriptions, memberships, fees, or other restrictions. Two of mine are "Articles, Research, & Resources in Psychology" at http://kspope.com and "Accessibility & Disability Information & Resources in Psychology Training & Practice" at http://kpope.com.

For 29 years APA was my professional home. As chair of the APA Ethics Committee and a Fellow of nine APA Divisions, I worked with many people who became close friends and gave so much to my professional and personal life. I was honored to receive the APA Award for Distinguished Contributions to Public Service "for rigorous empirical research, landmark articles and books, courageous leadership, fostering the careers of others, and making services available to those with no means to pay"; the Division 12 Award for Distinguished Professional Contributions to Clinical Psychology; the Division 42 Award for Mentoring; and other forms of recognition.

In 2008, with great regret and sadness I resigned from the APA. My respect and affection for the members, which continues to this day, made this a hard and reluctant step. I respectfully disagreed with decisive changes that APA made in its ethics codes and related policies after 9/11. In my view, those changes moved APA far from its ethical foundation, historic traditions, and basic values, and beyond what I could in good conscience support with my membership. I presented my view of these policy changes in my letter of resignation, which is online at http://kspope.com/apa/index.php, and in articles such as "Are the American Psychological Association's Detainee Interrogation Policies Ethical and Effective? Key Claims, Documents, and Results" in *Zeitschrift für Psychologie/Journal of Psychology*, 219(3), 150–158 (2011), which is online at http://kspope.com/apa/detainee.php; "Psychologists and Detainee Interrogations: Key Decisions, Opportunities Lost, and Lessons Learned," *Annual Review of Clinical Psychology*, 7, 459–481 (2011), which is online at http://kspope.com/interrogation.php; "Contrasting Ethical Policies of Physicians and Psychologists Concerning Interrogation of Detainees," *British Medical Journal*, 338, 1178–1186 (2009, with T. G. Gutheil), which is online at http://kspope.com/detainee/interrogation.php; and "Psychologists Abandon the Nuremberg Ethic: Concerns for Detainee Interrogations," *International Journal of Law and Psychiatry*, 32(3), 161–166 (2009, with T. G. Gutheil), which is online at http://kspope.com/nuremberg.php. (Please see Appendix A, "The Hoffman Report and the American Psychological Association Meeting the Challenge of Change," for a more recent discussion of these issues.)

The events of 9/11 cast all of us into a tangle of complex issues, dangerous realities, and hard choices. My decision to resign from APA reflected my effort to judge what was right for me. I respect those who saw the policy issues differently, held other beliefs, and took other paths.

We can each give so much to each other and to our communities. Sometimes just a word or gesture helps someone to keep going, overcome an obstacle, or see new vistas. An example: During that second year at Harvard I signed up for an advanced course in the med school. The first day I was already lost. The professor kept asking if we saw various structures in our microscopes. Everyone nodded yes, but I had no idea what he was talking about. I was too embarrassed to admit I couldn't see any of them. Finally I raised my hand and confessed. He looked at me a long time, then came down the aisle, put his hand on my back, leaned down to the floor, and plugged in my electronic microscope. Sometimes that's all it takes.

MELBA J. T. VASQUEZ

Why am I interested in ethics? When I trace the path of my professional development, it becomes clear that themes of social justice, empowerment, and fairness have informed every step of those processes.

The oldest of seven children, I grew up surrounded by the unconditional love of a large, Latino/a family in central Texas. I believe that this supportive environment provided by my immediate and extended family and community created a strong foundation to face the world. I grew up in a working class family during a period when people of color were socially segregated from White population. Despite having only elementary educations, and despite being working class, both my parents were politically involved at the grassroots level, and engaged in civil rights activities, modeling the importance of involvement and empowerment. I am very grateful to them for many values that they imparted, including articulating a strong belief in and support for education. My first jobs were picking cotton, babysitting, and cleaning people's houses. I also worked as a teacher aide during the summers of my high school years for one of the first Head Start programs in the state. During my adolescence and young adulthood, my family and those of many in my community moved into the middle class, partly as a result of Lyndon Johnson's War on Poverty initiatives. I was very much influenced by seeing that carefully designed and managed programs can make a positive difference in people's lives. I also witnessed the importance of dignity and integrity in people who often had little material wealth but who had so much to offer humanity through acts of kindness and compassion.

I obtained a Bachelor's degree with degrees in English and Political Science, and a teaching certificate at Texas State University, in my hometown. I was surprised and gratified to get positive messages from faculty members that I was capable of achievement, and learned firsthand how important it is to validate and communicate students' and others' strengths to them. I taught middle school for two years as I worked on a Master's degree in school counseling. As a first-generation college student coming from that rising middle class, I had never considered obtaining a doctorate but am grateful that my professor, Dr. Colleen Conoley, perceived me to be a "good fit" for the profession of counseling psychology. I obtained my doctorate from the APA accredited, scientist-practitioner Counseling Psychology program at the University of Texas at Austin in 1978.

I am also grateful to have been in the first cohort of the American Psychological Association's Minority Fellowship Program, which supported the last three years of my graduate study and which served as a powerful socializing process into the profession. It taught me the importance of effective strategies for addressing injustices in psychology.

After receiving my doctorate, I worked for 13 years at two university counseling centers; I also served as internship training director at both Colorado State University and the University of Texas at Austin. I am grateful to Dr. Donna McKinley and Dr. Suinn at CSU and Dr. David Drum at UT for being such great mentors. I am especially grateful to my spouse, Jim H. Miller, who has helped to support my career. He has been my best consultant, especially during challenging times. He helped to evoke integrity and to identify the "healthiest behavior" possible with a variety of dilemmas over my career. We have taken turns prioritizing our careers and goals over a 40-year period. We've had a very long-term and mutually supportive relationship. He is my best friend!

In 1991, I entered full-time independent practice, initially planning to do so temporarily, with plans to return to university administration at some point. However, I found that I was able to continue active involvement in professional leadership, advocacy, and scholarship and enjoyed the work in independent practice.

Early in my career, I was encouraged by Directors of the APA Minority Fellowship Program, Drs. Dalmas Taylor and then James Jones, to run for APA office. I was elected to the Board of Social and Ethical Responsibility for Psychology (BSERP). It was a transformational experience. I learned much in those days, as the BSERP led APA in divesting our investments in Apartheid South Africa and raised awareness in the association about what was then a new disease, HIV/AIDS. This board, considered the social conscience of psychology, was later merged with the Board of Ethnic Minority Affairs, to become the Board for the Advancement of Psychology in the Public Interest (BAPPI), and I was the first chair of that new board. Thus, my first governance experiences in APA were focused on social justice and the importance of ethical, moral choices of the APA.

My interests led me to seek leadership roles in other areas of the APA. I served as a member of the Committee of Women in Psychology and of various task forces. After helping to found Division 45, Society of the Psychological Study of Ethnic Minority Issues, I was its first Council representative (governing body of APA); I helped to organize and served as chair of the Ethnic Minority Caucus of the Council. I have also been a member of the Council of Representatives for Division 17 (and served as chair of the Public Interest Caucus) and for Division 42 (and served as chair of the Women's Caucus). The theme of engagement with social justice issues persisted as I became more involved in the inner workings of APA. When I have had concerns about directions of the Association, my response has been to continue to be involved in an attempt to voice the values I cherish.

In the 1980s, I became interested in professional ethics and was elected to serve on the APA Ethics Committee. Ken Pope was a member of that group at the same time, and, over the years, the two of us became coauthors on several ethics publications, including this book. I participated on the last two Ethics Committee Task Forces for revision of the Ethics Code (resulting in the 1992 and 2002 Ethics Codes).

I also served on practice-oriented bodies, including the Board of Professional Affairs, including as Chair, and on the Committee for the Advancement of Professional Practice. I was pleased to see the association so dedicated to developing quality, evidence-based services to meet the needs of psychologists to provide services to clients in independent practice, Veterans Affairs, community mental health centers, prison, medical and hospital settings, and others. I have been involved in developing psychology's legislative advocacy through activities sponsored by the APA's Practice Organization and the Association for the Advancement of Psychology.

I provided more leadership service when I was elected president of APA Division 35, Society for the Psychology of Women, the first Latina to hold that position. As my presidential project, I helped to cofound the 1999 National Multicultural Conference and Summit (with Rosie Bingham, Derald Wing Sue, and Lisa Porche Burke, who became great friends!). The NMCS is now held every 2 years. I have also served as president of APA Division 17, Society of Counseling Psychology, and of the Texas Psychological Association, again being the first Latina in each of these roles. I was elected to the APA Board of Directors (2007–2009), and then became the first woman of color to be elected as APA president (2011). It took a great deal of encouragement from colleagues over a ten-year period to believe that I could serve in that role. My passion for infusing psychology with social justice, fairness, and ethics fueled my decision to do so.

Serving as president of APA reflected love for and commitment to all the work I have described. It was an incredible opportunity that allowed me to represent the APA at various national and international conferences and events. I facilitated two meetings of the Council of Representatives, and was able to introduce "Social Justice" as one of the themes of the 2011 Conference of the APA. My three presidential projects involved appointing task forces of experts who worked hard to produce cutting edge reports about discrimination, immigration, and educational disparities.

My career has been rich, stimulating, and rewarding at many levels, and I feel very lucky to have been at the right place at the right time to benefit from numerous opportunities. I have been so lucky to have wonderful mentoring and guidance from wonderful psychologists too numerous to mention here, including many peers. I feel very fortunate to have been highly productive in my psychotherapy and consulting work, scholarship, mentoring of others, and leadership activities!

I believe in the ability of each person to be involved and provide input in a variety of ways to have influence in shaping the policies and direction of the association and/or the profession. I also believe that together we can continue to identify concrete strategies to meet the needs of psychologists and to promote psychological knowledge and ethical strategies to address the grand challenges of society at very critical times.

AUTHOR INDEX

Page references followed by *t* indicate a table.

SUBJECT INDEX

Page references followed by followed by *t* indicate a table.